COOK'S

ILLUSTRATED

~ 2014 ~

$35.00

Published by
America's Test Kitchen
17 Station Street
Brookline, MA 02445

ISBN-13: 978-1-940352-04-6
ISSN: 1933-639X

To get home delivery of *Cook's Illustrated* magazine, call 800-526-8442 inside the U.S., or 515-247-7571 if calling from outside the U.S., or subscribe online at www.cooksillustrated.com.

In addition to *Cook's Illustrated* Annual Hardbound Editions available from each year of publication (1993–2014), America's Test Kitchen offers the following cookbooks and DVD sets:

THE COOK'S ILLUSTRATED COOKBOOK SERIES
The Cook's Illustrated Meat Book
The Cook's Illustrated Cookbook
The Cook's Illustrated Baking Book
The Science of Good Cooking
The America's Test Kitchen Menu Cookbook
Soups, Stews & Chilis
The Best Skillet Recipes
The Best Slow & Easy Recipes
The Best Chicken Recipes
The Best International Recipe
The Best Make-Ahead Recipe
The Best 30-Minute Recipe
The Best Light Recipe
The Cook's Illustrated Guide to Grilling and Barbecue
Best American Side Dishes
The Best Cover & Bake Recipes
The New Best Recipe
Steaks, Chops, Roasts, and Ribs
Baking Illustrated
Perfect Vegetables
Italian Classics
The Best American Classics
The Best One-Dish Suppers

AMERICA'S TEST KITCHEN ANNUALS
The Best of America's Test Kitchen (2007–2015 Editions)
Cooking for Two (2009–2013 Editions)
Light & Healthy (2010–2012 Editions)

THE AMERICA'S TEST KITCHEN SERIES DVD SETS
(featuring each season's episodes from our hit public television series)
The *America's Test Kitchen* 4-DVD Set (2002–2014 Seasons)
The *America's Test Kitchen* 2-DVD Set (2001 Season)

THE AMERICA'S TEST KITCHEN SERIES COMPANION COOKBOOKS
America's Test Kitchen: The TV Companion Cookbook (2011–2015 Editions)
The Complete America's Test Kitchen TV Show Cookbook (2010)
America's Test Kitchen: The TV Companion Cookbook (2009)
Behind the Scenes with America's Test Kitchen (2008)
Test Kitchen Favorites (2007)
Cooking at Home with America's Test Kitchen (2006)
America's Test Kitchen Live! (2005)
Inside America's Test Kitchen (2004)
Here in America's Test Kitchen (2003)
The America's Test Kitchen Cookbook (2002)

THE AMERICA'S TEST KITCHEN LIBRARY SERIES
The How Can It Be Gluten-Free Cookbook
The Make-Ahead Cook
The America's Test Kitchen Do-It-Yourself Cookbook
Slow Cooker Revolution
Slow Cooker Revolution 2: The Easy Prep Edition
Comfort Food Makeovers
The Best Simple Recipes
Best Grilling Recipes
From Our Grandmothers' Kitchens

ADDITIONAL BOOKS FROM AMERICA'S TEST KITCHEN
The America's Test Kitchen New Family Cookbook
The Complete Cooking for Two Cookbook
The America's Test Kitchen Quick Family Cookbook
The America's Test Kitchen Healthy Family Cookbook
The America's Test Kitchen Family Cookbook
The America's Test Kitchen Family Baking Book
The America's Test Kitchen Cooking School Cookbook
Pressure Cooker Perfection
The Complete Cook's Country TV Show Cookbook
Cook's Country Annual Hardbound (2005–2014 Editions)
1993–2014 Cook's Illustrated Master Index

Visit our online bookstore at www.cooksillustrated.com to order any of our cookbooks and DVDs listed above. You can also order subscriptions, gift subscriptions, and any of our cookbooks and DVDs by calling 800-611-0759 inside the U.S., or at 515-246-6911 if calling from outside the U.S.

COOK'S ILLUSTRATED INDEX 2014

COOK'S ILLUSTRATED INDEX 2014

NUMBER 126

JANUARY & FEBRUARY 2014

COOK'S
ILLUSTRATED

Best Chicken Breasts
Crackling-Crisp Skin

Easy Cheese Soufflé
Soufflé Myths Debunked

Pressure-Cooker Pot Roast

Cooking Oil Guide
Don't Sauté with Olive Oil

Quick Yeast Bread
90 Minutes Start to Finish

Shrimp Fra Diavolo
Actual Shrimp Flavor

Testing Baking Pans

Almond Cake
Moist, Not Heavy

Best Swiss Cheese
Roasted Butternut Squash
Vietnamese Beef-Noodle Soup

CooksIllustrated.com
$6.95 U.S. & CANADA

7 25274 62805 6

0 2>

CONTENTS

January & February 2014

COOK'S
ILLUSTRATED

Founder and Editor — Christopher Kimball
Editorial Director — Jack Bishop
Editorial Director, Magazines — John Willoughby
Executive Editor — Amanda Agee
Test Kitchen Director — Erin McMurrer
Managing Editor — Rebecca Hays
Executive Food Editor — Keith Dresser
Senior Editors — Lisa McManus
Dan Souza
Senior Editors, Features — Elizabeth Bomze
Louise Emerick
Copy Editors — Nell Beram
Megan Ginsberg
Associate Editors — Hannah Crowley
Andrea Geary
Amy Graves
Andrew Janjigian
Chris O'Connor
Test Cooks — Daniel Cellucci
Lan Lam
Assistant Editors — Shannon Friedmann Hatch
Lauren Savoie
Assistant Test Cooks — Cecelia Jenkins
Sarah Mullins
Assistant Test Kitchen Director — Leah Rovner
Senior Kitchen Assistants — Michelle Blodget
Meryl MacCormack
Kitchen Assistants — Maria Elena Delgado
Shane Drips
Ena Gudiel
Executive Producer — Melissa Baldino
Co-Executive Producer — Stephanie Stender
Production Assistant — Kaitlin Hammond
Contributing Editor — Dawn Yanagihara
Consulting Editor — Scott Brueggeman
Science Editor — Guy Crosby, PhD
Managing Editor, Web — Christine Liu
Senior Editor, Cooking School — Mari Levine
Associate Editors, Web — Eric Grzymkowski
Roger Metcalf
Assistant Editors, Web — Jill Fisher
Charlotte Wilder
Senior Video Editor — Nick Dakoulas

Design Director — Amy Klee
Art Director — Julie Cote
Deputy Art Director — Susan Levin
Associate Art Director — Lindsey Timko
Deputy Art Director, Marketing — Jennifer Cox
Associate Art Directors, Marketing — Melenie Gryboski
Mariah Tarvainen
Designer, Marketing — Judy Blomquist
Staff Photographer — Daniel J. van Ackere
Photo Editor — Steve Klise

Vice President, Marketing — David Mack
Circulation Director — Doug Wicinski
Circulation & Fulfillment Manager — Carrie Fethe
Partnership Marketing Manager — Pamela Putprush
Marketing Assistant — Marina Tomao

VP, Technology, Product Development — Barry Kelly
Director, Project Management — Alice Carpenter
Production & Traffic Coordinator — Britt Dresser
Development Manager — Mike Serio

Chief Operating Officer — Rob Ristagno
Production Director — Guy Rochford
Workflow & Digital Asset Manager — Andrew Mannone
Senior Color & Imaging Specialist — Lauren Pettapiece
Production & Imaging Specialists — Heather Dube
Lauren Robbins
Director of Sponsorship Sales — Anne Traficante
Client Services Associate — Kate May
Sponsorship Sales Representative — Morgan Ryan
Customer Service Manager — Jacqueline Valerio
Customer Service Representatives — Jessica Haskin
Andrew Straaberg Finfrock

Retail Sales & Marketing Director — Emily Logan
Human Resources Director — Adele Shapiro
Publicity — Deborah Broide

THAI FRUIT Fruit in Thailand is as abundant as it is colorful and varied. GUAVA is prized when it's green and crunchy like an apple. Cracking open the pods of SWEET TAMARIND reveals sticky sweet-and-sour pulp with a texture similar to that of fruit leather. The liquid of YOUNG COCONUT is often sipped straight from the shell, while the tender meat inside is silky, rich, and milky-sweet. CUSTARD APPLE yields to slight pressure when ripe. Scoop out the soft flesh with a spoon; the hard black seeds are inedible. Eye-catching DRAGON FRUIT is all flair and little flavor; avoid eating the bitter magenta skin. Hairy RAMBUTAN looks intimidating, but its top half easily peels away; chew the juicy, gummy fruit from around the seed. GREEN PAPAYA is the immature version of the familiar ripe orange fruit. MANGOSTEEN segments are juicy, floral, and sweet.

COVER (Lemons): Robert Papp; **BACK COVER** (Thai Fruit): John Burgoyne

RECIPES THAT WORK®

America's Test Kitchen is a very real 2,500-square-foot kitchen located just outside Boston. It is the home of *Cook's Country* and *Cook's Illustrated* magazines and the workday destination of more than three dozen test cooks, editors, and cookware specialists. Our mission is to test recipes until we understand how and why they work and arrive at the best version. We also test kitchen equipment and supermarket ingredients in search of products that offer the best value and performance. You can watch us work by tuning in to *Cook's Country from America's Test Kitchen* (CooksCountry.com) and *America's Test Kitchen* (AmericasTestKitchen.com) on public television.

A LICK OF COMMON SENSE

Folks used to have common sense. They didn't plant their potatoes too close together. They trained a new rabbit dog while the old one was still young enough to hunt. They parked their pickups facing toward home when logging, so they could get out of the woods quickly in case of an accident. They made hay when the sun was shining. They split and stacked wood in early summer, not early fall. They called in the cows after opening the barn doors. And they would never drive up an icy dirt road in winter without thinking long and hard about how they were going to get back home.

They also didn't spend what they didn't have. They were never tempted to see what lay on the other side of the hill. They didn't start to run if it rained. In fact, I've never seen a Vermonter run for anything. They just figure that whatever it is, they'll eventually catch up with it.

To a Vermonter, or any country person, common sense is what keeps you alive. Liars and cheats may not have been welcome, but you wouldn't tolerate a man without common sense; he would most likely get you killed. A man who was not dependable might shoot another man's dog when rabbit hunting. (Tom once hunted with a man who did just that and wrapped the offender's 12-gauge around a maple. The dog recovered.) And you would be careless if you asked him to help out in the sugarhouse;

he would be likely to burn your front pan every year. He might also siphon the diesel fuel out of your tractor, jack a deer off your land, or run off with your wife.

Common sense is just another way of saying you learn from your mistakes. Unfortunately, some people, and most animals, don't. Take a horse. Some will shy away from a puddle of water in the road every time—they keep thinking that it might be 10 feet deep. Chickens don't bother to look up at the sky, and that's why they make a good source of protein for red-tailed hawks. And how many times will a dog chase a skunk?

When I was young, I didn't learn from experience; I just kept trying. I'd go fishing in the middle of the day when the suckers in the Battenkill were easy to see but uninterested in feeding. I'd put up a tree stand without knowing whether a deer would ever walk by it. And I would go hiking in strange woods without a compass, a flashlight, or something warm in case I had to stay out all night.

Now that I am older, I am more likely to think about what happened the last time I tried to mow that wet corner of the lower field or let the International 404—the one with the broken

Christopher Kimball

emergency brake—idle on the top of a hill. There is a sweet spot there somewhere, halfway between lessons learned and adventure. It's the sense to know when to pack your bags and when to double down; when to speak up and when to shut up; when to read the signs and when to ignore them.

A few weeks ago, I had lunch with my 23-year-old, Caroline, who lives in Vermont. She is finishing up college after a two-year hiatus and her heart is on the farm: raising rabbits, pressing cider, growing vegetables, spinning wool—a poster child for *The Whole Earth Catalog*. I was giving her career advice, helping, I thought, to better frame the life choices that she will soon confront. Unexpectedly, she started giving *me* advice, and for the first time in my life, I listened. She pointed out that when I ran, I should have walked; when I stood my ground, I should have moved on.

Caroline finished. I thought for a bit and said, "Well, at least I don't mind making a fool of myself." She laughed and replied, "Yes, Dad, that's why we love you."

That's the problem with some people: They don't have a lick of common sense.

FOR INQUIRIES, ORDERS, OR MORE INFORMATION

CooksIllustrated.com
At CooksIllustrated.com, you can order books and subscriptions, sign up for our free e-newsletter, or renew your magazine subscription. Join the website and gain access to 21 years of *Cook's Illustrated* recipes, equipment tests, and ingredient tastings, as well as companion videos for every recipe in this issue.

COOKBOOKS
We sell more than 50 cookbooks by the editors of *Cook's Illustrated*, including *The Cook's Illustrated Cookbook* and *The Science of Good Cooking*. To order, visit our bookstore at CooksIllustrated.com/bookstore.

COOK'S ILLUSTRATED MAGAZINE
Cook's Illustrated magazine (ISSN 1068-2821), number 126, is published bimonthly by Boston Common Press Limited Partnership, 17 Station St., Brookline, MA 02445. Copyright 2014 Boston Common Press Limited Partnership. Periodicals postage paid at Boston, MA, and additional mailing offices, USPS #012487. Publications Mail Agreement No. 40020778. Return undeliverable Canadian addresses to P.O. Box 875, Station A, Windsor, ON N9A 6P2. POSTMASTER: Send address changes to *Cook's Illustrated*, P.O. Box 6018, Harlan, IA 51593-1518. For subscription and gift subscription orders, subscription inquiries, or change of address notices, visit AmericasTestKitchen.com/support, call 800-526-8442 in the U.S. or 515-248-7684 from outside the U.S., or write to us at *Cook's Illustrated*, P.O. 6018, Harlan, IA 51593-1518.

FOR LIST RENTAL INFORMATION Contact Specialists Marketing Services, Inc., 777 Terrace Ave., 4th Floor, Hasbrouck Heights, NJ 07604; phone: 201-865-5800.
EDITORIAL OFFICE 17 Station St., Brookline, MA 02445; phone: 617-232-1000; fax: 617-232-1572. For subscription inquiries, visit AmericasTestKitchen.com/support or call 800-526-8442.

NOTES FROM READERS

⇒ BY ANDREA GEARY, LAN LAM & SARAH MULLINS ⇐

The Skinny on Skinny Avocados

I recently heard someone mention "skinny" avocados. Does such a thing really exist?

BECKY FRAZIER
CHAPEL HILL, N.C.

➤Yes, in fact, it does. Florida avocados are sometimes referred to as skinny avocados (and are actually labeled SlimCados by one producer). Florida avocados' fat by weight can be as little as half of that of common Hass avocados, which are grown primarily in California. You can tell the difference between them at first sight. On average, Florida avocados are 2.5 times the size of a typical Hass, with a shape similar to that of a papaya and a smooth, bright-green exterior. Besides being smaller, Hass avocados have a wrinkly skin that turns dark greenish black when ripe. We compared them three ways: plain, in guacamole, and in our recipe for Avocado Salad with Mango and Jícama (September/October 2012). Tasters noted that the plain Florida avocados were more watery, with a milder, more fruity flavor. In guacamole, they tasted more washed-out than the Hass. Since the Florida avocados have roughly six times the sugar of Hass avocados by weight, it's not surprising that tasters also found the Florida samples sweeter. Bottom line? We're sticking with nutty, buttery Hass avocados for guacamole, but the skinny variety is fine in salads or other dishes where a fresh, mild fruit flavor is desired. –S.M.

MORE FRUITY, LESS FATTY
"Skinny" avocados are fine in salads but a no-go for guacamole.

Going Dotty

Why do double-crust fruit pie recipes call for dotting the top of the filling with butter?

DONNA SMITH
GREYCLIFF, MONT.

➤Some say that scattering small bits of butter over a fruit filling keeps the juices from bubbling over in the same way that adding a bit of fat to simmering jam keeps it from foaming up in the preserving pan. The theory is that the fat disrupts the formation of bubbles on the surface of the viscous fruit mixture. Others claim that the butter simply enriches the flavor and texture of the pie filling.

To see which of these theories might be true, we baked six particularly juicy double-crust fruit pies—two each of blueberry, strawberry-rhubarb, and cherry—and dotted the filling of one of each pair with 2 tablespoons of butter. The butter neither encouraged nor hindered boilovers: Both the plain and the butter-dotted strawberry-rhubarb pies overflowed, but none of the blueberry and cherry pies did. As far as flavor and texture, tasters could not consistently identify which pies had added fat.

Our conclusion? If your favorite family recipe calls for dotting the filling with butter, you can certainly continue to do so out of deference to tradition, but it probably won't have much of an effect. –A.G.

Best Way to Save Leftover Wine

You have suggested freezing leftover wine in ice cube trays to use later in pan sauces, but is freezing a good way to store it for drinking?

MARY HOYLE
LITTLE ROCK, ARK.

➤To answer your question, we tried freezing Sauvignon Blanc, Pinot Noir, and Cabernet Sauvignon. We poured each of these wines into Mason jars, leaving just ¾ inch of space between the wine and the top of the jar. After one week, we thawed and compared each one against week-old samples that we had stored in the refrigerator, sealed the same way in Mason jars. All the samples tasted flat and less vibrant compared with freshly opened bottles of the same wines—but the previously frozen samples seemed to have even less flavor than the refrigerated wines. Furthermore, we noticed something we hadn't in the past when freezing wine for pan sauces: There was a layer of sediment at the bottom of the jar of each frozen sample. It turns out that the freeze/thaw process causes tannins, polyphenols, and other aromatic compounds in the wine to form crystals that fall out of solution. We found that heating reintegrates these compounds—fine if you are making a pan sauce, but obviously not an option for wine that you intend to drink.

To store wine (both red and white) for drinking, your best bet is to keep it in the refrigerator in an airtight container with as little air space as possible at the top and for no more than two or three days. Minimizing air space will limit the wine's exposure to oxygen and its dulling effect on flavor, while the refrigerator will slow what oxidation does occur. Besides using a Mason jar, we also recommend pouring leftovers into an empty wine half bottle or resealing the bottle with a vacuum wine sealer (our favorite is the VacuVin Vacuum Wine Saver, $14.99). –L.L.

Caffeine Content of Coffee

I recently switched from dark to light roast coffee. Does one have more caffeine than the other?

MICHAEL HENDERSON
HONOLULU, HAWAII

➤Coffee beans are roasted to different degrees to produce specific flavors, but whether the process affects caffeine level is a question many of us in the test kitchen have also had. We rounded up a bag of green coffee beans and a home coffee roaster and then brought half of the beans to a classic light roast and the rest to a dark roast. After grinding the batches separately in a burr grinder, we brewed two pots of coffee, using the same volume of ground coffee per batch (½ cup per 3½ cups of water), and sent both to a lab for testing. When the results came back, we learned that the light roast had much more caffeine than the dark roast—60 percent more in this particular case. Perplexed, we decided to see what would happen if we measured the ground coffee by weight instead. We made two more pots to send to the lab, measuring out 1½ ounces of ground coffee per 3½ cups of water. As we added ground coffee to the scale, we noticed that it took 2½ more tablespoons of dark roast than light roast to reach 1½ ounces. Nevertheless, when the results came back, we saw that both pots had virtually the same amount of caffeine.

It turns out that as the beans roast, they lose water and also puff up slightly—and the longer the roast time the more pronounced these effects. Dark roast beans will thus weigh less (and be slightly larger) than light roast beans. When the ground beans are measured by volume, the light roast particles will be denser, weigh more, and contain more caffeine than the dark grinds, producing a more caffeinated brew.

In sum: The only way to ensure that you're getting the same amount of caffeine with different roasts (all other variables being equal) is to weigh coffee. If you measure by volume, you'll end up with more buzz with a light roast than with a dark roast. –A.G.

LIGHT ROAST = HEAVY CAFFEINE
Because light roast coffee is roasted for less time, it's denser and heavier than dark roast. As a result, each particle of ground light roast contains more caffeine than a particle of ground dark roast. When equal volumes are measured, the light roast will thus pack more caffeine.

Black Walnuts

How do black walnuts compare with regular walnuts?

MARY COSTA
SAN DIEGO, CALIF.

➤ Not long ago, black walnuts were available only via mail order. But Diamond has recently started offering this cousin of the more familiar English walnut in supermarkets.

We sampled multiple bags of Diamond black walnuts out of hand and in cookies. Tasters had a mixed reaction to the nuts when eating them plain. Some described the nuts as "grassy" and "floral," while others found them unpleasantly bitter—even questioning whether the nuts were rancid. But a taster who grew up with a black walnut tree in his neighborhood assured us that the strong, even bitter flavor of the Diamond nuts was spot-on. The black walnuts were more likable in shortbread, where their strong taste complemented the buttery richness of the cookie.

In sum: Black walnuts are expensive ($1.55 per ounce versus $0.69 per ounce for English walnuts), probably because their tough outer hulls are extremely difficult to crack. And note that their unique flavor is not for everyone. We recommend that you sample a few before mixing them into a recipe. –A.G.

A Handy Buttermilk Substitute

I've tried adding lemon juice or vinegar to regular milk to approximate buttermilk for pancakes, but I never like how the pancakes taste. Are there any other options?

JAMES MORA
SAN FRANCISCO, CALIF.

➤ The acid in buttermilk helps baking soda do its job in recipes like biscuits and pancakes. To substitute regular milk in those recipes, the most common approach is to stir an acid like lemon juice or vinegar into it first. Though lemon is usually an acceptable flavor, we're with you on the questionable appeal of vinegar pancakes.

In researching alternatives, we discovered one that we'd never considered: cream of tartar, an acid with a less noticeable flavor that's often used to stabilize whipped egg whites.

When we used a mixture of cream of tartar and regular milk (1½ teaspoons of cream of tartar for each cup of milk), our biscuits and pancakes came out just as lofty and light as those made with buttermilk, with no off-flavors. But there was one problem: Unlike lemon juice and vinegar, powdery cream of tartar can clump when you stir it into milk. The solution? Whisk the cream of tartar into your dry ingredients instead.

UNOBTRUSIVE
Unlike vinegar or lemon juice, cream of tartar will acidify milk without adding flavor.

When you don't have buttermilk on hand (and the tartness of regular milk mixed with lemon juice isn't ideal), cream of tartar is an excellent alternative. –A.G.

Nut Butter Alternatives

Which makes a better nut-free substitute for peanut butter in baking and otherwise: sunflower seed butter or soy nut butter?

KATHRYN STURGES
ST. PAUL, MINN.

➤ To answer your question, we spread both alternative butters on bread, subbed them for peanut butter in cookies, and made some dipping sauces for crudités.

The soy nut butter was, in a word, terrible. Though its color made it look like a dead ringer for peanut butter, its flavor and texture bore no resemblance. It tasted too strongly of, well, soy when spread over bread, but its flavor then seemed to disappear entirely in recipes, such that the sugar in the cookies and the spices in the dipping sauce completely took over. Worse was its texture, which tasters described as chalky, gritty, and "mouth-coating in an extremely unpleasant way," both on bread and in sauce.

On the other hand, the sunflower seed butter was surprisingly good, especially to those of us who like sunflower seeds. In all three applications it boasted the pleasantly vegetal, slightly nutty flavor characteristic of the seeds, and though runny, its texture was still perfectly acceptable. We think it makes an interesting alternative to peanut butter, even if you aren't avoiding nuts. Like peanut butter, it comes in both smooth and crunchy varieties. –A.G.

Leaving in Celery Leaves

Can celery leaves be substituted for the stalks in recipes?

DOUG FITZPATRICK
FORT WORTH, TEXAS

➤ To get our bearings, we tasted the leaves on their own and found that they were much more intense and bitter-tasting than the stalks, especially the darker exterior ones. Next we made two batches of chicken salad, using minced stalks in one and an equal volume of minced leaves in the other. We preferred the crunch and sweeter flavor of the salad made with stalks; the leaves turned the salad too bitter. Finally, we made two batches of chicken stock, one with chopped stalks and the other with chopped leaves. Though cooking mellowed the flavor of the leaves somewhat, they still tasted too strong, leaving the soup with a slight medicinal taste. In sum, we don't recommend swapping in celery leaves for stalks. Treat celery leaves as you would an herb: Use a small amount to add complexity to soups and salads. –L.L.

SEND US YOUR QUESTIONS We will provide a complimentary one-year subscription for each letter we print. Send your inquiry, name, address, and daytime telephone number to Notes from Readers, *Cook's Illustrated*, P.O. Box 470589, Brookline, MA 02447, or to NotesFromReaders@ AmericasTestKitchen.com.

What Is It?

I couldn't resist buying this item tagged "Cooking Pin" at a flea market. Do you know what it's used for?

KATIE WIRTZ
JAMAICA PLAIN, MASS.

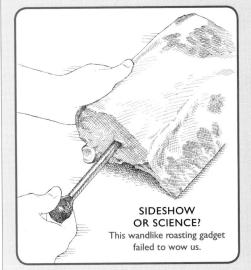

SIDESHOW OR SCIENCE?
This wandlike roasting gadget failed to wow us.

The manual of the Master Chef Cooking Pin makes a bold claim: Inserting the 14-inch-long metal rod through nearly any cut of meat will slash its cooking time by 50 percent. (From the looks of the manual, our guess is that this product was produced in the 1960s, but we have been unable to pinpoint its exact date of manufacture.) Per the manual, the "space age development" quickly conducts the oven's heat into the interior of the meat—a potential benefit as heat transfer usually happens only from the exterior in. We tested a pair of eye-round roasts and two half chickens, spearing the Cooking Pin through the center of one roast and both the thigh and breast of one chicken. We set the ovens to 325 degrees and kept our eyes on each one's internal temperature . . . and the clock. The roast and chicken with the instrument did cook more quickly, but only by 20 and 15 minutes, respectively, and impaling the meat left behind an unsightly gaping hole. And although we cooked the roast to medium-rare, we noticed an unattractive gray band around the spot where we had inserted the rod. The Cooking Pin is one gadget that we won't be stocking in our kitchen. –Shannon Friedmann Hatch

Quick Tips

⊰ COMPILED BY SHANNON FRIEDMANN HATCH ⊱

Preventing a Sticky Situation

Spraying plastic wrap with vegetable oil spray before using it to cover a bowl of rising dough is sometimes necessary to prevent sticking during proofing. But keeping the plastic from clinging to itself during spraying is a challenge. Jenny Johnson of River Falls, Wis., came up with this solution.

1. Drape the plastic over the bowl and spray it.

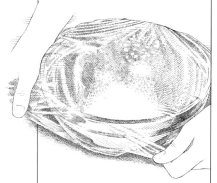

2. Quickly flip the plastic over so the sprayed side is facing the dough. Cover the bowl with the plastic.

A Peeling Idea

Hard-cooked eggs can be difficult to peel, especially when the shell shatters into tiny pieces. Judy Puckett of Seattle, Wash., uses this technique.

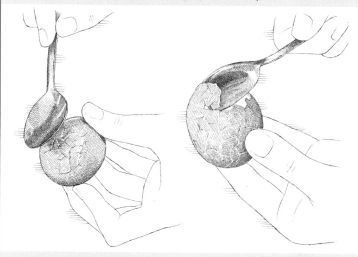

1. Tap the surface of a cooked egg with the back of a teaspoon to crack the shell.

2. Slip the edge of the spoon under the shell at the egg's base to loosen it. Then continue to move along the curve of the egg to remove the rest of the shell.

(Less) Time to Come Clean

With this trick, Kristin Cable of Las Vegas, Nev., has shortened her scrub time after kneading sticky dough.

1. Standing over the sink, "wash" your hands with a handful of flour instead of soap and water.

2. Rinse your hands with cold water. (Hot water causes the starches in the dough to gelatinize, thus requiring more scrubbing.)

Cupcake Topper

Cupcakes topped with swirled frosting may look like the work of a pro, but Robert Casillas of Los Angeles, Calif., has found a way to bring the method home.

1. Spoon a line of colored frosting down the center of a large piece of plastic wrap and then spoon a second color alongside it. Fold the plastic in half lengthwise.

2. Roll the frosting into a log, twisting and knotting one end of the plastic.

3. Insert the open end of the log into a pastry bag and pull the plastic tightly through the piping tip. Snip off the excess plastic.

4. Pipe the frosting onto cupcakes as usual.

SEND US YOUR TIPS We will provide a complimentary one-year subscription for each tip we print. Send your tip, name, address, and daytime telephone number to Quick Tips, *Cook's Illustrated*, P.O. Box 470589, Brookline, MA 02447, or to QuickTips@AmericasTestKitchen.com.

ILLUSTRATION: JOHN BURGOYNE

Fixing a Test-y Problem

Dennise Whitley of Norway, Maine, trusts her cake testers to tell her when her cakes are done—but only if she can find the thin metal rods in her drawers. Now she sticks them into the holes of a dedicated salt-shaker, where they are in plain sight and close at hand.

Foolproofing the Egg Roll

Even the most careful cook has placed a raw egg on the counter, only to watch it roll off and crack on the floor. Tamiko Azuma of Gilbert, Ariz., prevents the falls with the help of a small piece of a rubber mat. Its tacky surface keeps the eggs in place.

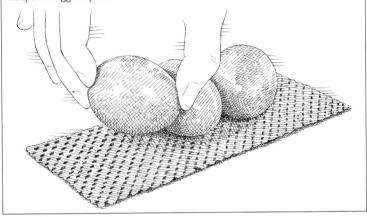

A Neat Trick for Straining Bacon Grease

Straining cooled bacon grease before saving it for future use helps avoid spoilage, but the potentially messy task often requires an extra set of hands. Sue Balcom of Mandan, N.D., has found a way to work alone: She sets a tea infuser over a Mason jar. Designed to rest in a mug, the infuser also sits securely on the jar's rim so that she can focus on careful pouring.

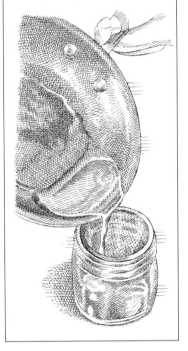

Racking Up Measuring Cups

Wendy Nicholls of San Francisco, Calif., has found the perfect way to store her metal measuring cups: on a magnetic knife strip. Not only are the cups easy to access but each measurement is also in view, as opposed to when the cups are nested together in a stack.

Measure for Measure

Always happy to have extra measuring spoons on hand, Craig Beach of Morgantown, W. Va., cleans and saves the plastic caps from cough syrup bottles and uses them to measure liquids. The caps, which hold 1 fluid ounce (the equivalent of 2 tablespoons), stack neatly for easy stowing.

Fuss-Free Polenta

To keep polenta from clumping, most recipes suggest pouring cornmeal in a thin stream into boiling water and whisking vigorously—a somewhat finicky process. But Ray Nazzai of Herndon, Va., has discovered that adding the cornmeal to cold water and stirring a bit to break up clumps before heating delivers the same creamy results. (The method works for coarse and fine cornmeals, as well as farina.)

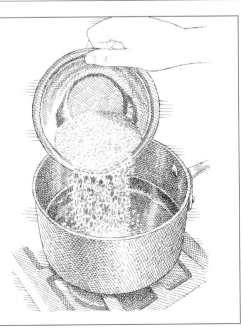

Homemade Bench Scraper

Bench scrapers make easy work of removing scraps of sticky dough from the counter or lifting chopped ingredients into a bowl or pan. Harry Lipman of Brooklyn, N.Y., found a way to fashion the tool from an old plastic cutting mat. After cleaning it well, he cut the flexible mat into 4 by 3-inch rectangles.

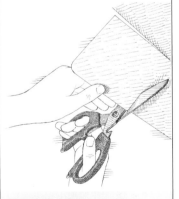

Ultimate Pan-Seared Chicken Breasts

The most effective approach to achieving chicken breasts with evenly golden, shatteringly crispy skin? Treat them like duck.

≫ BY ANDREW JANJIGIAN ≪

I'm always on the lookout for ways to get great skin on chicken. By that I mean skin that's paper-thin, deep golden brown, and so well crisped that it crackles when you take a bite. Such perfectly cooked skin, however, is actually a rarity. A good roast chicken may have patches of it, but the rotund shape of the bird means that uneven cooking is inevitable and that some of the skin will also cook up flabby and pale. And even on relatively flat chicken parts, there's the layer of fat beneath the skin to contend with: By the time it melts away during searing, the exterior often chars and the meat itself overcooks.

When I recently came across one of the best specimens of chicken I'd ever tasted, I had to figure out how to re-create it myself. The restaurant was Maialino (a Danny Meyer venture) in New York City, and the dish was Pollo alla Diavola. The tender meat and the tangy, spicy pickled cherry pepper sauce that was served with it had their own charms, but the chicken skin was incredible—a sheath so gorgeously bronzed and shatteringly crunchy that I'd swear it was deep-fried.

Our unique skin-crisping technique and bright pan sauce turn ho-hum pan-seared chicken breasts into a standout dinner for two.

Starting Small(er)

There were a number of hurdles to achieving the same chicken-skin nirvana at home, not the least of which was the cut of meat itself. At Maialino, the kitchen serves half of a chicken per person, removing all but the wing bones from the meat before searing it. For the sauce, the pickling liquid from the peppers is reduced and then used to deglaze the pan.

The point of all that butchery is to flatten out the bird so that its entire surface makes direct, even contact with the pan—a must for producing thoroughly rendered, deeply crisped skin. But since few home cooks can do that kind of knife work confidently and quickly, I decided to keep things simple and work with only breast meat, which would eliminate more than half of the butchering. Removing the breast bones required just a few quick strokes of a sharp knife (see "Boning a Split Chicken Breast," page 31). Moreover, switching from half chickens to split breasts made for more reasonable portions; the plate at Maialino is more than one person can possibly finish. I would serve a pair of breasts—enough for

two people—and keep things simple so that the dish would work as a weeknight meal.

Of course, the drawback to working with breast meat would be its tendency to overcook, particularly once I'd removed the bones—poor conductors of heat and, therefore, good insulators. My very basic initial cooking technique was placing the boned breasts skin side down in a hot, oiled skillet to crisp up their surface and then flipping the meat to let it color briefly on the other side. This gave me fairly crispy skin but meat that was dry and chalky. When I tried a slightly gentler approach, briefly pan-searing the chicken skin side down and then transferring the pan to the more even heat of a 450-degree oven until the breasts were cooked through, the meat was only somewhat more moist and tender. Clearly, some form of pretreatment was essential if I wanted the meat to be as succulent as the skin was crispy.

Brining was out, since it introduces additional water to the meat and inevitably leaves the skin slightly waterlogged. Salting would be the way to

go. Besides seasoning the meat deeply and helping it retain moisture as it cooks, salt would assist in drying out the skin. To further encourage the skin's dehydration (as well as the salt's penetration), I used one of the test kitchen's favorite techniques for chicken: poking holes in both the skin and meat with a sharp knife before applying the salt. (We have also had great success drying out the skin with a dusting of baking powder, but that trick requires an overnight stay in the fridge—too much to ask for a weeknight dish.)

Worth the Weight

Salting and slashing helped, but they got me only so far with the skin, which indicated that my simple searing technique needed further tweaking. Thus far, the best I'd accomplished was unevenly cooked skin, as I'd anticipated early on: patches that were gorgeously crispy and brown and adjacent patches that were inedibly pale and flabby. What's more, the skin tended to shrink away from the edges of the breast as it cooked, which, apart from the unsightly appearance, also caused the now-exposed meat to brown and turn dry and leathery in the process. Finally, the thin end of the breast still cooked up a bit dry by the time the thick end had fully cooked.

Evening out the thickness of the meat was easy: I simply pounded the thick end of the breast gently so that the entire piece cooked at the same rate. As for evening out the browning of the skin, I adapted a classic Italian technique that the chef at Maialino also uses: pinning the bird to the cooking surface with bricks. I figured that I could mimic that technique by weighing down the chicken breasts with a heavy Dutch oven. (Since I had no interest in transferring the weighty duo of pans to the oven, I'd switch to cooking the breasts entirely on the stovetop and see if I could manage without the oven's more even heat.) After 10 minutes over medium heat, I removed the pot and surveyed the chicken skin, which, for the most part, was far crispier than ever before and not at all shrunken. But maddeningly, pockets of fat persisted under the surface at the center and along the edges. And the meat? It was way overcooked now that the lean meat was pressed hard against the hot surface.

Amid my frustration, I had noticed something curious: When I removed the Dutch oven, a puff of steam arose from the pan—moisture from the chicken that had been trapped beneath the pot. That moisture was thwarting my skin-crisping efforts, so I wondered if the weight was necessary for the entire duration of the cooking time or if I could remove it partway through to prevent moisture buildup.

I prepared another batch, this time letting the breasts cook in the preheated oiled skillet under the pot for just 5 minutes before uncovering them. At this stage the skin was only just beginning to brown, and I feared that it might shrink without the weight, but I needn't have worried. As it continued to cook for another 2 to 4 minutes, the skin remained anchored to the pan, crisping up nicely without contracting in the least. Removing the pot early also allowed the meat to cook a bit more gently, as the heat that had been trapped around the chicken was released. But it wasn't quite gentle enough; dry meat still persisted.

The core problem—that it takes longer to render and crisp chicken skin than it does to cook the meat beneath it—had me feeling defeated until I realized a way to give the skin a head start: a "cold" pan. The idea wasn't my invention; it's a classic French technique for cooking duck breasts—the ultimate example of delicate meat covered with a layer of fatty skin. Putting the meat skin side down in the oiled pan before turning on the heat allows more time for the skin to render out its fat layer before the temperature of the meat reaches its doneness point. I hoped this approach would apply to chicken.

Initially, I thought I'd hit a roadblock: The breasts were sticking to the skillet—a nonissue when adding proteins to a hot pan, which usually prevents sticking. Fortunately, by the time the skin had rendered and fully crisped up, the breasts came away from the surface with just a gentle tug. Once the skin had achieved shattering crispiness, all it took was a few short minutes on the second side to finish cooking the meat.

Try a Little Tanginess

Chicken with skin this bronzed and brittle was tasty enough as is, but to pay homage to Maialino (and dress things up a bit), I set my sights on developing a few sauces.

My own rendition of Maialino's alla diavola sauce was nothing more than a reduction of pickled-pepper vinegar and chicken broth, thickened with a little flour and butter and garnished with a few chopped pickled peppers. Since it's the tanginess of that sauce that makes it the perfect accompaniment to the skin's ultrameaty flavor, I came up with a pair of variations on the same acid-based theme: lemon-rosemary and maple–sherry vinegar.

Satisfying my inner chicken skin perfectionist was gratifying in and of itself. But coming up with a quick and elegant way to dress up ordinary old chicken breasts? That was even better.

Secrets to Stunningly Crispy Skin

We did a little knife work and borrowed a pair of cooking techniques, one French and one Italian, to produce skin that's so crispy it crackles.

REMOVE BONE; FLATTEN
Boning and flattening the chicken ensures that it makes even contact with the pan's surface—a must for rendering the fat and crisping the skin. (For detailed directions, see "Boning a Split Chicken Breast," page 31.)

START "COLD"
Placing the chicken breasts skin side down in a "cold" (not preheated) skillet, a classic French technique for pan-searing duck breasts, gives the skin enough time to render its fat before the meat overcooks.

ADD WEIGHT
Using bricks to weigh down chicken so that every inch of skin stays flat and crisps up evenly is a common Italian technique. We achieved equally good results by pinning down the breasts with a Dutch oven.

CRISPY-SKINNED CHICKEN BREASTS WITH VINEGAR-PEPPER PAN SAUCE
SERVES 2

This recipe requires refrigerating the salted meat for at least 1 hour before cooking. Two 10- to 12-ounce chicken breasts are ideal, but three smaller ones can fit in the same pan; the skin will be slightly less crispy. A boning knife or sharp paring knife works best to remove the bones from the breasts. To maintain the crispy skin, spoon the sauce around, not over, the breasts when serving. For our free recipes for Crispy-Skinned Chicken Breasts with Lemon-Rosemary Pan Sauce and Crispy-Skinned Chicken Breasts with Maple–Sherry Vinegar Pan Sauce, go to CooksIllustrated.com/feb14.

Chicken
- 2 (10- to 12-ounce) bone-in split chicken breasts
  Kosher salt and pepper
- 2 tablespoons vegetable oil

Pan Sauce
- 1 shallot, minced
- 1 teaspoon all-purpose flour
- ½ cup chicken broth
- ¼ cup chopped pickled hot cherry peppers, plus ¼ cup brine
- 1 tablespoon unsalted butter, chilled
- 1 teaspoon minced fresh thyme
  Salt and pepper

1. FOR THE CHICKEN: Place 1 chicken breast, skin side down, on cutting board, with ribs facing away from knife hand. Run tip of knife between breastbone and meat, working from thick end of breast toward thin end. Angling blade slightly and following rib cage, repeat cutting motion several times to remove ribs and breastbone from breast. Find short remnant of wishbone along top edge of breast and run tip of knife along both sides of bone to separate it from meat. Remove tenderloin (reserve

for another use) and trim excess fat, taking care not to cut into skin. Repeat with second breast.

2. Using tip of paring knife, poke skin on each breast evenly 30 to 40 times. Turn breasts over and poke thickest half of each breast 5 to 6 times. Cover breasts with plastic wrap and pound thick ends gently with meat pounder until ½ inch thick. Evenly sprinkle each breast with ½ teaspoon kosher salt. Place breasts, skin side up, on wire rack set in rimmed baking sheet, cover loosely with plastic, and refrigerate for 1 hour or up to 8 hours.

3. Pat breasts dry with paper towels and sprinkle each breast with ¼ teaspoon pepper. Pour oil in 12-inch skillet and swirl to coat. Place breasts, skin side down, in oil and place skillet over medium heat. Place heavy skillet or Dutch oven on top of breasts. Cook breasts until skin is beginning to brown and meat is beginning to turn opaque along edges, 7 to 9 minutes.

4. Remove weight and continue to cook until skin is well browned and very crispy, 6 to 8 minutes. Flip breasts, reduce heat to medium-low, and cook until second side is lightly browned and meat registers 160 to 165 degrees, 2 to 3 minutes. Transfer breasts to individual plates and let rest while preparing pan sauce.

5. FOR THE PAN SAUCE: Pour off all but 2 teaspoons oil from skillet. Return skillet to medium heat and add shallot; cook, stirring occasionally, until shallot is softened, about 2 minutes. Add flour and cook, stirring constantly, for 30 seconds. Increase heat to medium-high, add broth and brine, and bring to simmer, scraping up any browned bits. Simmer until thickened, 2 to 3 minutes. Stir in any accumulated chicken juices; return to simmer and cook for 30 seconds. Remove skillet from heat and whisk in peppers, butter, and thyme; season with salt and pepper to taste. Spoon sauce around breasts and serve.

See How to Crisp It
Video available FREE for 4 months at CooksIllustrated.com/feb14

Bringing Back Cheese Soufflé

The first thing to know about cheese soufflé is that while it should *look* dramatic, making it shouldn't be. (Don't worry: It won't fall.)

⇒ BY ANDREW JANJIGIAN ⇐

Soufflé *au fromage*—ethereally light eggs and nutty, tangy Gruyère cheese combined and lifted to startlingly tall heights—can't help but impress. So why don't many people make it anymore?

Maybe because most people assume that it's a dish fraught with disaster, ready to collapse with the slightest disturbance. Classic French cookbooks intimidate with pages upon pages devoted to how to perfectly whip and fold in egg whites and precisely time the dish for your guests ("A soufflé can be waited for, but it can never wait," declares *La Bonne Cuisine de Madame E. Saint-Ange: The Original Companion for French Home Cooking*). Then there's the matter of fashioning a parchment collar around the dish to contain the batter as it rises, not to mention the mystery of determining when the soufflé is done—more concerns that make soufflé seem like a dish best left to the experts.

As I tried out a few recipes, I realized the truth: Soufflés are neither complicated nor finicky. In fact, a cheese soufflé is nothing more than a sauce that's transformed into dinner through the addition of egg whites and air. The sauce, typically a béchamel made of milk thickened with a paste (or roux) of equal parts butter and flour, provides the soufflé with stability. Grated cheese is added for flavor, and egg yolks introduce richness and a silky texture. Stop here and you'd have something that might dress up steamed broccoli or poached chicken. But fold in stiffly beaten egg whites and the dish stands on

Adding lots of Gruyère and Parmesan, and beating, not folding, the whites into the base mixture, delivers a soufflé that's light yet substantial.

its own, literally and figuratively. After this batter is poured into a round, straight-sided soufflé dish and baked in a hot oven, the water in the mixture rapidly turns to steam, inflating air bubbles and raising the soufflé to high heights.

But that doesn't mean all recipes for soufflés lead to optimal results. Some of the recipes I tried turned out

soufflés that were overly heavy and dense; others were so light and ethereal that they were hardly substantial enough for a meal. Still others had negligible cheese flavor. I wanted a cheese soufflé boasting not only stature but also enough substance to serve as a main course. It needed a balanced but distinctive cheese flavor and contrasting textures in the form of a crispy, nicely browned crust and a moist, almost custardy center.

The Big Cheese

I cobbled together a basic recipe—six eggs, 6 tablespoons each of butter and flour, a little more than a cup of milk, and 4 ounces of grated Gruyère (the classic choice)—and got down to testing. The resulting soufflé wasn't terrible, but it had a long way to go. It didn't have loads of cheese flavor; its texture was closer to that of a quiche than that of a soufflé; and it rose only about an inch or so above the lip of the dish.

I wondered if the béchamel might be the cause of multiple problems. Flour has a tendency to mute flavors, and its thickening power, while essential to providing the soufflé with stability, can also weigh things down. When I dialed back the amounts of butter and flour to 4 tablespoons each (anything less than that and the soufflé verged on soupy), the flavor of the cheese came through more clearly and the texture lightened up. This gave me enough wiggle room to add more cheese. But beyond a certain point (6 ounces) the texture began to suffer and my soufflé turned out squat. In order to increase the cheese flavor without causing damage, I turned to more intensely flavored yet feathery grated Parmesan. Adding 5 tablespoons, along with the 6 ounces of Gruyère, gave the soufflé the cheese flavor that it needed without the weight. I also dusted the sides and bottom of the soufflé dish and the top of the batter with a few more tablespoons of Parmesan.

As for baking temperature, recipes that I consulted varied from 300 degrees to 400 degrees. I wanted a soufflé with a crispy mahogany crust; nicely set edges; and a moist, barely set core. When the soufflé was cooked at too-low temperatures, the crust resisted browning and the interior set too evenly. Excessively high temperatures, on the other hand, cooked it too fast: When the crust was nicely browned, the interior

Soufflé Myths Debunked

MYTH: The soufflé will collapse from loud noises or sudden movements.
REALITY: Steam will keep a hot soufflé fully inflated. No loud noise or slamming of the oven door can change that.

MYTH: The egg whites must be gently folded into the base.
REALITY: Egg whites whipped to stiff peaks will have ample structure to handle aggressive beating, even in a stand mixer.

MYTH: Prodding to check doneness will make it collapse.
REALITY: A soufflé is not a balloon; it's a matrix of very fine bubbles. No tool can pop enough of them to cause it to fall.

MYTH: You can't make a fallen soufflé rise again.
REALITY: Yes, your soufflé will fall after it's been out of the oven for about 5 minutes. But returning it to a 350-degree oven will convert the water back into steam and reinflate it (it will lose about ½ inch of height).

FALLEN FROM GRACE

RETURNED TO GLORY

was still soupy. I found that 350 degrees worked best. Another key discovery: Rather than deal with the fussy step of greasing a parchment collar and securing it around the lip of the dish to create a taller soufflé and also prevent overflow as the soufflé rises, I simply left about 1 inch of headspace between the top of the batter and the lip of the dish. (For more on this topic, see "Avoid a Soufflé Meltdown," page 31.)

Knowing when the soufflé was done turned out to be very straightforward. Some recipes tell you that it should be "slightly jiggly" at the center, while others say to insert a skewer (or knitting needle) and look for a moist but not wet batter. I liked using two spoons to pry open the middle of the soufflé to check that it looked barely set but not soupy. Even better, though, was using an instant-read thermometer. I found that when inserted into the soufflé's core, the thermometer should reach about 170 degrees.

Peak Conditioning

I was making progress, but the interior consistency of the soufflé was still not exactly where I wanted it to be. The soufflé was rising nearly 3 inches when cooked, making it a bit too light and delicate. I already knew that more cheese wasn't the answer (plus I already had the cheese flavor down), so what could I do to create a soufflé that was light but not featherweight?

Up until now I'd been following soufflé convention and whipping the egg whites to stiff peaks in order to create maximum volume. I wondered whether I could dial back the lightness by not working them so hard. For my next test, I whipped the whites to soft peaks instead. While the resulting soufflé had a denser consistency, it was a little too dense and squat. Here was my Goldilocks moment: Stiff peaks provided a bit too much lift and airiness, and soft peaks provided not quite enough. "Medium" peaks would probably be perfect—if I only knew of a way to call for such a thing. Soft peaks retain some shape but droop slowly from the end of a whisk, while stiff peaks are glossy and firm and hold their shape entirely. But the midway point between the two is a nebulous thing; there just isn't a good visual indicator for such a stage.

But maybe there was another way. Most recipes insist that you fold the whites gradually and gently into the cheese-béchamel mixture to ensure that the soufflé rises properly. I wondered if that was really important. Next time around, I whipped the whites to stiff peaks and then stirred them vigorously rather than folded them into the cheese mixture. I didn't hold back: I hoped that I could break down some of the structure by whipping out just enough air from the whites. I worried that such manhandling might be overkill and ruin the soufflé completely, but it seemed to have plenty of volume going into the oven. And it baked up better than ever. The soufflé had risen beautifully (if not quite as high as before), and its consistency was perfect: light and airy but with the extra heft that it had been missing. I did one more test to see if I could streamline things even further and found that I could simply whip the cheese mixture into the whites right in the stand mixer.

Before wrapping things up, I wanted to find out if other cheeses could stand in for the Gruyère. Softer or milder cheeses, like goat, blue, and mild cheddar, were not good alternatives, since they either added too much moisture to the soufflé or were simply not potent enough. But cheeses with a similar depth of flavor, consistency, and meltability, like Comté, sharp cheddar, and gouda, made equally great-tasting soufflés.

At last, I had a richly flavored, entrée-worthy cheese soufflé that was as easy to prepare as it was impressive.

Serve this soufflé with a green salad for a light dinner. Comté, sharp cheddar, or gouda cheese can be substituted for the Gruyère. To prevent the soufflé from overflowing the soufflé dish, leave at least 1 inch of space between the top of the batter and the rim of the dish; any excess batter should be discarded. The most foolproof way to test for doneness is with an instant-read thermometer. To judge doneness without an instant-read thermometer, use two large spoons to pry open the soufflé so that you can peer inside it; the center should appear thick and creamy but not soupy.

- 1 ounce Parmesan cheese, grated (½ cup)
- ¼ cup (1¼ ounces) all-purpose flour
- ¼ teaspoon paprika
- ¼ teaspoon salt
- ⅛ teaspoon cayenne pepper
- ⅛ teaspoon white pepper
  - Pinch ground nutmeg
- 4 tablespoons unsalted butter
- 1⅓ cups whole milk
- 6 ounces Gruyère cheese, shredded (1½ cups)
- 6 large eggs, separated
- 2 teaspoons minced fresh parsley
- ¼ teaspoon cream of tartar

1. Adjust oven rack to middle position and heat oven to 350 degrees. Spray 8-inch round (2-quart) soufflé dish with vegetable oil spray, then sprinkle with 2 tablespoons Parmesan.

2. Combine flour, paprika, salt, cayenne, white pepper, and nutmeg in bowl. Melt butter in small saucepan over medium heat. Stir in flour mixture and cook for 1 minute. Slowly whisk in milk and bring to simmer. Cook, whisking constantly, until mixture is thickened and smooth, about 1 minute. Remove pan from heat and whisk in Gruyère and 5 tablespoons Parmesan until melted and smooth. Let cool for 10 minutes, then whisk in egg yolks and 1½ teaspoons parsley.

3. Using stand mixer fitted with whisk, whip egg whites and cream of tartar on medium-low speed until foamy, about 1 minute. Increase speed to medium-high and whip until stiff peaks form, 3 to 4 minutes. Add cheese mixture and continue to whip until fully combined, about 15 seconds.

4. Pour mixture into prepared dish and sprinkle with remaining 1 tablespoon Parmesan. Bake until risen above rim, top is deep golden brown, and interior registers 170 degrees, 30 to 35 minutes. Sprinkle with remaining ½ teaspoon parsley and serve immediately.

Watch Andrew Make Magic
Video available FREE for 4 months at CooksIllustrated.com/feb14

Pressure-Cooker Pot Roast, Perfected

Pressure cookers are back and better than ever. Too bad one of the appliance's most classic dishes hasn't seen the same improvement.

> BY DAN SOUZA

Recently, pressure cooking has made a comeback on the culinary scene. Sales of pressure cookers have grown by double digits in the past three years. More than 3 million were sold between July 2012 and July 2013 alone. Home cooks are rediscovering that with the pressure cooker's superheated environment, meals with deep, slow-cooked flavor that would normally take a full afternoon to cook can be transformed into weeknight options.

Surprisingly, though, one of the most classic recipes to make in a pressure cooker, pot roast, isn't nearly as impressive as the appliance itself. At least that's what I found when I set out to make pot roast in the test kitchen. I tried a half-dozen different recipes. They all pretty much followed the same approach: Brown the roast, add liquid and vegetables, lock on the lid, bring to high pressure, and cook for the prescribed amount of time. The results were also the same: While the meat turned tender, it was also torn apart at the edges; the gravy was watery; and the vegetables were mushy.

Why would making pot roast in a pressure cooker be so likely to fail? I came up with a few good reasons. For one, the pot traps steam (this is how pressure is built), so sauces don't reduce and concentrate the way that they would in an open pot. Second, a pressure cooker doesn't lend itself to the staggered addition of ingredients. If you want to add something to the pot, you must depressurize before you can remove the lid, and then you have to bring the pot back up to pressure before continuing. But even hardy vegetables like carrots and potatoes can't handle the cooking time required to tenderize the meat. And finally, since a pressurized pot is a closed environment, there is no way to monitor cooking by sight or smell—timing is everything. With these issues in mind, I set about getting supertender, deeply flavorful pot roast on the table in half of its normal 4-hour cooking time.

Separating the roast at its natural seam allows us to eliminate interior fat. We then tie the roasts so that they cook evenly.

Meat and Potatoes

Putting one of our established pot roast practices into action, I grabbed a 4-pound chuck-eye roast (the test kitchen's preferred cut for pot roast) and split it at its natural seam into two pieces. This allowed me to carve out the knobs of fat that would otherwise mar the interior slices. And more important, it would further speed cooking by creating two smaller roasts. While most of the recipes that I'd tried in my initial tests called for browning the meat on the stovetop, a few didn't. There was no noticeable flavor difference between these two approaches, so I decided to skip this messy step. I simply seasoned both pieces of meat with salt and pepper and then set them aside while I built my cooking liquid. I melted some butter in the pot and then stirred in thickly sliced onion and celery. After adding 2 cups of beef broth (about two-thirds of what a traditional recipe would use to account for the lack of reduction), I turned my attention to the main challenge: cooking the vegetables alongside the meat.

I asked our science editor if there are any tricks for keeping vegetables from falling apart during extended cooking, and it turns out that there is one. Certain vegetables (and fruits), including potatoes and carrots, contain an enzyme that enables them to remain firm during long cooking if given a low-temperature "pretreatment" first. When these vegetables are heated to between 130 and 140 degrees and held there for about 30 minutes, the enzyme alters the pectin in their cell walls, allowing it to cross-link with calcium ions to form a more durable structure. I experimented with the approach, bringing carrots and potatoes and a couple of quarts of water to 140 degrees and holding them there before draining the vegetables and proceeding with the recipe.

The results were impressive. Even after the hour of pressurized cooking that the meat required to turn tender, the carrots were intact and the potatoes were firm. But this pretreatment step was fussy and time-consuming. More important, I found after subsequent tests that this technique worked well only in some models of pressure cookers. When we tested pressure cookers last year, we found that the internal temperature of pots at high pressure varied as much as 23 degrees from one brand to the next (see "Problems Under Pressure"). This isn't a big problem for long-cooked roasts since the window of doneness is relatively wide, but it makes consistent timing nearly impossible for vegetables.

The other option was to cook the roasts on their own; depressurize the pot and set them aside; and then add the vegetables, repressurize, and cook until done. But this would add time—and hassle—to the process.

I resolved to go back to square one. I ditched the potatoes and, taking a cue from one of our traditional pot roast recipes, embraced the mushy carrots. After cooking the roast and a sliced carrot together, I pureed the cooking liquid and carrot in a blender into a thickened sauce. This eliminated my vegetable woes, and it also improved the body and flavor of the sauce. That said, the sauce still had a long way to go.

Browning Points

To help concentrate the flavor of the sauce, my next move was to cut back the amount of broth that I was adding to the pot to a single cup and to reduce

PHOTOGRAPHY: CARL TREMBLAY

A Great Pot Roast for Every Cooker

Most recipes don't take into account that internal pressure and evaporation loss vary from one pressure cooker to the next. For a pot roast recipe that works in every cooker, here's what we do.

➤ DITCH POTATOES; PUREE CARROT

Even when we used our best test kitchen tricks, getting the vegetables to cook consistently in different cookers was nearly impossible. So we add only carrot to the pot with the meat and then puree it with the final cooking liquid for a sauce with much-improved body and flavor.

➤ USE NATURAL RELEASE

Letting the pressure drop naturally is gentler than quick-releasing the pressure, which can cause the tender meat to fray. But pots don't naturally release pressure at the same rate, and the food continues to cook as the pressure drops. To ensure consistent results, we let the pressure naturally drop for 10 minutes and then quick-release any remaining pressure (at this point, it won't be enough pressure to do harm to the roasts).

➤ FINISH SAUCE ON STOVETOP

The amount of steam vented during cooking varies from one pot to the next, and the amount of liquid that the food releases will change from one attempt to the next. For a sauce with just the right consistency (and a deeper flavor), we reduce the pureed cooking liquid and carrot mixture in a saucepan on the stovetop under a watchful eye.

---

the pureed sauce for just a few minutes back on the stovetop; at that point I also added a few pats of butter to improve body, along with a bit of red wine and a sprig of thyme for depth. When this wasn't enough, I called on one of the test kitchen's favorite *umami* boosters. A couple of teaspoons of soy sauce lent meatiness without making the sauce taste like a stir-fry. Things were definitely looking up, but I felt that I could do better still.

Even though I wasn't browning the meat at the outset, the roasts were still developing some browning, despite the wet environment inside the pot. This might sound confusing. After all, ordinarily you need to thoroughly dry meat before searing so that its surface will brown properly. But in those cases it's not so much the water itself that's the problem but rather its impact on temperature and the amount of cooking time that the meat requires. Browning can take place at temperatures as low as 160 degrees but only very, very slowly. For something like a quick-cooking steak, browning needs to happen at a higher temperature (around 300 degrees) to ensure that the steak doesn't overcook before it browns.

With my pressure-cooker pot roast, the cooking time was fairly long, and the water and steam were reaching almost 250 degrees. So some browning of both the meat and the aromatics (and even the gravy) was in fact occurring. It just wasn't enough. In the past we've used baking soda to create an alkaline environment, which enables the Maillard reaction to work more rapidly. Could it help my pot roast recipe? When I added ¼ teaspoon of baking soda to the pot with my aromatics, I noticed almost immediately that the aromatics were softening and browning faster. But the real benefit wasn't clear until I tasted the final sauce, after the baking soda had had almost an hour of pressurized cooking time to do its work. This sauce was dark, rich, and incredibly meaty—a remarkable improvement for such a small ingredient change.

Frayed Not

The last detail to address was how to release the pressure when the cooking time was up. Most recipes seemed to call for a quick release, and while this sped things up, I realized that the fast release of steam and pressure was causing the ultratender meat to fray at the edges, or even fall apart. For roasts that stayed intact and could be cut into neat slices, a gentler natural release, done by simply moving the pot off the heat and letting the pressure drop naturally, was the way to go.

Finally I had a pressure-cooker pot roast that held its own against the best of the traditional versions. Even better, it took less than 2 hours from start to finish.

Problems Under Pressure

Modern pressure cookers are safer, quieter, and more intuitive than the models from 50 years ago. But that doesn't mean that all models perform the same. When we tested a dozen best-selling stovetop and electric pressure cookers last year, we made a key discovery: No two pots reached the same internal temperature. At high pressure the internal temperature should be 250 degrees (this is because at increased pressure more energy is required to make liquid boil, and more energy translates into a higher temperature). Yet temperatures varied from as low as 230 degrees to as high as 253 degrees.

This variance can make a huge difference not only on the cooking time but also on the final results of a recipe. In most cases, you'll need to do some trial and error before you get perfect results from your pot. (Note: In the test kitchen, we use our Best Buy, the Fagor Duo 8-Quart Stainless Steel Pressure Cooker.) –D.S.

PRESSURE-COOKER POT ROAST
SERVES 6 TO 8

If using an electric pressure cooker, turn off the cooker immediately after the pressurized cooking time and let the pressure release naturally for 10 minutes; do not let the cooker switch to the warm setting. To adjust for differences among pressure cookers, cook the roasts for the recommended time, check for doneness, and, if needed, repressurize and cook up to 10 minutes longer. A half teaspoon of red wine vinegar can be substituted for the wine.

- 1 (3½- to 4-pound) boneless beef chuck-eye roast, pulled into 2 pieces at natural seam and trimmed of large pieces of fat
  Kosher salt and pepper
- 4 tablespoons unsalted butter, cut into 4 pieces
- 1 onion, sliced thick
- 1 celery rib, sliced thick
- 1 carrot, peeled and sliced thick
- ¼ teaspoon baking soda
- 1 cup beef broth
- 2 teaspoons soy sauce
- 2 bay leaves
- 1 tablespoon red wine
- 1 sprig fresh thyme

1. Using 3 pieces of kitchen twine per roast, tie each roast crosswise at equal intervals into loaf shape. Season roasts with salt and pepper and set aside.

2. Melt 2 tablespoons butter in pressure cooker over medium heat; refrigerate remaining 2 tablespoons butter. Add onion, celery, carrot, and baking soda to pot and cook until onion breaks down and liquid turns golden brown, about 5 minutes. Stir in broth, soy sauce, and bay leaves, scraping up any browned bits. Nestle roasts side by side on top of vegetables in cooker.

3. Lock lid in place and bring pot to high pressure over high heat, 3 to 8 minutes. As soon as indicator signals that pot has reached high pressure, reduce heat to medium-low and cook for 55 minutes, adjusting heat as needed to maintain high pressure.

4. Remove pot from heat and let pressure release naturally for 10 minutes. Quick-release any remaining pressure, then remove lid, allowing steam to escape away from you. Transfer roasts to carving board, tent with aluminum foil, and let rest for 20 minutes.

5. Meanwhile, strain liquid through fine-mesh strainer into fat separator; discard bay leaves. Transfer vegetables in strainer to blender. Let liquid settle for 5 minutes, then pour defatted liquid into blender with vegetables. Blend until smooth, about 1 minute. Transfer sauce to medium saucepan. Add wine, thyme sprig, and 2 tablespoons chilled butter and bring to boil over high heat. Cook until sauce is thickened and measures 3 cups, 5 to 8 minutes.

6. Remove twine from roasts and slice against grain into ½-inch-thick slices. Transfer meat to serving platter and season with salt to taste. Remove thyme sprig from sauce and season sauce with salt and pepper to taste. Spoon half of sauce over meat. Serve, passing remaining sauce separately.

Vietnamese Beef and Noodle Soup

To make this one-pot meal at home, we'd need to figure out a way to build a broth as clear and beefy as the South Asian original but in a fraction of the time—no bones about it.

≥ BY ERIN McMURRER ≤

I can't think of an Asian cuisine that doesn't lay claim to a brothy noodle soup, but I also can't think of one that's as universally popular as *pho bo*. This Vietnamese beef and noodle soup's biggest selling point is its killer broth—a beefy, fragrant, faintly sweet concoction produced by simmering beef bones and water for hours with aromatics like ginger and onions and warm spices like cinnamon and star anise. Notably, those bones are often the only form of meat added to the cooking liquid; actual pieces of beef aren't introduced until serving, when the broth is strained and ladled onto very thin slices of raw steak (typically sirloin) and thin rice noodles in large individual serving bowls. Fresh herbs and a few aromatic vegetables are presented as garnishes. Pouring hot broth over the contents cooks the meat just enough and softens the noodles and vegetables. Condiments such as salty-sweet hoisin sauce, chili sauce, and fish sauce and lime wedges are passed at the table for individual flavor tinkering.

Those exotic yet approachable flavors are what fuel my frequent cravings for this dish, but like most soups built on long-simmered stocks, it's not something I've ever attempted at home. Who has the time to spend a day eking out a full-flavored beef stock, much less running around town trying to track down hard-to-find beef bones? But if I could devise an equally intense, complex-tasting broth in less time (and with easier-to-find ingredients), pho would surely become my ultimate beef and noodle soup to make at home.

Getting Grounded

Ditching the bones was an obvious first move, but finding an equally beefy substitute wasn't so simple. The easiest shortcut, I figured, would be to doctor store-bought beef broth with typical pho flavors. I threw together a working recipe based on that: 14 cups of beef broth (since pho is a one-bowl

Rather than simmer the meat in the cooking liquid, thinly slice the steak and place it raw into large serving bowls, where it cooks in the hot broth.

meal, this amount of liquid feeds four to six people), a handful of quartered onions, peeled and thinly sliced ginger, a cinnamon stick, six each star anise pods and whole cloves, a couple of teaspoons of salt, and a teaspoon of black peppercorns, all simmered for about 1½ hours. To say the result was a failure would be an understatement. The soup tasted exactly like what it was: spiced-up commercial broth. I tried adding a little fish sauce and sugar to the cooking liquid, and both were keepers—easy additions that rounded out the salty-sweet profile I was after. But the broth needed more help, so I made another batch in which I charred the onions and ginger under the broiler before adding them to the cooking liquid—a traditional technique for building savory depth in pho. Alas, the flavor boost was too subtle to warrant the extra step and certainly didn't compensate for the lack of meat. Pho made without beef bones was turning out to be more challenging than I'd thought.

But at that point it dawned on me that doing without beef bones didn't mean I had to do without

beef altogether. My reference point was the test kitchen's trick for making an ultrameaty sauce for steak without going to the trouble of sourcing and roasting bones for the base. Instead, we build rich, meaty flavor in a hurry by simmering some ground beef with the cooking liquid and then discarding the solids. We discovered that ground meat works well because its muscle fibers are broken up in the grinding process and, therefore, release meaty flavor very quickly.

Feeling hopeful, I pulled together another batch of broth, but this time I added 2 pounds of ground beef along with the commercial broth, aromatics, and spices. While that simmered, I used a sharp knife to peel ⅛-inch-thick slices off of a 1-pound piece of beef sirloin (a placeholder until I did further testing with other cuts). I also soaked strands of thin dried rice noodles in warm water and then briefly boiled them. Soaking helped them slough off excess starch and made them soften evenly and quickly in the boiling water. Then I loaded up individual bowls with the noodles and meat, as well as chopped cilantro and thin-sliced raw onion and scallions, before pouring hot broth over each serving.

The good news was that this broth was in a different league compared with my previous attempts: It was remarkably more savory and full-bodied, thanks to the ground beef. The downsides were that the ground beef had released "scum" into the liquid that turned it cloudy; the liquid retained a touch of that commercial broth tinniness and vegetal flavor; and, frankly, I wasn't thrilled about throwing away 2 pounds of beef. But fortifying the broth with ground meat had improved its flavor so dramatically that I couldn't resist pursuing the technique further.

As someone who's made her fair share of stock when cooking in restaurants, I was familiar with that pesky layer of scum, which forms any time you boil meat or bones. Traditional stock recipes, pho included, call for blanching the bones before adding them to the cooking liquid, a step that washes away much of their surface proteins and fat, which form the scum. I gave it a try with the ground beef and was glad to see that the technique was effective: Covering the meat with water, bringing it up to a boil for 2 minutes, and then quickly draining and rinsing it (to remove clingy bits of protein and fat)

before adding it to the beef broth made for a clearer, cleaner-tasting beef stock. (For more information, see "Best Route to Clear Stock.") Of course, it's not as easy to strain bits of ground meat as it is large beef bones, so I broke the 2-pound mass of meat into 1-inch chunks that weren't hard to fish out of the water. Swapping out a couple of cups of the broth for an equal amount of water took care of the tinny, vegetal notes without noticeably dampening the beefy flavor.

Making do with less beef broth also tempted my frugal side: Could I get away with less ground beef, too? Indeed, making my broth with 1½ pounds and 1 pound of ground beef, respectively, proved that the latter put up plenty of meaty flavor—and that the flavor payoff for 1 pound of meat was worth the sacrifice.

I had to admit that this broth had a lot going for it: all the flavor and complexity of real-deal beef broth without the fuss. My only hang-up was the 1½-hour simmer. For this pho to be part of my regular dinner rotation, not just a special-occasion dish, I'd need to hurry it along, so I tried skimping on the simmer time. To my delight, after testing various times, I discovered that the beef flavor peaked around the 45-minute mark—a change that put this soup on the table for a weeknight meal.

Meaty Matters

Some pho shops throw tough cuts like brisket and tripe into their long-simmered broths and offer them as garnishing options, but thin slices of raw, relatively tender steak are the most common and would do fine for my purposes. The question was which cut exactly, so I tried all the options I could think of: tenderloin, rib eye, strip steak, tri-tip, blade steak, flank, and eye of round. Tenderloin was favored for its supple texture, and its uniform cylindrical shape made thin-slicing it a breeze. But its prohibitive price meant that it was ill-matched for this humble soup. Plus, it offered nothing in the way of beefy flavor.

Strip steak, tri-tip, and blade steak all offered good beefiness and reasonable tenderness at a fraction of the price. I chose to work with strip since it is usually the easiest to find. To make the steak less challenging to slice thin, I employed the test kitchen's favorite trick for prepping stir-fry meat: briefly freezing the whole steak, which firms it up enough for the blade to make clean cuts. As a bonus, freezing also ensured that the steak didn't overcook when it came in contact with the hot broth.

I also pared down the list of tableside garnishes and condiments to the essentials. The must-haves—bean sprouts for crunch, basil (preferably Thai basil, though Italian basil will work), lime wedges, hoisin and chile sauces, and additional fish sauce—balanced the straightforward meatiness and mellow sweetness of the broth with heat, acidity, and freshness.

As I ladled the fragrant broth into serving bowls, my colleagues and I remarked at how easily and quickly the complex flavors of pho had come together and how this seemingly exotic dish suddenly felt much closer to home.

VIETNAMESE BEEF PHO
SERVES 4 TO 6

Our favorite store-bought beef broth is Rachael Ray Stock-in-a-Box All-Natural Beef Flavored Stock. Use a Dutch oven that holds 6 quarts or more. An equal weight of tri-tip steak or blade steak can be substituted for the strip steak; make sure to trim all connective tissue and excess fat. One 14- or 16-ounce package of rice noodles will serve four to six. Look for noodles that are about ⅛ inch wide; these are often labeled "small." Don't use Thai Kitchen Stir-Fry Rice Noodles since they are too thick and don't adequately soak up the broth.

1	pound 85 percent lean ground beef
2	onions, quartered through root end
12	cups low-sodium beef broth
¼	cup fish sauce, plus extra for seasoning
1	(4-inch) piece ginger, sliced into thin rounds
1	cinnamon stick
2	tablespoons sugar, plus extra for seasoning
6	star anise pods
6	whole cloves
	Salt
1	teaspoon black peppercorns
1	(1-pound) boneless strip steak, trimmed and halved
14–16	ounces (⅛-inch-wide) rice noodles
⅓	cup chopped fresh cilantro
3	scallions, sliced thin (optional)
	Bean sprouts
	Sprigs fresh Thai or Italian basil
	Lime wedges
	Hoisin sauce
	Sriracha sauce

1. Break ground beef into rough 1-inch chunks and drop in Dutch oven. Add water to cover by

BEEF SO THIN THAT IT COOKS IN THE BOWL

Traditionally, the steak for *pho* is sliced very thin and placed raw in the serving bowl. (It cooks, but ideally remains slightly rare, in the hot broth.) To cut thin slices against the grain, freeze the meat until it's very firm (this also prevents the meat from overcooking). Then stand the meat on its cut end and, using the sharpest, thinnest blade you have, point the tip downward and push the blade down and away from you in one stroke.

1 inch. Bring mixture to boil over high heat. Boil for 2 minutes, stirring once or twice. Drain ground beef in colander and rinse well under running water. Wash out pot and return ground beef to pot.

2. Place 6 onion quarters in pot with ground beef. Slice remaining 2 onion quarters as thin as possible and set aside for garnish. Add broth, 2 cups water, fish sauce, ginger, cinnamon, sugar, star anise, cloves, 2 teaspoons salt, and peppercorns to pot and bring to boil over high heat. Reduce heat to medium-low and simmer, partially covered, for 45 minutes.

3. Pour broth through colander set in large bowl. Discard solids. Strain broth through fine-mesh strainer lined with triple thickness of cheesecloth; add water as needed to equal 11 cups. Return broth to pot and season with extra sugar and salt (broth should taste overseasoned). Cover and keep warm over low heat.

4. While broth simmers, place steak on large plate and freeze until very firm, 35 to 45 minutes. Once firm, cut against grain into ⅛-inch-thick slices. Return steak to plate and refrigerate until needed.

5. Place noodles in large container and cover with hot tap water. Soak until noodles are pliable, 10 to 15 minutes; drain noodles. Meanwhile, bring 4 quarts water to boil in large pot. Add drained noodles and cook until almost tender, 30 to 60 seconds. Drain immediately and divide noodles among individual bowls.

6. Bring broth to rolling boil over high heat. Divide steak among individual bowls, shingling slices on top of noodles. Pile reserved onion slices on top of steak slices and sprinkle with cilantro and scallions, if using. Ladle hot broth into each bowl. Serve immediately, passing bean sprouts, basil sprigs, lime wedges, hoisin, Sriracha, and extra fish sauce separately.

Best Route to Clear Stock
Boiling ground beef (or, more traditionally, beef bones) for stock coaxes out great beef flavor but also soluble proteins and melted fat that render the liquid cloudy and leave a layer of scum on its surface. Frequently skimming away those impurities as the liquid cooks is one way to clear up the stock, but it's a tedious chore (especially when there are solids, like onions or spices, that you don't want to remove) and it never completely clarifies the stock. Blanching and rinsing the meat before adding it to the cooking liquid is a far more efficient method. The brief (2-minute) boil thoroughly agitates the meat so that its proteins and fat slough off but doesn't cook it long enough to wash away much flavor. A quick rinse rids the surface of any stubborn clingy bits. –E.M.

Really Good Shrimp Fra Diavolo

For a dish that didn't remind us of rubbery seafood in spicy marinara, we started by getting the shrimp's briny flavor to come out of its shell.

⇒ BY ANDREA GEARY ⇐

If the devil wanted to trick me into relinquishing my soul, I'd be insulted if he showed up for the occasion sporting a shiny red jump-suit, pointy horns, and a slick goatee. I like to think that it would take a bit more subtlety and finesse to tempt me. Yet many dishes with "devilish" names are so in-your-face spicy and pungent and so obvious that they're about as suavely enticing as a cartoon Beelzebub.

Consider shrimp fra diavolo, the 20th-century Italian American combo of shrimp, tomatoes, garlic, and hot pepper, often served over spaghetti or with crusty bread. At its best, it's lively and piquant, the tangy tomatoes countering the sweet and briny shrimp, and the pepper and garlic providing a spirited kick. Unfortunately, the spice is often so heavy-handed that it completely overwhelms the other flavors.

What's more, the fragile shrimp are often flambéed (for flavor or fiery effect, I've never been sure which) or pan-seared before being cooked further in the sauce, transforming them into chunks of overcooked, flavorless protein, identifiable only by their shape.

Simply taming the heat of shrimp fra diavolo would be as easy as cutting back on the spice (usually red pepper flakes), but that would make it another dish entirely: more like shrimp marinara. No, I intended to not only preserve the fiery character of fra diavolo but also heighten the other flavors—particularly the brininess of the shrimp—so that they could stand up to the heat. And I'd make sure that those shrimp remained succulent.

In Defense of Poaching

I started with the simplest sauce recipe I could find: a goodly amount of both garlic and red pepper flakes and a bit of dried oregano—all sautéed in a few tablespoons of vegetable oil until fragrant—plus chopped canned whole tomatoes and their juice, cooked down for a few minutes until thickened. My question was how to cook the shrimp. Recipes

What's missing from most shrimp fra diavolos? Seafood flavor. We build a quick shrimp stock—and add a pair of unlikely ingredients—for brininess.

that I found called for one of three techniques: sautéing the peeled shrimp (1½ pounds would yield four servings) along with the aromatics in oil before adding the sauce components; flambéing the sautéed shrimp by adding a few glugs of cognac to the pan and waving a lit match over the surface; and, the simplest method, slipping raw shrimp into the simmering tomato sauce, where they poached until just opaque and cooked through.

Flambéing turned out to be more impressive for its pyrotechnic display than for its flavor contribution. Besides, the technique produced rubbery shrimp. I hoped that by simply sautéing the shrimp I could coax out good briny flavor without overcooking them. Even more important, I hoped that the method would yield a valuable byproduct: the flavorful browned bits known as fond, which would serve as a rich shrimp base for the sauce. But alas, even browning the shrimp enough to develop fond had them teetering on the edge of overcooked, and stirring them back into the sauce before serving to meld their flavors sealed the deal.

Poaching, meanwhile, produced the tender shrimp that I was after, but with little briny seafood flavor to speak of. The finished product tasted like what I was trying to avoid: spicy shrimp marinara. If only I could use this poaching method but along the way boost the flavor presence of the shrimp.

Waste Not

I considered sacrificing a small portion of the shrimp by searing them to build fond and then throwing them away. That way, I'd develop a rich seafood backbone for the sauce before gently poaching the remaining raw shrimp in the sauce. But then it occurred to me that I already had a flavor-building ingredient at my disposal.

Crustacean shells contain loads of proteins, sugars, and flavor-boosting compounds called glutamates and nucleotides that are ideal for building the flavorful browning known as the Maillard reaction—a discovery we capitalized on in our recipes for roasted shrimp (January/February 2013), in which roasting the shrimp shell-on considerably amped up their savory seafood flavor. Searing these smaller shell-on shrimp would only overcook them, but browning the to-be-discarded shells as a foundation for the sauce was a possibility. The concept is a classic first step when making shrimp bisque—but oddly not a technique that I found during my fra diavolo research.

I started a new batch, this time sautéing the shrimp shells in a little oil until they and the surface of the pan were spotty brown. Then I deglazed the pan with wine—another pickup technique from seafood bisques. The puff of heady, seafood-rich steam that rose up from the pan indicated that I was on the right track. From there, I added the juice from a can of whole tomatoes (I'd add the solids later) and let the shells simmer, essentially creating a tomatoey shrimp "stock," which I strained from the shells about 5 minutes later (for more information, see "Secret's in the Stock"). When I took a whiff of the cooking liquid, the intensity of its seafood aroma impressed me—but not as much as the flavor did. A spoonful was remarkably rich and savory, like shrimp pot liquor.

The rest of the sauce was quick to pull together. I wiped out the skillet and sautéed the garlic, pepper flakes, and oregano in a couple of teaspoons of oil

PHOTOGRAPHY: CARL TREMBLAY

Secret's in the Stock

The sauce in most versions of shrimp fra diavolo tastes largely of cooked tomato and chile, but not really of seafood. To amp up savory shrimp flavor and brightness, we took a cue from classic seafood bisques and eked out a shrimp stock by browning the shells—an ingredient we would have otherwise discarded—deglazing the pan with white wine, and simmering the mixture with the juice from canned tomatoes. In just minutes, the shells give up remarkably rich flavor, which the wine and tomato juice balance with acidity. –A.G.

FLAVOR FOUNDATION
Briefly simmering browned shrimp shells in white wine and the juice from canned tomatoes produces a surprisingly complex stock to bolster the flavor of the sauce.

until fragrant and then added the reserved tomato solids. To break up the large chunks, I pummeled the pieces with a potato masher until I had a pulpy puree. In went the tomato stock, which needed more body, so I cranked up the heat a bit and let the mixture simmer for about 5 minutes, by which time it had thickened. Finally, I added the shrimp, turning them a few times to ensure that they cooked evenly, and finished the dish with handfuls of chopped basil and parsley and a drizzle of fruity extra-virgin olive oil.

I was almost satisfied: The shrimp were plump and juicy, and the sauce boasted true (but not overwhelming) heat. Searing the shells had paid off; there was more than a hint of rich shrimp flavor and brininess. And yet I hadn't nailed the intensity of either one of those flavors, so I pawed through the test kitchen pantry for something that might help.

Picker-Uppers

Minutes later, I had an answer in each hand. The first: a jar of anchovies. Don't underestimate the potential of these little fish. Mincing a pair of fillets (rinsed first to reduce their saltiness) and browning them with the aromatics added remarkably savory, not fishy, depth. The second, more unexpected find was a jar of pepperoncini. When I stirred in two of these minced pickled peppers at the end with the herbs, the acidity—and heat—of the sauce perked up just a bit more. On a whim, I stirred in a teaspoon of the brine from the jar, too, which amplified the effect.

This version of shrimp fra diavolo had enough fire from the garlic and pepper to please the most daring of diners and—thanks to the browned shells and anchovies—a round, rich seafood flavor, too. Served with warm, crusty bread, it made a meal that would tempt the devil himself.

If the shrimp you are using have been treated with salt (check the bag's ingredient list), skip the salting in step 1 and add 1/4 teaspoon of salt to the sauce in step 3. Adjust the amount of pepper flakes depending on how spicy you want the dish. Serve the shrimp with a salad and crusty bread or over spaghetti. If serving with spaghetti, adjust the consistency of the sauce with some reserved pasta cooking water. For our free recipe for Shrimp Fra Diavolo for Two, go to CooksIllustrated.com/feb14.

- 1½ pounds large shrimp (26 to 30 per pound), peeled and deveined, shells reserved
  Salt
- 1 (28-ounce) can whole peeled tomatoes
- 3 tablespoons vegetable oil
- 1 cup dry white wine
- 4 garlic cloves, minced
- ½–1 teaspoon red pepper flakes
- ½ teaspoon dried oregano
- 2 anchovy fillets, rinsed, patted dry, and minced
- ¼ cup chopped fresh basil
- ¼ cup chopped fresh parsley
- 1½ teaspoons minced pepperoncini, plus 1 teaspoon brine
- 2 tablespoons extra-virgin olive oil

1. Toss shrimp with ½ teaspoon salt and set aside. Pour tomatoes into colander set over large bowl. Pierce tomatoes with edge of rubber spatula and stir briefly to release juice. Transfer drained tomatoes to small bowl and reserve juice. Do not wash colander.

2. Heat 1 tablespoon vegetable oil in 12-inch skillet over high heat until shimmering. Add shrimp shells and cook, stirring frequently, until they begin to turn spotty brown and skillet starts to brown, 2 to 4 minutes. Remove skillet from heat and carefully add wine. When bubbling subsides, return skillet to heat and simmer until wine is reduced to about 2 tablespoons, 2 to 4 minutes. Add reserved tomato juice and simmer to meld flavors, 5 minutes. Pour contents of skillet into colander set over bowl. Discard shells and reserve liquid. Wipe out skillet with paper towels.

3. Heat remaining 2 tablespoons vegetable oil, garlic, pepper flakes, and oregano in now-empty skillet over medium heat, stirring occasionally, until garlic is straw-colored and fragrant, 1 to 2 minutes. Add anchovies and stir until fragrant, about 30 seconds. Remove from heat. Add drained tomatoes and mash with potato masher until coarsely pureed. Return to heat and stir in reserved tomato juice mixture. Increase heat to medium-high and simmer until mixture has thickened, about 5 minutes.

4. Add shrimp to skillet and simmer gently, stirring and turning shrimp frequently, until they are just cooked through, 4 to 5 minutes. Remove pan from heat. Stir in basil, parsley, and pepperoncini and brine and season with salt to taste. Drizzle with olive oil and serve.

Essential Guide to Oil

Just because supermarket shelves are crammed with dozens of different oils doesn't mean you need them all. For most of our cooking needs, we rely on just three.

BY SHANNON FRIEDMANN HATCH & ANDREW JANJIGIAN

❶ Vegetable Oil Blend

Vegetable oil should have a neutral taste that highlights (rather than masks) the flavors of other ingredients. Some varieties, such as corn and canola, take on subtle but distinct flavors in certain applications, so we make a point of avoiding them and go for a blend instead; that way, no one flavor will dominate.

FAVORITE:

Crisco Natural Blend Oil ($6.89 for 48 oz) A mix of canola, sunflower, and soybean oils, this oil tastes "very clean" even in high-heat applications.

❷ Everyday Extra-Virgin Olive Oil

In recent tests we've found that the flavors of extra-virgin olive oil (or EVOO) are driven off more thoroughly—and rapidly—by heat than we ever knew. So for cooking Mediterranean dishes like tomato sauce, moussaka, and paella in which olive oil is traditional, we stock the cheapest bottle we can find.

❸ Premium Extra-Virgin Olive Oil

The hallmark of a truly superior-quality EVOO is a pronounced flavor profile that can range from richly fruity, to grassy, to peppery and sharp. We reserve this good stuff for cold applications like dressings and for drizzling on food after cooking.

FAVORITES:

Columela Extra Virgin Olive Oil ($15.90 for 17 oz)
California Olive Ranch Arbequina ($16.69 for 500 ml)

SHOPPING TIPS:

If you can't buy one of our recommended products, prioritize freshness. Look for a harvest date on the label; try to buy oils from only this year's crop. Alternatively, look for a "best by" date as far away as possible. (Unopened olive oil is good for up to 18 months from the time it was bottled.)

UNDERSTUDY OILS

These two oils are also worth keeping on hand.

TOASTED SESAME OIL We drizzle this nutty-tasting Asian oil over everything from dumplings to stir-fries to noodles and soups.

PEANUT OIL Though not a must, this neutral-flavored oil has a high smoke point, which means that it's able to withstand prolonged heating without breaking down. Its high smoke point makes it an excellent choice for deep frying.

➤ STORING OIL

Store all oils in a cool, dark place. Store nut and seed oils in the refrigerator to help stave off rancidity, but avoid refrigerating olive oil. According to olive oil experts, repeatedly chilling olive oil and rewarming it to room temperature can create condensation in the bottle that degrades the flavor.

➤ CHECKING FOR FRESHNESS

Properly stored, vegetable oil should last six months once opened and EVOO at least three months. If you're unsure whether an oil is past its prime, heat a few tablespoons in a skillet. If vegetable oil smells anything other than neutral—and if olive oil smells musty rather than fruity—discard it.

Does It Pay to Cook with Extra-Virgin Olive Oil?

In Mediterranean countries, good olive oil has historically been plentiful and cheap and so used for almost everything. The health benefits of cooking with extra-virgin olive oil are well documented, but how much flavor does it add to a dish once it has been heated? And does high-end EVOO keep more of its flavor than cheaper EVOO?

TASTE TESTS We had 10 of our top tasters sample three oils straight out of the bottle: Crisco Natural Blend Oil, our favorite premium EVOO from Columela, and a much more affordable EVOO from Filippo Berio. We then had these same tasters try the oils again after we'd heated them to 350 degrees (the temperature typically reached by oil during frying) and held them there for 10 minutes. Finally, we had tasters sample tomato sauces made with the oils and potatoes tossed in the oils and then roasted.

RESULTS Tasters were easily able to distinguish the bold fruity and grassy flavors of both EVOOs compared with vegetable oil in the raw tasting. These differences lessened once the oils were heated. Some tasters were able to detect a faint grassiness and peppery finish in the EVOOs but little else. The three oils were indistinguishable from one another when cooked with tomato sauce and roasted potatoes.

BOTTOM LINE Cooking with EVOO may be healthy, but don't expect even a premium EVOO to add much flavor once it's heated.

SAUTÉING TIPS

We use a vegetable oil blend for nearly all our sautéing needs.

➤ Get a Cold Start

Cooks debate whether oil should be added to the pan before or after the pan is preheated. We strongly prefer adding oil to the cold (unheated) pan for three reasons: First, the oil serves as a reminder that the pan is heating (visually, a dry heated pan looks no different from a cold pan). Second, hot oil gives visual cues about when it's time to add food to the pan. Third, heating an empty nonstick pan can damage its coating and emit fumes.

➤ Let Oil Shimmer and Then Sauté

For proper browning, the oil must be moderately hot before you add food to the pan. Checking the oil's temperature is impractical, as sautéing requires such a small amount that your thermometer won't get an accurate reading. Instead, use the visual cue of "shimmering." When the oil starts to ripple, start cooking.

➤ Mind Smoking More Than Smoke Points

Most sautéing falls below an oil's smoke point, so you won't see smoke unless the pan gets too hot. (An exception: When searing food in a very hot skillet, wisps of smoke indicate that it's time to cook.) It's more important to be vigilant of vigorous smoking—if you see it, immediately remove the pan from the heat and let it cool. Dispose of the oil, wipe the pan clean, and start again.

FRYING KNOW-HOW

When deep-frying food in batches in which the oil will be heated for longer than 15 minutes, we may seek out peanut oil. But for shallow frying, which happens at a lower temperature, vegetable oil blend is our go-to.

➤ Shallow versus Deep Frying

We reserve shallow frying, in which the oil reaches only partway up the food, for bulky items like breaded cutlets or bone-in chicken pieces. These foods cook slowly enough that they can be browned in the oil one side at a time without risk of overcooking. With deep frying, food is completely submerged in the oil, which enables smaller, quick-cooking items like French fries to brown on all sides simultaneously.

➤ Oil Amount

When shallow-frying, make sure the oil reaches halfway up the sides of the food; otherwise, you'll end up with a pale band around the exterior. When deep-frying, you'll need at least 1 quart of oil to completely cover the food—but don't fill the pot more than half full to avoid splattering once food is added.

SHALLOW FRYING

DEEP FRYING

➤ Monitor the Temperature

When deep-frying, use a clip-on candy/deep-fry thermometer to guarantee that the oil reaches—and remains at—the target temperature (generally between 325 and 375 degrees). Don't let the thermometer touch the bottom or sides of the pot; if it does, you may get a false reading.

➤ Include Some "Recycled" Oil

When deep-frying, the first batch is often paler and less crispy than those that follow. But by mixing strained, previously used frying oil into fresh oil, you can get golden, crispy results from the start. Why? Oil that's already been exposed to heat produces surfactants that can penetrate the water barrier that surrounds food as it fries. This increased contact promotes browning and a nice crust. We use a 1:5 ratio of used oil to fresh.

➤ Rules for Reusing Oil

- Never reuse oil that smoked or that was used for fish.
- Let the oil cool completely.
- Strain the used oil through at least two layers of cheesecloth or paper coffee filters.
- Refrigerate the oil until ready to use.
- Discard the oil after three uses; in tests we found that the smoke point of peanut oil dropped 28 degrees after three rounds of frying.

DRESSING GUIDELINES

A premium extra-virgin olive oil is typically our first choice in vinaigrettes.

➤ Get the Ratio Right

For a vibrant but balanced dressing, we prefer a 3:1 ratio of oil to vinegar.

➤ Take Time to Emulsify

In tests, we found that coating greens with an emulsified dressing, rather than with separate hits of oil and vinegar, prevented the greens from quickly turning soggy; binding the oil in the vinegar prevents the fat from penetrating the waxy cuticle layer on salad greens (water-based liquids, like vinegar, can't cross through that film).

➤ Avoid Motorized Mixing

Never emulsify extra-virgin olive oil in a blender or food processor. The whirring blades will break the oil into very small droplets, releasing bitter-tasting compounds into the mix. (Note: In recipes that contain lots of other robust flavors, such as pesto, we have found that any bitter taste goes unnoticed.)

➤ Mix In a Little Mayo or Mustard

Whisking together oil and vinegar will make an emulsified dressing, but it won't hold well unless you add a helper ingredient. Mayonnaise and mustard both contain emulsifying agents—lecithin and mucilage, respectively—that keep the dressing stable for longer. Add ½ teaspoon of mayonnaise or mustard for every 3 tablespoons of oil and 1 tablespoon of vinegar.

BAKING BENEFITS

Butter is traditional in baking, but in many applications, oil can improve flavor and texture.

TENDERNESS Oil and butter both coat flour proteins and prevent them from bonding with water and developing tough gluten, but oil does it better. Many recipes that require tenderness but not added flavor, such as quick breads and muffins, rely on vegetable oil.

MOISTURE When butter's high water content—about 20 percent—evaporates in the oven, it can leave baked goods dry. While developing our Fluffy Yellow Layer Cake (March/April 2008), we discovered that using a combination of butter and vegetable oil makes our cake moister than if we were using all butter.

CLEAN TASTE While butter adds its own rich flavor, neutral-tasting oil allows other flavors to come to the fore. We use oil in recipes ranging from brownies and chocolate cupcakes to French apple cake.

Pasta with Sausage and Cream Sauce

In Italy, the star of this creamy pasta dish is handmade sausage from a tiny Umbrian village.
Where does that leave the rest of us?

> BY DAN SOUZA <

In the Middle Ages, butchers in the Umbrian village of Norcia became so adept at cutting, salting, and curing pork that the products they produced—sausage, bacon, prosciutto, and capocollo salami, to name a few— became legendary. Still named after the small town to this day, most pork butcher shops throughout Italy are called *norcinerie*, and pork butchers bear the title of *norcino*. It's no surprise, then, that *pasta alla norcina*—featuring fresh sausage—is widely considered to be the ultimate pasta and sausage dish.

On a recent trip to the region, I sampled many versions, the best of which featured crumbled fresh sausage, juicy and tender as could be, napped in cream and tossed with a small, chunky pasta. While some plates were fancied up with black truffles or other garnishes, sausage was always the focus. Made with the prized meat of Umbrian black pigs, the sausage tasted first and foremost of rich pork with hints of garlic and sometimes rosemary. I typically avoid trying to replicate dishes so deeply connected to their birthplace for fear that I won't do them justice, but my persistent cravings for this pasta dish won out. My goal was to come up with a version possessing all the virtues of the ones I'd savored in Italy.

Sorting Out Sausage

Whipping up a cream-based sauce would be relatively easy, so I focused my efforts on getting the sausage just right. And here I ran into a predictable obstacle: Store-bought Italian sausage made a poor substitute for the true handmade Italian stuff. Depending on the brand, I found that the grind size and fat and salt contents varied considerably. Even more problematic was that the overwhelming majority of mild Italian sausage in this country is the fennel-spiked type, which was all wrong for this recipe. Undeterred, I decided to simply follow Norcian tradition: I would make my own sausage.

See the Sausage Made

Video available FREE for 4 months at
CooksIllustrated.com/feb14

We brighten the cream sauce with white wine and lemon juice and reserve some pasta cooking water for adjusting its consistency.

Making fresh sausage at home may sound daunting, but it's actually pretty easy. At its simplest, sausage is nothing more than a humble mixture of chopped or ground meat (in this case pork), fat, and salt. The typical procedure is to rub a tough cut like pork shoulder with salt and allow it to sit for at least a few hours, during which time the salt pulls water from the meat. The water then mixes with the salt and forms a shallow brine on the meat's surface. The brine is then reabsorbed by the flesh, and it starts to dissolve some of the protein fibers. Finally, the salted meat is ground with fat and then kneaded by hand or by machine. During kneading, the proteins cross-link and bind together, and a strong protein network develops—much like the gluten network that is created when bread dough is kneaded. This network traps moisture and fat and produces the satisfying snappy texture of a good sausage. Easy enough, but I wanted to find a way

Don't Get Stuck

Orecchiette is prone to nest and stick. To keep the pieces separate, just stir—often.

around the extended salting time, which seemed beyond the pale for what was basically a weeknight pasta dish.

Grinding my own meat was too much trouble, so I jumped straight to an 8-ounce package of preground pork. Luckily, store-bought ground pork already has the 4:1 ratio of meat to fat typically used for pork sausage. I mixed kosher salt into several different batches and let them sit for various lengths of time, hoping that the greater surface area of the preground pork would significantly reduce the salting time (from hours to just minutes) and allow me to start kneading right away. Unfortunately, it took a full 30 minutes for the salt to dissolve, form a brine, and reabsorb. I needed to speed up the salting process. What if, instead of waiting for the salt to dissolve in the pork juices, I made the brine myself?

I did just that for my next batch, dissolving the salt in a spoonful of water and folding the solution into the pork. After 10 minutes, I could see the surface of the meat darken, a sure sign that the proteins were dissolving (as proteins dissolve they reflect light differently, causing a color shift). To this base, I added the simple flavorings I recalled from the sausage back in Norcia: minced garlic, ground black pepper, and chopped fresh rosemary. The pork was also quite soft; 10 seconds of mixing with a spoon efficiently brought the meat together into a thick, sticky mass, which meant that a strong protein network had developed.

I eagerly fried a small patty to check for seasoning. This stuff had the springy texture of well-made sausage, and it also tasted pretty good. My colleagues suggested adding a warm background spice, and a few tests proved that a little grated nutmeg accented the garlic and rosemary nicely. Still, for my imitation to compete with the real Umbrian sausage, I'd need to brown it well to develop as much meaty complexity as possible. And here I ran into another common problem: Thoroughly browning crumbled sausage deepens its flavor, but it practically guarantees tough, dry, meat. Was there a way to produce sausage that was well browned yet still moist?

How to Make Juicy, Flavorful Sausage

Store-bought Italian sausage didn't have the right flavors for the dish, so we made our own. Our unusual (but easy) approach produces meat that browns thoroughly on the outside and also stays tender and juicy within.

BRINE GROUND PORK
Brine in salt water to dissolve the pork's proteins and help the meat retain moisture. Add baking soda to further increase the meat's ability to hold water.

WORK IN SEASONINGS
After brining, use a rubber spatula to smear herbs and spices into the pork—a method that makes it springy.

BROWN ONE LARGE PATTY
Pat the pork into a 6-inch "burger" that can withstand a hard sear. Later, chop it and finish cooking the meat in the sauce.

How the Sausage Crumbles

Since ground pork sausage, like ground beef, has a tendency to dry out when crumbled and seared in a hot skillet, perhaps I needed to stop breaking it apart; instead, I'd try cooking it in one big piece, as I would a hamburger. I pressed the sausage into a 6-inch disk and browned it in a hot skillet slicked with oil. About 3 minutes per side was all it took to develop a crusty exterior, at which point the interior was still pink. I transferred the patty to a cutting board, chopped it into ⅛- to ¼-inch pieces, added the pieces back to the skillet, poured in some cream, and gently cooked them through. The good news: This sausage had terrific meaty flavor. The bad: It was still a bit drier than I would have liked. Could I do even better?

The test kitchen recently discovered the powerful effect that baking soda can have on moisture retention in meat, putting soda to good use in everything from pork stir-fries to turkey burgers. The alkaline soda raises the pH of the meat and dramatically improves its water-holding capacity by tenderizing its muscle fibers and giving them a looser structure. It was worth giving it a try in my sausage. I mixed up a few more batches of my recipe with increasing amounts of baking soda added to the brine. I then seared each batch on both sides, chopped them into rough bites, and simmered them for a few minutes in cream until they were no longer pink. With ¼ teaspoon of soda in the mix, the meat stayed incredibly juicy and tender—finally, American-made sausage was a reasonable facsimile of the Italian stuff.

Getting Saucy

With the sausage squared away, I focused on adding complementary flavors to the sauce. After chopping the browned sausage patty, I transferred it to a bowl with cream, where it could infuse its flavor, while I built the rest of the sauce (I would add the sausage-cream mixture back to the skillet later to cook the meat through). Super-pricey black truffles were out of the question, but I thought that a little background flavor from a much more common (and affordable) variety of fungi—cremini mushrooms—would be nice. I roughly chopped 8 ounces of

cremini mushrooms and sautéed them in the skillet until they were nicely browned. Tasters liked the flavor but felt that the pieces of mushroom competed for attention with the sausage. Easy enough to fix: A quick spin in the food processor reduced them to a fine consistency that blended discreetly into the dish. To mirror the flavors in the sausage, I added garlic, black pepper, and rosemary to the mushrooms. Then, to balance the richness of the dish, I deglazed the skillet with white wine and stirred in the sausage and cream to finish cooking. As is tradition, I also stirred in a handful of grated Pecorino Romano.

After tossing the sausage-speckled sauce with al dente orecchiette—this cupped, ear-shaped pasta cradled the chunky sauce nicely—I sprinkled it with chopped parsley and a squeeze of lemon juice for a fresh-tasting finish. I'd finally met my objective: a true tribute to the dish that I'd eaten abroad, complete with the requisite homemade sausage.

PASTA ALLA NORCINA
SERVES 6

White mushrooms may be substituted for the cremini, and short pasta such as mezzi rigatoni or shells for the orecchiette. For our free recipe for Pasta alla Norcina for Two, go to CooksIllustrated.com/feb14.

	Kosher salt and pepper
¼	teaspoon baking soda
8	ounces ground pork
3	garlic cloves, minced
1¼	teaspoons minced fresh rosemary
⅛	teaspoon ground nutmeg
8	ounces cremini mushrooms, trimmed
7	teaspoons vegetable oil
¾	cup heavy cream
1	pound orecchiette
½	cup dry white wine
1½	ounces Pecorino Romano cheese, grated (¾ cup)
3	tablespoons minced fresh parsley
1	tablespoon lemon juice

1. Grease large dinner plate with vegetable oil spray. Dissolve 1⅛ teaspoons salt and baking soda in 4 teaspoons water in medium bowl. Add pork and fold gently to combine; let stand for 10 minutes.

2. Add 1 teaspoon garlic, ¾ teaspoon rosemary, nutmeg, and ¾ teaspoon pepper to pork and smear with rubber spatula until well combined and tacky, 10 to 15 seconds. Transfer pork mixture to greased plate and form into rough 6-inch patty. Pulse mushrooms in food processor until finely chopped, 10 to 12 pulses.

3. Heat 2 teaspoons oil in 12-inch skillet over medium-high heat until just smoking. Add patty and cook without moving it until bottom is browned, 2 to 3 minutes. Flip patty and continue to cook until second side is well browned, 2 to 3 minutes longer (very center of patty will be raw). Remove pan from heat, transfer sausage to cutting board, and chop into ⅛- to ¼-inch pieces. Transfer sausage to bowl and add cream; set aside.

4. Bring 4 quarts water to boil in large Dutch oven. Add pasta and 2 tablespoons salt and cook, stirring often, until al dente. Reserve 1½ cups cooking water, then drain pasta and return it to pot.

5. While pasta cooks, return now-empty skillet to medium heat. Add 1 tablespoon oil, mushrooms, and ⅛ teaspoon salt; cook, stirring frequently, until mushrooms are browned, 5 to 7 minutes. Stir in remaining 2 teaspoons oil, remaining garlic, remaining ½ teaspoon rosemary, and ½ teaspoon pepper; cook until fragrant, about 30 seconds. Stir in wine, scraping up any browned bits, and cook until completely evaporated, 1 to 2 minutes. Stir in sausage-cream mixture and ¾ cup reserved cooking water and simmer until meat is no longer pink, 1 to 3 minutes. Remove pan from heat and stir in Pecorino until smooth.

6. Add sauce, parsley, and lemon juice to pasta and toss well to coat. Before serving, adjust consistency with remaining reserved cooking water as needed and season with salt and pepper to taste.

Better Roasted Butternut Squash

For great caramelization, don't drown squash in sugar or syrup. Instead, sharpen your knife.

⇒ BY DAN SOUZA ⇐

When it comes to preparing winter squash, I'm as guilty of taking the familiar route as the next person. I sprinkle the halves with some brown sugar, dot them with butter, and slide them into a hot oven. Or I cube the squash and toss it with oil before roasting to help it develop a bit more color and flavorful caramelization. Comforting, yes, but not all that inspiring.

A recipe in London-based chef Yotam Ottolenghi's book *Plenty* introduced me to an alternative squash universe. He slices the squash (skin and all) into thin half-moons to create more surface area for browning. And rather than add more sweetness, he tosses the roasted squash with savory ingredients, from chiles and lime to toasted nuts and spiced yogurt, which serve as a surprisingly successful foil to the squash's natural sweetness. I decided to bring this approach into the test kitchen and put my own spin on it.

My tasters were equally smitten with Ottolenghi's approach, but they also had a few comments. While they liked the toppings, most found the texture of the roasted squash skin unappealing, and they noted that the squash wasn't especially caramelized.

My first move was to lose the skin. I could have bought prepeeled squash, but we've found that the flavor of whole squash that you peel yourself is superior. As for the roasting method, Ottolenghi uses a relatively hot oven but a short cooking time of 15 minutes—sufficient to tenderize but not long enough for caramelization. I found that when the squash slices were roasted on the middle oven rack, they turned a light golden brown in about 40 minutes—but only on the side in contact with the baking sheet. For deeper caramelization on both sides, the solution was simple. I moved the sheet to the lowest oven rack, where it would absorb even more heat from the main heating element on the oven's floor. I then flipped the squash (and rotated the baking sheet) partway through roasting so that both sides could caramelize.

So far so good, but I had another idea. I had been tossing the squash with olive oil before roasting, but melted butter produced better browning, thanks to its milk proteins that undergo the Maillard reaction, leading to more complex flavors and aromas. These slices emerged perfectly caramelized, wonderfully

sweet, and tender—until I got to the edge of each slice. Despite my having removed the skin, the outer edge of each slice was tough.

The reason is this: Below the skin sits a white layer of flesh laced with greenish fibers, and I discovered that this rugged matrix resists turning tender, even with prolonged cooking. The fix? A few more swipes with my vegetable peeler revealed a pumpkin-orange interior that baked up tender from the center to the outer edge of each slice.

My last step was to come up with toppings that provided a mix of contrasting textures and bold flavors—including one with brown butter, hazelnuts, lemon juice, and chives. With my new approach I felt emboldened to add a little sweetness in the form of maple syrup to another savory topping, this one featuring goat cheese and pecans. You may not immediately recognize these dishes as the familiar roasted butternut squash, but actually, that's the point.

Peel deep and slice thin for squash that's well caramelized and tender from edge to edge.

ROASTED BUTTERNUT SQUASH WITH BROWNED BUTTER AND HAZELNUTS
SERVES 4 TO 6

For plain roasted squash omit the topping. This dish can be served warm or at room temperature. For the best texture it's important to remove the fibrous flesh just below the squash's skin. For our free recipes for Roasted Butternut Squash with Radicchio and Parmesan and Roasted Butternut Squash with Tahini and Feta, go to CooksIllustrated.com/feb14.

Squash
- 1 large (2½- to 3-pound) butternut squash
- 3 tablespoons unsalted butter, melted
- ½ teaspoon salt
- ½ teaspoon pepper

Topping
- 3 tablespoons unsalted butter, cut into 3 pieces
- ⅓ cup hazelnuts, toasted, skinned, and chopped coarse
- 1 tablespoon water
- 1 tablespoon lemon juice
- Pinch salt
- 1 tablespoon minced fresh chives

1. FOR THE SQUASH: Adjust oven rack to lowest position and heat oven to 425 degrees. Using sharp vegetable peeler or chef's knife, remove skin and fibrous threads from squash just below skin (peel until squash is completely orange with no white flesh remaining, roughly ⅛ inch deep). Halve squash

lengthwise and scrape out seeds. Place squash, cut side down, on cutting board and slice crosswise ½ inch thick.

2. Toss squash with melted butter, salt, and pepper until evenly coated. Arrange squash on rimmed baking sheet in single layer. Roast squash until side touching sheet toward back of oven is well browned, 25 to 30 minutes. Rotate sheet and continue to bake until side touching sheet toward back of oven is well browned, 6 to 10 minutes. Remove squash from oven and use metal spatula to flip each piece. Continue to roast until squash is very tender and side touching sheet is browned, 10 to 15 minutes longer.

3. FOR THE TOPPING: While squash roasts, melt butter with hazelnuts in 8-inch skillet over medium-low heat. Cook, stirring frequently, until butter and hazelnuts are brown and fragrant, about 2 minutes. Immediately remove skillet from heat and stir in water (butter will foam and sizzle). Let cool for 1 minute; stir in lemon juice and salt.

4. Transfer squash to large serving platter. Drizzle butter mixture evenly over squash. Sprinkle with chives and serve.

ROASTED BUTTERNUT SQUASH WITH GOAT CHEESE, PECANS, AND MAPLE

Omit topping. Stir 2 tablespoons maple syrup and pinch cayenne pepper together in small bowl. Before serving, drizzle maple mixture over squash and sprinkle with ⅓ cup crumbled goat cheese; ⅓ cup pecans, toasted and chopped coarse; and 2 teaspoons fresh thyme leaves.

Quinoa Pilaf for Nonbelievers

Could we turn this superfood into a dish we'd really want to eat?

> BY DAN SOUZA <

In the span of a decade, quinoa, a seed with humble South American roots, has gone from obscurity to mass consumption in America. I've always assumed its rapid ascent is mainly due to awareness of its health benefits (it's a nearly complete protein that's rich in fiber). While in theory the cooked grain (almost no one calls quinoa a seed) has an appealingly nutty flavor and crunchy texture, in practice it more often turns into a mushy mess with washed-out flavor and an underlying bitterness.

Pilaf recipes that call for cooking the grain with onion and other flavorings don't help matters. If it's blown out and mushy, quinoa pilaf is no better than the plain boiled grain on its own. I was determined to develop a foolproof approach to quinoa pilaf that I'd want to make not because it was healthy but because it tasted great.

My first clue into what might go wrong with the usual quinoa pilaf surfaced as soon as I gathered up recipes to try. All called for softening onion in butter or oil, adding quinoa to the pan and toasting it in the same fat, then pouring in liquid, and simmering covered until the grains were cooked through and the liquid was absorbed. Almost without exception, these recipes used a 2:1 ratio of liquid to quinoa. Could that be the problem?

To find out, I put together a basic working recipe: Soften finely chopped onion in butter in a saucepan, stir in quinoa and water, cover, and cook until tender. I then tested a range of water-to-quinoa ratios and found that, while 2 to 1 might be the common rule, 1 to 1 was nearly perfect. To allow for evaporation, I tweaked this ratio just slightly, using a bit more water than quinoa (1¾ cups water to 1½ cups quinoa). After about 20 minutes of covered simmering, the quinoa was tender, with a satisfying bite.

Or at least most of it was. There was a ½-inch ring of overcooked seeds around the pot's circumference. The heat of the pot was cooking the outer grains faster than the interior ones. To even things out, my first thought was to stir the quinoa halfway through cooking, but I feared that I would turn my pilaf into a starchy mess, as so easily happens with rice. But I needn't have worried. A few gentle stirs at the midway point gave me perfectly cooked quinoa, with no ill effects. Why? While quinoa is quite starchy—more

so than long-grain white rice—it also contains twice the protein of white rice. That protein is key, as it essentially traps the starch in place so you can stir it without creating a gummy mess.

The texture of the quinoa improved further when I let it rest, covered, for 10 minutes before fluffing. This allowed the grains to finish cooking gently and firm up, making them less prone to clump.

It was time to think about the toasting step. While the majority of quinoa on the market has been debittered, some bitter-tasting compounds (called saponins) remain on the exterior. We have found that toasting quinoa in fat can exacerbate this bitterness, so I opted to dry-toast the grains in the pan before sautéing the onion. After about 5 minutes in the pan, the quinoa smelled like popcorn. This batch was nutty and rich-tasting, without any bitterness.

Finally, I turned to seasonings. For a simple take, I finished the quinoa with herbs and lemon juice. Next, I looked to quinoa's birthplace for a combination with chile, *queso fresco*, lime juice, and peanuts. And to highlight quinoa's versatility, I developed a Mediterranean-inspired recipe with apricots, pistachios, and aged gouda. I always kept a judicious hand with additions, ensuring that my quinoa stayed in the spotlight—right where it belonged.

Using less water than is typical, plus stirring during cooking, delivers fluffy, evenly cooked quinoa.

QUINOA PILAF WITH HERBS AND LEMON
SERVES 4 TO 6

If you buy unwashed quinoa, rinse the grains in a fine-mesh strainer, drain them, and then spread them on a rimmed baking sheet lined with a dish towel and let them dry for 15 minutes before proceeding with the recipe. For more information on quinoa, see page 31. Any soft herbs, such as cilantro, parsley, chives, mint, and tarragon, can be used. For our free recipes for Quinoa Pilaf with Olives, Raisins, and Cilantro and Quinoa Pilaf with Shiitakes, Edamame, and Ginger, go to CooksIllustrated.com/feb14.

1½	cups prewashed quinoa
2	tablespoons unsalted butter, cut into 2 pieces
1	small onion, chopped fine
¾	teaspoon salt
1¾	cups water
3	tablespoons chopped fresh herbs
1	tablespoon lemon juice

1. Toast quinoa in medium saucepan over medium-high heat, stirring frequently, until quinoa is very fragrant and makes continuous popping sound, 5 to 7 minutes. Transfer quinoa to bowl and set aside.

2. Return now-empty pan to medium-low heat and melt butter. Add onion and salt; cook, stirring frequently, until onion is softened and light golden, 5 to 7 minutes.

3. Increase heat to medium-high, stir in water and quinoa, and bring to simmer. Cover, reduce heat to low, and simmer until grains are just tender and liquid is absorbed, 18 to 20 minutes, stirring once halfway through cooking. Remove pan from heat and let sit, covered, for 10 minutes. Fluff quinoa with fork, stir in herbs and lemon juice, and serve.

QUINOA PILAF WITH APRICOTS, AGED GOUDA, AND PISTACHIOS

Add ½ teaspoon grated lemon zest, ½ teaspoon ground coriander, ¼ teaspoon ground cumin, and ⅛ teaspoon pepper with onion and salt. Stir in ½ cup dried apricots, chopped coarse, before letting quinoa sit for 10 minutes in step 3. Substitute ½ cup shredded aged gouda; ½ cup shelled pistachios, toasted and chopped coarse; and 2 tablespoons chopped fresh mint for herbs.

QUINOA PILAF WITH CHIPOTLE, QUESO FRESCO, AND PEANUTS

Add 1 teaspoon chipotle chile powder and ¼ teaspoon ground cumin with onion and salt. Substitute ½ cup crumbled queso fresco; ½ cup roasted unsalted peanuts, chopped coarse; and 2 thinly sliced scallions for herbs. Substitute 4 teaspoons lime juice for lemon juice.

See How We Made It Better
Video available FREE for 4 months at CooksIllustrated.com/feb14

Easy Sandwich Bread

A tasty, even crumb and a tender crust, requiring minimal kneading and no shaping, in less than 2 hours. Fantasy? Or the best thing since sliced bread?

> BY ANDREA GEARY

A freshly baked loaf of bread is one of life's great pleasures. But these days, most people don't have 4 hours to devote to mixing dough, waiting for it to rise for an hour or so—twice—plus kneading (even if it's the stand mixer approach of most recipes today), shaping, and baking. While I can appreciate the classic bread-making process, I wondered: Could I find a way to make a yeasted loaf of bread in about half of the time? Furthermore, could I possibly avoid, or at least shortcut, some of the work?

I began by scouring cookbooks and websites for clever bread-making tricks and came across an old-fashioned type of loaf: batter bread. As its name implies, the yeasted loaf begins with a fluid batter (not a thick dough) that's made of all-purpose flour, yeast, salt, sugar, and quite a bit of water. Since its hydration level is so high (80 to 85 percent), the batter is beaten with a paddle instead of a dough hook (usually for about 5 minutes) and is transferred straight from the mixing bowl to a prepared loaf pan, no shaping required. And some recipes call for only one rise rather than the two needed to make most traditional loaves. They all promised tender loaves with great flavor—homemade sandwich bread without all the work. Was it too good to be true?

Well, yes and no. The few batter bread recipes I tried featured quick and easy aspects—less time being kneaded in the mixer (some even relied on just a wooden spoon and bowl), abbreviated or fewer proofs, and no shaping—that met my requirements. But that speed and simplicity came at a price. The loaves were generally squat and dumpy-looking, with bumpy, sunken tops instead of smooth, tender domes. Slicing revealed damp, fragile interiors that were exceedingly yeasty but otherwise bland. I wanted great-tasting bread with a soft, uniform crumb sturdy enough to support sandwich fillings. To get a loaf that justified even a modest effort, I'd have to make some serious modifications.

Building Character

I decided to solve the easiest problem first: that single-note yeast flavor. For quick rising, all the batter bread recipes that I found rely on more

An old-fashioned way to make bread inspires a loaf perfect for toast or sandwiches in about half of the time a conventional yeast bread requires.

than twice as much yeast as traditional loaf recipes do: 2¼ teaspoons versus 1 teaspoon. But all that yeast was giving the breads an overly yeasty, not "bready," flavor. Nevertheless, I was committed to sticking with the large amount since it made such a huge time savings.

My elementary but effective strategy was to cover up part of the yeastiness by working in some more flavorful ingredients. Adding a few tablespoons of melted butter was a good start toward a tastier loaf, and substituting whole-wheat flour for a portion of the all-purpose flour provided nutty, wheaty depth. I also traded 1 tablespoon of honey for the sugar, which was a twofer: It contributed complexity, and because heat causes honey to break down into simple sugars that encourage browning, it also gave the crust a bit more color.

Next up: building that complexity. In traditional bread, complexity develops by way of fermentation, which happens during the first and second rises. In these two proofing stages (each of which takes about an hour) the yeast consumes the sugars

that are created as the starches in the flour break down, producing the gases essential for making the dough rise. Along the way, a multitude of flavorful byproducts are generated: sugars, acids, and alcohol. Knowing this, I decided that there was no way that I could get by with just one rise. Two 20-minute proofs—one after mixing the batter and one after transferring it to the pan—would allow for at least some flavor development.

My bread, which was coming together in about 90 minutes, now had quite a bit more depth, and the yeast flavor was much less noticeable than in previous versions. But it still wasn't winning points for its damp, fragile texture or sunken appearance.

Network Failure

Yeasted breads derive their light, airy structure from gluten, a stretchy protein network that forms only when wheat flour is combined with water. That network traps the gases given off by the yeast, inflating the dough and causing it to rise. (If the gluten structure is weak, the network can't hold enough gas and the bread will collapse in the heat of the oven.) When a dough is initially mixed, the proteins that form the

PHOTOGRAPHY: CARL TREMBLAY; ILLUSTRATION: JOHN BURGOYNE

What Makes It Faster—and Easier?

The dough, or batter, for our bread is made with more than double the amount of yeast used in a typical sandwich bread, and it has 20 percent more water by weight. We also use the paddle attachment of our stand mixer instead of the dough hook employed for almost all other bread doughs.

MORE YEAST		HIGHER HYDRATION		PADDLE ATTACHMENT
WHY IT HELPS	+	**WHY IT HELPS**	+	**WHY IT HELPS**
Lots of yeast means a faster rise—20 minutes versus up to 2 hours for a standard loaf.		More water in the dough (up to a point) enhances gluten structure without requiring as much kneading; it also results in pourable dough that doesn't need shaping.		Using a paddle (more typically used to beat heavy cookie dough) instead of a dough hook allows for more aggressive, faster kneading.

network are weak and disorganized. They need to align in order to link up and acquire strength. Given enough time, they will line up on their own, or they can be physically encouraged to do so by kneading.

You'd think that my bread would have had a mighty strong gluten network since I had been beating the batter in the mixer for 5 minutes. Yet the loaf's inadequate volume, sunken top, and fragile crumb suggested otherwise.

Before launching an in-depth investigation into the disappointing structure and crumb, I made a quick adjustment: I swapped the all-purpose flour for higher-protein bread flour. More gluten-forming proteins in the bread-flour dough would surely result in a more robust structure. This switch was a step in the right direction, but my loaf still had a long way to go.

My batter had so much water in it that the loaf was damp. Maybe that was too much liquid? I knew that the hydration level of a dough (or batter, in this case) affects gluten strength: Generally, the more water, the stronger and more extensible the gluten strands are and the better able they are to provide support. That translates into a sturdier, airier bread. But there's a tipping point: Unless you are planning on a long fermentation—which I wasn't—too much water can actually inhibit the formation of gluten. I had been using 1¾ cups warm water (using warm, rather than room-temperature, water helps jump-start the yeast's activity, ensuring a faster rise). Guessing that my existing batter was too wet, I reduced the water in my next batch to 1¼ cups. I hoped that the resulting loaf would have a slightly drier crumb and that the gluten framework would be sturdier.

I attached the paddle to the mixer, beat the batter for 5 minutes on medium speed, and then set it aside to rise. (The hydration level was still notably high—the dough was still pourable.) After 20 minutes, I transferred the mixture to a greased loaf pan, smoothed the top with a spatula, and let it rise again briefly before baking it for 40 minutes. After the loaf cooled, I evaluated it for signs of improvement. It had a better top: not quite domed, but at least it wasn't lumpy or sunken. When I sliced it, I found a crumb that was not as damp as those of my earlier versions, but it was still fragile. I had made modest progress but not enough.

I thought back to other test kitchen bread recipes in which we have waited to add the salt until later in the mixing process. Why? Salt inhibits both the ability of flour to absorb water and the activity of the enzymes that break down proteins to begin the process of forming gluten. By delaying the addition of salt, I hoped that my bread would be able to develop a stronger gluten network. I mixed the flours, yeast, honey, water, and butter until everything was evenly combined and let the batter rise for 20 minutes. Then I added the salt (dissolved in 2 tablespoons of water for even distribution) and proceeded with mixing, rising, and so on.

At last I had a complete success. The resulting loaf was crowned with a rounded top, and the crumb was more resilient and no longer wet. I had a flavorful sandwich bread that could be made start to finish in about 90 minutes. But I had to admit that its parched surface was not really showcasing my success. To highlight my crowning achievement, I brushed the risen loaf with a shine-enhancing egg wash before baking. As a finishing touch, I brushed the warm loaf with melted butter after turning it out on the cooling rack, which augmented the sheen and made the thin crust even more tender and delicious.

This bread is so easy and quick that fitting it into my weekly schedule will be no problem. But considering how quickly it disappears, I think I'd better make it twice a week.

Flavor Fix

One downside of cutting back on rising time is a sacrifice in flavor, since the trademark taste of a classic loaf develops as fermentation occurs during two slow rises. We compensate for this by adding butter and honey to the batter as well as a bit of nutty whole-wheat flour.

The test kitchen's preferred loaf pan measures 8½ by 4½ inches; if using a 9 by 5-inch pan, check for doneness 5 minutes early. To prevent the loaf from deflating as it rises, do not let the batter come in contact with the plastic wrap. This loaf is best eaten the day it is made, but leftovers may be wrapped in plastic wrap and stored for up to two days at room temperature or frozen for up to one month.

- 2 cups (11 ounces) bread flour
- 6 tablespoons (2 ounces) whole-wheat flour
- 2¼ teaspoons instant or rapid-rise yeast
- 1¼ cups plus 2 tablespoons warm water (120 degrees)
- 3 tablespoons unsalted butter, melted
- 1 tablespoon honey
- ¾ teaspoon salt
- 1 large egg, lightly beaten with 1 teaspoon water and pinch salt

1. In bowl of stand mixer, whisk bread flour, whole-wheat flour, and yeast together. Add 1¼ cups warm water, 2 tablespoons melted butter, and honey. Fit stand mixer with paddle and mix on low speed for 1 minute. Increase speed to medium and mix for 2 minutes. Scrape down bowl and paddle with greased rubber spatula. Continue to mix 2 minutes longer. Remove bowl and paddle from mixer. Scrape down bowl and paddle, leaving paddle in batter. Cover with plastic wrap and let batter rise in warm place until doubled in size, about 20 minutes.

2. Adjust oven rack to lower-middle position and heat oven to 375 degrees. Spray 8½ by 4½-inch loaf pan with vegetable oil spray. Dissolve salt in remaining 2 tablespoons warm water. When batter has doubled, attach bowl and paddle to mixer. Add salt-water mixture and mix on low speed until water is mostly incorporated, about 40 seconds. Increase speed to medium and mix until thoroughly combined, about 1 minute, scraping down paddle if necessary. Transfer batter to prepared pan and smooth surface with greased rubber spatula. Cover and leave in warm place until batter reaches ½ inch below edge of pan, 15 to 20 minutes. Uncover and let rise until center of batter is level with edge of pan, 5 to 10 minutes longer.

3. Gently brush top of risen loaf with egg mixture. Bake until deep golden brown and loaf registers 208 to 210 degrees, 40 to 45 minutes. Using dish towels, carefully invert bread onto wire rack. Reinvert loaf and brush top and sides with remaining 1 tablespoon melted butter. Let cool completely before slicing.

 Watch: The Batter Becomes Bread
Video available FREE for 4 months at
CooksIllustrated.com/feb14

Best Almond Cake

To perfect this elegant European dessert, we deepened its flavor and lightened its texture—and did it all in a food processor.

⇒ BY SARAH MULLINS ⇐

Almond cake is elegantly simple, consisting of a single layer so rich in flavor that it requires no frosting. That nearly every European country has a version of the cake—from Sweden's visiting cake to Italy's *torta di mandorle* to Spain's *tarta de Santiago* (which harks back to the Middle Ages)—is a testament to its appeal.

In addition to its great taste, a reason for the cake's popularity in Europe may be that it's almost impossible to screw up. Putting one together is a straightforward matter. First you cream almond paste or ground almonds with sugar and then butter. Eggs go into the bowl next, followed by a small amount of flour, a bit of salt, and perhaps some almond extract. The batter is poured into a prepared pan and baked, and the dessert is ready to eat as soon as it's cool.

Since recipes for almond cake typically call for little flour and rarely include a leavening agent, the texture of the cake is usually quite dense—the opposite of a fluffy American yellow cake. And when almond paste is used instead of ground almonds, the cake becomes even more solid, bearing a particularly smooth, almost fudgelike consistency. While this is exactly what European cooks intend, I've always found this style a bit too heavy to nibble with tea or to enjoy after a rich dinner. I didn't want an ultrafluffy crumb, but I did want a dessert that was more cake than confection—without sacrificing the trademark rich almond flavor and simplicity of the original.

Going Nutty

My first decision was to nix the almond paste. Store-bought almond paste is usually made up of a 1:1 ratio of ground almonds to sugar, along with a binding agent, such as glucose syrup. But its high sugar content is at least partially responsible for the candylike texture that I wanted to eliminate. That said, commercial almond paste

Toasted sliced almonds topped with sugar and lemon zest dress up and add satisfying crunch to this simple cake.

does have one thing going for it: great nutty flavor. Could I replace the almond paste without losing that?

Using a basic recipe calling for 1¼ cups of sugar, 10 tablespoons of butter, four eggs, and ½ cup of flour, I tried the most convenient substitute first: store-bought almond flour (which is just very finely ground blanched almonds), which I added to the batter with the other dry ingredients. Unfortunately, almond flour's only benefit was accessibility: The cake that it produced had weak almond flavor, plus the flour was so finely milled that the crumb was still quite dense. Since nuts are commonly toasted to improve their taste, I whipped up one more cake using almond flour that I'd browned in a skillet, but it was tricky to get the small particles to toast evenly, and the browning did nothing to help the textural issue.

Next up: toasted whole almonds ground in a food processor. The flavor of this cake was miles ahead of the almond-flour cake, but the pulverized skins of the nuts looked unappealing and tasted somewhat

bitter, so I switched to blanched almonds. For depth, I stirred in a drizzle of almond extract. These changes did the trick. This cake had the concentrated almond flavor of an almond-paste cake, and though it was still rather dense, the cake was now dotted with tiny nut particles that at least broke up the crumb a little. With the almonds settled, I went on to find other ways to lighten the cake.

Supporting Structure

I considered the flour first. When butter and sugar are creamed, the airy mixture can help give a cake lift—but only if the batter contains enough gluten to support air pockets. My cake had so little flour (and therefore so little gluten development) that it was unable to hold on to air, hence its short, dense form. I tried substituting higher-protein bread flour for all-purpose flour, hoping that I could stick with ½ cup and still produce a cake with a strong structure. The bread flour created structure all right—so much that the crumb turned tough and chewy. The best option turned out to be a simple one: adding an extra ¼ cup of all-purpose flour (for a total of ¾ cup), which helped my cake rise a bit higher. Another consideration was leavener, so I stirred a bit of baking powder into my next batch. Just ¼ teaspoon helped inflate the air pockets, resulting in a taller rise. But the cake needed even more lift.

I knew that whipped eggs can give a cake—particularly a low-flour cake like this one—great structure since their protein network can trap air, so I gave it a shot. Using a stand mixer, I whipped the four eggs and 1¼ cups of sugar for 2 minutes. I lit up when the pale yellow mixture nearly tripled in volume. With high hopes, I added the butter (melted this time so it would be easy to incorporate) and then the remaining dry ingredients, poured the batter into a prepared pan, and slid the pan into a 325-degree oven. Sure enough, the cake that came out of the oven was the tallest yet. In fact, it was even loftier than I had intended: Now it was on the high end of the fluffiness spectrum, with the domed top and superlight, aerated crumb typical of an American layer cake. Using fewer eggs wasn't the answer; a two-egg cake was squat and dense.

How We Got the Best Almond Flavor—and Cake Texture

For a rich, nutty taste and a consistency that's not too dense, we toast blanched almonds (we dislike the slight bitterness imparted by skin-on almonds) to deepen their flavor. Then we grind them in the food processor. The ground nuts give the crumb an open, rustic texture.

START WITH BLANCHED ALMONDS

TOAST UNTIL GOLDEN BROWN

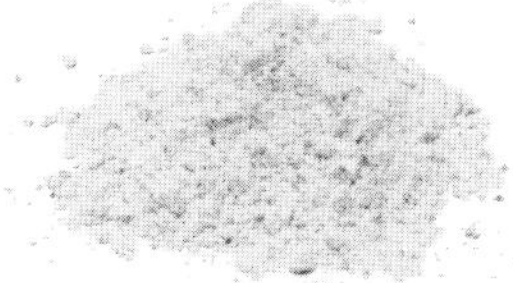

GRIND WITH FLOUR, SALT, AND LEAVENERS

A Simple Process

Feeling as though I was at the end of my rope, I decided to take a break from ingredient testing to consider the equipment. Given that this was a cake known for its simplicity, I wasn't happy calling for two large kitchen appliances—a food processor and a stand mixer. The food processor was a must, as there was no way my stand mixer was going to grind almonds. But what would happen if I tried to whip my ingredients in the food processor instead of in the mixer?

I cracked my eggs into the food processor, added the sugar, and hit the on button. I was excited to see the mixture turn pale and gain some height in the bowl. But when I turned off the machine, the foam partially deflated. Still, I pressed on, adding the melted butter and finally the flour, ground almonds, salt, and baking powder to the food processor bowl. I put the cake in the oven, worried that I'd wasted my time and ingredients. But when I pulled out the finished cake, things were looking up. The unwanted doming hadn't happened, leaving the nicely level top that I was looking for. Once the cake had cooled, I eagerly took a taste. The crumb was no longer reminiscent of an American layer cake. Instead, it was rich and rustic—neither too fluffy nor too dense. Even better, I had used only one appliance to make the cake.

It turns out that a mixer gently unfolds the protein strands of eggs, creating a strong foam that holds on to air. The sharp blade of a food processor is more damaging to protein strands, so the foam that it creates is less sturdy. Lucky for me, this meant that I got exactly the moderately risen crumb and elegant level top that I was looking for.

Now for a few tweaks. The perimeter of the cake was baking through before the middle was set, resulting in slightly dry edges. Knocking down the oven temperature by 25 degrees and substituting vegetable oil for half of the butter solved the problem. The lower oven temperature allowed the cake to bake more slowly, so it cooked more evenly, and since oil, unlike butter, contains no water that evaporates during baking, it produced a moister crumb.

But the lower oven temperature created a new problem. Now the cake wasn't browning as well, emerging pale instead of golden brown. Once again, a seemingly small change had a dramatic impact. Just ⅛ teaspoon of baking soda, which encourages browning reactions, brought back the color without noticeably altering the crumb.

Finally, I wanted to create a crunchy, flavorful topping with a hint of citrus to play off of the great almond flavor. In keeping with the nearly effortless adornment of traditional almond cakes (usually just a dusting of confectioners' sugar), I decided on a sprinkling of sliced almonds and lemon-infused granulated sugar. To echo the lemony flavor of my topping, I also added some lemon zest to the cake batter itself. These easy additions produced a delicate crunch and a pop of citrus flavor. And for those who really want to dress up the dessert, I also developed an orange-spiked crème fraîche.

With its rich taste, lighter texture, and lovely flat top, my almond cake had all the great flavor of the European version with a texture more suited to my American palate.

SCIENCE Egg Foams: Mixer versus Food Processor

The goal when mixing most cake batters is to incorporate a lot of air into the eggs so that the cake will bake up light and tall, and a mixer is usually the best tool to get the job done. For our Best Almond Cake, however, we wanted a flat, level top; just a moderate rise; and a texture that was neither too fluffy nor too dense. Ditching the mixer in favor of a food processor did the trick. Here's why: When eggs and sugar are whipped in a mixer, the whisk gently unfolds the protein strands in the eggs while incorporating lots of air, producing a foam with a strong network that holds on to that air. The outcome? A tall, well-risen, domed cake. A food processor, with its high rpm and very sharp blade, similarly unravels the eggs' protein strands and incorporates air, but it also damages some strands along the way. The result is just what we were after: a flatter, slightly denser cake. –S.M.

MIXER
Tall and domed.

FOOD PROCESSOR
Perfectly flat.

BEST ALMOND CAKE
SERVES 8 TO 10

If you can't find blanched sliced almonds, grind slivered almonds for the batter and use unblanched sliced almonds for the topping. Serve plain or with Orange Crème Fraîche.

- 1½ cups plus ⅓ cup blanched sliced almonds, toasted
- ¾ cup (3¾ ounces) all-purpose flour
- ¾ teaspoon salt
- ¼ teaspoon baking powder
- ⅛ teaspoon baking soda
- 4 large eggs
- 1¼ cups (8¾ ounces) plus 2 tablespoons sugar
- 1 tablespoon plus ½ teaspoon grated lemon zest (2 lemons)
- ¾ teaspoon almond extract
- 5 tablespoons unsalted butter, melted
- ⅓ cup vegetable oil

1. Adjust oven rack to middle position and heat oven to 300 degrees. Grease 9-inch round cake pan and line with parchment paper. Pulse 1½ cups almonds, flour, salt, baking powder, and baking soda in food processor until almonds are finely ground, 5 to 10 pulses. Transfer almond mixture to bowl.

2. Process eggs, 1¼ cups sugar, 1 tablespoon lemon zest, and almond extract in now-empty processor until very pale yellow, about 2 minutes. With processor running, add melted butter and oil in steady stream, until incorporated. Add almond mixture and pulse to combine, 4 to 5 pulses. Transfer batter to prepared pan.

3. Using your fingers, combine remaining 2 tablespoons sugar and remaining ½ teaspoon lemon zest in small bowl until fragrant, 5 to 10 seconds. Sprinkle top of cake evenly with remaining ⅓ cup almonds followed by sugar-zest mixture.

4. Bake until center of cake is set and bounces back when gently pressed and toothpick inserted in center comes out clean, 55 to 65 minutes, rotating pan after 40 minutes. Let cake cool in pan on wire rack for 15 minutes. Run paring knife around sides of pan. Invert cake onto greased wire rack, discard parchment, and reinvert cake onto second wire rack. Let cake cool, about 2 hours. Cut into wedges and serve. (Store cake in plastic wrap at room temperature for up to 3 days.)

ORANGE CRÈME FRAÎCHE
MAKES ABOUT 2 CUPS

- 2 oranges
- 1 cup crème fraîche
- 2 tablespoons sugar
- ⅛ teaspoon salt

Remove 1 teaspoon zest from 1 orange. Cut away peel and pith from oranges. Slice between membranes to release segments and cut segments into ¼-inch pieces. Combine orange pieces and zest, crème fraîche, sugar, and salt in bowl and mix well. Refrigerate for 1 hour.

Baking Pans Prove Their Mettle

Could it possibly make much difference which metal 13 by 9-inch pan you use? Several dozen rounds of baking later, the answer was an unequivocal yes.

⪔ BY DAVID PAZMIÑO ⪕

We can't think of a piece of cookware that's more basic than the 13 by 9-inch metal baking pan, but we also can't think of one that's more essential. It's the vessel that we pull out for everything from sheet cakes and sticky buns to cornbread and bar cookies (though it can't do everything, so we use glass and ceramic baking dishes, too; see "Completing the Trio"). At first glance it might seem as though any one of the generic-looking metal boxes on store shelves would do just fine. But you'd be surprised: Choose the wrong one and your brownies will be overbaked and dry at the edges, and the sticky part of your sticky buns will stick to the pan, not the buns.

Out of the gate we knew that we would only consider pans with sharp, 90-degree (rather than sloped or curved) corners. These are actually harder to find—manufacturers more often opt to make pans with rounded edges since it's a cheaper process. But decades of experience have taught us that pans with straight sides not only produce bars with well-defined, professional-looking edges but also, and more important, ensure that batter sits level and thus bakes evenly. Consider a batch of brownies baked in a pan with rounded corners (we've all had them): Their thin, overbaked edges and domed, underbaked middle happen because the batter can't pool as deep at the shallower curved edges of the pan.

But sharp corners alone don't guarantee perfect results, as we discovered when we set out to find our ideal 13 by 9-inch metal baking pan. We were looking for a sturdy, durable pan that would easily release food and yield baked goods with crisp, tidy corners; uniform color; and a tender crumb from edge to center. In fact, in the eight pans we tested (priced from $9.99 to $32.95), batches of cornbread, brownies, and sticky buns baked up in remarkably different ways. So what exactly makes a pan worth seeking out—or avoiding?

If the pan's surface is too dark in color, as is the case with the Chicago Metallic Non-Stick Bake & Roast Pan, it can be problematic. We found that the dark surface of this pan browned cornbread nicely,

but when it came to brownies, the surface conducted heat just a little too well, and the resulting brownies had tough, cracked edges by the end of the baking time. Sticky buns fared even worse: The buns overbrowned and ended up glued together by the rock-hard, nearly burnt glaze. Pans with lighter surface colors didn't have such extreme problems—none that we tested had issues with undercooking—but a surface that is too light may not deliver browning when you want it. Light, shiny silver vessels, such as those from Fat Daddio's and Parrish, produced decently tanned cornbread, but the loaf turned out by our front-runner, a pan whose color falls somewhere in between dark and light, was so gorgeously bronzed that it garnered oohs and aahs in the test kitchen.

A nonstick coating isn't always required—we line pans with a foil sling when making brownies and bars, guaranteeing easy removal—but it is essential for any recipe for which you might need to invert the pan to release the food once baked, such as an upside-down cake or sticky buns. We found that

Completing the Trio

While a metal baking pan is ideal for making bar cookies, cornbread, sheet cakes, and sticky buns, glass and ceramic dishes are a must for certain jobs.

GLASS

Why You Need It: Tempered glass won't react with acidic foods such as tomatoes and is safe for use with metal utensils. Its transparency lets you track browning, and the rounded corners make it easy to scoop out soupy desserts and casseroles.

Our Favorite: Pyrex Bakeware 9 x 13 Baking Dish

CERAMIC

Why You Need It: Unlike glass and metal pans with nonstick coatings, some ceramic baking dishes are broiler-safe, making this material the only option for dishes that cook entirely or finish browning under the broiler's intense heat.

Our Favorite: HIC Porcelain Lasagna Baking Dish

sticky buns baked in pans without nonstick coatings either had to be chiseled out one by one or, if they did release from the pan, left behind nearly all their glaze. Meanwhile, most pans with nonstick coatings easily released the caramel glaze, including our favorite pan up to this point, which left not a trace behind.

The sticky bun test also highlighted a different issue with two pans boasting innovative features that we initially held high hopes for. One was the Fat Daddio's cheesecake pan, a pan with a removable bottom. We thought that this pan would make recipes like sticky buns easier to manage. Not so. Instead, it leaked the buns' sugary glaze, filling the kitchen with smoke and leaving the buns bare; it also allowed cornbread batter to ooze out. We experienced the same leakage problems with the Focus Foodservice pan extender, a metal frame used by bakeries that sits in a 13 by 9-inch sheet pan to create an instant baking dish.

Cleaning and durability are also important considerations. Nonstick pans that released food readily were also simpler to clean. While we knew that cutting with a metal utensil is generally a bad idea in these pans, it's something we all admittedly do at one time or another. So we cut and served cobblers with metal utensils, and we dragged a knife across the surface as if we were cutting brownies, slicing a grid shape into each empty pan 12 times. Every pan became scratched, the worst being the Chicago Metallic Non-Stick Bake & Roast Pan, whose dark finish chipped off in spots. Aluminum is a comparatively soft material for cookware and bakeware, so we weren't surprised that uncoated aluminum pans didn't fare all that well, becoming deeply grooved. Our front-runner did well in this test, with scratches that felt slightly shallower than the rest and a finish that showed no signs of chipping. But the corrugated surface of the nonstick-coated USA Pan cake pan fared best in our durability tests: Its textured surface disguised scratches and also prevented the knife from penetrating as deeply.

In the end, we had a clear winner. The Williams-Sonoma Goldtouch Nonstick Rectangular Cake Pan gave us moist, evenly baked brownies that required no trimming for crisp, uniform edges; perfectly tender and browned gooey sticky buns with no mess left behind to clean up; and cornbread with star quality. Plus, its reasonably durable finish released baked goods beautifully. At $32.95 it was the most expensive pan in our testing, but the outstanding results it produced make it worthwhile.

See How the Pans Perform

Video available FREE for 4 months at CooksIllustrated.com/feb14

TESTING 13 BY 9-INCH METAL BAKING PANS

We tested eight metal baking pans measuring 13 by 9 inches, baking our chewy brownies, sticky buns with pecans, and cornbread in them and assessing the pans on their performance, design, cleanup, and ability to withstand scratches. Prices shown were paid online, and a source for the winner is on page 32.

DISHWASHER-SAFE

This is the manufacturer's washing recommendation.

PERFORMANCE

We baked brownies, sticky buns, and cornbread in each pan, observing the degree of browning, evenness of cooking from edge to center, and release from the pan. Scores of good, fair, and poor were assigned to each test, and the aggregate score determined the overall rating.

DESIGN

We gave high marks to pans that were easier to move in and out of the oven and flip while still warm and full of food.

CLEANUP

Pans received higher marks if we found it easy to remove baked-on food.

SCRATCHING

As an abuse test, we served cobbler with a metal utensil and used a paring knife to cut each pan as if we were slicing brownies, repeating each stroke 12 times. Pans were downgraded for deep grooves and damage.

	CRITERIA		TESTERS' COMMENTS

HIGHLY RECOMMENDED

WILLIAMS-SONOMA Goldtouch Nonstick Rectangular Cake Pan, 9" x 13"
Model: 1984723 Price: $32.95
Material: Aluminized steel
Nonstick Coating: Yes
Dishwasher-Safe:
Yes, but hand washing recommended

Performance	★★★
Design	★★★
Cleanup	★★★
Scratching	★★

Producing the most evenly cooked, professional-looking baked goods of all the pans we tested, this model made brownies that were level and moist from center to edge and cornbread that was deeply golden and uniformly browned. Not even sticky bun glaze stuck to the pan. Despite becoming slightly scratched in abuse tests, its surface released perfectly and was easy to clean.

RECOMMENDED

USA PAN Rectangular Cake Pan
Model: 1110RC Price: $19.99
Material: Aluminized steel
Nonstick Coating: Yes
Dishwasher-Safe: No

Performance	★★★
Design	★★
Cleanup	★★★
Scratching	★★½

This pan was a strong performer in all tests, though its corrugated-looking bottom ridges were controversial: They left marks that some testers found unappealing on baked goods, but the ridges helped minimize scratches. The pan's nonstick coating released flawlessly. (Note: USA Pan is also the maker of our top-rated Goldtouch pan, though the two have different nonstick finishes.)

RECOMMENDED WITH RESERVATIONS

FAT DADDIO'S 9- by 13- by 2-Inch Sheet Cake Pan
Model: POB-9132 Price: $12.94
Material: 14-gauge anodized aluminum
Nonstick Coating: No
Dishwasher-Safe: No

Performance	★★
Design	★★★
Cleanup	★½
Scratching	★½

The large rolled lip on this pan made it extra-easy to handle. It baked evenly, but the lack of nonstick coating was problematic for gooey sticky bun recipes. The surface showed every scratch, and the pan is not dishwasher-safe.

PARRISH Magic Line 9- by 13- by 2-Inch Oblong Cake Pan
Model: POB-9132 Price: $20
Material: 14-gauge 3003 aluminum alloy
Nonstick Coating: No
Dishwasher-Safe: Yes, but finish will stain and discolor

Performance	★★
Design	★★★
Cleanup	★½
Scratching	★

Bakers appreciated the broad, extended rims that formed handles on this pan, making flipping hot sticky buns easier. This pan baked evenly for great-looking cakes and brownies. Too bad there isn't any nonstick coating, since sticky buns nearly cemented to the bottom. The surface scratched deeply.

NOT RECOMMENDED

CHICAGO METALLIC Non-Stick Bake & Roast Pan
Model: 16945 Price: $13.49
Material: Aluminized steel
Nonstick Coating: Yes
Dishwasher-Safe:
Yes, but hand washing recommended

Performance	★
Design	★★
Cleanup	★★★
Scratching	★

The darkest pan in the testing produced the deepest browning, which gave us a flavorful crust on cornbread but created a challenge with other recipes. We learned to check for doneness early: Brownies had tougher, drier edges; sticky bun glaze hardened into candy. The pan's coating released well, but the knife scratched it deeply, and tiny pieces of coating chipped off.

CHICAGO METALLIC Commercial II Traditional Uncoated Bake & Roast Pan
Model: 49945 Price: $13.17
Material: Aluminized steel
Nonstick Coating: No
Dishwasher-Safe:
Yes, but hand washing recommended

Performance	★
Design	★★
Cleanup	★½
Scratching	★

This sturdy pan underperformed due to its lack of a nonstick coating: Almost all the glaze from the sticky buns was left behind in the bottom of the pan, and cornbread stuck to it like glue. The bottom of the pan scratched deeply.

FAT DADDIO'S Anodized Aluminum Sheet Cheesecake Pan with Removable Bottom
Model: P0BCC-9133 Price: $23.79
Material: 14-gauge anodized aluminum
Nonstick Coating: No
Dishwasher-Safe: No

Performance	★
Design	★★
Cleanup	★
Scratching	★

We had high hopes for this pan with a removable bottom (like a tart pan), looking forward to not having to flip out a cake. But sticky bun glaze leaked and burned, and cornbread batter oozed under and baked the removable bottom right into the bread. The surface scratched deeply.

FOCUS FOODSERVICE Aluminum Sheet Pan Extender, Quarter Size
Model: FSPA811 Price: $9.99
Material: Aluminum
Nonstick Coating: No
Dishwasher-Safe: No

Performance	★
Design	★
Cleanup	★
Scratching	N/A

For bakeries, this product may be a great way to get another use out of a rimmed baking sheet, but it was a flop for us: Sticky glaze leaked all over the oven and burned, and cornbread rose on both sides of the extender and glued it to the sheet. Brownie batter stayed put because of the aluminum sling we'd made to lift the bars from the pan.

In Search of a Better Swiss

We scoured supermarket cases, the deli counter, and specialty cheese shops for Swiss that would shine on a cheese plate, not just melt on a sandwich.

⇒ BY AMY GRAVES ⇐

A pockmarked wedge of Swiss may be instantly recognizable as the icon of "cheese," but it's rarely celebrated for its flavor. Often rubbery and bland, most Swiss—stateside, at least—may be fine as a gooey layer in a Reuben but would never star on a cheese plate. In fact, there was only one sample that we enjoyed eating out of hand the last time we tasted Swiss cheese, in 2005. That genuine Emmentaler from Switzerland made by Emmi (Emmentaler is the real name for the cheese Americans call Swiss) boasted a nuanced, sweet hazelnut flavor. It also comes with a hefty price tag ($18.99 per pound), thanks to processing standards that go along with its Appellation d'Origine Contrôlée (AOC), or Controlled Term of Origin. This prompted us to shop for comparable, but more affordable, cheeses this time around. But since we were so impressed by the flavors of traditionally made Swiss, we also singled out two high-end mail-order cheeses.

The eight cheeses we came away with spanned a wide spectrum of price points and presentations—and even naming conventions. Three were pre-sliced and five were in wedges. Five were called Swiss and one Jarlsberg, the Norwegian version of Swiss-style cheese. Two were genuine Emmentalers from Switzerland, which wear the full moniker of Emmentaler Switzerland AOC (the word "Emmentaler" itself is not protected, meaning that cheeses with that label can come from anywhere). One of those was our previous winner from Emmi; the other, also from Emmi, was a cave-aged product available only via mail order. Finally, we included an Emmentaler from Wisconsin made according to Swiss tradition and available only via mail order.

Flavor Makers

Served plain at room temperature, the cheeses revealed a wide range of flavors and textures—from rubbery, moist, and bland "like string cheese" to drier and more crumbly, with "savory," "grassy," "almost gamy" notes that were unexpected in Swiss cheese and had us swooning.

The ingredient labels helped explain these differences. The three strongest-flavored cheeses were all made from raw milk—an ingredient that is part of the centuries-old and now legally enforced recipe for Emmentaler Switzerland AOC. As we knew from previous cheese research, raw milk's native microflora and enzymes work in tandem with the added cheese cultures to develop the fullest flavor spectrum. The fact that raw milk is so key to a cheese's flavor development might lead you to wonder why so many producers—including five with cheeses in our lineup—go to the trouble of pasteurizing, but it turns out that there's a flavor argument for that, too. The native bacteria in raw milk can also produce unpleasant off-flavors, so large companies (which often buy from multiple dairies and therefore have a harder time controlling milk quality) eliminate possible lows—and, by extension, highs—by pasteurizing the milk, relying solely on the starter culture for flavor. Another reason that cheesemakers pasteurize: cost. Strict U.S. Food and Drug Administration regulations require that raw-milk cheeses be aged for 60 days before sale in the United States, and aging is an expensive process.

Of course, aging cheese also improves its flavor. All but one of the cheeses we sampled was aged for at least 60 days, and our preferences generally fell in line with age. The longer a cheese ripened—at least a year for the two top-rated products—the more complex and nuanced its flavor, and the more we liked it. Meanwhile, tasters compared some of the younger samples with Monterey Jack—or even "plastic." Notably, salt was only a factor for two of the young cheeses. High sodium content is not a characteristic of real Emmentaler, but in these cases it helped mitigate the samples' blandness.

The age of Swiss cheese is also directly related to its most recognizable feature: the holes. These "eyes" are gas bubbles that form inside the wheels when cultures consume lactic acid in the cheese and release it in the form of carbon dioxide. Young cheeses might have gaps the size of peas, whereas the craters in Emmentaler Switzerland AOC can grow as large as walnuts. We put that theory to the test by measuring the diameter of an average-size hole in each cheese and lining up the samples in ranking order. The correlation was obvious: The more mature cheeses had holes that measured roughly 25 millimeters (about 1 inch) on average, while the cheese that wasn't aged at all, a low-ranking sample from Kraft, had a single hole less than one-quarter of that size.

Melting Down Preconceptions

There is a downside to buying aged cheeses, however: They don't melt well—a big problem for a cheese like Swiss that's routinely melted in sandwiches. Instead, older cheeses become oily and separated when heated, as their proteins break down and release casein molecules that bind together with age to form a tough network that doesn't melt smoothly.

Given that, we anticipated texture flaws in the older cheeses when we melted all the samples in grilled cheese sandwiches, but we figured that at least their rich, complex flavors would hold up nicely. So imagine our surprise when tasters panned the sandwiches made with the longest-aged wedges—the darlings of our plain tasting—not so much for their texture but for their unpleasant "funky," "lingering metallic" flavors. Even stranger, heat improved the younger cheeses: Not only did most of them melt beautifully but several young cheeses—including the nonaged Kraft—suddenly gave up "nutty tang."

Baffled, we contacted Mark E. Johnson, senior scientist at the Wisconsin Center for Dairy Research, who offered a scientific explanation for the flavor transformation: Any cheese will taste sharper as it

Signs of a Great Swiss for Snacking

A few visual cues on the packaging—and on the cheese itself—make it easy to pick a top-quality wedge.

⇒ **RAW MILK** The native microflora and enzymes in raw milk add far more complexity than pasteurized milk does.

⇒ **MATURITY** Cheeses that ripen longer will be drier, with richer, grassy, nutty flavors.

⇒ **BIG "EYES"** The bigger the holes the older (and more flavorful) the cheese.

⇒ **"TEARS OF JOY"** These salty, flavorful beads are condensation formed by the gases that produce Swiss cheese's holes.

TASTING SWISS CHEESE

Twenty-one *Cook's Illustrated* staff members sampled eight Emmentaler and Emmentaler-style Swiss cheeses at room temperature and in grilled cheese sandwiches, rating them on flavor, texture, and overall appeal. Products were selected from among top sellers at supermarkets, recent winners of American Cheese Society awards, and recommendations from high-end cheesemongers. Products are listed in order of preference. Sodium levels were based on label information. The hole diameter listed in the chart is based on measuring an average-size hole in a single sample of each cheese. A source for the winner appears on page 32.

HIGHLY RECOMMENDED FOR CHEESE PLATE ONLY	TASTERS' COMMENTS
EDELWEISS CREAMERY Emmentaler Switzerland Swiss Cheese **Price:** $12.99 for 1¼ lb ($0.65 per oz) **Aged:** Up to 12 months **Style:** Raw milk, American-made **Sodium:** 60 mg per oz **Hole Diameter:** 23.7 mm 	We think that Wisconsin-based Edelweiss Creamery, which emulates traditional Swiss methods, including the use of copper vats for flavor development, makes a better Swiss cheese than the Swiss—and for a lot less money. This cheese's "grassy" nuttiness makes it worth mail-ordering, but don't melt it. Those flavors turned "funky" in grilled cheese.
EMMI Kaltbach Cave-Aged Emmentaler Switzerland AOC **Price:** $12.99 for 8 oz ($1.62 per oz) **Aged:** 12 to 18 months **Style:** Raw milk, Swiss import **Sodium:** 50 mg per oz **Hole Diameter:** 26.5 mm 	The rich "savory," "almost gamy" flavors that make this cave-aged raw-milk Swiss import eminently worthy of a cheese plate (and command a high price tag) also render it unsuitable for melting. It made for an "oily" grilled cheese with a "lingering metallic taste."

RECOMMENDED FOR CHEESE PLATE AND COOKING	
EMMI Emmentaler Cheese AOC **Price:** $18.99 for 1 lb ($1.19 per oz) **Aged:** 120 days (4 months) **Style:** Raw milk, Swiss import **Sodium:** 50 mg per oz **Hole Diameter:** 22.9 mm	Thanks to its relative youth and raw-milk base, this Swiss import offered the best of both worlds: a texture that turned "creamy" when melted in a grilled cheese and enough "pleasantly pungent" character for eating out of hand.

RECOMMENDED FOR COOKING ONLY	
BOAR'S HEAD Gold Label Switzerland Swiss Cheese **Price:** $9.75 for 1 lb ($0.61 per oz) **Aged:** More than 120 days **Style:** Pasteurized milk, Swiss import **Sodium:** 60 mg per oz **Hole Diameter:** 13.7 mm	Its "mild nutty flavor" made tasters dub this product a "generic Swiss" straight out of the package, but it soared to the top of the heap in grilled cheese, where it boasted a "great mineral" taste in addition to a "smooth" texture.
NORSELAND Jarlsberg **Price:** $6.99 for 1 lb ($0.44 per oz) **Aged:** 60 days **Style:** Pasteurized milk, Norwegian import **Sodium:** 180 mg per oz **Hole Diameter:** 17.4 mm	This Norwegian version of Swiss shared the relatively bland flavor profile of many of the other cheeses in the lineup, but heat drew out its "nicely salty" flavor (Jarlsberg typically contains more sodium than other Swiss-style cheeses) and also turned it pleasantly "gooey."
KERRYGOLD Swiss Cheese **Price:** $5.99 for 7 oz ($0.86 per oz) **Aged:** 90 days or longer **Style:** Pasteurized milk, Irish import **Sodium:** 110 mg per oz **Hole Diameter:** 11.4 mm	As with the Norseland Jarlsberg, relatively high sodium bolstered the flavor of this Irish-made Swiss; some likened it to a mild "cheddar" straight out of the package. Heated in grilled cheese, it gained "nuttiness." Though its texture was "stretchy" to some, it was still "a good melt."

NOT RECOMMENDED	
KRAFT Natural Cheese Big Slice Swiss **Price:** $2.68 for 8 oz ($0.34 per oz) **Aged:** 0 days **Style:** Pasteurized milk, American-made **Sodium:** 49 mg per oz **Hole Diameter:** 4.8 mm	Without raw milk or any aging at all, this cheese couldn't help tasting like "bland city." Though it developed "some nutty tang" when melted, its texture was also unappealingly "chewy."
SARGENTO Natural Aged Swiss Deli Style Sliced Swiss Cheese **Price:** $4.29 for 7 oz ($0.61 per oz) **Aged:** 60 days or longer **Style:** Pasteurized milk, American-made **Sodium:** 55 mg per oz **Hole Diameter:** 12.12 mm	"Kids' cheese," "generic," "plasticky"—pick your descriptor. This cheese was downright "bland" when eaten plain. Warming it in grilled cheese made it "extremely melty and oozy," but the flavor was still "Blandsville."

ages because of the breakdown in its protein matrix, he said, but Emmentaler is different. Byproducts of the very bacteria that provide its unique flavor can also make it too pungent at higher temperatures. In other words, heat was a bane to older Swiss that boasted good flavor straight out of the package but a boon to younger products that took on some character-building nuttiness when melted.

The Emmi Emmentaler was the exception: Because it was made from raw milk and aged just a little (four months), it had enough complexity to function as a good snacking cheese and also melted nicely. Otherwise, we recommend shopping for Swiss with a purpose: For heated applications, the younger Emmi and Boar's Head cheeses are excellent options, but almost any young Swiss will do. For cheese plates, go for aged raw-milk cheeses like the imported Kaltbach Cave-Aged Emmentaler by Emmi or our favorite (and considerably cheaper) Emmentaler Swiss Cheese from the Edelweiss Creamery—a Wisconsin-based producer that we think out-Swisses the Swiss.

TASTING Baby Swiss

The "baby" in baby Swiss doesn't just refer to the small size of the wheel. To suit Americans' taste for milder cheese, Swiss-born cheesemakers in the 1960s changed the recipe for regular Swiss to reduce its flavor, too: They used pasteurized milk and shortened the culturing step and aging time. Of the four baby Swiss cheeses we tried, our favorite, from Organic Valley, tasted more "nutty," but any of them will function fine as a gooey sandwich layer. For complete tasting results, go to CooksIllustrated.com/feb14. –A.G.

BABY BOOMER
Organic Valley Baby Swiss has more "mineral" Swiss flavor than other brands do.

⇒ BY ANDREW JANJIGIAN & DAN SOUZA ⇐

Reviving Stale Bread

The staling of bread and other starch-based foods is due to a process called retrogradation. In the bread-making process, water hydrates the starches in the flour and then, as the loaf bakes, the starches gelatinize and soften. Over time, the starches in that baked loaf crystallize and incorporate water into the crystalline structure, leading to an apparently dry, stale loaf. The good news is that the water doesn't travel very far: Most of it remains trapped within the starch crystals. This proximity makes the retrogradation process reversible, at least for a little while.

Toasting slices of bread is one way to release water from the starch crystals and thus revive the bread. But what if you want to reverse the staling of an entire loaf? That requires a more gentle touch because in order to avoid water loss due to evaporation, you need to gradually heat the entire loaf to the gelation point (about 140 degrees)—but without heating it to the boiling point of water (212 degrees). In addition, with drier crusty breads like baguettes and *boules*, you also need to supply water to the exterior of the loaf to ensure that all the starches can properly soften.

Here's our method: If the bread is crusty, briefly pass it under a running faucet of cold water (for softer loaves, skip this step). Wrap the loaf tightly with aluminum foil, place it on the middle rack of a cold oven, and set the temperature to 300 degrees. After about 30 minutes (15 to 20 minutes for small or narrow loaves like baguettes), remove the foil and return the loaf to the oven for about 5 more minutes to crisp up the crust.

But note that because reheating a stale loaf doesn't free the starches to move around the way that they can in a just-baked loaf, they recrystallize much more quickly. The effect lasts for only a few hours or so, so make sure to serve or use your revived bread immediately. –A.J.

Bursting the Bubble on Champagne Stemware

Wide, shallow goblets (or *coupes*) were once the stemware of choice for champagne, but these days you're more likely to get a glass of bubbly in a tall, narrow flute. Is one better than the other, or is it just a matter of aesthetics?

In addition to the fact that the compact shape of a flute can keep champagne from warming too fast, a flute limits the exposed surface area of the champagne, which slows the release of carbon dioxide. The bubbles deliver much of champagne's flavor (by way of smell); as the bubbles rise through the liquid, they carry aromatic compounds to the surface and deliver them to your nose. So slowing down the production of bubbles ensures good flavor from first sip to last. The larger exposed surface area of champagne in a coupe would logically translate into the faster release of bubbles and thus a more quickly dissipated flavor.

FAVOR THE FLUTE

Naturally, we had to see (and taste) for ourselves, so we compared champagne served in flutes with bubbly served in wider goblets. Most tasters found the champagne in wider glasses to be fizzier yet flatter in taste; they described the champagne as "sweet" and "acidic," with little complexity. The flutes delivered champagne with "citrusy," "floral," and "fruity" aromas. So while your grandmother's goblets may look retrochic, we suggest that you serve your champagne in flutes. –A.J.

The Science of Cooking: Bubbles in Beverages
Video available FREE for 4 months at CooksIllustrated.com/feb14

SCIENCE Use Salt to Speed Cooling

In the test kitchen we rely on salt for many applications beyond seasoning, but one of the niftiest is adding it to an ice bath to lower the freezing point of water and turn the bath into a superfast freezer.

How is this possible? When ice and water are combined, the exteriors of the ice cubes immediately start to melt. Dissolving salt in the ice water causes individual salt ions to form. These particles disperse throughout the ice water and physically reduce the tendency of water molecules to form ordered crystals of ice at 32 degrees. In other words, the salt depresses the freezing point of the mixture so that more of the ice cubes turn to liquid. Since ice cubes out of most home freezers can be as cold as zero degrees (the temperature that most home freezers are set to), this process introduces very cold water to the ice bath. In the test kitchen we were able to achieve slushy ice baths with temperatures as low as 17 degrees.

In the past, we've found that a well-salted ice bath can chill a bottle of room-temperature wine in less than 40 minutes (compared with the hour plus required to chill one in the freezer). We decided to adapt the technique for several additional applications.

FORMULA FOR FASTER CHILLING
A salty ice bath will quickly cool everything from wine to meat to hot liquids.

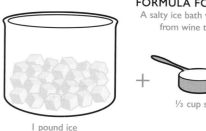

I pound ice   ⅓ cup salt   ⅓ cup water (omit for cooling hot liquid as ice will quickly melt)

FREEZING MEAT FOR STORAGE

When freezing steaks, pork chops or tenderloins, or chicken parts for long-term storage, the faster the meat freezes the smaller the ice crystals. Smaller ice crystals translate into less cellular damage and less loss of juices during cooking. For the juiciest frozen steaks, pork, or chicken, wrap the meat in plastic wrap, place the pieces in a zipper-lock bag, and submerge the bag in the ice, salt, and water. Once the meat is frozen solid (thick cuts will take longer than thin ones), remove the bag from the ice bath and transfer it to the freezer. (In general, we recommend using frozen meat within a few months.)

FREEZING MEAT FOR GRINDING

We often grind our own meat for burgers or other uses, starting with whole cuts that we cube and then partially freeze to facilitate grinding them in a food processor. With this method, meat cubes take about 40 minutes to sufficiently harden. By putting the meat in a single layer in a zipper-lock bag and submerging it in a salted ice bath, the meat freezes 10 times faster—in just 4 minutes.

COOLING HOT LIQUIDS

To bring hot soups and stews to room temperature for storage in the fridge or to quickly chill hot coffee or tea destined to be iced, we place the liquid in a metal container, set it in a second container, and surround it with ice and salt (there's no need to add water since some of the ice melts instantly).

When we used this method to chill 190-degree chicken broth, the salted ice bath hit a frigid 17 degrees, whereas a standard ice bath registered 32 degrees. In our tests, broth allowed to cool in a salted ice bath reached room temperature (72 degrees) in less than 5 minutes. In contrast, broth allowed to cool with ice alone hadn't reached room temperature even after 20 minutes. –D.S.

Why would you want to bone chicken breasts when they're available in every supermarket already boned? Answer: Because you want to cook boneless breasts with skin (which are far harder to find). In our recipe for crispy-skinned chicken breasts (page 7), removing the bones allows the entire surface of the meat to lie flat and even against the pan—a must for perfectly crispy skin. –A.J.

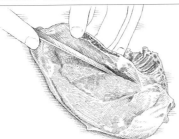
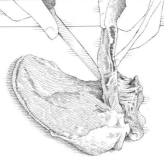

1. With chicken breast skin side down, run tip of boning or sharp paring knife between breastbone and meat, working from thick end of breast toward thin end.

2. Angling blade slightly and following rib cage, repeat cutting motion several times to remove ribs and breastbone from breast.

3. Find short remnant of wishbone along top edge of breast and run tip of knife along both sides of bone to separate it from meat.

Why Color Matters for Roux

A roux, a cooked mixture of flour and fat, works primarily as a thickener or structural agent for sauces and stews, but it also provides the dish with flavor and color. Notably, the flavoring and thickening properties don't work independently.

Roux are always cooked to a specific shade that can range from white to blond to peanut butter—and even darker. The darker the color the more pronounced the roux's flavor. But at the same time that a roux darkens, its thickening power lessens. This is because the intense heat from frying the flour in fat causes its starch chains to break down, and these smaller pieces are less efficient thickeners. So the longer a roux is cooked, the less effective at thickening it will be.

To quantify more precisely how cooking influences a roux's thickening power, we borrowed a specialized tool for measuring viscosity from Brookfield Engineering Laboratories in Middleboro, Massachusetts. We prepared three roux cooked to white, blond, and peanut butter using 4 tablespoons of butter and ¼ cup of all-purpose flour for each batch. We then added 2 cups of water to each roux and simmered the mixtures for 20 minutes. Holding each batch at the same temperature, we then tested their viscosities with the borrowed viscometer. Using the white roux (cooked for just 1 minute) as our baseline, we found that the blond roux (cooked for 3 minutes) had 14 percent less thickening power. The peanut butter–colored roux (cooked for 5 minutes) had 26 percent less thickening power.

The takeaway? These aren't small differences; it's important to cook a roux to the right color. Cook the béchamel for a soufflé too long and it won't have the same thickening power or structural integrity—and your soufflé won't rise as much. And if you shortchange the cooking time for the roux in a stew recipe, you could end up with a gloppy, overly thickened dish. –D.S.

Avoid a Soufflé Meltdown

Soufflé recipes traditionally require attaching a greased parchment collar around the lip of the soufflé dish. Extending the collar several inches above the dish keeps the soufflé contained so that it rises up rather than spills over. But we found that the old-fashioned approach isn't necessary. The key is giving the fluid batter enough room to set up before it rises above the dish's lip. It takes about 20 minutes for the batter to reach the rim, at which point it's set and will continue to rise up, rather than spill over. In our Cheese Soufflé recipe (page 9), we call for leaving an inch of space between the top of the batter and the rim of the dish. Because soufflé dishes vary a bit in capacity, you may not need all the batter in our recipe, so discard any left over after filling your dish to the proper level. (For more information about soufflé dishes, see our testing on page 8.) –A.J.

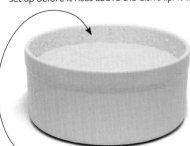

SHOOT FOR BELOW THE RIM
Leaving 1 inch of space between the batter and the rim gives the batter room to set.

Handle with Care

When we tested nonstick skillets in 2010, the manufacturer of our winner, the T-fal Professional Non-Stick Fry Pan, 12.5 Inches, informed us that the pan was ovensafe to 450 degrees. The company recently updated this limit, stating that the silicone covering on the handle could be damaged if heated above 350 degrees. Since we have recipes that require putting a nonstick skillet in an oven hotter than that, we wanted a method for protecting the handle in ovens running up to 450 degrees.

We tried simply wrapping the handle with a double layer of aluminum foil, but in a 450-degree oven this bought us only a few extra minutes before the handle exceeded 350 degrees. A better approach was to wrap the handle in a double layer of wet paper towels and then cover the towels with a double layer of foil. As long as there was water within the foil jacket (it will eventually boil away), the temperature of the handle couldn't exceed 212 degrees (the boiling point of water). We found that the handle stayed safely below 350 degrees for a solid 30 minutes in a 450-degree oven and for well over an hour in a 425-degree oven, after which the water boiled away.

This trick will also work with any pot or pan—not just our winning T-fal skillet—that needs to go into a hot oven and has a handle that is oven-safe only up to 350 degrees. –A.J.

THAT'S A WRAP
Wet paper towels and a double layer of foil can make a skillet handle more heat-resistant.

The Many Colors of Quinoa

WHITE
Most commonly available.

RED
Can be used interchangeably with white quinoa.

BLACK
Use only when specified in recipes.

White quinoa is the most commonly found variety of these tiny seeds native to South America, but red and black varieties are increasingly available. To see if color made a difference, we put together batches of our quinoa pilaf recipes (page 21) using all three types. White quinoa, the largest seeds of the three, had a slightly nutty, vegetal flavor with a hint of bitterness; it also had the softest texture of the three quinoas. The medium-size red seeds offered a heartier crunch, thanks to their additional seed coat and a predominant nuttiness. Black quinoa seeds, the smallest of the three, have the thickest seed coat. They were notably crunchy in our recipe and retained their shape the most during cooking, but many tasters disliked their slightly sandy texture. These seeds had the mildest flavor, with a hint of molasses-like sweetness.

We'll definitely use white and red quinoa interchangeably in our quinoa pilaf recipes and other side dishes or salads, but black quinoa is better off in recipes specifically tailored to its distinctive texture and flavor. –D.S.

⇒ BY AMY GRAVES, LISA McMANUS & SARAH SEITZ ⇐

NEW Reusable Food Wrap

Bee's Wrap, a beeswax-coated cloth, touts itself as an environmentally friendly alternative to plastic wrap. Pliable, reusable for about 1 year with regular (twice per week) usage, and mildly sweet-smelling, the wrap seals to a container or adheres to itself. It comes in three sizes ($16 to $19 for three sheets, depending on size), plus bread wrap ($15 each) for wrapping an entire loaf. We used it to cover serving bowls and to wrap sandwiches and bread. The cloth avoided our

BEE PLUS
Use eco-friendly Bee's Wrap to seal anything but meat.

major pet peeve with plastic—that it clings to itself—and kept food just as tightly sealed. But the wrap isn't recommended for use with meat, since it can't be washed in hot water. The cloth left a light waxy residue on hands and dishes (but not on food), though it came off easily with soap and water. Plastic still trumps beeswax for convenience, but if you're trying to cut down on how much plastic you use, Bee's Wrap can help. –S.S.

UPDATE Blender

When we rated blenders in our September/October 2012 issue, we highly recommended the Hemisphere Control Blender ($199.99) by Breville; it was the co-winner with our high-end favorite, the Vitamix 5200 ($449). But we promised to keep an eye on the

BLENDING IN
Hundreds of smoothies later, Breville's Hemisphere Control Blender is still going strong—with a caveat.

Breville's long-term durability. Since then, we've made more than 400 smoothies in a single copy of the Breville blender, choosing a motor-challenging combination of juice, chunks of frozen fruit, and raw kale. We also purchased six more models for routine use in the test kitchen. The blender that made hundreds of smoothies is still going strong; however, we did have some issues with three of the six kitchen machines. In all cases, the motors worked fine, but problems centered on a tiny button on the base. It's a secondary safety device, which starts the motor when activated by pressure from a slim plastic rib on the inside bottom of the jar. One jar had a broken rib, keeping it from pressing the button. But other faulty machines with intact ribs were more puzzling: If we pressed hard on the outside of the jar, the switch engaged.

Breville engineers examined the machines and concluded that food had dribbled into the button, making the switch sticky, so it failed to engage—so we will be sure to try not to let food drip in that area. Given that our blenders experience unusually heavy use, we still recommend this machine. That said, if you subject your blender to heavy-duty use, you should consider investing in the Vitamix, a powerful commercial-style blender with a seven-year warranty. –L.M.

NEW Red Wine Stain Removers

Embarrassing as it is to spill a glass of red wine, that's a minor concern compared with getting the stain out. We rounded up three red-wine-stain-removal products and used them to treat stains on khakis, white dish towels, and a beige carpet made of polyester shag fibers. All three products lightened the stains on the khakis and towels to a grayish green that disappeared completely after one laundry cycle. The shag carpet sample required more work with each of the products—a few more spritzes or

WINE BEGONE
Wine Away completely eliminated stains from our clothing, towels, and carpeting.

splashes, plus some blotting, drying, and reapplying. Even then, one product, Vino 911, left a faint blemish. Only Wine Away Red Wine Stain Remover completely erased the stain from the carpet without help from water or another cleaner. We purchased two 12-ounce bottles of Wine Away for $21. –A.G.

NEW Innovative Biscuit Cutter

When you roll out and cut biscuit dough with a conventional cutter, you always need to reroll and recut the scraps multiple times. This overworks the dough, leading to biscuits that are tough, dense, and chewy. Enter the Hexagon Biscuit Cutter by Ateco ($9.49), a grid of six hexagonal cutters (each 2⅝ inches across) linked like a honeycomb that allows you to cut nearly all the biscuit dough in one go. Wondering if the cutter was a gimmick or a real solution, we tried it—with great success. The first six biscuits were cut in one swoop. After gently gathering and rerolling scraps from the periphery, we cut the

BETTER BISCUITS
The Hexagon Biscuit Cutter by Ateco cuts biscuits efficiently.

last two biscuits with one more push. The sturdy stainless-steel cutter sliced crisply, producing tall, tender, flaky pastries. –L.M.

For complete testing results of each item, go to CooksIllustrated.com/feb14.

Sources

Prices were current at press time and do not include shipping. Contact companies to confirm information or visit CooksIllustrated.com for updates.

PAGE 8: SOUFFLÉ DISH
- Emile Henry 2-Quart Soufflé Dish: $46.95, item #B0000636WU, Amazon (**amazon.com**).

PAGE 15: TABLET STAND
- Arkon Portable Fold-Up Stand for Tablets: $10.16, item #IPM-TAB1, Amazon.

PAGE 27: 13 BY 9-INCH METAL BAKING PAN
- Williams-Sonoma Goldtouch Nonstick Rectangular Cake Pan, 9" by 13": $32.95, item #1984723, Williams-Sonoma (877-812-6235; **williams-sonoma.com**).

PAGE 29: SWISS CHEESE
- Edelweiss Creamery Emmentaler Switzerland Swiss Cheese: $12.99 for 1¼ lb, Wisconsin Cheese Shop (877-947-2439; **wischeese.com**).

PAGE 32: REUSABLE FOOD WRAP
- Bee's Wrap: $16 to $19 for three sheets or $15 for one bread wrap, Bee's Wrap (**beeswrap.com**).

PAGE 32: BLENDER
- Breville Hemisphere Control Blender: $199.99, item #BBL605XL, Breville (866-273-8455; **brevilleusa.com**).

PAGE 32: RED WINE STAIN REMOVER
- Wine Away Red Wine Stain Remover: $21 for two 12-oz bottles, item #20WA, Wine Away (888-946-3292; **wineaway.com**).

PAGE 32: INNOVATIVE BISCUIT CUTTER
- Ateco Hexagon Biscuit Cutter: $9.49, item #1445151, The WEBstaurant Store (717-392-7472; **webstaurantstore.com**).

U.S. POSTAL SERVICE STATEMENT OF OWNERSHIP, MANAGEMENT AND CIRCULATION

1. Publication Title: Cook's Illustrated; 2. Publication No. 1068-2821; 3. Filing Date: 9/24/13; 4. Issue Frequency: Jan/Feb, Mar/Apr, May/Jun, Jul/Aug, Sep/Oct, Nov/Dec; 5. No. of Issues Published Annually: 6; 6. Annual Subscription Price: $41.70; 7. Complete Mailing Address of Known Office of Publication: 17 Station Street, Brookline, MA 02445; 8. Complete Mailing Address of Headquarters or General Business Office of Publisher: 17 Station Street, Brookline, MA 02445; 9. Full Names and Complete Mailing Address of Publisher, Editor and Managing Editor: Publisher: Christopher Kimball, 17 Station Street, Brookline, MA 02445; Editor: Jack Bishop, 17 Station Street, Brookline, MA 02445; Managing Editor: Rebecca Hays, 17 Station Street, Brookline, MA 02445; 10. Owner: Boston Common Press Limited Partnership, Christopher Kimball, 17 Station Street, Brookline, MA 02445; 11. Known Bondholders, Mortgagees, and Other Securities: None; 12. Tax Status: Has Not Changed During Preceding 12 Months; 13. Publication Title: Cook's Illustrated; 14. Issue Date for Circulation Data Below: September/October 2013; 15a. Total Number of Copies: 1,038,371 (Sep/Oct 2013: 1,060,273); b. Paid Circulation: (1) Mailed Outside-County Paid Subscriptions Stated on PS Form 3541: 790,208 (Sep/Oct 2013: 818,393); (2) Mailed In-County Paid Subscriptions Stated on PS Form 3541: 0 (Sep/Oct 2013: 0); (3) Paid Distribution Outside the Mail Including Sales Through Dealers and Carriers, Street Vendors, Counter Sales, and Other Paid Distribution Outside the USPS: 63,113 (Sep/Oct 2013: 60,347); (4) Paid Distribution by Other Classes of Mail Through the USPS: 0 (Sep/Oct 2013: 0); c. Total Paid Distribution: 853,321 (Sep/Oct 2013: 878,740); d. Free or Nominal Rate Distribution: (1) Free or Nominal Rate Outside-County Copies Included on PS Form 3541: 4,522 (Sep/Oct 2013: 4,547); (2) Free or Nominal Rate In-County Copies Included on Form PS 3541: 0 (Sep/Oct 2013: 0); (3) Free or Nominal Rate Copies Mailed at Other Classes Through the USPS: 0 (Sep/Oct 2013: 0); (4) Free or Nominal Rate Distribution Outside the Mail: 515 (Sep/Oct 2013: 515); e. Total Free or Nominal Rate Distribution: 5,037 (Sep/Oct 2013: 5,062); f. Total Distribution: 858,357 (Sep/Oct 2013: 883,802); g. Copies Not Distributed: 180,014 (Sep/Oct 2013: 176,471); h. Total: 1,038,371 (Sep/Oct 2013: 1,060,273); i. Percent Paid: 99.41% (Sep/Oct 2013: 99.43%).

INDEX
January & February 2014

ONLINE EXCLUSIVES
Available free for 4 months at
CooksIllustrated.com/feb14
Crispy-Skinned Chicken Breasts with
  Lemon-Rosemary Pan Sauce
Crispy-Skinned Chicken Breasts with
  Maple–Sherry Vinegar Pan Sauce
Pasta alla Norcina for Two
Quinoa Pilaf with Olives, Raisins, and Cilantro
Quinoa Pilaf with Shiitakes, Edamame,
  and Ginger
Roasted Butternut Squash with Radicchio
  and Parmesan
Roasted Butternut Squash with Tahini and Feta
Shrimp Fra Diavolo for Two
Tasting Baby Swiss
Testing Innovative Biscuit Cutter
Testing Red Wine Stain Removers
Testing Reusable Food Wrap
Testing Soufflé Dishes
Testing Tablet Stands and Covers

🎥 WATCH NEW VIDEOS
Available free for 4 months at
CooksIllustrated.com/feb14
Best Almond Cake
Cheese Soufflé
Crispy-Skinned Chicken Breasts
Easy Sandwich Bread
Pasta alla Norcina
Pressure-Cooker Pot Roast
Quinoa Pilaf with Herbs and Lemon
Roasted Butternut Squash
Shrimp Fra Diavolo
Testing 13 by 9-Inch Metal Baking Pans
The Science of Cooking: Bubbles in
  Beverages
Vietnamese Beef Pho

AMERICA'S TEST KITCHEN COOKING SCHOOL

Let us help you become a better cook. Offering more than 100 courses for cooks at every level, our school combines personalized instruction from America's Test Kitchen test cooks with leading-edge technology to provide a unique and effective learning experience. Start a 14-day free trial at OnlineCookingSchool.com.

COOK'S ILLUSTRATED IS NOW AVAILABLE ON iPAD!

Download the *Cook's Illustrated* app for iPad and start a free trial subscription or purchase a single issue. Issues are enhanced with recipe videos, full-color step-by-step slide shows, and expanded reviews and ratings. Go to CooksIllustrated.com/iPad to download our app through iTunes.

 Find us on Facebook: facebook.com/CooksIllustrated
Follow us on Twitter: twitter.com/TestKitchen

Best Almond Cake, 25

Shrimp Fra Diavolo, 15

Pressure-Cooker Pot Roast, 11

Quinoa Pilaf with Herbs and Lemon, 21

Roasted Butternut Squash, 20

Crispy-Skinned Chicken Breasts, 7

Cheese Soufflé, 9

Easy Sandwich Bread, 23

Vietnamese Beef Pho, 13

Pasta alla Norcina, 19

Sweet
Tamarind

Guava

Custard
Apple

Mangosteen

Rambutan

Green
Papaya

Young Coconut

Dragon
Fruit

THAI FRUIT

NUMBER 127

MARCH & APRIL 2014

COOK'S
ILLUSTRATED

Shredded Beef Tacos
Faster, Easier, Meatier

A Whole New Way to Poach Chicken

Higher, Lighter Scones
Traditional British Technique

Complete Guide to Classic Sauces
Translated for the Home Cook

Best Orange Juice
How Fresh Is "Fresh"?

Thai Chicken Curry
Simplified, Not Dumbed Down

Lemon Pudding Cake
Perfecting Both Layers

Sesame-Crusted Salmon
Testing Colanders
Pasta with Cauliflower

CooksIllustrated.com
$6.95 U.S. & CANADA

CONTENTS

March & April 2014

COOK'S
ILLUSTRATED

Founder and Editor	Christopher Kimball
Editorial Director	Jack Bishop
Editorial Director, Magazines	John Willoughby
Executive Editor	Amanda Agee
Test Kitchen Director	Erin McMurrer
Managing Editor	Rebecca Hays
Executive Food Editor	Keith Dresser
Senior Editors	Lisa McManus
	Dan Souza
Senior Editors, Features	Elizabeth Bomze
	Louise Emerick
Copy Editors	Nell Beram
	Megan Ginsberg
Associate Editors	Hannah Crowley
	Andrea Geary
	Amy Graves
	Andrew Janjigian
	Chris O'Connor
Test Cooks	Daniel Cellucci
	Lan Lam
Assistant Editors	Shannon Friedmann Hatch
	Lauren Savoie
Assistant Test Cooks	Cecelia Jenkins
	Sarah Mullins
Assistant Test Kitchen Director	Leah Rovner
Senior Kitchen Assistants	Michelle Blodget
	Meryl MacCormack
Kitchen Assistants	Maria Elena Delgado
	Shane Drips
	Ena Gudiel
Executive Producer	Melissa Baldino
Co-Executive Producer	Stephanie Stender
Production Assistant	Kaitlin Hammond
Contributing Editor	Dawn Yanagihara
Consulting Editor	Scott Brueggeman
Science Editor	Guy Crosby, PhD
Managing Editor, Web	Christine Liu
Senior Editor, Cooking School	Mari Levine
Associate Editors, Web	Eric Grzymkowski
	Roger Metcalf
Assistant Editors, Web	Jill Fisher
	Charlotte Wilder
Senior Video Editor	Nick Dakoulas
Design Director	Amy Klee
Art Director	Julie Cote
Deputy Art Director	Susan Levin
Associate Art Director	Lindsey Timko
Deputy Art Director, Marketing	Jennifer Cox
Associate Art Directors, Marketing	Melanie Gryboski
	Mariah Tarvainen
Designer, Marketing	Judy Blomquist
Staff Photographer	Daniel J. van Ackere
Photo Editor	Steve Klise
Vice President, Marketing	David Mack
Circulation Director	Doug Wicinski
Circulation & Fulfillment Manager	Carrie Fethe
Partnership Marketing Manager	Pamela Putprush
Marketing Assistant	Marina Tomao
VP, Technology, Product Development	Barry Kelly
Director, Project Management	Alice Carpenter
Production & Traffic Coordinator	Britt Dresser
Development Manager	Mike Serio
Chief Operating Officer	Rob Ristagno
Production Director	Guy Rochford
Workflow & Digital Asset Manager	Andrew Mannone
Senior Color & Imaging Specialist	Lauren Pettapiece
Production & Imaging Specialists	Heather Dube
	Lauren Robbins
Director of Sponsorship Sales	Anne Traficante
Client Services Associate	Kate May
Sponsorship Sales Representative	Morgan Ryan
Customer Service Manager	Jacqueline Valerio
Customer Service Representatives	Jessica Haskin
	Andrew Straaberg Finfrock
	Juliet Tierney
Retail Sales & Marketing Director	Emily Logan
Human Resources Director	Adele Shapiro
Publicity	Deborah Broide

PRINTED IN THE USA

GULF COAST FISH REDFISH, or red drum, has copper scales, a white belly, and dark splotches on its tail. Rubbing fillets with Cajun blackening spices and then grilling is a popular preparation. Both redfish and BLACK DRUM are sometimes sold as "puppy drum," a label that indicates that the fish is young and small in size and good for eating. The SOUTHERN KINGFISH is also known as sea mullet. Whole or filleted, this firm, white fish is frequently breaded and pan-fried until crispy. The meaty, mild, firm flesh of RED SNAPPER is adaptable to nearly any cooking method. GULF FLOUNDER'S subtle flavor and tender, delicate flesh make it equally versatile. BLACK GROUPER'S skin is thick and tough, but its flesh is moist and flaky. Iridescent POMPANO has a mild fish flavor and a moderately oily texture.

COVER (*Mangos*): Robert Papp; **BACK COVER** (*Gulf Coast Fish*): John Burgoyne

GULF COAST FISH

America's TEST KITCHEN

RECIPES THAT WORK®

COLD RAIN AND SNOW

It was a cold rain. Not the kind that splashes off a jaunty baseball cap and onto a summer cattail. This was a chilling rain, a damp that seeped under my collar, trickled down my back; a rain that melted the snow into fog that rolled up from the hollow, into the upper meadow, and then up toward my hunting cabin on the mountaintop. The 100-mile view of overlapping ranges turned into a whiteout; even the stand of trees at the bottom of the meadow faded to gauzy white and was swallowed as if I were observing through a sinking porthole.

If you asked me what I was up to on that November Sunday, I would have said hunting, but I was wondering what was over the far ridge to the southeast, past the pine-strewn ledges where big bucks are known to bed down during the day, past the stand of dead chestnut trees on the steep sidehill over and down toward Chunks Brook Road. I had been turned around more than once on top of that ridge, looking out west when I thought it was east. When unsure of location, I sit and do nothing except observe one gray squirrel chasing another over a matter of nuts. Civilization retreats and nature has its moment. Bears, deer, rabbits, and bobcats live in these woods through the winter, making their way through deep snowfall, eating bark and digging up greens from under drifts. There's a thought for modern man.

Some of us—there is a name for it, I'm sure—awake in the fall, when the gunmetal November skies return, the cold rain falls, and an icy swirl forms on the insides of storm windows in the old farmhouse.

The frost is on the pumpkin and the mud freezes to ruts. The soft cushion of fall leaves turns to a stiff crunch underfoot, layered with a top frosting of first snowfall. The woods quiet down, the helter-skelter of noisy summer heads south, and we are left with whatever sound rings true—the rush of a brook, the squeak and skid of strong oak limbs in an upsurge of wind, and the hoot of an owl, or perhaps it was actually a bear calling out across the ridgelines. I wait for the response.

There are times in these dark woods when you imagine that cities have never been built, that the era of humans has come and gone. You notice the direction of the wind—a southerly blow means a change of weather—and you know just how much daylight is left after what weakly passes for the sun drops down below the western ridgeline.

At first, I thought that the winter woods were about nothing—an antidote to a world stuffed with everything. The winter makes you work for it, makes you reach out and grab whatever truth is buried in the hills and swales like verse from T. S. Eliot: "There will be time to murder and create, / And time for all the works and days of hands / That lift and drop a question on your plate." Summer offers itself glibly, like some garishly suited hawker of entertainment. The winter work is worth it for those who can sift

Christopher Kimball

through the stanzas of triple meaning, how a leaden sky offers release from quotidian burdens.

You think, as the poet did, of disturbing the universe with a new thought. Maybe all that has come before has no meaning, or perhaps there is no meaning at all. The signs of human ignorance are everywhere: a dead fox decomposing into an upper pasture, bear tracks in soft snow, a great horned owl gliding silently through a thickly wooded hollow. I sift through clues to observe what lies behind the dark curtain of forest.

Just before sleep, this ocean of cold rain and snow offers lovelorn visions, like the mermaids of J. Alfred Prufrock.

I have seen [the mermaids] riding seaward on
   the waves
Combing the white hair of the waves blown back
When the wind blows the water white and black.

We have lingered in the chambers of the sea
By sea-girls wreathed with seaweed red and brown
Till human voices wake us, and we drown.

I fall asleep, dreaming of November woods, with no fear of waking. Let others drown in what might have been.

FOR INQUIRIES, ORDERS, OR MORE INFORMATION

CooksIllustrated.com
At CooksIllustrated.com, you can order books and subscriptions, sign up for our free e-newsletter, or renew your magazine subscription. Join the website and gain access to 21 years of *Cook's Illustrated* recipes, equipment tests, and ingredient tastings, as well as companion videos for every recipe in this issue.

COOKBOOKS
We sell more than 50 cookbooks by the editors of *Cook's Illustrated*, including *The Cook's Illustrated Cookbook* and *The Science of Good Cooking*. To order, visit our bookstore at CooksIllustrated.com/bookstore.

COOK'S ILLUSTRATED MAGAZINE
Cook's Illustrated magazine (ISSN 1068-2821), number 127, is published bimonthly by Boston Common Press Limited Partnership, 17 Station St., Brookline, MA 02445. Copyright 2014 Boston Common Press Limited Partnership. Periodicals postage paid at Boston, MA, and additional mailing offices, USPS #012487. Publications Mail Agreement No. 40020778. Return undeliverable Canadian addresses to P.O. Box 875, Station A, Windsor, ON N9A 6P2. POSTMASTER: Send address changes to *Cook's Illustrated*, P.O. Box 6018, Harlan, IA 51593-1518. For subscription and gift subscription orders, subscription inquiries, or change of address notices, visit AmericasTestKitchen.com/support, call 800-526-8442 in the U.S. or 515-248-7684 from outside the U.S., or write to us at *Cook's Illustrated*, P.O. 6018, Harlan, IA 51593-1518.

FOR LIST RENTAL INFORMATION Contact Specialists Marketing Services, Inc., 777 Terrace Ave., 4th Floor, Hasbrouck Heights, NJ 07604; phone: 201-865-5800.

EDITORIAL OFFICE 17 Station St., Brookline, MA 02445; phone: 617-232-1000; fax: 617-232-1572. For subscription inquiries, visit AmericasTestKitchen.com/support or call 800-526-8442.

⇒ BY ANDREA GEARY, LAN LAM & SARAH MULLINS ⇐

Stabilizing Whipped Cream

Is there a way to keep whipped cream from weeping if you want to make it ahead of time?

RACHEL TAYLOR
ANNAPOLIS, MD.

➤ Unlike other dessert toppings and frostings, whipped cream doesn't keep well if made in advance. After a few hours it begins to weep out liquid and eventually loses the air bubbles that have been whipped into it. In the past, we've held whipped cream in a fine-mesh strainer set over a bowl for up to 8 hours. To see if we could stabilize the topping to avoid the strainer setup and hold it even longer, we tried a slew of additives we'd heard might help: marshmallow crème, xanthan gum, cream of tartar, confectioners' sugar, nonfat dry milk powder, instant dry vanilla pudding mix, gelatin, and buckwheat flour. Some ingredients, like cream of tartar, worked well but added unwanted flavors. Others, like xanthan gum, made the whipped topping more dense and reminiscent of sour cream. The best of the bunch proved to be gelatin, which we first heated in a bit of water to liquefy it and ensure even distribution in the cold cream. It kept liquid from weeping for a full day, contributed no additional flavors, and didn't noticeably change the texture of the whipped cream.

To make 3 cups of whipped cream in advance, sprinkle ½ teaspoon of unflavored powdered gelatin over 1½ tablespoons of water in a microwave-safe bowl and let it stand for 3 minutes. Microwave the mixture in 5-second increments until the gelatin is dissolved and liquefied. Whip 1½ cups of chilled heavy cream (along with 1½ teaspoons of sugar and ½ teaspoon of vanilla extract, if desired) in a stand mixer, staying on low speed until small bubbles form and then increasing the speed to medium. When the beaters begin to leave a trail in the cream, slowly pour in the gelatin mixture and then increase the speed to high and continue to beat until soft peaks form. If well covered, the whipped cream will retain its moisture and airiness for up to 24 hours. –S.M.

DEFLATED
After 2 to 3 hours, liquid (and air) escapes from whipped cream.

FULL OF AIR
A little gelatin whipped with the dairy keeps things stable for 24 hours.

▶ The Science of Cooking: Beer Batter
Video available free for 4 months
at CooksIllustrated.com/apr14

The Role of Beer in Beer Batter

What does the beer in a beer batter coating do? Can I substitute something else?

ROGER PLANT
BON AIR, ALA.

➤ Beer batter—made by combining beer (usually a lighter style such as a lager), egg, and flour—is often used to coat fish, onion rings, and other types of pub-style fare before deep-frying. Though we've found that including hard liquor in the batter can lead to more-tender results in tem-

PICK YOUR BUBBLY
Any of these carbonated drinks will lead to a light, tender batter-fried crust.

pura, the alcohol in most lagers and pilsners is so low (about 5 percent by volume) that its effect would be minimal at best. Far more important is the fact that beer is carbonated, which affects the batter in two ways. First, the bubbles provide lift as they escape from the batter during frying. Second, the carbonation makes the batter slightly more acidic, which limits how much gluten can form when the beer and flour mix, preventing the batter from turning tough. This is because gluten forms most readily in a pH of 5 to 6, while most carbonated beverages share a similar pH of 4 (unless they contain a strongly acidic ingredient). In theory any bubbly drink with a neutral or appropriate flavor profile could serve as a substitute. To prove this point, we fried fish in batters made with beer, nonalcoholic beer, seltzer, and water and found that all the batches with a carbonated beverage did indeed lead to noticeably lighter, lacier crusts than the batter made with plain water. In sum, carbonation and pH are the biggest factors in delivering a better batter-fried crust, so feel free to use bubbly substitutes such as nonalcoholic beer or seltzer water. –L.L.

Storing Cream Cheese Frosting

Can I leave a cake with cream cheese frosting out on the counter, or do I have to refrigerate it?

DONALD TURNER
VENTURA, CALIF.

➤ Because we don't particularly enjoy eating cold cake, whenever possible we like to leave cake out on the counter and consume it within a couple of days. One exception is cake with cream cheese frosting. The U.S. Food and Drug Administration advises refrigerating any food made with cream cheese after 2 hours (that includes time spent making the food). In general, that seems like sound advice. However, we feel comfortable leaving the frosting for our Simple Carrot Cake with Cream Cheese Frosting (March/April 2003) out for up to 8 hours, since we know that sugar acts as a preservative and that the amount we use is more than 50 percent of the weight of the cream cheese.

Bottom line: Cake with cream cheese frosting does need to be refrigerated—and generally within 2 hours after you've made it. To serve the cake after it's been chilled, remove only the slices you plan to serve from the refrigerator, rather than the whole cake, since individual slices will warm up more quickly. This will also minimize any food safety risks. –A.G.

Mechanically Tenderized Meat

Most of the beef at my local wholesale club is labeled "blade tenderized." What does that mean?

GLORIA ALLEN
PHOENIX, ARIZ.

➤ Blade-tenderized (also known as "mechanically tenderized" or "needled") meat has been passed through a machine that punctures it with small, sharp blades or needles to break up the connective tissue and muscle fibers with the aim of making a potentially chewy cut more palatable (or an already tender cut more so). Because the blades can potentially transfer illness-causing bacteria such as *E. coli* from the surface of the meat into the interior, meat processed in this way should be cooked to 160 degrees (well-done) to ensure that any potential bacteria is no longer viable. Unfortunately, blade-tenderized meat can be difficult to identify because the punctures are nearly invisible to the naked eye. While the U.S. Department of Agriculture has published guidelines suggesting that all mechanically tenderized meat be labeled and accompanied by a reminder to cook the meat to 160 degrees, these do not become mandatory until January 2016. A handful of retailers, including Costco, label their tenderized beef, but if you're concerned, you can ask your supermarket butchers to see if they can confirm the processing of their meat.

As for the effectiveness of blade tenderizing, we compared tenderized top sirloin steaks and rib-eye steaks from Costco with traditional steaks, and we found that the blade-tenderized steaks were indeed more tender when all the steaks were cooked to a safe 160 degrees. But we prefer our steaks cooked to medium-rare, and—since that isn't advisable with blade-tenderized beef—we'll be seeking out traditional meat. –A.G.

More Mileage from Basil Bunches

You've said that cilantro stems can be used in recipes. Is this also the case with basil stems?

LOUISE HEARD
DOVER, MASS.

➤ We have found that cilantro stems have the same fresh flavors as their leaves and can be used as long as their crunchier texture is acceptable. To see if basil stems could also be put to use, we first got our bearings by asking tasters to sample basil leaves as well as various portions of the stems raw. All agreed that the tender, thinner, younger stems tasted clean and sweet, comparable to the leaves. However, as tasters reached thicker, older portions of stem, particularly the lower portion of the central stem, bitter flavors began to dominate.

With that in mind, we made two batches of a classic basil pesto in our food processor, one with leaves that had been destemmed and another with equal volumes of both leaves and tender stems. Tasters were unable to tell one batch from the other.

The takeaway? While we don't recommend using the thicker stems from a bunch of basil, it's perfectly fine to make the most of your basil bunch and put the younger, more tender stems to use. –L.L.

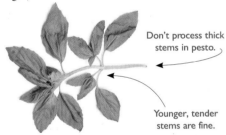

Don't process thick stems in pesto.

Younger, tender stems are fine.

STEM EDUCATION

Does Apricot Origin Matter?

Can I use California and Mediterranean dried apricots interchangeably?

MARY ADAMS
WESTBOROUGH, MASS.

➤ California and Mediterranean dried apricots begin with two different varieties of fruit that are also processed differently—factors that help give each type a distinctive taste, texture, and appearance. Deep orange in color, California apricots are halved before drying, resulting in flesh that's thin and shriveled. Yellowish-orange Mediterranean (also known as Turkish) apricots are dried whole and then pitted. Their flesh is thicker and plumper than that of the California variety—not surprising since fruit dried whole will retain more moisture than halved fruit. Both types are sold sulfured (which preserves color and prevents the growth of mold) and unsulfured.

We compared both kinds in sulfured form from the same brand (Sun-Maid). When eaten on their own, the Mediterranean apricots were described as juicy, plump, and more sweet than tart, while the California apricots were deemed slightly chewy but praised for their lively, ultraconcentrated flavor.

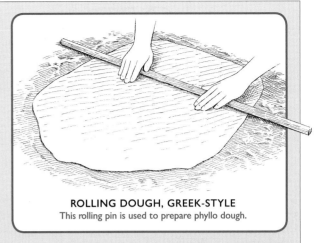

WHAT IS IT?

I inherited this from my Greek grandmother. Can you tell me what it's for?

ALEXANDER TRAMPAS
BROOKLINE, MASS.

Though it looks like a broom handle, it's a rolling pin traditionally used to flatten phyllo dough into tissue-thin sheets for baklava, spanakopita, and the like. In Greece it's called *plasti*, and in Turkey it's an *oklava*. About a yard in length, it's thin (the one we looked at was ½ inch in diameter), with straight ends rather than the tapered ones many French pins have. Its shape allows the cook closer contact with the dough to ensure even rolling and thin, wide sheets. The dough is rolled out with the pin over a floured cotton cloth (akin to an extra-large pastry cloth) and then gently hand-stretched to the table's span before being cut. The result is delicate, fine sheets. Store-bought phyllo dough is even thinner since it's mechanically pressed; recipes we referenced recommended using one handmade sheet for every three store-bought. –Shannon Friedmann Hatch

ROLLING DOUGH, GREEK-STYLE
This rolling pin is used to prepare phyllo dough.

When used in a chutney, the drier California fruit absorbed the recipe's liquid early on. We had to add more water to cook the sauce properly, but the apricots made a bright, complex chutney. The same recipe made with Mediterranean apricots yielded a chutney that was juicier and sweeter and that had the expected consistency without any modifications.

We also tasted unsulfured versions of both kinds of apricots and found them to be sweeter and less "apricot-y" across the board. Tasters felt that the variety of the apricot had a much bigger influence on the flavor of the dried fruit than did sulfuring.

To avoid having to tweak recipes on the fly, we recommend using Mediterranean apricots in cooking and baking (unless a recipe specifies the California variety). They're less expensive and more widely available, and most recipes calling for dried apricots are designed to work with their plump, juicy sweetness. But for eating out of hand, we'll be reaching for the tart, chewy California variety. –A.G.

Minimizing Static in Burr Grinders

No matter how careful I am when emptying the grind chamber of my burr-style coffee grinder, ground coffee sticks to the chamber and flies all over the counter. Any solutions?

MICHAEL PHILLIPS
ST. LOUIS, MO.

➤ The problem is static electricity. When beans pass through the grinding mechanism, they pick up an electrical charge that causes the ground coffee to "jump" out of the grinder or stick stubbornly to the sides of the container that captures the ground coffee (often called the grind chamber). This problem becomes worse when the chamber is made of plastic; it's a very poor conductor of electrical charge, so these particular grind chambers don't encourage the

---

electricity in the ground coffee to dissipate quickly.

An online search turned up several possible fixes, but most of them didn't work. Since dry conditions encourage static buildup, water seemed like a logical antidote. But adding a couple of drops of water to the beans before grinding made no difference, and misting the chamber with water prevented the jumping problem but exacerbated sticking. Many coffee fans suggest running a strip of aluminum foil from the inside of the plastic container to the outside to provide an escape route for the static, but this not only was ineffective but also trapped grinds behind the foil, making it messy to empty them into our coffee filter. We were intrigued by one suggestion: stirring the ground coffee with a metal fork to "gather" the electricity before lifting the lid. We found that a fork certainly gathered the static—as well as an abundance of the ground coffee with it. We even flirted with the suggestion of running a copper wire from the base of the grind chamber to the outside of the machine but ultimately rejected it since it required drilling a hole in our machine.

In the end, the best solution was the simplest: Give the static time to dissipate on its own. For medium-grind coffee (appropriate for a regular drip coffee maker), grind the coffee, wait for 5 minutes, and then remove the grind chamber from the machine. Rap the chamber firmly on the counter before opening the lid to send any stray grinds to the bottom of the container with the others. For finer grinds like espresso, add a few minutes to the waiting period; for coarser grinds for a French press, subtract a few minutes. –A.G.

Quick Tips

⇒ COMPILED BY SHANNON FRIEDMANN HATCH ⇐

Single-Serve Steel-Cut Oats

Anna Smith of Auburn, Ala., enjoys steel-cut oats, but preparing a full batch in the morning takes too long and produces more than she needs. Our Ten-Minute Steel-Cut Oatmeal (September/October 2012) is quick, but it serves four. Here's how she cooks just one serving in minutes.

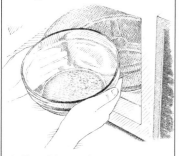

1. Place ⅔ cup of water, a pinch of salt, and 3 tablespoons of steel-cut oats in a 1-quart bowl. Microwave for 1½ minutes.

2. Cover the dish with plastic wrap and refrigerate overnight.

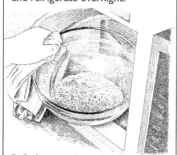

3. Before serving, microwave at 50 percent power for 5 minutes.

Bar Back(up)

When Reese Lloyd of Superior, Colo., entertains, he likes to make cocktails to order without the hassle of stopping to wash the cocktail shaker between drinks. Instead of buying multiple shakers, he fashioned an extra with a widemouthed 1-quart Mason jar and two corresponding lids.

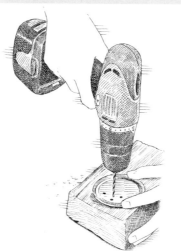

1. Drill several holes in one lid. File down any raised metal.

2. Screw on the band over the unpunctured lid and shake. To pour, replace the lid with the one with holes in it.

Impromptu Cutlery Carrier

When Mary Liz Towne of Sheboygan, Wis., needs to transport a knife, she takes care to sheathe the sharp blade. Because she doesn't own a guard for each knife in her set, she uses this unlikely alternative: lint roller tape. She unrolls the sheet to accommodate the length of her blade and folds it in half to cover the blade. (Trim any excess width, if necessary.)

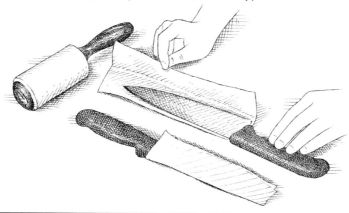

Sog-Free PB&J

Joel Esposito of Jacksonville, Fla., often packs peanut butter and jelly sandwiches, only to find that by lunchtime the slice of bread in contact with the jelly has gotten soggy. To avoid the unpleasant texture, he spreads peanut butter on both bread slices and then tops the peanut butter on each side with jelly.

Keeping Salad Greens Fresher

We've verified that blowing into a bag of salad greens (thereby increasing the carbon dioxide level) keeps the contents fresh longer (September/October 2011), but we don't recommend this method for sanitary reasons. Looking for another carbon dioxide source, David Griffith of Somerville, Mass., turned to his seltzer maker. A few puffs before he seals the bag do the trick.

SEND US YOUR TIPS We will provide a complimentary one-year subscription for each tip we print. Send your tip, name, address, and daytime telephone number to Quick Tips, *Cook's Illustrated*, P.O. Box 470589, Brookline, MA 02447, or to QuickTips@AmericasTestKitchen.com.

Second Liners

While in the middle of baking cupcakes, Leila Rieder of Providence, R.I., ran out of liners. Thinking quickly, she devised an easy substitute.

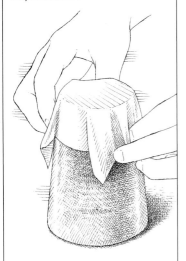

1. Cut 5-inch squares from a sheet of parchment paper and firmly press them over the base of an inverted drinking glass to shape them.

2. Place the shaped liners into the muffin cups. Fill and bake as directed.

Popping Difficult Lids

When Kate Chuprevich of Chestnut Hill, Mass., has trouble opening a stubborn jar, she reaches for a thin metal spoon. Using the spoon as a lever, she slides its tip between the lid and the jar—avoiding the lid's notches—and gently presses down on the handle until the seal releases.

Eating All Your Veggies

Rather than allow vegetable scraps to wither (or get lost) in her crisper drawer, Ellen Quinn of Oakland, Calif., tosses any leftovers into a reserved clamshell container. This way, she can easily find them if she needs a small amount of chopped vegetables, such as for an omelet or a salad.

Better Broiled Grapefruit

Broiled grapefruit is quick and easy: Halve the grapefruit, top the cut halves with honey or brown sugar, and place them under the broiler element. The problem? The citrus's curved base makes the fruit prone to tip, spilling the topping and the juice. Sue Switenki of Medina, Minn., sets each half in a canning jar lid band to keep them stable and upright.

Minimizing Flour Spray

No matter how gingerly you try to open a new bag of flour, the results are the same: A cloud of fine white dust rains down on the counter. For a no-mess fix, David Lowery of Pittsburgh, Pa., slaps the top of the bag a few times before opening it to settle the flour so that it stays inside.

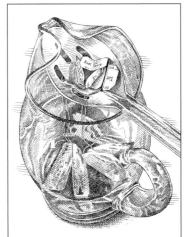

Keeping Tabs on Tea Bags

When brewing iced tea in a pitcher, Dan McCoy of Brooklyn, N.Y., found that the weight of the tea bags often pulled the attached short strings and tabs into the hot water. Fed up with fishing out the bags, he now crimps the strings' tabs to fit through the holes of a slotted spoon and props it across the opening while the tea steeps. The strings aren't pulled in, and removing the bags is as simple as lifting the spoon.

Mastering Kitchen Towel Hang-Ups

Tired of her kitchen towels falling to the floor from her oven door handle, Linda Satzger of Pittsburgh, Pa., came up with an off-course solution: a golf towel. Its grommet allows it to easily hang from golf bags and—with the help of a shower curtain ring—her oven handle.

A New Way to Poach Chicken

Hardly anyone poaches chicken anymore—and with good reason:
The classic technique is fussy and leads to bland meat. We set out to change that.

> BY DAN SOUZA <

I hear it all the time: Boneless, skinless chicken breasts are dry and stringy. I always reply that it's not the chickens' fault. Sure, modern chicken breasts are lean and mild. But the same can be said for most fish, and we don't pass the buck to our finned friends. Instead, we adjust our cooking techniques. Yet we throw delicate chicken breasts onto a white-hot grill, sear them hard in a skillet, and even toss them under the broiler—all potential paths to leathery flesh. Meanwhile we ignore one of the most obvious methods for delivering tender, moist chicken: poaching.

This old-school technique has a reputation for being fussy—and it is. The traditional method calls for maintaining a pot of water just below a simmer (between 160 and 180 degrees); it's not exactly hands-free or foolproof since you have to be vigilant about keeping the heat level just so. Furthermore, it rarely does much for flavor.

That said, it has the potential to deliver meat that's exceptionally moist and succulent. If I could take away some of the fussiness and figure out how to use the method to boost flavor, I might just be able to kick-start a poaching renaissance.

Poaching the Approach

I already had a head start: When we developed a chicken salad recipe a few years ago, we came up with an easier, more hands-free poaching method. Instead of heating water in a pot and then tossing in cold chicken breasts and fiddling constantly with the burner until the breasts are done, we combine the water and chicken from the beginning. Four boneless, skinless chicken breasts go into a Dutch oven with 6 cups of salted cold water; we heat the pot over medium heat until the water temperature reaches 170 degrees; and then we remove the pot from the heat and allow it to sit, covered, until the breasts are cooked through.

The beauty of this technique is that it's incredibly

Our poached chicken is so flavorful and tender that it needs only a simple, bright-tasting sauce to make it entrée-worthy.

gentle and mostly hands-off. It results in moist meat that's ready to be cubed and tossed with mayonnaise and seasonings for chicken salad. I adopted this basic approach as my starting point, hoping that a few adjustments would produce breasts with meatier, richer flavor and that were even more moist, if possible. I was after chicken breasts that could stand alone on a dinner plate with nothing more than a simple sauce.

The first change I made was increasing the water to 4 quarts. More water translates to a larger reserve of heat and thus better assurance that the breasts will hit the desired internal temperature of 160 degrees, even if you are using a thin pot or a poorly calibrated thermometer. And since the sides of the breasts in contact with the bottom of the pan could potentially cook faster, I also raised the breasts off the bottom of the pot—the additional liquid allowed me to put them in a steamer basket while still keeping them fully submerged. And finally, I used a meat mallet to lightly pound the thicker end of the breasts to promote more even cooking. These adjustments worked well, so I moved on to amping up flavor.

Breast Augmentation

My primary goal was to add richer, more complex flavor to the breasts during cooking, but keep the flavors neutral enough that my chicken could still pair with a range of sauces for a versatile main course. Over the years we've learned that it's difficult for most flavorings to penetrate very far into a piece of poultry or meat. During marinating, brining, and even cooking, most flavors travel only a few millimeters into meat. There are, luckily, some exceptions. Many recipes, including my working one here, testify to the fact that given sufficient concentration and time, salt can penetrate much farther into the interior of a chicken breast. Sugar also works in this way, so I added a few tablespoons to my salted poaching water. Tasters approved; the chicken didn't taste sweet—just a bit rounder and fuller.

I then looked to two other categories of ingredients for more flavor: alliums and foods rich in glutamate. The latter, a common amino acid, gives food a savory, meaty flavor. In addition to being found in ingredients like tomatoes, Parmesan cheese, and mushrooms, glutamates are in many fermented seasonings, such as miso, soy sauce, and fish sauce. I tried adding quantities of all three seasonings to my poaching liquid. Used in a relatively dilute concentration, the soy won out, adding meatiness and depth without giving itself away.

Alliums (such as onions, scallions, shallots, and garlic) not only offer potent flavor but, due to their solubility in water, can also move passively into meat along with water. I tried adding each of the aforementioned alliums to separate pots of poached chicken and asked tasters to pick a favorite. Garlic took first for the complex, sweet background flavor that it added; I smashed six cloves with the side of my knife, peeled away the skins, and tossed the cloves into the pot.

Beyond the Surface

I was making good progress in the flavor department, and the salt was penetrating decently into each chicken breast, though not as much as I would have liked. Quantity and time are the key players in how far the salt could get, and the poaching time wasn't all that long. This got me thinking about brining and salting, two techniques that give salt time to diffuse deeper into pieces of meat or poultry. Salting is a longer process than brining, and it's a technique that we typically use when we want to develop browning and crispy skin on the meat—not something that I was going for here. But I'd just finished crafting the perfect salty, flavorful poaching liquid. Could it also serve as a brine? Our standard brine for boneless, skinless chicken breasts is ¼ cup salt to 2 quarts water. With ¼ cup salt and ½ cup soy sauce to 4 quarts water, my poaching solution was just below that ratio. My instinct was that it could serve as a gentle brine and double as the poaching liquid without making the chicken overly salty.

I gave it a shot, adding the chicken breasts to the poaching liquid and letting them sit for 30 minutes at room temperature, which allowed the breasts' internal temperature to slowly start to rise. Then I turned on the heat and proceeded with the recipe. Tasters declared this batch the most evenly seasoned and flavorful thus far, as well as the most juicy and tender. Those 30 minutes had given the salt time to dissolve some proteins in the chicken, resulting in a tenderizing effect. At the same time, the water, glutamate, and garlic flavor compounds had time to make their way deeper into the flesh. Even my skeptical "anti–white meat" colleagues had to admit that this was really good, flavorful chicken.

Now all I needed was a couple of simple sauces that would complement the chicken's mild, meaty flavor and juicy, tender texture. The first was a yogurt-based sauce with cumin, garlic, and fresh cilantro. For the second sauce I took inspiration from an Indian chutney and made a warm vinaigrette with tomato, ginger, fennel, and brown sugar.

With a technique so easy, foolproof, and good, I bet that even the most skeptical of cooks will never again doubt the power of poaching.

PERFECT POACHED CHICKEN BREASTS
SERVES 4

To ensure that the chicken cooks through, don't use breasts that weigh more than 8 ounces each. If desired, serve the chicken with one of our sauces (recipes follow) or in a salad or sandwiches. For our free recipes for Perfect Poached Chicken Breasts for Two and Parsley Sauce with Cornichons and Capers, go to CooksIllustrated.com/apr14.

    4   (6- to 8-ounce) boneless, skinless chicken
        breasts, trimmed
    ½   cup soy sauce
    ¼   cup salt
    2   tablespoons sugar
    6   garlic cloves, smashed and peeled

1. Cover chicken breasts with plastic wrap and pound thick ends gently with meat pounder until ¾ inch thick. Whisk 4 quarts water, soy sauce, salt,

Tender, Juicy Poached Chicken That Tastes Good, Too

Traditional poaching is a fussy procedure that requires constant monitoring of the cooking liquid and fiddling with the stove to ensure that it stays at a subsimmer—the main hallmark of this method. Our approach is gentler, requires no monitoring, and even adds flavor to mild chicken.

USE LOTS OF WATER
In traditional poaching, only an inch or two of water is used. We use a full 4 quarts.

ADD FLAVOR BOOSTERS
Most flavorings in a cooking liquid can't migrate very far into meat. We add a few that can: soy sauce, salt, sugar, and garlic.

PROP UP CHICKEN
Elevating the chicken on a steamer basket ensures that none of the meat will be in contact with the bottom of the pot and all sides will cook evenly.

COOK COVERED, OFF HEAT
Bringing the cooking liquid to 175 degrees, covering the pot, and cooking the chicken in residual heat is foolproof and hands-off.

sugar, and garlic in Dutch oven until salt and sugar are dissolved. Arrange breasts, skinned side up, in steamer basket, making sure not to overlap them. Submerge steamer basket in brine and let sit at room temperature for 30 minutes.

2. Heat pot over medium heat, stirring liquid occasionally to even out hot spots, until water registers 175 degrees, 15 to 20 minutes. Turn off heat, cover pot, remove from burner, and let stand until meat registers 160 degrees, 17 to 22 minutes.

3. Transfer breasts to carving board, cover tightly with aluminum foil, and let rest for 5 minutes. Slice each breast on bias into ¼-inch-thick slices, transfer to serving platter or individual plates, and serve.

CUMIN-CILANTRO YOGURT SAUCE
MAKES ABOUT 1 CUP

Mint may be substituted for the cilantro. This sauce is prone to curdle and thus does not reheat well; prepare it just before serving.

    2   tablespoons extra-virgin olive oil
    1   shallot, minced
    1   garlic clove, minced
    1   teaspoon ground cumin
    ⅛   teaspoon red pepper flakes
    ½   cup plain whole-milk yogurt
    ⅓   cup water
    1   teaspoon lime juice
        Salt and pepper
    2   tablespoons chopped fresh cilantro

Heat 1 tablespoon oil in small skillet over medium heat until shimmering. Add shallot and cook until softened, about 2 minutes. Stir in garlic, cumin, and pepper flakes and cook until fragrant, about 30 seconds. Remove from heat and whisk in yogurt, water, lime juice, and remaining 1 tablespoon oil. Season with salt and pepper to taste and cover to keep warm. Stir in cilantro just before serving.

WARM TOMATO-GINGER VINAIGRETTE
MAKES ABOUT 2 CUPS

Parsley may be substituted for the cilantro.

    ¼   cup extra-virgin olive oil
    1   shallot, minced
    1½   teaspoons grated fresh ginger
    ⅛   teaspoon ground cumin
    ⅛   teaspoon ground fennel
    12   ounces cherry tomatoes, halved
         Salt and pepper
    1   tablespoon red wine vinegar
    1   teaspoon packed light brown sugar
    2   tablespoons chopped fresh cilantro

Heat 2 tablespoons oil in 10-inch nonstick skillet over medium heat until shimmering. Add shallot, ginger, cumin, and fennel and cook until fragrant, about 15 seconds. Stir in tomatoes and ¼ teaspoon salt and cook, stirring frequently, until tomatoes have softened, 3 to 5 minutes. Off heat, stir in vinegar and sugar and season with salt and pepper to taste; cover to keep warm. Stir in cilantro and remaining 2 tablespoons oil just before serving.

Poaching Liquid That Doubles as a Brine

We use our well-seasoned poaching liquid not only to impart flavor to the chicken as it cooks but also as a solution in which to brine the meat before turning on the heat. Letting the breasts sit in this liquid for 30 minutes at room temperature has its benefits: The salt (along with the sugar and flavorings) gets a jump-start on seasoning the meat and breaking down proteins to create more-tender chicken. Furthermore, the chicken loses its chill, so it needs less exposure to the heat to come up to temperature.

Taqueria Beef Tacos at Home

Classic shredded beef tacos are known for their robust meatiness. So why do most recipes use a marginally beefy cut and throw a ton of meaty flavor down the drain?

⇒ BY ANDREW JANJIGIAN ⇐

When Americans think of shredded meat tacos, we tend to think of those filled with pork carnitas. But in Mexico, the saucy beef filling called *carne deshebrada* (which translates as "shredded meat") is also hugely popular. A *taqueria* standard as well as a home-cooked favorite, it's made by braising a large cut of beef (usually brisket, chuck roast, or even flank or skirt steak) until ultratender and then shredding the meat and tossing it with either a *rojo* sauce made with tomatoes and/or dried chiles or a *verde* sauce made with tomatillos. My preference is for the robust rojo style, particularly those versions that feature warm, earthy spices. Instead of having to seek out a good local taqueria every time I get a craving for this Mexican comfort food, I wondered how hard it would be to make a great version at home.

Getting Saucy

The handful of carne deshebrada recipes that I found didn't look complicated. They started with the same basic procedure: covering the cut of choice with water in a large pot, adding some flavorings (onion, garlic, cilantro, and sometimes various others), and braising the meat for several hours until tender. The meat is then removed, shredded, and combined with a sauce prepared separately. The sauce recipes showed more variation. Some were as simple as canned whole or diced tomatoes simmered quickly with onion and garlic, while others went on to add a mix of spices as well as dried and sometimes fresh chiles. Some sauces were pureed, while others were left a bit chunky.

No matter the sauce used, one flaw was clear: For a dish known for its meatiness, the beef flavor was noticeably wan. One contributing factor seemed obvious: Once the roast or steak was cooked and removed from the pot, the cooking liquid, along with all the flavor released by the beef, was poured

Opting for beef short ribs over more traditional chuck roast cuts the cooking time by hours and delivers a seriously meaty, rich taco filling.

▶ **See the Setup**
Video available free for 4 months
at CooksIllustrated.com/apr14

down the drain. My goal was clear: I wanted a recipe for this shredded meat filling that really emphasized beef flavor. For the rojo sauce, I wasn't sold on any particular style, but I wanted it to boast meaty depth and complexity.

Since discarding the cooking liquid was clearly detracting from my goal of meaty flavor, my first move was to put the braising liquid to use in the sauce. Having it pull double duty would not only ensure more flavor but also streamline things by allowing me to skip preparing a sauce separately.

It made sense to swap out the water for beef broth. I wanted to add only as much broth as I'd need to adequately sauce the beef; my guess was that 2 cups would be about right. I added it to the pot with the meat (I went with a chuck roast for the moment), along with diced canned tomatoes, chopped onion, a little minced jalapeño, and garlic. At this point, I opted not to use dried chiles, which allowed me to skip pureeing the sauce. I cooked the meat until tender before shredding it and returning it to the pot to toss with the sauce. The filling was definitely

meatier but still not nearly meaty enough.

I took a step back. What about the cut of meat? Chuck roast is reasonably flavorful, but there are definitely cuts that are beefier, plus it took a full 5 hours of cooking to turn tender. Other popular choices, flank and skirt steak, held promise in terms of flavor and are fairly quick-cooking, but because they don't have much marbling, they tended to dry out. Ditto for brisket. So I turned to a test kitchen favorite for braising: boneless beef short ribs. While not traditional to the dish, tasters agreed that short ribs delivered the meatiest, richest taco filling yet. And cutting them into 2-inch cubes reduced the cooking time by half, to a comparatively quick 2½ hours. Because short ribs are fairly fatty, the filling was a little greasy, but trimming the meat well before cooking and skimming the cooking liquid before saucing the meat were easy fixes.

Depth Perception

My recipe was shaping up nicely: The flavor was much improved, it used easy-to-find ingredients, and its preparation was fairly simple. The meat required trimming before cooking and shredding afterward, but it was hands-off for most of the cooking time. I wanted to keep it that way, but I had to wonder if I couldn't develop even more meaty flavor.

I didn't want to tack on the extra step of browning the meat at the start, but I'd developed enough braising recipes to know that meat that isn't submerged in liquid will brown during cooking. My short ribs were just peeking above the liquid and thus barely browning. What if I gave the meat a lift so that more of it was exposed? I sliced an onion into thick rounds, arranged them in the pot with the cooking liquid, and placed the chunks of short ribs on top. When I pulled the pot from the oven about 2½ hours later and removed the lid, at first glance I wasn't hopeful about the results. The onion rounds had softened and sunk, taking the meat down with them. But when I removed the meat from the sauce to shred it, I noticed that it had stayed afloat long enough to develop really good browning, and the beef had tons of meaty flavor. What about the sauce? I fished the onion slices out of the pot and gave it a taste. It was certainly good and meaty—but it wasn't much else.

The Right Blend

I wondered if broth really made the best choice for the cooking liquid, which was now incredibly meaty but lacking in depth and brightness. My recipe was really nothing more than a braise, and many braises use some form of alcohol to provide both traits that my sauce was missing. Wine didn't seem appropriate for this Mexican braise, but beer did, and when I swapped in a bottle of good ale for most of the broth, tasters found the sauce much improved. It still lacked acidity, so I ditched the remaining broth in favor of cider vinegar. I also decided to swap out the canned tomatoes for the concentrated *umami*-rich flavors of tomato paste.

The switch to tomato paste whetted my appetite for a smoother sauce; without the chunks of tomatoes, the sauce was incorporating much more thoroughly with the shreds of meat. For the next batch, I gave the cooking liquid a quick whiz in the blender before combining it with the shredded meat. This sauce was better still, with a silky, unctuous texture.

Now that I was pureeing the sauce, there was no reason not to use dried chiles. Recipes called for a wide variety, from fruity, moderately hot guajillos; to mildly flavored, slightly spicy New Mexican reds; to smoky-sweet anchos and earthy, raisiny pasillas. While each variety had its merits, anchos came out on top. By the end of the cooking time, they were plenty soft and easily pureed into the sauce, giving it the smoky, spicy kick it needed.

Up to this point, I hadn't been adding herbs or spices to the sauce. Traditional choices ranged from only a little dried oregano to up to 10 different seasonings. For increased complexity without going overboard, I settled on the warm notes of ground cumin, cinnamon, and cloves, along with dried oregano and bay leaves.

Top This

For taco toppings, we usually stick with reliable standbys like salsa, pico de gallo (chopped fresh tomatoes, onions, and chiles), guacamole, and cheese, but I felt that given the filling's richness, a topping that was bright and added crunch would provide perfect contrast.

To that end, I looked past Mexico to El Salvador and homed in on *curtido,* a crunchy, tart cabbage-carrot slaw with a spicy kick that's a specialty of that country. While the slaw is often fermented to develop flavor (a process that takes several days or even weeks), I found that a quick version tossed together while the meat was braising and then refrigerated for 1 hour had all the punch that my tacos required. The key was marinating the shredded vegetables, onion, and jalapeño in a fruity cider vinegar–based pickling liquid before draining and serving them. In addition to the curtido, a sprinkling of crumbled *queso fresco* (or feta if you're in a pinch) introduced the right salty, creamy finish to the tacos.

With that, I had a carne deshebrada taco that could hold its own against the best of the rest.

Giving Beef(iness) a Boost

We found that many recipes for the shredded beef taco filling known as *carne deshebrada* produced results that weren't actually all that beefy. To improve meatiness, we used short ribs, one of the most flavorful braising cuts we know, and cut them into 2-inch cubes for faster cooking. We also propped up the cubes on onion rounds so that the exposed portions would brown during the 2-plus hours of cooking—thus avoiding the fuss of searing the meat before cooking.

Sliced onion lifts the short ribs above the braising liquid, which delivers more browning—and more meaty flavor.

SHREDDED BEEF TACOS (CARNE DESHEBRADA)
SERVES 6 TO 8

Use a full-bodied lager or ale such as Dos Equis or Sierra Nevada. If you can't find *queso fresco,* substitute feta. If your Dutch oven does not have a tight-fitting lid, cover the pot tightly with a sheet of heavy-duty aluminum foil and then replace the lid. To warm the tortillas, place them on a plate, cover them with a damp dish towel, and microwave them for 60 to 90 seconds. The shredded beef also makes a great filling for empanadas, tamales, and chiles rellenos.

Beef

1½	cups beer
½	cup cider vinegar
2	ounces (4 to 6) dried ancho chiles, stemmed, seeded, and torn into 1-inch pieces
2	tablespoons tomato paste
6	garlic cloves, lightly crushed and peeled
3	bay leaves
2	teaspoons ground cumin
2	teaspoons dried oregano
	Salt and pepper
½	teaspoon ground cloves
½	teaspoon ground cinnamon
1	large onion, sliced into ½-inch-thick rounds
3	pounds boneless beef short ribs, trimmed and cut into 2-inch cubes

Cabbage-Carrot Slaw

1	cup cider vinegar
½	cup water
1	tablespoon sugar
1½	teaspoons salt
½	head green cabbage, cored and sliced thin (6 cups)
1	onion, sliced thin
1	large carrot, peeled and shredded
1	jalapeño chile, stemmed, seeded, and minced
1	teaspoon dried oregano
1	cup chopped fresh cilantro
18	(6-inch) corn tortillas, warmed
4	ounces queso fresco, crumbled (1 cup)
	Lime wedges

1. FOR THE BEEF: Adjust oven rack to lower-middle position and heat oven to 325 degrees. Combine beer, vinegar, anchos, tomato paste, garlic, bay leaves, cumin, oregano, 2 teaspoons salt, ½ teaspoon pepper, cloves, and cinnamon in Dutch oven. Arrange onion rounds in single layer on bottom of pot. Place beef on top of onion rounds in single layer. Cover and cook until meat is well browned and tender, 2½ to 3 hours.

2. FOR THE CABBAGE-CARROT SLAW: While beef cooks, whisk vinegar, water, sugar, and salt in large bowl until sugar is dissolved. Add cabbage, onion, carrot, jalapeño, and oregano and toss to combine. Cover and refrigerate for at least 1 hour or up to 24 hours. Drain slaw and stir in cilantro right before serving.

3. Using slotted spoon, transfer beef to large bowl, cover loosely with aluminum foil, and set aside. Strain liquid through fine-mesh strainer into 2-cup liquid measuring cup (do not wash pot). Discard onion rounds and bay leaves. Transfer remaining solids to blender. Let strained liquid settle for 5 minutes, then skim any fat off surface. Add water as needed to equal 1 cup. Pour liquid in blender with reserved solids and blend until smooth, about 2 minutes. Transfer sauce to now-empty pot.

4. Using two forks, shred beef into bite-size pieces. Bring sauce to simmer over medium heat. Add shredded beef and stir to coat. Season with salt to taste. (Beef can be refrigerated for up to 2 days; gently reheat before serving.)

5. Spoon small amount of beef into each warm tortilla and serve, passing slaw, queso fresco, and lime wedges separately.

For Maximum Flavor, Keep the Cooking Liquid

Many recipes for *carne deshebrada* call for braising the meat, shredding it, and tossing it in a sauce made separately. Meanwhile, the braising liquid is thrown out. We use a lesser amount of cooking liquid; add dried chiles, tomato paste, garlic, herbs, and warm spices to it; and puree it—and all its meaty flavor—into a sauce. For depth and brightness, we forgo water (or even broth) as the braising liquid in favor of a combination of beer and vinegar.

Italian Milk-Braised Pork

In Italy, cooks like to braise pork roasts in milk because it creates an exceptionally rich, savory sauce. But there's a trade-off: The result is not pretty.

> BY LAN LAM

Maiale al latte, or pork cooked in milk, is not only one of the most delicious roasts in the Italian canon but also one of the simplest. Traditionally, it's a boneless pork roast, usually from either the loin or the shoulder, that's seasoned with salt and pepper, browned in a little fat, and then braised in milk, often with a few garlic cloves and some fresh sage. The idea behind cooking the meat in milk is that it tenderizes the pork. While the meat indeed turns out supple and juicy, the milk's impact on this outcome is dubious—in most recipes, only the bottom third or so of the roast is in contact with the milk. More impressive is that the milk cooks down to form a lush, deeply savory sauce.

But the dish has one major drawback: The sauce looks downright homely—not only drab in color but full of lumps created when the milk curdles. Both typical cuts of meat also present challenges: A fat- and collagen-streaked shoulder roast is ideal for braising, except that in the recipes I tried, my tasters found that it made the already-rich dish overwhelming. Meanwhile, the lean loin was guaranteed to dry out.

For my version, I wasn't worried about the meat; the test kitchen has tackled plenty of pork cooking problems before. As for the sauce, if I could come up with a way to smooth out those lumps (and maybe add brightness and complexity to the one-note savoriness), I'd have gone far toward making this a standard roast for the American home kitchen.

Mechanical Intervention

There wasn't much to do about making a shoulder roast less fatty and rich, but a dry loin roast I could fix with a brine. Submerging it in the salt and sugar solution for 90 minutes or so—our usual pretreatment for this cut—would help it stay moist during cooking and give it a nice seasoning boost, too.

After patting the brined roast dry, I seared it in

Our version of the dish features a center-cut loin roast, which cooks relatively quickly and slices neatly, and a sauce that looks as good as it tastes.

Look: It's Smooth
Video available free for 4 months at CooksIllustrated.com/apr14

a Dutch oven in a little oil until all the sides were nicely brown. Then I poured in 3 cups of whole milk—enough to go about halfway up the meat—along with a handful of peeled garlic cloves and a teaspoon of minced fresh sage. As the milk bubbled, I scraped the bottom of the pot to dislodge the fond (flavorful bits left over from browning the meat) and then covered the pot and slid it into a 275-degree oven, where the meat would cook more evenly than if I were to braise it on the stovetop. Not even an hour had passed before the center of the pork hit its target 140 degrees (relatively fast cooking was another boon to using the loin), at which point I transferred it to a cutting board while I considered what to make of the sauce—right now, a liquid that was unattractively strewn with curdled bits.

The reason behind this effect: The slightly acidic juices shed by the pork cause the milk's casein proteins to bind together into curdlike clusters, a reaction that speeds up when the milk is heated. Some recipes recommend whisking the milk vigorously after braising to break up the clumps. To my

surprise, the whisk actually did a halfway-decent job of this, though the sauce was still far from smooth. Thinking that whisking the milk as it cooked might be more effective, I removed the seared roast from the pot, leaving the vessel on the stove; added the milk; and stirred as it simmered. Once the milk had thickened to a batter-like consistency about 20 minutes later, I returned the pork and its juices to the pot and the pot to the oven to finish cooking. This time, I also made sure to flip the roast halfway through cooking, since the first test indicated that the side in contact with the pot was cooking faster.

I was on the right track; the curds were smaller for sure. But they were still distracting—and frankly, I'd hoped for a better payoff for all that stirring.

Smooth Move

A chat with our science editor pointed me in a new direction: Add fat to the milk. This makes it less likely to curdle in acidic conditions, since the fat molecules wedge themselves between the casein proteins, literally preventing them from bonding. I considered switching from the loin to the fattier shoulder roast but realized that would do me no good: The fat needed to be in the milk before its exposure to the acidic pork juices; otherwise, it would still curdle.

Instead, I seared another loin roast and removed it from the pot so that I could still stir the milk as it reduced, but this time I also added 2 tablespoons of heavy cream to the pot. With more fat in the milk, I felt confident enough to wait to stir the milk until after it had thickened a bit and turned pale brown. To my delight, the sauce remained smooth. Even my tasters marveled at the liquid's improved appearance. But when they tasted it, their enthusiasm dampened; the extra fat had dulled the best part of the sauce: its deep porky flavor.

Rendered pork fat really would be a good option, I realized: It could provide the same anticurdling function as the fat in the cream and also offer a meaty boost. Launching another test, I chopped up 2 ounces of bacon and placed it in the Dutch oven with ½ cup of water—a technique that we've recently discovered prevents the rendered fat from burning. Once the water evaporated and the bacon had taken on a bit of color, I fished the pieces out of the pot and discarded them, leaving only the rendered fat. I then proceeded as before: searing the roast, removing it from the pot, adding the milk, and building the sauce. This time, the sauce wasn't just smooth and rich but a lot meatier, too—though, unfortunately, not in a good way. The smoky bacon overwhelmed the mild porky flavor of the roast itself. No problem; I simply switched to an equal amount of cleaner-tasting salt pork and tried the test again. Now the sauce boasted straightforward porky richness. But could I eke out even more savory depth?

Baking soda may sound like an odd addition to a braising sauce, but we've discovered that this alkaline ingredient has considerable powers beyond leavening. When I added just a pinch to the Dutch oven with the milk and seasonings, its high pH encouraged deeper browning, which not only added to the sauce's savoriness but also deepened its color a bit.

As for brightening its flavor, my first thought was to cut the sauce with some white wine. I worried that such an acidic ingredient would prove too much for the milk—even with the extra fat—and undo all I'd done to prevent curdling. But there was only one way to find out: Once I'd removed the pork to rest, I whisked ½ cup of wine into the sauce. Happily, the sauce remained perfectly smooth. Encouraged, I added a spoonful of tart Dijon mustard (and some chopped parsley) off heat for even more complexity and color, and the sauce still didn't curdle.

When I peeled thin slices off of this last roast (the thinner the slice, the shorter the muscle fibers and the more tender the meat), dressed them with my lush, ultrasavory milk sauce, and scattered a bit more chopped parsley over the platter, I couldn't help thinking that maybe I'd even outdone many of the Italian originals.

MILK-BRAISED PORK LOIN
SERVES 4 TO 6

The milk will bubble up when added to the pot. If necessary, remove the pot from the heat and stir to break up the foam before returning it to the heat. We prefer natural pork, but if your pork is enhanced (injected with a salt solution), do not brine. Instead, skip to step 2.

> Salt and pepper
> ¼ cup sugar
> 1 (2- to 2½-pound) boneless pork loin roast, trimmed
> 2 ounces salt pork, chopped coarse
> 3 cups whole milk
> 5 garlic cloves, peeled
> 1 teaspoon minced fresh sage
> ¼ teaspoon baking soda
> ½ cup dry white wine
> 3 tablespoons chopped fresh parsley
> 1 teaspoon Dijon mustard

1. Dissolve ¼ cup salt and sugar in 2 quarts cold water in large container. Submerge roast in brine, cover, and refrigerate for at least 1½ hours or up to 2 hours. Remove roast from brine and pat dry with paper towels.

2. Adjust oven rack to middle position and heat oven to 275 degrees. Bring salt pork and ½ cup water to simmer in Dutch oven over medium heat. Simmer until water evaporates and salt pork begins to sizzle, 5 to 6 minutes. Continue to cook, stirring frequently, until salt pork is lightly browned and fat has rendered, 2 to 3 minutes. Using slotted spoon, discard salt pork, leaving fat in pot.

3. Increase heat to medium-high, add roast to pot, and brown on all sides, 8 to 10 minutes. Transfer roast to large plate. Add milk, garlic, sage, and baking soda to pot and bring to simmer, scraping up any browned bits. Cook, stirring frequently, until milk is lightly browned and has consistency of heavy cream, 14 to 16 minutes. Reduce heat to medium-low and continue to cook, stirring and scraping bottom of pot constantly, until milk thickens to consistency of thin batter, 1 to 3 minutes longer. Remove pot from heat.

4. Return roast to pot, cover, and transfer to oven. Cook until meat registers 140 degrees, 40 to 50 minutes, flipping roast once halfway through cooking. Transfer roast to carving board, tent with aluminum foil, and let rest for 20 to 25 minutes.

5. Once roast has rested, pour any accumulated juices into pot. Add wine and return sauce to simmer over medium-high heat, whisking vigorously to smooth out sauce. Simmer until sauce has consistency of thin gravy, 2 to 3 minutes. Off heat, stir in 2 tablespoons parsley and mustard and season with salt and pepper to taste. Slice roast into ¼-inch-thick slices. Transfer slices to serving platter. Spoon sauce over slices, sprinkle with remaining 1 tablespoon parsley, and serve.

SCIENCE How Fat Keeps Milk from Curdling

Most recipes for milk-braised pork yield a sauce that's rich and meaty but also curdled. That's because the pork's slightly acidic juices lower the pH of the milk, causing the clusters of casein proteins in milk that normally repel one another to suddenly attract one another and form clumps. Heating the milk speeds up this reaction.

The easy fix: Add a little fat to the 3 cups of milk in our recipe before it simmers. The fat molecules—we use rendered salt pork fat to boost meaty flavor—surround the casein clusters, preventing them from bonding. Fat's ability to prevent curdling is so effective that we were even able to brighten the flavor of the cooked sauce with highly acidic wine and Dijon mustard without affecting its smooth consistency. –L.L.

LUMPY AND FRUMPY
Whole milk doesn't have enough fat to prevent curdling in the presence of slightly acidic pork juices and heat.

SMOOTH AND SILKY
A couple of tablespoons of fat added to the whole milk keeps it from curdling—even when superacidic wine and mustard are introduced.

TESTING Waiter's Corkscrews

Lever-style corkscrews make uncorking bottles of wine effortless, but when our favorite from Oggi broke after limited use, we sought out a more durable favorite. The "waiter's friend," a slim, ungimmicky style that is simple to use once you master the technique, is what wine professionals call on, so we rounded up five openers priced from $12.99 to a staggering $225.

More money didn't buy a better opener. Pricey models by Code-38 and Laguiole lacked leverage compared with top models; the worm on the Code-38 loosened a bit by the end of testing; and the last-place Laguiole slipped off the bottle. Cheaper models, from Pulltap's and Trudeau, featured ergonomically curved bodies and hinged fulcrums that made easy work of pulling the cork, but what justifies the extra $27 for the Pulltap's is its Teflon-coated worm, which considerably reduced friction as we twisted. For more information and a demo on how to use a waiter's corkscrew, go to CooksIllustrated.com/apr14. –Amy Graves

SMOOTH OPERATOR
PULLTAP'S Classic Evolution Corkscrew by Pulltex

Price: $39.95
Comments:
Our winner's chrome body was easy to grip, and its hinged fulcrum provided great leverage. Its Teflon-coated worm produced hardly any friction going into the cork.

CHEAP AND STURDY
TRUDEAU Double Lever Corkscrew
Price: $12.99
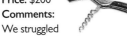
Comments:
This second-place bargain model's hinged steel fulcrum offered solid leverage, and its grippy body and thin, grooved worm made it easy to twist into the cork.

BEST BUY

STUBBORN AND SLIPPERY
LAGUIOLE en Aubrac Sommelier
Price: $200

Comments:
We struggled to twist this last-place opener's thick worm into corks—and also to pull out the cork: The fulcrum's sloped ledge easily slipped off the lip of the bottle.

Pasta with Cauliflower and Bacon

How to make this restaurant favorite at home? Crowd the pan and consolidate pots.

⇒ BY LAN LAM ⇐

In restaurants, the combination of pasta, cauliflower, bacon, and bread crumbs can be transformed into a dish far greater than the sum of its parts: lush and creamy, a wonderfully balanced combination of nutty florets, meaty bacon, and crunchy crumbs. At home, however, the promise of the dish is often overshadowed by the sinkful of dirty pots and pans left after cooking. This is because most times, the cauliflower and bread crumbs are roasted or toasted in different pans in the oven, while the bacon is crisped in a skillet and a pot of water is set to boil for the pasta. Four pans for what should be an easy weeknight dish? No thanks. To make this restaurant dish at home, a little streamlining was definitely in order.

Some recipes that I found tried to cut down on pots by forgoing the roasting of the cauliflower and cooking it and the pasta in the same pan. Others called for steaming the florets in the same skillet that was used to cook the bacon and toast the bread crumbs. But without roasting, the texture and flavor of the vegetable was compromised. This is because raw cauliflower is more than 90 percent water, so when it is blanched or steamed, much of that water is retained—resulting in mushy florets that easily fade into the background.

Roasting the cauliflower seemed critical, since it would not only encourage moisture to escape but also create browning and enhance the nutty flavor of the florets. Wanting to avoid turning on my oven and using another pan, I tried browning the florets in batches in a skillet. But the sheer volume of florets (one head yields about 8 cups) meant that it took a long time to cook them all.

Generally we avoid crowding the pan because it causes the food to steam more than brown. But even in a crowded pan, I reasoned, some of the food will brown; maybe in this dish, that's all I'd need for an extra boost of flavor. Plus, if I kept the heat high enough, a lot of the water from the cauliflower would still evaporate. So the next time, instead of cooking the cauliflower in batches, I loaded up the skillet with the entire crop of florets and let it rip over medium-high heat. After about 10 minutes, a fair number of the florets were nicely browned and the whole lot was crisp-tender, too. Sold.

Now on to the last problem: When I stirred some

Bread crumbs toasted with bacon add a little bit of crunch and meaty flavor.

of the pasta cooking water into the nearly finished dish to help create a sauce, I found that the pasta sucked most of it right up, and what little liquid was left was thin and unsatisfying. Restaurants don't have this problem. Their pasta cooking liquid is so viscous and superstarchy from boiling batch after batch in the same pot that it easily creates a creamy sauce when tossed with cooked pasta. The idea of adding starch to my finished dish seemed unappealing—but what if I just didn't throw any away? I switched cooking methods, adapting one usually reserved for making risotto, in which only the amount of liquid needed to cook the rice and create a starchy sauce is added to the pot and no more. This would mean that I wouldn't have to discard any water, and thus all the pasta starch would make it into the final dish.

I toasted some panko bread crumbs in a skillet, which I then wiped clean and used to brown my cauliflower in one heaping batch. In a Dutch oven, I crisped my bacon and then softened chopped onion and some thyme in the rendered fat. Then I added the pasta and a measured amount of water. As soon as the pasta was al dente and nearly all the water had been absorbed, I added the cauliflower and gave the mixture a stir. The resulting dish? Lush and well dressed. When I tried swapping in a mixture of wine and chicken broth for the water, tasters agreed: The flavor was even more complex.

It still tasted more bacon-y than I wanted, however, and the panko had become a bit soggy. I had a simple solution for that: Instead of cooking the pasta with the bacon, I made a bacon and bread-crumb garnish to sprinkle on the finished dish by cooking

the bacon, toasting the bread crumbs in the bacon fat, and then mixing them with the bacon. A final addition of parsley and lemon juice enlivened the dish, and there it was: restaurant flavor at home—with only two pots.

PASTA WITH CAULIFLOWER, BACON, AND BREAD CRUMBS
SERVES 4 TO 6

Farfalle, orecchiette, or gemelli can be substituted for the campanelle. If the pasta seems too dry, stir in up to ¼ cup of hot water. For our free recipe for Pasta with Cauliflower, Bacon, and Bread Crumbs for Two, go to CooksIllustrated.com/apr14.

- 3 slices bacon, cut into ¼-inch pieces
- ½ cup panko bread crumbs
  Salt and pepper
- 2 tablespoons vegetable oil
- 1 large head cauliflower (3 pounds), cored and cut into 1-inch florets
- 1 onion, chopped fine
- ½ teaspoon minced fresh thyme
- 1 pound campanelle
- 5½ cups chicken broth
- ½ cup dry white wine
- 3 tablespoons minced fresh parsley
- 1 teaspoon lemon juice, plus lemon wedges for serving

1. Cook bacon in 12-inch skillet over medium-high heat until crispy, 5 to 7 minutes. Add panko and ¼ teaspoon pepper and cook, stirring frequently, until panko is well browned, 2 to 4 minutes. Transfer panko mixture to bowl and wipe out skillet.

2. Heat 5 teaspoons oil in now-empty skillet over medium-high heat until shimmering. Add cauliflower and 1 teaspoon salt; cook, stirring occasionally, until cauliflower is crisp-tender and browned in spots, 10 to 12 minutes. Remove pan from heat and cover to keep warm.

3. Heat remaining 1 teaspoon oil in Dutch oven over medium heat until shimmering. Add onion, thyme, and ½ teaspoon salt; cook, stirring frequently, until onion has softened, 4 to 7 minutes. Increase heat to high, add pasta, broth, and wine, and bring to simmer. Cook pasta, stirring frequently, until most of liquid is absorbed and pasta is al dente, 8 to 10 minutes.

4. Remove pot from heat; stir in parsley, lemon juice, and cauliflower; and season with salt and pepper to taste. Serve, passing panko mixture and lemon wedges separately.

▶ Look, Ma: Only Two Pots
Video available free for 4 months
at CooksIllustrated.com/apr14

Improving Sesame-Crusted Salmon

For a rich, full-flavored coating, we looked to Japan—and the Middle East.

⇒ BY LAN LAM ⇐

The fish and sesame duo gets around, showing up in cuisines from Asia to California to the Middle East. The simplest approach is to coat fillets with the seeds (they stick easily) and then pan-sear the fish. Tuna is often used, but so is less-expensive salmon—my preference for a weeknight meal. When I first tasted salmon prepared this way, I thought that only minor tweaks would be necessary to correct the ho-hum sesame flavor and slightly dry, unevenly cooked fish. But halfway through dinner, I realized that the problems ran deeper. Both salmon and sesame have a monotonous richness, so finishing a whole serving was a chore. I wanted a lively dish in which the salmon and sesame would be offset with bolder, brighter flavors.

Brining the fish for just 15 minutes took care of any dryness. It may seem odd to brine something that basically lived in a brine, but the saltwater soak seasons the flesh and subtly changes its protein structure, helping it retain moisture. I blotted the brined fillets with paper towels, applied the seeds to both sides, and eased the fillets into an oil-slicked nonstick skillet. When the seeds turned golden, I transferred the skillet to the oven for more-gentle, even cooking. Flawlessly cooked, moist fish? Check.

On to the dull sesame flavor. While chatting with a fellow cook about possible solutions, he mentioned Japanese *gomashio*. The term translates as "sesame salt" and at its most basic is just those two ingredients. To make the savory blend, you toast the seeds and then mix or grind them with salt.

Maybe salt and a little toasting were just what the seeds needed. But instead of grinding the seeds with salt after toasting them, I submerged them in some of the brine that I had mixed up for the fish, drained them, and toasted them whole in a skillet. The brine woke up the nutty flavor of the seeds by infusing each one with salt. What's more, because the starch in the seeds absorbed water from the brine and then gelatinized during toasting, the seeds were now crispier than ever.

But I wanted an even more potent sesame punch. I experimented with cooking the fillets in sesame oil, but most of the oil's flavorful compounds vaporized in the hot skillet. I scanned the test kitchen pantry and spotted a Middle Eastern staple: tahini, which is basically ground sesame seeds. The only problem was its runny consistency—it would slide right off the slippery fillets. Before experimenting with thickeners, I decided to enliven the tahini with some lemon juice. I drizzled in the juice a little at a time, tasting after each addition. Oddly, the more juice I added

the more viscous the tahini became. Two teaspoons of juice produced great tang and a misolike texture. (See "A Surprising Tahini Thickener" on page 30 for more about this.) Happily, the thick paste was ideal for adhering other flavorful elements to the salmon, so I added minced scallion whites, lemon zest, grated fresh ginger, and a dash of cayenne. I smeared the flavor-packed mixture onto the fillets, pressed on the sesame seeds, seared the fish, and popped the pan into the oven. Now I had a real winner. The contrasting flavors shone through—and the last bite was as interesting as the first.

SESAME-CRUSTED SALMON WITH LEMON AND GINGER
SERVES 4

For even cooking, purchase fillets that are about the same size and shape. If any of your fillets have a thin belly flap, fold it over to create a more even thickness (see page 31). For our free recipes for sesame-crusted salmon for two, go to CooksIllustrated.com/apr14.

	Salt
¾	cup sesame seeds
4	(6- to 8-ounce) skinless salmon fillets
2	scallions, white parts minced, green parts sliced thin
1	tablespoon grated lemon zest plus 2 teaspoons juice
4	teaspoons tahini
2	teaspoons grated fresh ginger
⅛	teaspoon cayenne pepper
1	teaspoon vegetable oil

1. Adjust oven rack to middle position and heat oven to 325 degrees. Dissolve 5 tablespoons salt in 2 quarts water. Transfer 1 cup brine to bowl, stir in sesame seeds, and let stand at room temperature for 5 minutes. Submerge fillets in remaining brine and let stand at room temperature for 15 minutes.

2. Drain seeds and place in 12-inch nonstick skillet. Cook seeds over medium heat, stirring constantly, until golden brown, 2 to 4 minutes. Transfer seeds to pie plate and wipe out skillet with paper towels. Remove fillets from brine and pat dry.

3. Place scallion whites and lemon zest on cutting board and chop until whites and zest are finely minced and well combined. Transfer scallion-zest mixture to bowl and stir in lemon juice, tahini, ginger, cayenne, and ⅛ teaspoon salt.

4. Evenly distribute half of paste over bottoms (skinned sides) of fillets. Press coated sides of fillets in

Brining and then toasting the sesame seeds accentuates their rich, nutty taste and crunchy texture.

seeds and transfer, seed side down, to plate. Evenly distribute remaining paste over tops of fillets and coat with remaining seeds.

5. Heat oil in now-empty skillet over medium heat until shimmering. Place fillets in skillet, skinned side up, and reduce heat to medium-low. Cook until seeds begin to brown, 1 to 2 minutes. Remove skillet from heat and, using 2 spatulas, carefully flip fillets over. Transfer skillet to oven. Bake until center of fish is translucent when checked with tip of paring knife and registers 125 degrees, 10 to 15 minutes. Transfer to serving platter and let rest for 5 minutes. Sprinkle with scallion greens and serve.

SESAME-CRUSTED SALMON WITH LIME AND CORIANDER

Substitute 4 teaspoons lime zest for lemon zest, lime juice for lemon juice, and ¼ teaspoon ground coriander for cayenne.

SESAME-CRUSTED SALMON WITH ORANGE AND CHILI POWDER

Substitute orange zest for lemon zest, orange juice for lemon juice, and ¼ teaspoon chili powder for cayenne.

▶ **See Our Sesame Tricks**
Video available free for 4 months at CooksIllustrated.com/apr14

Thai Chicken Curry with Potatoes

Green and red curries offer big heat and bracing acidity, but the milder variety known as *massaman* tempts with deeper, more complex flavors.

> BY LAN LAM

There are as many interpretations of Thai curries as there are cooks who prepare them, but the versions served in stateside restaurants tend to fit a similar profile: a coconut milk–based sauce that's flavored and thickened with a concentrated spice paste, filled out with meat or fish and vegetables, and served over plenty of steamed jasmine rice. Hot and tangy red and green curries, which get their respective colors from the type of chile in the paste, are most familiar to Americans, along with curries tinted golden yellow by spices like turmeric. And then there's my favorite: a somewhat less well-known variety called *massaman*.

Unlike many Thai dishes that feature hot, sour, salty, and sweet elements, massaman curry trades on a warm, faintly sweet, and not overly spicy profile, thanks to the mix of warm spices like cinnamon, cloves, cardamom, and cumin, as well as roasted dried chiles and aromatics like shallots, garlic, and fresh galangal (a sweet-spicy cousin of ginger) that make up its paste. A last-minute addition of either shrimp paste or fish sauce and a few teaspoons of tangy tamarind balance the rich sauce, which is typically paired with chicken (or beef), potato chunks, and roasted peanuts.

Massaman is a dish that I've always wanted to tackle at home, but it presents challenges in an American kitchen. Ingredients like galangal and tamarind are hard to track down. Plus, precooking dried chiles and aromatic vegetables and toasting and grinding whole spices (another traditional step) make for one heck of a prep job—and that's just for the paste. I was determined to produce a massaman curry as fragrant and rich-tasting as any Thai restaurant would make, but with less work.

Cuts and Pastes

Pulling together the curry at the end would be easy, so I skipped right to streamlining the paste. To see

> ▶ **Watch from Start to Finish**
> Video available free for 4 months
> at CooksIllustrated.com/apr14

Once the curry paste is made (which can be done up to a week in advance), this rich, fragrant dish can be on the table in about half an hour.

what would happen if I cut the precooking step for both the dried chiles and the aromatics, I compared the dish with two different batches of paste. The first I made the traditional way, using oven-toasted dried red chiles (I chose the New Mexican kind for their relatively moderate heat and wide availability) along with broiled skin-on shallots and garlic. In the second batch, the same ingredients (this time the alliums were peeled) went into the blender without precooking. Both pastes also got a knob of fresh ginger (the most obvious substitute for galangal), as well as a dash of fish sauce. As for the spices, some recipes I found called for up to a dozen different kinds—and just a little of each one—but to stick with my streamlining goal, I knocked down the list to whole cloves, cinnamon, cardamom, and cumin, all toasted and ground per tradition for now.

To finish both curries, I browned the pastes in a little oil to deepen their flavors, poured in chicken broth and coconut milk, and simmered the mixtures with Yukon Gold potatoes, onion, peanuts, and a little salt until the potatoes were tender. Finally I slipped

in pieces of boneless, skinless chicken thighs. (Dark meat was a must for its rich flavor.)

The flavor difference between the two batches wasn't just noticeable. My tasters declared the paste made with precooked chiles and alliums in a different league altogether from its uncooked counterpart: richer-tasting, with rounder, more complex flavor, thanks to the caramelization of the sugars in these ingredients. I'd also discovered that there was a textural advantage to precooking: The heat had softened the vegetables, making them a bit easier to blend into a uniform paste, especially when I added a little water and several teaspoons of vegetable oil to the blender jar.

That meant that my only hope for a shortcut rested on the spices. Since they would end up blooming in oil, which also brings out their flavors, I wondered if toasting them beforehand was necessary—or if I could even sub in preground spices. I ran more tests, comparing whole spices that I'd toasted and ground against their preground equivalents. Fortunately, this timesaver worked: The depth and intensity of the preground spice paste was a little less potent, but the basic effect I was going for—warmth with faint sweetness—came across just fine.

In fact, I wondered if I could take this streamlining one step further and use a commercial spice blend instead of measuring out individual spices. After trying pumpkin pie spice (too much cinnamon) and curry powder (too much turmeric), I landed on five-spice powder. Though not an exact match with the traditional massaman lineup, the generally warm, fragrant profile of this blend (which typically includes

For Complex Curry, Turn on the Oven

Massaman curry is richer-tasting and more complex than other varieties of Thai curry not just because of the mix of ingredients in its paste but also because of how they're prepared. By toasting the dried chiles and broiling the aromatic vegetables, we get a paste with a rounder and mellower flavor than we would if we added those components raw, as is done in sharper-tasting red and green curries.

Thai Curry by Color and Spice

Several of the typical curries you'll see on a Thai menu are identifiable by their color—a reflection of the type and amount of chiles, aromatic vegetables, herbs, and spices in the curry paste. *Massaman*, a relative of yellow curry, is better known for its depth and fragrance from warm spices, which makes it stand out from other varieties.

RED

This curry, which has moderate salty sweetness, is fairly spicy and sour, thanks to lots of dried red chiles and a big hit of lime at the end.

GREEN

A high ratio of fresh green chiles plus raw aromatics and very little sugar typically makes this variation the hottest and most pungent type of Thai curry.

YELLOW

Stateside versions tend to be mild, though authentic yellow curries can be quite hot. All are heavy on turmeric—hence the color.

MASSAMAN

Though one of the mildest Thai curries, massaman is also one of the most complex. Traditionally, the paste combines cinnamon, star anise, cloves, cardamom, and cumin—all introduced to Thailand by Muslim merchants around the 12th century—as well as dried chiles and aromatics. To cut down on ingredients, our recipe swaps some of the individual spices for five-spice powder.

---

fennel, cinnamon, star anise, cloves, and either pepper or ginger) made a nice stand-in, and its flavor was potent enough that just a teaspoon got the job done. Some cumin and a little extra black pepper went into the mix, and I was done.

A Bright Spot

From there, I had only a couple of technique and flavor issues to work through. Traditional Thai curry recipes call for frying the paste in coconut cream (either skimmed from the top of a can of coconut milk or bought separately) that's first heated until its oil separates out, or "cracks." I pitted a batch of curry in which I had fried the paste in the skimmed, cracked cream against my working recipe, which called for simply frying the paste in vegetable oil. Admittedly, a few tasters picked up on the more concentrated flavor of the cracked cream curry, but most agreed that vegetable oil worked fine. (If you want to try cracking coconut cream yourself, see "How to 'Crack' Coconut Cream," page 30.)

My colleagues were also clamoring for a bit of brightness, so I tried finishing the curry with a few teaspoons of lime juice—my best guess for a tamarind substitute. Alas, its effect was too sharp for massaman, and scaling back on the juice flattened its effect altogether.

What did work: changing *when* I added the lime juice rather than the amount. When I replaced some of the water in the paste with a few teaspoons of juice, the lime's acid mellowed as it cooked in the curry but didn't disappear. Finishing the curry with lime zest and cilantro freshened it even more.

Served with a heap of fragrant jasmine rice, my version of massaman curry captured everything I love about this dish: richness and depth from the roasted chiles and aromatics, warmth from the spices, crunch from the peanuts, and a touch of freshness from the lime and cilantro, all brought together in a manageable amount of time.

TASTING Jasmine Rice

A staple in Southeast Asian cuisine, jasmine rice is becoming a favorite in America, too: Its consumption shot up by 15 percent in the United States between 2011 and 2012, according to the USA Rice Federation. Unlike ordinary white rice, it carries a delicate scent that's not a byproduct of jasmine flowers but the result of an elevated level of the flavor compound 2-acetyl-1-pyrroline. The scent is detectable even when the rice is covered with bold sauces, and it boasts a soft, delicate texture.

Of the six jasmine rice products that we tasted, both plain and with Thai-style curry, the lone microwavable contender, from Uncle Ben's, ranked dead last for tasting like "plastic," while the pricey mail-order grains from Lotus Foods lost points for disintegrating in the curry. Top honors went to widely available Dynasty Jasmine Rice for its floral fragrance and separate, toothsome grains. For complete tasting results, go to CooksIllustrated.com/apr14. –Naomi Kooker

NICEST RICE
DYNASTY Jasmine Rice
Price: $4.59 for 2 lb
(14 cents per oz)
Comments: Even covered with curry, the "clean" flavor and "finishing hit of jasmine" stood out in this rice, which was also praised for "tender, distinct" grains.

THAI CHICKEN CURRY WITH POTATOES AND PEANUTS
SERVES 4 TO 6

Serve the curry with jasmine rice. The ingredients for the curry paste can be doubled to make extra for future use. Refrigerate the paste for up to one week or freeze it for up to two months.

Curry Paste

- 6 dried New Mexican chiles
- 4 shallots, unpeeled
- 7 garlic cloves, unpeeled
- ½ cup chopped fresh ginger
- ¼ cup water
- 4½ teaspoons lime juice
- 4½ teaspoons vegetable oil
- 1 tablespoon fish sauce
- 1 teaspoon five-spice powder
- ½ teaspoon ground cumin
- ½ teaspoon pepper

Curry

- 1 teaspoon vegetable oil
- 1¼ cups chicken broth
- 1 (13.5-ounce) can coconut milk
- 1 pound Yukon Gold potatoes, unpeeled, cut into ¾-inch pieces
- 1 onion, cut into ¾-inch pieces
- ⅓ cup dry-roasted peanuts
- ¾ teaspoon salt
- 1 pound boneless, skinless chicken thighs, trimmed and cut into 1-inch pieces
- 2 teaspoons grated lime zest
- ¼ cup chopped fresh cilantro

1. FOR THE CURRY PASTE: Adjust oven rack to middle position and heat oven to 350 degrees. Line rimmed baking sheet with aluminum foil. Arrange chiles on prepared sheet and toast until puffed and fragrant, 4 to 6 minutes. Transfer chiles to large plate. Heat broiler.

2. Place shallots and garlic on foil-lined sheet and broil until softened and skin is charred, 6 to 9 minutes.

3. When cool enough to handle, stem and seed chiles and tear into 1½-inch pieces. Process chiles in blender until finely ground, about 1 minute. Peel shallots and garlic. Add shallots, garlic, ginger, water, lime juice, oil, fish sauce, five-spice powder, cumin, and pepper to blender. Process to smooth paste, scraping down sides of blender jar as needed, 2 to 3 minutes. You should have 1 cup paste.

4. FOR THE CURRY: Heat oil in large saucepan over medium heat until shimmering. Add curry paste and cook, stirring constantly, until paste begins to brown, 2½ to 3 minutes. Stir in broth, coconut milk, potatoes, onion, peanuts, and salt, scraping up any browned bits. Bring to simmer and cook until potatoes are just tender, 12 to 14 minutes.

5. Stir in chicken and continue to simmer until chicken is cooked through, 10 to 12 minutes. Remove pan from heat and stir in lime zest. Serve, passing cilantro separately.

Essential Sauces for the Modern Cook

There's a reason certain sauces never go out of style. A great sauce can transform a dish, adding intense flavor and pulling all the elements into balance. Here's how we updated some of the classics. BY SHANNON FRIEDMANN HATCH

RED WINE PAN SAUCE
MAKES ½ CUP

The beauty of a pan sauce is that it needs only a few ingredients and a little bit of time to taste deeply savory. The key is incorporating the browned bits (or fond) left in the pan after searing the protein by dissolving them with wine. The sauce is then enriched with butter. Red wine pan sauce's best mates are steaks and chops.

WHAT CAN GO WRONG: The wine can make the sauce taste harsh and boozy.

HOW WE FIXED IT: We reduce the wine separately from the broth. In experiments, we found that wine and broth reduced together had as much as eight times more alcohol than wine reduced on its own first. Less booziness allows more wine flavors to come to the fore: While the alcohol burns off, the wine's nonvolatile flavor compounds concentrate, making it taste richer and more complex. Wine choice is also important: A medium-bodied fruity wine made from a blend of grapes, such as a Côtes du Rhône, offers the most well-rounded flavor.

1	large shallot, minced
½	cup red wine
¾	cup chicken broth
2	teaspoons packed brown sugar
3	tablespoons unsalted butter, cut into 3 pieces and chilled
1	teaspoon minced fresh rosemary
¼	teaspoon balsamic vinegar
	Salt and pepper

Pour off all but 2 teaspoons fat from pan used to cook meat. Add shallot to pan and cook over medium-high heat, stirring frequently, until softened, 1 to 2 minutes. Add wine and simmer rapidly, scraping up any browned bits, until liquid is reduced to glaze, about 30 seconds. Stir in broth and sugar and simmer until reduced to ⅓ cup, 4 to 6 minutes. Stir in any accumulated meat juices. Off heat, whisk in butter, 1 piece at a time, until melted and sauce is thickened and glossy. Stir in rosemary and vinegar. Season with salt and pepper to taste, spoon over meat, and serve.

Choose the right wine.

Reduce it separately.

WHITE WINE PAN SAUCE
MAKES ½ CUP

Lighter and brighter in taste than its red wine sibling, white wine pan sauce makes plain pan-seared chicken breasts or pork tenderloin seem special.

WHAT CAN GO WRONG: As with red wine pan sauce, a white wine pan sauce, too, can taste boozy and flat.

HOW WE FIXED IT: For a more complex taste, we follow our method in Red Wine Pan Sauce and reduce the wine before adding the broth. As for wine choice, Sauvignon Blanc is your best bet. In tests, we found that it boils down to a "clean" yet sufficiently acidic flavor that plays nicely with the other ingredients. Dry vermouth is a close second—and it has the advantage of a long shelf life. Chardonnay is too oaky, and Pinot Grigio is so mild that its flavor quickly fades into the background. Note: Expensive wine is never necessary for cooking purposes, but the wine you cook with should be good enough to drink on its own.

1	large shallot, minced
2	garlic cloves, minced
½	cup dry white wine
¾	cup chicken broth
3	tablespoons unsalted butter, cut into 3 pieces and chilled
1	teaspoon minced fresh thyme
¼	teaspoon white wine vinegar
	Salt and pepper

Pour off all but 2 teaspoons fat from pan used to cook meat. Add shallot and garlic to pan and cook over medium heat, stirring frequently, until softened, 1 to 2 minutes. Add wine and simmer rapidly, scraping up any browned bits, until liquid is reduced to glaze, about 30 seconds. Stir in broth and simmer until reduced to ⅓ cup, 4 to 6 minutes. Stir in any accumulated meat juices. Off heat, whisk in butter, 1 piece at a time, until melted and sauce is thickened and glossy. Stir in thyme and vinegar. Season with salt and pepper to taste, spoon over meat, and serve.

Combine yolks and butter first.

HOLLANDAISE
MAKES ABOUT 2 CUPS

This lush, lemony butter sauce isn't just for eggs Benedict. Its richness is a great counterpoint to steamed vegetables like asparagus; it can also dress up steak, crab cakes, and roasted potatoes.

WHAT CAN GO WRONG: Hollandaise is prone to break quickly. This is because its emulsion—in this case, the dispersal of tiny fat droplets in water that are held in place by the yolks—is weak.

HOW WE FIXED IT: The trick is to make a stronger emulsion by rearranging the usual order of operations. Instead of combining the egg yolks with the water from the start, which dilutes the yolks' emulsifying powers, we whisk the yolks with the butter and then introduce the water. The resulting sauce is so stable that it can be chilled and reheated.

12	tablespoons unsalted butter, softened
6	large egg yolks
½	cup boiling water
2	teaspoons lemon juice
⅛	teaspoon cayenne pepper
	Salt

Whisk butter and egg yolks together in large heatproof bowl set over medium saucepan filled with ½ inch barely simmering water, making sure that water does not touch bottom of bowl. Slowly add boiling water (for accuracy, bring 1 cup to a boil and then measure ½ cup) and cook, whisking constantly, until thickened and sauce registers 160 degrees, 7 to 10 minutes. Off heat, stir in lemon juice and cayenne. Season with salt to taste. Serve.

TO MAKE AHEAD: Hollandaise can be refrigerated for up to 3 days. Microwave at 50 percent power, stirring every 10 seconds, until heated through, about 1 minute.

BEURRE BLANC

MAKES ABOUT ⅔ CUP

Use this delicately flavored butter sauce to add richness to simply prepared fish, shellfish, chicken, and vegetables.

WHAT CAN GO WRONG: Like hollandaise, beurre blanc is a fat-in-water emulsion that breaks easily. If the butter gets too hot, its own emulsion "breaks" and its butterfat leaks out of the sauce, turning it greasy.

HOW WE FIXED IT: Taking a cue from modern versions of this sauce, we add cream to stabilize the emulsion; its casein proteins surround the butterfat droplets, keeping them suspended in the liquid.

    3   tablespoons dry white wine
    2   tablespoons white wine vinegar
    1   small shallot, minced
        Pinch salt
    1   tablespoon heavy cream
    8   tablespoons unsalted butter, cut into 8
        pieces and chilled

Bring wine, vinegar, shallot, and salt to boil in small, heavy-bottomed saucepan over medium-high heat. Reduce heat to medium-low and simmer until reduced by two-thirds, about 5 minutes. Whisk in cream. Add butter, 1 piece at a time, whisking vigorously after each addition until butter is incorporated and forms thick, pale yellow sauce, 30 to 60 seconds. Remove pan from heat and serve.

AÏOLI

MAKES ABOUT ¾ CUP

This garlicky mayonnaise adds kick to sandwiches, vegetables, bouillabaisse, and seafood.

WHAT CAN GO WRONG: The sauce can taste overly harsh and bitter.

HOW WE FIXED IT: We minced a single clove of garlic to a paste on a rasp-style grater for an aïoli with full but even garlic flavor and no harsh-tasting bits. A mix of vegetable and extra-virgin olive oils leads to clean flavor that's still fruity.

    2   large egg yolks
    4   teaspoons lemon juice
    1   garlic clove, minced to paste
        Salt and white pepper
    ⅛   teaspoon sugar
    ½   cup vegetable oil
    ¼   cup extra-virgin olive oil

In large bowl, combine egg yolks, lemon juice, garlic, ¼ teaspoon salt, and sugar. Whisking constantly, very slowly drizzle oils into egg mixture until thick and creamy. Season with salt and pepper to taste.

TO MAKE AHEAD: Aïoli can be refrigerated for up to 3 days.

BASIL PESTO

MAKES ¾ CUP; ENOUGH FOR 1 POUND PASTA

Pesto's most familiar application is dressing pasta, but a dollop of its bright, nutty flavor can enliven everything from soup to stew to chicken, sandwiches, and steamed potatoes.

WHAT CAN GO WRONG: The sharpness of raw garlic can overpower more delicate, aromatic basil. The basil also quickly turns a drab, unappealing dark green.

HOW WE FIXED IT: To mellow the garlic's flavor, we briefly toast the whole, unpeeled cloves in a dry skillet before chopping and processing. A small amount of parsley, which doesn't discolor as easily as basil, helps keep the pesto green. Finally, pounding the herbs before pureeing them releases more of their flavorful oils so that they stand up better to the garlic.

    3   garlic cloves, unpeeled
    2   cups fresh basil leaves
    2   tablespoons fresh parsley leaves
    7   tablespoons extra-virgin olive oil
    ¼   cup pine nuts, toasted
        Salt and pepper
    ¼   cup finely grated Parmesan or Pecorino
        Romano cheese

1. Toast garlic in small, heavy skillet over medium heat, shaking pan occasionally, until fragrant and color of cloves deepens slightly, about 7 minutes. Let garlic cool slightly, then peel and chop.

2. Place basil and parsley in heavy-duty 1-gallon zipper-lock bag. Pound bag with flat side of meat pounder or rolling pin until all leaves are bruised.

3. Process oil, pine nuts, ½ teaspoon salt, garlic, and herbs in food processor until smooth, scraping down sides of bowl as needed, about 1 minute. Stir in Parmesan and season with salt and pepper to taste.

TO MAKE AHEAD: Pesto can be covered with thin layer of oil (1 to 2 tablespoons) and refrigerated for up to 4 days or frozen for up to 1 month.

Toast garlic; add parsley.

Process with toasted bread.

SALSA VERDE

MAKES 1½ CUPS

This potent green sauce boasts a fresh grassy taste along with tangy, garlicky, fruity flavor. Use it on steak, chicken, pork, or shrimp.

WHAT CAN GO WRONG: With so many assertive flavors in the mix, the sauce can come on too strong, and it typically separates easily.

HOW WE FIXED IT: We add an unusual ingredient—bread—and process it with the oil and lemon juice before adding the other ingredients. Bread doesn't just mellow the assertive flavors in the mix; its starches stabilize the emulsified sauce by increasing its viscosity (more viscous mixtures are more stable) as well as absorbing the lemon juice so it doesn't separate from the oil.

    2   slices hearty white sandwich bread
    1   cup extra-virgin olive oil
    ¼   cup lemon juice (2 lemons)
    4   cups fresh parsley leaves
    4   anchovy fillets, rinsed
    4   tablespoons capers, rinsed
    1   garlic clove, minced
    ¼   teaspoon salt

Toast bread in toaster at lowest setting until surface is dry but not browned, about 15 seconds. Remove crusts and cut bread into rough ½-inch pieces (you should have about 1½ cups). Process bread pieces, oil, and lemon juice in food processor until smooth, about 10 seconds. Add parsley, anchovies, capers, garlic, and salt. Pulse until mixture is finely chopped (mixture should not be smooth), about 5 pulses, scraping down sides of bowl with rubber spatula after 3 pulses. Transfer mixture to small bowl before serving.

TO MAKE AHEAD: Salsa verde can be refrigerated for up to 2 days. Bring to room temperature and stir to recombine before serving.

Ultimate Thick-Cut Sweet Potato Fries

Classic French fries made with white potatoes—crispy on the outside, creamy on the inside—set a high bar. We wanted sweet potato fries that could truly compete.

⋟ BY DAN SOUZA ⋞

Though they're both called potatoes, white potatoes and sweet potatoes couldn't be more different. Sweet potatoes come from a completely different plant family than white potatoes like russets and contain far less starch, more water, and a lot more sugar. As a result, they cook very differently—a fact that is nowhere more apparent than when making fries: It's very hard to make sweet potato fries that rival classic French fries made from russets.

Sweet potato fries are typically soggy or burnt—and often they hit both marks at once. Occasionally a restaurant manages to deliver crispy sweet potato fries, but they never taste much like the tuber. These fries are usually not even house-made: They're frozen fries purchased from a food processing plant. Furthermore, they're frequently cut too thin for my liking, offering little in the way of a supercreamy, sweet-tasting interior—in my opinion, the biggest selling point of this vegetable. Fueled by a serious hunger for good thick-cut sweet potato fries, I ordered 50 pounds of the orange spuds and got to work.

The Perfect Coat

While commercial frozen sweet potato fries lack flavor, I have to respect their ability to turn (and stay) supercrispy. How do they do it? When I compared the ingredient lists of a few products, I found a common theme: starch. A starchy coating on these frozen fries makes all the difference. This discovery didn't come entirely by surprise. After all, it's the high-starch composition of russet potatoes that makes them so suited to frying, and we use starchy coatings to give all kinds of low-starch foods (like chicken) a crispy fried exterior. Meanwhile, sweet potatoes don't just contain less starch than white potatoes do; a little research informed me that they also contain an enzyme that, when heated, converts some of the starch in the sweet potatoes into sugars. All this translates into a serious handicap in the world of deep frying.

Cutting the potatoes into wedges rather than skinny fries means more creamy, flavorful sweet potato interior in every bite.

So would adding a starchy coating to my fries be the fix that allowed them to crisp up? I rounded up a group of easy-to-find starches—potato starch, cornstarch, arrowroot, and all-purpose flour (while not a pure starch, it's often used for coating foods when deep-frying)—and ran a test to compare. After heating 2 quarts of vegetable oil in a large Dutch oven to 350 degrees, I dusted four batches of ¾-inch-wide peeled sweet potato wedges (which I'd cut in half crosswise for a more manageable shape) with each type of starch and fried them until tender and, in theory, crispy.

What a disappointment. None of the starches formed anything resembling a crispy crust: They clung meekly to the sweet potatoes as a dry, flaky, dusty coating. It turns out that cut sweet potatoes—unlike, say, chicken—don't exude much moisture. Instead, almost all the water that they contain stays trapped within their cell walls. Why is liquid so important in a coating when frying? In hot oil the food's surface moisture quickly turns into steam, and as the steam escapes the food, the outer starchy coating dries out and crisps. The escaping steam leaves behind small holes, and oil fills those holes, helping create a crispy brown crust. These little holes also break up the texture of the coating so that it's crunchy when bitten into rather than hard or leathery—think of a porous Nestlé Crunch bar versus a dense, hard bar of solid chocolate. (For more information, see "Why Starch Gets Crispy When Fried," page 30.)

Given that, the solution seemed easy: I simply added some water to each of the starches, creating thin slurries that I could dip the wedges into before frying. This was a promising step forward. All the fries emerged with at least a modicum of crust. In the end, cornstarch won out, producing the best crust, with a nicely crisped texture.

But there were still some issues to deal with. For one, my fries looked more like sweet potato tempura—the fried coating was wispy and puffed away from the wedges. In addition, the coating, while crispy right out of the oil, had a tendency to quickly turn soft and soggy. And finally, the interiors of the sweet potatoes were more chalky than smooth, creamy, and sweet.

Blanching to the Rescue

Thinking that I should switch gears, I turned my focus away from the coating and toward achieving the perfect creamy interior. The cause of the problem was quite clear: The short time that it took to dry and crisp the slurry on the outside wasn't sufficient to cook the thick wedges all the way through.

My first thought was to go the classic French fry route and treat my uncoated wedges to a quick blanch in lower-temperature (around 250-degree) oil before dipping them in the slurry and frying them again at the proper higher temperature to crisp the coating. I gave it a try, and while it resulted in a big difference for the interior texture—which turned soft and sweet—the oil slick on the outside of the blanched fries made it hard to get good slurry coverage. So I switched to blanching in water rather than in oil, simmering the wedges in a couple of quarts of salted water until their exteriors were tender but their very centers remained slightly firm. (Blanched any further, my fries tended to break apart when mixed with the slurry.) Then I proceeded with the

Sweet Potato Fries Gone Wrong

The typical sweet potato fry is cut thin, which means too little creamy sweet potato interior. Cutting our fries into wedges was a good fix, but their shape wasn't the only hurdle. Because sweet potatoes are low in starch—and a portion of what starches they do possess converts into sugars when heated—most sweet potato fries end up limp or burnt. Giving our sweet potato fries a starchy coating ensures a crust with a crispy texture.

LIMP, BURNT LOSERS
Low-starch sweet potatoes often burn before they crisp up.

coating and frying as before. This adjustment made a big difference. Without an oily barrier, the slurry clung evenly to each blanched wedge. Plus, adding the salt created better-tasting interiors. This was the best batch yet.

It was time to return to the issues with the coating—namely, it was too thin (and thus prone to sog out) and didn't cling to the fries very well. Was there a way to thicken the coating and at the same time make it adhere better to the wedges? In the past, we've found that adding baking soda to the cooking water for white potatoes breaks down their exteriors, turning them pasty and starchy while their interiors remain firm. In many cases this would, of course, be a bad thing, but I wondered if using baking soda here would be a plus, creating a tacky exterior that the slurry would bind to more firmly.

I gave it a shot, adding 1 teaspoon of baking soda to the blanching water. After about 5 minutes of simmering, the water turned orange and the potatoes' exteriors were mushy, just as I'd expected. Once I'd folded these spuds into the slurry, a thick, gloppy orange paste coated the wedges. It looked promising—and it delivered. These wedges had a substantial, crispy coating that clung close to the potatoes, and my fries remained crispy for a long time out of the oil. What's more, they had visual appeal, with great orange color both inside and out. Finally I'd made exactly the fries that I'd been after.

Less Is More

My last move was to try to simplify and foolproof the frying process. Up to this point I'd been using our standard setup: frying in batches in 2 quarts of oil in a large Dutch oven and keeping the fries warm in a low oven. But my supersticky coating mixture meant that now my fries were pretty likely to stick to one another, as well as to the bottom of the pot. To eliminate the bottom-sticking issue, I opted for nonstick cookware. At first a skillet seemed like an odd choice, but I found that I could drop the oil from 2 quarts to just 3 cups and still keep the wedges fully submerged.

To limit how much the fries stuck to one another, I added them to the pan individually with tongs to ensure that there was good spacing around them—a simple step, considering I was using thick-cut wedges rather than shoestring fries. Any fries that did manage to stick together were easily pried apart with tongs or two forks either during or after frying.

While many restaurants serve ketchup with their sweet potato fries, I always find the combination cloyingly sweet. Instead, I took a cue from the Belgians and whipped up a creamy, spicy mayonnaise-based sauce. Into the mayonnaise base I stirred spicy Asian chili-garlic sauce and white vinegar.

Supercrispy, ultracreamy, and complete with a spicy sauce, these thick-cut sweet potato fries would be the reason I save russets for baking and mashing.

THICK-CUT SWEET POTATO FRIES
SERVES 4 TO 6

If your sweet potatoes are shorter than 4 inches in length, do not cut the wedges crosswise. We prefer peanut oil for frying, but vegetable oil may be used instead. Leftover frying oil may be saved for further use; strain the cooled oil into an airtight container and store it in a cool, dark place for up to one month or in the freezer for up to two months. We like these fries with our Spicy Fry Sauce (recipe follows), but they are also good served plain.

- ½ cup cornstarch
  Kosher salt
- 1 teaspoon baking soda
- 3 pounds sweet potatoes, peeled and cut into ¾-inch-thick wedges, wedges cut in half crosswise
- 3 cups peanut oil

1. Adjust oven rack to middle position and heat oven to 200 degrees. Set wire rack in rimmed baking sheet. Whisk cornstarch and ½ cup cold water together in large bowl.

2. Bring 2 quarts water, ¼ cup salt, and baking soda to boil in Dutch oven. Add potatoes and return to boil. Reduce heat to simmer and cook until exteriors turn slightly mushy (centers will remain firm), 3 to 5 minutes. Whisk cornstarch slurry to recombine. Using wire skimmer or slotted spoon, transfer potatoes to bowl with slurry.

3. Using rubber spatula, fold potatoes with slurry until slurry turns light orange, thickens to paste, and clings to potatoes.

4. Heat oil in 12-inch nonstick skillet over high heat to 325 degrees. Using tongs, carefully add one third of potatoes to oil, making sure that potatoes aren't touching one another. Fry until crispy and lightly browned, 7 to 10 minutes, using tongs to flip potatoes halfway through frying (adjust heat as necessary to maintain oil temperature between 280 and 300 degrees). Using wire skimmer or slotted spoon, transfer fries to prepared wire rack (fries that stick together can be separated with tongs or forks). Season with salt to taste and transfer to oven to keep warm. Return oil to 325 degrees and repeat in 2 more batches with remaining potatoes. Serve immediately.

SPICY FRY SAUCE
MAKES ABOUT ½ CUP

For a less spicy version, use only 2 teaspoons of Asian chili-garlic sauce. The sauce can be made up to four days in advance and stored, covered, in the refrigerator.

- 6 tablespoons mayonnaise
- 1 tablespoon Asian chili-garlic sauce
- 2 teaspoons white vinegar

Whisk all ingredients together in small bowl.

KEY STEPS | MAKING GOOD ON SWEET POTATO FRIES

Here's how we turned sweet potatoes into impressively crispy fries with perfect creamy interiors.

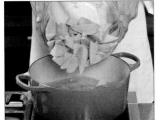

BLANCH
Blanching the wedges helps ensure that their interiors fully cook and turn creamy when fried. Adding baking soda to the water makes them tacky on the outside.

COAT
The cornstarch slurry stays put thanks in part to the parcooked wedges' tacky exteriors, and it crisps up beautifully in the hot oil.

FRY
Frying the wedges in a nonstick skillet prevents them from sticking to the bottom of the pan. The change in vessel also allows us to use far less oil.

Proper British Scones

Buttery rich American scones are a coffeehouse staple, but the fluffy and tender British original has a refined appeal all its own.

> BY ANDREA GEARY <

"This is fantastic. But it's not a scone." The setting was a café in Cambridge, Massachusetts, and the speaker was an English customer who was emphatically brandishing a pastry that I had made. It was a large, rustic triangle with a craggy, sugary exterior and a buttery, fruit-studded middle. At the time, I naively believed it to be a scone.

Years later, on a visit to the United Kingdom, I understood what he meant—mine were American, not British, scones. The two are like cousins who have grown up in very different environments. Though they share the same name and a lot of the same DNA, they are, as the Brits might say, as different as chalk and cheese.

Proper British scones are round and tall, with a light, cakelike crumb and a soft, tender crust. They're not as sweet or as rich as American scones, but that's because they're usually split in half, lavishly spread with butter or clotted cream, and piled high with jam at teatime.

While I love American-style scones, that cozy British teatime ritual holds tremendous appeal. And because rich, buttery American scones would be a bit over-the-top in that context, I resolved to develop a recipe for light, fluffy scones, suitable for serving in the British style.

Cookie-Cutter Cousins

Here's how I've made American scones for almost two decades: I combine all-purpose flour, sugar, baking powder, and salt in a bowl; then I rub in a very generous amount of cold butter until it is distributed throughout the dry ingredients in thin, broad flakes. I whisk together milk and eggs and gently stir that mixture into my dry ingredients to form a shaggy dough. At that point I add some flavorings (fresh or dried fruit, nuts, chocolate chips, spices, maple syrup—the sky's the limit), and then, working gently and quickly, I form the dough into disks, which I cut into wedges. A bit of egg wash, maybe a sprinkling of coarse sugar, and the scones go into the oven. They emerge somewhat crumbly, squat, and whimsical in shape, but they have a buttery charm that has ensured their spot in my baking repertoire.

Plenty of leavener, ample kneading, and a start in a hot oven give these scones the impressive height expected of a classic British scone.

The recipes that I collected for British scones featured the same basic ingredients as mine, minus all the add-ins and with two key differences. First, British recipes call for self-raising flour, which is like American all-purpose flour with a leavening agent already added. (Don't confuse it with American self-rising flour, which is lower in protein and has added salt.) It's ubiquitous in the United Kingdom but harder to find here. For authenticity's sake, I tracked down a couple of bags locally, knowing that I would devise a substitution later.

The second difference was more clear-cut: British recipes call for about one-third of the amount of butter that my recipe requires. So I lowered the butter content in my recipe, and I also cut back on the sugar to make my scones more jam-compatible. I followed my trusty mixing method, but instead of forming the dough into wedges, I used a cookie cutter to make round scones. No egg wash, no sugar—just straight into a 425-degree oven. The result looked familiar. In fact, here in America we have a special name for such a thing: a biscuit.

Rub It In

A bite confirmed my suspicions: These scones tasted great, but they lacked the tender, cakelike crumb of British scones. Strange: They were made with the same ingredients and in the same ratios. How had I ended up with a bready biscuit?

Realizing that the difference had to be in the methods, I compared them closely to see what didn't line up: dry ingredients combined—check; dairy and egg whisked—check; butter worked into the dry ingredients—aye, there's the rub, so to speak.

I was still working the cold, hard fat quickly into the dry ingredients, leaving noticeable bits of butter in the mixture per the usual approach with American scones. But a close reading of traditional British scone recipes reveals a significant difference in technique: The butter is rubbed into the dry ingredients so completely that it is no longer visible—no lumps, no flakes. In fact, British cooks often use soft, room-temperature butter to make the process even easier, quicker, and more thorough. This approach promises a finer, more even crumb because the structure is not disrupted by those large pieces of fat. It also produces a crumb that is more tender. Why? Because with more of the flour particles coated with fat, and thus protected from the wet ingredients, a lot of the proteins in the flour are prevented from linking up to form gluten. The result is a fine-textured and tender scone, much more cakelike than biscuitlike.

So I made up another batch, this time thoroughly working softened butter into the dry ingredients before mixing the dough lightly. (I also switched to using a food processor to blend in the butter, which many cooks prefer to using their hands.) And indeed, this subtle change in tactics was enough to give me the cakelike texture I was after.

This discovery led to another equally compelling one. My method called for rolling out the dough once, cutting eight scones from it, and then rerolling the scraps to make four more scones. I noticed that the scones from the second roll consistently rose a bit higher in the oven than those from the first roll, which seems counterintuitive when you consider all those dire warnings about overmixing that are so often a feature of baking recipes. The fear in those cases is

A Tale of Two Scones

While rich, dense American scones are no-holds-barred, cakelike British scones show restraint.

THE AMERICAN

THE BRIT

THE AMERICAN		THE BRIT
1½ cups, chilled	BUTTER	½ cup, softened
1 tablespoon of baking powder	LEAVENER	2 tablespoons of baking powder
The more the better	ADD-INS	A smattering of currants
Egg wash and lots of coarse sugar	TOPPING	Light milk-and-egg wash

that the gluten network will overdevelop and become tighter if it is overworked when it comes in contact with moisture, leading to tougher texture and a hampered rise. But in this case, so much of the flour was coated in fat that it was effectively waterproofed, making it harder for gluten bonds to form. This meant that working the dough a bit more was actually beneficial since it offered those proteins still available (i.e., from any uncoated flour) a chance to link together, giving the scones a little more structure to support more lift. With this in mind, I upped the number of times that I kneaded the dough from a dozen to 25 to 30 for maximum lift and rerolled the scraps with no qualms.

I was encouraged by my progress, but my scones still lacked the impressive height of those that I had enjoyed in Britain. I knew that I could do better.

Raising Hopes

It was time to find a substitute for that self-raising flour. I had seen recommendations for adding anywhere from 1 to 2 teaspoons of baking powder per cup of all-purpose flour to approximate the lift of self-raising, and the issue was further complicated because most British scone recipes go on to boost the lift even more with additional baking powder, which varied in amount from recipe to recipe as well. I had to start somewhere, so I added 3 tablespoons of baking powder to my 3 cups of flour. In doing so, I seriously overshot the mark. Though the scones were indeed light and tall, they also had that telltale flavor of excess leavening, which some tasters described as soapy and others metallic.

In search of maximum lift and no leavening flavor, I made four more batches, decreasing the baking powder by 1 teaspoon per batch and tracking scone height and negative flavor comments. I found my sweet (or at least nonsoapy) spot at 2 tablespoons.

Aspiring to even greater heights, I considered the oven temperature. Yeast-leavened breads often start in an extremely hot oven to maximize "oven spring," the growth spurt that happens when water vaporizes into steam and the air in the dough heats up and expands. Then the heat is lowered to ensure that the crust does

not burn before the interior is cooked through. Would this approach work with chemically leavened scones? It did. When I preheated my oven to 500 degrees and then turned it down to 425 degrees after putting in the scones, I got the lightest, fluffiest batch yet.

A couple more tweaks brought my scones to the level of those that I had enjoyed in England. I added currants rather than raisins because their smaller size meant better distribution within each scone, and they seemed more appropriate. And I reserved a small amount of the milk and egg mixture to brush on top of the scones before baking. It made the dough a little less soft so it was easier to handle, and it helped the scones brown a bit more. It also gave my scones the soft, tender crust that I wanted.

The words "stately" and "fluffy" are rarely used together, but they both described my scones perfectly. And while they looked quite impressive piled on a plate, they really came into their own when split and topped with plenty of butter—or clotted cream—and jam, served alongside a mug of tea. If I ever meet another Englishman who's keen to talk scones, I'm confident that I'll be able to hold my own in both English and American.

When a Second Roll Doesn't Produce Second-Best

For many baked goods that require rolling out the dough (biscuits, pie dough), rerolling scraps produces a tougher, more squat result. This is because just as with kneading, the action of rolling creates a stronger, tighter gluten network—and too much gluten can negatively influence texture and rise. But our British-style scones offer more leeway. The butter is worked into the flour so thoroughly that it prevents many of the proteins from ever linking up to form gluten in the first place. Far from being a hazard, rerolling the second batch of dough merely encourages a little more of the proteins to link together, leading to a bit more structure and more lift in the oven.

BRITISH-STYLE CURRANT SCONES
MAKES 12 SCONES

We prefer whole milk in this recipe, but low-fat milk can be used. The dough will be quite soft and wet; dust your work surface and your hands liberally with flour. For a tall, even rise, use a sharp-edged biscuit cutter and push straight down; do not twist the cutter. These scones are best served fresh, but leftover scones may be stored in the freezer and reheated in a 300-degree oven for 15 minutes before serving. Serve these scones with jam as well as salted butter or clotted cream.

- 3 cups (15 ounces) all-purpose flour
- ⅓ cup (2⅓ ounces) sugar
- 2 tablespoons baking powder
- ½ teaspoon salt
- 8 tablespoons unsalted butter, cut into ½-inch pieces and softened
- ¾ cup dried currants
- 1 cup whole milk
- 2 large eggs

1. Adjust oven rack to upper-middle position and heat oven to 500 degrees. Line rimmed baking sheet with parchment paper. Pulse flour, sugar, baking powder, and salt in food processor until combined, about 5 pulses. Add butter and pulse until fully incorporated and mixture looks like very fine crumbs with no visible butter, about 20 pulses. Transfer mixture to large bowl and stir in currants.

2. Whisk milk and eggs together in second bowl. Set aside 2 tablespoons milk mixture. Add remaining milk mixture to flour mixture and, using rubber spatula, fold together until almost no dry bits of flour remain.

3. Transfer dough to well-floured counter and gather into ball. With floured hands, knead until surface is smooth and free of cracks, 25 to 30 times. Press gently to form disk. Using floured rolling pin, roll disk into 9-inch round, about 1 inch thick. Using floured 2½-inch round cutter, stamp out 8 rounds, recoating cutter with flour if it begins to stick. Arrange scones on prepared sheet. Gather dough scraps, form into ball, and knead gently until surface is smooth. Roll dough to 1-inch thickness and stamp out 4 rounds. Discard remaining dough.

4. Brush tops of scones with reserved milk mixture. Reduce oven temperature to 425 degrees and bake scones until risen and golden brown, 10 to 12 minutes, rotating sheet halfway through baking. Transfer scones to wire rack and let cool for at least 10 minutes. Serve scones warm or at room temperature.

Perfecting Lemon Pudding Cake

During baking, this dessert's batter separates into two distinct layers.
To ensure top-notch cake and pudding, we'd have to unravel its culinary chemistry.

⋟ BY SARAH MULLINS ⋞

Pudding cakes have been around, in one form or another, since the 1700s. But the kind we know today really took off in the 1860s, probably due to the advent of egg beaters with rotating parts that made whipping the egg whites for the batter easier. At the same time, cooks began experimenting with flavorings, including a lemon version that has never gone out of style. Part of the dessert's appeal is its seemingly magical transformation during baking: A single batter goes into the oven but comes out as a twofer—an airy, soufflélike cake resting on top of a silky lemon pudding. Of course, that's assuming it's executed correctly. The reality is that most of the lemon pudding cakes I've sampled have been subpar, often featuring wet, underbaked cake or grainy, curdled pudding, or both. What would it take to fix the problems associated with this dessert?

Beginning with the Basics

I got my bearings by preparing a fairly typical recipe, whisking together ¾ cup of sugar, two egg yolks, fresh lemon juice and zest, and ½ cup of flour. Next I stirred in 1 cup of whole milk plus ½ cup of cream for richness and then gradually folded in four egg whites whipped with a bit more sugar. Finally, I poured the batter into six ramekins. (Baking the pudding in a single dish is more typical, but individual ramekins would be more elegant.) This dessert always bakes in a water bath, which helps insulate the pudding layer from the heat of the oven and helps prevent it from curdling. Following the test kitchen's approach, I arranged a folded dish towel in the bottom of a roasting pan as an anchor and then nestled the ramekins into the towel. I poured boiling water into the pan and transferred the assembly to a 350-degree oven. Once baked, the batter separated into distinct tiers of cake and pudding. So what causes the batter to do its trademark split? The answer is surprisingly straightforward: The whipped egg whites are less

The amount of flour in the batter and the stiffness of the whipped egg whites help determine the ratio of cake to pudding in this lush dessert.

dense than the other ingredients and thus rise to the top of the dessert during baking, taking some of the flour with them. The egg white proteins coagulate and set to a "solid" cakelike structure, while the denser ingredients settle to the bottom of the baking dish, where they thicken into a pudding.

Simple enough, but I wanted to better understand the role that the egg whites play. I made two desserts, one in which I whipped my egg whites only very slightly and another in which I beat them to firm, dry peaks that stood up on my whisk. How much would the quantity of air incorporated into the whites affect the end result? As it turned out, quite a bit. Though the pudding layers were unsurprisingly near identical in both samples, the cake layers had stark differences. The barely whipped whites produced a dense, rubbery cake that was less than ¼ inch tall. The stiff whites, on the other hand, produced a firm, almost tough layer that rose higher than an inch. I now knew that the height of the cake was directly related to the amount of air in the whites. I wanted a tender cake with moderate lift, so I would whip my

whites to the midway point between loose and stiff: soft, glossy peaks.

Next up: the flour. Since pudding cakes contain so little flour, I wondered if adjusting the quantity might shed even more light on the mechanics of this dessert. Sure enough, when I doubled the amount of flour to 1 cup, the pudding disappeared entirely and the dessert baked into a single claylike mass. On the other hand, when I tried ¼ cup of flour instead of the ½ cup I had been using, the amount of pudding increased, producing a 1:4 pudding to cake ratio that my tasters thought was ideal.

Getting in Sync

I now had a better understanding of the nuts and bolts of the dessert, and I was ready to make some other improvements. There were two big problems. First, my recipe was producing cake that lacked structure. Second, the pudding cooked faster than the cake, and even with the water bath, it was still curdling when I baked the dessert until the cake was done.

I decided to tackle the texture of the cake first. Though somewhat unconventional for lemon pudding cake, using baking powder to create and expand gas pockets might give the top layer a little more lift and make it seem more cakelike. When I added various amounts to my batter, tasters agreed that ½ teaspoon of baking powder did the trick. As an added bonus, the baking powder also helped produce a gorgeous golden top, since it made the acidic batter slightly more alkaline, and an alkaline cake browns better than an acidic one.

Now what could I do to prevent the pudding layer from cooking more quickly than the cake and curdling? Reducing the oven temperature from 350 to 325 degrees helped a little bit, but not enough.

Would it help to alter the water bath? In most recipes that use the technique, including those for lemon pudding cake, the water added to the pan is typically boiling. I wondered if I could slow things down with a cool bath instead of a hot one. I baked pudding cakes in pans filled with cold water, ice water, and (as a control) boiling water. I made sure to pour the water only one-third of the way up the sides of the ramekins, so the water insulated only the pudding portion, giving the slow-baking cake a little extra

▶ Watch the Magic Happen
Video available free for 4 months
at CooksIllustrated.com/apr14

Water baths insulate food from the heat of the oven, helping custards and other delicate desserts cook more slowly. Typically, the bath gets filled with boiling water. Because the bottom pudding layer in this dessert cooks more quickly than the cake layer, we found that cold water works better, allowing the pudding to set slowly and without curdling, giving the cake time to bake through.

A large roasting pan accommodates more water, which takes longer to heat, providing more protection.

Water reaches just one-third of the way up, insulating only the pudding layer. Unaffected by insulation, the slow-to-cook cake layer bakes at a higher temperature.

A towel lining the bottom of the pan secures the ramekins.

exposure to the heat. As it had been doing, the pudding in the boiling-water bath continued to curdle, even at the lower oven temperature. However, the desserts baked in cold and ice water boasted smooth pudding. Since it took longer to bake, the cake layer could now fully cook without risk of overdone pudding. Because cold and ice water produced nearly identical results, I chose to use cold since it baked the desserts a little faster.

The size of the water bath also made a difference. By using probes to record the temperatures of the baths, I learned that the cake layers in a smaller bath baked in 40 minutes (at which point the water was 186 degrees), but the puddings curdled. The cakes in a larger pan required 53 minutes of baking and their puddings were as silky as could be. I checked the final temperature of this water bath: 179 degrees. Going back to my data, I found that the smaller water bath had reached the same temperature a whole half-hour earlier, at 23 minutes. The bigger bath was better, delivering a gentler cooking environment so that the layers finished in tandem.

Finessing Flavor

With the consistency of the dessert right where I wanted it, I was ready to focus on the lemon flavor. After some tinkering, I determined that ½ cup of lemon juice and 3 tablespoons of zest struck just the right balance. The only problem was that the zest ruined the texture of the silky pudding, riddling it with tiny, gritty threads.

Seeking to capture the flavor of the zest but not its abrasive texture, I tried infusing it into the warmed milk/cream mixture for 15 minutes and then straining out the solids. And because I thought that lots of fat might be necessary to extract flavor, I also steeped some zest in a small amount of warm melted butter (I figured that I could incorporate this into the cake if necessary). In a side-by-side taste test, the tart, floral notes were more present in the milk/cream mixture than in the infused butter. After a little research, this result made total sense.

Lemon peel contains numerous flavor compounds. Some are water-soluble and others are fat-soluble. Butter has such a low water content that the zest's water-soluble compounds could not be effectively extracted in it. In contrast, the more hydrated (but still fatty) milk and cream mixture was able to extract a better balance of the fat-soluble and water-soluble flavor compounds.

My last move was to embellish the dessert with a colorful, flavorful garnish. Taking a classic, simple approach, I whipped up a quick blueberry compote that meshed well with the dessert's tart notes.

With a few tweaks, I'd turned a rather humble classic into a dessert that consistently delivered a smooth, silky pudding and a light cake every time.

LEMON PUDDING CAKES
SERVES 6

To take the temperature of the pudding layer, touch the probe tip to the bottom of the ramekin and pull it up ¼ inch. The batter can also be baked in an 8-inch square glass baking dish. We like this dessert served at room temperature, but it can also be served chilled (the texture will be firmer). Spoon Blueberry Compote (recipe follows) over the top of each ramekin or simply dust with confectioners' sugar.

1	cup whole milk
½	cup heavy cream
3	tablespoons grated lemon zest plus ½ cup juice (3 lemons)
1	cup (7 ounces) sugar
¼	cup (1¼ ounces) all-purpose flour
½	teaspoon baking powder
⅛	teaspoon salt
2	large eggs, separated, plus 2 large whites
½	teaspoon vanilla extract

1. Adjust oven rack to middle position and heat oven to 325 degrees. Bring milk and cream to simmer in medium saucepan over medium-high heat. Remove pan from heat, whisk in lemon zest, cover pan, and let stand for 15 minutes. Meanwhile, fold dish towel in half and place in bottom of large roasting pan. Place six 6-ounce ramekins on top of towel and set aside pan.

2. Strain milk mixture through fine-mesh strainer into bowl, pressing on lemon zest to extract liquid; discard lemon zest. Whisk ¾ cup sugar, flour, baking powder, and salt in second bowl until combined. Add egg yolks, vanilla, lemon juice, and milk mixture and whisk until combined. (Batter will have consistency of milk.)

3. Using stand mixer fitted with whisk, whip egg whites on medium-low speed until foamy, about 1 minute. Increase speed to medium-high and whip whites to soft, billowy mounds, about 1 minute.

Gradually add remaining ¼ cup sugar and whip until glossy, soft peaks form, 1 to 2 minutes.

4. Whisk one-quarter of whites into batter to lighten. With rubber spatula, gently fold in remaining whites until no clumps or streaks remain. Ladle batter into ramekins (ramekins should be nearly full). Pour enough cold water into pan to come one-third of way up sides of ramekins. Bake until cake is set and pale golden brown and pudding layer registers 172 to 175 degrees at center, 50 to 55 minutes.

5. Remove pan from oven and let ramekins stand in water bath for 10 minutes. Transfer ramekins to wire rack and let cool completely. Serve.

BLUEBERRY COMPOTE
MAKES ABOUT 1 CUP

To use fresh blueberries, crush one-third of them against the side of the saucepan with a wooden spoon after adding them to the butter and then proceed as directed.

1	tablespoon unsalted butter
10	ounces (2 cups) frozen blueberries
2	tablespoons sugar, plus extra for seasoning
	Pinch salt
½	teaspoon lemon juice

Melt butter in small saucepan over medium heat. Add blueberries, 2 tablespoons sugar, and salt; bring to boil. Lower heat and simmer, stirring occasionally, until thickened and about one-quarter of juice remains, 8 to 10 minutes. Remove pan from heat and stir in lemon juice. Season with extra sugar to taste.

SCIENCE
Maximizing Citrus Flavor

To produce bold citrus flavor in our pudding without marring its silky-smooth texture with pieces of lemon zest, we steep the zest in liquid (and then strain it out). Some of the flavor compounds in the zest are fat-soluble, such as d-limonene. Others, like citric acid, are water-soluble. To extract the most flavor, we infuse the zest into a mixture of two liquids that we use in our batter—milk and heavy cream—that together contain goodly amounts of both water and fat.

Tropical Fruit Salads

Making a vibrant fruit salad with peak summer produce is a cinch, but what are we supposed to do the rest of the year?

> BY KEITH DRESSER

When aromatic stone fruit, plump berries, and juicy, crisp melons are at the peak of ripeness, it doesn't require much skill to put together a stunning fruit salad. But as summer fades, so do the options: Stone fruit disappears, berries have as much flavor as the packaging they come in, and melons are rock hard and dry. By late winter even apples and pears are not at their best. Salads based on citrus are easy to come by, but I wanted something different.

After a trip to the market, I saw clearly that I should work with tropical fruits. Mango, papaya, and pineapple are easy to find in the winter and early spring, plus they boast sweetness and nuanced flavors that are ideal for building a salad.

But for a fruit salad to be successful it needs a range of flavors, so the sweet, floral tropical fruits alone wouldn't suffice. Bright citrus was the answer. Pairing oranges with the mangos, clementines with the papayas, and grapefruit with the pineapple meant that each salad had complementary tangy notes. A ratio of 1 part citrus to 4 parts tropical fruit produced juicy—but not waterlogged—salads.

To dress the fruit, I heated modest amounts of sugar, lime juice, and lime zest (along with a pinch of salt) in a small saucepan until the sugar dissolved, and I let the mixture cool completely. When drizzled over the salads, the lime syrup blended with the fruits' natural juices to create a sweet-tart balance, and the salt worked its usual magic of bringing all the flavors into focus.

With the foundations of my salads complete, I explored the idea of adding more complexity. My first thought was to scatter in some fragrant chopped fresh herbs like mint or basil, but while they contributed visual appeal, many tasters felt that the herbs moved the salads into salsa territory. For my next try, I sprinkled in a small amount of a potent dried spice or aromatic. Red pepper flakes, grated fresh ginger, and ground cardamom all worked well, subtly highlighting the fruit. The only problem was that since I was using such a small amount, it was hard to get the seasonings to distribute evenly. When I infused the spice or aromatic into the lime syrup instead of

sprinkling it on the fruit, my problem was solved.

At this point I was more than satisfied with my flavor combinations, but I thought that the salads could use an additional ingredient to contrast with the soft fruit. I hoped that a handful of unsalted nuts or seeds would be the way to go, but their crunch was too jarring.

I was stumped until I happened upon a Mexican recipe that combined silky mango slices with chunks of crisp jícama. The pairing of tender fruit and a mild-flavored, crunchy vegetable seemed like an excellent idea. I diced up a small bulb of jícama and tossed it into my mango-orange salad. Success! Well, sort of. The jícama's mild sweetness was a nice backdrop for the fruit, but it was actually a little too crisp. It dawned on me that I could take advantage of my hot syrup: I could use it to soften the jícama. Instead of tossing the raw vegetable with the fruit, I added it to the still-hot syrup and allowed the mixture to sit as the syrup cooled to room temperature.

Now I had true success. The hot syrup took the raw edge off of the vegetable while preserving a modest amount of crispness. In my last round of tests, I discovered that even slightly softer cucumber and chayote (a relative of the cucumber) benefited from a soak in the hot syrup for, respectively, my pineapple-grapefruit salad and my papaya-clementine salad. These were cool-weather fruit salads to rival summer's best.

Jícama contributes a bit of crunch to a salad of tender mango and orange pieces.

MANGO, ORANGE, AND JÍCAMA SALAD
SERVES 4 TO 6

Make sure that the syrup has cooled before pouring it over the fruit.

- 3   tablespoons sugar
- ¼   teaspoon grated lime zest plus 3 tablespoons juice (2 limes)
- ¼   teaspoon red pepper flakes
      Pinch salt
- 12 ounces jícama, peeled and cut into ¼-inch dice (1½ cups)
- 2   oranges
- 2   mangos, peeled, pitted, and cut into ½-inch dice (4 cups)

1. Bring sugar, lime zest and juice, pepper flakes, and salt to simmer in small saucepan over medium heat, stirring constantly, until sugar is dissolved, 1 to 2 minutes. Remove pan from heat, stir in jícama, and

let syrup cool for 20 minutes.

2. Meanwhile, cut away peel and pith from oranges. Slice into ½-inch-thick rounds, then cut rounds into ½-inch pieces. Place oranges and mangos in large bowl.

3. When syrup is cool, pour over oranges and mangos and toss to combine. Refrigerate for 15 minutes before serving.

PAPAYA, CLEMENTINE, AND CHAYOTE SALAD

Chayote, also called mirliton, is often sold with other tropical fruits and vegetables. If you can't find chayote, substitute an equal amount of jícama.

Substitute 2 teaspoons grated fresh ginger for red pepper flakes; 1 chayote, peeled, halved, pitted, and cut into ¼-inch dice, for jícama; 3 clementines, peeled and each segment cut into 3 pieces, for oranges; and 2 large papayas, peeled, seeded, and cut into ½-inch dice, for mangos.

PINEAPPLE, GRAPEFRUIT, AND CUCUMBER SALAD

Substitute ground cardamom for red pepper flakes; 1 cucumber, peeled, halved lengthwise, seeded, and cut into ¼-inch dice, for jícama; 1 grapefruit for oranges; and 1 pineapple, peeled, cored, and cut into ½-inch dice, for mangos.

The Truth About Orange Juice

Is the sunny image of our favorite breakfast juice actually just pulp fiction?

⊰ BY HANNAH CROWLEY ⊱

Orange juice is America's most popular juice, a breakfast staple with a sunny, wholesome image. Package labels tempt us with phrases like "fresh squeezed" and "grove to glass" and with images of oranges speared with straws. Even brand names like Simply Orange and Florida's Natural suggest that these juices are just a notch away from freshly picked fruit squeezed into a glass. There's financial proof that these companies' fresh-focused marketing pays off. According to a 2010 report published by the University of Florida Institute of Food and Agricultural Sciences Extension, Americans will shell out $1 to $2 more per gallon for juice that they perceive to be fresher.

But the truth is, commercial orange juice can't be that simple an enterprise because of the complex challenge that manufacturers face. What's at stake: how to produce (and profit from) a juice that has fresh and consistent flavor 365 days a year and a shelf life long enough to withstand transport to and storage in supermarkets. Mind you, this is all from a seasonal fruit crop with natural variation in flavor and that is susceptible to the whims of disease, bugs, and volatile weather patterns.

Given that, technology is the core focus of companies trying to engineer the most natural-tasting product. Case in point: Coca-Cola, which owns the major players Simply Orange and Minute Maid, has developed a staggeringly precise algorithm to aid in processing juice, according to a 2013 *Bloomberg Businessweek* investigation. Called Black Book, it reportedly analyzes 1 quintillion variables that affect the juice-making process, including the 600-plus volatiles responsible for optimal juice flavor, as well as erratic weather patterns, crop yields, and cost. The company also uses satellites to track when it should harvest the fruit. The upshot: If a hurricane barrels through Florida (or any other global region) or a cold snap threatens the trees, the company can remap its production model in less than 10 minutes.

These systems certainly turn a profit: Last year, Coca-Cola and Pepsi, which owns the other major producer, Tropicana, each pulled in $1 billion of the $3.9 billion spent on orange juice in the United States. But as for the real question—whether these high-tech advances make for better-tasting juice—we'd have to see for ourselves.

To find out, we built a tasting lineup around five nationally available refrigerated orange juices. (We selected medium pulp when available, as it's the style most akin to fresh squeezed and often the most popular.) We also included two frozen concentrates, from Minute Maid and Tropicana, because in previous tastings they've rated surprisingly high. (For more about this, see "Does Frozen Concentrate Deserve a Second Look?" on page 27.) And we threw in two lower-calorie juices—an increasingly popular subcategory made by cutting juice with water and sweetening it with stevia. All nine juices were served lightly chilled and evaluated for freshness, flavor, texture, and overall appeal.

Label Sleuthing

Tasters panned the two lower-calorie juices, Minute Maid Pure Squeezed Light Orange Juice Beverage and Tropicana Trop50 Orange Juice Beverage, for tasting "ridiculously sweet" and "cloying"—evidence that these producers may have overdone it with the stevia, which is up to 300 times sweeter than granulated sugar. As for the other juices, three self-described "gourmet" or "pure" products earned the highest marks, with tasters touting their "nice balance of acidity and sweetness" and "fresh," "honest" flavors. These juices were followed by the two frozen concentrates and a straightforward supermarket brand, and then by an outlier: our previous winner, Tropicana Pure Premium Orange Juice.

However, the buzzwords on the labels didn't help explain why some juices performed better, as none of those terms are industry-regulated. Also not helpful were the juices' nutrition labels, which indicated that all seven full-calorie samples had the same single ingredient—orange juice—and nearly identical nutritional makeups. That left us looking to processing methods for clues—an investigation that showed us just how far from fresh squeezed most commercial orange juice really is.

A Lengthy Process

We figured that pasteurization would be an obvious place to start, particularly because a couple of the top-ranking products, Simply Orange Not from Concentrate 100% Pure Squeezed Pasteurized Orange Juice and Minute Maid Pure Squeezed Never from Concentrate Pasteurized 100% Orange Juice, advertised that their juices were "gently pasteurized." But in most cases we

Fresh Flavor Hype

Manufacturers have long tried to convince consumers that processed orange juice is no different from juice squeezed directly into a glass.

were thwarted in our efforts to tie better flavor to juice being subjected to lower heat. It turns out that the U.S. Food and Drug Administration (FDA) doesn't recognize the term "gently pasteurized," and most producers won't elaborate on what they mean by it either. Only Natalie's 100% Florida Orange Juice, another top performer, shared a pasteurization detail with us that indicated that the company is being gentler with its juice. The manufacturer heats it to around 160 degrees, which is the minimum pasteurization temperature recommended by the FDA to ensure safety and shelf-life stability. It's a temperature that industry experts say is, in fact, lower than what most juice makers use.

Still in search of other reasons for the flavor differences we perceived, we moved on to examine the next stage of orange juice processing: storage. Because different varieties of oranges are in season at different times, most manufacturers squeeze the juice immediately and store it for months to maintain a year-round supply of particular varieties. To keep the juice from turning rancid, they must prevent it from oxidizing. These days, the answer for most companies is deaeration, a process in which they strip away the juice's oxygen and store the juice, sometimes for as long as a year, in million-gallon tanks—so-called tank farms—topped with a layer of nitrogen to prevent further deterioration. (When used to replace air in a container, nitrogen provides effective protection against oxidation.)

The downside is that stripping the oxygen out of juice also strips out the juice's flavor-providing compounds. That's where blend technicians, who correct for flavor deficiencies, come in. Their job isn't simply a matter of blending multiple batches of juice to balance sweetness and acidity (though this is part of their process, and experts told us that blending likely contributed to some of the flavor differences that we detected). The technicians also restore taste to the juice through the addition of "flavor packs." These highly engineered additives are made from essential orange flavor volatiles that have been harvested from the fruit and its skin and then chemically reassembled by scientists at leading fragrance companies: Givaudan, Firmenich, and

Two Paths from the Grove to Your Glass

Don't be fooled by sunny marketing slogans: Most commercial orange juice is far from "fresh-squeezed." In fact, the juice can sit around for as long as a year in holding tanks before it's bottled and shipped for sale—and, consequently, it must undergo a number of harsh processing steps to allow for long-term storage. First, manufacturers pasteurize the juice, which kills off harmful bacteria—and flavor. Next, they strip the oxygen from (or deaerate) the juice, which prevents it from rotting during storage and zaps more flavor. Then, to compensate for the flavor loss, they hire scientists to doctor the juice with flavor packs: blends of orange flavor volatiles that they have stripped from the fruit and its skin and chemically reassembled to give the impression of fresh, sweet, natural orange flavor.

Natalie's, our winning orange juice, takes a different, more natural approach. Rather than store squeezed juice, the company stores whole oranges in climate-controlled rooms, squeezes the juice to order, pasteurizes it at the lowest possible temperature, and ships it within 24 hours. As a result, Natalie's is able to skip the deaeration and flavor-correction steps, which explains why its juice tastes naturally fresher and sweeter than juice from other brands.

SQUEEZED
shortly
after harvest.

PASTEURIZED
at higher temperatures.

DEAERATED
and held in tanks
for up to a year.

SHIPPED
after flavor packs
are added to simulate
freshness.

SQUEEZED
shortly after harvest
or stored whole
in climate-controlled
rooms.

PASTEURIZED
at 160 degrees.

SHIPPED
within 24 hours.

MOST BRANDS
Deaeration strips
most brands' juice
of fresh flavor that
must be added back in.

NATALIE'S
Squeezing just before
shipping and no deaeration
give Natalie's juice a more
naturally fresh taste.

International Flavors and Fragrances, which make perfumes for the likes of Dior, Justin Bieber, and Taylor Swift. By reorganizing these compounds, scientists are able to compensate for the flavor-destroying effects of pasteurization and deaeration, and to tailor the flavor of the packs—and by extension the flavor of the juice—to each juice company's exact specifications.

The Fresh Maker

But while the blending process and the addition of flavor packs enable juice companies to develop a distinct flavor profile and guarantee that flavor from bottle to bottle, those factors don't make a company unique. Juice blending is an industry-wide practice, and most of the juices that we tasted were enhanced by flavor packs. What we learned is that the makers of our top-ranking juices did a better job of figuring out and executing the exact flavor profile that consumers wanted.

That's no small task, as orange juice expert Alissa Hamilton explains in her book, *Squeezed: What You Don't Know About Orange Juice*. In it, she cites Russell Rouseff, a longtime researcher at the Citrus Research and Education Center at the University of Florida, who points out that fresh orange juice flavor is one of the toughest to imitate because none of the compounds that contribute to the orange's aroma "individually smell of orange." Hence, blend technicians do the best they can, piecing together compounds that add up to orange flavor.

To make matters more complicated, consumer preferences vary across different cultures when it comes to orange juice flavor. Hamilton goes on to suggest that what North Americans want their juice to taste like differs from what consumers in South America and Mexico prefer, so juice companies often tweak their flavor pack formulas to vary the levels of perceived sweetness, freshness, and acidity.

In the United States, fresh flavor is paramount, so juice makers include a compound called ethyl butyrate in the flavor packs. This compound isn't an artificial flavor: It occurs naturally in fresh-squeezed orange juice as an aroma, but because it's volatile, much of it is driven off during pasteurization and deaeration. Adding more ethyl butyrate to the juice after these processes actually restores the impression of freshness. (Humans are far more sensitive to smell than to taste; 80 to 85 percent of what we characterize as flavor is actually due to aroma.)

We wanted to see for ourselves if ethyl butyrate was boosting our impression of freshness in the top-ranking juices, so we sent samples of all nine juices to an independent laboratory to get them analyzed for the compound. The results were convincing: Three of the juices that ranked highest for fresh flavor—Minute Maid Pure Squeezed Never from Concentrate Pasteurized 100% Orange Juice, Simply Orange Not from Concentrate 100% Pure Squeezed Pasteurized Orange Juice, and Florida's Natural 100% Pure Florida Orange Juice—contained relatively high levels of ethyl butyrate (as high as

4.92 milligrams per liter), indicating that their respective companies were adding plenty of it to their flavor packs. (One note: While ethyl butyrate is technically natural, boosting fresh flavor in orange juice with flavor packs certainly is not, and there are currently multiple class action cases against orange juice companies for engineering products that are far more processed than they're advertised to be.)

Notably, there were two exceptions to the lab results and how they tracked with our preferences. First, the juice containing the highest level of ethyl butyrate (8.53 milligrams per liter), Minute Maid Pure Squeezed Light Orange Juice Beverage, was panned for its lack of fresh flavor—a discrepancy that we chalked up to this lower-calorie juice's overwhelming sweetness, which masked any impression of freshness. (The other lower-calorie juice in our lineup, Tropicana Trop50 Orange Juice Beverage, also ranked high for sweetness and tanked for fresh flavor.)

Second, the other juice that ranked high for freshness, Natalie's 100% Florida Orange Juice, contained a much lower amount of ethyl butyrate (1.01 milligrams per liter) compared with other "fresh-tasting" juices. But as it turns out, fresh-squeezed orange juice naturally contains about 1.19 milligrams of ethyl butyrate per liter, so the amount in Natalie's isn't far off from what occurs naturally in the fruit.

Just Juice

That statistic made even more sense when we learned that Natalie's is, in fact, a genuinely much fresher product than other orange juices. Rather than create an illusion of freshness by treating juice that's been deaerated with flavor packs, Natalie's squeezes oranges to order and ships its juice within 24 hours. Short storage times also allow the company to forgo deaeration.

Because the company squeezes oranges year-round, the flavor of its juice shifts as different varieties come into season; tasters reported that the batch we sampled was "superfresh" and pleasantly "tropical," with hints of mango, guava, and pineapple. It also has a much shorter shelf life than most commercial orange juices—26 days compared with about a year for juice that's been deaerated. However, Natalie's has a system in place to minimize dramatic seasonal flavor change: When Valencia season ends and early varieties like Hamlin are harvested in September and October, the company holds extra whole Valencias just above freezing in special climate-controlled rooms and blends their juice with juice from early oranges in October and November.

That kind of flavor variability might not be what consumers expect from their orange juice, but it doesn't bother us. In fact, we named Natalie's our favorite because we think a juice that actually is fresher, not just engineered to taste that way, is worth seeking out—and paying a bit more for (it costs about 38 percent more than other high-ranking orange juices do).

TASTING ORANGE JUICE

We tasted nine nationally available supermarket orange juices, including two frozen concentrates; we rated them on freshness, sweetness, acidity, and overall appeal. An independent lab assessed levels of ethyl butyrate, a compound that occurs naturally in oranges and that is added back to most commercial orange juice to make its flavor seem fresher, as well as the Brix (sugar content) and acidity percentages. Scores were averaged and the products appear in order of preference.

RECOMMENDED

NATALIE'S 100% Florida Orange Juice, Gourmet Pasteurized
Price: $5.99 for 64 oz (9 cents per oz)
Ethyl Butyrate: 1.01 mg per liter
Brix: 12% **Acidity:** 0.71%
Comments: Because Natalie's squeezes its juice within 24 hours of shipping it and doesn't manipulate its flavor, the juice tasted "superfresh" and also exhibited a level of ethyl butyrate consistent with fresh fruit. Less processing also made its flavor more variable; tasters found the batch we sampled "almost tropical," with notes of guava and mango.

SIMPLY ORANGE Not from Concentrate 100% Pure Squeezed Pasteurized Orange Juice, Medium Pulp
Price: $3.99 for 59 oz (7 cents per oz)
Ethyl Butyrate: 3.22 mg per liter
Brix: 12.7% **Acidity:** 0.7%
Comments: Blend technicians nailed an appealing balance of flavors for this juice. A generous amount of ethyl butyrate helped it taste "fresh squeezed," and its "intensely sweet" orange flavor was tempered by a "bright," "mildly sour" tang.

MINUTE MAID Pure Squeezed Never from Concentrate Pasteurized 100% Orange Juice, Some Pulp
Price: $3.79 for 59 oz (6 cents per oz)
Ethyl Butyrate: 3.7 mg per liter
Brix: 11.8% **Acidity:** 0.71%
Comments: Its "full, round" flavor, which was "very orangey" and "fresh" (thanks to plenty of ethyl butyrate), put this juice near the top of the chart. Tasters' only complaint was that this juice carried a bit "more tartness" than they wanted.

MINUTE MAID Original Frozen Concentrated Orange Juice
Price: $2.99 for 64 oz (5 cents per oz)
Ethyl Butyrate: 0.92 mg per liter
Brix: 11.6% **Acidity:** 0.64%
Comments: With its "vibrant," "sweet," "balanced" flavor and only "a hint of bitterness," this top-rated frozen product challenged frozen concentrate's bad rap. That it has a shelf life of three to five years and a lower price point than ready-to-serve juices makes it worth considering.

FLORIDA'S NATURAL 100% Pure Florida Orange Juice, with Pulp
Price: $3.79 for 59 oz (6 cents per oz)
Ethyl Butyrate: 4.92 mg per liter
Brix: 12.5% **Acidity:** 0.71%
Comments: Lots of ethyl butyrate gave this juice a "fragrant," "blossoming orange" aroma, but some tasters picked up on a "processed" taste, suggesting that its flavor wasn't quite as fresh. The juice was big on pulp, which some likened to fresh squeezed, though others found it too thick.

RECOMMENDED CONTINUED

TROPICANA 100% Frozen Concentrated Orange Juice
Price: $1.89 for 48 oz reconstituted (4 cents per oz)
Ethyl Butyrate: None detected
Brix: 11.6% **Acidity:** 0.64%
Comments: Some tasters called out this frozen concentrate for its "bitter," "metallic" flavor, while others found it sweet without being "cloying." Its "perfect amount of pulp" was also a draw that made it seem "close to freshly squeezed OJ," and we can't argue with its rock-bottom price.

RECOMMENDED WITH RESERVATIONS

TROPICANA Pure Premium Orange Juice, Homestyle
Price: $3.99 for 59 oz (7 cents per oz)
Ethyl Butyrate: 1.71 mg per liter
Brix: 11.9% **Acidity:** 0.75%
Comments: Tropicana's flagship juice (and our previous winner) tasted "slightly sweet" and "reasonably fresh" but comparatively acidic (lab results confirmed that it was the most acidic juice we tasted), with "tart" flavor that was "bitter, like grapefruit."

NOT RECOMMENDED

MINUTE MAID Pure Squeezed Light Orange Juice Beverage
Price: $3.39 for 59 oz (6 cents per oz)
Ethyl Butyrate: 8.53 mg per liter
Brix: 6.5% **Acidity:** 0.68%
Comments: "Tang or Sunny D, right?" guessed one taster. Others suggested "Pez." No wonder: This low-cal juice was cut with water and sweetened with stevia. That not only made it downright "sugary" but also overwhelmed the fresh-tasting effect of a high dose of ethyl butyrate.

TROPICANA Trop50 Orange Juice Beverage
Price: $3.99 for 59 oz (7 cents per oz)
Ethyl Butyrate: None detected
Brix: 5.7% **Acidity:** 0.58%
Comments: Another "sugar bomb," this stevia-sweetened low-calorie juice was "abrasively sweet," "cloying," and "artificial." More important: "It doesn't taste like it was made from oranges." It was also "watery" and "thin."

DID YOU KNOW? All products reviewed by America's Test Kitchen, home of *Cook's Illustrated* and *Cook's Country* magazines, are independently chosen, researched, and reviewed by our editors. We buy products for testing at retail locations and do not accept unsolicited samples for testing. We do not accept or receive payment or consideration from product manufacturers or retailers. Manufacturers and retailers are not told in advance of publication which products we have recommended. We list suggested sources for recommended products as a convenience to our readers but do not endorse specific retailers.

But if you're in the market for a juice that's consistent from bottle to bottle and costs a bit less, our runner-up from Simply Orange tastes "very fresh" and does a nice job of balancing sweetness and acidity. Unfortunately, we can no longer say the same of our previous winner, Tropicana's flagship Pure Premium juice. Tasters deemed this sample comparatively "tart" and "bitter"—comments that were confirmed by lab tests, in which it rated highest for acidity. It also appears that the U.S. marketplace agrees. Sales of this juice have fallen in recent years as both Simply Orange and Minute Maid have taken on a larger share.

Does Frozen Concentrate Deserve a Second Look?

Last year, frozen orange juice concentrate accounted for just 3.3 percent of total orange juice sales in the United States. That's probably because consumers think of the concentrate as a tinny, thin juice that they drank as kids—hardly comparable to the ready-to-serve (RTS) juices popular today. But our tasting results indicate that frozen concentrate has changed for the better: The two that we tasted, from Minute Maid and Tropicana, not only earned our recommendation but actually beat out some of the RTS juices in our lineup.

Juice-blending and flavor packs have long been used to improve the flavor of concentrates. Nowadays, experts told us, manufacturers are also adding back pulp for more natural body and using newer evaporation methods that don't heat the juice as long, which preserves more of its natural flavor. Plus, these products cost roughly 35 percent less than most RTS juices do. All this makes a good case for giving frozen concentrates a try.

The Drainage Games

A colander is just a bowl with holes, right? Chasing loose pasta around the sink may change your mind about that.

≥ BY ADAM RIED ≤

Italian chefs on TV dip their tongs into pots of boiling water to retrieve strands of pasta. The rest of us drain our pasta like mere mortals: in a colander. Our favorite has long been the RSVP International Endurance Precision Pierced 5 Qt. Colander ($25.99), a stainless-steel model covered from rim to base in holes that allow water to escape easily. But with many newcomers on the market, we decided that a rematch was in order: the RSVP International versus 15 new colanders, priced from about $18 to $60. Our lineup included larger (roughly 5-quart) colanders made from both stainless and enameled steel and wire mesh, as well as collapsible silicone baskets set in stiff plastic frames. One such model even had extending arms, allowing it to span a sink.

Watering Holes

Right off the bat we eliminated eight models that were so fundamentally flawed that we didn't consider them worthy contenders—collapsible models in particular. The annoying tendency of these supposedly innovative colanders, such as those from Joseph Joseph and Progressive International, to come unclipped or tip over and dump pasta all over the sink canceled out their flat storage appeal. The sturdier example from Rösle had issues of its own—namely, broad flat handles where water collected and turned the metal slippery and ripping hot—that made its sky-high price seem even more ridiculous.

With the remaining eight colanders, we started by taking a closer look at the most obvious feature: the holes. Big holes might seem advantageous for speedy drainage, but they can backfire when dealing with slender or small foods. The colander from Reston Lloyd, as well as both Squish models, illustrated this when we used them to drain rice-shaped orzo. Water streamed out of their large (3.36- to 8.02-millimeter) perforations—followed by as much as ½ cup of orzo.

Ironically, though, none of these large-holed models drained water all that quickly. That's because their holes were arranged in clusters surrounded by solid, unperforated areas that thwarted drainage. Those inferior designs put them at a considerable disadvantage

▶ **Watch the Drainage Games**
Video available free for 4 months at CooksIllustrated.com/apr14

against the fine-wire-mesh colander by Excel Steel and the stainless-steel products from RSVP International and OXO. With tiny (1.90- to 2.28-millimeter) all-over perforations, these colanders not only drained more effectively but also contained every last grain of orzo. The RSVP International colander drained water particularly well; when we shook the bowl to drain any excess water, barely a drop came out.

Bowled Over

As for the bottoms of the colanders, most of the models sporting feet or ring bases proved sufficiently stable. They also provided crucial clearance between the base of the colander and the sink floor. In a colander without feet or a base, the food in the bowl can come into contact with a backwash of drained liquid (and whatever grunge may have escaped your last sink scrubbing). Such was the biggest downfall of the Squish 4-Quart Collapsible Colander, a model with no base at all that allowed the bottom half of the drained pasta to get soaked with water bubbling back up the drain. (Sure, you can mitigate this effect by pouring out the water and pasta slowly—but who thinks of that when they're holding a pot full of scalding water?) Meanwhile, the model's sibling, the Squish Expanding Over-the-Sink Colander, made this a nonissue.

That might argue for buying an over-the-sink colander, or one with the tallest, most substantial base you can find, except that a too-beefy base can get in the way of another core colander task: resting over a bowl

while salted produce sheds excess moisture. When we loaded up each model with 2 cups of diced tomatoes tossed with salt and set the colanders over 9-inch bowls to collect the juices (as you would when making salsa), we encountered a few fit issues. Suddenly, the Squish Over-the-Sink Colander was no longer convenient, as its oblong frame didn't come close to fitting over the mouth of the bowl. Likewise, the placement of the feet on the wire-mesh Excel Steel caused it to sit unsteadily on the bowl rim (though its medium-size sibling, included in the set of three, fit fine).

When it came to cleaning, we noted which models could go in the dishwasher—a feature that we consider essential, so we automatically downgraded the two models that weren't dishwasher-safe: the Norpro and the Reston Lloyd. We ran the other six colanders through 26 cycles in a residential dishwasher (normal wash, with heated drying) and found that the stainless-steel and mesh colanders emerged in much the same condition as they went in. That wasn't so for the silicone models, all of which emerged looking noticeably faded and dingy.

By the end of testing, we had found several colanders that we wouldn't want in our kitchens and none that we'd want more than our old stalwart, the RSVP International Endurance Precision Pierced 5 Qt. Colander. It boasts an excellent combination of small, all-over perforations, a wide base for great stability, and a decent amount—1⅛ inches—of ground clearance. All these features add up to class-leading draining performance.

Poking Holes in Flawed Colander Designs

Innovative designs don't always pay off, especially in a colander. These quirky models didn't make the final cut.

POP-UP PROBLEMS
Barely any pasta slipped through the small, shallow holes on the Dexas Popware Collapsible 10" Pop Colander ($30), but this model had a fatal flaw: Shaking it to drain excess cooking water caused the silicone bowl to pop up, sending pasta up and over the sides.

HOT, SLICK, AND SPENDY
The gleaming stainless-steel base on the Rösle Collapsible Colander ($60) became scorching hot from the draining pasta, burning us when we tried to loosen stuck-on orzo. Water pooled on its shelflike handles, making them slick. And then there was its ridiculously high price.

(UN)STEADY AS SHE GOES
A wide 12¼-inch mouth and narrow 5½-inch base caused the Progressive International 5-Quart Collapsible Colander ($17.49) to rock and roll when we poured boiling water and pasta into it too fast or at the wrong angle. It even tipped over once.

TESTING COLANDERS

We tested eight colanders, each roughly 5 quarts. All were purchased online and are listed below in order of preference. A source for the winner is on page 32. We eliminated the following models in pretesting for a variety of design flaws, including flimsy or poor construction, difficulty cleaning, and cramped size: Architec Gripper Colander, Dexas Popware Collapsible 10" Pop Colander, Joseph Joseph Folding Colander, Norpro Stainless Steel Expanding Over-the-Sink Colander with Base Frame, OXO Good Grips 3-Piece Large Bowl and Colander Set, Progressive International 5-Quart Collapsible Colander, Rösle Collapsible Colander, and Tovolo Stainless Steel Perforated Colander.

PERFORMANCE We drained 1 pound of angel hair and 1 pound of orzo, each cooked in 1 gallon of boiling water, in each colander, looking for efficient, thorough draining and noting when any pasta escaped. We also drained 2 cups of diced tomatoes tossed with ¼ teaspoon of salt in each model, setting each colander over a 9-inch bowl for 30 minutes.

DESIGN We evaluated each colander's perforation coverage, stability, and elevation from the sink floor (noting whether backwash from draining liquid was able to reach the colander bowl), as well as the material, size, and placement of the handles.

CLEANUP After each pasta and tomato draining test, colanders were left to sit for 15 minutes and then washed by hand under warm running water with a sponge/scrubber and liquid dish soap. Testers then evaluated how easy it was to remove residual pasta starch and tomato seeds. Dishwasher-safe colanders were run through 26 cycles in a residential dishwasher (normal cycle, with heated drying), and their condition was evaluated after each cycle. Colanders not described by manufacturers as dishwasher-safe were noted as such in the chart (and downgraded because of it).

	CRITERIA	TESTERS' COMMENTS

HIGHLY RECOMMENDED

RSVP INTERNATIONAL Endurance Precision Pierced 5 Qt. Colander
Model: PUNCH-5 Price: $25.99
Material: Stainless steel
Hole Size: 2.28 mm
Dishwasher-Safe: Yes

Performance ★★★
Design ★★★
Cleanup ★★★

With all-over tiny perforations that don't allow small foods to escape, our longtime favorite colander has a draining performance that remains unmatched. Its 1⅛ inches of ground clearance was enough to keep nearly all the drained pasta from getting hit with backwash. The model cleans up nicely in the dishwasher, and its handles are slim but still substantial enough to grip easily.

RECOMMENDED

OXO Good Grips 5-Quart Stainless Steel Colander
Model: 1134700 Price: $29.99
Material: Stainless steel; nonslip plastic rim and feet
Hole Size: 2.28 mm
Dishwasher-Safe: Yes

Performance ★★★
Design ★★½
Cleanup ★★★

Testers appreciated this colander's beefy rim, its point at the center of the base to drive liquid down and out the bottom perforations, and its nonskid feet, though we wish they raised the bowl more than ⅜ inch off the sink floor to combat the backwash effect.

CUISINOX 24 Cm Footed Colander
Model: COL-2 Price: $19.90
Material: Stainless steel
Hole Size: 2.98 to 3.58 mm
Dishwasher-Safe: Yes

Performance ★★½
Design ★★½
Cleanup ★★★

Though its larger perforations allowed a few strands of angel hair and 1½ teaspoons of orzo to escape, this reasonably priced colander had other redeeming traits—namely, a deep bowl and large, easy-to-grip handles. But it felt lightweight and a bit chintzy, which made us worry about long-term durability.

RECOMMENDED WITH RESERVATIONS

EXCEL STEEL Cook Pro Stainless Steel Mesh Colanders with Silicone Handles, Set of 3
Model: 29030 Price: $39.95
Material: Steel mesh, with silicone-covered handles
Hole Size: 1.90 mm
Dishwasher-Safe: Yes

Performance ★★★
Design ★★
Cleanup ★★

Each of the fine-mesh colanders in this set of three drained just as efficiently as our winner but lacked its sturdy frame: Their delicate walls dented easily. Orzo grains became lodged between the mesh and the frame. The largest colander didn't fit well over the bowl in our tomato test, but the medium size worked fine.

NORPRO Krona Stainless Steel 9.5" Deep Colander
Model: 227 Price: $32.27
Material: Stainless steel
Hole Size: 2.72 to 4.18 mm
Dishwasher-Safe: No

Performance ★★½
Design ★★½
Cleanup ★★

No strand pasta slipped through the larger holes on this deep colander, but 2 tablespoons of orzo did. Its patchy clusters of holes didn't allow water to drain as easily as did top-performing models. The deep bowl cleaned up readily with a soapy sponge—though we'd really prefer it if the model were dishwasher-safe.

NOT RECOMMENDED

SQUISH 4-Quart Collapsible Colander
Model: 41000 Price: $19.99
Material: Plastic and silicone
Hole Size: 3.36 to 8.02 mm
Dishwasher-Safe: Yes

Performance ★½
Design ★★
Cleanup ★★

With some holes in this colander measuring almost ¼ inch, it's no wonder that a whopping 5 tablespoons of orzo escaped. This collapsible model has no base and, therefore, practically no elevation from the bottom of the sink. Its silicone body became faded and dingy after the dishwasher cycles.

SQUISH Expanding Over-the-Sink Colander
Model: 41006 Price: $24.99
Material: Plastic and silicone
Hole Size: 4.53 to 6 mm
Dishwasher-Safe: Yes

Performance ★½
Design ★★
Cleanup ★★

While there's plenty of clearance when this model is anchored over the sink, there's almost none when it sits on the sink floor. Several tablespoons of orzo slipped through its large holes. Its oblong frame was awkward to maneuver and didn't fit over the draining bowl. The colorful silicone looked faded after being run through the dishwasher.

RESTON LLOYD Calypso Basics 5-Quart Colander
Model: 88100 Price: $25.99
Material: Enameled steel
Hole Size: 5.59 to 7 mm
Dishwasher-Safe: No

Performance ★
Design ★★
Cleanup ★★

This model's only perk: its 1¾-inch base, which raised it high off the sink floor. But since it allowed a whopping ½ cup of orzo to escape, was not dishwasher-safe, and required vigorous scrubbing to remove stuck-on bits of pasta, we'll pass.

⇒ BY ANDREW JANJIGIAN, LAN LAM, SARAH MULLINS & DAN SOUZA ⇐

TECHNIQUE How to "Crack" Coconut Cream

Traditional Thai curry recipes call for frying the spice paste in coconut cream that's been "cracked"—that is, simmered until its oil separates out. Besides drawing out the oil, simmering the coconut cream also forces water to evaporate, making for a slightly more concentrated curry. We skip this step in our Thai Chicken Curry with Potatoes and Peanuts (page 15) and fry the paste in vegetable oil to keep things simple, but if you want to achieve a slightly richer-tasting curry, follow the steps below and then proceed with step 4 of the recipe, adding the curry paste to the saucepan and omitting the oil. (Add the remaining coconut milk with the broth.) In step 5, add up to ¾ cup of water to ensure that the chicken pieces are just submerged in the liquid.

Note that some products contain emulsifiers and stabilizers that discourage the formation of the cream layer. We have found that Thai Kitchen Coconut Milk works best for this process. –L.L.

1. Skim solid layer of cream from can of coconut milk to yield roughly ¾ cup.

2. Simmer cream in large saucepan over medium heat, stirring constantly, until cream is texture of yogurt and sizzles at edges, 7 to 12 minutes.

A Surprising Tahini Thickener

For our sesame-crusted salmon recipes (page 13), a smear of tahini on each fillet helps boost the sesame flavor. But tahini has a thin consistency, which means that it won't stay put on the moist, slick surface of a fish fillet. To thicken the tahini and give it some holding power, the solution is a bit surprising: We stirred in 2 teaspoons of lemon juice.

You'd think that adding a liquid would thin tahini rather than thicken it. Why the opposite? Tahini is simply sesame-seed butter, made by grinding hulled sesame seeds into a paste. Much of its makeup is carbohydrates, and when a small amount of lemon juice (or any water-containing liquid) is added to tahini, a portion of each carbohydrate molecule is drawn to the water. As a result, clumps of carbohydrates appear. As the amount of water is increased, more clumps develop, causing the tahini to thicken overall. If you keep adding water, eventually you'll cross over the threshold of thickening it; enough water in the system will cause the tahini to loosen and thin out. This is similar to what happens when chocolate seizes. A small amount of added water acts like a glue, wetting particles just enough to get them to stick together, but eventually if you add too much water, the mixture turns into an evenly thinned-out liquid.

This same process also occurs with peanut butter (both all-natural and commercial varieties of the stuff): For example, if you make satay sauce for grilled meat, peanut dipping sauce for spring rolls, or dan dan noodles, you will notice that clumps appear when you first add liquid to the peanut butter. But as you keep adding liquid to reach the required consistency for these sauces, the lumps disappear. –L.L.

SCIENCE Why Starch Gets Crispy When Fried

While you can certainly fry food in hot oil as is (think skin-on chicken pieces), we often dip food in a coating first. Such coatings provide a few benefits: They help protect the food from moisture loss, and they shield the food from direct contact with the hot frying oil for more gentle cooking. And perhaps most important, we know that these coatings—starchy coatings, specifically—become incredibly crispy when fried. But until now we've never really asked ourselves the deeper question: What exactly is happening that makes starch the key?

Here's what we've learned. First, the starch granules in the coating absorb water, whether from the wet surface of the food itself or because they are combined with a liquid to make a slurry before coating the food (as we do for our Thick-Cut Sweet Potato Fries; see page 19). The hydrated granules swell when they are initially heated in the oil, allowing the starch molecules to move about and separate from one another. As water is driven away during the frying process, these starch molecules lock into place, forming a rigid, brittle network with a porous, open structure.

Furthermore, the two types of starch molecules (amylose and amylopectin) form some cross-links with one another at high frying temperatures, further reinforcing the coating's structure. Thus, the molecules in this porous network have room to compress and fracture, providing the sensation of crispiness. Interestingly, cornstarch contains 25 to 28 percent amylose, which is higher than the amount in wheat or potato starch (which are 20 to 22 percent amylose), and this is why cornstarch works the best for making crispy coatings on fried foods.

–D.S.

Running Hot and Cold on Water Baths

The success of many custard recipes (crème brûlée, flan, cheesecake) depends on baking in a water bath, which allows these delicate desserts to cook more evenly and slowly. We've always called for adding boiling water to the roasting pan for the bath, but when we were developing our recipe for Lemon Pudding Cakes (page 23), we found that pouring cold water into the pan delivered better results: a bottom pudding layer that was gently and evenly cooked, and a top cake layer that was perfectly baked and nicely browned.

Intrigued, we decided to revisit classic recipes calling for water baths to find out if boiling water was really the ideal. We baked three batches each of crème brûlée (prepared in 4-ounce ramekins) and cheesecake (prepared in a 9-inch springform pan), with three different starting temperatures for the water bath: boiling, room-temperature, and ice-cold. In the baths that started with boiling water, not only did both desserts cook the fastest but these samples had a smoother, more uniform texture. The desserts baked in baths that started with ice water did not cook uniformly; the bottom half was perfectly done while the top half was overcooked. The results weren't as extreme with baths that started with room-temperature water, but the desserts were still unevenly baked and not satisfactory.

The reason is this: The temperature of boiling water is much closer to the temperature of the oven, which means that the lower portion sitting in the bath and the upper exposed portion start in environments of similar temperature and thus cook evenly. Meanwhile, it will take a bath started with cold or room-temperature water a period of time to heat up, thus slowing the cooking of the submerged portion. While our Lemon Pudding Cakes benefit from this staggered cooking, when it comes to desserts that are one consistency throughout, like crème brûlée and cheesecake, we recommend taking the time to bring a pot of water to a boil for the water bath. –S.M.

For Even Cooking, Give Salmon a Tummy Tuck

The salmon fillets we get from our fishmonger often have the belly portion still attached. With oven roasting or pan searing, this thinner section will inevitably overcook by the time the thicker meaty portion of the salmon fillet is done. Instead of wastefully cutting it off, fold over the flap and secure it in place with a toothpick. This will ensure that it cooks on pace with the rest of the fillet. –L.L.

Courting Yeast Disaster, with No Advantage

We recently noticed that the instructions on some instant and rapid-rise yeast products recommend using 120- to 130-degree water for making bread doughs—curious, since those temperatures are dangerously close to the range at which yeast rapidly dies: 130 to 140 degrees.

According to the manufacturers, their reasoning is to "guarantee yeast activity." However, we suspect that the true intent is to guarantee yeast activity that is both rapid and visible. We know that yeast is perfectly active when combined with water at far colder temperatures (we use ice water when proofing doughs for days to develop flavor)—the yeast just "wakes up" very slowly. Using hotter water would appeal to bakers for whom seeing dough bubble and rise (and seeing this happen quickly) is believing.

We advise patience, not only because such hot water can kill the yeast, which means that your dough won't rise, but also because at the very least it can negatively affect the structure and flavor of the finished bread by encouraging overproofing or overheating during mixing. Both result in overactive yeast, which creates sour flavors and loss of dough structure (i.e., less rise) through overproduction of acids and carbon dioxide.

To see the impact of too-hot water on dough for ourselves, we made dinner rolls, pizza *bianca*, and cinnamon swirl bread using 130-degree water and compared these baked goods with control batches made with water at the temperatures called for in our recipes (none of which went higher than 110 degrees). The higher-temperature water affected the rolls the least: These rolls were pretty close in appearance to the control batch, although several tasters picked up on a sour flavor. The pizza bianca and cinnamon swirl bread made with 130-degree water suffered significantly. Both were more dense and squat than their controls and tasted slightly sour. But perhaps most notably, while initially the proofing for all three recipes happened more quickly using 130-degree water, by the second hour or so, these hot doughs had cooled down, the proofing had slowed, and all the control versions had caught up. In other words, there's no real timesaver in using water that's above 120 degrees in yeasted doughs—and there's a real risk of ruining them. –A.J.

OVERHEATED
130-degree water stunts rise.

SAFE AND SURE
Room-temperature water lets yeast do its job.

SCIENCE Low-Sugar Lemonade That's Just as Sweet

When using citrus juice in recipes, we often introduce zest as well since it provides a deeper, rounder citrus flavor without contributing additional acidity. We've also found that steeping the zest in liquid pulls out its flavors; the distracting shreds of zest can then be strained out, leaving behind a liquid with a bolder, better citrus taste. We wondered if this steeping-and-straining technique could deliver a better lemonade.

EXPERIMENT

We made two batches of lemonade, each for four 8-ounce servings. For one batch, we zested and juiced five lemons, let the zest soak in the juice for 5 minutes, and then strained out the zest and combined the juice with 10 tablespoons of sugar, 2½ cups of water, and a pinch of salt. For our second batch (the control), we followed the same procedure but skipped the zest.

RESULTS

Sure enough, soaking the zest delivered lemonade with a deeper, rounder citrus flavor than we got from a control batch made without the soaking step. And more notably, the lemonade actually tasted sweeter—cloyingly sweet, in fact. Reducing the sugar by at least 10 percent and up to 25 percent (depending on personal taste) was a must. (Letting the zest soak for longer periods of time didn't make any further difference in terms of sweetness.)

EXPLANATION

Though no research has been done on lemon zest and its effect on perceived sweetness, certain plant compounds known as flavanones have been found to enhance the perceived sweetness of food by masking bitterness. Lemon zest contains flavanone compounds that have chemical structures very similar to those of sweetness-enhancing flavanones, so it stands to reason that they're having the same effect: masking the bitter taste of the lemonade and thereby enhancing the sweetness.

TAKEAWAY

While 32 ounces of lemonade made the classic way can call for upwards of 10 tablespoons of sugar, soaking the zest in the juice for 5 minutes would allow you to cut up to 3 tablespoons of sugar and deliver an equally sweet drink. –S.M.

WITHOUT ZEST
10 tablespoons of sugar.

WITH ZEST
Only 7 tablespoons of sugar but just as sweet.

TECHNIQUE How to Reheat Fish

Fish is notoriously susceptible to overcooking, so reheating previously cooked fillets is something that makes nearly all cooks balk. But since almost everyone has leftover fish from time to time, we decided to figure out the best approach to warming it up.

As we suspected, we had far more success reheating thick fillets and steaks than thin ones. Both swordfish and halibut steaks reheated nicely, retaining their moisture well and with no detectable change in flavor. Likewise, salmon reheated well, but be aware that, thanks to the oxidation of its abundant fatty acids into strong-smelling aldehydes, doing so brought out a bit more of the fish's pungent aroma. There was little we could do to prevent trout from drying out and overcooking when heated a second time.

To reheat thicker fish fillets, use this gentle approach: Place the fillets on a wire rack set in a rimmed baking sheet, cover them with foil (to prevent the exteriors of the fish from drying out), and heat them in a 275-degree oven until they register 125 to 130 degrees, about 15 minutes for 1-inch-thick fillets (timing varies according to fillet size). We recommend serving leftover cooked thin fish in cold applications like salads. –A.J.

EQUIPMENT CORNER

≥ AMY GRAVES, LISA MCMANUS & LAUREN SAVOIE ≤

UPDATE Garlic Presses

Since some might balk at the nearly $40 price of our top garlic press, the Kuhn Rikon Stainless Steel Epicurean Garlic Press, we tested new, cheaper models that seemed promising. Our hopes were short-lived. The clunky pressing mechanism and short handles of the Kuhn Rikon Easy-Clean ($16) made for hard work, and its crevices trapped garlic. The same manufacturer's Easy-Squeeze ($24.95), a redesigned version of a former test kitchen favorite, was indeed comfortable to use, but it was difficult to clean, plus the quibble we had with the previous version—garlic oozing out the sides—remained. The long handles on the innovative Garject by Dreamfarm ($34.95) provided great leverage for pressing. But its pressed garlic was wet and mashed (not minced), and its "eject" function for cleaning the hopper worked only occasionally. Our hopes for a favorite slightly cheaper press will have to wait; once again, nothing beats the Epicurean press. –L.M.

PRESS CREDENTIALS
The sturdy and efficient Kuhn Rikon Epicurean Garlic Press is still our main squeeze—and worth its high price.

UPDATE Bench Scrapers

A bench scraper should effortlessly scrape sticky dough off the counter, cut through dough, and scoop up chopped food. When we recently ordered new copies of our winner, the OXO Good Grips Stainless Steel Multi-Purpose Scraper & Chopper ($9.99), instead of having the sharp edge we expected, the scrapers were blunt and struggled to cut through dough. An OXO representative said that the model had not changed, but clearly something in the manufacturing had. So we rounded up six scrapers, including the OXO, for a fresh round of testing. Testers preferred thin, deeply beveled edges, which made it easier to dislodge pie dough from the counter and neatly portion bread and pizza doughs. One model's extra-long plastic blade was an advantage for speedy cleanup, but its ultrathin handle made it unwieldy. A dustpan-shaped scraper scooped up diced vegetables in a snap, but its edge was too dull for dough. A model that we'd liked in the past proved best. The Dexter-Russell 6" Dough Cutter/Scraper—Sani-Safe Series ($7.01) has a deeply beveled edge that quickly slid under pie dough and effortlessly cut through bread and pizza dough. Its textured polypropylene handle is just slender enough to make it easy to grasp and keep flat to the work surface for fast and efficient cleanup. –A.G.

A CLOSE SCRAPE
The Dexter Russell 6" Dough Cutter/Scraper easily dislodges pie dough and cleanly cuts bread and pizza doughs.

NEW Travel Tea Infusers

For tea aficionados who want loose-leaf tea on busy mornings, travel tea infusers, with either removable or retractable baskets for the leaves, offer a solution. We tested four models priced from $15.99 to $22.99. Three used baskets that had to be removed manually; we had to open the lid, remove the basket, and find somewhere to discard the leaves. The same three leaked during bumpy commutes. Knowing that we all lose our grip once in a while, we dropped the full mugs from waist height onto the pavement. One broke on the first drop, and another shattered on the third. The best performer was the Aladdin Tea Infuser Mug ($18.99). Flipping a lever lifts its basket and tucks it under the lid. It survived shaking and tossing, and we appreciated that it was microwave- and dishwasher-safe. But it, too, was flawed: The basket came loose a few times when we used the lever to lift it, releasing leaves into the brew. We're still looking for a travel mug that can reliably make loose-leaf tea. –L.S.

LOOSE LEAVES
Though a rugged traveler, the Aladdin Tea Infuser Mug let tea leaves tumble when we lifted the lever to stop steeping.

NEW Greek Yogurt Maker

Add this to the list of kitchen DIY projects: making your own Greek yogurt. Milk containing live cultures (usually added in the form of powdered culture or a little store-bought yogurt) must be held at 110 degrees for 8 to 12 hours and then cooled and strained. Many recipes rely on makeshift means for maintaining the proper temperature—an oven with its light turned on, a slow cooker, an insulated mug—plus jury-rigging a setup for straining. Enter the Dash Greek Yogurt Maker, an electric vessel that maintains a constant 110-degree temperature for up to 12 hours and uses a built-in timer that shuts off the heat after a preset time. It also comes with two containers and a fine-mesh strainer. After about 14 hours, it delivered a perfectly thick, creamy batch of Greek yogurt and the process was almost entirely hands-off. That said, we did have a couple of issues with the model: It has a stubby 15-inch power cord, and at $49.99 it's a significant splurge that's only worthwhile if you eat a lot of Greek yogurt. –L.S.

DIY GREEK YOGURT
The Dash Greek Yogurt Maker takes some of the guesswork out of homemade yogurt. But for $49.99, maybe it should harvest honey and drizzle it on top, too.

NEW 12.5-Inch Pan Lids

Our top-rated nonstick skillet, the 12.5-inch T-fal Professional Non-Stick Fry Pan, has always had one drawback: no lid. So tackling any recipe that calls for a cover, such as fried eggs, pan-roasted root vegetables, or skillet lasagna, was a problem. Most universal pan lids are too small to fit the T-fal's 12.5-inch diameter, so we went shopping for 12.5-inch lids. We found six models, priced from $10.80 to $32.16, made from a variety of materials. The Homichef, the Cuisinox, and the Swiss Diamond were disqualified out of the gate. Despite the proper measurement, they didn't fit our skillet. Instead, the lids' lips rested on the skillet's top edge. Of the three contenders left, an all-aluminum lid with a recessed center closed off almost an inch of space inside, which was all right for fried eggs but not skillet lasagna. The other two lids, both stainless steel and domed in shape, performed better. In the end, our top pick was the Paderno Stainless Steel 12.5 Inch Lid, which fit snugly and trapped steam reliably, ensuring flawless cooking. The only drawback: At $32.16, it costs almost as much as the skillet we bought it to fit. On the plus side, its shape lets it fit on our favorite 12-inch pans. –A.G.

FITS TO A T(FAL)
The slightly indented perimeter of the Paderno Stainless Steel 12.5 Inch Lid made it a perfect fit our favorite nonstick skillet, and some of our other favorite skillets as well.

For complete testing results, go to CooksIllustrated.com/apr14.

Sources

Prices were current at press time and do not include shipping. Contact companies to confirm information or visit CooksIllustrated.com for updates.

PAGE 11: WAITER'S CORKSCREWS
- Pulltap's Classic Evolution Corkscrew by Pulltex: $39.95, item #1036573, Sur La Table (800-243-0852, **surlatable.com**).
- Trudeau Double Lever Corkscrew: $12.99, item #B000RAWVPK, Amazon (866-216-1072, **amazon.com**).

PAGE 29: COLANDER
- RSVP International Endurance Precision Pierced 5 Qt. Colander: $25.99, item #B000BUDDVM, Amazon.

PAGE 32: GARLIC PRESS
- Kuhn Rikon Stainless Steel Epicurean Garlic Press: $39.95, item #2315, Cutlery and More (800-650-9866, **cutleryandmore.com**).

PAGE 32: BENCH SCRAPER
- Dexter-Russell 6" Dough Cutter/Scraper—Sani-Safe Series: $7.01, item #S196, Food Service Warehouse (877-877-5655, **foodservicewarehouse.com**).

PAGE 32: GREEK YOGURT MAKER
- Dash Greek Yogurt Maker: $49.99, item #DGY001PK, Amazon.

PAGE 32: 12.5-INCH PAN LID
- Paderno Stainless Steel 12.5 Inch Lid: $32.16, item #B001CU7AT6, Amazon.

INDEX
March & April 2014

Thai Chicken Curry with Potatoes, 15

British-Style Currant Scones, 21

Milk-Braised Pork Loin, 11

Shredded Beef Tacos, 9

Mango, Orange, and Jícama Salad, 24

Sesame-Crusted Salmon, 13

Lemon Pudding Cakes, 23

Thick-Cut Sweet Potato Fries, 19

Pasta with Cauliflower and Bacon, 12

Perfect Poached Chicken Breasts, 7

  Find us on Facebook: facebook.com/CooksIllustrated
Follow us on Twitter: twitter.com/TestKitchen

PHOTOGRAPHY: CARL TREMBLAY; STYLING: MARIE PIRAINO

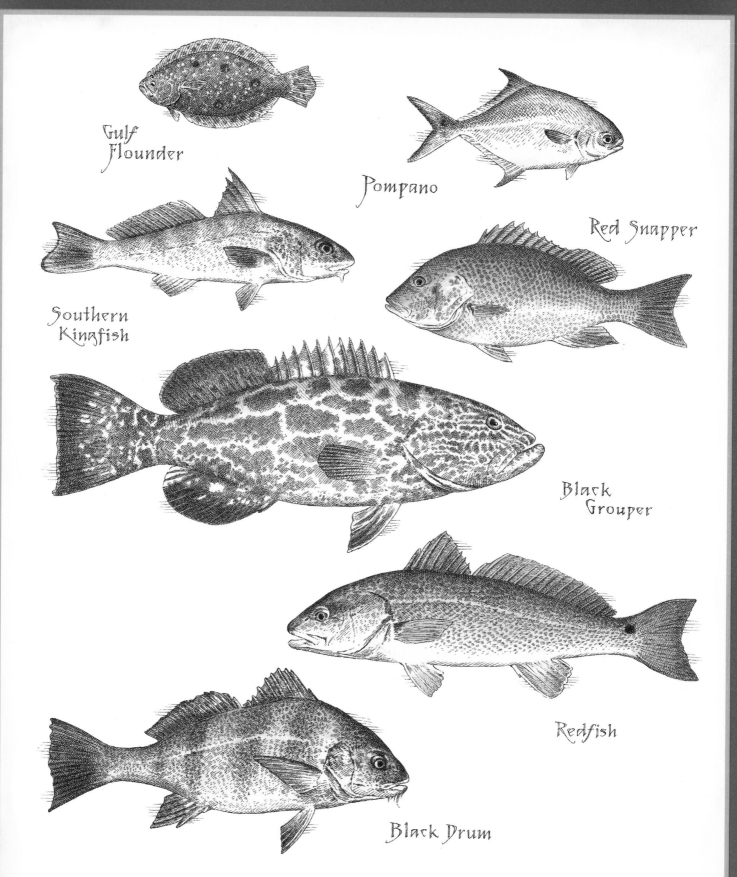

Gulf Flounder

Pompano

Red Snapper

Southern Kingfish

Black Grouper

Redfish

Black Drum

GULF COAST FISH

COOK'S
ILLUSTRATED

A New Way to Grill Pork Tenderloin
Better Char, More Even Cooking

Carrot-Ginger Soup
Two Ingredients, Four Ways

Best Grilled Steak
Step-by-Step Guide

Gluten-Free Pizza Worth Eating

Tasting White Beans
Are Canned Better than Dried?

Strawberry Mousse
Lush Texture, Real Berry Flavor

Chinese Braised Beef
Streamlined Comfort Food

Roast Cornish Game Hens
Testing Mandolines
Pasta with Spinach and Ricotta

CooksIllustrated.com
$6.95 U.S. & CANADA

7 25274 62805 6

06>

CONTENTS
May & June 2014

COOK'S
ILLUSTRATED

Founder and Editor	Christopher Kimball
Editorial Director	Jack Bishop
Editorial Director, Magazines	John Willoughby
Executive Editor	Amanda Agee
Test Kitchen Director	Erin McMurrer
Managing Editor	Rebecca Hays
Executive Food Editor	Keith Dresser
Senior Editors	Hannah Crowley
	Andrea Geary
	Lisa McManus
	Dan Souza
Senior Editors, Features	Elizabeth Bomze
	Louise Emerick
Senior Copy Editor	Megan Ginsberg
Copy Editors	Nell Beram
	Krista Magnuson
Associate Editors	Amy Graves
	Shannon Friedmann Hatch
	Andrew Janjigian
	Chris O'Connor
Test Cooks	Daniel Cellucci
	Lan Lam
Assistant Editors	Lauren Savoie
	Kate Shannon
Assistant Test Cooks	Cecelia Jenkins
	Sarah Mullins
Assistant Test Kitchen Director	Leah Rovner
Senior Kitchen Assistants	Michelle Blodget
	Alexxa Grattan
Kitchen Assistants	Maria Elena Delgado
	Shane Drips
	Ena Gudiel
Executive Producer	Melissa Baldino
Co-Executive Producer	Stephanie Stender
Associate Producer	Kaitlin Hammond
Contributing Editor	Dawn Yanagihara
Consulting Editor	Scott Brueggeman
Science Editor	Guy Crosby, PhD
Managing Editor, Web	Christine Liu
Associate Editors, Web	Jill Fisher
	Eric Grzymkowski
	Roger Metcalf
Assistant Editor, Web	Charlotte Wilder
Senior Video Editor	Nick Dakoulas
Product Manager, Cooking School	Anne Bartholomew
Senior Editor, Cooking School	Mari Levine
Design Director	Amy Klee
Photography Director	Julie Cote
Art Director	Susan Levin
Associate Art Director	Lindsey Timko
Art Director, Marketing	Jennifer Cox
Associate Art Directors, Marketing	Melanie Gryboski
	Mariah Tarvainen
Designer, Marketing	Judy Blomquist
Staff Photographer	Daniel J. van Ackere
Associate Art Director, Photography	Steve Klise
Vice President, Marketing	David Mack
Circulation Director	Doug Wicinski
Circulation & Fulfillment Manager	Carrie Fethe
Partnership Marketing Manager	Pamela Putprush
Marketing Assistant	Marina Tomao
Chief Operating Officer	Rob Ristagno
VP, Digital Products	Fran Middleton
Production Director	Guy Rochford
Workflow & Digital Asset Manager	Andrew Mannone
Senior Color & Imaging Specialist	Lauren Pettapiece
Production & Imaging Specialists	Heather Dube
	Lauren Robbins
Director, Project Management	Alice Carpenter
Development Manager	Mike Serio
Director of Sponsorship Sales	Anne Traficante
Client Services Manager	Kate Zebrowski
Senior Controller	Theresa Peterson
Customer Service Manager	Jacqueline Valerio
Customer Service Representatives	Jessica Haskin
	Andrew Straaberg Finfrock
	Juliet Tierney
Executive Director, Book Marketing	Beth Ineson
Retail Sales & Marketing Director	Emily Logan
Human Resources Director	Adele Shapiro
Publicity	Deborah Broide

PRINTED IN THE USA

MANGOS Though mangos are native to South Asia, they are now cultivated in most tropical climates around the world. Varieties abound in India, where the fragrant, custard-smooth ALPHONSO is touted as the country's finest example. Small, rotund MANCURAD is enjoyed for its floral notes, while the hefty BANGANPALLI boasts hints of coconut. KEITT, a variety that originated in Florida, remains green even when ripe; like all varieties, it's ready to eat when it yields to gentle pressure. Haitian mangos, also known as FRANCIQUE, follow a ripening spectrum similar to that of bananas—starting out lime-colored and then changing to golden. TOMMY ATKINS, a variety native to Florida and a year-round U.S. supermarket staple, is more tart than sweet and often stringy in texture. In contrast, the flesh of the kidney-shaped ATAULFO, or champagne mango, is smooth and honey-sweet.

COVER (Onions): Robert Papp; BACK COVER (Mangos): John Burgoyne

RECIPES THAT WORK®

America's Test Kitchen is a very real 2,500-square-foot kitchen located just outside Boston. It is the home of *Cook's Country* and *Cook's Illustrated* magazines and the workday destination of more than three dozen test cooks, editors, and cookware specialists. Our mission is to test recipes until we understand how and why they work and arrive at the best version. We also test kitchen equipment and supermarket ingredients in search of products that offer the best value and performance. You can watch us work by tuning in to *Cook's Country from America's Test Kitchen* (CooksCountry.com) and *America's Test Kitchen* (AmericasTestKitchen.com) on public television.

THE LAST WE'LL SEE

It's been 30 years since I saw a team of mules driving a corn binder in the field next to the Methodist Church on the banks of the Green River. It's been even longer since I saw Freddie Woodcock test the syrup at Junior Bentley's saphouse. The shack has now sunk into the ground, disappearing quietly while nobody was looking. And the bachelor farm suppers on Friday night at the corner house are over. The last time I went, back in the 1980s, our unofficial town mayor, Susie Depeyster, rented a film on growing rutabaga, which was the main source of entertainment if you don't count the stories told by the farmers in green work pants strung out like blue jays on the spare bed turned couch. They remembered every detail of who kissed whom 50 years ago at the dance hall that burned down during FDR's administration.

I have also seen the last of Marie Briggs, the town baker and the doyen of the Yellow Farmhouse, the first farmhouse on the left as you drive into town. I have had the final bite of her nutmeg doughnuts, molasses cookies, baking powder biscuits, and anadama bread. I have shot my last rat in Floyd's barn, the one behind the farmhouse, where he milked his one Holstein, the creamy white liquid frothy and fly-specked in the pail. And I have said goodbye to John, our headstrong neighbor, who would give you the shirt off his back while maintaining a gruff demeanor. I have served him his final cup of coffee "with a snort" and listened to his last story about Normandy, June 1944. I've seen the last of Marie, Floyd, and John, but it doesn't mean they don't haunt the barns and kitchens and woods of my childhood—they pop up when least expected and then old conversations continue.

If one tends toward curiosity, one wonders what will disappear next. A neighbor sitting in his garage in a rose chintz recliner watching his potatoes grow across the street. Tom, Nate, Joe, and Dave grilling venison steaks over a wood fire below a ridgeline in February, taking a break from tapping trees. The sound of coyotes going in for the kill on a moonless night in late summer. A yearling with outstretched ears, stepping out of the treeline to take a closer look at me, the intruder. Teenagers sleeping in hammocks in 4-H barns at the Washington County fair trying to win a blue ribbon with their Ayrshire or Jersey named Winnie, Brittany, or Bramble. Or the stories. The hermit up in Beartown who got rid of his troublesome neighbors by haunting their cabin at night using a violin to mimic ghostly sounds. Or the time Axel Blomberg finally hooked that big fish he had been after all summer and when it flopped off the hook, he dove headlong after it into the cold Green River pool. He limped for a month.

We are seeing the last of places where people are born, live, and are buried. Where every hollow and brook has a name: Blind Buck Stream, Beattie Hollow, Swearing Hill (which faces Minister Hill), Juniper Swamp Road, and Trout Run. Where every person in town has a purpose. They volunteer for the fire department, run the country store, fix trucks, or grow corn for the dairy farmer down the street. Intimacy breeds storytelling and from the stories, legends are born. My favorite is the Haunted Chimney: A murdered wife rides through the woods on a white horse haunting her burnt-out homestead.

Most of all, I hope I haven't seen the last of a race of men and women who don't care a lick about what others think of them. The bachelor farmer who, after a stroke, was strapped every Sunday afternoon onto his riding mower with crisscross seat belts so he could be useful. The woman who attended her own

Christopher Kimball

memorial service just before she died—she didn't want to miss her own party. Harley and Dorothy who showed up at Tom and Nancy's farmhouse every Friday night for 20 years just for dessert. (Harley always took two ice cubes in his hot cup of tea.) The widow who kept having her husband dug up out of the cemetery to fit him with a new suit of clothes.

The world we leave behind is small and peculiar. Its map is local not global. We aren't bilingual; we speak only the local patois. History is made in the churches, fire departments, hollows, and town halls, not in books. One can garden stark naked (one of my neighbors still has a taste for this) or ride an electric golf cart up and down the back roads just for the heck of it. It is a small universe—the granite obelisks on the town line mark the edges of our Milky Way. But we always know where we are from the stars above, the rush of a brook, a haze of wood smoke, or the sharp odor of liquid manure. The faces at Sherman's store tell you everything about the seasons—in late March, eyes are hollow and the stubble on the chin faded. Even the farmer's caps seem loose as if the heads have shrunk a bit in the cold.

I have a black and white photograph from the 1920s of a school outing at the Haunted Chimney. The girls are well-turned out in white frocks, the boys in pressed pants and collared shirts. The chimney is still there, at the end of Chambers Road past two dairy farms. It's just into the tree line on the left—the foundation intact and the chimney standing tall. Someday, I may be the last person to look for a woman on a white horse. That's the day that the old foundation turns to ruin and we are all lost, lost to history and imagination.

FOR INQUIRIES, ORDERS, OR MORE INFORMATION

CooksIllustrated.com
At CooksIllustrated.com, you can order books and subscriptions, sign up for our free e-newsletter, or renew your magazine subscription. Join the website and gain access to 21 years of *Cook's Illustrated* recipes, equipment tests, and ingredient tastings, as well as companion videos for every recipe in this issue.

COOKBOOKS

We sell more than 50 cookbooks by the editors of *Cook's Illustrated*, including *The Cook's Illustrated Cookbook* and *The Science of Good Cooking*. To order, visit our bookstore at CooksIllustrated.com/bookstore.

COOK'S ILLUSTRATED MAGAZINE

Cook's Illustrated magazine (ISSN 1068-2821), number 128, is published bimonthly by Boston Common Press Limited Partnership, 17 Station St., Brookline, MA 02445. Copyright 2014 Boston Common Press Limited Partnership. Periodicals postage paid at Boston, MA, and additional mailing offices, USPS #012487. Publications Mail Agreement No. 40020778. Return undeliverable Canadian addresses to P.O. Box 875, Station A, Windsor, ON N9A 6P2. POSTMASTER: Send address changes to *Cook's Illustrated*, P.O. Box 6018, Harlan, IA 51593-1518. For subscription and gift subscription orders, subscription inquiries, or change of address notices, visit AmericasTestKitchen.com/support, call 800-526-8442 in the U.S. or 515-248-7684 from outside the U.S., or write to us at *Cook's Illustrated*, P.O. 6018, Harlan, IA 51593-1518.

FOR LIST RENTAL INFORMATION Contact Specialists Marketing Services, Inc., 777 Terrace Ave., 4th Floor, Hasbrouck Heights, NJ 07604; phone: 201-865-5800.

EDITORIAL OFFICE 17 Station St., Brookline, MA 02445; phone: 617-232-1000; fax: 617-232-1572. For subscription inquiries, visit AmericasTestKitchen.com/support or call 800-526-8442.

⇒ BY ANDREA GEARY, LAN LAM & DAN SOUZA ⇐

Egg Substitutes for Breading

I'm allergic to eggs. Is there anything I can substitute for the beaten egg when breading foods like chicken and eggplant?

KELLY BATES
AUSTIN, TEXAS

➤ The traditional process for breading foods like chicken cutlets and eggplant slices requires three steps (known as a bound breading): Dredge the food in flour, dip in beaten egg, and then coat

CREAM IS BEST

If you can't use eggs, use heavy cream to hold breading in place.

in bread crumbs. The egg behaves like a glue, holding the crumbs in place. On occasion we've employed mustard to do the job, but we wanted to find a more neutral-tasting, all-purpose replacement.

We compared batches of chicken cutlets and eggplant dipped in egg to those in which we swapped in heavy cream, gelatin, and store-bought Ener-G Egg Replacer, a powdered mixture of starches, gums, and leaveners that gets hydrated before use. Cream could be used as is, while the gelatin required blooming in cold water for 5 minutes and then melting the mixture in boiling water and letting it cool before use.

The breading on the egg replacer sample came off in patches during frying. The gelatin worked and didn't add flavor but was fussy to use. Luckily cream worked well, adhering the crumbs nicely.

In conclusion: We recommend using heavy cream when breading foods if you cannot use eggs. –L.L.

The Hull Story on Sesame Seeds

What are unhulled sesame seeds, and can I use them like regular sesame seeds?

BRYAN HOLMES
PORTLAND, ORE.

➤ When just harvested from sesame plants, sesame seeds are embedded in a seed coat, or hull. Most sesame seeds in this country are sold with the seed coat removed, but the unhulled kind (also labeled natural) is a staple in Japan and becoming increasingly available in natural foods stores in the United States. We tasted hulled and unhulled seeds raw and toasted and found in both cases that the unhulled seeds were crunchier and almost hard. Unhulled seeds also tasted slightly bitter, which is due to the oxalates (the same compounds in

spinach) in the hull. In sesame cookies, most tasters preferred the hulled seeds for nutty, clean flavor, although a few tasters liked the added complexity that the faint bitterness of the unhulled seeds provided.

The takeaway: Unhulled seeds will work fine in recipes calling for hulled (conventional) sesame seeds, but be aware that they will have a firmer texture and a slightly bitter flavor. –L.L.

Salt and Frying Oil

I've heard that getting salt in frying oil is bad. Why?

PETE LEE
SAN FRANCISCO, CALIF.

➤ The theory is that ionic substances, such as table salt, can initiate the formation of small amounts of free radicals when heated in oil to high temperatures. These free radicals spur reactions that create impurities in the oil and, as a result, lower the oil's smoke point, which means it can't be reused for frying. The free radicals can also speed the development of rancid aromas and flavors.

To find out how much of an issue it can be, we added ⅛ teaspoon of table salt (an amount you would use to season potatoes before frying) to 2 quarts of peanut oil, heated the oil to 325 degrees, and fried French fries. After letting the oil sit overnight, we repeated the process two more times. We also prepared a control batch of peanut oil following the same steps but without the salt. After each round, we smelled both samples blind to see if we could detect any off or rancid aromas. Next, we fried cubes of white bread in the two oils (since they are a blank canvas and soak up oil so well) and tasted them for traces of rancidity. Finally, we heated both samples and noted at what temperature they each began to smoke.

None of our tasters were able to detect rancid aromas or flavors, and the salted oil started to smoke within a couple of degrees of the unsalted sample, both right around 415 degrees.

Our conclusion? Problems caused by salt in frying oil are more likely an issue for restaurants, where the oil is held at high temperatures for an extended time and is used heavily. For home cooks it shouldn't present a problem, especially since we recommend using a batch of frying oil at most three times before discarding it. –D.S.

Don't Brine Water-Chilled Chicken

The label on my chicken breasts says they may contain up to 5 percent retained water. Does that affect their ability to soak up a brine?

STEVEN SIMPSON
HOUSTON, TEXAS

➤ This label indicates that the chicken was chilled in water rather than in cold air during processing. The chicken absorbs water as it soaks, so it does raise the question of whether it can absorb a brine as well as air-chilled chicken.

When we brined both air-chilled and water-chilled boneless skinless chicken breasts for 45 minutes, we found that the air-chilled chicken absorbed 3½ times as much brine as the water-chilled chicken did. After cooking, the air-chilled samples retained 25 percent more moisture and were notably juicier and more well seasoned than water-chilled samples.

Why? Since the chicken with retained water is limited in its ability to take up brine, it is also unable to absorb much of the brine's salt, which not only seasons the meat but enables it to retain more moisture during cooking, too. The water absorbed during processing simply drains off during cooking, leaving the meat almost as dry and unseasoned as chicken that isn't brined at all.

Our favorite chicken, from Bell & Evans, is air-chilled, so we prefer brining because it's very effective and it takes only 45 minutes for parts. But you aren't out of luck if only water-chilled breasts are available: Opt to salt rather than brine. Sprinkle the water-chilled boneless, skinless chicken breasts with kosher salt (1½ teaspoons per pound) and refrigerate for 1 hour. During that time, some of the excess water in the chicken will be drawn out of the meat, where it will dissolve the salt on the surface, and then be reabsorbed as brine. The chicken will not take on additional moisture, but salting will ensure that it loses less moisture during cooking and will season the meat. Our testing proved that salting water-chilled chicken for an hour will deliver meat that retains just as much water as brined air-chilled chicken. –A.G.

OPT TO SALT

Treat water-chilled chicken breasts with kosher salt (1½ teaspoons per pound) for 1 hour.

Chillin' with Dry Ice

Is there a benefit to using dry ice instead of regular ice when packing a cooler?

JANA DODSON
TAMPA, FLA.

To answer your question, we first packed two coolers with various cold items (beer, steaks, and salad greens) and equal weights of ice and dry ice. We quickly ran into a problem: The dry ice chilled the food so well that it froze it. Pinpointing the exact amount of dry ice that would chill versus freeze food proved difficult since there are so many variables at play (how full the cooler is and the density and temperature of the food, for starters).

We decided to change course and look at how dry ice compares with regular ice in keeping ice cream frozen. Four half-gallons of ice cream stored with 5 pounds of regular ice in a midsize cooler were soupy after 3 hours, while a similarly packed container kept cold with dry ice took 9 hours to reach the same state. The dry ice also took up half the space and required no cleanup since, unlike water-based ice, dry ice (made by cooling and compressing carbon dioxide) changes from a solid to a gas as the temperature rises and simply dissipates into the air.

We recommend using dry ice with only frozen foods. It's important to have a full cooler when using dry ice since the rate at which dry ice disappears is dependent on the amount of empty space in the cooler (using empty covered food-storage containers to fill empty space works well). Be sure to follow the retailer's instructions for how to handle dry ice. –L.L.

A COOLER OPTION
Dry ice will keep frozen foods frozen three times longer than regular ice, plus there's no cleanup.

Sparking Kale

I tried your method for making kale chips in the microwave (November/December 2013), and the pieces actually sparked during cooking. What's going on?

MARIANNE DONAHOE
PARADISE VALLEY, ARIZ.

Sparking never happened when we were developing the recipe, but your question certainly sparked our curiosity. When we got letters from other readers, we revisited our microwave method for kale chips, making batches in 10 different microwaves. But try as we might, we couldn't get sparks to fly. That said, research informed us it can in fact happen, and the phenomenon even has a name: arcing. There are a few theories about what causes it. It could be that the mineral or moisture content of certain vegetables makes them more prone to spark. Others say it's more likely to happen when pieces of food with sharp (rather than rounded) edges are arranged too closely together in the microwave.

Using a reduced power level won't solve the issue. Waves can be emitted by a microwave at only one energy level, so the appliance just cycles on and off when set on a lower power setting—one burst of waves can still cause arcing. We suggest you make sure your kale is dried thoroughly and that the pieces are spread out on the plate. If this doesn't help, your best bet is to stop using your microwave to make kale chips (according to the U.S. Department of Agriculture, prolonged arcing can damage your microwave). –L.L.

Adding Water to Whisky

I've always heard that adding water to whisky improves its flavor. Can you tell me why?

HAROLD CHENEY
ATLANTA, GA.

The burning, pungent qualities contributed by the high proportion of alcohol in whisky can make it hard to evaluate nuances. Adding water dilutes the alcohol, which reduces the burn and allows other properties to reveal themselves. But there's also something significant happening on a molecular level. Aroma molecules share more chemical likenesses with alcohol than they do with water. As such, they tend to bind with alcohol. Adding water frees up more of the aroma molecules to evaporate into the taster's nose. Since appreciation of flavors happens at least as much in the nose as on the tongue, "watered-down" spirits actually seem more flavorful.

To experience the science at work, we had tasters sip 1½-ounce samples of 80 proof whisky neat and then with water added in increasing 1-teaspoon increments. While they noted that the neat sample of whisky had aromas of honey and caramel, flavor comments fell mostly in line with descriptions like "boozy" and "lots of burn." With just 1 teaspoon of water added, the alcohol receded and tasters picked up on sweet, vegetal flavors and subtle aromas like hay and apple. Most tasters preferred the addition of 2 teaspoons (which diluted the alcohol to 65 proof), allowing flavors such as vanilla, apple, and pear to really come to the fore. By 3 teaspoons the whisky began to taste watered down to many tasters, though one found it beneficial to add up to 5 teaspoons.

The takeaway? Adding a little water to whisky will open up the nose and bring out more nuanced flavors, but the ideal amount of water will vary depending on the drinker. –A.G.

WHAT IS IT?

I can tell this is a cutting tool given the blade, but can you tell me what it is used for?

KATE EDEKER
QUINCY, MASS.

What you have is a traditional Alaskan knife called an ulu (pronounced "OO-loo"). These knives are still in use today. Native Alaskans originally fashioned the arc-shaped blade from slate or jade and the handle from wood, bone, or ivory. Although today's blades are made from steel, the design hasn't changed much over time. It's said to excel at filleting fish, but modern cooks tout its versatility for everything from chopping nuts to slicing pizza.

Curious how the ulu tackled routine knife work, we used it to chiffonade basil and chop almonds. Rocking the blade back and forth, we found that it worked fine in both cases, although the basil was slightly bruised. The ulu excelled at our final challenge: filleting whole trout. It cut through bone to remove the head and sliced through scales effortlessly, and the curved blade allowed us to remove the flesh in broad, even strokes. The result was tidy, gorgeous fillets. If you prep whole fish, the ulu is for you. –Shannon Friedmann Hatch

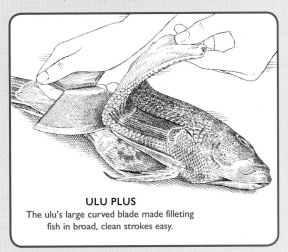

ULU PLUS
The ulu's large curved blade made filleting fish in broad, clean strokes easy.

Quick Tips

⇒ COMPILED BY SHANNON FRIEDMANN HATCH ⇐

Easier French Press Cleaning

French presses are hard to clean as the spent grounds cling to the bottom of the carafe. To easily get rid of all the grounds without having any go down her disposal (usually considered inadvisable), Janet Lazrow of Philadelphia, Pa., fills the carafe with water, pours its contents into a fine-mesh strainer over the sink, and dumps the grounds into the trash.

Tangle-Free Tongs

Spring-loaded tongs without a locking mechanism catch on other equipment and create a jumbled mess. To keep the arms closed when not in use, Eugene Parvin of Elmhurst, Ill., reserves the plastic ring from the screw top of a plastic container of orange juice or milk and slips it around the tool.

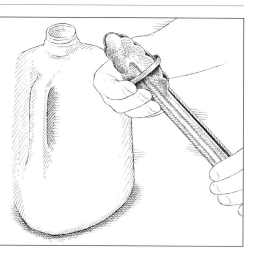

Shear Brilliance

Plucking the individual leaves from fresh herbs like parsley and dill can be time-consuming, especially when you need a large amount. Eric Scalavino of North Providence, R.I., has a quicker method: He holds the bunch with one hand and, using a downward stroke, shaves what he needs from the stem. (Be sure to discard any large, woody stems that get cut off before proceeding with the recipe.)

Digital Display

Mary Aman of Melbourne, Fla., often uses her tablet computer to view recipes while cooking, but its flat design means that it doesn't stand on its own. Rather than invest in a tablet stand, she puts her plate stand to use. The easel-like tool secures the tablet and keeps it upright for easy reading. (The stand also works for cookbooks.)

Breaking Up Rock-Hard Brown Sugar

If Joyce Goldberg of Montvale, N.J., discovers that her brown sugar has dried out and formed rock-hard clumps, she uses her coffee grinder to quickly break up what she needs (up to ¼ cup at a time) so that she can proceed with her recipe.

Twist-Tie Tepee

Transporting frosted cakes or cream pies without a cake carrier means covering the dessert with plastic wrap, but if the plastic is not propped up, it will smudge the topping. Toothpicks keep the plastic at bay—if their sharp points don't poke through it. Instead, Anne Walbridge of Sausalito, Calif., creates a blunt-edged prop by folding twist ties in half. Just before serving, she touches up the topping.

SEND US YOUR TIPS We will provide a complimentary one-year subscription for each tip we print. Send your tip, name, address, and daytime telephone number to Quick Tips, *Cook's Illustrated*, P.O. Box 470589, Brookline, MA 02447, or to QuickTips@AmericasTestKitchen.com.

Reheating Leftover Rice

For leftover rice that tastes just as fluffy and moist as a fresh-made pot, Jim Smith of Rockville, Md., uses this method.

1. Fill a saucepan with ½ inch of water. Place a steamer basket lined with a damp coffee filter in the pan.

2. Add chilled rice; cover and cook until heated through, about 5 minutes. Fluff with a fork and serve.

Broken-Cupcake Parfait

Instead of panicking when her cupcakes stick to the muffin tin, Sally McQuail of Downingtown, Pa., improvises with the crumbly (but still tasty) pieces by alternating cake and frosting to fill small, individual plastic cups.

Better Baking Mat Storage

Silicone baking mats are often stored rolled, but without a way to secure them, they quickly unfurl. Cynthia Kaufmann of Silver Spring, Md., uses this solution.

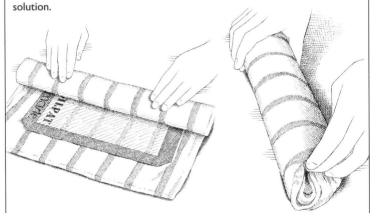

1. Lay a large, clean dish towel that's at least as big as the mat on a flat surface. Place the baking mat on top.

2. Starting at a short end, roll the towel over the mat. Tuck the ends of the towel into the tube to secure.

Storing Extra Eggs

It's not uncommon for Ken Burnham of Marco Island, Fla., to purchase a new carton of eggs before he's used up the old one. To save fridge space, he places the newer carton upside down on a shelf and sets the older eggs in the now-inverted cups on the bottom of the carton.

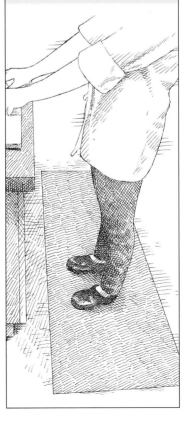

Taking the Cake (Layers)

When Kristina Feigin of Andover, Mass., made a cake that called for halving the layers, she realized that she had no way to transfer the delicate slices to the stand for frosting. She found that a rimless baking sheet easily slides between the layers.

Om in the Kitchen

Specially designed chefs' floor mats offer cooks comfort when standing in the kitchen—but at a steep price. Tara Powers of Sisters, Ore., uses a yoga mat instead. Its surface prevents slips and offers a surprising amount of cushioning, plus it easily rolls up for storage when not in use.

Grilled Pork Tenderloin Steaks

When grilling delicate pork tenderloin, the best approach is to treat it roughly.

⇒ BY DAN SOUZA ⇐

One of the most common—and, in my view, pointless—ways to grill pork tenderloin is to turn it into medallions. You start with an oblong, easy-to-manage roast but cut it into coins that require constant attention lest they overcook or, worse, slip through the grates. That said, I understand why folks do it. Pork tenderloin is a mild cut, so it makes sense to build up as much flavor as possible on the exterior. Cutting the roast into smaller pieces is an obvious way to accomplish that because it creates much more exposed surface area to absorb seasonings or a marinade, not to mention char from the grill.

My job would be to take the spirit of the medallion approach but find a shape and a technique that, while it reliably delivered a maximum amount of flavorful, nicely browned crust, still kept this lean cut tender.

Getting into Shape

My first thought: Cut the roast into fewer but taller medallions, the idea being that not only would I have fewer pieces of meat to manage on the grill, but their thickness would give them more time to char over high heat without overcooking. It would also prevent them from falling through the grate. But by paring down the roast into 2-inch-tall medallions, I'd essentially created a bunch of small tenderloin roasts that didn't offer much more surface area than the whole roast.

If more surface area was my goal, perhaps slicing was the wrong approach. What I really needed to do was pound the roast into wider, flatter swatches that would maximize the exterior surface area. So I cut each tenderloin in half to create two shorter cylinders and then pounded the halves into "steaks" that were ¾ inch thick. Those cutting and pounding steps had taken just minutes and had produced—I did some quick calculations—almost 30 percent more surface area.

From there I seasoned the steaks simply, with salt and pepper, and then spread a full chimney of lit coals over half of the kettle in order to create areas for both direct and indirect cooking. This setup allowed me to sear the steaks (on both sides for maximum browning) over high heat and then pull them across the grate to the cooler side of the grill to cook until they had reached the target 140 degrees,

Cutting shallow slits on both sides of the steaks helps them soak up more of the marinade and creates more surface area for browning.

making sure that the wider end of each steak was pointed toward the fire for even cooking.

The good news was that my tasters unanimously preferred this unusual tenderloin treatment to a roast that I'd simply cooked whole and sliced; the pork steaks delivered much more flavorful browned crust per bite. But my tasters' compliments came with constructive feedback, too—specifically, that searing the steaks had turned the exterior on this fat-deficient cut somewhat leathery and tough. They also said that they wanted the pork to taste meatier. Dressing up the flavor of mild-mannered pork tenderloin was a must.

Soaking It Up

Bold seasonings and fat would help solve flavor and texture problems, so I turned to a treatment that offers both: a marinade. Putting the test kitchen's knowledge into practice, I grabbed marinade must-haves, starting with salt. In addition to seasoning the meat, salt dissolves proteins within the meat, which helps it trap moisture and become more tender. I also included oil, as most of the aromatics, herbs, and spices that we add to marinades are soluble in

fat; plus, oil helps the marinade evenly coat the meat. For flavor, I tossed in minced garlic, plus lime juice for brightness, as we've found that the strong flavor of acids in marinades usually comes through in the cooked meat quite well. The final core ingredient was honey, which adds complexity and encourages browning. (I also mixed up marinades with orange juice and with lemon juice to create a couple of variations.)

After whisking together those ingredients (plus salt and pepper), I marinated the steaks for 30 minutes and then wiped off the excess marinade and proceeded with my two-phase grilling method. But the flavor boost wasn't much. Tasters reported good garlic flavor, but the lime was faint. Also, while the crust was decently browned, it was still tough.

Thinking that a longer marinade time would help, I let the next batch of pork steaks soak for 45 minutes—still well within the 1-hour limit that the test kitchen sets for marinating meats in acidic liquids. (After that point, acids break down surface proteins and turn meat mushy.) This time, my tasters and I noticed that the salt had penetrated further into the meat, improving seasoning and tenderness, but the other flavors of the marinade—from the lime in particular—were still barely detectable.

I doubted that extending the marinating time another 15 minutes would bring out much more lime flavor or boost meatiness, so I tried enhancing the citrus presence by adding a tablespoon of grated lime zest—a fairly large amount so that its flavor would come through even after the meat had been cooked. (Unlike juice, citrus zest doesn't boost acidity, nor does it affect the texture of meat.) As for ramping up meaty flavor, I traded a portion of the salt in the marinade for a splash of *umami*-rich fish sauce, which, in small quantities, heightens savory flavor without making foods taste distinctly Asian or fishy.

My tasters deemed this batch brighter and meatier but wanted more of those flavors—a request that made me think twice about wiping off the excess marinade. My only concern was that leaving all that moisture on the meat would thwart my browning efforts. On the contrary: When I gave it a shot, the results were surprisingly good. Not only was the flavor deeper, but the water in the marinade burned off quickly enough that the pork required, at most, an extra 45 seconds to achieve the deep brown color that I was looking for. Leaving excess marinade on the meat had another benefit: Its extra fat and moisture kept the crust from drying out and toughening during cooking.

This simple tweak had been so effective that I wanted to see if I could get even more of the marinade to cling to the meat. With a sharp knife, I cut ⅛-inch-deep crosshatch marks into the steaks—thin channels that trapped more of the marinade, giving the pork bolder flavor. The slits also beefed up the crust, since they created more surface area for browning.

All Dressed Up

The marinade made the outside of my steaks taste so bright and meaty that I couldn't help but wish that their milder interior did, too. Thinking that this was the perfect job for a sauce, I set aside ½ cup of the marinade before adding the pork to the liquid and poured it over the cooked steaks just before serving. This was a little better—but all that lime juice and raw garlic made the uncooked marinade taste too harsh. Its body was also too thin to function as a sauce. A few teaspoons of mayonnaise fixed both issues, giving the sauce lightly creamy body and balanced flavor. Stirring in some chopped cilantro freshened it up nicely.

I had one last thought: Pouring the sauce over the whole steaks put it in contact with only the exterior. To ensure that its flavor reached the inside of the pork, too, I sliced the steaks before serving, drizzled them with some sauce, and passed the rest at the table. I also sprinkled the meat with flake sea salt (such as Maldon), a small touch that added bursts of crunch and seasoning to each bite.

My grilled pork tenderloin looks and tastes nothing like most versions—and I couldn't be happier about that.

MAYO MAKES IT A SAUCE

To add a last-minute burst of flavor to our Garlic-Lime Grilled Pork Tenderloin Steaks, we reserve a portion of the garlic-citrus marinade to use as a sauce. But pouring the punchy liquid over the steaks resulted in a too-sharp taste; plus, its consistency was thin and runny. Adding mayonnaise solved both problems. A few teaspoons balanced the marinade's sharp acidity and contributed much-needed body.

The Geometry of Pounding Pork

Cylindrical pork tenderloin doesn't have much surface area for browning. Pounding the roast into a flat steak seemed like an obvious way to increase the amount of meat that comes in contact with the grill—and as a result, the flavor in every bite—but we didn't realize how significant the difference actually was until we did the math. Flattening a cylindrical piece of pork tenderloin into a ¾-inch rectangular steak increased its surface area by almost 30 percent.

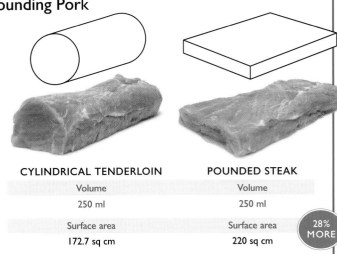

CYLINDRICAL TENDERLOIN	POUNDED STEAK
Volume	Volume
250 ml	250 ml
Surface area	Surface area
172.7 sq cm	220 sq cm

28% MORE

GARLIC-LIME
GRILLED PORK TENDERLOIN STEAKS
SERVES 4 TO 6

Since marinating is a key step in this recipe, we don't recommend using enhanced pork. For our free recipe for Garlic-Lime Grilled Pork Tenderloin Steaks for Two, go to CooksIllustrated.com/june14.

- 2 (1-pound) pork tenderloins, trimmed
- 1 tablespoon grated lime zest plus ¼ cup juice (2 limes)
- 4 garlic cloves, minced
- 4 teaspoons honey
- 2 teaspoons fish sauce
- ¾ teaspoon salt
- ½ teaspoon pepper
- ½ cup vegetable oil
- 4 teaspoons mayonnaise
- 1 tablespoon chopped fresh cilantro
  Flake sea salt (optional)

1. Slice each tenderloin in half crosswise to create 4 steaks total. Pound each half to ¾-inch thickness. Using sharp knife, cut ⅛-inch-deep slits spaced ½ inch apart in crosshatch pattern on both sides of steaks.

2. Whisk lime zest and juice, garlic, honey, fish sauce, salt, and pepper together in large bowl. Whisking constantly, slowly drizzle oil into lime mixture until smooth and slightly thickened. Transfer ½ cup lime mixture to small bowl and whisk in mayonnaise; set aside sauce. Add steaks to bowl with remaining marinade and toss thoroughly to coat; transfer steaks and marinade to large zipper-lock bag, press out as much air as possible, and seal bag. Let steaks sit at room temperature for 45 minutes.

3A. FOR A CHARCOAL GRILL: Open bottom vent completely. Light large chimney starter filled with charcoal briquettes (6 quarts). When top coals are partially covered with ash, pour evenly over half of grill. Set cooking grate in place, cover, and open lid vent completely. Heat grill until hot, about 5 minutes.

3B. FOR A GAS GRILL: Turn all burners to high, cover, and heat grill until hot, about 15 minutes. Leave primary burner on high and turn off other burner(s).

4. Clean and oil cooking grate. Remove steaks from marinade (do not pat dry) and place over hotter part of grill. Cook, uncovered, until well browned on first side, 3 to 4 minutes. Flip steaks and cook until well browned on second side, 3 to 4 minutes. Transfer steaks to cooler part of grill, with wider end of each steak facing hotter part of grill. Cover and cook until meat registers 140 degrees, 3 to 8 minutes longer (remove steaks as they come to temperature). Transfer steaks to carving board and let rest for 5 minutes.

5. While steaks rest, microwave reserved sauce until warm, 15 to 30 seconds; stir in cilantro. Slice steaks against grain into ½-inch-thick slices. Drizzle with half of sauce; sprinkle with sea salt, if using; and serve, passing remaining sauce separately.

LEMON-THYME
GRILLED PORK TENDERLOIN STEAKS

Substitute grated lemon zest and juice (2 lemons) for lime zest and juice. Add 1 tablespoon minced fresh thyme to lemon mixture with garlic. Omit cilantro.

SPICY ORANGE-GINGER
GRILLED PORK TENDERLOIN STEAKS

Reduce lime zest to 1½ teaspoons and juice to 2 tablespoons. Add 1½ teaspoons grated orange zest plus 2 tablespoons juice, 2 teaspoons grated fresh ginger, and ¼ teaspoon cayenne to lime mixture with garlic.

▶ **Look: Tenderloin? No, Steak.**
Video available free for 4 months at CooksIllustrated.com/june14

Gluten-Free Pizza Worth Eating

Most gluten-free pizza tastes like wet cardboard. By examining every detail, we eventually came up with a crust that's crispy outside and light and airy inside.

⇒ BY ANDREW JANJIGIAN ⇐

It made sense that I was asked to develop a gluten-free pizza crust. Baking bread has been my passion for nearly 30 years. But I've always embraced gluten as the magic ingredient in bread. It's the source of its structure and, as a result, much of its texture. So this was the bread baker's ultimate challenge: Develop a gluten-free pizza crust that everyone would want to eat, whether they were avoiding gluten or not.

My first forays into the world of gluten-free pizza were, in an odd way, encouraging. I sought out every pizza joint that sold a gluten-free pie, and every crust was awful. Some were rubbery and dense. Others were stiff and flavorless. And none bore any resemblance to the real thing, which needs to be—at the very least—crispy on the underside and airy and tender within. I also tried a handful of recipes from various gluten-free cookbooks and websites; the results were no better.

Clearly, the world of gluten-free pizza was so dismal that almost any improvement would be welcome. But I didn't want to settle for just passable. I wanted to make a crust with an airy texture and good chew, a crust that could hold its own against the wheat-flour versions.

Network Solutions

The first thing I needed was a substitute for the wheat flour. This isn't an easy swap since there isn't a single wheat-free flour that can supply the same characteristics as wheat flour's makeup of protein, starch, and fat. A blend was a must. Fortunately, some of my colleagues had recently developed just such a blend (see page 10 for more information) for the test kitchen's new gluten-free cookbook. With

Almond flour, baking soda, and psyllium husk deliver a crust that is crispy on the exterior and tender and airy within—just like a traditional one.

the substitute on hand, I got down to business.

Given the numerous flaws that I'd encountered in those early samples, I decided to start from the ground up. For two 12-inch pizzas, I figured that roughly 3 cups of the flour blend would be right. To this I added a teaspoon of instant yeast, 2 teaspoons of salt, and a teaspoon of xanthan gum.

Why xanthan gum? The gluten-free flour blend's protein network is weak in comparison with the gluten network of wheat flour, and xanthan gum (made by fermenting simple sugars using the microorganism *Xanthomonas campestris*) behaves like glue in many gluten-free baked goods, strengthening the weak network and improving elasticity. That's exactly what my gluten-free dough would need. Without such reinforcement, the carbon dioxide produced by the yeast would simply escape from the dough and the resulting crust would be tough, dense, and squat. If xanthan gum is so effective at holding gluten-free baked goods together, you might wonder why we didn't include it in the test kitchen's flour blend. We left it out because not all recipes need it, and those that do require varying amounts.

I placed my dry ingredients in the bowl of a stand mixer fitted with a dough hook and poured in 1½ cups of water and ¼ cup of oil (typical amounts for standard pizza dough). I let the machine work the dough until it started to pull away from the sides of the bowl—the signal that there was decent structural development. (In a wheat-based dough you'd say "gluten development," but I was obviously dealing with a different protein network.) Then I put my dough in a lightly oiled bowl, covered it with plastic wrap, and waited for it to proof.

And waited. Even after 90 minutes, the dough showed no signs of expanding. When I cut into it, I found a network of tiny bubbles, but hardly the airy holes that I'd hoped for. But I forged ahead anyway, rolling out the dough (even with the xanthan gum, the dough was still too fragile to stretch like wheat-based pizza dough), topping the rounds with sauce and cheese, and baking them in a hot oven. The result? A crust that was dense and flat, with a tough underside and gummy interior. This was far from passable.

A Gluten-Free Crust That Doesn't Fall Flat

With psyllium husk and plenty of water, our dough has the structure and elasticity that others lack.

OUR CRUST: Airy and tender

TYPICAL GLUTEN-FREE CRUST: Dense and rubbery

Calling on Reinforcements

The obvious question to address was why the dough didn't rise. In traditional yeasted doughs, the rise and the yeast tend to go hand in hand since yeast produces gas (as well as flavor compounds) as it ferments. So I tried adding more yeast in increasing amounts. But no matter how much I added, the dough refused to budge. In fact, the only noticeable difference was that in high amounts, the yeast gave the dough a sour, overproofed flavor.

Maybe the dough lacked the structure necessary to contain the gases; that pointed to the xanthan gum. For the next few tests, I added increasing amounts of xanthan gum, from 1½ teaspoons up to 3 tablespoons. While the greater amount increased the dough's ability to expand, it also gave the dough an unappealing rubbery consistency.

Could it be that xanthan gum wasn't the best choice? Maybe I should have been using one of the other two structural-reinforcement options that I'd seen called for: guar gum (produced by grinding the endosperm of Indian guar plant seeds) or powdered psyllium seed husks (most commonly used as a dietary fiber). The guar gum performed no better than the xanthan gum, and it also contributed an off-flavor. However, psyllium husk was a definite improvement. One and a half tablespoons delivered a dough that rose visibly during proofing and a final crust that had a more open crumb. Our science editor explained that psyllium husk is far more effective at attracting and holding on to water molecules than the other gums are, which allows it to create a thick gel. This gel, combined with psyllium husk's insoluble fiber and protein, was providing incredibly strong structural reinforcement for my dough's protein network, making it capable of trapping lots of gas during proofing as well as steam during baking.

Nevertheless, the crust was far from the light and airy crust that I'd set my sights on.

Watered Down

I'd been noticing something. While the dough now rose well during proofing, when I rolled it out to shape the crust, much of the gas was expelled. The dough never recovered like a wheat-flour dough, even when I tried letting it rise a second time post-shaping. If the crust couldn't hold on to gas as well as I needed it to, maybe I could give it a little boost. To this end I turned to an ingredient used in countless baked goods, though less often in yeasted ones: baking powder. Sure enough, a couple of teaspoons of the leavener, activated by the heat of the oven, gave the dough a bit more of the lift that it had been missing.

Still, it wasn't enough. Many traditional wheat-based pizza doughs can be rather stiff right after mixing yet end up open and airy after proofing, making them easy to stretch. This elasticity also translates into a dough that can puff up with steam in the oven, and thus a crust that bakes up light and airy. But in the case of my gluten-free dough, the dough

started out stiff and stayed stiff. Thinking about how, in the past, I've gotten some unworkably stiff wheat-based doughs to stretch more, I landed on water. Increasing the water in a wheat-based dough allows the protein network to be more fluid and thus more flexible and stretchable. Would the same rule apply to the network in my gluten-free pizza dough? To find out, I made a series of doughs using increasing amounts of water.

Even before I topped the pizzas with tomato sauce, Parmesan cheese, and mozzarella cheese and baked them off, I could tell that I was onto something: The more water the dough contained the more it rose during proofing. As it happened, my dough seemed to benefit from the additional water far more than I'd expected: The most tender crust and open crumb came when I'd added so much water that it went from being a dough to more of a thick batter.

Of course, this added liquid created some new problems. For one, mixing the dough with the dough hook was now ineffective: The dough was so wet that the hook just spun around. Switching to the paddle attachment was an easy fix. Second, the additional water made shaping the crust with a rolling pin, as I had been doing, impossible. Instead, I spread it out on a baking sheet with a rubber spatula into an 8-inch circle, much like spreading frosting on a cake, and then misted the dough with vegetable oil spray, covered it with a piece of plastic wrap, and pressed it into an even, large round with a properly thick edge around the perimeter. Last, and most important, while the final crust had the perfect tender texture and open, airy crumb around the outer edge, the added water had made it gummy toward the center.

To remove the excess water, I tried parbaking the rounds without any topping in a hot oven just until they'd started to brown. This produced crusts that looked nice and dry on the exterior, but they were still gummy inside. To drive off enough water without overbaking the exterior, I tested incrementally lower oven temperatures and increased baking times. I finally got it just right when I started the crust in a cold oven, set the temperature to 325 degrees, and let it cook through slowly for about 45 minutes. I then sauced the parbaked crust, sprinkled it with mozzarella and a little Parmesan, and put it back in a 500-degree oven briefly to melt the cheese and finish browning the crust.

That's Nuts

Now that I had a pizza crust with a light and airy (but not gummy) interior, there was only one obstacle: The underside of the crust was more tough than crispy. No problem, I thought: Adding more oil to the dough would get it to fry up a bit. Alas, while this did help it crisp, it also left the pizza greasy. Gluten-free flours, I learned, don't absorb fats as readily as wheat flour does, and clearly I'd gone over the maximum.

The solution turned out to be almond flour. Adding just 2½ ounces to the dough boosted the overall fat content and gave my crust the crispiness that it needed without causing any noticeable change in flavor. And because almonds (and nuts in general) don't shed all their oil when heated, the crust wasn't greasy.

As for the toppings, I liked keeping it simple with just cheese and sauce, but I did find that additional toppings were fine as long as I limited them to no more than 6 ounces of vegetables and 4 ounces of meat per pie. (Thinly slice hearty vegetables, such as peppers and onions, and sauté them before using, and precook meats like pepperoni to drain them of fat.) Finally, I had a gluten-free pizza crust that I could serve proudly, even to those who didn't have to avoid gluten.

THE BEST GLUTEN-FREE PIZZA

MAKES TWO 12-INCH PIZZAS

This recipe requires letting the dough rise for 1½ hours and prebaking the crusts for about 45 minutes before topping and baking. If you don't have almond flour, you can process 2½ ounces of blanched almonds in a food processor until finely ground, about 30 seconds. Psyllium husk is available at health food stores. You can substitute 16 ounces (2⅔ cups plus ¼ cup) King Arthur Gluten-Free Multi-Purpose Flour or 16 ounces (2⅔ cup plus ½ cup) Bob's Red Mill GF All-Purpose Baking Flour for the America's Test Kitchen Gluten-Free Flour Blend. Note that pizza crust made with King Arthur will be slightly denser and not as chewy, and pizza crust made with Bob's Red Mill will be thicker and more airy and will have a distinct bean flavor.

Crust

16	ounces (3⅓ cups plus ¼ cup) America's Test Kitchen Gluten-Free Flour Blend (recipe follows)
2½	ounces (½ cup plus 1 tablespoon) almond flour
1½	tablespoons powdered psyllium husk
2½	teaspoons baking powder
2	teaspoons salt
1	teaspoon instant or rapid-rise yeast
2½	cups warm water (100 degrees)
¼	cup vegetable oil
	Vegetable oil spray

Sauce

1	(28-ounce) can whole peeled tomatoes, drained
1	tablespoon extra-virgin olive oil
1	teaspoon red wine vinegar
1	garlic clove, minced
1	teaspoon dried oregano
½	teaspoon salt
¼	teaspoon pepper
1	ounce Parmesan cheese, grated fine (½ cup)
8	ounces whole-milk mozzarella cheese, shredded (2 cups)

1. FOR THE CRUST: Using stand mixer fitted with paddle, mix flour blend, almond flour, psyllium, baking powder, salt, and yeast on low speed until combined. Slowly add warm water and oil in steady stream until incorporated. Increase speed to medium and beat until dough is sticky and uniform, about 6 minutes. (Dough will resemble thick batter.)

2. Remove bowl from mixer, cover with plastic wrap, and let stand until inside of dough is bubbly

► **You've Got to See This**
Video available free for 4 months at CooksIllustrated.com/june14

(use spoon to peer inside dough), about 1½ hours. (Dough will puff slightly but will not rise.)

3. Adjust oven racks to middle and lower positions. Line 2 rimmed baking sheets with parchment paper and spray liberally with oil spray. Transfer half of dough to center of 1 prepared sheet. Using oil-sprayed rubber spatula, spread dough into 8-inch circle. Spray top of dough with oil spray, cover with large sheet of plastic, and, using your hands, press out dough to 11½-inch round, about ¼ inch thick, leaving outer ¼ inch slightly thicker than center; discard plastic. Repeat with remaining dough and second prepared sheet.

4. Place prepared sheets in oven and heat oven to 325 degrees. Bake dough until firm to touch, golden brown on underside, and just beginning to brown on top, 45 to 50 minutes, switching and rotating sheets halfway through baking. Transfer crusts to wire rack and let cool.

5. FOR THE SAUCE: Process all ingredients in food processor until smooth, about 30 seconds. Transfer to bowl and refrigerate until ready to use.

6. One hour before baking pizza, adjust oven rack to upper-middle position, set baking stone on rack, and heat oven to 500 degrees.

7. Transfer 1 parbaked crust to pizza peel. Using back of spoon or ladle, spread ½ cup tomato sauce in thin layer over surface of crust, leaving ¼-inch border around edge. Sprinkle ¼ cup Parmesan evenly over sauce, followed by 1 cup mozzarella. Carefully slide crust onto stone and bake until crust is well browned and cheese is bubbly and beginning to brown, 10 to 12 minutes. Transfer pizza to wire rack and let cool for 5 minutes before slicing and serving. Repeat with second crust, ½ cup tomato

sauce (you will have extra sauce), remaining ¼ cup Parmesan, and remaining 1 cup mozzarella.

TO MAKE AHEAD: Extra sauce can be refrigerated for up to 1 week or frozen for up to 1 month. Parbaked and cooled crusts can sit at room temperature for up to 4 hours. Completely cooled crusts can be wrapped with plastic wrap and then aluminum foil and frozen for up to 2 weeks. Frozen crusts can be topped and baked as directed without thawing.

AMERICA'S TEST KITCHEN GLUTEN-FREE FLOUR BLEND

MAKES 42 OUNCES (ABOUT 9⅓ CUPS)

Be sure to use potato starch, not potato flour, with this recipe. Tapioca starch is also sold as tapioca flour; they are interchangeable. We strongly recommend that you use Bob's Red Mill white and brown rice flours; see page 31 for more information on rice flours. We also recommend that you weigh your ingredients; if you measure by volume, spoon each ingredient into the measuring cup (do not pack or tap) and scrape off the excess. Check out our book *The How Can It Be Gluten-Free Cookbook* for more recipes using the blend.

24	ounces (4½ cups plus ⅓ cup) white rice flour
7½	ounces (1⅔ cups) brown rice flour
7	ounces (1⅓ cups) potato starch
3	ounces (¾ cup) tapioca starch
¾	ounce (¼ cup) nonfat dry milk powder

Whisk all ingredients in large bowl until well combined. Transfer to airtight container and refrigerate for up to 3 months.

Building Our Own Gluten-Free Flour Blend

When developing our gluten-free pizza recipe, we wanted a wheat-free substitute for all-purpose flour that would work in our pizza dough as well as in cookies, muffins, and cakes. We found that store-bought gluten-free blends perform inconsistently; one product might deliver great cookies but subpar cakes. For that reason, we decided to create our own.

To start, we reviewed how wheat flour works. When hydrated, starch granules in the flour swell, and with the help of mixing or kneading (or sufficient time), the proteins in the flour link up to form long elastic strands called gluten. These strands surround the gelled starch granules, creating a network that enables rise and a sturdy structure. Since no single gluten-free flour or starch performs in this way, a blend was necessary. We found that two flours—white rice flour and brown rice flour—provided the right baseline of protein, starch, and flavor. And since different starches absorb water, swell, and gel at different temperatures and to different degrees, we enlisted two kinds—potato starch and tapioca starch—to create the right amount of chew and structure. Finally, the proteins and sugars in milk powder ensure that baked goods brown properly.

Be aware: A gluten-free flour blend is a complicated mixture, and thus brands aren't easily interchangeable. It's best to work with recipes that have been developed around a particular blend.

WHITE RICE FLOUR
Provides a neutral-tasting, refined protein/starch base.

BROWN RICE FLOUR
Supplies proteins that, along with those in the white rice flour, create a network that mimics gluten. Also provides a nutty, wheaty flavor.

POTATO STARCH
Contributes large starch granules that gel at higher temperatures and set to a more extensive, open network when cool, thus providing tenderness.

TAPIOCA STARCH
Provides smaller granules that gel at lower temperatures, forming a more compact network when cool, thus providing chew and elasticity.

MILK POWDER
Contributes proteins that help improve structure and, along with its sugars, undergo the Maillard browning reaction, which leads to more complex flavor.

Fusilli with Ricotta and Spinach

To successfully combine ricotta and spinach outside pasta (instead of stuffed into it), you need to know when to add the cheese.

> BY ANDREW JANJIGIAN

Every so often I come across a recipe that teams simple boiled pasta with spinach and ricotta as a sort of quick "deconstructed" version of stuffed shells, manicotti, or ravioli. Since the labor involved in cooking a stuffed pasta dish makes it the sort of project that most of us reserve for special occasions, a no-fuss dish created by simply tossing the same ingredients together has a lot of appeal.

But when I gave a few recipes of this sort a try, my enthusiasm faded. The authors all seemed to forget that the stuffed pasta is only one component of the dish: Ravioli and the like are typically served with a bright marinara, a meaty ragu, or even a nutty browned butter. When you take these contrasting flavors away, the dish loses complexity, and the richness of the ricotta hijacks the mild spinach and pasta. My goal was to punch up the flavor to make up for what a sauce contributes to a stuffed pasta.

Most of the recipes I found employ one of two basic methods: The first calls for buzzing raw spinach and ricotta in a food processor along with bold ingredients like garlic, Parmesan, and toasted nuts to create a "pesto." The uncooked puree is then tossed with hot pasta just prior to serving. The second approach requires sautéing chopped, blanched spinach with aromatics; stirring in the ricotta; and cooking it just long enough to create a uniform sauce. Unfortunately, the pesto tasted neither of mineral-y spinach nor of milky ricotta. Pureed together, the two components seemed to cancel each other out. The result of the latter method also tasted somewhat wan, but I could at least discern the ingredients, so that's where I began my testing.

First I set out to tackle the sauce's gritty, chalky texture. Heat causes the ricotta curds to release water and coagulate, rendering the sauce grainy. I tried cooking the cheese as briefly as possible in order to prevent this from happening, but it doesn't take much heat to induce the effect, and I had to at least bring the sauce to a simmer before dressing the pasta.

Adding cream would minimize grittiness (the fat in the cream coats the milk proteins in the cheese to slow down coagulation), but to prevent curdling entirely, I had to either add an excessive amount of cream or dial down the ricotta to the point that its presence was lost completely. Then I had a better idea: Simply withhold most of the cheese and dollop it onto the finished dish. This would prevent graininess while keeping the ricotta presence distinct.

To bring out the best from the cheese, I seasoned

Toss just a little ricotta and cream with the pasta; then drop large spoonfuls of cheese over the serving bowl.

it with extra-virgin olive oil, salt, and pepper. And to make sure it didn't go onto the pasta cold, I let it sit out on the counter to warm up to room temperature while the pasta cooked. After combining a small amount of ricotta with cream and using it to dress the pasta, I spooned the remaining seasoned ricotta on top of the dish. This worked perfectly: Instead of a dilute amount of cheese in each bite, tasters got concentrated hits here and there, much as they would when eating filled pasta.

With the ricotta sorted out, I turned my attention to the spinach. I wanted to use baby spinach since it requires very little prep. Figuring that it was worth trying the most straightforward approach to cooking it, too, I simply threw the coarsely chopped leaves into the pot with the pasta (curly fusilli nicely trapped the sauce) once it was al dente. This worked like a charm: In just 30 seconds, the spinach was wilted yet still brilliant green.

To make the flavors pop, I opted for a healthy dose of sautéed garlic mixed into the ricotta and cream mixture, along with sprinklings of nutmeg and cayenne for an underlying warmth. A generous dusting of grated Parmesan cheese provided additional depth, and lemon zest and lemon juice introduced welcome brightness. Finally, in order to produce a nice, velvety texture, I employed a dead-simple trick we've used in the past: Let the dressed pasta sit for a few minutes, stirring it occasionally, to draw out some of the pasta's starches. Together, these elements combined to give me a dish that was as easy to make as it was delicious.

FUSILLI WITH RICOTTA AND SPINACH
SERVES 4 TO 6

We like fusilli for this recipe since its corkscrew shape does a nice job of trapping the sauce, but penne and campanelle also work well.

- 11 ounces (1⅓ cups) whole-milk ricotta cheese
- 3 tablespoons extra-virgin olive oil
  Salt and pepper
- 1 pound fusilli
- 1 pound (16 cups) baby spinach, chopped coarse
- 4 garlic cloves, minced
- ¼ teaspoon ground nutmeg
- ⅛ teaspoon cayenne pepper
- ¼ cup heavy cream
- 1 teaspoon grated lemon zest plus 2 teaspoons juice
- 1 ounce Parmesan cheese, grated (½ cup), plus extra for serving

1. Whisk 1 cup ricotta, 1 tablespoon oil, ¼ teaspoon pepper, and ⅛ teaspoon salt in medium bowl until smooth; set aside.

2. Bring 4 quarts water to boil in large pot. Add pasta and 1 tablespoon salt and cook, stirring often, until al dente. Reserve 1 cup cooking water. Stir spinach into pot with pasta and cook until wilted, about 30 seconds. Drain pasta and spinach and return them to pot.

3. While pasta cooks, heat remaining 2 tablespoons oil, garlic, nutmeg, and cayenne in saucepan over medium heat until fragrant, about 1 minute. Remove pan from heat and whisk in remaining ⅓ cup ricotta, cream, lemon zest and juice, and ¾ teaspoon salt until smooth.

4. Add ricotta-cream mixture and Parmesan to pasta and toss to combine. Let pasta rest, tossing frequently, until sauce has thickened slightly and coats pasta, 2 to 4 minutes, adjusting consistency with reserved cooking water as needed. Transfer pasta to serving platter, dot evenly with reserved ricotta mixture, and serve, passing extra Parmesan separately.

▶ **Watch the Pasta Process**
Video available free for 4 months at CooksIllustrated.com/june14

Bringing Home Cioppino

Fish and shellfish piled high in a flavorful broth make this San Francisco stew a project.
Could we simplify the shopping and cooking and still maintain its indulgent appeal?

⪧ BY LAN LAM ⪦

When I think of stew, words like "humble" and "simple" usually come to mind. The seafood stew known as cioppino, however, is a different matter. True, it has modest origins. Brought to San Francisco by Italian immigrants, the earliest versions were uncomplicated affairs made by fishermen, featuring the catch of the day in a simple broth created from little more than water, tomato paste, and garlic. Today's restaurant versions have taken it to another level. Showcasing an assembly of fish and shellfish piled high in a bright, complex broth and anointed with fruity olive oil, cioppino is an indulgence for a seafood lover like me. From the first whiff of briny clams and mussels to the last drops of the flavorful broth, mopped up with a crust of bread, this stew is a serious treat—but it's also a production that can intimidate the home cook. Many recipes call for up to a half-dozen different types of seafood and a tomatoey fish stock that is simmered for hours. I did find shortcut versions, but these proved disappointing: The broth tasted thin and there wasn't enough variety to make a dish that felt special. My goal: a restaurant-worthy cioppino in which every component was perfectly cooked and the broth was rich-tasting but which could be on the table quickly and with minimal fuss.

Fishing for Answers

I began by selecting the seafood. I needed to scale down the list to a choice few that presented a good mix of textures and flavors. For the fish, a white variety is most traditional and the best choice, since oily varieties like salmon muddy the stew's light flavors. Swordfish seemed promising, but tasters found its texture too meaty. Sea bass was acceptable, although it fell apart slightly. Halibut fillets worked perfectly—they were tender and had just enough heft. As for the shellfish, even though just about all the cioppino

Placing the cooked halibut in serving bowls and then ladling the shellfish and broth on top ensures tender, intact chunks of fish.

recipes from San Francisco feature Dungeness crab, I decided to omit it. Other seafood options offer enough briny-sweet flavor—plus the sourcing, cooking, cracking, and shelling of it just complicated things. We also agreed that the sweetness of shrimp seemed out of place. But a combination of briny littleneck clams and savory-sweet mussels had just the flavors I was looking for.

With the seafood lineup ready to go, I moved on to the cooking method. Recipes that I found typically followed one of two approaches. The first method called for putting everything in the broth at the same time—submerging the fish in the broth so that it could poach while also serving as a raft for the shellfish, which rested on top to steam. I quickly discovered the flaw here: To generate enough steam to cook the shellfish, I had to bring the broth (a placeholder mixture for now) to a boil. That left me with overcooked,

wrung-out halibut, not to mention chewy mussels, since they take less time to cook than clams do. The second approach, staggered additions, seemed much more promising. I put the halibut in the Dutch oven first, let it simmer until about halfway done, and then added the clams, followed by the mussels a few minutes later. The big problem here was that there's little leeway if one component happens to cook more quickly or more slowly than expected. A minute or two on either end makes a huge difference for seafood, and if one component strayed from my projected cooking time, the others suffered. This one-pot approach was clearly not going to work. The only way to perfectly cook three varieties of seafood was to cook each one separately and bring them all together in the hot broth to serve.

With this in mind, I poached the halibut in the broth and then turned off the heat and let it sit while I steamed the clams and then the mussels in water and butter in a separate pan. Removing them as they opened ensured ideal doneness for each one, and using a shallow skillet made the task easy. The cooked shellfish stayed warm in the pot of broth until they were all done.

This was a huge improvement: Finally each seafood component was perfectly cooked. But there was still a small problem that had plagued every version I'd made. When I went to serve the cioppino, no matter how careful I was when ladling the stew into bowls, it was impossible to avoid knocking the clams and mussels around, and their hard shells broke the halibut into unappealing shreds. The solution? I transferred the halibut to a plate as soon as it was done and kept it covered with foil while I steamed the shellfish. (Keeping the halibut in large pieces ensured that it was easy to remove from the pot.) Then I divided the still-warm halibut among serving bowls and ladled the broth and shellfish on top. This worked seamlessly, so I moved on to fine-tuning the broth. It was taking too long, and it seemed more like pasta sauce than like the base for a seafood stew.

Cleaning Clams

Most clams these days are cultured. After being dug, they are usually held on flats submerged in salt water for several days. During this time they expel grit they have ingested; scrubbing is only necessary to remove exterior sand and grit before cooking.

▶ **Watch the Progression**
Video available free for 4 months at CooksIllustrated.com/june14

One at a Time

Cooking the halibut, then the clams, and finally the mussels ensures that each component is perfectly done.

SIMMER HALIBUT IN POT

The halibut needs just 15 minutes in the pot; set the cooked fish aside before adding the cooked shellfish.

STEAM CLAMS AND THEN MUSSELS IN SKILLET

Transfer the clams and mussels to the pot as they open; using a skillet makes it easy to leave grit behind when pouring the cooking liquid into the pot.

Wine and Brine

Up to this point, I had been sautéing onions in oil until golden and then stirring in garlic and a few spices (bay leaves, dried oregano, and red pepper flakes) and, finally, canned tomatoes and water. Following precedent set by the recipes I'd found, I simmered this mixture for about an hour before adding the halibut.

I decided to start my revision of the broth with the flavor. As the clams and mussels opened, they released their briny juices into the steaming water. Why not put that to use? For my next test I cut back on the water in the broth and poured the clams' and mussels' cooking liquid into the pot once they were done. As long as I poured slowly, it was easy to leave any sand and grit from the clam shells behind in the skillet. This was a definite improvement, but the stew really hit the mark when I replaced the rest of the water in the broth with bottled clam juice.

Now my stew had a clean, briny flavor appropriate to a seafood stew, but tasters wanted a bit more acidity and complexity. The answer was using white wine to steam the shellfish.

Flavor squared away, I moved on to seeing what I could do about the broth's lengthy simmer. The idea was to concentrate and meld the broth's components, but I wondered how essential that really was. After all, I wasn't making a stock or a tomato-based pasta sauce. As it turned out, a long simmer was entirely unnecessary. In fact, once I poured the clam juice and tomatoes into the sautéed onions and aromatics, the broth tasted just right after a mere 5 minutes of cooking. I added the halibut and let it poach in the broth for 15 minutes.

A little parsley stirred into the pot and a generous drizzle of olive oil were the finishing touches. In an hour, I had restaurant-worthy cioppino in my own kitchen.

CIOPPINO
SERVES 4 TO 6

Any firm-fleshed, ¾- to 1-inch-thick whitefish (such as cod or sea bass) can be substituted for halibut. Discard clams or mussels with unpleasant odors, cracked shells, or shells that won't close. If littlenecks are not available, substitute Manila or mahogany clams, or use 2 pounds of mussels. If using only mussels, skip step 3 and cook them all at once with the butter and wine for 3 to 5 minutes. For our free recipe for Cioppino for Two, go to CooksIllustrated.com/june14.

¼	cup vegetable oil
2	large onions, chopped fine
	Salt and pepper
¼	cup water
4	garlic cloves, minced
2	bay leaves
1	teaspoon dried oregano
⅛–¼	teaspoon red pepper flakes
1	(28-ounce) can whole peeled tomatoes, drained with juice reserved, chopped coarse
1	(8-ounce) bottle clam juice
1	(1½-pound) skinless halibut fillet, ¾ to 1 inch thick, cut into 6 pieces
1	pound littleneck clams, scrubbed
1¼	cups dry white wine
4	tablespoons unsalted butter
1	pound mussels, scrubbed and debearded
¼	cup chopped fresh parsley
	Extra-virgin olive oil

1. Heat vegetable oil in Dutch oven over medium-high heat until shimmering. Add onions, ½ teaspoon salt, and ½ teaspoon pepper; cook, stirring frequently, until onions begin to brown, 7 to 9 minutes. Add water and cook, stirring frequently, until onions are soft, 2 to 4 minutes. Stir in garlic, bay leaves, oregano, and pepper flakes and cook for 1 minute. Stir in tomatoes and reserved juice and clam juice and bring to simmer. Reduce heat to low, cover, and simmer for 5 minutes.

2. Submerge halibut in broth, cover, and gently simmer until fish is cooked through, 12 to 15 minutes. Remove pot from heat and, using slotted spoon, transfer halibut to plate, cover with aluminum foil, and set aside.

3. Bring clams, wine, and butter to boil in covered 12-inch skillet over high heat. Steam until clams just open, 5 to 8 minutes, transferring them to pot with tomato broth as they open.

4. Once all clams have been transferred to pot, add mussels to skillet, cover, and cook over high heat until mussels have opened, 2 to 4 minutes, transferring them to pot with tomato broth as they open. Pour cooking liquid from skillet into pot, being careful not to pour any grit from skillet into pot. Return broth to simmer.

5. Stir parsley into broth and season with salt and pepper to taste. Divide halibut among serving bowls. Ladle broth over halibut, making sure each portion contains both clams and mussels. Drizzle with olive oil and serve immediately.

Roast Cornish Game Hens

Getting crispy skin on a roast bird that spends an hour in the oven is challenging enough.
What do you do with one that cooks in just 20 minutes?

⇒ BY ANDREW JANJIGIAN ⇐

Since they first appeared on American tables in the 1950s, Cornish game hens have typically been more of a special-occasion meal than a weeknight family dinner. But to me, these Lilliputian birds have attributes that make them appealing to serve any night of the week. For starters, they typically weigh about 1¼ to 1½ pounds, so they cook quickly—in less than 30 minutes. What's more, the exteriors of their smaller breasts aren't prone to dry out before the interiors cook through, a perennial hurdle when roasting regular chickens. The hens also boast a higher skin-to-meat ratio than regular chickens, which makes them both more forgiving and more flavorful. The skin shields the meat from the oven's heat, and its fatty underbelly bastes the meat throughout cooking, leaving not just the dark portions but the white meat juicy and rich in a way that the breast on a chicken rarely is. Finally, hens offer the benefit of elegant presentation: Everyone at the table gets an entire bird on his or her plate.

That's not to say that Cornish game hens don't come with challenges. In fact, their combination of small stature and abundant skin makes getting the exterior crispy and golden at the same time that the meat comes up to temperature even trickier than when working with a larger bird. Why? Because in order for the skin to brown and crisp, it must first render its fat and moisture, a process that takes more time than the meat beneath it takes to cook through. With a regular chicken, the bird spends the better part of an hour in the oven (so it's doable though still a challenge); with a Cornish game hen, you're working with less than half of that time, which barely gives the skin a chance to render, much less brown and crisp.

With that in mind, I set my sights on roasting moist, juicy Cornish game hens with the same beautifully browned, cracklingly crisp skin that I expect on larger birds.

To get the hens deeply brown and crispy, we remove their backbones, halve the hens so they lie flat, and finish them under the broiler.

▶ **Andrew Cooks the Birds**
Video available free for 4 months at CooksIllustrated.com/june14

Speeding the Way to Crispy Skin

The good news: When we developed our recipe for Crisp Roast Chicken (March/April 2008), we devised a few tricks that hasten the skin-crisping process and guarantee a bird with moist meat.

First, we attack the layer of fat under the skin before cooking, since fat can thwart crisping as much as moisture can. By loosening the skin and poking holes in the thickest pockets of fat, we essentially create channels through which the fat can drain.

Then we go after the skin's moisture: We rub the surface with a mixture of kosher salt and baking powder. Salt helps pull moisture to the skin's surface so that it can evaporate more quickly. And baking powder is slightly alkaline, which helps it break down the proteins in the skin to further promote crisping and browning. (For the hens, I also added a little vegetable oil to the salt before mixing in the powder, which helped the latter cling to the salt grains and, in turn, to the skin. For more information, see "Add Oil for an Evenly Distributed Rub" on page 30.) Finally, we air-dry the salt-rubbed chicken uncovered

in the fridge for a number of hours. It's a step that requires some forethought, but the results are worth it, as the naturally dry environment evaporates moisture from the skin.

Hot on the Trail

I applied this three-pronged pretreatment to four hens, air-drying them for 4 hours, and compared them with another batch of birds that went straight from the package to the oven. The cooking method for both (which I adapted from that same roast chicken recipe) was simple: Roast the hens, breast side down on a cooling rack set in a rimmed baking sheet, in a 450-degree oven for 10 minutes; flip them and roast them 10 minutes longer; and then crank the heat to 500 degrees for the final 5 to 10 minutes of cooking, until the white and dark meat hit 160 and 175 degrees, respectively.

To my disappointment, the skin on the pretreated poultry, while improved, was still far from ideal. Extending the air-drying time all the way to 24 hours (so that more moisture would evaporate) helped, but not enough, so I moved on to the cooking method. I thought that roasting the birds low and slow might give the skin time to render, at which point I could blast them under high heat to develop color. But when I dropped the heat to 300 degrees, not enough moisture evaporated from the skin and it didn't crisp. And at that rate the birds took an hour to cook.

Next I took it to the opposite extreme. I tried roasting the hens really high, at 500 degrees, the entire time—and when that still didn't even out the skin color, I tried pushing things even further. I left the birds in the oven past when the meat was up to temperature. My logic was that if there was all that extra fat and moisture, the meat might not suffer much if it was a little overcooked. That turned out to be true—to a point. The meat, including the breast, was still relatively juicy and tender at 180 degrees, but even then the skin was unimpressive. I continued to roast the hens until the skin was finally evenly browned, but by that point the meat was compromised.

What did get me closer was a blast under the broiler after the birds' initial 10-minute stint at 500 degrees. After about 5 minutes, their white and dark portions were up to temperature, the meat

Because the meat on Cornish game hens finishes cooking long before their skin crisps, we devised a few tricks to accelerate the skin's progress.

SPATCHCOCK
For each bird, cut through the bones on either side of the backbone; discard the backbone.

SPLIT
Cutting through the center of the breast makes two halves that lie flat for better browning.

SEPARATE AND POKE
Loosening and poking holes in the skin allows the fat to drain during cooking, aiding crisping.

SALT AND AIR-DRY
Rubbing the birds with salt and baking powder and then chilling them evaporates moisture.

SEAR Starting the birds skin side down on a preheated baking sheet effectively (and efficiently) crisps their skin.

---

was juicy, and the skin was almost evenly burnished. Well, almost. The problem, I realized, was the birds' rotund shape, which was keeping some of the surface at a greater distance from the heating element. A little knife work was in order.

Split Decision

Before pretreating my next batch, I removed the hens' backbones so that they could lie flat, giving their skin even exposure to the heating element. They looked really good now—golden from edge to edge. But the flattened birds spanned an entire dinner plate—not the elegant presentation I had in mind. Splitting them in half after removing the backbones made them more manageable to serve.

Admittedly, I had high standards for crackly-crisp skin, so as a last-ditch move I went for the extreme and seared a couple of the halves skin side down in a skillet before transferring the pan to a 500-degree oven to finish cooking. At last, the skin was gorgeously brown and crispy. Of course, cooking four hens, two halves at a time, in a skillet was impractical, so I switched to using a baking sheet preheated in the oven. I spritzed the skin of each bird with vegetable oil spray and sprinkled it with pepper. Then I placed all the halves skin side down on the hot sheet and slid it into the oven. When I flipped the halves 10 minutes later, the skin looked almost as good as that on the batch I'd seared in the skillet. Blasting the birds skin side up under the broiler for 5 minutes easily finished the job.

All that remained to consider was flavor. The overnight salt rub was seasoning the tops of the birds; rubbing a bit more kosher salt on their undersides evened it out. I also realized that I could dress up the salt rub by adding dried herbs and spices. After a few flavor experiments, I settled on combinations of cumin, coriander, and paprika; thyme, marjoram, and rosemary; and oregano, anise, and hot smoked paprika.

Now that I had a recipe for roasted poultry that guaranteed great meat and skin and, once pretreated, could be on the table in well under half an hour, Cornish game hens were looking more appealing than ever for any day of the week.

ROASTED CORNISH GAME HENS
SERVES 4

This recipe requires refrigerating the salted meat for at least 4 hours or up to 24 hours before cooking (a longer salting time is preferable). If your hens weigh 1½ to 2 pounds, cook three instead of four, and extend the initial cooking time in step 5 to 15 minutes. We prefer Bell & Evans Cornish Game Hens. For our free recipes for Cumin-Coriander Roasted Cornish Game Hens, Herb-Roasted Cornish Game Hens, Oregano-Anise Roasted Cornish Game Hens, and Roasted Cornish Game Hens for Two, go to CooksIllustrated.com/june14.

> 4 (1¼- to 1½-pound) Cornish game hens, giblets discarded
> Kosher salt and pepper
> ¼ teaspoon vegetable oil
> 1 teaspoon baking powder
> Vegetable oil spray

1. Using kitchen shears and working with 1 hen at a time, with hen breast side down, cut through bones on either side of backbone; discard backbone. Lay hens breast side up on counter. Using sharp chef's knife, cut through center of breast to make 2 halves.

2. Using your fingers, carefully separate skin from breasts and thighs. Using metal skewer or tip of paring knife, poke 10 to 15 holes in fat deposits on top of breasts and thighs. Tuck wingtips underneath hens. Pat hens dry with paper towels.

3. Sprinkle 1 tablespoon salt on underside (bone side) of hens. Combine 1 tablespoon salt and oil in small bowl and stir until salt is evenly coated with oil. Add baking powder and stir until well combined. Turn hens skin side up and rub salt–baking powder mixture evenly over surface. Arrange hens skin side up and in single layer on large platter or plates and refrigerate, uncovered, for at least 4 hours or up to 24 hours.

4. Adjust oven racks to upper-middle and lower positions, place rimmed baking sheet on lower rack, and heat oven to 500 degrees.

5. Once oven is fully heated, spray skin side of hens with oil spray and season with pepper. Carefully transfer hens, skin side down, to preheated sheet and cook for 10 minutes.

6. Remove hens from oven and heat broiler. Flip hens skin side up. Transfer sheet to upper rack and broil until well browned and breasts register 160 degrees and drumsticks/thighs register 175 degrees, about 5 minutes, rotating sheet as needed to promote even browning. Transfer to platter or individual plates and serve.

Not Just a Little Chicken

Cornish game hens are neither from Cornwall nor wild game, and they can be hens or roosters. They were reportedly first bred in the 1950s by a Connecticut couple, Jacques and Alphonsine Makowsky, who crossed breeds of domestic chickens with a Cornish gamecock and sold the hybrid when it was very young. As a result, Cornish game hens typically weigh less than 2 pounds, so they cook faster than larger chickens and look nice on a plate—traits that make them popular with consumers. They also feature small breasts and a high ratio of fatty skin to meat. The fatty underside bastes the meat as it cooks, which might explain why we found both their white and dark portions more tender, juicy, and flavorful than those on regular chickens.

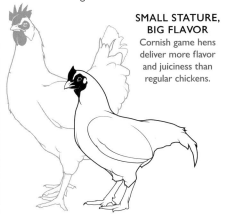

SMALL STATURE, BIG FLAVOR
Cornish game hens deliver more flavor and juiciness than regular chickens.

How to Grill a Great Steak

Knowing a few methods for pretreating steaks—and a universal grilling technique—will allow you to produce great results from a variety of cuts. BY SHANNON FRIEDMANN HATCH

SAVVY SHOPPING

Inspect the Meat
➤ Buy bright red or pink steaks with fine streaks (not clumps) of pure white intramuscular fat. Dark red/purple meat indicates an older, tougher animal.
➤ Juices should be in the meat, not in the package. The latter, known as purge, may be a sign of botched freezing, and the meat will cook up dry and cottony.

➤ **TIP:** To measure the thickness of a steak, hold it up to your index finger. The distance between the tip and your first knuckle is about 1 inch.
"Organic" Means Something; "Natural" Doesn't
➤ Organic is a government term that means the meat is antibiotic-free, has no added hormones, and that the animal ate an organic diet. Natural is simply advertising.

Grass-Fed May Not Be Worth the Money
➤ Grass-fed steaks can cost at least twice as much as the same grain-fed cuts, but when we tasted the two styles in strip and rib-eye steaks, we generally found the flavor differences between them to be negligible. Save your money for premium cuts.

PREMIUM STEAKS

STRIP STEAK
Alternative names: Top loin, shell, sirloin strip, Kansas City strip, New York strip
Tenderness: ★★★
Flavor: ★★★

RIB EYE
Alternative names: Spencer steak (West Coast), Delmonico steak (East Coast)
Tenderness: ★★★
Flavor: ★★★

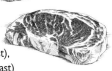

T-BONE
Tenderness: ★★★
Flavor: ★★★

Before Grilling: Season and Then Rest or Freeze

Inherently flavorful and tender, premium cuts need little more than salt and pepper. That said, applying either of these simple techniques will make a great steak even better.

When Time Allows: Salt and Rest
Given time, salt will travel into the meat, seasoning it deeply and altering its protein structure to make it even more tender. Prolonged salting will also dry out the meat's surface and encourage better browning.

Two hours before grilling, pat the steaks dry, season them with 1½ teaspoons of kosher salt per pound of meat (kosher salt is easier to distribute than table salt), and let them rest in the fridge.
➤ **TIP:** For milder heat, add pepper before cooking (the heat will temper its bite); for more punch, sprinkle it on the meat directly after grilling.

When Time Is Short: Rub and Freeze
To season and boost browning in a hurry, coat steaks with a mixture of cornstarch and salt and freeze them briefly. Both substances absorb surface moisture—crucial for achieving a substantial crust. Freezing the coated meat evaporates even more moisture.

For every pound of steak, combine 1½ teaspoons of kosher salt and ¾ teaspoon of cornstarch. Apply a thin coat of the rub all over the steaks' exteriors. Freeze the meat on a wire rack set in a rimmed baking sheet for 30 minutes.
➤ **TIP:** Don't let the steaks warm up before you cook them. Grilling them cold from the freezer lets the meat develop a deep crust before the interior overcooks.

EVERYDAY STEAKS

SKIRT STEAK
Alternative names: Fajita steak, Philadelphia steak
Tenderness: ★★
Flavor: ★★★

FLANK STEAK
Alternative name: Jiffy steak
Tenderness: ★
Flavor: ★★★

FLAP MEAT SIRLOIN STEAK
Alternative names: Sirloin tips, flap meat, steak tips
Tenderness: ★★
Flavor: ★★★

BONELESS SHELL SIRLOIN
Alternative names: Top butt, butt steak, top sirloin butt, top sirloin steak, center-cut roast
Tenderness: ★★
Flavor: ★★

Before Grilling: Marinate or Rub

Applied properly, a marinade or spice rub will boost flavor and tenderness in less expensive cuts.

FREE RECIPES
Better than A.1. Steak Marinade
New Mexican Chile Rub
CooksIllustrated.com/june14

Score Meat Before Marinating or Rubbing
Cutting crosshatch slits (1/16 inch deep) on both sides of the meat creates more surface area, which allows seasonings to penetrate faster and causes the meat to release sticky proteins that give marinades or rubs a strong foothold.

Mix Up an Effective Marinade
Both salt (or a salty liquid like soy sauce) and oil are critical to a marinade. Salt increases juiciness by pulling moisture from the marinade into the meat. Oil activates the fat-soluble flavor compounds in herbs and spices. A little sugar or honey boosts browning.

Prepare a soy-based marinade (such as our Better than A.1. Steak Marinade), reserving ¼ cup. Marinate scored steaks in a 1-gallon zipper-lock bag for 1 hour in the refrigerator, flipping them after 30 minutes. Discard the bag and the marinade, pat the steaks dry, and grill. Slice the grilled, rested steaks and toss the slices in the reserved marinade to further boost their flavor.

Apply a Salty Spice Rub
A rub made with toasted, coarsely ground whole spices delivers bolder flavor and a more substantial crust than a rub made from preground spices. To boost tenderness, mix kosher salt into the rub.

Briefly toast whole spices (such as cumin seeds, coriander seeds, and black peppercorns; use 2 to 3 tablespoons per pound of meat) in a dry skillet. Grind spices, add 1½ teaspoons of kosher salt per pound of meat, and press the rub onto dry, scored steaks. Refrigerate the steaks for 2 hours. Just before grilling, mist the steaks with vegetable oil spray to help the rub cling and encourage the spices' fat-soluble compounds to "bloom" on the grill.

BUILD A HALF-GRILL FIRE

Any steak can be grilled by creating a hotter side for quickly developing the crust and, if needed, a cooler side to finish cooking over gentle radiating heat.

Charcoal Setup

Open bottom vent completely. Light large chimney starter filled with charcoal briquettes (6 quarts). When top coals are partially covered with ash, pour evenly over half of grill. Set cooking grate in place, cover, and open lid vent completely. Heat grill until hot, about 5 minutes.

Gas Setup

Turn all burners to high, cover, and heat grill until hot, about 15 minutes. Leave primary burner on high and turn off other burner(s).

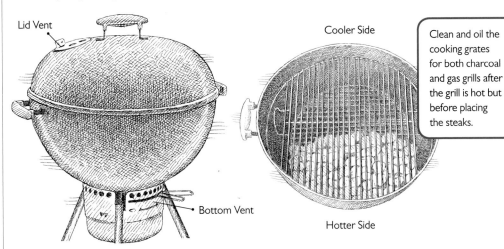

Lid Vent

Cooler Side

Clean and oil the cooking grates for both charcoal and gas grills after the grill is hot but before placing the steaks.

Bottom Vent

Hotter Side

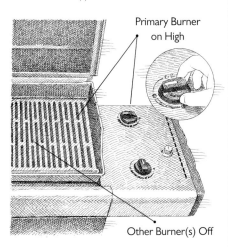

Primary Burner on High

Other Burner(s) Off

FOOLPROOF GRILLING METHOD

1. SEAR AND FLIP Grill steaks over hotter side, without moving them, for 2 to 4 minutes. Once first side is well browned, flip steaks and cook 2 to 4 minutes longer.
➤ **TIP:** The meat will release when it's time to cook the other side—wiggle it and if it resists, keep cooking.

2. TAKE TEMPERATURE Lift each steak off grill and insert thermometer through its side to check for desired doneness: rare (120 degrees), medium-rare (125 degrees), or medium (135 degrees).

3. TRANSFER IF NECESSARY Drag any unfinished steaks to cooler side of grill to finish cooking.
➤ **TIP:** Steaks less than 1 inch thick may cook to the desired temperature during the initial sear on the hotter side of the grill.

4. REST Muscle fibers in meat contract during cooking. To allow them to relax and some expelled juices to move back in, let steaks rest on wire rack set in rimmed baking sheet (to keep crust dry) loosely covered with aluminum foil for 10 minutes (5 minutes for steaks less than 1 inch thick).

5. SLICE Slicing thin and against grain shortens muscle fibers, making tougher cuts seem more tender. Using sharp chef's knife, slice tougher steaks (skirt, flank, sirloin steak tips, and boneless shell sirloin) against grain into thin pieces.

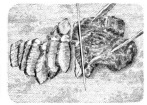

Toppings for Top Steaks

Premium steaks don't need much adornment. Try a sprinkle of flake sea salt (such as Maldon), the large crystals of which add a delicate crunch to the meat's crust. We also like the Tuscan tradition of finishing grilled T-bone or porterhouse steaks with a drizzle of high-quality extra-virgin olive oil and a squeeze of fresh lemon juice. Alternatively, you can add richness and more assertive flavor to any type of plain grilled steak by topping it with a compound butter.

SHALLOT-HERB BUTTER

MAKES ABOUT ½ CUP; ENOUGH FOR 3 POUNDS STEAK

The butter can be prepared up to 48 hours in advance. If the butter is cold, place it on the steaks after grilling; if the butter is at room temperature, place it on the steaks after they have rested.

4	tablespoons unsalted butter, softened
2	tablespoons minced shallot
2	tablespoons minced fresh parsley
1	garlic clove, minced
¼	teaspoon salt
¼	teaspoon pepper

Combine all ingredients in medium bowl. Divide butter evenly among steaks and serve.

Superior Steak Knives

Don't be tempted by serrated steak knives that promise to tackle tough meat. We've found that these blades actually make jagged tears, not smooth cuts. Our favorite steak knives, the six-piece Victorinox Rosewood Straight Edge Steak Knife Set ($109.99), feature 4¾-inch blades that are exceptionally sharp and nimble, not to mention comfortable (and handsome) wood handles.

BEST BLADES
Supersharp straight-edge steak knives from Victorinox slice through even tough cuts with ease.

Chinese Braised Beef

With tender chunks of beef in a potent, exotically fragrant sauce, red-cooked beef is Asian comfort food at its best. Problem is, there's little comfort in fussy recipes.

⇒ BY ANDREA GEARY ⇐

Every culture has its own version of slow-cooked, satisfying, warm-you-from-the-inside-out comfort food, and Chinese red-cooked beef is a prime example of the genre. While the dish shares some of the same homey appeal of American beef stew, the Chinese take is arguably more appealing. What you get: chunks of ultratender meat moistened in a modest amount of sauce that makes up for what it lacks in volume with its potent flavor. Red-cooked beef also differs from American stews in that it doesn't have add-ins like carrots or potatoes. Instead, the focus is exclusively on the beef and the sauce, which is redolent with flavorings like ginger, cinnamon, star anise, Sichuan peppercorns, and cardamom. The meal is typically rounded out with plenty of steamed vegetables and rice, which provide a neutral background for the intensity of the sauce.

I learned quickly not to get hung up on the name. "Red-cooked" (or *hong shao*) comes from the notion that a protein (beef, pork, poultry, or fish) simmered in a lightly sweetened broth of soy sauce and spices takes on a ruddy hue, but every version that I've seen has a deep, rich brown color.

There are two approaches to red cooking. The first calls for braising the food in plenty of liquid and saving that liquid to be used repeatedly for the same purpose, imparting deeper flavor with each use. As appealing as that sounded, it wasn't really practical. I centered my attention on the second approach, in which the meat is braised in liquid and then removed from the pot, after which the braising liquid is reduced to an intensely flavored, demi-glace-like consistency.

All the recipes in this style that I'd rounded up started out the same way: Cube a large cut of beef (shank is the most traditional), blanch the cubes in water (a step that's said to remove impurities), and then set them aside while you make the braising liquid. The most basic of these stocks called for simply

We streamline an already simple dish by adding five-spice powder instead of whole spices and using molasses instead of caramelizing sugar.

combining water with soy sauce, a bit of sugar, rice wine (or sherry), ginger, scallions, garlic, and one or two spices. But even when such stocks were reduced, I found that they didn't have the layers of flavor that are key to the dish. On the other hand, more-elaborate recipes that incorporated caramelized sugar, pungent fermented condiments such as chili bean paste, and lengthy lists of whole spices were beautifully nuanced. My challenge, then, would be maintaining the complex, aromatic flavor profile of this comfort food while making it as fuss-free as possible—no trips to an Asian market required.

The Meat of the Matter

To determine which cut of beef would be best, I blanched several braising cuts in boiling water (I'd revisit whether this step was really necessary later) and then simmered them in separate pots of water flavored with soy sauce, sugar, scallions, garlic, sherry, fresh ginger, and cinnamon sticks (likewise, I'd figure out the full spectrum of spices that I'd want to use when I was farther along). The shank

worked beautifully. It was amazingly tender and moist, and it imparted a silky fullness to the sauce. But since shank can be hard to find in American supermarkets, I set it as the benchmark to be matched and made my way through a list of alternatives.

Brisket was tender but dry. Chuck roast and blade steak were tender and rich but required a lot of trimming before going into the pot. In the end, I opted for boneless short ribs, which had enough fat and collagen to cook up moist but required minimal prep before I put them in the pot. True, short ribs didn't produce a sauce with the richness of that made with shank, but I would address that later. On the upside, short ribs cooked in about half the time of shank. After bringing the pot to a simmer, I moved the bulk of the cooking to the oven, where the meat could simmer without constant monitoring. I left the meat in large pieces to make it easier to remove from the pot when it came time to strain out the aromatics and reduce my sauce, and I simply used a pair of forks to pull apart the tender meat into bite-size chunks before I added them to the reduced sauce.

About that blanching step: Briefly cooking the meat in boiling water removes free proteins from the surface, which produces a clearer stock—but since I was reducing the stock to a concentrated, opaque sauce, I realized that this probably wasn't important. One test confirmed that blanching not only made no difference in the appearance of my red-cooked beef but didn't affect its flavor or texture either, so I happily eliminated that step.

And what about browning? In the West we are very influenced by French cooking, which often means browning meat to deepen its flavor. However, I decided that this wasn't necessary here. While browning could provide a moderate boost to the meatiness of the dish, short ribs are plenty beefy, and in the case of red cooking, the complex, potently flavored sauce would—or should—overshadow it. Which brought me to my next task: Improving the rather one-dimensional flavor of the sauce.

Sugar and Spice

To balance the saltiness of the soy sauce and impart a subtle sweetness, thus far I had been using white sugar. Brown sugar added a little more depth, but

I was still intrigued by recipes that incorporated caramelized sugar. For my next batch, I cooked ¼ cup of sugar with a bit of water until it turned dark brown; then I added the other ingredients to the pot. Its slight bitterness contributed interesting new flavor notes. Could I get the same effect without the extra step? When I tried substituting 2 tablespoons of molasses straight out of the jar for the sugar, I was pleased to find that it provided a similarly bittersweet flavor. Some thick hoisin sauce introduced complementary sweetness and flavor and a bit of body, too.

Now for the spices. Though tasters had loved the versions I had made that called for a slew of whole spices, were the spices really necessary? Some recipes required just one spice—preground five-spice powder. It was here that I suffered a crisis of conscience. I had ditched the blanching step and opted for molasses over caramelized sugar (with, it must be said, no detrimental effect in either case), but surely substituting a ground mixture of spices was going a step too far.

Not at all. In fact, I found that with just 1½ teaspoons of five-spice powder, the flavors in the braise really came together, shifting from a subtle infusion to a more developed and powerful punch. A bit of heat was the only thing missing, so I added 1 teaspoon of red pepper flakes.

Now the sauce had all the deep, nuanced flavor that I was after, but the consistency was wrong. Because you know what you get when you boil down a water-based stock? Very flavorful water.

The Stock Thickens

I wanted a sauce that would cling to the meat and accompanying rice rather than flow to the bottom of the bowl, and this wasn't it. I tried flour—the most common thickener in recipes for Western-style beef stews—but it produced a gravy rather than the lacquer-like glaze I wanted. Cornstarch wasn't quite right here either: It gave the sauce that slick texture often found in a stir-fry sauce, and it seemed a bit lightweight for this application. What I really wanted was that rich glazelike texture I had gotten when I had braised the beef shanks for 5 hours. When I considered that it was the meat's collagen that really made that version such a success, the answer was obvious: Add gelatin, since collagen converts to gelatin during cooking.

I admit that I went a bit overboard at first: 2 tablespoons of gelatin gave the sauce a tacky consistency. Backing down to 1½ tablespoons, added at the beginning of cooking, and introducing a mere teaspoon of cornstarch at the end produced a sauce that coated the meat nicely without forming a gel.

With its tender meat and satisfying heartiness, this version of red-cooked beef had all the appeal of an American-style stew, but the warmth of the sweet spices and the deep savory flavor made it a welcome change from my usual cool-weather offerings. Best of all, with fussy steps like blanching meat and caramelizing sugar eliminated, this dish had come together with an ease that made it comfort food in every sense.

CHINESE BRAISED BEEF
SERVES 6

With its generous amount of soy sauce, this dish is meant to taste salty, which is why we pair it with plain white rice. For our free recipe for Basic White Rice, go to CooksIllustrated.com/june14. A simple steamed vegetable like bok choy or broccoli completes the meal. Boneless beef short ribs require little trimming, but you can also use a 4-pound chuck roast. Trim the roast of large pieces of fat and sinew, cut it across the grain into 1-inch-thick slabs, and cut the slabs into 4 by 2-inch pieces.

1½ tablespoons unflavored gelatin
2½ cups plus 1 tablespoon water
½ cup dry sherry
⅓ cup soy sauce
2 tablespoons hoisin sauce
2 tablespoons molasses
3 scallions, white and green parts separated, green parts sliced thin on bias
1 (2-inch) piece ginger, peeled, halved lengthwise, and crushed
4 garlic cloves, peeled and smashed
1½ teaspoons five-spice powder
1 teaspoon red pepper flakes
3 pounds boneless beef short ribs, trimmed and cut into 4-inch lengths
1 teaspoon cornstarch

1. Sprinkle gelatin over 2½ cups water in Dutch oven and let sit until gelatin softens, about 5 minutes. Adjust oven rack to middle position and heat oven to 300 degrees.

2. Heat softened gelatin over medium-high heat, stirring occasionally, until melted, 2 to 3 minutes. Stir in sherry, soy sauce, hoisin, molasses, scallion whites, ginger, garlic, five-spice powder, and pepper flakes. Stir in beef and bring to simmer. Remove pot from heat. Cover tightly with sheet of heavy-duty aluminum foil, then lid. Transfer to oven and cook until beef is tender, 2 to 2½ hours, stirring halfway through cooking.

3. Using slotted spoon, transfer beef to cutting board. Strain sauce through fine-mesh strainer into

fat separator. Wipe out pot with paper towels. Let liquid settle for 5 minutes, then return defatted liquid to now-empty pot. Cook liquid over medium-high heat, stirring occasionally, until thickened and reduced to 1 cup, 20 to 25 minutes.

4. While sauce reduces, using 2 forks, break beef into 1½-inch pieces. Whisk cornstarch and remaining 1 tablespoon water together in small bowl.

5. Reduce heat to medium-low, whisk cornstarch mixture into reduced sauce, and cook until sauce is slightly thickened, about 1 minute. Return beef to sauce and stir to coat. Cover and cook, stirring occasionally, until beef is heated through, about 5 minutes. Sprinkle scallion greens over top. Serve.

Beef Shank—Even Better than Short Ribs

Shank is a cut from the lower leg of the steer. Though it is very sinewy, it is actually quite lean. In the United States, it's often used to make low-fat ground beef. This is a shame because with braising, it becomes meltingly tender, and its liquefied connective tissue imparts a silky richness to a sauce that requires little, if any, defatting. If you can find shank and have an extra hour or two, it's the best and most economical choice for red-cooked beef. You'll find shank sold as both long cut and cross cut (with or without the bone). If using cross cut, decrease the gelatin to 2¼ teaspoons and increase the cooking time in step 2 to 4 hours. If using long cut, cut it crossways into 1-inch-thick slabs, omit the gelatin, and increase the cooking time in step 2 to 5 hours.

LONG-CUT SHANK
Lots of connective tissue; cooks in 5 hours.

CROSS-CUT SHANK
Less connective tissue; cooks in 4 hours.

Great Carrot-Ginger Soup

For a soup that tastes like its namesakes, use two forms of carrot and two forms of ginger.

> BY SARAH MULLINS <

The coupling of sweet carrots and pungent ginger has the potential to produce an elegant, flavorful soup. It's troubling, then, that I've been unable to truly taste either ingredient in most of the versions I've tried. That's due primarily to the hapless addition of other vegetables, fruits, or dairy—all of which mask the starring flavors. Another irritating problem is a grainy consistency; I like my pureed soups to be perfectly smooth and creamy. Could I bring this soup to its full potential, producing a version with a smooth, silken texture and pure, clean flavors?

I started by making a bare-bones soup, sweating minced onion and garlic in butter and then adding peeled, sliced carrots, fresh grated ginger, and vegetable broth. I simmered the mixture until the carrots were tender and then gave it a whirl in the blender. Unfortunately, the carrot flavor seemed muddled. And while the soup had a fiery kick, it had not even a hint of the fresh, bright flavor associated with ginger. What's more, even though they'd been cooking for 20 minutes and seemed sufficiently tender, the carrots hadn't completely broken down, so the soup was riddled with fibrous bits. Not a promising start.

First up for repair: flavor. For unadulterated carrot flavor, it made sense to ditch the broth in favor of plain water, which I augmented with a couple of complementary sprigs of fresh thyme. This was a vast improvement, eliminating the blurred vegetable background of my first batch. Next, trying for an even more concentrated, caramelized taste, I whipped up two more soups—one with roasted carrots and another with slices sautéed in butter until caramelized. Unfortunately, neither method added quite the right flavor. Roasting brought an undesirable earthiness and sautéing yielded a soup that tasted like sweet potatoes.

But these tests made me realize that what was really missing in my soup was ultrafresh carrot flavor. That in turn made the solution seem obvious: Just use raw carrots—in the form of carrot juice. After a few tries, I settled on swapping ¾ cup of carrot juice for some of the water and stirring in another ¾ cup (along with a tablespoon of cider vinegar for sweet tang) right before serving. Between the earthy, sweet cooked carrots and the bright, raw carrot juice, this was a well-balanced soup.

⊙ Look: It's Velvety
Video available free for 4 months
at CooksIllustrated.com/june14

Sour cream, chives, and croutons increase the complexity of this simply made soup.

On to the ginger. My soup had the peppery heat associated with the root but almost none of its vibrant fruitiness. I rounded up the different forms of ginger—fresh juice, fresh grated, ground, and crystallized—and started sampling. Ginger juice offered plenty of heat but little flavor. Ground ginger simply tasted bitter. A combo of fresh and crystallized ginger was the best of the bunch, with the former supplying spiciness and the latter delivering the almost citrusy freshness that ginger is prized for.

I sautéed 1 tablespoon of finely grated fresh ginger and ¼ cup of minced crystallized ginger (plus 1 teaspoon of sugar to counter their spiciness) with the other aromatics and then continued with my recipe. In the finished soup, the duo struck an ideal balance of flavor and heat.

For the silkiest possible consistency, I tried cooking the carrots longer, until they were mushy and breaking apart. After I pureed it, the soup was better but still not smooth enough. I wanted to avoid straining, so it only made sense to turn to one of the test kitchen's secret weapons: baking soda. We have used it on numerous occasions to break down the cell walls of a vegetable as it cooks in water. Sure enough, with just ½ teaspoon of baking soda and 20 minutes of simmering, the soup was smoother than any I'd ever had. In fact, it was downright velvety—all without the need for lengthy cooking or fussy straining.

As finishing touches, a sprinkle of fresh chives and a swirl of sour cream provided subtle onion flavor and mild tang. A few crispy, buttery croutons for textural contrast and my retooled classic was complete.

CARROT-GINGER SOUP
SERVES 6

In addition to sour cream and chives, serve the soup with Buttery Croutons (recipe follows).

- 2   tablespoons unsalted butter
- 2   onions, chopped fine
- ¼   cup minced crystallized ginger
- 1   tablespoon grated fresh ginger
- 2   garlic cloves, peeled and smashed
-      Salt and pepper
- 1   teaspoon sugar
- 2   pounds carrots, peeled and sliced ¼ inch thick
- 4   cups water
- 1½   cups carrot juice
- 2   sprigs fresh thyme
- ½   teaspoon baking soda
- 1   tablespoon cider vinegar
-      Chopped chives
-      Sour cream

1. Melt butter in large saucepan over medium heat. Add onions, crystallized ginger, fresh ginger, garlic, 2 teaspoons salt, and sugar; cook, stirring frequently, until onions are softened but not browned, 5 to 7 minutes.

2. Increase heat to high; add carrots, water, ¾ cup carrot juice, thyme sprigs, and baking soda and bring to simmer. Reduce heat to medium-low and simmer, covered, until carrots are very tender, 20 to 25 minutes.

3. Discard thyme sprigs. Working in batches, process soup in blender until smooth, 1 to 2 minutes. Return soup to clean pot and stir in vinegar and remaining ¾ cup carrot juice. (Soup can be refrigerated for up to 4 days.) Return to simmer over medium heat and season with salt and pepper to taste. Serve with sprinkle of chives and dollop of sour cream.

BUTTERY CROUTONS
MAKES ABOUT 2 CUPS

- 3   tablespoons unsalted butter
- 1   tablespoon olive oil
- 3   large slices hearty white sandwich bread, cut into ½-inch cubes
-      Salt

Heat butter and oil in 12-inch skillet over medium heat. When foaming subsides, add bread cubes and cook, stirring frequently, until golden brown, about 10 minutes. Transfer croutons to paper towel–lined plate and season with salt to taste.

Perfecting Rice and Pasta Pilaf

How do you get rice and pasta to cook up fluffy and tender in one pot? With a good soak.

> BY ANDREW JANJIGIAN

For some, rice and pasta pilaf conjures up images of streetcars ascending steep hills to the tune of that familiar TV jingle. But for me, it's not the "San Francisco Treat" that comes to mind but Sunday dinners at my Armenian grandmother's. As it turns out, the two memories are not so disparate: Rice-A-Roni owes its existence to a fateful meeting in 1940s San Francisco. Lois DeDomenico, daughter of Italian immigrants, learned to make rice and pasta pilaf from her Armenian landlady, Pailadzo Captanian. The dish became a staple of the DeDomenico household and would eventually inspire Lois's husband, Tom, whose family owned a pasta factory, to develop a commercial version. They named the product after its two main ingredients—rice and macaroni (pasta)—and the rest is history.

The original dish is a simple affair: A fistful of pasta (usually vermicelli) is broken into short pieces and toasted in butter. Finely chopped onion and/or minced garlic is added next, followed by basmati rice. Once the grains are coated in fat, chicken broth is poured in. After simmering, the pilaf is often allowed to sit covered with a dish towel under the lid to absorb steam—a trick that yields superfluffy results. In a well-executed version, the rice and pasta are tender and separate, boasting rich depth from the butter and nuttiness from the toasted noodles.

Sadly, I never learned my grandmother's recipe, and the cookbook versions I tried fell short. Some featured mushy, overcooked vermicelli; in others, the rice was the problem, either sticking together in a mass or cooking up firm. Using both garlic and onion (shredded on a box grater so that it would add flavor but not a distracting texture), I patched together a recipe and mostly resolved the under- or overcooked rice problem simply by nailing the appropriate amount of liquid: 2½ cups to 1½ cups rice and ½ cup pasta.

But even with this ratio, my pilaf was plagued by a thin layer of somewhat raw, crunchy rice just beneath the pasta, which always floated to the top of the pot during simmering. What's more, the pasta was too soft and mushy. The quicker-cooking vermicelli seemed to absorb broth more rapidly than the rice, thereby denying the rice that surrounded it sufficient liquid to cook through. My theory was confirmed when I reduced the water by ¼ cup and deliberately left the pasta out of a batch: The rice cooked up tender as could be.

Adding more broth would make the dish soggy. Stirring during cooking helped, but it wasn't a reliable fix: Plenty of grains still emerged underdone.

I needed every last grain of rice to absorb the broth at the same rate as the pasta did. I considered removing the toasted vermicelli from the pot, starting the rice, and then adding back the pasta when the rice was nearly tender, but that seemed unwieldy. Then I came up with a more viable solution: soaking. Starches absorb water at relatively low temperatures, so I guessed that I could hydrate, or sort of parcook, the rice in hot tap water ahead of time. Sure enough, when I saturated the grains in hot water for 15 minutes before continuing with the recipe, the finished rice and pasta both had an ideal tender texture.

With my foolproof approach at hand, I developed a classic herbed variation as well as versions incorporating spices, sweet ingredients, and nuts. I now had a nutty, buttery, perfectly cooked side dish that brought me right back to my grandmother's kitchen.

RICE AND PASTA PILAF
SERVES 4 TO 6 AS A SIDE DISH

For our free recipe for Rice and Pasta Pilaf with Crispy Shallots and Pistachios, go to CooksIllustrated.com/june14. Use long, straight vermicelli or vermicelli nests.

1½	cups basmati or other long-grain white rice
3	tablespoons unsalted butter
2	ounces vermicelli, broken into 1-inch pieces
1	onion, grated
1	garlic clove, minced
2½	cups chicken broth
1¼	teaspoons salt
3	tablespoons minced fresh parsley

1. Place rice in medium bowl and cover with hot tap water by 2 inches; let stand for 15 minutes.

2. Using your hands, gently swish grains to release excess starch. Carefully pour off water, leaving rice in bowl. Add cold tap water to rice and pour off water. Repeat adding and pouring off cold water 4 to 5 times, until water runs almost clear. Drain rice in fine-mesh strainer.

3. Melt butter in saucepan over medium heat. Add pasta and cook, stirring occasionally, until browned, about 3 minutes. Add onion and garlic and cook, stirring occasionally, until onion is softened but not browned, about 4 minutes. Add rice and cook, stirring occasionally, until edges of rice begin to turn translucent, about 3 minutes. Add broth and salt and bring to boil. Reduce heat to low, cover, and cook until all liquid is absorbed, about 10 minutes. Off heat, remove lid, fold dish towel in half, and place over pan; replace lid. Let stand for 10 minutes. Fluff rice with fork, stir in parsley, and serve.

A simple technique allows both the pasta and the rice to cook up perfectly tender.

HERBED RICE AND PASTA PILAF

Stir ¼ cup plain whole-milk yogurt, ¼ cup minced fresh dill, and ¼ cup minced fresh chives into pilaf with parsley.

RICE AND PASTA PILAF WITH GOLDEN RAISINS AND ALMONDS

Place ½ cup golden raisins in bowl and cover with boiling water. Let stand until plump, about 5 minutes. Drain and set aside. Stir 2 bay leaves and 1 teaspoon ground cardamom into rice with chicken broth. Discard bay leaves and stir raisins and ½ cup slivered almonds, toasted and chopped coarse, into rice with parsley.

RICE AND PASTA PILAF WITH POMEGRANATE AND WALNUTS

Omit onion and garlic. Add 2 tablespoons grated fresh ginger to pan with rice. Stir ½ teaspoon ground cumin into rice with chicken broth. Omit parsley and stir ½ cup walnuts, toasted and chopped coarse; ½ cup pomegranate seeds; ½ cup chopped fresh cilantro; and 1 tablespoon lemon juice into fluffed rice.

▶ See Real Rice-A-Roni
Video available free for 4 months at CooksIllustrated.com/june14

The Best Way to Cook Artichokes

The most common way to cook artichokes—in a pot of boiling water—is also the worst. We wanted to add flavor, not wash it away.

> BY ADAM RIED <

There's a reason that steaming became a classic way to cook an artichoke: Because the vegetable goes into the pot whole, there's almost no prep work involved, which keeps the method dead simple. But steaming has its faults, too—mainly that cooking an artichoke in water washes out the vegetable's delicate nuttiness rather than accentuating it. Plus, some diners are as daunted by an untrimmed artichoke's pointy leaves and fuzzy interior choke (which has to be removed to get to the best part, the heart) as they are by manhandling a lobster at the table.

A dry heat method like roasting seemed like a much better approach. There's a bit more knife work to do upfront—roasted artichokes are typically well trimmed and halved from the start—but the payoff is worth it. The method allows you to remove the choke so those at the table don't have to. What's more, halving the artichokes and cooking them cut side down on a hot sheet pan concentrates their nutty richness and encourages caramelization and the flavorful Maillard browning reaction. Ideally, the method delivers an almost entirely edible product: a rich, velvety stem and heart surrounded by fully tender inner leaves and partially softened outer leaves that are chewy at the top but contain a patch of creamy meat at their base—the part you typically scrape off with your teeth.

But that's not always what you get. Artichokes dry and toughen easily in the oven, meaning that they can't be simply tossed onto a hot baking sheet and blasted until they're brown. To come up with a roasting method that produced artichokes that tasted nutty and rich and also boasted fully tender hearts and stems, as well as outer leaves that were at least nicely softened, would take some tinkering.

Trimming and Bathing

Members of the thistle family, artichokes look like—and technically are—flower buds that range

▶ **Watch It Step by Step**
Video available free for 4 months at CooksIllustrated.com/june14

Our hybrid steam-and-roast method yields artichokes that are tender, deeply flavorful, and nicely browned.

considerably in size. I decided to stick with widely available medium (8- to 10-ounce) specimens. Larger and smaller artichokes present challenges: The former can be tough and fibrous, while the latter make for more prep work.

Before I started in on my roasting method, I gave myself a refresher course on the knife work involved, including trimming away the woody exterior of the stem, splitting the bulb down the middle, and scooping out the choke (for detailed directions, see "Preparing Artichokes for Roasting").

There was one other precooking step to consider: whether to submerge the halved artichokes in lemon water to prevent them from discoloring. Many artichoke recipes call for this pretreatment, since the acid (vinegar is also common but I prefer lemon for its cleaner flavor) neutralizes the enzyme that causes the cut surfaces of artichokes to quickly discolor when exposed to oxygen. It occurred to me that this cosmetic fix might be unnecessary since the artichokes would be browning in the oven, but a quick test convinced me it was worth doing.

When artichokes oxidize, they develop drab gray-brown patches that are unlike (and not camouflaged by) the deep, rich brown color produced by caramelization and the Maillard reaction. Besides, preparing a water bath is a simple thing to do, so I plunged four halved artichokes (enough for four people) into a bowl of lemon water and moved on to the oven.

Going Under Cover

Artichokes are prone to dry out not because they have significantly less moisture than other good roasting vegetables like carrots and broccoli but because their leaves open and separate as they cook, exposing much more surface area and allowing their moisture to evaporate quickly. They're also fibrous, which makes them challenging to roast because there's only a short window between the time the texture of the inner leaves goes from softly chewy to leathery. Knowing that, I fished the halved artichokes out of the water bath, shook off a bit of the excess water, and proceeded to toss them with a couple of tablespoons of extra-virgin olive oil (plus a little salt and pepper) as we always do when roasting vegetables—making sure to work the oil deep into the leaves to keep them lubricated.

Those factors also compelled me to skip uncovered roasting tests, during which the artichokes would dry out, and start with a hybrid steaming-roasting technique that we've applied to other roasted vegetables. I arranged the halves cut side down on a rimmed baking sheet and then crimped aluminum foil over the tray, creating a steam chamber out of the moisture escaping from the artichokes that I hoped would soften even the more-fibrous outer leaves and also preserve more of their flavor since they'd be steaming in their own "juice." I let the artichokes steam for about 15 minutes in a 500-degree oven, at which point I pulled back the foil cover and let them roast for another 10 to 15 minutes so that the moisture would burn off, allowing the artichokes to develop deeper color and flavor.

It had been an OK start: Though the artichokes' inner leaves, stems, and hearts were just about tender, the meat on some of the outer leaves was still rather dry and chewy. Also, in some spots the cut sides in contact with the pan were verging on burnt.

A bit of knife work before roasting will lead to more concentrated flavor—and eliminate the messy scooping work at the table.

   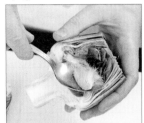 

TRIM TOP AND BOTTOM
Using sharp chef's knife, cut away most of stem, leaving about ¾ inch attached. Cut off top quarter of leaves.

SNAP OFF OUTER LEAVES
Pull tough outer leaves downward and break off at base. Repeat with leaves in first 3 or 4 rows from base.

TIDY UP STEM
Use paring knife to trim away tough outer layer of stem and base, removing dark green parts.

SPLIT AND SCOOP
Halve artichoke lengthwise with chef's knife. Using spoon, scoop out fuzzy choke.

REMOVE LEAVES AROUND CHOKE
Pull out tiny purple-tinged leaves around choke, leaving small cavity.

I had a few tweaks in mind that I thought might help: lowering the oven temperature to 475 degrees and switching from a rimmed baking sheet to a 3-quart baking dish, the taller sides of which would trap more moisture. Those quick fixes took care of the overbrowning issue (brushing oil inside the baking dish helped, too)—but not the texture of the flesh on the outer leaves. I tried doubling the layer of foil (in case steam was escaping) and adding a layer of parchment paper between the foil and the artichokes to concentrate the steam, but with little effect.

Foiling Dryness

Clearly, the artichokes needed to retain more moisture, but I hesitated to leave the foil on the whole time—surely that would just steam them and prevent any browning. But I was fresh out of other ideas and figured that I had nothing to lose by trying.

This go-round, I left the foil on the baking dish for the full 25 minutes. The artichokes' color wasn't as burnished as it had been, but I actually didn't mind the slight cosmetic compromise given the artichokes' considerably better texture. Now, the inner leaves, stems, and hearts were fully tender, while the outer layers were a notch shy of softly chewy. Also good news: After steaming in their own trapped moisture, the artichokes had a noticeably more concentrated and nutty flavor.

My tasters gobbled up these rich-tasting, tender pieces so quickly that I wondered if I even needed to whip up a dipping sauce. But I had an idea that made use of my cooking technique: a roasted lemon vinaigrette, which I prepared by simply tossing a pair of lemon halves in the baking dish along with the artichokes and then whisking their juicy pulp with finely grated garlic, Dijon mustard, extra-virgin olive oil, and a couple of tablespoons of parsley. The punchy but not sharp dressing was a natural pairing with the artichokes, as was the more classic artichoke condiment I threw together: a garlicky butter sauce.

I suppose steamed artichokes will never go out of style, but now that I had a roasting technique that produced results that are more flavorful—and almost entirely edible—I can't imagine ever going back.

ROASTED ARTICHOKES
SERVES 4

If your artichokes are larger than 8 to 10 ounces, strip away another layer or two of the toughest outer leaves. Use your teeth to scrape the flesh from the cooked tough outer leaves. The inner tender leaves, heart, and stem are entirely edible. Serve the artichokes plain with a squeeze of lemon or pair them with Aïoli or Garlic Butter Sauce. For these free recipes as well as our free recipe for Roasted Artichokes for Two, go to CooksIllustrated.com/june14.

1 lemon, plus lemon wedges for serving
4 artichokes (8 to 10 ounces each)
3 tablespoons extra-virgin olive oil
Salt and pepper

1. Adjust oven rack to lower-middle position and heat oven to 475 degrees. Cut lemon in half, squeeze halves into 2 quarts water, and drop in spent halves.

2. Cut off most of stem of 1 artichoke, leaving about ¾ inch attached. Cut off top quarter. Pull tough outer leaves downward toward stem and break off at base; continue until first three or four rows of leaves have been removed. Using paring knife, trim outer layer of stem and rough areas around base, removing any dark green parts. Cut artichoke in half lengthwise. Using spoon, remove fuzzy choke. Pull out inner, tiny purple-tinged leaves, leaving small cavity in center of each half. Drop prepped halves into lemon water. Repeat with remaining artichokes.

3. Brush 13 by 9-inch baking dish with 1 tablespoon oil. Remove artichokes from lemon water, shaking off some excess lemon water (some should be left clinging to leaves). Toss artichokes with remaining 2 tablespoons oil and ¾ teaspoon salt and season with pepper to taste, gently working some oil and seasonings between leaves. Arrange artichoke halves cut side down in baking dish and cover tightly with aluminum foil.

4. Roast until cut sides of artichokes start to brown and both bases and leaves are tender when poked with tip of paring knife, 25 to 30 minutes.

Transfer artichokes to serving dish. Serve artichokes warm or at room temperature, passing lemon wedges separately.

ROASTED ARTICHOKES WITH LEMON VINAIGRETTE

Cut very thin slices off both ends of 2 lemons and cut lemons in half crosswise. Place lemon halves, flesh side up, in baking dish with artichokes before covering with foil in step 3. Roast artichokes as directed. Once roasted lemon halves are cool enough to handle, squeeze into fine-mesh strainer set over bowl. Press on solids to extract all pulp; discard solids. Measure 1½ tablespoons strained lemon pulp into small bowl. Whisk in ½ teaspoon finely grated garlic, ½ teaspoon Dijon mustard, and ½ teaspoon salt and season with pepper to taste. Whisking constantly, gradually drizzle 6 tablespoons extra-virgin olive oil into lemon mixture. Whisk in 2 tablespoons minced fresh parsley. Serve with artichokes.

Assessing Artichokes

When selecting fresh artichokes at the market, examine the leaves for some clues that will help you pick the best specimens. The leaves should look tight, compact, and bright green; they should not appear dried out or feathery at the edges. If you give an artichoke a squeeze, its leaves should squeak as they rub together (evidence that the artichoke still possesses much of its moisture). And while we don't advocate abusing the produce in the store, the leaves should also snap off cleanly; if they bend, the artichoke is old. –A.R.

PASS ON THIS

Fresh Strawberry Mousse

Here's a juicy problem: how to get a creamy mousse with bright, concentrated fruit flavor out of bland, watery supermarket strawberries.

> BY SARAH MULLINS <

When it comes to mousse desserts, recipes for the chocolate kind—or even citrus versions—abound. But it's not often that you see recipes for mousses that feature strawberries—which, in my opinion, is a sad omission. The berry's bright, sweet flavor is a natural fit in other creamy desserts and would surely make a light and refreshing variation. Plus, mousse is great for warm-weather entertaining: It doesn't require turning on the oven, it looks elegant once it's portioned into bowls and dressed up with a simple garnish, and it's entirely make-ahead.

With a little digging, I managed to find a few recipes for strawberry mousse. Most followed the same simple steps: Puree fresh berries, strain the mixture, add sugar and a stabilizer (most often gelatin), and then fold the puree into whipped cream and allow it to set in the refrigerator. But once I tried these recipes, I realized why this type of mousse isn't more common: Not one of the resulting mousses tasted much like strawberries. The reason wasn't hard to determine. Even in season, the average supermarket strawberry is watery and just doesn't have a lot of flavor. Cooking the berries to drive off some of their moisture and concentrate flavor, as a few recipes suggest, wasn't the answer. While these mousses had more discernible strawberry flavor, they also tasted cooked and jamlike, with none of the fresh taste of a berry eaten out of hand. Meanwhile, those recipes that didn't call for cooking down the fruit also suffered textural problems: The large amount of juice given up by the berries made these desserts loose and runny.

A strawberry mousse that lived up to the name would need to have a lush yet light texture and the sweet flavor of the best fresh summer berries.

Filling Up on Fruit

My strategy would be to get the flavor of the mousse tasting genuinely like fresh strawberries and then figure out how to deal with what would

▶ Sarah Makes the Mousse
Video available free for 4 months at CooksIllustrated.com/june14

Diced fresh strawberries add another punch of bright fruit flavor (and color) to this creamy mousse.

inevitably be an overly wet, soft texture.

Because this was strawberry season, I indulged myself with one quick test, splurging on the best farmers' market berries I could find. This batch did taste brighter and sweeter, but it was a predictably impractical solution. Besides the high price and limited availability of the fruit, the texture of the dessert was a disaster. Thanks to these superjuicy berries, the dessert was more akin to melted ice cream than mousse.

I went back to supermarket berries, figuring I'd ramp up the amount of puree until I had something that tasted sufficiently fruity. I started by softening 1¾ teaspoons of gelatin in a few tablespoons of water. Then I pulsed 2 pounds of strawberries—nearly twice the amount called for in most recipes—to create about 2 cups of puree. I strained out the seeds and added the softened gelatin and ½ cup of sugar. I folded the fruit mixture into 1 cup of heavy cream

It's OK to Eat a Few

Supermarket strawberries are often sold in containers labeled "1 pound," but we discovered that a package can weigh up to 4 ounces more than that. For accuracy when cooking, weigh the berries first and save the extras for snacking.

that I'd whipped to stiff peaks, portioned it into serving bowls, and let the mousse chill for about 4 hours to set up.

Frustratingly, this puree-heavy mousse wanted for still more concentrated fruit flavor. And the texture was worse than I thought—so loose that it practically dribbled off the spoon.

Breaking the Mold

Putting the flavor issue on hold, I reviewed my options for tightening up the texture. My recipe already contained gelatin, which acts as a stabilizer by forming a gel network that traps liquid. Adding more only made the mousse go from soupy to so overly set that it jiggled like Jell-O. I tried other common mousse stabilizers: pectin, whipped egg whites, and even white chocolate.

Pectin was a quick strikeout. It acts like gelatin when exposed to heat, its molecules linking up and forming a water-trapping matrix, and it made the mousse springy. Also a fail were whipped egg whites, as we disliked their eggy flavor and foamy texture. Melted white chocolate made the mousse taste chalky, and its rich flavor overpowered the delicate taste of the strawberries.

What if I replaced some of the whipped cream with another dairy product that contributed thicker body? Sour cream, mascarpone, and cream cheese came to mind, and after another round of tests, I settled on the latter. The soft but dense cream cheese (I swapped in 4 ounces for ½ cup of heavy cream) was a big step in the right direction. It firmed up the mousse's texture and didn't mask strawberry flavor.

Reduction Deduction

And yet the mousse was still softer than I liked. It also lacked depth—an important part of great strawberry flavor. Cooking the berries would only destroy that brightness, but there was an approach that could allow me to keep the fresh berry taste while still concentrating its flavor: macerating the berries and then reducing their shed liquid to a fixed amount. This would also allow me to limit the amount of juice going into the mousse without wasting it.

Getting the Most out of Supermarket Strawberries

Supermarket strawberries rarely deliver the bright flavor and concentrated sweetness that you find in farmers' market specimens. By macerating the finely chopped berries and then using both fresh and cooked forms of the fruit, we were able to capture the bright, deep strawberry flavor that we wanted.

A LITTLE CONCENTRATED JUICE
By reducing the shed berry juice (about ⅔ cup) to just 3 tablespoons, we were able to deepen its flavor and control the amount of liquid we're adding to the mousse.

A LOT OF FRESH PUREE
Pureeing and straining the macerated chopped berries yields about 1⅔ cups of puree—enough for a punch of bright, fresh berry flavor.

Instead of immediately pureeing the berries for my next batch, I pulsed them just a bit (to produce small pieces with lots of surface area) and then tossed them with sugar and a pinch of salt. After 45 minutes, I strained them, which left me with an impressive ⅔ cup of juice. I then pureed the drained berries and strained the resulting pulp to get rid of the seeds. From there I reduced the juice until it measured about 3 tablespoons—I'd essentially made a berry syrup—and then I whisked in the softened gelatin until it was dissolved, followed by the softened cream cheese and the berry puree. I folded the enriched fruit puree into the whipped cream and chilled it.

This batch was wonderfully rich and creamy and not runny in the least, and the strawberry flavor was the best yet. Thanks to the tandem effect of the berry syrup and the fresh puree, my mousse tasted both bright and concentrated (but not "cooked"). Happily, the results were just as good when I made the mousse with frozen berries, which turned this into a year-round dessert. (Frozen berries actually have a perk of their own: Freezing causes them to naturally exude quite a bit of moisture, so the macerating step is unnecessary.)

I made just two more adjustments. Instead of softening the gelatin in water, I dissolved it in a little of the drained strawberry juice—a tweak that enhanced the berry flavor a bit more. (I still reduced the remaining liquid to 3 tablespoons.) Replacing berry juice with strawberry (or raspberry) liqueur, a colleague's suggestion, was a great option for when I wanted more-complex berry flavor.

The other adjustment addressed a lingering complaint from my tasters: The mousse had always been a bit streaky—that is, folding the fruit mixture into the cream with a spatula didn't thoroughly marry the two components. Using a whisk to more thoroughly combine the cream with the puree–cream cheese mixture gave the mousse uniform flavor and color.

Finally, to make this dessert more elegant and give it one more boost of fresh berry flavor, I scattered extra diced fresh strawberries over the top. And since frozen strawberries don't make for a pretty garnish, I also came up with a topping that would work whether you're using fresh or frozen fruit: a lemon-zest-and-juice-spiked whipped cream, which underscored the bright, lightly tangy flavor in the berries.

FRESH STRAWBERRY MOUSSE
SERVES 4 TO 6

This recipe works well with supermarket strawberries and farmers' market strawberries. In step 1, be careful not to overprocess the berries. If you like, substitute 1½ pounds (5¼ cups) of thawed frozen strawberries for fresh strawberries. If using frozen strawberries skip step 1 (do not process berries). Proceed with the recipe, adding the ½ cup of sugar and the salt to the whipped cream in step 4. For more-complex berry flavor, replace the 3 tablespoons of raw strawberry juice in step 2 with strawberry or raspberry liqueur. In addition to the diced berries, or if you're using frozen strawberries, you can serve the mousse with Lemon Whipped Cream (recipe follows). For our recipe for Fresh Strawberry Mousse for Two, go to CooksIllustrated.com/june14.

- 2 pounds strawberries, hulled (6½ cups)
- ½ cup (3½ ounces) sugar
  Pinch salt
- 1¾ teaspoons unflavored gelatin
- 4 ounces cream cheese, cut into 8 pieces and softened
- ½ cup heavy cream, chilled

1. Cut enough strawberries into ¼-inch dice to measure 1 cup; refrigerate until ready to garnish. Pulse remaining strawberries in food processor in 2 batches until most pieces are ¼ to ½ inch thick (some larger pieces are fine), 6 to 10 pulses. Transfer strawberries to bowl and toss with ¼ cup sugar and salt. (Do not clean processor.) Cover bowl and let strawberries stand for 45 minutes, stirring occasionally.

2. Strain processed strawberries through fine-mesh strainer into bowl (you should have about ⅔ cup juice). Measure out 3 tablespoons juice into small bowl, sprinkle gelatin over juice, and let sit until gelatin softens, about 5 minutes. Place remaining juice in small saucepan and cook over medium-high heat until reduced to 3 tablespoons, about 10 minutes. Remove pan from heat, add softened gelatin mixture, and stir until gelatin has dissolved. Add cream cheese and whisk until smooth. Transfer mixture to large bowl.

3. While juice is reducing, return strawberries to now-empty processor and process until smooth, 15 to 20 seconds. Strain puree through fine-mesh strainer into medium bowl, pressing on solids to remove seeds and pulp (you should have about 1⅔ cups puree). Discard any solids in strainer. Add strawberry puree to juice-gelatin mixture and whisk until incorporated.

4. Using stand mixer fitted with whisk, whip cream on medium-low speed until foamy, about 1 minute. Increase speed to high and whip until soft peaks form, 1 to 3 minutes. Gradually add remaining ¼ cup sugar and whip until stiff peaks form, 1 to 2 minutes. Whisk whipped cream into strawberry mixture until no white streaks remain. Portion into dessert dishes and chill for at least 4 hours or up to 48 hours. (If chilled longer than 6 hours, let mousse sit at room temperature for 15 minutes before serving.) Serve, garnishing with reserved diced strawberries.

LEMON WHIPPED CREAM
MAKES ABOUT 1 CUP

If preferred, you can replace the lemon with lime.

- ½ cup heavy cream
- 2 tablespoons sugar
- 1 teaspoon finely grated lemon zest plus 1 tablespoon juice

Using stand mixer fitted with whisk, whip cream on medium-low speed until foamy, about 1 minute. Add sugar and lemon zest and juice, increase speed to medium-high, and whip until soft peaks form, 1 to 3 minutes.

Cream Cheese for Consistency

In addition to using whipped cream and gelatin, we fortify our Fresh Strawberry Mousse with an unusual ingredient: cream cheese. The rich, soft-but-dense texture of the cultured dairy lends the mousse just enough body and a bit of subtle tang.

BODY BUILDER
Cream cheese gives mousse a thick, creamy texture without turning it dense.

Beans You Can Count On

Think canned cannellini beans are no match for dried beans cooked from scratch?
Today's canning processes might just prove that notion full of beans.

≽ BY LISA McMANUS ≼

We go through a lot of cannellini beans in the test kitchen. Their creamy texture and mildly nutty flavor round out soups, casseroles, pasta dishes, and salads, and they make appealing dips. Our readers love them, too. Seventy-one percent say that they regularly buy cannellini beans, outstripping the next two most popular white beans: great Northern and navy. We've always appreciated the convenience of canned beans for use in quick recipes and for their ability to be pureed into perfectly creamy spreads. That said, we've also always been a little prejudiced in favor of dried beans, considering their flavor and texture superior. They've been our top choice for bean-centric recipes like cassoulet and, in particular, soups, where they also lend richness and velvety texture to the broth.

As we surveyed the market to select five brands of each type, we spotted some trends. Recently, dried beans have been enjoying something of an image makeover, with home cooks and chefs snapping up mail-order heirloom varieties. We included two, from Rancho Gordo and Zürsun Idaho, to see if they were truly better than plain-Jane supermarket dried beans. (Frustratingly, Rancho Gordo was sold out of its popular cannellini; instead, we included a similar bean recommended by the company.) When it came to canned beans, we were happy to find that our options had grown since 2003; back then we couldn't even find enough nationally distributed brands of cannellini beans to make a tasting, so we opened it up to all white beans. This time we had no problem assembling a lineup of cannellini beans, including one organic version that eschews preservatives and salt. Separating our lineups of dried and canned beans, we invited 21 editors, test cooks, and other staffers to gather for blind tastings six times, serving two rounds each of the beans plain, in dip, and in soup. To avoid any prejudices, we didn't tell participants whether the beans they were evaluating were canned or dried.

A Hill of Beans

When we tallied the final results, we were shocked. Top scores for canned beans actually edged out top scores for dried beans. Sure, we disliked a few brands of canned, whose mushy textures and tinny flavors lived up to our preconceptions, but the best canned beans were excellent: firm and intact, with meltingly tender skins, creamy texture, and clean bean flavor. And above all, they were perfectly uniform.

When it came to the dried beans, the heirloom varieties stood out for flavor; tasters noticed a "clean," "sweet" taste, almost like "chestnuts." Supermarket dried beans were more ordinary in taste but still appealing. It was their texture that really drove down their ratings. With every batch, we followed our tested process, soaking the dried beans for 8 to 24 hours in a brine of 2 tablespoons of salt and 4 quarts of cool water and then rinsing and gently simmering them in plenty of water. But even after this careful effort, some brands of beans, despite having years left before their "best by" dates, cooked unevenly. While some brands' beans had tender skins, others had coatings that were tough, thick, or fell off in plasticky curls. In the end, we could fully recommend only one brand of dried beans.

To confirm the results, we pitted our top canned bean against our top and bottom ranked dried beans, prepared in our Hearty Tuscan Bean Stew (March/April 2008). The result? Our top dried bean, an heirloom variety from Rancho Gordo, and our favorite canned bean, by Goya, were neck and neck. And what about the lowest-ranked dried bean—oddly, also by Goya? It was left in the dust when it came to both taste and texture. We had our final proof: Today's best canned beans can match—and even greatly surpass—the quality of dried beans. How? We realized we didn't know beans about beans.

Perfect Under Pressure

Today, about 1.35 million acres of beans intended for drying are planted in the United States annually. On this scale, experts informed us, considerations of flavor are far less important compared with keeping yields high and production cheap. And remarkably, these beans are still processed pretty much the way they always have been. Bean plants themselves signal when they are ready to harvest by turning from green to gold as they dry on the stalk. Plants are cut down to finish drying and then threshed to separate the now-dried beans from pods. Historically, this was done by hand; today, machines collect the beans and chop the rest into compost. Beans to be sold dried are never washed since this would introduce moisture that could make them sprout or rot. Instead, they are passed over screens to remove stunted beans, stones, and dirt; color-sorted; and then stored in giant totes until they're ready to be packaged.

Meanwhile, modern canning practices take bean processing to a whole new level. The exact procedure varies from brand to brand, but generally it starts with a thorough cleaning and then automatic size sorting and computerized optical inspection. In some cases if the computer spots a subpar bean, a puff of air will literally blow it right out of the production line. Then the beans are quickly blanched in hot water (similar in function to an overnight soak for dried beans) and sealed in cans with water and often salt. The salt works like a brine, not only improving flavor but also helping tenderize the skins. All but one of the canned brands we tasted add calcium chloride, which maintains firmness and prevents splitting, and calcium disodium EDTA, a preservative that binds iron in the water and prevents white beans from turning brown. (Not surprisingly, beans from Eden Organic, the only brand that skipped the salt and preservatives, hit rock bottom in our rankings for being "inedibly" bland, with serious textural woes.) The final step is pressure-cooking the beans right in their cans. Assuming the manufacturer carefully calibrates the contents, cooking times, and temperatures, the result is consistent: perfectly cooked and intact beans.

Dried beans have another disadvantage. When their condition deteriorates, it happens invisibly. During

Don't Shun the Can

Goya dried beans were at the absolute bottom of our tasting of dried beans, yet the company's canned beans—which are the same variety of bean as the dried—not only won top marks in the canned category but also soundly trounced their dried cousins. Why the big difference? Manufacturers like Goya put canned beans through rigorous (and proprietary) quality controls and precisely calibrated processing, while dried beans go from stalk to store with minimal sorting and easily deteriorate if stored too long or under poor conditions.

GOYA CANNED
High-tech inspection ensures top-notch beans.

GOYA DRIED
Fewer quality controls lead to bland, blown-out beans.

months of storage, they can dry out too much, and this can lead to hairline cracks that split open during cooking, and it can also cause loss of flavor volatiles, leaving beans bland. In fact, the moisture level in dried beans should not drop much below 10 percent or top 18 percent, or they won't cook evenly. Lab tests showed that only our top-rated dried bean landed within this range; all the others fell below 10 percent.

In addition to length of storage, storage conditions (including during transportation to market) also play a major role in bean quality. If dried beans are kept in a warm, moist place, they can absorb moisture and off-flavors. Heat and moisture encourage pectin and calcium to bind and harden inside the bean, a process called polymerization, while the cell walls of the skins toughen, a process known as lignification. If either of these things happens, beans cook unevenly or take forever to turn tender.

Some of our dried beans also crumbled or turned mushy too readily in the pot. This is because of the calcium content. Just as canners add calcium chloride to retain the beans' structure, natural calcium in dried beans (determined by genetics of the beans and environmental factors like soil conditions and weather) helps them hold their shape during cooking. Lab tests confirmed that our top-ranked dried bean contained more than twice the calcium of the lowest-ranked. So it made sense that our winner stayed intact during cooking while the low-ranked beans consistently crumbled.

Beans to Buy

While tasters praised the nutty flavor and uniformly tender, intact texture of our favorite dried bean, Rancho Gordo's Classic Cassoulet Bean, our overall favorite bean proved to be canned Goya Cannellini. These well-seasoned beans (the saltiest in the lineup) were tender, creamy, and intact. But we had one last question: Could canned beans impart the same velvety richness to soups and stews that we were used to getting from dried beans?

We made two more batches of Hearty Tuscan Bean Stew with our favorite canned bean. For one batch, we followed the typical procedure, draining and rinsing the beans before adding them to the pot. For the other, we introduced the entire contents of the can, without draining. In a blind test, tasters clearly preferred the soup that included the can liquid. Soup made with drained and rinsed beans was noticeably thinner and less rich. In the batch to which we had added the whole can, the starchy liquid imparted the kind of body comparable to what we'd get when using dried beans (and the stew was not too salty). It made sense given that, essentially, the can serves as a mini cooking pot during processing. (We'll be following up with more tests about using the can liquid.)

Our takeaway? When we really want beans with superior flavor, we'll be glad to mail-order heirloom beans from Rancho Gordo. (And when their cannellini beans are back, we'll try those and post an update on our website.) That said, from here on we're going to be using canned beans more often.

TASTING
CANNED CANNELLINI BEANS

We tasted five nationally distributed supermarket brands of canned cannellini beans—plain, in dip, and in soup—rating their flavor, texture, and overall appeal. Results were averaged and brands of canned beans appear below in order of preference. Sodium levels of canned beans are taken from labels and were adjusted to a ½-cup (130-milligram) serving size. (We also tasted five brands of dried cannellini and cassoulet beans. For the complete results of that tasting, go to CooksIllustrated.com/june14.)

RECOMMENDED

GOYA Cannellini
Price: $1.49 for 15.5 oz (10 cents per oz)   **Sodium:** 416 mg per ½-cup serving
Comments: Tasters' favorite canned beans were "well seasoned" (they had the highest sodium level of the lineup), "big and meaty," and "very satisfying," with both "earthy sweetness" and "savory flavor." Their texture was consistently "ultracreamy and smooth," with a "nice firm bite"—all evidence of carefully calibrated processing.

BUSH'S BEST Cannellini Beans White Kidney Beans
Price: $1.19 for 15.5 oz (8 cents per oz)   **Sodium:** 270 mg per ½-cup serving
Comments: "Creamy and firm," these beans had a "beautiful appearance." They were "plump," "meaty" and "plush," and "smooth and intact," with a "nice nutty flavor and very clean bean taste." In soup, the beans were "perfect" and kept their creamy texture and "hearty," "beany" flavor. But these beans lost a few points because they tasted less seasoned than our winner did and had a slightly chalkier texture in the dip.

RECOMMENDED WITH RESERVATIONS

PROGRESSO Cannellini White Kidney Beans
Price: $1.59 for 19 oz (8 cents per oz)   **Sodium:** 340 mg per ½-cup serving
Comments: With a "mild, vegetal" flavor deemed "a tad bland and blah," these beans were also "a bit mealy." "Almost every bean is broken, with tough skins and grainy flesh—like mashed russet potatoes," noted one taster. A few tasters detected a "slight sharp, canned/metallic finish." Their softness helped make the dip "richer and creamier," but "bits of skin" got in the way.

CENTO Cannellini White Kidney Beans
Price: $2.58 for 19 oz (14 cents per oz)   **Sodium:** 360 mg per ½-cup serving
Comments: "Creamy but blown-out," these beans were "too mushy" and "too broken," even in dip, where the texture resembled "baby food," a sign that they may have been processed too long or at too high of a temperature. Some tasters found them "supermellow," "delicate," and even slightly "herbal," but others said that the flavor was "pretty absent." Tasters sometimes noted slight off-flavors of chlorine or mustiness.

NOT RECOMMENDED

EDEN ORGANIC Cannellini White Kidney Beans, No Salt Added
Price: $2.19 for 15 oz (15 cents per oz)   **Sodium:** 40 mg per ½-cup serving
Comments: Tasters hated these beans, which have no added salt, calcium chloride for firmness, or preservatives, rejecting them in every tasting. We found them "very sour," "watery," "flat," "rank," and "icky," with "grainy interiors" and "leathery," "tough skins." At best, they were "inedibly bland." Even with fresh lemon, parsley, garlic, and olive oil, the dip tasted like "chalk dip."

Pride of the Dried

The problem with most dried beans is that they don't undergo the same level of quality controls as canned beans do. One dried white bean of the five in our tasting was the exception: an heirloom bean, Rancho Gordo Classic Cassoulet Bean ($5.95 plus shipping per pound). The company's smaller yield of heirloom beans seems to be the key. It gives more attention to the beans, and higher turnover ensures freshness. (This also meant that Rancho Gordo was sold out of cannellini beans at the time of our tasting and recommended its cassoulet beans as a substitute.) Also, heirloom beans feature varieties that have been more critically selected for superior flavor and texture. Our tasters found the beans from Rancho Gordo "creamy and smooth, nutty and sweet," with a "fresh, clean" taste and a "lovely texture and appearance." One taster raved: "I could curl up with a bowl of these." When we want dried white beans, we'll make the effort to mail-order them from Rancho Gordo. A source for these beans is on page 32.

RANCHO GORDO

The Mandoline You'll Actually Use

Too often, these precision slicers sit tucked away in a cupboard. We wanted one so easy to use, clean, and store that we'd reach for it every day.

≥ BY LISA McMANUS ≤

You don't have to be a restaurant chef to appreciate a good mandoline. These tools can thin-slice, julienne, and (in some cases) waffle-cut produce far faster than a skilled cook wielding a sharp knife can, and with utter precision. That uniformity is at least as valuable as the time savings—and not just for cosmetic reasons. When cuts are uneven, so is cooking.

But for a mandoline to be truly useful in a home kitchen, not just an appliance you break out for the occasional vegetable gratin or elegantly shingled fruit tart, it must be easy to set up, clean, and store. And given that you're working with sharp blades, it must also be as safe to use as it is efficient.

We came to these conclusions when we evaluated mandolines in 2008, passing on those that required fussy setups and maintenance or that came with blades for making every conceivable cut—a level of operation that most home cooks just won't use.

We thought that we found everything we wanted—a compact, intuitive, reasonably priced slicer that would expedite everyday cutting tasks—in the OXO Good Grips V-Blade Mandoline ($39.99). Compared with the pricey professional models in the lineup, the OXO was also relatively easy to set up. Yet over time and with repeated use, we've realized that the device is somewhat inconvenient. Our biggest gripe: Extra blades are stored under the body, and unless you remove them first—an annoying step—food rains down on them during slicing, making it necessary to pull them out anyway for cleaning.

Sharp—and Sharply Designed

Besides its top-notch blade performance, our winning mandoline, the Swissmar Börner, includes a few features that make it so user-friendly that you might just keep it out for daily use.

ACCOMMODATES ALL PRODUCE
The unobstructed 4 by 13¾-inch platform lets you slice big tomatoes and cut fries and zucchini planks without pretrimming to fit.

KEEPS HANDS OUT OF HARM'S WAY
Adjusting slice thickness or changing julienne blades is easy and safe: They're on plastic plates—no blade handling required.

Plus, unfolding the blade storage tray and then reassembling this gadget can feel like acrobatics; as one tester noted, it's like playing with a Transformers toy that changes from a car to a robot.

Those flaws have heightened our appreciation for our previous Best Buy, the Kyocera Ceramic Slicer ($24.95), an utterly simple, ultracompact paddle that slices food into four thicknesses. The catch: That's all it does. But if we could find a mandoline that offered multiple cuts and similar convenience, we'd have an even more useful tool at our disposal. From a new crop of supposedly more user-friendly slicers, we selected seven models priced under $50 to pit against our old favorites.

Novel Failures
We quickly realized that most of these contenders weren't more convenient than the OXO—and that several were actually fussier. Most mandolines operate similarly: You hold the food with a hand guard and push it along the surface to the blade, adjusting slice thickness by changing the distance between the platform and the blade. One model, by Chef'n, takes a different approach: To keep your hand away from the cutting edge, this device has you pull a handle that moves the blade to the food, which waits in a 3½-inch chamber on the platform. Of course, to fit a larger item like a russet potato in that chamber, we had to dramatically trim the spud, creating work and waste, not to mention some really stumpy French fries.

The Kuhn Rikon's novel design also failed. This device does away with slice thickness adjustment

SAVES SPACE
A caddy that stands vertically, not horizontally, limits the footprint to mere inches. It also allows the parts to air-dry and includes a hook for the hand guard.

by lining up two blades, one for thin cuts and one for deep ones, about 3 inches apart on its platform. Problem is, you want to make long strokes when you're slicing, and that setup makes it hard to avoid bumping into the cover of the unused blade. Plus, this model's platform is so skinny that it can barely accommodate the width of a potato, much less a tomato.

Finally, there were storage issues, particularly with the Norpro. Its body doesn't house its many extra parts (which carry out nontraditional mandoline functions like juicing and shredding—most of which didn't work well), so we had to toss them in a zipper-lock bag.

Staying Safe
Most models didn't feel all that safe. In some cases, particularly with the paddle slicers, that was because the hand guards did a poor job. Whereas the OXO and Swissmar Börner mandolines featured broad guards that offered maximum protection and held food securely on long prongs, paddle slicers usually came with dinky guards featuring shallow spikes that mangled food more than they gripped it.

In other cases, swapping out blades felt more perilous than operating the slicer. Doing so brought our hands dangerously close to sharp edges, especially unsnapping the Microplane's julienne blade to move it from its holding spot. Even the designed-for-safety Chef'n felt unsafe when we switched blades; the force needed to remove the blade platform made the whole mandoline snap and jerk.

The only models that did feel safe were those that limited, or eliminated, the need for handling blades, such as the Progressive International. Flip a switch on its handle and the slicer goes from thin to thick; flip another one on the tool's side and julienne spikes pop up. The Zyliss paddle also offers a built-in julienne blade, as well as a switch that adjusts thickness—features that would have elevated it in our rankings if its dull blade hadn't torn apart a tomato.

Sharpest Tool in the (Vertical) Box
Built-in blades weren't the only design that kept hands away from blades. The Swissmar slicer has you change slice thickness by easily popping out,

TESTING MANDOLINES

We tested nine mandolines, cutting firm russet potatoes and soft ripe tomatoes with all available slice thicknesses. We julienned potatoes and carrots, sliced zucchini lengthwise, and made wavy/waffle slices when available. We observed how easy the slicers were to set up, how safe they felt, and how hard they were to clean and reassemble. Products are listed in order of preference. A source for the winner appears on page 32. For the dimensions of the cuts made by each mandoline, go to CooksIllustrated.com/june14.

CUTS The number and style of available cuts is listed.

EASE OF USE We preferred models that required less effort and felt more comfortable to set up, slice a variety of foods to specific thicknesses, change blades, clean, and reassemble.

SAFETY Mandolines received higher scores if they had large, comfortable hand guards that securely gripped foods and kept fingers away from blades, as well as other features to keep the user safer at all stages of handling.

CLEANUP We gave high marks to models that had few nooks and crannies or design elements that trapped food, making them easier to wash.

PERFORMANCE We preferred models that produced crisp, uniform, intact slices and juliennes on every setting and sliced smoothly and quickly.

	CRITERIA		TESTERS' COMMENTS
HIGHLY RECOMMENDED			

SWISSMAR Börner Original V-Slicer Plus Mandoline
Model: V-1001 Price: $29.99
Cuts: 2 slices, 2 juliennes

Ease of Use ★★★
Safety ★★★
Cleanup ★★★
Performance ★★★

This simple device made cuts effortlessly with stunningly precise results. Its hat-shaped guard protects well; cleanup and storage is a breeze, thanks to its compact vertical caddy. Even with just four cuts, all this adds up to a slicer that we'll use every day.

KYOCERA Adjustable Slicer with Handguard
Model: CSN-202-RD Price: $24.95
Cuts: 4 slices

Ease of Use ★★★
Safety ★★
Cleanup ★★★
Performance ★★★

This paddle continues to be a terrific choice for cooks looking only for fast, precise slicing (it doesn't julienne). Changing the thickness requires no blade handling, and it stows in a drawer. We'd prefer a more secure hand guard.

RECOMMENDED

PROGRESSIVE PREPWORKS Julienne and Slicer
Model: HG-53 Price: $22.25
Cuts: 3 slices, 1 julienne (3 thicknesses)

Ease of Use ★★½
Safety ★★
Cleanup ★★★
Performance ★★½

A built-in julienne blade and slice adjustment settings make this paddle efficient, compact, and supereasy to use. One quibble: The thinnest slice setting was almost flush with the platform and worked best with firm foods that could push down the platform.

OXO Good Grips V-Blade Mandoline Slicer
Model: 1155700V2 Price: $39.99
Cuts: 4 slices, 2 juliennes, 1 wavy/waffle

Ease of Use ★★
Safety ★★★
Cleanup ★½
Performance ★★★

Our former favorite adjusts slice thickness with a dial, includes a broad hand guard, and makes crisp cuts. But blades stored beneath its platform get dirty during cutting, forcing us to clean and reassemble them—a tricky task akin to playing with a Transformers toy.

RECOMMENDED WITH RESERVATIONS

NORPRO Mandoline Slicer/ Grater with Guard
Model: 306 Price: $24.25
Cuts: slices adjustable up to 7 mm, 2 juliennes, 2 graters, 1 shredder, 1 wavy/waffle, 1 citrus juicer

Ease of Use ★★
Safety ★★½
Cleanup ★★
Performance ★★½

A dial adjusts slice thickness—no blade handling required—but gauging thickness requires a ruler. Though it slices and juliennes well, other nonessential "bonus" attachments proved disappointing, and there is no place to store them. The lock switch to change blades also jams when the slicer is wet.

NOT RECOMMENDED

ZYLISS 2-in-1 Handheld Slicer
Model: 11960 Price: $19.99
Cuts: 3 slices, 1 julienne (3 thicknesses)

Ease of Use ★★½
Safety ★★½
Cleanup ★★★
Performance ★

Pushing a button to switch tasks makes this paddle easy to operate, and its contoured hand guard worked a bit better than those of other paddle slicers. Too bad the blade dulled by the end of testing, and its mini serrations scarred food.

KUHN RIKON Thick & Thin Mandoline
Model: 22339 Price: $25
Cuts: 2 slices

Ease of Use ★
Safety ★★½
Cleanup ★★
Performance ★

Two blades—one thick, one thin—built into this slicer's platform were set too close together to allow for long slices. The skinny platform forced us to trim down a potato and squeeze in a tomato. Its mini hat-shaped hand guard imitated the OXO hand guard's larger design but was less effective.

CHEF'N Pull'n Slice Mandoline
Model: 104-622-120 Price: $49.95
Cuts: 4 slices, 2 juliennes

Ease of Use ★½
Safety ★½
Cleanup ★
Performance ★½

To keep hands safe, this model moves the blade to the food—but that's only useful if the food fits in the 3½-inch holding chamber. Thicker slices were uneven. Changing blades made the body jolt. Nooks and crannies around the blades never got clean.

MICROPLANE Adjustable Slicer with Julienne Blade
Model: 34040 Price: $29.95
Cuts: 3 slices, 1 julienne (3 thicknesses)

Ease of Use ★
Safety ★
Cleanup ★½
Performance ★

Handling this paddle's julienne blade felt dicey. An ill-placed support bar broke long slices. Long spikes on the guard mangled food. Slicing firm potatoes was fine, but softer tomatoes turned to mush.

rotating, and sliding a smooth plastic plate into place; the blade itself never moves. Two additional plates with julienne spikes keep your fingers at a safe distance from their edges. These and other pluses helped make this tool our favorite. First, it was effortless to push food through its razor-sharp blades, and every piece of produce that we sliced or julienned emerged with stunning, diamond-cut edges. Its lone shortcoming is that it makes just four cuts—two thicknesses each of slicing and julienning—but the julienne feature makes it a more versatile upgrade to the Kyocera. The Swissmar is also one of the few models with a long, unobstructed platform, which enabled us to produce long, graceful zucchini planks and full-length French fries. We never had to pretrim foods, so waste was minimal.

Finally, there's its unique perk: a caddy that stands vertically, which limits the mandoline's footprint to inches. That setup is a boon to cleanup and safety, too. After washing, simply load the parts into the caddy to air-dry, where sharp edges are covered, and hang the hand guard on its hooks like a hat. Just don't pack the Swissmar into a cupboard; you'll be breaking it out again in no time.

Making the Most of Your Mandoline

During our testing of mandolines (see page 28), we came up with a few tips for use.

For Added Safety, Get a Glove

Even though we found the guard on our winning mandoline, the Swissmar Börner Original V-Slicer Plus Mandoline, very effective and safe, nicking the tips of your fingers on the blades might still be a fear. For the nervous (or for those who own another mandoline with a less-safe guard), we recommend investing in the winner of our protective glove testing, the Microplane Specialty Series Cut Resistant Glove ($14.95), for an extra level of protection.

Halve Large or Awkward Foods First

It's difficult to get the prongs of the guard to insert evenly into big, round foods like potatoes or onions. Because of this, food won't feel securely gripped. It not only makes the task more difficult but also will likely produce uneven slices. Halving food first and then starting with the cut side down on the mandoline will ensure it sits steady, giving you even slices and better efficiency.

Put the Guard on the Food, Not Vice Versa

Whenever possible, put food on the cutting board and push the guard down onto it to attach it to the guard's prongs, rather than holding the guard with prongs upward and pushing the food onto it. This guarantees that the guard goes on straight, fits snugly, and holds food level with the blade.

Use It to Dice, Not Just Slice

We've always thought of the mandoline as a slicing tool, but we recently discovered a clever trick that allows you to make perfect dice on our winning mandoline. Here's how. –L.M.

1. Remove julienne blade from mandoline and place flat on cutting board. Holding blade panel with one hand, use other hand to run vegetable, attached to guard, across blade once, making parallel scores in one direction.

2. Replace julienne blade. Turn vegetable 90 degrees and run it across blades to make crosswise cuts, giving you dice. Repeat as desired.

▶ **THE SCIENCE OF COOKING: GLUTEN-FREE** Creating a great gluten-free pizza crust required weeks of thinking and experimenting. Dan shows us the science behind the success. Video available free for 4 months at CooksIllustrated.com/june14.

Why Cold Butter Keeps Sauces from Breaking

Many home cooks are intimidated by classic butter sauces like beurre blanc because they are notoriously finicky preparations; the high butter content means that the sauces have a tendency to break. Classic French cookbooks call for slowly whisking in cold pieces of butter, a little at a time. We wanted to confirm if this is really necessary. We set out to answer two questions: Does the temperature of butter matter? And does it need to be added incrementally, or can it be whisked in all at once? Before we got to work, we needed to review a few points about butter.

Unlike oils, which are 100 percent fat, butter is an emulsion of water in butterfat (16 to 18 percent water to 80 percent butterfat). It's known as a water-in-fat emulsion because the water is dispersed in tiny droplets throughout the fat. But when butter is whisked into a small amount of liquid, as happens when making a butter sauce, the butter inverts to a fat-in-water emulsion. You can easily taste the difference: We perceive butter as being fatty and greasy because the fat coats all the water and makes direct contact with our tongues. In a butter sauce, we notice plenty of richness, but it doesn't taste greasy, thanks to the thin coating of liquid surrounding the fat. This ability to convert from one type of emulsion to the other is what allows such a large amount of butter to turn into a sauce; if you swapped in oil for the butter, the oil would immediately separate and float on the top of the liquid.

EXPERIMENT

We made several batches of a white butter sauce that calls for 8 tablespoons of butter. We tested whisking the butter into a wine and vinegar base, one tablespoon at a time, both softened at room temperature and cold from the fridge. We also tested whisking in the butter, cut into four 2-tablespoon pieces, all at once. We tested this approach twice as well, with cold and then softened butter.

RESULTS

The only sample that thickened into a proper butter sauce was the one made by whisking in cold butter one tablespoon at a time. The other sauces remained thin and broke. Why the difference?

EXPLANATION

Cold butter melts slowly, which allows you to thoroughly break the butterfat into tiny droplets that can be dispersed throughout the water. And gradually adding the butter one piece at a time slows down the process even further. Together, these steps ensure a stable emulsion. If you add the fat warm and/or too quickly, the fat will end up as larger droplets, which translates to a weaker emulsion (and thinner sauce) that is more prone to break. So tradition has it right. For a successfully thickened butter sauce, make sure to start with cold butter cut into small pieces, add it gradually, and whisk constantly. –D.S.

Add Oil for an Evenly Distributed Rub

To give our Roasted Cornish Game Hens (page 15) shatteringly crispy skin, we rub them with a mixture of two ingredients: kosher salt, which removes moisture, and baking powder, which promotes browning and crisping. Combining the baking powder and salt in a bowl before applying the rub works OK, but it isn't ideal. That's because the finer grains of baking powder settle out from the coarser salt, which makes even distribution tricky. To prevent them from separating, we mix the salt with a little oil and then add the baking powder. The oil creates a moist, tacky surface on the salt, giving the baking powder something to cling to, thus ensuring that it distributes evenly and our game hens have evenly crispy skin. –A.J.

How Much Sodium Is in Brined Food?

There are a number of foods that we typically soak in a saltwater solution, or brine, before cooking. The salt in the brine doesn't just season the food; in the case of meat, poultry, and fish, it improves juiciness and tenderness. It also helps dried beans cook faster and gives them a creamier texture and more tender skin. That said, we've often wondered just how much sodium ends up in brined food. To find out, we sent cooked samples of boneless, skinless chicken breasts, boneless center-cut pork chops, skinless salmon fillets, and black beans that we brined for our standard recommended times to an independent lab for sodium analysis. We also analyzed plain water–soaked samples so that we could then subtract any naturally occurring sodium. Here's how much sodium brining adds to each food. (Note: The Dietary Guidelines for Americans recommend less than 2,300 milligrams daily for people under 51 and less than 1,500 milligrams for those 51 and older.) –D.S.

	BRINING FORMULA	ADDED SODIUM	SALT EQUIVALENT
6 ounces cooked boneless, skinless chicken breast	2 quarts water 1/4 cup salt 1 hour	270 milligrams	Less than 1/8 teaspoon
6 ounces cooked boneless center-cut pork chop	2 quarts water 1/4 cup salt 1 hour	218 milligrams	Less than 1/8 teaspoon
6 ounces cooked skinless salmon fillet	2 quarts water 5 tablespoons salt 15 minutes	173 milligrams	Just over 1/16 teaspoon
3 ounces (1/2 cup) cooked black beans	2 quarts water 1 1/2 tablespoons salt 24 hours	52 milligrams	Less than 1/32 teaspoon

TECHNIQUE | ONIONS WORTH THEIR SALT

When raw onion slices are used as a pizza topping, they tend to char in the fierce, dry heat of the oven. This is because an onion's moisture is trapped within its cell walls, and in the short amount of time that it takes to bake a pizza, the cells don't have long enough to break down and release their moisture to prevent the onion from burning. Sautéing the onion slices before topping the pizza is one way to jump-start the breakdown process and thus help prevent burning, but cooking them in oil or butter changes their flavor and texture, making them softer and sweeter—and that's a different topping altogether.

We recently discovered a technique that retains more of the raw onion flavor and crunch while preventing burning: tossing the onion slices with a little bit of salt and sugar. Both ingredients draw water out of the onion cells, and the combination (we like a 1:2 ratio of salt to sugar) ensures that the onion slices don't become too salty or too sweet. You can also use this approach to soften red or sweet onions before using them in salads or sandwiches. –A.J.

1. Toss 1 teaspoon salt and 2 teaspoons sugar with 1 sliced onion in bowl.

2. Let slices sit for 15 minutes, then rinse in 3 changes of water.

3. Dry onions using salad spinner or paper towels.

TECHNIQUE | EMERGENCY ROUX TO THE RESCUE

Roux, a cooked mixture of flour and fat, is often used to thicken sauces and stews. It makes an appealing thickener because cooking takes the raw edge off the flour and gives it a nutty, toasted flavor. But a roux is prepared at the start of a recipe, before liquids and other ingredients are added to the pot. What happens if you get to the end and find that your stew or sauce is too thin? You could whisk in a cornstarch slurry, but this tends to produce a tacky, shiny result (think stir-fry sauces). An uncooked roux, or beurre manié, is also less than ideal, since it brings a raw flour taste to the dish.

A better option: Make a quick roux in the microwave, which is easier than using the stovetop for cooking small amounts. We tested "emergency roux" made with oil and butter and settled on the oil version since it required less stirring. To make 1/4 cup, follow the steps below. Make sure to use a microwave-safe measuring cup or bowl. We recommend placing it on a dry dish towel when you remove it from the microwave since it's best to avoid placing very hot tempered glass directly onto a cold surface. –S.M.

1. Mix 2 tablespoons flour with 2 tablespoons oil.

2. Microwave for 1 1/2 minutes. Stir, then microwave for 45 seconds. Stir, microwave for 45 seconds, and stir again.

3. For darker roux, continue microwaving and stirring in 15-second increments.

4. Stir 1 tablespoon at a time into stew or gravy until desired consistency is reached.

White Rice Flour for Gluten-Free Baking

The America's Test Kitchen Gluten-Free Flour Blend, which we use in our pizza recipe on page 10 and in our new book *The How Can It Be Gluten-Free Cookbook*, requires five ingredients, one of which is white rice flour. When developing the blend, we discovered that the grind size of white rice flour is not uniform across brands. The flour from Arrowhead Mills was more coarse (with grains the size of semolina), while flours from Bob's Red Mill, EnerG, and Living Now were more fine (with grains similar to all-purpose flour). This difference can dramatically affect the final results of baked goods, since coarse-ground flour absorbs liquid more slowly than fine-ground flour.

We found that using a flour blend prepared with coarse white rice flour from Arrowhead Mills is most problematic for quick breads, cakes, and cookies. Because these items are baked shortly after mixing, the flour doesn't fully absorb the liquid and fat before baking. Doughs and batters will be soupy, and the cookies will be flat; quick breads will sink; and muffins and cupcakes won't dome. The long proofing times required for yeasted loaves allow for better liquid absorption, which alleviates many of these problems, but the loaves still won't dome perfectly. In all these cases, we recommend preparing the blend with fine-ground white rice flour (Bob's Red Mill is our favorite and most widely available). However, we found both batches of blend delivered acceptable pizza crusts, due to the combination of the dough's proofing time and being rolled thin. If you are mixing up our blend to make only our gluten-free pizza, you'll be fine using either coarse or fine rice flour. –A.J.

COARSE-GROUND
Liquids are absorbed slowly, a problem for most baked goods but fine for pizza dough.

FINE-GROUND
Liquids are absorbed more quickly into baked goods, delivering proper structure.

EQUIPMENT CORNER

§ AMY GRAVES & LAUREN SAVOIE ≤

NEW Pizza Grilling Kits

Most home ovens can't reach the 700 plus–degree temperatures of commercial ovens. Enter KettlePizza kits, which are designed to turn 18.5- and 22.5-inch kettle-style charcoal grills into wood-fired ovens. All kits include a metal collar that elevates the grill's lid and has a cutout that lets you insert pizzas without losing heat. We tried the brand's most popular model, the Deluxe USA Kit ($239.95), which also comes with a round baking stone and aluminum peel. The results were underwhelming: The maximum temperature reached in the dome was about 650 degrees, and pizzas cooked unevenly. When the flames died down, we had to remove the hot equipment to refuel. The higher-end kit, the Pro 22 Kit ($299.95), performed better. A grate replacement holds the tombstone-shaped baking stone and features openings in the sides, which made refueling easy. A metal fire basket that holds wood chips alongside the stone helped boost temperatures in the dome to more than 900 degrees. Pizzas had evenly cooked toppings, perfectly charred crusts, and great wood-fired flavor. It's a whopping amount to pay for outdoor pizza, but it's still far cheaper than a backyard wood-fired oven. –L.S.

MAKING CONVERTS
The KettlePizza Pro 22 Kit turns a 22.5-inch charcoal kettle grill into a backyard pizza oven.

NEW Keep-Crisp Box

Warm, humid weather quickly sogs out crispy foods like potato chips, crackers, and cereal, which is where the Brisker Elite comes in. This stainless-steel box promises to banish moisture by maintaining temperatures in the high 90s inside. We compared two sets of opened bags of snack foods, putting one on the counter, sealed with clips, and the other in the Brisker. While the humidity wasn't very high in the test kitchen, it took only a few days for popcorn on the counter to turn soggy, while popcorn in the Brisker was good for longer than a week. Graham crackers, cereal, potato chips, and cookies on the counter went south in seven days but stayed crispy and fresh-tasting for more than three times that long in the metal box. Pretzels, however, fared for the worse in the heat of the appliance, turning chalky and crumbly—albeit after nine days. A $149 price tag is high for protecting snack food, though it might be worth it if you live in a humid environment. –L.S.

SOG, BE GONE
The Brisker Elite keeps warm, humid air from turning chips, crackers, and cereal stale.

UPDATE 12-inch Skillets

For everything from searing steaks to shallow frying, a 12-inch traditional skillet is our go-to pan. But recently, All-Clad replaced our favorite tri-ply Stainless 12-Inch Fry Pan, and our favorite inexpensive 12-inch skillet from Tramontina also changed. The revamped All-Clad 12-Inch Stainless Fry Pan ($154.95) delivered the good news: Its slightly more steeply angled handle provided better leverage, and its thicker aluminum core sped up cooking (it does require a little more vigilance). For even heating, it was the old pan's match. The pan is also induction-compatible.

Now the bad news. Although the updated Tramontina 12-Inch Tri-Ply Clad Open Frying Pan ($49.97) sports a comfortable new handle, its 8-inch cooking surface is 1½ inches smaller than that of the old pan. It couldn't hold eight pieces of chicken, and two 12-ounce steaks were a tight squeeze. Its new brushed-finish interior was also hard to clean. Luckily, our second-ranked inexpensive skillet can step up: The shorter handle on the Emeril Pro-Clad Stainless Steel Tri-Ply 12-Inch Fry Pan ($34.99) brought our hands a little close to the heat, but the roomy pan uniformly browned and sautéed foods and produced a quick, dark sear on steaks and chicken (it's also induction-compatible). For cooks looking for a cheaper pan, the Emeril Pro-Clad is a solid choice. –A.G.

TURBO MODEL
The steeper handle on the All-Clad 12" Fry Pan improves its maneuverability, and its thicker aluminum core speeds up cooking.

NEW Grill Flare Spray

Grill flare-ups, caused by dripping fat, can ruin food. Our usual remedies are either to move the food away from the flames or spritz the flames with water. Recently, we found another possibility: FlareDown ($8.49), a food-safe liquid containing water, potassium salts, and grease-cutting surfactants in a spray bottle. We spritzed FlareDown onto flames when grilling fatty pork and found that the product fared no better than a spray bottle of water. The powerful spray of the FlareDown kicked up ashes onto the meat and tamed the flames for only a few seconds. Worse, we could taste its bitter, salty residue on the food. –A.G.

FLAMEOUT
FlareDown tames grill flare-ups for only a few seconds and leaves residue on food.

UPDATE Soup Ladles

Serving soup seems straightforward—until you try to do it with a poorly designed ladle. Our favorite, the Rösle Hook Ladle with Pouring Rim, won our top spot a few years ago for its long, offset handle, a 5.4-ounce bowl with a pouring rim, and a hook for resting on the rim of a tall pot. But $34 is

BIG DIPPER
The angled handle on the OXO Good Grips Ladle makes it easy to control; at $9.99, it's also easy on the budget.

a lot to spend for easy drip-free serving, so we rounded up four new, cheaper models to see if any could match it. The critical factor turned out to be the angle of each ladle's offset handle. Some, like our favorite, from Rösle, were deeply bent, offering a better grip and maximum control. In the end, the Rösle ladle kept its first-place status, but we did find a worthy Best Buy: the OXO Good Grips Brushed Stainless Steel Ladle. While its handle nearly matches the Rösle's 45-degree-angled handle, the OXO is ½ inch shorter, making scooping broth out of a tall stockpot more difficult. Still, at $9.99, it's a solid bargain alternative. –A.G.

For complete testing results, go to CooksIllustrated.com/june14.

Sources

Prices were current at press time and do not include shipping. Contact companies to confirm information or visit CooksIllustrated.com for updates.

PAGE 13: WINE SAVERS
- Coravin Wine Access System: $299, item #100001, Coravin (855-692-6728, **coravin.com**).
- The Wine Preserver: $24.95, Aircork (866-321-7861, **aircork.com**).

PAGE 27: WHITE BEANS
- Rancho Gordo Classic Cassoulet Bean: $5.95, item #CAS-01, Rancho Gordo (707-259-1935, **ranchogordo.com**).

PAGE 29: MANDOLINES
- Swissmar Börner V-1001 Original V-Slicer Plus Mandoline: $29.99, item #B0000632QE, Amazon (866-216-1072, **amazon.com**).

PAGE 32: PIZZA GRILLING KIT
- KettlePizza Pro 22 Kit: $299.95, item #KPPK-22, Kettle Pizza (888-205-1931, **kettlepizza.com**).

PAGE 32: KEEP-CRISP BOX
- Brisker Elite: $149, item #678B, Brisker The Electric Crisper (513-871-5475, **brisker.com**).

PAGE 32: 12-INCH SKILLETS
- All-Clad 12-Inch Stainless Fry Pan, Model 4112: $154.95, item #8701004401, Amazon.
- Emeril Pro-Clad Stainless Steel Tri-Ply 12-Inch Fry Pan: $34.99, item #2100059328, Amazon.

PAGE 32: SOUP LADLES
- Rösle Hook Ladle with Pouring Rim: $34, item #10009, Rösle USA (302-326-4801, **rosleusa.com**).
- OXO Good Grips Brushed Stainless Steel Ladle: $9.99, item #1057952, OXO (800-545-4411, **oxo.com**).

INDEX
May & June 2014

Find us on Facebook:
facebook.com/CooksIllustrated

Follow us on Twitter:
twitter.com/TestKitchen

 WATCH NEW VIDEOS

America's Test Kitchen
COOKING SCHOOL

Let us help you become a better cook!

Offering more than 100 courses for cooks at
every level, our school combines personalized
instruction from America's Test Kitchen test
cooks with leading-edge technology to provide
a unique and effective learning experience.

➤ **Start a 14-Day Free Trial at**
OnlineCookingSchool.com.

Fusilli with Ricotta and Spinach, 11

Carrot-Ginger Soup, 20

Roasted Artichokes, 23

Chinese Braised Beef, 19

Garlic-Lime Grilled Pork Tenderloin Steaks, 7

Rice and Pasta Pilaf, 21

Fresh Strawberry Mousse, 25

Cioppino, 13

The Best Gluten-Free Pizza, 10

Roasted Cornish Game Hens, 15

PHOTOGRAPHY: CARL TREMBLAY; STYLING: MARIE PIRAINO

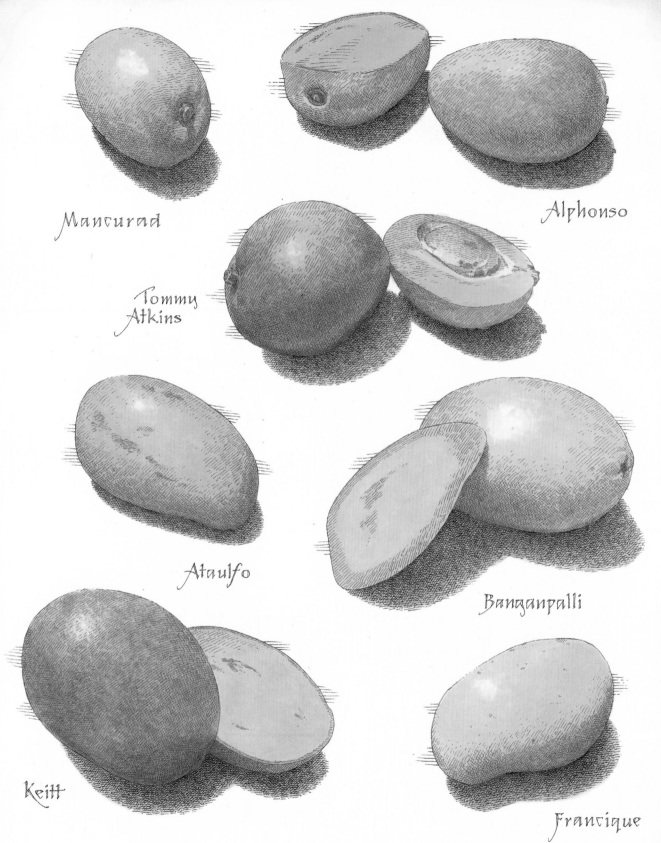

Mancurad

Alphonso

Tommy
Atkins

Ataulfo

Banganpalli

Keitt

Francique

MANGOS

COOK'S
ILLUSTRATED

Best Grilled Burger
Steak Tips, Butter, and Salt

Chicken Souvlaki
Moist Meat, Bright Lemon Flavor

Cream Cheese Brownies
The Secret's in the Swirl

Smoky Pulled Pork (on a Gas Grill)

Singapore Noodles
Hong Kong Favorite at Home

What's the Best Food Storage Bag?

How to Cook Eggs
Five Foolproof Recipes

Frozen Yogurt Tasting
Reinventing Zucchini Bread
Pasta Frittata

CooksIllustrated.com
$6.95 U.S. & CANADA

CONTENTS
July & August 2014

COOK'S
ILLUSTRATED

Founder and Editor	Christopher Kimball
Editorial Director	Jack Bishop
Editorial Director, Magazines	John Willoughby
Executive Editor	Amanda Agee
Test Kitchen Director	Erin McMurrer
Managing Editor	Rebecca Hays
Executive Food Editor	Keith Dresser
Senior Editors	Hannah Crowley
	Andrea Geary
	Lisa McManus
	Dan Souza
Senior Editors, Features	Elizabeth Bomze
	Louise Emerick
Senior Copy Editor	Megan Ginsberg
Copy Editors	Nell Beram
	Krista Magnuson
Associate Editors	Amy Graves
	Shannon Friedmann Hatch
	Andrew Janjigian
	Chris O'Connor
Test Cooks	Daniel Cellucci
	Lan Lam
Assistant Editors	Lauren Savoie
	Kate Shannon
Assistant Test Cooks	Cecelia Jenkins
	Sarah Mullins
Assistant Test Kitchen Director	Leah Rovner
Senior Kitchen Assistants	Michelle Blodget
	Alexxa Grattan
Kitchen Assistants	Maria Elena Delgado
	Ena Gudiel
Executive Producer	Melissa Baldino
Co-Executive Producer	Stephanie Stender
Associate Producer	Kaitlin Hammond
Contributing Editor	Dawn Yanagihara
Science Editor	Guy Crosby, PhD
Managing Editor, Web	Christine Liu
Associate Editors, Web	Jill Fisher
	Eric Grzymkowski
	Roger Metcalf
Assistant Editor, Web	Charlotte Wilder
Senior Video Editor	Nick Dakoulas
Product Manager, Cooking School	Anne Bartholomew
Senior Editor, Cooking School	Mari Levine
Design Director	Amy Klee
Photography Director	Julie Cote
Art Director	Susan Levin
Associate Art Director	Lindsey Timko
Art Director, Marketing	Jennifer Cox
Associate Art Directors, Marketing	Melanie Gryboski
	Mariah Tarvainen
Designer, Marketing	Judy Blomquist
Staff Photographer	Daniel J. van Ackere
Associate Art Director, Photography	Steve Klise
Vice President, Marketing	David Mack
Circulation Director	Doug Wicinski
Circulation & Fulfillment Manager	Carrie Fethe
Partnership Marketing Manager	Pamela Putprush
Marketing Assistant	Marina Tomao
Chief Operating Officer	Rob Ristagno
VP, Digital Products	Fran Middleton
Production Director	Guy Rochford
Workflow & Digital Asset Manager	Andrew Mannone
Senior Color & Imaging Specialist	Lauren Pettapiece
Production & Imaging Specialists	Heather Dube
	Lauren Robbins
Director, Project Management	Alice Carpenter
Development Manager	Mike Serio
Senior Controller	Theresa Peterson
Customer Loyalty & Support Manager	Amy Bootier
Customer Service Representatives	Jessica Haskin
	Andrew Straaberg Finfrock
	Juliet Tierney
VP, New Business Development	Michael Burton
Director of Sponsorship Sales	Anne Traficante
Client Services Manager	Kate Zebrowski
Executive Director, Book Marketing	Beth Ineson
Retail Sales & Marketing Director	Emily Logan
Human Resources Director	Adele Shapiro
Publicity	Deborah Broide

PRINTED IN THE USA

BEETS are closely related to chard, which explains why many cooks value the leafy greens in addition to the root. The youngest burgundy shoots of the **BULL'S BLOOD** variety are especially prized since they offer the sweetest greens, so if the beet itself is sold, it's often of diminutive size. Boasting one of the highest sugar contents of any vegetable, the sweetness of the supermarket staple **RED** beet intensifies with cooking. Despite their red skin, **CHIOGGIA** beets, an Italian heirloom breed, are striped inside. Cooks often shave them thin and serve them raw in salads. **GOLDEN** beets offer a dense, meaty texture. **WHITE** beets are savory and reminiscent of turnips. Creamy, rich **CHAMPAGNE** beets have a carrot-like sweetness.

COVER (Peaches): Robert Papp; **BACK COVER** (Beets): John Burgoyne

America's
TEST KITCHEN
RECIPES THAT WORK®

A BUCKET LIST OF LITTLE THINGS

I do not want to climb Everest or see the Great Wall of China. Nor do I want to drive at Le Mans, compete at the World Series of Poker, or try to beat Joey Chestnut, the competitive eater, who can devour 69 hot dogs with buns in just 10 minutes.

I do, however, have a list of little things that I would like to complete before my time is up. I have listed them in reverse order.

20. A friend of a friend lent me $20 in Vienna in the summer of 1971 during a backpacking trip to Turkey. I said that I would pay it back but lost his address. Does anyone know a young American architect who lived in Vienna in 1971 and who was down $20? Just post onto my Facebook account.

19. When I was a kid, Marie Briggs was the official baker at the Yellow Farmhouse in Vermont. Her molasses cookies and nutmeg doughnuts were legendary. I promise myself I'll bake up a big batch of both items and bring them to Charlie Bentley, the only surviving bachelor farmer from that era.

18. I have at least 1,000 thank-you notes that I never wrote, so I just bought an old Underwood typewriter as a form of penance. The first one will be to the plumber who, on Easter Sunday 1996, came out to fix our furnace.

17. I never flossed properly and would like to learn.

16. I love books but am running out of time. I have assembled my "book bucket list" of 72 books (including *Middlemarch*, which I have tried to read on three separate occasions but failed). You can find the list at CooksIllustrated.com/72books.

15. I have read hundreds of terrible books (more than a few from Oprah's Book Club) in my life and I want the time back. Since this is impossible, I will assemble paperback editions of these books and burn them this summer at an al fresco conflagration I have named The Flaming Bridges of Madison County. Everyone is invited; bring your own worst books.

14. It used to be the mark of an educated person to be able to recite from memory. The five items I would like most to know by heart are Elizabeth Barrett Browning's "How Do I Love Thee"; Lewis Carroll's "Jabberwocky"; "Now is the winter of our discontent" from *Richard III;* "The Minstrel Boy" from "The Man Who Would Be King"; and the short first paragraph of *Tropic of Cancer* that reads, "I am living at the Villa Borghese. There is not a crumb of dirt anywhere, nor a chair misplaced. We are all alone here and we are dead." Plus, I can never remember the theme music from *The Man from U.N.C.L.E.*

13. Many friends have passed before I got a chance to say a proper goodbye. Most have been cremated, so there is no headstone to commemorate with flowers. You know who you are, so, from the bottom of my heart, goodbye, and know that I still love you.

12. I want to write a free cookbook for folks who know nothing about cooking. It would contain just 25 simple recipes, just about all one needs to know to be a good cook.

11. I have always wanted to tie a decent clove hitch.

10. I will lobby the federal government to reinstate home economics classes in elementary schools across the United States. A good education includes knowing how to cook.

9. I would like to engage in an entirely frivolous but arguably noble political act of will, protesting something that will never change: war, campaign

Christopher Kimball

money, junk food, grown-ups who dress like their teenage children, or bad cooking. It's comforting to be on the losing side once in a while.

8. I have spent a lifetime thinking that I should enjoy shad roe, hundred-year eggs, durian, *rognons de veau* (kidneys), and *saag paneer*. I will no longer eat foods I don't like.

7. I would love to help my four kids discover the infinite joys of hard work. Since this cannot be taught, only learned, I will settle for a lifetime of mostly fruitless encouragement from the sidelines.

6. I would like to make pretied bow ties illegal. Tying one's own bow tie is the most elemental form of self-respect.

5. I know that Dunkin' Donuts' coconut doughnuts are bad for me and I would love to give them up, but I won't.

4. I want to build a monument to things that are becoming obsolete but will be missed terribly: libraries, downtowns, typewriters, drive-ins, fountain pens, full-service gas stations, shoelaces, suspenders, Sunday suppers, big breakfasts, galoshes, and phones connected by landlines.

3. I would like to live long enough to see my kids have kids who are as noble in spirit and kind as my kids are.

2. I will never give in to reality, whatever that is. Everything is possible if you simply ignore what cannot be done. As my mother once commented, "What's so good about reality anyway?"

1. I will stop making lists and start living day by day, enjoying each and every bite of that occasional coconut doughnut.

FOR INQUIRIES, ORDERS, OR MORE INFORMATION

CooksIllustrated.com
At CooksIllustrated.com, you can order books and subscriptions, sign up for our free e-newsletter, or renew your magazine subscription. Join the website and gain access to 21 years of *Cook's Illustrated* recipes, equipment tests, and ingredient tastings, as well as companion videos for every recipe in this issue.

COOKBOOKS
We sell more than 50 cookbooks by the editors of *Cook's Illustrated*, including *The Cook's Illustrated Cookbook* and *The Science of Good Cooking*. To order, visit our bookstore at CooksIllustrated.com/bookstore.

COOK'S ILLUSTRATED MAGAZINE
Cook's Illustrated magazine (ISSN 1068-2821), number 129, is published bimonthly by Boston Common Press Limited Partnership, 17 Station St., Brookline, MA 02445. Copyright 2014 Boston Common Press Limited Partnership. Periodicals postage paid at Boston, MA, and additional mailing offices, USPS #012487. Publications Mail Agreement No. 40020778: Return undeliverable Canadian addresses to P.O. Box 875, Station A, Windsor, ON N9A 6P2. POSTMASTER: Send address changes to *Cook's Illustrated*, P.O. Box 6018, Harlan, IA 51593-1518. For subscription and gift subscription orders, subscription inquiries, or change of address notices, visit AmericasTestKitchen.com/support, call 800-526-8442 in the U.S. or 515-248-7684 from outside the U.S., or write to us at *Cook's Illustrated*, P.O. 6018, Harlan, IA 51593-1518.

FOR LIST RENTAL INFORMATION Contact Specialists Marketing Services, Inc., 777 Terrace Ave., 4th Floor, Hasbrouck Heights, NJ 07604; phone: 201-865-5800.

EDITORIAL OFFICE 17 Station St., Brookline, MA 02445; phone: 617-232-1000; fax: 617-232-1572. For subscription inquiries, visit AmericasTestKitchen.com/support or call 800-526-8442.

⇛ BY ANDREA GEARY, LAN LAM & SARAH MULLINS ⇚

Spatula Stain Remover

Is there a way to remove stains from silicone spatulas?

LILA TULLOCK
NEW HAVEN, CONN.

➤ When silicone spatulas pick up stains from tomato sauce, turmeric, or pesto, often even an aggressive soapy scrubbing won't get them completely clean. So we set out to find a better cleaner.

JUST CLEAN
Soap washes away oil but not colored stains.

CLEAN AND CLEAR
Oxidants break down and remove color compounds.

After staining one set of white silicone spatulas bright yellow with a turmeric-and-water paste and another set red with tomato sauce, we soaked each one in potential stain fighters: white vinegar, a slurry of dish soap and baking soda, 3 percent hydrogen peroxide, a bleach solution (made by diluting 2½ tablespoons of bleach in 2 cups of water), and a control mixture of soapy water. After 24 hours of soaking, only the spatulas soaked in hydrogen peroxide or the bleach solution were back to their original white.

Our science editor explained that while soap can help break up and wash away oil, to remove intensely colored stains, the compounds that provide the color need to be broken down into colorless molecules. Hydrogen peroxide and bleach are both oxidants, a type of compound that excels at this task. Just remember to wash your stain-free spatulas in warm soapy water before use. –S.M.

Reusing Pickle Brine

I hate throwing out the leftover brine when I finish a jar of pickles. Can I use it to make a batch of homemade pickles?

CAROL FOX
FAIR OAKS, CALIF.

➤ We tried quick-pickling fresh cucumber slices in leftover brine using two common methods. For the first batch, we put fresh cucumber slices right into the leftover brine. For the second, we brought the leftover brine to a boil and then poured it over cucumber slices that we had salted and left to drain for 1 hour. We refrigerated both batches for 24 hours before sampling them.

Although the untreated cucumbers picked up a little tang from the brine, for the most part they retained their fresh cucumber flavor. The treated cucumbers, on the other hand, produced good results. They had the right dense texture and deeper color, and they were brightly flavored and well seasoned with garlic and dill from the brine.

To make quick pickles from leftover brine, toss cucumber slices in a colander with salt (1½ teaspoons per pound of cucumbers) and let them sit for 1 hour; then transfer them to a jar. Bring the brine to a boil and pour it over the pickles. Seal the jar and refrigerate the pickles for 24 hours before eating. The pickles can be kept for up to two weeks. (We don't recommend reusing the brine more than once.) –S.M.

Creaming Without a Mixer

I don't have an electric mixer. Is there an easy way to cream butter and sugar by hand?

PATRICIA PATTERSON
NEW HAMBURG, ONTARIO

➤ Creaming does more than just combine the two ingredients. As sugar is rapidly mixed into fat, it creates millions of tiny air pockets that expand in the heat of the oven, giving baked goods lift. Skip the creaming step and your cakes and cookies may turn out squat and dense.

Creaming softened butter and sugar by hand using just a bowl and a wooden spoon is hard labor: It'll take you 20 minutes compared with the mere 3-minute hands-off stint in the mixer. Our search for an easier way led us to an unlikely product: whipped butter.

READY WHIP
Whipped butter simplifies creaming by hand.

We selected two recipes—one cookie and one cake—that started with a creaming step and made each according to the recipe using a stand mixer. Then we made each by hand, substituting an 8-ounce tub of whipped unsalted butter for the two sticks each recipe called for. To our surprise, the cookies were indistinguishable, and the cake made with whipped butter was every bit as fluffy as the one made according to the recipe.

A few caveats: Make sure you're using pure whipped butter, not "light" butter or butter spread. Also, because it contains so much air, whipped butter must be substituted by weight, not volume. Lastly, cold whipped butter is relatively brittle and must be softened at room temperature before using; trying to speed things up in the microwave will cause both your butter and your baked goods to fall flat. –A.G.

A Simple Syrup Solution

I make simple syrup with a 2:1 ratio of sugar to water since it sweetens drinks without diluting them, but sugar crystals always form. Is there a way to prevent this?

VIRGINIA MIMMACK
DALLAS, TEXAS

➤ Simple syrup crystallizes when enough of the sugar molecules stick to one another that they become insoluble in the water. In a syrup prepared with such a high ratio of sugar to water (often referred to as a rich syrup), as yours is, the chance of sugar molecules clustering and crystallizing is high.

We made three batches of rich syrup by bringing 2 cups of sugar and 1 cup of water to a boil, and then we added ingredients that allegedly prevent crystallization—¼ teaspoon of lemon juice and ¼ teaspoon of cream of tartar—to two batches, respectively, and left the third alone. Within 24 hours we saw crystals in the control. The additives bought us more time, but after 48 hours crystals still began to appear. Adding these ingredients in larger amounts helped, but they changed the flavor profile too much.

To find a more effective solution, we had to understand why these additives helped. The cream of tartar and lemon juice are both acids that are able to break down sugar molecules into glucose and fructose in a process called inversion. So not only were fewer sugar molecules available to cluster together in our doctored syrups but the newly present glucose and fructose were physically blocking the remaining sugar molecules from one another.

So we just needed a way to invert enough of the sugar without changing the flavor. After some research, we landed on prolonged exposure to heat. Simmering the syrup for 10 minutes, instead of merely bringing it to a boil, inverted enough of the sugar without affecting flavor.

Here's our method: Bring 2 cups of granulated sugar and 1 cup of water to a simmer in a medium saucepan. Continue to simmer the syrup, covered, for 10 minutes, and then let it cool completely. The syrup can be refrigerated for at least two weeks without crystallization. –L.L.

Hull-Less Barley

What is hull-less barley, and how does it compare with pearl barley?

DANA BERSON
JAMAICA PLAIN, MASS.

➤ With increasing interest in whole grains, hull-less barley is cropping up more frequently in supermarkets alongside pearl barley. While the variety of barley used to produce pearl barley has a tough, inedible hull that must be polished off, a process that wears away most of the bran and germ beneath, a different variety of barley is used to produce hull-less barley. Its hull is attached so loosely that it falls off without abrasion, leaving the bran and germ intact.

When we prepared hull-less barley using the pilaf method, we found that it had an appealingly chewy texture and nutty flavor more similar to those of wheat berries than to the familiar soft, slightly fuzzy exterior and al dente core of pearl barley. And while we like to prepare pearl barley risotto-style, we learned that the more intact grains of hull-less barley couldn't soak up broth and wine and didn't release starch to create a creamy sauce.

The takeaway: While it shouldn't be used as a substitute for pearl barley, hull-less barley has a firm texture and nutty flavor that makes it a great choice for grain salads and hearty side dishes. –A.G.

How to Store Tofu

I always store leftover tofu in water, but I've heard that changing the water can help it last a little longer. Is that true?

SARA McCABE
ARLINGTON, MASS.

➤ Like you, we've always stored tofu in water. But we spoke to an artisanal tofu maker who recommended changing the water daily. We also read that storing it in lightly salted water is the best method. To find out which approach kept tofu tasting fresh the longest, we tried each using extra-firm, firm, and silken tofu, storing the samples in plastic containers. As controls, we also placed a sample of each style in a zipper-lock bag with as much air pressed out as possible.

The samples without any liquid lasted only four to six days. We don't recommend storing tofu in salted water: Although these samples stayed fresh for two weeks, they also picked up a noticeable salty flavor almost immediately. The samples stored in water that we changed daily were edible for 10 days, after which they began losing flavor. However, in the end, our preferred method was our old standard: Submerging the tofu in plain tap water (and not changing it) kept the tofu as fresh-tasting as straight-from-the-package tofu for 10 days and didn't require any maintenance. Just make sure that the water is clear; cloudy water can be a sign of bacterial growth and the tofu should be discarded. –L.L.

UNDERWATER WINNER
Tofu stored in tap water keeps for up to 10 days.

WHAT IS IT?

We discovered this item in a storage box and have no idea what it is. Any clues?

LOIS McANALLEN
ORO VALLEY, ARIZ.

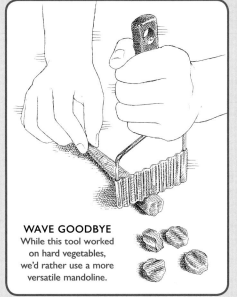

WAVE GOODBYE
While this tool worked on hard vegetables, we'd rather use a more versatile mandoline.

What you have is a garnisher. There are two popular styles: Either the blade comes straight out from the handle like a shovel (like yours), or the blade is set off to the side of the handle (like an axe). Its hallmark is the corrugated-style blade, intended to produce wavy slices. Garnishers, as the name indicates, were designed for aesthetic purposes—picture radishes or cucumbers on a mid-century crudités platter or carrots in a luncheon salad.

When we used it to cut radishes and carrots, our results were mixed. While it did produce the promised wavy shape, it was difficult to produce slices of consistent thickness and nearly impossible to make thin cuts. We came across a few sources that also touted the tool as a waffle-fry cutter, so we tried pushing it through a potato. Not only did we experience similar problems with controlling the size of the cuts but the tool also snagged on the potato's skin, leaving a jagged edge. (Peeling the potato before cutting and frying, as we often do, would at least solve that issue.)

After these less-than-impressive initial tests, we predicted that the tool would smash softer foods, but overall, it produced clean undulating slices of pickled beets and cheddar cheese, perhaps a nice touch for antipasti or cheese plates (we did find that the cheese needed to be cold for clean slicing). That said, we're more likely to reach for a mandoline, which can take care of most slicing tasks and produce consistent results both thick and thin. –Shannon Friedmann Hatch

Potato Nails

Do potato nails, rods that are inserted into baking potatoes to decrease the cooking time, really work?

KATHERINE GRICE
CLAYTON, GA.

➤ Here's the theory: Baked potatoes typically cook from the outside in, requiring about 75 minutes in a 350-degree oven to cook through. A piece of metal stuck through to its center will conduct heat, thus speeding up the process. Though most potato nails are made of aluminum, there are also stainless-steel versions available.

To test the theory, we selected three potatoes of the same weight. We left one alone as a control, impaled one on an aluminum potato nail, and threaded the third on a stainless-steel skewer (an easy stand-in for a stainless-steel potato nail). We baked them all in the same 350-degree oven, rotating them after 30 minutes. True enough, the aluminum-studded potato finished first, the stainless-steel assist came in second, and the control potato took the longest. The surprise? There was only a 7-minute difference between the speediest potato and the slowest.

We wondered if more nails would speed things up enough to make it worthwhile. Unfortunately, no. Even a potato that had been run through with an

NOT SO STUDLY
Even five nails made little difference in baking time.

absurd five nails cooked only 11 minutes faster than an intact potato.

The takeaway: Potato nails aren't really worth the investment. If you want to quickly cook a potato, here's what we recommend. Poke a potato several times with a fork and then microwave it until it is slightly soft, 6 to 12 minutes, flipping it halfway through microwaving. Transfer the potato to a 450-degree oven and bake it directly on the middle rack until a skewer glides easily through the flesh, about 20 minutes. –A.G.

SEND US YOUR QUESTIONS We will provide a complimentary one-year subscription for each letter we print. Send your inquiry, name, address, and daytime telephone number to Notes from Readers, *Cook's Illustrated*, P.O. Box 470589, Brookline, MA 02447, or to NotesFromReaders@ AmericasTestKitchen.com.

Quick Tips

⇒ COMPILED BY SHANNON FRIEDMANN HATCH ⇐

Hang Up Your Gloves

Eliza Cleveland of Branford, Conn., prefers to hang her dishwashing gloves so that they're always at hand, but her pair lacks tabs to do so. Undeterred, she created her own by folding a piece of duct tape over the top edge of each one and then piercing the tape with a hole puncher.

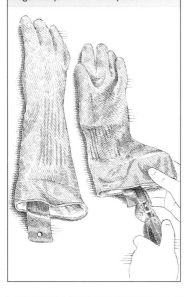

Steadying Tippy Tacos

The rounded base of a hard taco shell usually requires one hand to steady it while the other stuffs. Olivia Tipton of Carlisle, Ohio, frees up both hands by cleverly wedging the shell between the tines of a fork to keep it upright.

Corn Kernel Catcher

Corn kernels have a tendency to ricochet across the kitchen as they are cut from the cob. Elise Bayard-Franklin of Belmont, Mass., devised this setup to contain them.

1. Place a small bowl upside down inside a larger bowl.

2. Steady the wide end of a corn cob on top of the overturned bowl and slice downward to remove kernels. The smaller bowl elevates the cob so you can get a clean slice, and the larger bowl catches the kernels.

A Hole New Way to Pluck Herbs

Plucking the leaves from a bunch of tender herbs like cilantro and dill can be tedious and time-consuming. Carly Helmetag of Somerville, Mass., has found that threading the stems through the holes of her colander (starting from the inside and pulling them through) makes quick work of the task—plus, the bowl collects the leaves.

A Sharp Trick for Scooping Hard Ice Cream

When faced with a container of ice cream that is too hard to scoop, Doug Jeffers of Cambridge, Mass., uses this method.

1. Warm the blade of a sharp paring knife under hot water.

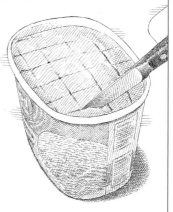

2. Make 1-inch-deep cuts, spaced 1 inch apart, from side to side. Turn the container 90 degrees and repeat to form a checkerboard pattern.

3. Warm the ice cream scoop under hot water before scooping. Repeat as necessary.

SEND US YOUR TIPS We will provide a complimentary one-year subscription for each tip we print. Send your tip, name, address, and daytime telephone number to Quick Tips, *Cook's Illustrated*, P.O. Box 470589, Brookline, MA 02447, or to QuickTips@AmericasTestKitchen.com.

ILLUSTRATION: JOHN BURGOYNE

Pineapple (Prep) Express

Michelle Emond of Worthington, Ohio, makes double use of her strawberry huller to remove the spiny eyes from a pineapple. The tool's prongs pluck out the fruit's tough spots with minimal waste.

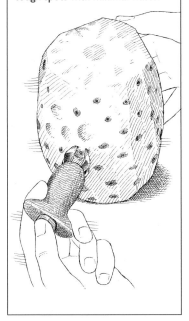

Keeping 'shrooms Submerged

When Linda Miller of Stowe, Pa., rehydrates dried mushrooms in hot liquid, they tend to bob on the surface of the broth instead of staying submerged, leaving some parts tough or even crunchy. She now anchors them by nesting a 1-cup liquid measuring cup inside a 2-cup vessel. The 2-cup measure holds the liquid and mushrooms, while the 1-cup measure (a small bowl would work, too) ensures that the mushrooms stay below the surface while they soak.

Rinsing Out Clingy Ingredients

When a rubber spatula is too big to use to scrape clingy bits of tomato sauce or paste from emptied jars and cans, Catherine Camden of Cumberland, R.I., uses this trick: She adds a tablespoon or two of liquid to the container, swirls it around to wash the bottom and sides, and then empties it into the pot. A bonus: Rinsing with a splash of wine or broth adds extra flavor.

Neat Meat Grinder

In many recipes that call for ground beef, such as burgers, we find that grinding the meat at home offers better flavor; however, it can be a messy step. Mary Goldman of Berkeley, Calif., drapes plastic wrap over the grinder spout and attaches it to the sides of the catch bowl below to keep the bits of raw meat contained as they fall.

Clip for a Tighter Fit

The compost bags that Ellis Hawes of Seattle, Wash., uses are too wide for his narrow pail. To keep the top secure and open, he gathers and twists the excess to one side and fastens it in place with a bread bag clip.

Lost Power Indicator

Joe Novotny of Coupeville, Wash., offers this solution for gauging whether his refrigerator lost power while he was on vacation: He places three ice cubes in a zipper-lock bag on a freezer shelf before leaving. If the cubes have melted together upon his return, he knows the fridge shut off while he was away.

On Guard Against Cuts

After injuring her finger on her box grater one too many times, Ellie Sweeney of Melrose, Mass., now spears the food she is prepping with the long prongs of her mandoline guard. Just as it grips food and protects hands from that tool's sharp blade, it also prevents painful nicks on the grater and allows her to prep without worry. (To prevent the tines of the guard from snagging on the grater, stop an inch or so from the end of the food.)

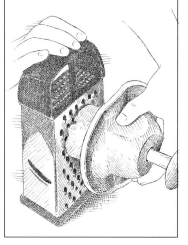

DIY Ice Pack

Whenever she's short on ice packs for her large cooler, Eileen Jones of Lawrence, Kan., improvises with clean half-gallon waxed cardboard juice containers that she keeps on hand for this purpose. Filled with water and frozen, the block shapes take up minimal space and make for easy packing.

The Best Grilled Burger

Preground chuck patties may be easy to throw on the grill, but if you want ultrabeefy, tender, juicy burgers, start with steak tips—and open the freezer.

⇒ BY ANDREW JANJIGIAN ⇐

To me, one of the best things about summer is the chance to eat a really great burger off the grill. By that I mean a burger with an ultracraggy charred crust, a rich beefy taste, and an interior so juicy and tender that it practically falls apart at the slightest pressure.

The problem is, such a burger is actually pretty hard to come by. While the typical specimen may have a nicely browned crust, it's also heavy and dense with a pebbly texture. The reason is no mystery: Most cooks use preground meat from the supermarket, which is usually ground so fine that a certain amount of graininess is inevitable. Furthermore, they tend to shape the meat into tightly packed disks that, while easier to flip on the grill, guarantee dense texture. Forming loose patties produces that prized open texture, but it's a far riskier proposition on a grill than in a skillet or on a griddle. On a flat uniform surface, a loosely packed patty is fully supported, and once that patty forms a crust, carefully sliding a spatula beneath it and gently flipping it over is relatively easy. On the open grates of a grill, however, that same patty is likely to wind up on the coals before a crust can form to hold it together.

This summer I decided to tackle these issues head on and find an approach to a truly excellent backyard burger. I'd look at every possible variable, from how and when to season the meat, to how best to form the patties and what size to make them, and of course, how to get them on and off the grill in one piece. The perfect burger might take a little more work, but it would definitely be worth it.

A Real Grind

It was a given that I'd need to grind my own meat. Besides being ground too fine, commercial burger meat is also manhandled during processing and compressed inside tightly wrapped packages. This overmanipulation draws out a lot of the sticky

These burgers develop great char and stay perfectly medium-rare at the center because we freeze them before putting them on the grill.

▶ **See the Proper Texture**
Video available free for 4 months at CooksIllustrated.com/aug14

protein myosin, so even if you form your patties with a gentle hand at home, your results have already been compromised—a denser texture is inevitable. And while chuck (the cut that's often preground for supermarkets) might make a decent burger—I would certainly consider it—I wanted to decide for myself which cut would deliver the best flavor.

In the test kitchen, we've found it easy to grind meat ourselves with a food processor. The method we've developed (no matter the cut) calls for trimming gristle and excess fat from the meat, cutting the meat into ½-inch pieces, freezing it for about 30 minutes to firm it up so that the blades cut it cleanly instead of smashing and smearing it (which leads to pasty, dense results), and finally processing it in small batches to ensure an even, precise grind.

I narrowed the cut of meat to three options: chuck, boneless short ribs, and sirloin steak tips (aka flap meat). Each of these choices is relatively inexpensive, decently tender, and contains a sufficient amount of fat to ensure burgers that are reasonably moist and flavorful. Chuck had great flavor and ample marbling,

but it contained a lot of sinewy connective tissue that had to be painstakingly removed before grinding (something the mass-market preground versions easily take care of during processing). Deeply marbled short ribs were gloriously fatty and rich—but a bit too rich for several tasters, so they were also out. Somewhat leaner steak tips had great meaty flavor and required virtually no trimming. They came up a bit short in terms of richness, but I had a trick up my sleeve for fixing that.

In our Juicy Pub-Style Burgers recipe (May/June 2011), we call for tossing the ground meat with melted butter. The burgers don't taste of butter, but they gain deeper flavor and richness. However, pouring melted butter over my near-frozen meat was somewhat problematic; the butter started to solidify on contact, making it tricky to evenly distribute. I realized that there was a way to incorporate the butter that would not only enable even distribution but also be easier: adding it to the food processor when grinding the meat. Cut into ¼-inch cubes and frozen, 4 tablespoons of butter ground perfectly into pieces the same size as the beef and were scattered uniformly throughout the mixture.

A Sticky Situation

Now I was ready to sort out the mechanics of shaping and grilling. I determined that 6 ounces was the ideal portion size: generous but not excessive. A patty that was 4½ inches across would fit perfectly on the average bun once cooked. This gave me patties that were ¾ inch thick, which I figured were just thick enough to allow decent char on the exterior without overcooking at the center (any thicker and they'd be too hard to eat). I also knew from experience that I would need to make a small depression in the center of each patty before grilling to ensure that they finished flat instead of ballooning outward.

But before I could even add those divots, I had to sort out my biggest obstacle: How could I form my burgers so that they wouldn't fall apart on the grate but at the same time achieve that essential open texture? Too much manipulation of ground meat translates to tough burgers, but maybe a little handling of it could work in my favor. If I could draw out just a little sticky myosin, maybe it would help hold the burgers together without making them tough. First I tried kneading the ground meat lightly as if it were dough. Unfortunately, with this approach knowing exactly when to stop was difficult; it was far too easy to under- or overshoot the mark. What if I heavily kneaded only a small portion of the mixture until it was very sticky and then combined that with the remainder? This wasn't much better; it was a challenge to evenly incorporate the sticky, tightly packed portion into the rest without eventually overworking the lot of it.

Salt, like kneading, also draws out myosin. For this reason, I've always avoided adding it to ground meat before shaping, instead seasoning the patties just before putting them on the grill. I wondered if there was a middle ground. It would certainly be easier to control how much salt I added compared with how much I kneaded, so I made batches of burgers containing increasing amounts of salt, from ¼ teaspoon up to 1 teaspoon per pound of meat. Adding the salt and then using a fork to toss the meat allowed me to evenly distribute the salt without overworking the meat. Sadly, small amounts did little to help bind the meat together, and by the time I'd added enough to give them the necessary structure, the resulting burgers were tough and springy.

However, working salt into the interior of the meat did have an upside: It thoroughly seasoned the meat and made it juicier. This made good sense: Just as the salt in a brine helps meat retain moisture as it cooks (salt alters the structure of the proteins to allow them to hold on to water more efficiently), the salt mixed into the ground meat ensured that it stayed juicy and moist on the grill. I just had to be precise, adding only as much salt as I could get away with before adversely affecting the burgers' texture. That turned out to be ½ teaspoon per pound.

Chill Out and Loosen Up

I had made great progress, but if I couldn't find a way to keep my burgers intact, it didn't matter how good they tasted. My loosely formed patties held together pretty well for the first few seconds on the grill, but as soon as the meat lost its chill from the refrigerator, the patties started to fall apart. I needed an approach that would hold the patties together long enough for them to develop a crust (which would then take over the job). When I thought about it that way, the answer became obvious: Freeze them. For my next test, I placed the burgers in the freezer until they were just firm but not frozen solid (which took about 30 minutes) and then headed out to the grill. As I'd hoped, by the time they'd thawed at their centers, they had developed enough crust to ensure that they held together. In fact, because they were cold, I found that they could stay on the grill a few minutes longer per side—gaining even more tasty char and making flipping all the more fail-safe—without going beyond medium-rare.

All that remained were the details of the fire itself.

To ensure that the burgers charred on the exterior dramatically and quickly, a hot fire proved best. Since they took up very little real estate on the grate, I corralled a few quarts of charcoal inside a disposable aluminum roasting pan (perforated to let in oxygen so that they would burn) underneath the burgers to guarantee a cooking space that was plenty hot. (On a gas grill, this translated to setting all the burners to high and preheating the grill for 15 minutes.)

Whether served with the classic fixings like lettuce and tomato or something fancier—I developed three different creamy grilled-vegetable toppings—this was a grilled burger that actually lived up to my ideal.

TENDER, JUICY GRILLED BURGERS
SERVES 4

This recipe requires freezing the meat twice, for a total of 65 to 80 minutes, before grilling. When stirring the salt and pepper into the ground meat and shaping the patties, take care not to overwork the meat or the burgers will become dense. Sirloin steak tips are also sold as flap meat. Serve the burgers with your favorite toppings or one of our grilled-vegetable toppings (for our free recipes for Grilled Scallion Topping, Grilled Shiitake Mushroom Topping, and Grilled Napa Cabbage and Radicchio Topping, go to CooksIllustrated.com/aug14).

- 1½ pounds sirloin steak tips, trimmed and cut into ½-inch chunks
- 4 tablespoons unsalted butter, cut into ¼-inch pieces
  Kosher salt and pepper
- 1 (13 by 9-inch) disposable aluminum pan (if using charcoal)
- 4 hamburger buns

1. Place beef chunks and butter on large plate in single layer. Freeze until meat is very firm and starting to harden around edges but still pliable, about 35 minutes.

2. Place one-quarter of meat and one-quarter of butter cubes in food processor and pulse until finely ground into pieces size of rice grains (about 1/32 inch), 15 to 20 pulses, stopping and redistributing meat around bowl as necessary to ensure beef is evenly ground. Transfer meat to baking sheet. Repeat grinding with remaining 3 batches of meat and butter. Spread mixture over sheet and inspect carefully, discarding any long strands of gristle or large chunks of hard meat, fat, or butter.

3. Sprinkle 1 teaspoon pepper and ¾ teaspoon salt over meat and gently toss with fork to combine. Divide meat into 4 balls. Toss each between hands until uniformly but lightly packed. Gently flatten into patties ¾ inch thick and about 4½ inches in diameter. Using thumb, make 1-inch-wide by ¼-inch-deep depression in center of each patty. Transfer patties to platter and freeze for 30 to 45 minutes.

Add Salt for Juicier Burgers

Mixing ground meat with too much salt will make burgers tough, but ¾ teaspoon helps the meat retain its juices.

Make a Burger That Goes Splat

Store-bought burger meat can't help but cook up dense and tough. It's ground very fine and then wrapped up tightly for retail—factors that cause too much of the sticky protein myosin to be released, literally gluing the meat together. By grinding meat ourselves, we can keep it coarse and pack it gently into patties that stay fall-apart tender.

A TOUGH SELL
This burger made with preground meat held together even when we dropped a 10-pound Dutch oven on it.

SMASHINGLY TENDER
Meat ground at home delivers a much more tender burger, one that splattered easily under the Dutch oven's weight.

4A. FOR A CHARCOAL GRILL: Using skewer, poke 12 holes in bottom of disposable pan. Open bottom vent completely and place disposable pan in center of grill. Light large chimney starter filled two-thirds with charcoal briquettes (4 quarts). When top coals are partially covered with ash, pour into disposable pan. Set cooking grate in place, cover, and open lid vent completely. Heat grill until hot, about 5 minutes.

4B. FOR A GAS GRILL: Turn all burners to high, cover, and heat grill until hot, about 15 minutes. Leave all burners on high.

5. Clean and oil cooking grate. Season 1 side of patties liberally with salt and pepper. Using spatula, flip patties and season other side. Grill patties (directly over coals if using charcoal), without moving them, until browned and meat easily releases from grill, 4 to 7 minutes. Flip burgers and continue to grill until browned on second side and meat registers 125 degrees for medium-rare or 130 degrees for medium, 4 to 7 minutes longer.

6. Transfer burgers to plate and let rest for 5 minutes. While burgers rest, lightly toast buns on grill, 1 to 2 minutes. Transfer burgers to buns and serve.

Eggplant Involtini

The classic approach to these cheese-filled eggplant rolls—breading and frying—is tedious, and it obscures the signature ingredient. We ditched both steps for a lighter, less fussy dish.

⪼ BY ANDREA GEARY ⪻

The first recipe I made for eggplant *involtini* ("little bundles" in Italian) was so complicated and messy that I wondered if it was the malicious invention of someone who wanted cooks to suffer.

It started innocently enough with a homemade tomato sauce. While that simmered, I cut two eggplants lengthwise into ½-inch-thick planks and fried them. Frying sounds like one step, but in this case it was actually several: Before frying, I had to salt the planks for 45 minutes to remove excess moisture, pat them dry, and coat them in flour, eggs, and bread crumbs. After doing that with four batches, I was still only halfway done.

I mixed up a ricotta filling, spread a dollop of it on each slice, rolled up the slices, and arranged them in a baking dish. I poured the sauce over the bundles, topped the assembly with mozzarella and Parmesan, and baked it for 30 minutes—barely enough time to clear up the devastation my project had left in its wake.

The resulting dish was rich and hefty, similar to classic eggplant Parmesan, though the process had been slightly more arduous, thanks to that rolling-rather-than-layering step. While eggplant Parmesan is justifiably popular, both the making and the eating are a bit heavy going for the height of summer.

But I was charmed by those tidy little involtini, and the combination of eggplant, tomato sauce, and cheese has timeless appeal. My goal: Come up with a version of involtini that would emphasize the eggplant and minimize the fuss.

The (Not So) Bitter Truth

Many eggplant recipes begin by treating the cut fruit with a heavy dose of salt to draw out excess moisture. It supposedly pulls out bitterness, too.

Let's start with the second claim: It's true that unsalted eggplant can taste a tad bitter from compounds called alkaloids that are found under the skin and in the seeds, but salt doesn't really draw

To save on cleanup, we simmer the eggplant rolls in the skillet used to make the sauce and then slide the skillet under the broiler to brown the cheese.

many of those compounds out. As we've found with other bitter-tasting foods, like coffee and grapefruit, salt merely masks bitter flavors; it doesn't eliminate them. And though eggplants were once very bitter indeed, as food scientist Harold McGee points out in *On Food and Cooking*, this trait has been significantly reduced through selective breeding methods. In short, bitterness is less of an issue than it once was. But the excess water problem? That's real.

The flesh of an eggplant is made up of millions of tiny air-filled compartments enclosed by water-fortified walls. If you fry eggplant without removing some of that water beforehand, two things happen: First, those air sacs flood with oil, turning the eggplant greasy. Second, when heat turns the water to steam, some of it will become trapped in the eggplant's flesh. And as the steam forcibly tries to escape, it will damage the structure of the fruit. The result? Mushy, oily, and entirely unappetizing eggplant.

When you salt eggplant, some of that potentially destructive water is removed, so the walls of the air sacs weaken and collapse. That sounds bad, but it's

actually good: The end result is eggplant with a more compact, meatier consistency. And a denser texture means that there are fewer places for oil to get trapped.

But I didn't want to devote 45 minutes to drying out the eggplant if I didn't have to. Instead, I tried a test kitchen shortcut: microwaving the planks in a single layer for about 6 minutes. Unfortunately, the microwave's limited capacity meant that I could work with only one-quarter of the eggplant at a time, so 12 slices of eggplant required almost half an hour of intermittent engagement. It wasn't ideal.

Bake It Better

By this time there was a rebellious thought lurking in the back of my mind: Maybe I wouldn't fry the eggplant. True, most recipes I found required frying the planks, either breaded or plain, but I was after a simpler, lighter, cleaner-tasting dish. And if I didn't fry, maybe I wouldn't have to salt.

Recipes for grilled eggplant rarely call for preliminary salting. That's because there's little oil on the grill for the flesh to soak up, and the eggplant's excess water quickly evaporates. I wasn't about to fire up the grill, but I wondered if other dry-heat cooking methods might offer the same benefits.

I peeled two eggplants and cut them into ½-inch-thick planks. Broiling the plain slices (I skipped the breading to lighten the dish and its workload) on a wire rack set in a rimmed baking sheet worked pretty well but demanded near-constant vigilance and flipping halfway through to prevent burning. It also required working in two batches. Hoping for a hands-off method, I tried baking instead.

I brushed the planks with oil, seasoned them with salt and pepper, and then baked them on two greased parchment-lined baking sheets in a 375-degree oven for about 30 minutes. Happily, they emerged light brown and tender, with a compact texture that was neither mushy nor sodden. Though the tops and sides of the slices had dried out nicely, there was still a bit of residual moisture on the undersides, so I let the planks cool and firm up on the baking sheet for 5 minutes and then flipped them to allow the remaining steam to escape. These slices were meaty and tender, but not at all squishy, and I didn't miss frying. It was time to move on to the filling.

We trade the salting, breading, and frying steps that classic recipes employ for a lighter, no-fuss approach.

1. SLICE Lay each peeled eggplant on its side and slice it lengthwise into ½-inch-thick planks (you should have 12 planks).

2. BAKE Brush both sides of slices with oil, season with salt and pepper, and bake until tender and lightly browned, about 30 minutes.

3. STUFF AND ROLL With widest end facing you, place portion of ricotta mixture on bottom third of slice. Roll into cylinder.

Less Cheese, More Flavor

Ricotta, which forms the base for most involtini fillings, is subtle, so you have to use a lot of it if you want it to stand up to the tomato sauce. But for these lighter involtini, I wanted to decrease the overall amount of cheese. Swapping some of the ricotta for a lesser amount of a more assertive cheese seemed like the way to go.

I limited myself to 1 cup of ricotta, which was half the amount required by that initial recipe. Adding ½ cup of grated Parmesan and a handful of chopped basil to bump up its flavor didn't cut it, though, and the texture of the filling was unexpectedly tight and bouncy. In my next batch, I used bolder Pecorino Romano instead of the Parmesan, and I stirred in a tablespoon of lemon juice. Things started looking (and tasting) brighter—but that resilient texture remained.

It was clear that the dry, aged cheese—whether Parmesan or Pecorino—was the source of that tight, granular texture. Just a small handful was fine, but when I added a full ½ cup to 1 cup of ricotta, the texture of the filling deteriorated from creamy to firm. In fact, it reminded me of ground meat that had been overcooked, and I wondered if it was indeed the same problem: an excessive linking of proteins. And that thought led me to the solution: bread crumbs.

When you add a paste of bread crumbs and milk (called a panade) to ground meat, it interferes with the linking of the meat proteins so that the cooked meat stays loose and soft. Bingo. When I incorporated just one slice of bread, whizzed to crumbs in the food processor, into the ricotta-Pecorino combo (no milk required), the filling remained creamy.

Streamlining the Sauce

It was time to circle back to the beginning: the tomato sauce. The placeholder recipe I had been working with called for sautéing onions and garlic, adding canned diced tomatoes and seasonings, and simmering the sauce for at least an hour. It wasn't all

that onerous, but my success with the eggplant and the filling had raised the bar, and now I demanded a sauce that could be made from start to finish while the eggplant had its 30-minute stint in the oven.

Diced tomatoes don't break down easily because they're treated with calcium chloride during processing to help them keep their chunky shape, hence the lengthy cooking time. I briefly flirted with the idea of going with fresh summer tomatoes, but blanching, peeling, and cooking them down wasn't consistent with my goals of speed and simplicity. Instead I swapped the diced tomatoes for more-tender canned whole tomatoes (where the calcium chloride works only on the exterior of the tomato) that I chopped roughly, and the sauce came together in about half the time. To trim a few more minutes, I stripped the sauce down to the bare bones: just garlic, oregano, tomatoes, and a pinch of red pepper flakes. This simpler sauce fit perfectly into my more streamlined dish.

Bread Crumbs: Outside to Inside

In most involtini recipes bread crumbs are used to coat the eggplant, but in our version we put them in the cheese. The bread crumbs keep the filling creamy by preventing the Pecorino Romano proteins from linking tightly.

Between ditching the salting, trading frying for baking, and making a quick- rather than long-simmered sauce, I had saved loads of time on prep, but it occurred to me that I could save a bit more time on cleanup, too. I made the sauce in a 12-inch skillet instead of a saucepan, and I nestled the filled eggplant rolls directly in the simmering sauce. When the rolls had begun to warm through, I moved the whole skillet to the broiler instead of the oven.

After about 5 minutes, the eggplant was nicely browned and the sauce was bubbly and hot. I let my creation cool slightly and then crowned it with an additional dusting of Pecorino and a sprinkling of basil before serving directly from the skillet.

No one would mistake this light, fresh skillet supper for rich and heavy eggplant Parmesan. The eggplant truly shines, and the cheese and sauce complement it rather than weigh it down. And the best part might just be how easy it is to make—no one will ever blame me for taking advantage of a cook's precious time.

EGGPLANT INVOLTINI
SERVES 4 TO 6

Select shorter, wider eggplants for this recipe. Part-skim ricotta may be used, but do not use fat-free ricotta. Serve the eggplant with crusty bread and a salad.

- 2 large eggplants (1½ pounds each), peeled
- 6 tablespoons vegetable oil
  Kosher salt and pepper
- 2 garlic cloves, minced
- ¼ teaspoon dried oregano
  Pinch red pepper flakes
- 1 (28-ounce) can whole peeled tomatoes, drained with juice reserved, chopped coarse
- 1 slice hearty white sandwich bread, torn into 1-inch pieces
- 8 ounces (1 cup) whole-milk ricotta cheese
- 1½ ounces grated Pecorino Romano cheese (¾ cup)
- ¼ cup plus 1 tablespoon chopped fresh basil
- 1 tablespoon lemon juice

1. Slice each eggplant lengthwise into ½-inch-thick planks (you should have 12 planks). Trim rounded surface from each end piece so it lies flat.

2. Adjust 1 oven rack to lower-middle position and second rack 8 inches from broiler element. Heat oven to 375 degrees. Line 2 rimmed baking sheets with parchment paper and spray generously with vegetable oil spray. Arrange eggplant slices in single layer on prepared sheets. Brush 1 side of eggplant slices with 2½ tablespoons oil and sprinkle with ½ teaspoon salt and ¼ teaspoon pepper. Flip eggplant slices and brush with 2½ tablespoons oil and sprinkle with ½ teaspoon salt and ¼ teaspoon pepper. Bake until tender and lightly browned, 30 to 35 minutes, switching and rotating sheets halfway through baking. Let cool for 5 minutes. Using thin spatula, flip each slice over. Heat broiler.

3. While eggplant cooks, heat remaining 1 tablespoon oil in 12-inch broiler-safe skillet over medium-low heat until just shimmering. Add garlic, oregano, pepper flakes, and ½ teaspoon salt and cook, stirring occasionally, until fragrant, about 30 seconds. Stir in tomatoes and their juice. Increase heat to high and bring to simmer. Reduce heat to medium-low and simmer until thickened, about 15 minutes. Cover and set aside.

4. Pulse bread in food processor until finely ground, 10 to 15 pulses. Combine bread crumbs, ricotta, ½ cup Pecorino, ¼ cup basil, lemon juice, and ½ teaspoon salt in medium bowl.

5. With widest ends of eggplant slices facing you, evenly distribute ricotta mixture on bottom third of each slice. Gently roll up each eggplant slice and place seam side down in tomato sauce.

6. Bring sauce to simmer over medium heat. Simmer for 5 minutes. Transfer skillet to oven and broil until eggplant is well browned and cheese is heated through, 5 to 10 minutes. Sprinkle with remaining ¼ cup Pecorino and let stand for 5 minutes. Sprinkle with remaining 1 tablespoon basil and serve.

Smoky Pulled Pork on a Gas Grill

We've always believed that a gas grill just can't match charcoal when it comes to flavor.
But after months of testing, our gas-grilled pulled pork didn't just match charcoal—it beat it.

⇒ BY LAN LAM ⇐

When it comes to making pulled pork on the grill, few would disagree that a charcoal grill is a better bet than a gas grill for creating meltingly tender meat full of pungent, sweet-sharp smoke flavor. As barbecue purists will tell you, it's hard—if not impossible—to produce the same quality of smoke on a gas grill as you can over charcoal. That said, a gas grill is infinitely more convenient. There's no messy setup or cleanup: Just flip a switch and you're good to go. Plus, you can cook a large pork roast on the grill the whole time instead of finishing it in the oven or dealing with refueling, which charcoal versions require.

This year, on behalf of those who embrace convenience (or simply don't have a charcoal grill), I decided to challenge the assumption that a gas grill is an inferior choice for smoking meat. I set out to nail down an ironclad method that would eliminate inconsistencies when smoking over gas, delivering pulled pork that would rival that made with a charcoal grill. I would take nothing at face value—even the idea that wood chips were the best source for smoke (see "What Were We Smoking?"). The only ground rule I set for myself: I would not resort to cheating by using liquid smoke or any presmoked material (such as smoked tea leaves).

Priming the Pork

One thing that wasn't up for debate was what cut of pork to use. Pork butt is ideal because it's collagen-rich and has the right amount of intramuscular fat. During cooking, that fat renders while the collagen transforms into water-retaining gelatin, together giving pulled pork its tender texture. I started by trimming a 5-pound roast of excess fat, and then I cut it into thirds. This would not only lessen the cooking time (which is usually about 7 hours) but also increase the number of surfaces that smoke could cling to.

With ample fat and collagen, pork butt is ideal for pulled pork. To maximize the surface area that smoke can cling to, we cut it into thirds.

And while I would add a spice rub later, for the time being I decided to sprinkle on just salt to make it easier to assess smoke flavor. I rubbed on plenty (5 teaspoons), wrapped the pieces tightly in plastic wrap, and left them to sit overnight in the refrigerator. This would give the meat time to absorb the salt, seasoning it and changing its protein structure so that it could retain more of its juices during cooking.

The next day, I moved out to the grill. I knew from experience that I would need to cook the pork until it reached an internal temperature of 195 degrees: If cooked any less, the meat would be chewy and tough, but if it went too much above 200 degrees, it would start to dry out. For the bulk of the cooking time, though, I wanted to keep the meat between 160 and 180 degrees, the range in which the connective tissue will slowly break down. To do this, a low-and-slow cooking method—using indirect heat and maintaining a grill temperature of around 300 degrees—would be key. A couple of water-filled pie plates under the cooking grate would catch any juices that dripped and prevent them from burning. The plates would also create a moist environment that would keep the exterior of the pork from drying out and help smoke stick to the meat. A few quick tests (without smoke at this point) established a cooking time of 4 to 5 hours. With the framework of my recipe settled, I was ready to face the main challenge: perfecting the smoke.

In Search of Smoke

I started by taking a close look at our procedures for using wood chips on a gas grill. The goal is to get chips to smolder slowly and consistently; if they ignite and burn up quickly, some of the compounds in the wood that would normally add desired flavor to the meat instead go up in flames, and what doesn't burn off adds a sooty, acrid flavor to the food. We usually address this concern by soaking the chips in water for 15 minutes and then wrapping the soaked chips in a foil packet and poking a few holes in it to let out the smoke. The packet is placed on the primary burner, below the cooking grate. Starting with the flame cranked up to high gets the smoke going (and preheats the grill), and then we adjust the heat to low to maintain the appropriate barbecuing temperature before putting on the food to cook.

While these directions have always delivered acceptable results, they also seemed open to interpretation—a hunch that was confirmed when I asked several kitchen interns to follow them. The packets they created were all different sizes and punctured with different-size openings. Not surprisingly, when we sampled the end results, the smoke flavor of the pork was also all over the map, ranging from decently smoky to basically nonexistent.

Obviously, one critical piece of business was to come up with a very specific set of instructions for making the packets that would ensure uniformity from cook to cook and, in turn, produce a consistent amount of smoke. The first step was to be as precise as possible about the quantity of chips. We've always measured chips by volume, but we've done plenty of tests that prove that volume measurements vary, depending on who is doing the measuring. As persnickety as it might sound, if I truly wanted consistency, I'd need to weigh the chips. When barbecuing

See How to Set It Up
Video available free for 4 months
at CooksIllustrated.com/aug14

meat over a long period of time, we have typically called for 4 cups of chips, so that seemed like the best amount to start my testing with. I settled on 4 cups of chips weighing 9½ ounces.

Next I experimented with the size of the foil packets. Though we've sometimes called for wrapping all the chips in a single packet, I found this setup unwieldy. I landed on dividing the chips between two packets that I folded into 8 by 4½-inch rectangles, each of which sat nicely over the burner. I then tried cutting a number of openings of various sizes and shapes into the foil. I poked holes in some packets and cut slits in others. An important point: The openings control how much smoke goes out as well as how much oxygen comes in. When the oxygen was too plentiful (i.e., the openings were too large), the chips quickly burned up instead of smoldering. But if the openings were too small or too few, the chips didn't get enough oxygen to even smolder. Two evenly spaced 2-inch slits were best, producing a consistent stream of smoke. I also realized that I needed to be careful about how I arranged the packets on the burner, since the bars of the cooking grate could block the slits and prevent smoke from escaping.

With a packet made to my specifications, I realized that soaking the chips wasn't preventing them from igniting; it was simply delaying the onset of smoke. Because I was so carefully controlling the oxygen availability, soaked or not, the chips in my packets weren't going up in flames, and in either case a packet filled with 2 cups of chips always produced about 45 to 60 minutes of smoke.

Knowing that I had a set amount of smoke to work with, my next question was, would it be better to use two packets of unsoaked chips, which would allow me to inundate the meat with smoke at the beginning of cooking, or would producing a smaller stream of smoke over a longer period by using one packet of soaked chips and one packet of unsoaked chips be better? Our recipe for Smoked Chicken (July/August 2011) had turned up a few important factors about smoking that could help argue for either case. First, more smoke flavor gets absorbed early in the cooking process. This is because smoke contains mostly water-soluble compounds, and a piece of meat contains more water at the beginning

What Were We Smoking?

In our quest to get the richest smoke flavor possible into pulled pork made on a gas grill, we experimented with other sources of smoke beyond the traditional wood chips. Our conclusion? Getting things like cinnamon sticks to smolder on the grill is fun and quirky, but wood chips still provide the best smoke flavor.

PANTRY FINDS

When wood smolders, the cellulose, hemicellulose, and lignin compounds that it contains break down and flavor food. So we looked for pantry items with a similar makeup to see if they would work any better. Cinnamon sticks, dried garbanzo beans, and walnut shells all produced smoke, but it was weak—almost sweet—rather than bold, as you'd expect with wood-smoked barbecue.

PUCKS, BRICKS, AND PELLETS

Made by compressing wood chips and sawdust, smoker pucks and bricks were hard to arrange on the gas grill, and they usually caught fire. Wood pellets and sawdust-type products, sealed in a foil packet according to their instructions, required frequent refueling for pulled pork—they would be fine for a quickly smoked pork chop but were not worth the effort here.

of cooking: As it cooks, water slowly evaporates. Second, a piece of food can absorb only so much smoke flavor at any given point. Finally, when the meat is at its smoke-absorption capacity in either situation, some smoke just drifts away through the grill vents, but some of it can break down on the food's surface, giving it a harsh, acrid taste.

The only way to know which approach was best was to smoke some pork. I cooked one batch over two packets of dry chips, and another batch over one packet of soaked chips and one dry. While it was a close call, a handful of tasters felt that the batch in which both packets were dry and thus inundated with smoke was acrid-tasting: Stretching out the smoke over a longer period of time ensured that the pork could absorb maximum smoke gradually without off-flavors.

The results were impressively smoky, but tasters still wondered if I could boost the smokiness just a little more. Since I was at the upper limit for how much wood I could fit on the grill, I focused on finding a way to get more of the existing smoke into the meat. As it cooked, the pork was releasing juices into the water-filled pan below—juices that were infused with smoky flavor. Why should it all go to waste? When the smoke petered out after the

first 1½ hours of cooking, I transferred the meat to a disposable aluminum roasting pan. This way, any juices that released during the remaining cooking time would be collected. I stirred a portion of the juices back into the meat after shredding it. (Stirring all the juices back in made the final consistency too liquidy.)

I also wondered if there was a way to get more smoke to cling to the meat, instead of letting it escape through the vents and into the air. A coworker with whom I was chatting about my dilemma noted that my clothes actually smelled smokier on cold days. She was onto something: On cooler days, the surface of my coat was cold, and when the smoke particles came in contact with it, they quickly changed from gas to solid, thus clinging to my coat rather than drifting off into the air above. Could the same logic be applied to the pork? For my next test, instead of pulling the pork from the fridge when I headed outside to set up the grill, which caused its surface temperature to rise about 10 degrees before I set it on the grates, I waited to pull it from the fridge until I was ready to start cooking. Once this final batch was cool enough to handle, I shredded the meat and waited for my tasters to comment. By their expressions, I could tell that with

The Importance of a Just-So Packet

In the past, we've found that sealing wood chips in a foil packet with a few slits cut into it is the best method for producing smoke on a gas grill. We confirmed that that's still the case, but we also found that our directions for making a packet have been too vague. By ironing out the details, we ensure consistent, steady smoke from one packet to the next.

➤ Eight by 4½-inch packets hold 4.75 oz of chips, the maximum amount that will fit on the burner.

➤ Two 2-inch-long slits let in just enough oxygen for a steady smolder. (Be careful that the slits don't get blocked by the grate's bars.)

➤ Weigh the chips—don't measure by volume—since chips vary greatly in size.

➤ Since the pork can absorb only so much smoke at any moment, soak half of the chips to draw out the smoke over a longer period.

these last tweaks I'd really nailed a deep smoke flavor.

It was time to focus on the dry rub and the sauce. I ruled out cumin, mustard, and chili powder for rub ingredients; these spices masked rather than enhanced the smoke's flavor. A simple mixture of paprika, brown sugar, and pepper rubbed onto the pork along with the salt added depth without taking over and also provided some color and helped create an appealing bark-like crust. As for the sauce, a combination of cider vinegar, ketchup, brown sugar, and red pepper flakes cut cleanly through the pork's richness and, like the rub, helped amplify the smoky flavor.

I had one final test to go: I asked my tasters to compare my gas-grilled pulled pork with pulled pork made on a charcoal grill in a blind tasting. The moment of truth: Tasters unanimously agreed that my gas-grilled version boasted not just as much smoke flavor but, in fact, more. That's right, barbecue purists: more smoke flavor.

With this method, gas grill owners—or at least those who are willing to be very precise in their method—never have to feel sheepish about making pulled pork. My pulled pork is as good and smoky as backyard barbecue gets.

SMOKY PULLED PORK ON A GAS GRILL
SERVES 8 TO 10

Pork butt roast is often labeled Boston butt in the supermarket. We developed this recipe with hickory chips, though other varieties of hardwood can be used. (We do not recommend mesquite chips.) Before beginning, check your propane tank to make sure that you have at least a half-tank of fuel. If you happen to run out of fuel, you can move the pork to a preheated 300-degree oven to finish cooking. Serve the pulled pork on white bread or hamburger buns with pickles and coleslaw.

Pork
	Kosher salt and pepper
2	teaspoons paprika
2	teaspoons packed light brown sugar
1	(5-pound) boneless pork butt roast, trimmed
9½	ounces wood chips (4 cups)
2	(9-inch) disposable aluminum pie plates
1	(13 by 9-inch) disposable aluminum roasting pan

Vinegar Sauce
2	cups cider vinegar
2	tablespoons ketchup
2	teaspoons packed light brown sugar
1	teaspoon red pepper flakes
1	teaspoon kosher salt

1. FOR THE PORK: Combine 5 teaspoons salt, 2½ teaspoons pepper, paprika, and sugar in small bowl. Cut pork against grain into 3 equal slabs. Rub salt mixture into pork, making sure meat is evenly coated. Wrap pork tightly in plastic wrap and refrigerate for at least 6 hours or up to 24 hours.

2. Just before grilling, soak 2 cups wood chips in water for 15 minutes, then drain. Using large piece of heavy-duty aluminum foil, wrap soaked chips in 8 by 4½-inch foil packet. (Make sure chips do not poke holes in sides or bottom of packet.) Repeat with remaining 2 cups unsoaked chips. Cut 2 evenly spaced, 2-inch slits in top of each packet.

3. Remove cooking grate and place wood chip packets directly on primary burner. Place disposable pie plates, each filled with 3 cups water, directly on other burner(s). Set grate in place, turn all burners to high, cover, and heat grill until hot and wood chips are smoking, about 15 minutes. Turn primary burner to medium and turn off other burner(s). (Adjust primary burner as needed to maintain grill temperature of 300 degrees.)

4. Clean and oil cooking grate. Place pork on cooler side of grill, directly over water pans; cover; and smoke for 1½ hours.

5. Transfer pork to disposable pan. Return disposable pan to cooler side of grill and continue to cook until meat registers 200 degrees, 2½ to 3 hours.

6. Transfer pork to carving board and let rest for 20 minutes. Pour juices from disposable pan into fat separator and let stand for 5 minutes.

7. FOR THE VINEGAR SAUCE: While pork rests, whisk all ingredients together in bowl. Using 2 forks, shred pork into bite-size pieces. Stir ⅓ cup defatted juices and ½ cup sauce into pork. Serve, passing remaining sauce separately.

Maximizing Smoky Flavor on a Gas Grill

In addition to getting the details of the wood chip packet just right, we made several other small adjustments that together paid off with big smoky flavor.

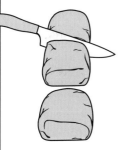

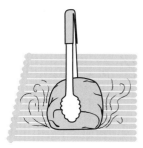

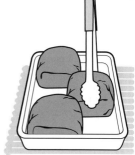

INCREASE SURFACE AREA
Cutting a 5-pound boneless pork butt roast into three equal slabs provides more total surface area for the smoke to cling to.

ADD HUMIDITY
Placing two water-filled pans in the grill creates a humid environment that keeps the surface of the meat moist, which allows for better absorption of water-soluble smoke compounds.

PUT COLD PORK ON GRILL
Smoke will condense more easily on a cold surface, so we put the pieces of pork on the grill straight from the fridge rather than bringing it to room temperature as many recipes suggest.

CATCH THE SMOKY JUICES
When the smoke peters out, putting the pieces of pork in a pan saves smoky juices that can be added back before serving.

Introducing White Gazpacho

Think you know gazpacho? Meet its rich and creamy—but still light—predecessor.

⇒ BY LAN LAM ⇐

My first introduction to Spanish white gazpacho, or *ajo blanco*, was a revelation. The silky soup arrived ice-cold in a small bowl, decorated with a delicate mosaic of almonds, sliced grapes, and vibrantly green olive oil. Its flavors were as intricate as its appearance: Some bites offered a nutty crunch, while others were sharply fruity and floral; in still others, peppery extra-virgin olive oil was at the fore. When I learned that the complexity had been coaxed from just a handful of ingredients, I was intrigued.

A little research taught me that white gazpacho predates the familiar red version since tomatoes didn't reach Spain until after Columbus. The rock-bottom-cheap ajo blanco was prepared by peasants with five ingredients at their disposal: stale bread, garlic, vinegar, oil, and salt. They pounded the bread and garlic with a mortar and pestle, added slugs of vinegar and oil with salt to taste, and either ate the gazpacho in that form or stirred in water to make it drinkable. When the dish migrated from the tables of laborers to those of aristocrats, upscale ingredients like almonds and grapes (or even fish or pickled vegetables) went into the mix, transforming a humble mush into a dish meant to impress.

And yet, the first couple of batches I whipped up from modern recipes were far from impressive. Some were watery and bland; others were grainy and salad dressing–esque. I decided to nail down my technique before figuring out the flavor.

Although traditionalists rely on a mortar and pestle (and elbow grease), I planned on putting a kitchen appliance to work. I pulled out a blender and a food processor and loaded each with placeholder amounts of bread, almonds, garlic, vinegar, and water. I pureed the ingredients and then streamed oil into each machine. When I strained the soups, I could plainly see that the blender had done the better job of breaking down the solids, but the soup was still marred by tiny almond bits.

I recalled that the recipes employing a mortar and pestle proceeded in a specific manner. First, the almonds were finely crushed. Meanwhile, the bread was soaked in water to facilitate grinding. The almonds and bread were then mixed into a paste and only then was liquid incorporated. I mimicked

Toasted almonds and grapes provide textural contrast.

the process in a blender: I buzzed the almonds until they were powdery and then added the soaked bread, garlic, a splash of vinegar, and salt and pepper. Once these ingredients were pureed, I drizzled in the olive oil and finally thinned the soup with more water. This soup was thicker, creamier, and smoother than ever.

Now that I had a foolproof procedure, I examined the ingredients. Stale bread never produced a soup that was significantly different from fresh, and plain old sandwich bread worked as well as (if not better than) fancy artisanal types. Blanched sliced almonds were best since they didn't create brown flecks in the ivory soup. Brightened with sherry vinegar and a pinch of cayenne, my gazpacho was tasty, but I had yet to capture the fruity, floral flavors that had drawn me to this unique recipe in the first place.

Switching from everyday extra-virgin olive oil to a premium brand added a fruity, peppery pop. I tried toasting the almonds but this darkened the soup and gave it a toasted flavor that was less than refreshing. Finally, I realized that the sharper, almost flowery profile of bitter almonds (found in almond extract) would be a better fit. I made another batch with just a drop of extract, and this hit the mark. However, even an extra drop of extract ruined the gazpacho. For foolproof measuring, I mixed ⅛ teaspoon of the extract into a tablespoon of soup and then stirred 1 teaspoon of the extract mixture into the soup.

As for garnishes, thinly sliced green grapes were a given. For crunch, I toasted a few almonds in oil and sprinkled them lightly with salt. After ladling the soup into bowls, I mounded the garnishes in the center and then drizzled on my oil. This gazpacho had the taste to back up its looks.

▶ Lan Makes the Soup
Video available free for 4 months at CooksIllustrated.com/aug14

SPANISH CHILLED ALMOND AND GARLIC SOUP
SERVES 6 TO 8

This rich soup is best when served in small portions (about 6 ounces). Use a good-quality extra-virgin olive oil. Our favorite is Columela Extra Virgin Olive Oil. Too much almond extract can ruin the soup. Hence, the unusual mixing technique in step 4.

- 6 slices hearty white sandwich bread, crusts removed
- 4 cups water
- 2½ cups (8¾ ounces) plus ⅓ cup sliced blanched almonds
- 1 garlic clove, peeled
- 3 tablespoons sherry vinegar
  Kosher salt and pepper
  Pinch cayenne pepper
- ½ cup extra-virgin olive oil, plus extra for drizzling
- ⅛ teaspoon almond extract
- 2 teaspoons vegetable oil
- 6 ounces seedless green grapes, sliced thin (1 cup)

1. Combine bread and water in bowl and let soak for 5 minutes. Process 2½ cups almonds in blender until finely ground, about 30 seconds, scraping down sides of blender jar as needed.

2. Using your hands, remove bread from water, squeeze it lightly, and transfer to blender with almonds. Measure 3 cups soaking water and set aside; transfer remaining soaking water to blender.

3. Add garlic, vinegar, 1¼ teaspoons salt, and cayenne to blender and process until mixture has consistency of cake batter, 30 to 45 seconds. With blender running, add olive oil in thin, steady stream, about 30 seconds. Add reserved soaking water and process for 1 minute. Season with salt and pepper to taste. Strain soup through fine-mesh strainer set in bowl, pressing on solids to extract liquid. Discard solids.

4. Measure 1 tablespoon of soup into second bowl and stir in almond extract. Return 1 teaspoon of extract mixture to soup; discard remainder. Chill for at least 3 hours or up to 24 hours.

5. Heat vegetable oil in 8-inch skillet over medium-high heat until oil begins to shimmer. Add remaining ⅓ cup almonds and cook, stirring constantly, until golden brown, 3 to 4 minutes. Immediately transfer to bowl and stir in ¼ teaspoon salt.

6. Ladle soup into shallow bowls. Mound an equal amount of grapes in center of each bowl. Sprinkle cooled almonds over soup and drizzle with extra olive oil. Serve immediately.

Bringing Home Singapore Noodles

The trademark of this Hong Kong stir-fry is its bold curry flavor, but all that curry powder creates a dusty texture. Time for a little innovation.

∋ BY ANDREA GEARY ∈

Nomenclature aside, Singapore noodles have nothing to do with Singapore and are virtually unknown there. In fact, this light, almost fluffy stir-fry of thin, resilient rice noodles, vegetables, and shrimp is native to Hong Kong, and nobody seems to know for sure how it came to be named for a city that's more than 1,500 miles away.

What makes Singapore noodles truly a Hong Kong invention isn't just that the dish includes typical Chinese ingredients like garlic, ginger, and soy. It's that it prominently features curry powder, a spice blend invented by the Brits that probably trickled into Hong Kong's cuisine when it was under British rule. The heady spice blend lends the dish a pervasive aroma of cumin and coriander and a pleasant chile burn—characteristics that make it a classic in Chinese restaurants outside Hong Kong, too, and one of my favorites.

But the curry powder can also be the most problematic element of Singapore noodles. Because this dish is not saucy, the dry powder doesn't distribute evenly, leading to patchy curry flavor (and color), not to mention gritty texture.

This was the core problem I set out to solve when I created my own version of Singapore noodles. And given that I wanted this dish to function as a light yet satisfying one-dish meal, I also vowed to revise the typical ratio of ingredients, which tends to be about 80 percent noodles, with the vegetables and protein acting almost as garnishes.

All Tangled Up

The ingredient list for Singapore noodles is simple—just dried rice noodles (usually thin vermicelli), ordinary vegetables, shrimp, a handful of seasonings, and maybe some eggs—and once the ingredients are prepped, the cooking takes all of 15 minutes.

The universal first step is to soak the rice noodles; you want them to be just pliable, but not fully

▶ See How It Comes Together
Video available free for 4 months
at CooksIllustrated.com/aug14

By bumping up the amount of shrimp and vegetables and adding scrambled eggs, we turn this noodle stir-fry into a one-dish meal.

softened since they'll continue to absorb liquid during cooking. Covering 6 ounces of noodles with boiling water, letting them soak for 2½ minutes, stirring them occasionally, and draining them produced exactly the texture I was hoping for.

From there, I broke out my large nonstick skillet for stir-frying. We've found that this vessel's wide, level surface makes more contact with flat domestic burners than the bowl shape of a wok does, allowing for quicker evaporation, so foods don't steam.

Over a medium-high flame, I heated a couple of teaspoons of vegetable oil and sautéed 12 ounces of large shrimp in a single layer until they'd browned on the bottom. Then I slid the cooked shrimp onto a plate, lowered the heat, added another spoonful of oil, and stir-fried some grated ginger and minced garlic until fragrant. In went some thin-sliced red bell pepper and shallots, which I cooked until tender but still verging on crisp, followed by the drained noodles, ⅔ cup of chicken broth, a couple of splashes of soy sauce, and 2 tablespoons of mild (or "sweet") curry powder—a generous amount that's

about par for the course in this dish. (While the spicier Madras variety of curry powder is common in Singapore noodles, I decided to start with the milder type and see if I needed to add heat.) Then I added back the shrimp, cranked the heat to high, and briefly tossed everything together until the mixture was relatively dry and the noodles were al dente.

At least, I tried to toss everything together. What actually happened was that the long noodles tangled, forming a tight ball that forced most of the vegetables and shrimp to the sides of the skillet. The dish was also still much too noodle-heavy, not to mention lean with just a few teaspoons of oil. And then there was the curry powder: It had given the whole ensemble a predictably gritty texture and a slightly bitter edge. The curious thing was that while those qualities would normally signal spice overload to me, I actually found the curry flavor lacking.

Coming into Bloom

Since increasing the amount of curry powder would only make the dish dustier, I tried switching from mild curry powder to the spicier Madras variety. But it turns out that brands of Madras curry vary widely in their heat output. I was better off using the mild variety and adding heat with a touch of cayenne. As for enhancing the curry flavor, I'd gotten nowhere.

Then it occurred to me to try changing not the amount or type of curry powder, but how I was treating it. We tend to think of spices as a fixed quantity: You get a specific amount of flavor from

Curry Powder: Mild versus Madras

Most curry powders fall into one of two categories: mild or "sweet" (often identified by the lack of any description on the label) and hotter Madras style (which usually is identified as such). Both types contain turmeric, which accounts for the yellow color, as well as warm spices like cumin, ginger, and cardamom. But Madras curry powder has a higher ratio of dried chile and black pepper, which makes it spicier.

a specific amount of spice. But that's not strictly true. It's possible to increase the flavor of a given amount of spice by heating it in oil or butter—a technique called "blooming." That's because the flavor compounds in most spices are fat-soluble, so they infuse readily into oil, and like most chemical interactions, this happens more quickly in a warm environment. As the compounds are drawn from the spice granules into the warm oil, they mix, producing stronger and more complex flavors. I also thought that making a curry-infused oil could provide the missing fat to the dish.

I heated 3 tablespoons of oil in the skillet and stirred in the 2 tablespoons of curry powder I had been using originally. Then I heated the spice oil for 4 minutes over medium-low heat. By that point I could smell that I was on the right track from the rich curry aroma, and my tasters confirmed as much when they tasted the curry oil–dressed noodles, noting the richer, more complex flavor. Even better, blooming the curry powder had caused the spice granules to disperse evenly in the oil, so their grittiness was no longer noticeable. Tasters' only lingering flavor complaint was that the curry was still a touch bitter, but it was nothing that a spoonful of sugar couldn't fix. On to tackling that ball of noodles.

Cuts and Adds

In Chinese tradition long noodles symbolize a long life, but in wrestling with them I'd grown short-tempered, so I made a drastic move. After soaking and draining the vermicelli, I cut across them twice to make them shorter and less tangle-prone.

I also cut the shrimp into ½-inch pieces that dispersed nicely throughout the noodles, and I bulked up the protein and vegetables by adding 4 eggs (scrambled with a little salt), 4 scallions cut into ½-inch pieces, and a couple of cups of bean sprouts.

Of course, adding more elements to the dish made it that much harder to toss everything together neatly in the confines of a skillet, so I moved the operation to a larger mixing bowl. Tossing the cut noodles with the curry oil, soy sauce, and sugar in the deeper vessel made it easier to distribute the dressing evenly throughout the noodles; the lubricating effect of the oil also helped the noodles combine with the rest of the ingredients.

Then, as each pair of components—shrimp and eggs, aromatics and vegetables—finished cooking, I collected them in a second large bowl. To finish softening the dressed noodles, I simmered them in the skillet with the chicken broth, tossing them for about 2 minutes until the broth had been absorbed. Finally, I slid the hot noodles into the bowl with the shrimp and vegetables and squeezed fresh lime juice over the bowl to brighten the flavor.

With bold, complex curry flavor and a more evenly balanced ratio of noodles, protein, and vegetables, my version of Singapore noodles was as satisfying as any I'd had in a Chinese restaurant and would slip easily into my weeknight lineup.

UNTANGLING SINGAPORE NOODLES

Two easy steps help avoid the usual ball of noodles that forms when you toss the rice vermicelli with the shrimp and vegetables.

SHORTEN THE STRANDS
Cutting the soaked and drained rice vermicelli into thirds makes them less tangle-prone.

LUBRICATE WITH CURRY OIL
Coating the noodles with curry oil prevents them from sticking. "Blooming" the spice in oil also boosts its flavor, softens its gritty texture, and adds richness.

SINGAPORE NOODLES
SERVES 4 TO 6

For spicier Singapore noodles, add the optional cayenne pepper. Look for dried rice vermicelli in the Asian section of your supermarket. A rasp-style grater makes quick work of turning the garlic into a paste. For our free recipe for Singapore Noodles for Two, go to CooksIllustrated.com/aug14.

- 4 tablespoons plus 1 teaspoon vegetable oil
- 2 tablespoons curry powder
- ⅛ teaspoon cayenne pepper (optional)
- 6 ounces rice vermicelli
- 2 tablespoons soy sauce
- 1 teaspoon sugar
- 12 ounces large shrimp (26 to 30 per pound), peeled, deveined, tails removed, and cut into ½-inch pieces
- 4 large eggs, lightly beaten
  Salt
- 3 garlic cloves, minced to paste
- 1 teaspoon grated fresh ginger
- 1 red bell pepper, stemmed, seeded, and cut into 2-inch-long matchsticks
- 2 large shallots, sliced thin
- ⅔ cup chicken broth
- 4 ounces (2 cups) bean sprouts
- 4 scallions, cut into ½-inch pieces
- 2 teaspoons lime juice, plus lime wedges for serving

1. Heat 3 tablespoons oil, curry powder, and cayenne, if using, in 12-inch nonstick skillet over medium-low heat, stirring occasionally, until fragrant, about 4 minutes. Remove skillet from heat and set aside.

2. Bring 1½ quarts water to boil. Place noodles in large bowl. Pour boiling water over noodles and stir briefly. Soak noodles until flexible, but not soft, about 2½ minutes, stirring once halfway through soaking. Drain noodles briefly. Transfer noodles to cutting board. Using chef's knife, cut pile of noodles roughly into thirds. Return noodles to bowl, add curry mixture, soy sauce, and sugar; using tongs, toss until well combined. Set aside.

3. Wipe out skillet with paper towels. Heat 2 teaspoons oil in skillet over medium-high heat until shimmering. Add shrimp in even layer and cook without moving them until bottoms are browned, about 90 seconds. Stir and continue to cook until just cooked through, about 90 seconds longer. Push shrimp to 1 side of skillet. Add 1 teaspoon oil to cleared side of skillet. Add eggs to clearing and sprinkle with ¼ teaspoon salt. Using rubber spatula, stir eggs gently until set but still wet, about 1 minute. Stir eggs into shrimp and continue to cook, breaking up large pieces of egg, until eggs are fully cooked, about 30 seconds longer. Transfer shrimp-egg mixture to second large bowl.

4. Reduce heat to medium. Heat remaining 1 teaspoon oil in now-empty skillet until shimmering. Add garlic and ginger and cook, stirring constantly, until fragrant, about 15 seconds. Add bell pepper and shallots. Cook, stirring frequently, until vegetables are crisp-tender, about 2 minutes. Transfer to bowl with shrimp.

5. Return skillet to medium-high heat, add broth to skillet, and bring to simmer. Add noodles and cook, stirring frequently, until liquid is absorbed, about 2 minutes. Add noodles to bowl with shrimp and vegetable mixture and toss to combine. Add bean sprouts, scallions, and lime juice and toss to combine. Transfer to warmed platter and serve immediately, passing lime wedges separately.

How to Cook Perfect Eggs

The two-part nature of eggs makes it maddeningly difficult to cook them just right. Understanding how heat affects each part is the key to better results. BY ELIZABETH BOMZE

The Egg Challenge: One Ingredient, Two Parts

The fundamental challenge in most egg cookery is that an egg is essentially not just one ingredient but two: the white and the yolk. Each has different types and ratios of proteins, fats, and water, which means that each reacts differently to heat, coagulating (or solidifying) at different temperatures. Furthermore, the white, being on the outside and in direct contact with the heat source, cooks much faster than the yolk. The goal of most basic forms of egg cookery (hard-cooking, soft-cooking, poaching, and frying) is to prevent the white from turning rubbery before the yolk has a chance to reach the desired consistency.

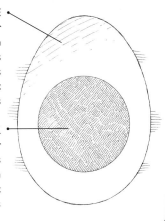

WHITE
88 percent water
11 percent protein
1 percent minerals
and carbohydrates
**Fully set
at 180 degrees**

YOLK
50 percent water
34 percent lipids
16 percent protein
**Fully set
at 158 degrees**

IDEAL HARD-COOKED
➤ **Common Problems:** Rubbery whites; dry, chalky yolks

OUR SOLUTIONS
➤ **Start in Cold Water:** Goal is to get whites and yolks to fully cook at same rates; starting in cold water ensures minimal temperature differential between outside of egg and inside.
➤ **Use Enough Water:** Covering eggs with 1 inch water ensures water has enough thermal capacity to cook them through.
➤ **Bring to Boil; Rest off Heat:** Taking pan off heat causes water temperature to quickly drop below boiling point.
➤ **Cover Pot:** A tight-fitting lid locks in enough heat to ensure that eggs are fully (and perfectly) cooked in 10 minutes.

TIP: Peeling Made Easier
Very fresh eggs are hard to peel because the relatively low pH of the white causes it to adhere strongly to the inner shell membrane. If you have fresh eggs, wait a few days to hard-cook them, or try one of the following tricks.
➤ Add ½ teaspoon of baking soda for every quart of cooking water to raise its pH, which raises the pH of the egg white.
➤ Crack the eggs on the broad end where there is an air pocket, and then roll them on their sides to fracture the shells all over before peeling.

START COLD
Bringing the water to a boil with the eggs—and then resting them off heat—cooks the white and yolk gently.

HARD-COOKED EGGS

6   large eggs

1. Place eggs in medium saucepan, cover with 1 inch water, and bring to rolling boil over high heat. Remove pan from heat, cover, and let rest for 10 minutes. Fill medium bowl with 1 quart water and 1 tray ice cubes.
2. Transfer eggs to ice bath with slotted spoon; let sit for 5 minutes. Serve.
ADJUSTING THE YIELD:
Works with any number of eggs, so long as they fit in a single layer covered by 1 inch of water.

FOOLPROOF SOFT-COOKED
➤ **Common Problems:** Inconsistently set whites and overdone yolks

OUR SOLUTIONS
➤ **Use Cold Eggs and High Heat:** Temperature extremes deliver steepest temperature gradient, ensuring that yolk stays fluid while white cooks through. Using refrigerator-cold eggs and boiling water—consistent temperatures—also makes recipe more foolproof.
➤ **Steam; Don't Boil:** Steaming isn't just faster than boiling; it's more flexible. With only ½ inch water in pan, you can cook anywhere from 1 to 6 eggs without altering timing. That's because curved eggs make very little contact with (and therefore don't lower temperature of) water.
➤ **Shock with Cold Water:** Transferring pot of eggs to sink and placing under cold running water halts carryover cooking, so yolks stay runny and whites stay tender.

GET UP A HEAD OF STEAM
With steam, the water temperature doesn't change when you add the eggs, allowing you to cook up to six.

SOFT-COOKED EGGS

6   large eggs, cold

1. Bring ½ inch water to boil in medium saucepan over medium-high heat. Place eggs in water. Cover and cook for 6½ minutes.
2. Remove cover, transfer saucepan to sink, and place under cold running water for 30 seconds. Serve.
ADJUSTING THE YIELD:
Works with 1 to 6 eggs.

TIP: Soft-Cooked Eggs Gone Cold? Reheat Them
Bring ½ inch water to boil in medium saucepan over medium-high heat. Steam eggs, covered, for 3½ minutes.

FLAWLESS FRIED

➤ **Common Problems:** Overcooked bottoms and raw tops; different cooking rates

OUR SOLUTIONS

➤ **Preheat Pan Gently:** Preheating skillet over low heat for 5 minutes eliminates hot spots and produces consistent temperature over surface.

➤ **Include Two Fats:** Oil can preheat without smoking. Butter delivers great flavor, contains milk proteins that encourage browning, and offers visual cue for pan's temperature: It should take about 1 minute to stop foaming; if it browns in that time, pan is too hot and you should start over.

➤ **Start Medium-High; Finish off Heat:** Briefly frying eggs, covered to trap heat, starts to set whites and brown edges. Finishing them off heat allows whites to cook through without overcooking yolks.

FRIED EGGS

2 teaspoons vegetable oil
4 large eggs
   Salt and pepper
2 teaspoons unsalted butter,
   cut into 4 pieces and chilled

1. Heat oil in 12-inch nonstick skillet over low heat for 5 minutes. Crack 2 eggs into bowl and season with salt and pepper. Repeat with remaining 2 eggs and second bowl.

2. Increase heat to medium-high and heat until oil is shimmering. Add butter and swirl to coat pan. Simultaneously pour both bowls of eggs into pan.

3. Cover and cook for 1 minute. Remove skillet from burner and let stand, covered, 15 to 45 seconds, depending on preferred doneness. Serve.

ADJUSTING THE YIELD:
To cook 2 eggs, use 8- or 9-inch nonstick skillet and halve oil and butter.

PUT A LID ON IT
Covering the pan ensures that the eggs cook from both the bottom and the top.

SOFT, TENDER SCRAMBLED

➤ **Common Problems:** Dry, tough curds

OUR SOLUTIONS

➤ **Add Fat:** Half-and-half and extra egg yolks raise coagulation temperature of egg proteins by keeping them from bonding together too tightly. Water in dairy turns to steam and helps eggs puff.

➤ **Season Before Cooking:** Salt tenderizes by preventing egg proteins from bonding too tightly.

➤ **Use Small(er) Skillet:** Relatively small 10-inch pan keeps eggs in thicker layer that traps more steam, producing billowy curds.

➤ **Start High; Finish Low:** Starting over medium-high heat creates puffy curds; lowering once eggs coagulate ensures that they won't overcook.

TIP: Electric Stove? Use Two Burners
Because electric stoves don't respond quickly to heat changes, it's best to heat one burner on low heat and the second on medium-high and to move the skillet between the burners for temperature adjustment.

SCRAMBLED EGGS

8 large eggs plus 2 large yolks
¼ cup half-and-half
⅜ teaspoon salt
¼ teaspoon pepper
1 tablespoon unsalted butter, chilled

1. Beat eggs and yolks, half-and-half, salt, and pepper together in bowl.

2. Heat butter in 10-inch nonstick skillet over medium-high heat until foaming subsides. Add egg mixture and, using rubber spatula, scrape along bottom and sides of skillet until eggs begin to clump, 1½ to 2½ minutes. Reduce heat to low and fold eggs until clumped and just slightly wet, 30 to 60 seconds. Serve.

---

	2 EGGS	4 EGGS	6 EGGS
Additional Yolk	1	1	1
Half-and-Half	1 tablespoon	2 tablespoons	3 tablespoons
Seasonings	pinch salt, pinch pepper	⅛ teaspoon salt, ⅛ teaspoon pepper	¼ teaspoon salt, ⅛ teaspoon pepper
Butter	¼ tablespoon	½ tablespoon	¾ tablespoon
Skillet Size	8 inches	8 inches	10 inches

PERFECT POACHED

➤ **Common Problems:** Under- or overcooked yolks; raggedy-looking whites

OUR SOLUTIONS

➤ **Use Skillet:** Shallow-sided skillet (nonstick eliminates risk of sticking) allows easier access than deep pot for sliding eggs into and retrieving them from water but holds enough water to keep eggs submerged.

➤ **Add Salt and Vinegar:** Salt seasons eggs, and vinegar (white distilled, white wine, rice, and cider all work) helps egg white proteins set quickly, reducing risk of fraying.

➤ **Crack Eggs into Teacups:** Portioning eggs into teacups (2 per cup) allows you to add as many as 8 eggs to skillet simultaneously so they cook at same rate.

➤ **Poach off Heat:** Since bubbles cause eggs to jostle and whites to fray, bring water to rolling boil, add eggs, cover skillet (to trap heat), and poach them gently off heat.

TIP: Make-Ahead Poached Eggs (Really)
Drop the poached eggs into ice water and refrigerate for up to three days. To reheat, bring 3 inches of water to a simmer in a large saucepan, remove pan from the heat, add the eggs, and let stand for 1 to 1½ minutes.

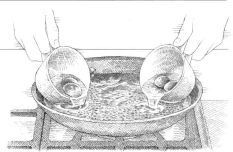

SYNCHRONIZE THE START
Use teacups to pour all the eggs in at once.

POACHED EGGS

1 teaspoon salt
2 tablespoons vinegar
4 large eggs, cracked into small
   handled cups (2 per cup)

1. Fill 12-inch nonstick skillet nearly to rim with water, add salt and vinegar, and bring mixture to boil over high heat.

2. Tip eggs into boiling water all at once, cover, and remove from heat. Let stand until yolks are medium-firm, 4 minutes. Drain eggs on paper towel–lined plate. Serve.

ADJUSTING THE YIELD: For 8 large eggs, poach 5 minutes; for 12, 6 minutes.

Grilled Chicken Souvlaki

Bright lemon flavor and charred-yet-moist, evenly cooked meat are the hallmarks of good souvlaki. They're also the hardest traits to get right.

> BY ANDREA GEARY <

Souvlaki is basically a Greek term for meat grilled on a stick. Just about every meat-eating culture has a version, but when it comes to being documented masters (if not the originators) of the technique, Greek credentials are hard to beat. Homer's *Iliad* and *Odyssey* are rich with detailed accounts of the heroes skewering meat and cooking it over fire, souvlaki-style.

In modern Greece, souvlaki is usually made with pork, but at Greek restaurants here in the United States, boneless, skinless chicken breast is common. The chunks of white meat are marinated (often overnight) in a tangy mixture of lemon juice, olive oil, oregano, parsley, and sometimes garlic before being skewered and grilled until nicely charred. Souvlaki may be served with rice and cooked vegetables or a salad, but just as often the chicken is placed on a lightly grilled pita, slathered with a yogurt-based *tzatziki* sauce, wrapped snugly, and eaten out of hand. This sandwich is my favorite way to eat souvlaki: The creamy sauce, freshened with herbs and cucumber, complements the char of the chicken, and the soft pita pulls it all together.

At least as appealing as the dish itself is how easily it translates to a home grill. The ingredients are readily available, and small chunks of boneless chicken cook quickly, making souvlaki a prime candidate for weeknight backyard fare. I just needed to come up with a good recipe.

Marinade Matters

Because boneless, skinless chicken breast easily turns dry and leathery on the grill, I wondered if I could buck tradition and substitute fattier and more forgiving boneless thighs instead. But when I experimented with grilling cubes of both thighs and breasts (marinated overnight first), wrapping them in warm pitas with a placeholder yogurt sauce, I had to admit that the richer flavor of the thighs actually seemed ill-suited for souvlaki. In the end, I decided

Swaddling the chicken and vegetables in a pita and wrapping it all in foil makes this sandwich less messy to eat.

Look: Perfectly Grilled Skewers
Video available free for 4 months at CooksIllustrated.com/aug14

to stick with white meat, which had a cleaner flavor that melded much more companionably with the other components.

Still, the breast meat was bland. It was also mushy on the outside and dry within, and I recognized that the long soak in the acidic marinade was to blame. Tests have shown us that, over time, acid weakens the protein bonds on the surface of meat, which causes that mushy texture. What's more, the marinade never penetrates much below the meat's surface, so its flavor is superficial at best. Bottom line: The long marinating step had to go.

In my next test, I went to the other extreme: I tossed the 1-inch cubes of chicken with lemon juice and olive oil and then immediately skewered and grilled them over very hot coals. It was only a modest success. The pasty exterior was gone, but the meat was still bland and dry, especially those more exposed chunks that had been on either end of each skewer.

Packing It In

So I mixed up a brine. We've long known that soaking meat in a saltwater solution before cooking encourages it to take up extra moisture, and the salt, some of which is also absorbed, not only seasons the meat but also changes its physical structure in such a way that it retains more moisture when cooked. Brining the chicken after cutting it into chunks would be particularly effective, as there would be more exposed surface area in contact with the solution.

I soaked the chicken for 30 minutes while the grill heated and then drained it, patted it dry, and tossed it with olive oil, lemon juice, dried oregano, parsley, and black pepper. I also added a bit of honey, which I had seen in a few souvlaki recipes; I suspected that a sweetener would add complexity and help with browning. The one thing I left out was garlic. In previous tests most of it had fallen off, and what had remained on the meat burned. I'd try to make up for it in the tzatziki. In the meantime, I threaded the dressed chunks onto skewers and grilled them over very hot coals for about 15 minutes, at which point they were cooked through and well charred.

The brine had helped, as most of the chicken was now moist, but those end pieces were still parched. That brought up a fundamental problem with the meat-on-a-stick method: Meat that's packed tightly on a skewer doesn't cook evenly. The middle pieces are insulated from the fierce heat, while the exposed end pieces cook faster. Poking around with my thermometer, I found that the end pieces reached the target 160 degrees at least 4 minutes before the middle ones did.

Spacing the pieces at intervals instead of packing them snugly helped even out the cooking, but it required more skewers (which meant more to watch and turn). Also, since the chunks weren't packed tightly, they spun around when I tried turning the skewers.

I had a better idea. Instead of packing only meat onto my skewers, I started each one with a stack of bell pepper chunks, then threaded on the chicken pieces, and finished each skewer with two chunks of red onion. The vegetables functioned as shields,

Marinate Twice

Briefly soaking the grilled chicken and vegetables in some reserved marinade before wrapping them in a pita rehydrates their dry exteriors and delivers bright citrus punch.

protecting the end pieces of chicken from the heat so they cooked at the same rate as the middle pieces. A bonus: They added more char flavor to the wrap and broke up the all-meat filling with some crunch.

What was missing from the chicken was the lemon punch that I associate with souvlaki, so I made a quick adjustment. Instead of using all the lemon–olive oil mixture to coat the raw chicken, I reserved ¼ cup of it to use postmarinade. When the skewers came off the grill, I unloaded the chicken and vegetables into a bowl with the reserved sauce. Covering the bowl and letting the contents steam for a bit to absorb the sauce resulted in bright-tasting chicken and vegetables.

That's a Wrap

Next up: the sauce. Tzatziki is plain yogurt flavored with garlic, cucumber, herbs, salt, and maybe a bit of acid like lemon juice or vinegar. Since raw garlic can be too assertive, I used a trick we discovered when making Caesar salad dressing: grating the garlic to a paste and briefly steeping it in lemon juice before adding both to the sauce. The acid converts the harsh-tasting garlic compound, allicin, into mellower compounds in the same way that cooking does.

Thick Greek yogurt is typically used and the cucumbers, either grated or minced, are usually pretreated with salt to remove excess moisture. But the mixture of yogurt and salted cucumbers was so heavy and thick that it dominated the wrap. To thin out the sauce, I skipped salting the cucumbers and relied on the salt in the tzatziki to pull water from the cucumbers into the yogurt as it sat (from that point on, I prepared the sauce before the chicken). When it came time to assemble the wraps, the tzatziki had a thinner consistency.

Finally, I made a subtle, but important, change to how I handled the pita bread. Traditionally, souvlaki is wrapped in soft pocketless pitas, which are hard to find at regular supermarkets. The trouble with conventional pocketed pitas was that when I warmed them on the grill the way I had seen Greek cooks do, they turned dry and brittle and were nearly impossible to fold around the cooked chicken. Brushing them with oil and water before grilling didn't help.

I was happy to trade char on the pita (the chicken had plenty) for a pillowy texture, so I wrapped my stack of four pitas tightly in foil after moistening the top and bottom surfaces of the stack with water. I placed the packet on a cooler side of the grill, so the bread could steam while the chicken cooked. By the time the chicken had rested, the pitas were soft, warm, and floppy—perfect for wrapping.

With my goals of charred, lemony chicken, creamy tzatziki, and soft bread met, I wrapped up my sandwich, and my testing.

GRILLED CHICKEN SOUVLAKI
SERVES 4

This *tzatziki* is fairly mild; if you like a more assertive flavor, double the garlic. A rasp-style grater makes quick work of turning the garlic into a paste. We like the chicken as a wrap, but you may skip the pita and serve the chicken, vegetables, and tzatziki with rice. You will need four 12-inch metal skewers. For tips on wrapping the sandwich in foil, see page 31. For our free recipe for Grilled Chicken Souvlaki for Two, go to CooksIllustrated.com/aug14.

Tzatziki Sauce
- 1 tablespoon lemon juice
- 1 small garlic clove, minced to paste
- ¾ cup plain Greek yogurt
- ½ cucumber, peeled, halved lengthwise, seeded, and diced fine (½ cup)
- 3 tablespoons minced fresh mint
- 1 tablespoon minced fresh parsley
- ⅜ teaspoon salt

Chicken
- Salt and pepper
- 1½ pounds boneless, skinless chicken breasts, trimmed and cut into 1-inch pieces
- ⅓ cup extra-virgin olive oil
- 2 tablespoons minced fresh parsley
- 1 teaspoon finely grated lemon zest plus ¼ cup juice (2 lemons)
- 1 teaspoon honey
- 1 teaspoon dried oregano
- 1 green bell pepper, quartered, stemmed, seeded, each quarter cut into 4 chunks
- 1 small red onion, ends trimmed, peeled, halved lengthwise, each half cut into 4 chunks
- 4 (8-inch) pita breads

1. FOR THE TZATZIKI SAUCE: Whisk lemon juice and garlic together in small bowl. Let stand for 10 minutes. Stir in yogurt, cucumber, mint, parsley, and salt. Cover and set aside.

2. FOR THE CHICKEN: Dissolve 2 tablespoons

Softening Supermarket Pita

To soften up dry, tough supermarket pita, we moisten two of the breads with a little water and then stack them on either side of two unmoistened pieces. Then we steam the breads in a foil-wrapped stack on the cooler side of the grill while the cooked chicken rests.

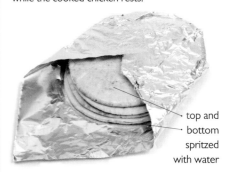

top and
bottom
spritzed
with water

salt in 1 quart cold water. Submerge chicken in brine, cover, and refrigerate for 30 minutes. While chicken is brining, combine oil, parsley, lemon zest and juice, honey, oregano, and ½ teaspoon pepper in medium bowl. Transfer ¼ cup oil mixture to large bowl and set aside to toss with cooked chicken.

3. Remove chicken from brine and pat dry with paper towels. Toss chicken with remaining oil mixture. Thread 4 pieces of bell pepper, concave side up, onto one 12-inch metal skewer. Thread one-quarter of chicken onto skewer. Thread 2 chunks of onion onto skewer, and place skewer on plate. Repeat skewering remaining chicken and vegetables on 3 more skewers. Lightly moisten 2 pita breads with water. Sandwich 2 unmoistened pita breads between moistened pita breads and wrap stack tightly in lightly greased heavy-duty aluminum foil.

4A. FOR A CHARCOAL GRILL: Open bottom vent completely. Light large chimney starter mounded with charcoal briquettes (7 quarts). When top coals are partially covered with ash, pour evenly over half of grill. Set cooking grate in place, cover, and open lid vent completely. Heat grill until hot, about 5 minutes.

4B. FOR A GAS GRILL: Turn all burners to high, cover, and heat grill until hot, about 15 minutes. Leave primary burner on high and turn off other burner(s).

5. Clean and oil cooking grate. Place skewers on hotter side of grill and cook, turning occasionally, until chicken and vegetables are well browned on all sides and chicken registers 160 degrees, 15 to 20 minutes. Using fork, push chicken and vegetables off skewers into bowl of reserved oil mixture. Stir gently, breaking up onion chunks; cover with foil and let sit for 5 minutes.

6. Meanwhile, place packet of pitas on cooler side of grill. Flip occasionally to heat, about 5 minutes.

7. Lay each warm pita on 12-inch square of foil. Spread each pita with 2 tablespoons tzatziki. Place one-quarter of chicken and vegetables in middle of each pita. Roll into cylindrical shape and serve.

A Vegetable Shield

The age-old problem with grilling meat on a stick: The end pieces overcook. We protect the chicken by threading pepper and onion pieces on the ends. The charred vegetables taste great in the sandwich, too.

MEAT IN THE MIDDLE

Perfecting Pasta Frittata

Throwing together eggs and last night's pasta is one way to make this dish. But for the ideal—a creamy interior encased in crispy strands—skip the leftovers and start from scratch.

> BY DAN SOUZA <

Leftovers get a bad rap. It's too bad, because they're the foundation of some of the best dishes out there. For me, one of the most underrated made-from-leftovers preparations is pasta frittata, in which leftover pasta is transformed into a thick, creamy, golden-brown omelet laced with noodles. The dish got its start in Naples, Italy. The classic Neapolitan pasta frittata starts with leftover cooked and sauced pasta (most often a long noodle shape) and half a dozen or so eggs beaten with salt, pepper, melted lard or butter, and grated Parmigiano-Reggiano cheese. The best versions I've eaten also featured small bites of meat or vegetables that contributed flavor without overly disrupting the creamy texture of the dish.

The only barrier I encounter in whipping up a quick pasta frittata for dinner is that I rarely find myself with leftover pasta. But why should that stand in the way? Cooking dried pasta would add a little more effort, but maybe I could streamline the process. And who knows? I might find a way to make a good dish even better.

The Basics

Since I wasn't dealing with leftovers, I had the whole world of pasta open to me. To see which particular type might work best, I boiled up a variety of shapes and sizes and tested them in a bare-bones recipe of eight beaten eggs, ½ cup of Parmesan cheese, and some salt and pepper. It was clear right off the bat that long noodles like spaghetti, linguine, and fettuccine were superior to short and tubular types. While the strands effortlessly blended with the eggs, chunky and tubular pastas created gaps and led to frittatas that broke apart during slicing. Among the long noodles, spaghetti was the winner, ensuring a more balanced ratio of pasta to egg in each bite compared with the wider linguine and fettuccine. If skinny was good, perhaps skinnier would be even better, so I made one more frittata, this time using angel hair pasta. These delicate strands proved ideal, bringing a satisfying web of pasta to every bite without marring the tender egg texture.

While most Italians will claim that there is only one way to cook pasta—in a large quantity of boiling water—we've actually found that the process is

Delicate angel hair pasta incorporates seamlessly into the frittata without disrupting its tender, creamy texture.

far more flexible. While a full pot of water does help keep pasta from sticking together, it turns out that a little water works just fine, provided you stir often. Perhaps even more surprising is that you can start pasta directly in cold water that is then brought to a boil and get results identical to those you'd get from throwing it into already boiling water. I decided to put these discoveries into practice in the name of convenience. Instead of pulling out a large Dutch oven, filling it with 4 quarts of water, and bringing it to a full boil, I tossed 6 ounces of halved angel hair pasta into a 10-inch nonstick skillet along with 3 cups of water and some salt. I placed the skillet over high heat and stirred occasionally as it came to a boil. Then I let it simmer, stirring occasionally, until the pasta was tender and the water had evaporated. All told it took about 15 minutes, and by cooking off the water, I could even skip dirtying a strainer. On to the egg mixture.

Beating together eight eggs (a number that provided the right balance and structure for 6 ounces of dried pasta) with salt, pepper, and Parmesan and

tossing in cooked angel hair is about as easy as it gets—but ensuring that this mixture cooks up creamy and tender takes a bit more thought. I knew that the final texture of my frittata would be determined by how gently it was cooked and the amount of fat in the mix. Gently cooking any egg preparation ensures that the exterior portions don't overcook and turn rubbery while the interior comes up to temperature. Turning my stove dial to medium, covering the frittata during cooking, and flipping it halfway through proved a winning formula. The top and bottom took on a burnished appearance while the inside stayed moist and relatively tender.

But I wanted it to be even more tender, so I turned my attention to fat. Fat keeps eggs tender by coating their proteins and preventing them from bonding together too firmly. Neapolitans would likely reach for lard, butter, or cream when making this dish, but after a series of tests, my tasters preferred extra-virgin olive oil since it produced a frittata that tasted more of egg and less of rich dairy. For eight eggs, 3 tablespoons of oil provided good richness and plenty of protection against toughness.

The Extras

I was feeling pretty pleased and nearly ready to close the file on the recipe but for one thing: All along, tasters had raved when they encountered the inevitable few strands of angel hair that had settled at the bottom or sides of the hot pan, turning brown and crispy. The contrast between the creamy eggs and these crispy strands was actually one of the best parts. Was there any way to get even more of these browned strands?

To this end, I started fiddling with how I layered the egg and the noodles, thinking that I could purposely leave some of the pasta on the bottom of the frittata to ensure contact with the pan. I got mixed results—sometimes the pasta would stay put and other times the egg would just seep under it and foil my plans. Up to this point I'd been boiling the pasta in the skillet and then pouring in the egg mixture. What I really needed to do was fry the pasta before incorporating the eggs. Why not just add a little oil to the skillet with the pasta and water and let it start frying once the water evaporated? This

Though it's usually whipped up with last night's noodles, pasta frittata can be just as simple using our from-scratch approach.

USE A SKILLET
Add water, broken angel hair, and oil to skillet—the only vessel you will need for this dish.

COOK OFF LIQUID
Once pasta is tender, keep cooking until water evaporates and pasta starts sizzling in oil.

LET IT CRISP
After about 5 minutes, pasta will start to crisp (check progress by lifting up the edge).

LIFT LOOSE STRANDS
Pour eggs over pasta, then gently pull up top strands to allow eggs to flow into center.

SLIDE AND INVERT
To brown second side, slide frittata onto plate, invert onto second plate, and return to skillet.

---

is the same technique that is used with potstickers and, to my delight, it worked just as well here. As soon as the last bit of water evaporated, the pasta started sizzling. I cooked it, swirling and shaking the pan to prevent sticking, until the strands at the bottom of the pan turned lightly crispy. Then I simply poured my egg mixture over the pasta and used tongs to mix the egg throughout the uncrisped strands, leaving the bottom layer as undisturbed as possible. Sure enough, the time that it took to cook the egg through resulted in a substantial, lacy layer of crispy, browned pasta that almost served as a crust, delivering satisfying crunch in every bite. Meanwhile, the rest of the pasta stayed tender, melding into the creamy eggs.

The frittata was ready to be flavored with some bold ingredients. I knew that the key to adding vegetables and meat was cutting everything into small pieces (which didn't disturb the interior texture). The add-ins also needed to precook in the skillet since they would just warm through in the frittata. My favorite combination was a mix of savory sweet Italian sausage and chopped hot cherry peppers. It

A TOASTY BOTTOM

A layer of crispy golden pasta on the bottom of the frittata (shown here after we flipped it to brown the top and before we reinvert it for serving) distinguishes our version.

offered richness and plenty of acidity and heat to balance. I also whipped up a version featuring broccoli rabe and a pinch of pepper flakes. Finally, I made one with thinly sliced cremini mushrooms, sage, and pungent Gorgonzola. No matter the flavor, my pasta frittata never lasted long in the kitchen. A shame—I like leftovers.

PASTA FRITTATA
WITH SAUSAGE AND HOT PEPPERS
SERVES 4 TO 6

To ensure the proper texture, it's important to use angel hair pasta. We like to serve the frittata warm or at room temperature, with a green salad. For our free recipe for Pasta Frittata with Mushrooms and Gorgonzola, go to CooksIllustrated.com/aug14.

- 8 large eggs
- 1 ounce Parmesan cheese, grated (½ cup)
- 3 tablespoons extra-virgin olive oil
- 3 tablespoons coarsely chopped jarred hot cherry peppers
- 2 tablespoons chopped fresh parsley
  Salt and pepper
- 8 ounces sweet Italian sausage, casings removed, crumbled
- 2 garlic cloves, sliced thin
- 3 cups water
- 6 ounces angel hair pasta, broken in half
- 3 tablespoons vegetable oil

1. Whisk eggs, Parmesan, olive oil, cherry peppers, parsley, ½ teaspoon salt, and ½ teaspoon pepper in large bowl until egg is even yellow color; set aside.

2. Cook sausage in 10-inch nonstick skillet over medium heat, breaking up sausage with wooden spoon, until fat renders and sausage is about half cooked, 3 to 5 minutes. Stir in garlic and cook for 30 seconds. Remove skillet from heat. Transfer sausage mixture (some sausage will still be raw) to bowl with egg mixture and wipe out skillet.

3. Bring water, pasta, vegetable oil, and ¾ teaspoon salt to boil in now-empty skillet over high

heat, stirring occasionally. Cook, stirring occasionally, until pasta is tender, water has evaporated, and pasta starts to sizzle in oil, 8 to 12 minutes. Reduce heat to medium and continue to cook pasta, swirling pan and scraping under edge of pasta with rubber spatula frequently to prevent sticking (do not stir), until bottom turns golden and starts to crisp, 5 to 7 minutes (lift up edge of pasta to check progress).

4. Using spatula, push some pasta up sides of skillet so entire pan surface is covered with pasta. Pour egg mixture over pasta. Using tongs, lift up loose strands of pasta to allow egg to flow toward pan, being careful not to pull up crispy bottom crust. Cover skillet and continue to cook over medium heat until bottom crust turns golden brown and top of frittata is just set (egg below very top will still be raw), 5 to 8 minutes. Slide frittata onto large plate. Invert frittata onto second large plate and slide it browned side up back into skillet. Tuck edges of frittata into skillet with rubber spatula. Continue to cook second side of frittata until light brown, 2 to 4 minutes longer.

5. Remove skillet from heat and let stand for 5 minutes. Using your hand or pan lid, invert frittata onto cutting board. Cut into wedges and serve.

PASTA FRITTATA WITH BROCCOLI RABE

Omit cherry peppers, parsley, and sausage. Heat 2 teaspoons vegetable oil in 10-inch nonstick skillet over medium heat until shimmering. Add garlic and ⅛ teaspoon red pepper flakes and cook for 1 minute. Stir in 8 ounces broccoli rabe, trimmed and cut into ½-inch pieces, 1 tablespoon water, and ¼ teaspoon salt; cover skillet and cook until broccoli rabe is crisp-tender, 2 to 3 minutes. Remove skillet from heat and add 1 tablespoon white wine vinegar. Transfer broccoli rabe to bowl with egg mixture. Proceed with recipe from step 3, cooking pasta with remaining 7 teaspoons vegetable oil.

▶ **Dan Shows You How**
Video available free for 4 months at CooksIllustrated.com/aug14

Tomatillo Salsa

For a top-notch tomatillo salsa, we take a half-raw, half-cooked approach.

⋟ BY SANDRA WU ⋞

In Mexico and the Southwest, the tomatillo—a small, green, tomato-like fruit with a thin, papery husk and tangy, juicy flesh—is widely used, particularly in salsa. The bright-tasting sauce is scooped up with tortilla chips or served as an accompaniment to everything from chicken to fish to pork. It shares many of the ingredients of its raw-tomato sibling, *salsa cruda*—fresh green chiles, onion, garlic, lime juice, and cilantro—but the tomatillos are often cooked to soften their crunch. Cooking also mellows the abundant citric acid in the fruit.

I jotted down a wish list for my ideal version of tomatillo salsa. Fire-roasted tomatillo salsas are commonplace, but I had in mind a superquick indoor recipe. I also wanted to highlight the unique lemony/herbal flavor of tomatillos. Finally, the salsa would have to have enough body to hold up nicely on a tortilla chip.

After husking several pounds of tomatillos and rinsing off the sticky material that coats their skin, I got to work. Before investigating cooking techniques, I tried an oddball approach, buzzing raw tomatillos in the food processor with some placeholder aromatics and seasonings. Unsurprisingly, this uncooked salsa left a lot to be desired; it was crunchy, with an astringent, mouth-puckeringly sour taste.

The fruit would have to be cooked, but by what method? I had high hopes for pan-roasting the tomatillos on the stovetop, but by the time the fruit was tender, the skin had turned leathery and tough. Another approach, processing all the ingredients (for now I was using just tomatillos, onion, and chiles) and then simmering the concoction, produced a sludge that could have come from a jar. Boiling the fruit prior to processing offered clean flavor but also a drawback: Whole tomatillos cooked unevenly as they bobbed in the bubbling water, and halving the fruit before boiling only exacerbated their already watery consistency.

Broiling, on the other hand, was a real winner. All it required was tossing the whole husked and rinsed tomatillos in vegetable oil and placing them under the broiler (I arranged them on a foil-lined baking sheet for easy cleanup) until they turned spotty brown. The blazing heat drove off some of the watery liquid in the tomatillos, producing a salsa with a thicker texture and a more concentrated taste.

▶ **See Salsa Happen**
Video available free for 4 months at CooksIllustrated.com/aug14

This was good progress, but the flavor of the salsa was still lackluster. I tried broiling the onions and chiles along with the tomatillos, but this contributed an overcooked taste. Left raw, the aromatics had a fresh, pungent bite. Still, something was missing. I recalled how I'd salvaged some of the less desirable salsas left over from my initial tests by mixing them with the tastier versions. One particular pairing came to mind. The raw salsa that wasn't very palatable on its own actually tasted pretty good when blended with one of the cooked salsas.

That sparked an idea: What if I left some of the tomatillos raw? I broiled half of the tomatillos and left the other half uncooked and then gave them a few quick pulses together in the food processor along with the other ingredients. It turned out to be a good move: The cooked tomatillos broke down into a thick, juicy base, while the uncooked tomatillos, onion, and chile provided a refreshingly crunchy, chunky foil.

With the base of the recipe solidified, I adjusted the remaining ingredients. White onion contributed a relatively mellow flavor that melded well with the tomatillos whereas yellow and red onion were a little too sharp; scallions were too grassy. A single clove of garlic was enough to add depth without imparting sting; 1/2 cup of chopped cilantro provided fresh, herbal notes; and 2 tablespoons of lime juice provided a measure of acidity to complement the tart tomatillos.

As for the chile component, I compared two of the most commonly available fresh green chiles: jalapeño and serrano. Side by side, it was difficult to tell a difference between salsa containing either one, so in the end, I elected to go with the slightly more widely available jalapeño, seeding it and giving the option to add the seeds (most of the heat resides in the ribs and seeds) back to the finished salsa to reach a desired level of spiciness.

Finally, because tomatillos vary in tartness, I seasoned the salsa to taste with a sprinkle of sugar in addition to the usual salt. I also stirred in a couple of teaspoons of extra-virgin olive oil to round out all the flavors and give the dip a little more body.

With a big bowl of tortilla chips at the ready, I dug in. A condiment this fresh-tasting and herbaceous meant there was no reason that tomatillo salsa would ever have to take a back seat to red salsa again.

TOMATILLO SALSA
MAKES 2 CUPS

This salsa can be served with chips or as an accompaniment for pork, chicken, or fish. For a spicier salsa, reserve and add the jalapeño seeds.

- 1   pound tomatillos, husks and stems removed, rinsed well and dried
- 1   teaspoon vegetable oil
- 1   small white onion, chopped
- 1   jalapeño chile, stemmed, halved, and seeded
- ½   cup fresh cilantro leaves
- 2   tablespoons lime juice
- 1   garlic clove, minced
-     Salt
- 2   teaspoons extra-virgin olive oil
-     Sugar

1. Adjust oven rack 6 inches from broiler element and heat broiler. Line rimmed baking sheet with aluminum foil. Toss half of tomatillos with vegetable oil and transfer to prepared sheet. Broil until tomatillos are spotty brown and skins begin to burst, 7 to 10 minutes. Transfer tomatillos to food processor and let cool completely.

2. Halve remaining tomatillos and add to food processor with broiled tomatillos. Add onion, jalapeño, cilantro, lime juice, garlic, and ¼ teaspoon salt. Pulse until slightly chunky, 16 to 18 pulses. Transfer to salsa bowl and let stand at room temperature for 15 minutes. Stir in olive oil and season with salt and sugar to taste. Serve.

Reinventing Zucchini Bread

What should be a light, moist snack is often a dense, greasy disappointment. Could we lighten the loaf?

≥ BY SARAH MULLINS ≤

In the health food–crazed 1960s and '70s, recipes for zucchini bread popped up everywhere. With bits of healthy green vegetable speckling the crumb, the bread was a sweet treat you could not only enjoy but also feel virtuous about eating. But while other food fads have come and gone, zucchini bread has remained hugely popular—and for an entirely different reason: The high water content of the vegetable makes it ideal for producing the soft, moist crumb that is the hallmark of a great quick bread.

But zucchini can also be a liability, as too much leads to a soggy loaf. That's why, in spite of the oft-stated goal of using up surplus squash, most recipes top out at a mere 10 to 12 ounces. And funnily enough, despite being associated with a health-food movement, the recipes tend to call for copious amounts of oil that turn the loaf greasy and overly rich.

Packing more zucchini into the bread would hopefully pave the way for scaling back the ½ to ¾ cup of oil that most recipes call for, so I set a goal of doubling the usual amount of squash. Simply folding coarsely grated zucchini shreds into the batter is common, but wringing them out in a towel first seemed like a better approach: The drier the zucchini was, the more I could squeeze into a loaf without sogging it out. Sure enough, a full ½ cup of pale green liquid dripped out of 1½ pounds of squash. Encouraged, I ran a few more zucchini along the fine holes of the grater before wringing them out, reasoning that the increased surface area of the smaller pieces would help expel more liquid. Indeed, I got ¾ cup of juice from this batch.

I used each type (both wrung out), as well as 1½ pounds of unsqueezed coarse shreds as a control, in a typical zucchini bread recipe minus most of the fat: all-purpose flour, generous amounts of baking soda and powder for lift, sugar, touches of salt and cinnamon, eggs, a handful of toasted walnuts, and just ¼ cup of oil. I scraped the batters into greased loaf pans before putting them into 325-degree ovens. The bread made with unsqueezed shreds emerged predictably wet and gummy, and the finely shredded loaf was just as dense—the thin shreds had clumped

► **Look: It Really Is Better**
Video available free for 4 months
at CooksIllustrated.com/aug14

Sprinkling sugar over the batter produces a crisp crust.

together, compressing the crumb. Fortunately, the coarsely grated squeezed squash produced a crumb that was supermoist, more open, and significantly less gummy. Plus, it wasn't greasy at all. I'd stick with the squeezed coarse shreds.

Now what about this loaf's flavor? Here I was pleasantly surprised. As low-key as zucchini may be, I had feared that an overload would give the bread a vegetal taste. But despite the significant amount, the bread had a sweet, mildly earthy taste; mineral or strong vegetal flavors were absent. It turns out that by removing much of the moisture, I had also removed some of the key compounds, called Amadori compounds, responsible for zucchini's vegetal flavor, which are concentrated in the juice, not the flesh.

I just needed to get rid of a remaining trace of gumminess. I swapped a portion of the all-purpose flour for whole-wheat flour, since the bran and germ in whole-wheat flour allow it to absorb more moisture than the all-purpose kind. I was gratified to find that not only was this latest loaf no longer sticky but it also boasted a nice coarseness from the whole wheat. It just needed some complexity. No problem: I simply switched from granulated sugar to molasses-y brown sugar, increased the cinnamon to 1 tablespoon, and added nutmeg and vanilla.

With its light, moist crumb that's low on oil and chock-full of zucchini (and even boasts a whole-grain element), this bread might even pass as a "health" food. I just consider it the best zucchini bread I've ever tasted.

ZUCCHINI BREAD
MAKES 1 LOAF

Use the large holes of a box grater to shred the zucchini. The test kitchen's preferred loaf pan measures 8½ by 4½ inches; if you use a 9 by 5-inch loaf pan, start checking for doneness 5 minutes early. For our free recipe for Zucchini Bread with Pistachios and Orange, go to CooksIllustrated.com/aug14.

- 1½ pounds zucchini, shredded
- 1¼ cups packed (8¾ ounces) brown sugar
- ¼ cup vegetable oil
- 2 large eggs
- 1 teaspoon vanilla extract
- 1½ cups (7½ ounces) all-purpose flour
- ½ cup (2¾ ounces) whole-wheat flour
- 1 tablespoon ground cinnamon
- 1½ teaspoons salt
- 1 teaspoon baking powder
- 1 teaspoon baking soda
- ½ teaspoon ground nutmeg
- ¾ cup walnuts, toasted and chopped (optional)
- 1 tablespoon granulated sugar

1. Adjust oven rack to middle position and heat oven to 325 degrees. Grease 8½ by 4½-inch loaf pan.

2. Place zucchini in center of dish towel. Gather ends together and twist tightly to drain as much liquid as possible, discarding liquid (you should have ½ to ⅔ cup liquid). Whisk brown sugar, oil, eggs, and vanilla together in medium bowl. Fold in zucchini.

3. Whisk all-purpose flour, whole-wheat flour, cinnamon, salt, baking powder, baking soda, and nutmeg together in large bowl. Fold in zucchini mixture until just incorporated. Fold in walnuts, if using. Pour batter into prepared pan and sprinkle with granulated sugar.

4. Bake until top bounces back when gently pressed and toothpick inserted in center comes out with few moist crumbs attached, 65 to 75 minutes. Let bread cool in pan on wire rack for 30 minutes. Remove bread from pan and let cool completely on wire rack. Serve.

ZUCCHINI BREAD WITH WALNUTS AND DRIED CHERRIES

Substitute cocoa powder for cinnamon and ground cloves for nutmeg. Prepare bread with walnuts and add ¾ cup dried cherries, chopped, to batter with walnuts.

Better Cream Cheese Brownies

Everyone loves a rich brownie. Tangy cheesecake is a slam dunk. It's too bad that when they're combined, you wind up with a cheesy center and watered-down chocolate.

≥ BY SARAH MULLINS ≤

Though I love the idea of cream cheese brownies, every one I've encountered has had serious flaws. In some, the cream cheese swirl is chalky and flavorless, overwhelmed by the chocolate brownie. In others, the cream cheese is properly creamy and moist but the brownie portion is wet and dense. And often the swirl is so uneven, one bite is all cream cheese and the next is all chocolate. No wonder I've always just stuck with a standard-issue brownie.

Still, the potential nagged at me: In one dessert, I could have moist, chocolaty richness balanced by a tangy, creamy cheesecake-like swirl. For a cream cheese brownie that lived up to that ideal, the key would be to develop a brownie batter and a cream cheese swirl that worked with, not against, each other.

Moisture Management

For my ideal moist, chocolaty brownie component, I started with a test kitchen recipe that relies on a combination of 2 ounces of unsweetened chocolate and 4 ounces of bittersweet for deep and complex chocolate flavor, plus just ¾ cup of flour and 1 cup of sugar—enough to tame any bitterness without making the dessert candy-like. As for the cream cheese portion, recipes I'd found called for anywhere from 8 to 16 ounces of cream cheese, so I split the difference, mixing 12 ounces of softened cream cheese with ¼ cup of granulated sugar and an egg (for both moisture and structure). I spread the brownie batter in the pan, dropped spoonfuls of the cream cheese mixture on top, and then swirled them together with a knife and baked it off.

Once cooled and cut, my brownies revealed a problem common to so many of the bad versions I'd tried: They were too wet. The cream cheese swirl was leaching liquid into the brownie portion. I needed to start with a cakier style of brownie so that once the brownies absorbed moisture from the cream cheese swirl, they would land just where I wanted them. So I switched to another test kitchen recipe, one that delivers cakier brownies by using proportionally more flour and less chocolate (just 3 ounces of unsweetened), as well as a little baking powder for lift.

Unsweetened chocolate gives the brownie portion bold chocolate flavor, while sour cream bolsters the tang in the cream cheese swirl.

This was a definite step in the right direction, but the brownies were still baking up too wet, and the chocolate flavor was a bit muted. Dropping the cream cheese down to 8 ounces helped with the moisture issue and also moved the chocolate flavor more to the front—but not enough. When I upped the unsweetened chocolate from 3 to 4 ounces, the brownies were more chocolaty, but they also turned overly bitter.

I wondered if another variety of chocolate would be a better choice. I made three pans of brownies, comparing batches made with cocoa powder and bittersweet chocolate with my working recipe. The two made with bittersweet chocolate definitely weren't bitter but they also lacked the assertive chocolate punch that my brownies needed for contrast with the cream cheese swirl. Cocoa powder produced a flat chocolate flavor and also went too far texturally, making the brownies way too dry. I thought briefly about reexamining the combination of bittersweet and unsweetened chocolate from my initial test, but buying two bars of chocolate only to use 2 ounces from each seemed beyond the pale. My best approach turned out to be simple: I stuck with the 4 ounces of unsweetened chocolate for depth of flavor and increased the sugar from 1 cup to 1¼ cups to tame the bitterness. A teaspoon of vanilla extract helped round out the flavors.

Giving the Swirl a Whirl

With the brownie portion where I wanted it, I moved on to the cream cheese swirl. Its texture was spot-on—perfectly creamy and not at all chalky—but the flavor was wan and it got lost in the rich chocolate. Cutting the sugar in the swirl mixture in half, down from ¼ cup to just 2 tablespoons, allowed the swirl's dairy profile to come out a bit more, but it needed more tang. Adding lemon juice made it more tart than tangy, so I tried substituting increasing amounts of sour cream for a portion of the cream cheese. I could tell I was on

Why the Swirling Technique Matters

CREAM CHEESE COLLAPSE
Most cream cheese brownies suffer from a wet center weighed down by too much cream cheese.

SWIRLED CHAMPION
Our version is well-balanced and fudgy through and through.

DOLLOP BROWNIE BATTER, NOT CREAM CHEESE

By rethinking the standard swirling process, we get a perfectly marbled brownie that bakes evenly from edge to center.

1. SPREAD CREAM CHEESE MIXTURE OVER BROWNIE BASE

Evenly spreading the cream cheese mixture prevents it from weighing down the brownie base.

2. WARM RESERVED BROWNIE BATTER, AND THEN DOLLOP AND SWIRL

Top with spoonfuls of reserved brownie batter—microwaved for a few seconds to make it more fluid and easier to work with—before swirling with a knife.

the right track, and eventually I settled on ½ cup of sour cream with 4 ounces of cream cheese. This gave the swirl enough refreshing tanginess to stand out against the chocolate (any more and it tasted sour). Of course, adding sour cream had reintroduced an old enemy: moisture. So I took out the egg and added 1 tablespoon of flour to return the body that the mixture had just lost. (The flour also helped absorb a tad more moisture.)

Finally, I was getting really close to my ideal—the two batters had the right texture and flavor—but the cream cheese swirl wasn't evenly distributed. It was more concentrated toward the center, which meant that almost every brownie had either too little or too much of the cream cheese. And beyond the aesthetics, this was causing structural problems. The brownies were sinking in the center because of the heavier, moister cream cheese batter, while the edges where the brownie batter dominated were puffed and overly dry. The cause, I realized, was my swirling approach—spreading the brownie batter in the pan, dolloping the cream cheese mixture on top, and then swirling them together. Only wisps of the swirl were getting to the very edges.

For my next test, I spread most but not all of the brownie batter evenly in the pan, and then topped it with the cream cheese mixture, this time spreading it into an even layer all the way to the edges of the pan. Then I dolloped the small amount of remaining brownie batter (microwaved briefly to loosen it up) on top and swirled it together with a knife. These brownies not only had a more evenly distributed layer of the cream cheese filling but also baked more evenly. My final tweak was to lower the oven temperature from 350 to 325 degrees, allowing the brownies to bake more slowly and gently to guarantee that the edges wouldn't dry out by the time the center had cooked through.

Finally I had a moist, chocolaty brownie with a rich, tangy cheesecake swirl—and now, old-fashioned brownies seemed a bit boring.

CREAM CHEESE BROWNIES
MAKES SIXTEEN 2-INCH BROWNIES

To accurately test the doneness of the brownies, be sure to stick the toothpick into the brownie portion, not the cream cheese. Leftover brownies should be stored in the refrigerator. Let leftovers stand at room temperature for 1 hour before serving.

Cream Cheese Filling
- 4 ounces cream cheese, cut into 8 pieces
- ½ cup sour cream
- 2 tablespoons sugar
- 1 tablespoon all-purpose flour

Brownie Batter
- ⅔ cup (3⅓ ounces) all-purpose flour
- ½ teaspoon baking powder
- ½ teaspoon salt
- 4 ounces unsweetened chocolate, chopped fine
- 8 tablespoons unsalted butter
- 1¼ cups (8¾ ounces) sugar
- 2 large eggs
- 1 teaspoon vanilla extract

1. FOR THE CREAM CHEESE FILLING: Microwave cream cheese until soft, 20 to 30 seconds. Add sour cream, sugar, and flour and whisk to combine. Set aside.

2. Adjust oven rack to middle position and heat oven to 325 degrees. Make foil sling for 8-inch square baking pan by folding 2 long sheets of aluminum foil so each is 8 inches wide. Lay sheets of foil in pan perpendicular to each other, with extra foil hanging over edges of pan. Push foil into corners and up sides of pan, smoothing foil flush to pan. Grease foil.

3. FOR THE BROWNIE BATTER: Whisk flour, baking powder, and salt together in bowl and set aside. Microwave chocolate and butter in bowl at 50 percent power, stirring occasionally, until melted, 1 to 2 minutes.

4. Whisk sugar, eggs, and vanilla together in medium bowl. Add melted chocolate mixture (do not clean bowl) and whisk until incorporated. Add flour mixture and fold to combine.

5. Transfer ½ cup batter to bowl used to melt chocolate. Spread remaining batter in prepared pan. Spread cream cheese filling evenly over batter.

6. Microwave bowl of reserved batter until warm and pourable, 10 to 20 seconds. Using spoon, dollop softened batter over cream cheese filling, 6 to 8 dollops. Using knife, swirl batter through cream cheese filling, making marbled pattern, 10 to 12 strokes, leaving ½-inch border around edges.

7. Bake until toothpick inserted in center comes out with few moist crumbs attached, 35 to 40 minutes, rotating pan halfway through baking. Let cool in pan on wire rack for 1 hour.

8. Using foil overhang, lift brownies out of pan. Return brownies to wire rack and let cool completely, about 1 hour. Cut into 2-inch squares and serve.

▶ **Look: Sarah Bakes Brownies**
Video available free for 4 months at CooksIllustrated.com/aug14

Bagging Up Better Food Storage

Crummy plastic food storage bags leak, rip, and are tricky to seal. We wanted a strong, leakproof bag that would close securely without a fuss and keep food fresher longer.

> BY LISA McMANUS ⋹

Why is it so hard to find a good plastic food storage bag? Too often the plastic is flimsy, the closure doesn't work without a fight, and when you finally get it closed, it leaks. Then there's the dizzying array of options. Do you need both "storage" and "freezer" bags? Do you want zipper locks or plastic sliders? Expandable bags for bulky foods or double-layer bags for extra protection? One thing, though, is clear: American consumers use a lot of these bags, spending $1.6 billion on them last year alone, according to Chicago market-research firm IRi. A few years ago we picked a favorite bag by Glad: a thick, protective freezer bag with an airtight double-grooved seal. Recently we received conflicting reports from the manufacturer about whether this product was being discontinued. Ultimately we decided that it could no longer hold our top spot, and we went back to the drawing board.

As in our previous testing, we focused on gallon-size bags, in which we store everything from herbs and cookie dough to meat and tomato sauce. We also opted exclusively for freezer bags this time, since past tests have taught us that freezer bags are generally made with thicker plastic, which can keep food fresh longer than the thinner plastic of storage bags. Our wish list: a bag that was easy to seal, leakproof, and durable and that excelled at protecting food. We bought eight products—four sold in supermarkets, two food-service bags sold in bulk via mail order, and two eco-friendly options. Five closed with zipper-lock tracks; three used sliders. Prices ranged from 10 cents all the way up to a staggering 49 cents per bag.

Holding the Bag

Our first criterion: simplicity. You shouldn't need extra hands to prop up a bag for filling or have to guess if it's really closed. Bags should swallow up plenty of food and still be easy to seal. To push the limits, we packed each bag with 4 pounds of large carrots. We were able to zip all the carrots into all the bags, and none poked holes in the plastic. But one bag had a petite zipper channel that was hard to match up, while another was tough to keep open

▶ **See the Splits and Saves**
Video available free for 4 months at CooksIllustrated.com/aug14

because of its dual layers of flimsy plastic; plus, when we flipped over the edges of this bag's opening (a handy trick to help prop open any bag), its side seams ripped. At least some bags came with useful features—one had a foldout bottom panel that helped it stand up and made it easier to fill. Two bags were particularly sturdy around the opening (one was made of sturdier plastic overall and the other had a wide band of thicker plastic around the top), which made them easy to prop open, and both had deep zipper channels that were effortless to seal.

Next we filled the bags with a gallon of water each and laid them on the counter, noting whether any leaked. To our chagrin, four bags bombed, leaking a few drops—or entire puddles—all over the counter. We didn't imagine any of them would turn around and prove their worth (and indeed none did, all four falling to the bottom of our rankings by the end of our testing), but we forged ahead with them anyway.

Freezing Out

Our next benchmark: an airtight bag that protects the food. The development of freezer burn, indicated by the appearance of brownish-white discoloration on the food and snowy ice crystals, is a visible sign of likely failure in this department. It happens when frozen food dehydrates and oxidizes when it is exposed to air. We froze bags filled with bone-in pork chops, hamburger patties, cookie-dough balls, and sandwich bread. Within two weeks, several bags revealed icy crystals forming on the food, some of which got progressively worse. But in the top-performing bags, scarcely any snowy residue appeared, even after two months.

We sent the bags to a lab to measure their thickness as well as how fast moisture travels through their plastic, called the water vapor transmission rate. A lower, or slower, rate would indicate better protection. But when the results came back, they didn't reveal a clear trend. Our front-runner, which exhibited only a little residue after two months, had the fastest transmission rate of all the bags, while bags with slower rates, which should translate to better protection, had food that iced up. What was going on? Well, if a bag has a leaky seal, it doesn't matter how impermeable the plastic is.

So we devised a follow-up test that would also factor in the seal. We weighed desiccant packs (the moisture-absorbing packets found in product packaging), enclosed them in each bag, submerged the bags in water for a week, and then reweighed the packs. One product failed outright—we found the pack

Anatomy of a Better Bag

The thickness and permeability of the plastic is important, but sturdy construction and a reliable seal are also key to a winning bag.

A deeply grooved zipper is easy to seal, and a double zipper adds insurance.

A thick plastic collar makes a bag easier to prop open for filling and provides a better barrier to air.

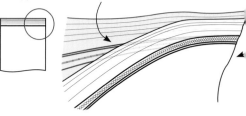

floating inside a water-filled bag. The packs in three other bags weighed about ½ gram more, indicating that some moisture had gotten in. But four sets—including in our front-runner—stayed remarkably dry, gaining only tenths or hundredths of a gram.

A Blowout Finish

Our last standard: bags that can hold up to abuse. We poured ¾ gallon of tomato sauce into each bag, sealed the bags, and pushed them off the counter. While we don't expect home cooks to throw around bags of sauce, bags can get knocked around in the fridge or freezer, and accidents do happen. Although four bags exploded, four—our front-runner among them—bounced to the floor without spilling a drop. And finally, we shook each bag briskly three times, both upright and upside down. Our top two bags didn't leak even a dribble. Interestingly, in both abuse tests, all the failures but one happened at the site of the seal.

Our conclusion: While thick plastic helps, strong seals are more important. The seal on our runner-up, a commercial bag by Elkay Plastics, never blew out; plus its plastic was the thickest in the lineup. It lost a few points in the desiccant test and burst a side seam during the extreme tomato sauce test, but it's a reliable option if you want to buy in bulk. Our winner, Ziploc Brand Double Zipper Gallon Freezer Bags, features a fail-safe dual zipper and a thick plastic collar that makes it easy to prop open and serves as an improved barrier to air. Leakproof and sturdy, it was also the cheapest bag we tested. And finally, we were pleased to find an environmentally friendly bag we can recommend, by Green'N'Pack.

TESTING FOOD STORAGE BAGS

We tested eight gallon-size freezer bags, evaluating freezer protection and whether they were leakproof, tough, and easy to handle. Scores were averaged and bags appear in order of preference. A source for the runner-up appears on page 32.

FREEZER PROTECTION

We froze four bone-in pork chops, 2 pounds of ground beef patties, one dozen balls of frozen chocolate-chip cookie dough, and a half-loaf of white sandwich bread for two months, checking them after two weeks, one month, and two months for freezer burn and ice crystals. Bags that kept food in the best condition the longest received high marks.

DURABILITY

We pushed bags filled with ¾ gallon of tomato sauce from kitchen counters and shook bags filled with 1 gallon of water (upright and upside down) to test strength. We checked for damage during routine handling.

LEAKPROOF

To assess bag permeability and the quality of the seal, we weighed packets of moisture-absorbing desiccant, sealed them in bags, and kept the bags submerged in water for one week. Then we reweighed the desiccant packs. Drier packets rated highest. Bags also lost points for leaking when filled with 1 gallon of water and laid flat on counter.

EASE OF USE

We preferred bags that were sturdily constructed, making them easier to prop open to fill, and that were easy to securely seal even when very full.

THICKNESS

The thickness of a single wall of the plastic bags, measured by an independent laboratory, in mils (¹⁄₁₀₀₀ of an inch).

	CRITERIA	TESTERS' COMMENTS

HIGHLY RECOMMENDED

ZIPLOC
Brand Double Zipper Gallon Freezer Bags with the Smart Zip Seal
Model: UPC #0-25700-00382-3
Price: $3.99 for 30 bags ($0.13 per bag)
Style: Zipper-lock
Thickness: 2.4 mil

Freezer Protection ★★★
Durability ★★★
Leakproof ★★★
Ease of Use ★★★

Frozen food stayed fresh in this bag even after two months. Its band of thicker plastic extending 2 inches below the zipper provided structure that made for easier filling and offered an extra barrier of protection. Its double zipper helped it remain leakproof and stand up to abuse.

ELKAY PLASTICS
Ziplock Heavy Weight Freezer Bag
Model: UPC #6-54866-01303-4
Price: $9.69 for 100 bags ($0.10 per bag), plus shipping
Style: Zipper-lock
Thickness: 3.7 mil

Freezer Protection ★★★
Durability ★★
Leakproof ★★½
Ease of Use ★★★

With the thickest plastic in the lineup and a tight seal, this bag provided excellent protection. Frozen cookie dough and pork chops had virtually no ice crystals and were fresh-looking after two months. A side seam split when we dropped this bag (full of tomato sauce), and the bag let in a little moisture when we submerged it.

RECOMMENDED

GREEN'N'PACK
Food Storage Freezer Gallon Bags
Model: UPC #8-54347-00303-9
Price: $11.90 for 30 bags ($0.40 per bag)
Style: Zipper-lock
Thickness: 2.7 mil

Freezer Protection ★★½
Durability ★★
Leakproof ★★½
Ease of Use ★★½

This eco-friendly bag, designed to biodegrade, performed well, though it didn't quite match our top bags. Frozen food stayed in excellent shape for a month but began to show a few signs of ice crystals after two months. Its seal could be a little bigger and stronger.

DIVERSEY, INC.
Ziploc Commercial Resealable Gallon Freezer Bags
Model: 94604
Price: $34.99 for 250 bags ($0.14 per bag), plus shipping
Style: Zipper-lock
Thickness: 2.5 mil

Freezer Protection ★★
Durability ★★
Leakproof ★★★
Ease of Use ★★½

This food-service version of our winner just wasn't as good. Frozen foods stayed in very good condition for the first two weeks but then began showing moderate amounts of ice crystals. While it has dual zippers like our winner, it lacks that bag's collar of thicker plastic, which meant it was not as easy to handle and delivered less freezer protection.

HEFTY
Slider Bag, Gallon Freezer
Model: UPC #0-13700-82413-5
Price: $3.29 for 13 bags ($0.25 per bag)
Style: Slider
Thickness: 2.5 mil

Freezer Protection ★★
Durability ★★★
Leakproof ★★½
Ease of Use ★★

Frozen food quickly acquired a moderate amount of "snow" around the edges. This bag claims to have "a stronger seal than Ziploc bags when shaken, dropped, or stacked," and it tied our top-ranked Ziploc when dropped and shaken, but its zipper leaked. It was also a bit too floppy.

RECOMMENDED WITH RESERVATIONS

ZIPLOC
Brand Gallon Freezer Slider Bags
Model: UPC #0-25700-02313-5
Price: $2.49 for 10 bags ($0.25 per bag)
Style: Slider
Thickness: 2.8 mil

Freezer Protection ★★★
Durability ★
Leakproof ★★
Ease of Use ★★★

We really liked this bag's gusseted, expandable bottom, and foods stayed in good condition in the freezer. We only wish its sliding seal were stronger: It failed during abuse testing, dripped when full, and let in some moisture when submerged.

NOT RECOMMENDED

NATURAL VALUE
Slider Gallon Freezer Bags
Model: UPC #7-06173-02019-6
Price: $2.35 for 10 bags ($0.24 per bag)
Style: Slider
Thickness: 3.3 mil

Freezer Protection ★
Durability ★★★
Leakproof ★★½
Ease of Use ★★

Frozen food became icy after two weeks; meat showed gray freezer burn spots after a month. The bags themselves are not particularly "green," as their manufacturer admits, but the box is made from recycled materials. While the bags survived abuse testing intact, the seal leaked when full of water.

ZIPLOC
Brand Double Guard Double Layer Gallon Freezer Bags
Model: UPC #0-25700-01261-0
Price: $6.37 for 13 bags ($0.49 per bag)
Style: Zipper-lock
Thickness: 2.0 mil outer layer, 1.0 mil inner layer

Freezer Protection ★★
Durability ★
Leakproof ★
Ease of Use ★

This pricey double-layer bag claims to provide a better barrier against freezer burn; we found it only middling. Floppy and flimsy, this bag was also hard to fill and its weak seal burst during abuse tests. The side seams above the zipper ripped as we filled bags and leaked steadily when filled with liquids. We found our desiccant packs floating inside the bags.

What's So Great About Frozen Yogurt?

These days, supermarket frozen yogurts are flying off the shelves. Is that because they're healthful and taste good—or because they simply sound that way?

⋑ BY AMY GRAVES & KATE SHANNON ⋐

Frozen yogurt has had its ups and downs since it debuted in the 1970s, but its recent comeback has been big. Sales of the low-fat ice cream alternative jumped 74 percent between 2011 and 2013 to rake in a total of $486 million. That's a staggering increase compared with the numbers for ice cream, which, though it still outsells frozen yogurt by more than 12-fold, grew about 4 percent. But the growth isn't hard to explain. By implying that their products have the indulgent taste of ice cream but still offer many of the same nutritional benefits as refrigerated yogurt, frozen yogurt manufacturers have convinced a growing population of health-conscious consumers that they're not sacrificing that much by switching to the dessert—and might actually be doing themselves a favor by eating it.

We wanted to judge for ourselves whether the huge popularity of this current generation of supermarket frozen yogurts is warranted, so we scooped up eight of the best-selling national products, both low-fat and nonfat versions, in the most straightforward flavor: vanilla. Whether a frozen yogurt had the flavor of traditional vanilla ice cream or the tartness of a refrigerated yogurt, we wanted it to deliver a rich, creamy texture and clean, not-too-sweet flavor.

Counter(ing) Culture

Before we dug in, we did a little research into how much these frozen desserts have in common with refrigerated yogurt—and it turns out, that's a very tricky question to answer. The U.S. Food and Drug Administration (FDA) has only a loose definition for refrigerated yogurt, and none whatsoever for frozen yogurt. In fact, the FDA doesn't even regulate how many live and active cultures the refrigerated product should contain—and of course, the presumption that yogurt contains a significant dose (specifically of *Lactobacillus bulgaricus* and *Streptococcus thermophilus*) is the main reason it's considered a health food in the first place.

We concluded that it's best to take the label "yogurt" on frozen yogurt packaging with a grain of salt, along with mentions of live and active cultures on the ingredient list. Even if a frozen yogurt starts out with lots of bacteria, that doesn't mean those bacteria will make it through the manufacturing process. For example, heat-treating the dairy after culturing (a practice used to prolong shelf life or reduce tartness) will kill off virtually all the bacteria—and since there are no regulations for frozen yogurt, manufacturers aren't required to tell you what they've done. What's more, even if a frozen yogurt hasn't been heat-treated, the vast majority of bacteria that it contains before it's frozen is likely to die off during freezing. According to Donald Schaffner, extension specialist in food science, director of the Center for Advanced Food Technology, and professor at Rutgers University, "It's possible, or even likely, that the freezing process might kill off anywhere from 90 to 99 percent of bacteria."

These aren't the only reasons to doubt frozen yogurt's value as a "healthy" dessert. While the product is generally much lower in fat compared with ice cream, it often contains nearly as much sugar. Most frozen yogurts are also loaded with a laundry list of additives and stabilizers that don't make their way into high-quality refrigerated yogurt or ice cream.

Smooth Operators

Those considerations aside, there's no denying the huge popularity of frozen yogurt, so we carried on with our tasting to see if any of the supermarket products offered at least good flavor and texture. But even the news on that front wasn't great. With a few exceptions, the yogurts either tested our tolerance for sweetness or exhibited odd off-flavors. Even more damning were their textures—no surprise, since when you remove fat from a frozen dairy product, it becomes more difficult to attain an ultrasmooth consistency. We could tell just by looking that some products were rock hard, while others were fluffy like whipped cream cheese. The better brands achieved "smooth," "light" creaminess thanks to a few key components. The first: corn syrup. As we discovered when developing our recipe for Vanilla Ice Cream (July/August 2011), corn syrup inhibits iciness by restricting the movement of the water molecules so that they are less likely to link up and form large crystals. Corn syrup also depresses the freezing point of frozen yogurt, which makes it less vulnerable to the constant thawing and refreezing involved in transporting a frozen dessert.

Stabilizers also help stave off ice crystal formation and boost the perception of creaminess. In fact, their role is even more crucial in frozen yogurt than it is in ice cream, since frozen yogurt's lower fat and higher moisture contents make it especially vulnerable to ice crystal formation. Some stabilizers, like carrageenan, are particularly effective. When combined with milk protein, this polysaccharide forms a custardy gel so strong that it replicates the texture of cream. The combination of carrageenan and corn syrup worked so well in the Turkey Hill frozen yogurt, which is fat-free, that the "soft," "smooth" product earned our recommendation. (The "gritty" textures of the other two fat-free yogurts, both from Stonyfield, moved them to the bottom of the chart.) But without corn syrup, carrageenan was unable to save the low-ranking Healthy Choice dessert, which tasters found "sludgy." It was also easy to spot the lone stabilizer-free frozen yogurt, from Häagen-Dazs, a product that went from rock hard to soup in minutes.

Frozen Yogurt versus Ice Cream

There's no denying that choosing frozen yogurt over ice cream saves on fat. But once you factor in sugar and additives, is frozen yogurt really that much better for you? After comparing some of the numbers from our favorite vanilla ice cream from Ben & Jerry's and the winning vanilla frozen yogurt from TCBY, we're not so sure that giving up the ice cream we love for a frozen yogurt that we merely like is worth the sacrifice in satisfaction.

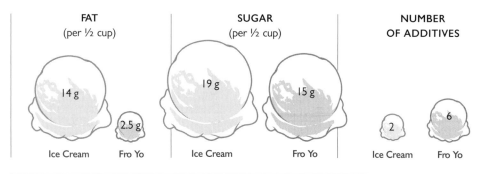

FAT (per ½ cup)		SUGAR (per ½ cup)		NUMBER OF ADDITIVES	
14 g	2.5 g	19 g	15 g	2	6
Ice Cream	Fro Yo	Ice Cream	Fro Yo	Ice Cream	Fro Yo

TASTING SUPERMARKET FROZEN YOGURT

Twenty-one America's Test Kitchen staff members tasted eight top-selling supermarket vanilla frozen yogurts. We rated the products on flavor, texture, and overall appeal. Fat and sugar per ½-cup serving were taken from package labels. An independent laboratory calculated overrun, listed as a percentage increase over the original volume of the frozen yogurt base. Results were averaged and frozen yogurts appear below in order of preference.

RECOMMENDED

TCBY Classic Vanilla Bean Frozen Yogurt
Price: $3.95 per 1.5-qt container ($0.08 per oz)
Fat: 2.5 g per ½ cup **Sugar:** 15 g per ½ cup **Overrun:** 78.4%
Ingredients: Skim milk, sugar, cream, corn syrup, vanilla bean flavoring (vanilla bean specks, natural flavor, xanthan gum), propylene glycol monoesters, mono and diglycerides, guar gum, locust bean gum, carrageenan, probiotic yogurt cultures (*S. thermophilus, L. bulgaricus, L. lactic, B. lactis, L. acidophilus, L. casei, L. rhamnosus*)
Comments: Tasters praised the "balanced sweetness" and "straightforward vanilla flavor" of this product. (We tested its supermarket-only formulation.) Its combination of corn syrup, carrageenan, and cream, not to mention its chart-topping overrun percentage, helped it achieve a smooth texture, though some tasters felt that it bordered on "bouncy."

BEN & JERRY'S Vanilla Greek Frozen Yogurt
Price: $6.50 per 1-pt container ($0.41 per oz)
Fat: 4.5 g per ½ cup **Sugar:** 19 g per ½ cup **Overrun:** 20.3%
Ingredients: Skim milk, Greek yogurt (cultured skim milk, natural flavor, carrageenan), liquid sugar (sugar, water), cream, water, corn syrup solids, egg yolks, nonfat yogurt powder (cultured nonfat milk), vanilla extract, sugar, locust bean gum
Comments: With a "pleasant tang" that was "recognizably like yogurt" and a "natural vanilla flavor," this frozen yogurt (available in Ben & Jerry's shops) was "appealing" and reminded some of "cheesecake." Tasters also praised its "smooth," if "a bit runny," texture.

TURKEY HILL Dairy Vanilla Bean Frozen Yogurt
Price: $3.69 per 1.5-qt container ($0.08 per oz)
Fat: 0 g per ½ cup **Sugar:** 14 g per ½ cup **Overrun:** 54.7%
Ingredients: Nonfat milk, sugar, cultured nonfat milk (contains live active cultures), corn syrup, maltodextrin, calcium carbonate, cellulose gel, cellulose gum, mono and diglycerides, vanilla, vanilla bean, polysorbate 80, carrageenan, vitamin A, vitamin D₃
Comments: Lots of stabilizers and emulsifiers (including carrageenan) created a "smooth" consistency in this nonfat yogurt, though some tasters found it "a little thin and icy," with "not enough milkfat." It was "not even vaguely tart"; rather, it tasted "clean," "appealing," and "sweet."

NOT RECOMMENDED

HÄAGEN-DAZS Vanilla Low Fat Frozen Yogurt
Price: $3.99 per 14-oz container ($0.29 per oz)
Fat: 2.5 g per ½ cup **Sugar:** 21 g per ½ cup **Overrun:** 9.6%
Ingredients: Skim milk (lactose reduced), corn syrup, sugar, egg yolks, cream, vanilla extract, active yogurt cultures
Comments: We had high hopes for this product, which has the shortest ingredient list of the bunch. But without any stabilizers, tasters bemoaned its chalky texture, which quickly melted into yogurt "soup." Its high sugar content gave it a "syrupy," "cloying" flavor that one taster compared to "eating liquid marshmallows."

NOT RECOMMENDED CONTINUED

HEALTHY CHOICE Vanilla Bean Greek Frozen Yogurt
Price: $3.99 per package of three 4-oz containers ($0.33 per oz)
Fat: 2 g per ½ cup **Sugar:** 11 g per ½ cup **Overrun:** 75%
Ingredients: Nonfat milk, cultured nonfat milk, sugar, cream, polydextrose, maltodextrin, milk protein concentrate, less than 2% of: vanilla extract, vanilla bean seed powder, gelatin, dextrose, cellulose gel, propylene glycol, monoesters, citric acid, mono and diglycerides, cellulose gum, carrageenan, calcium phosphate
Comments: Tasters found this "Greek" frozen yogurt "sludgy," perhaps due to a lack of corn syrup combined with a high overrun percentage. That texture, paired with "buttermilk" tang (which may have been enhanced by the addition of citric acid), was more reminiscent of "frozen cheesecake" than yogurt.

BLUE BELL Country Vanilla Lowfat Frozen Yogurt
Price: $5.75 per ½-gal container ($0.09 per oz)
Fat: 1.5 g per ½ cup **Sugar:** 16 g per ½ cup **Overrun:** 54.4%
Ingredients: Cultured lowfat milk, sugar, skim milk, corn syrup, high fructose corn syrup, natural vanilla flavor, cellulose gel, cellulose gum, vegetable gums (guar, carrageenan, carob bean), xanthan gum, annatto color; contains live yogurt culture (*L. bulgaricus* and *S. thermophilus*)
Comments: This product's "really yellow" color suggested eggy richness, but it "doesn't taste as rich and creamy as it looks." In fact, tasters found it "foamy," noting that it "just slumps in the cup." Its "supersweet" flavor was "cloying"—like "fake sugar"—and there was "not enough vanilla" flavor.

STONYFIELD Gotta Have Vanilla Organic Nonfat Frozen Yogurt
Price: $3.99 per 1-pt container ($0.25 per oz)
Fat: 0 g per ½ cup **Sugar:** 19 g per ½ cup **Overrun:** 44%
Ingredients: Cultured pasteurized organic nonfat milk, naturally milled organic sugar, organic rice syrup, organic whey protein concentrate, organic vanilla flavor, organic carob bean gum, organic guar gum, organic vanilla bean specks; contains live active cultures (*S. thermophilus, L. bulgaricus, L. acidophilus, bifidus,* and *L. casei*)
Comments: "Tastes like the worst qualities of low-cal dairy," said one taster. "Sweet, fake, lean." Without any fat, corn syrup, or carrageenan to aid smoothness, this product had a texture that was "more crystal-y than creamy."

STONYFIELD Greek Vanilla Organic Nonfat Frozen Yogurt
Price: $4.29 per 1-pt container ($0.27 per oz)
Fat: 0 g per ½ cup **Sugar:** 17 g per ½ cup **Overrun:** 52%
Ingredients: Cultured pasteurized organic nonfat milk, naturally milled organic sugar, organic whey protein concentrate, organic rice syrup, organic carob bean gum, organic guar gum, organic vanilla extract, organic vanilla bean specks; contains live active cultures (*S. thermophilus, L. bulgaricus, L. acidophilus, bifidus,* and *L. casei*)
Comments: This nonfat yogurt was plagued by a host of off-flavors that summoned comparisons to "spoiled milk" and "stinky tropical fruit." Like its sibling, this product lacked ingredients like corn syrup and carrageenan that promote smoothness, and its "grainy" and "gritty" texture helped secure its spot at the bottom.

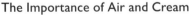

The Importance of Air and Cream

Another core, but less obvious, component of the texture of frozen desserts is air. Manufacturers aerate their products to increase the overall volume and to produce a lighter texture. "Overrun" refers to the percentage increase in volume from aeration, and by law it can be as high as 100 percent in frozen desserts. If that sounds like a cheap way to get consumers to pay more, it is—and the overrun in some of the yogurts we tasted, such as TCBY, ran as high as 78 percent. Some overrun is a must in frozen desserts, particularly lean frozen yogurts; without air, they would be rock solid and virtually inedible.

Finally, cream might sound like an unlikely ingredient in a low-fat dessert like frozen yogurt, but even in small quantities it made a big difference. Besides adding richness, it introduced additional milk solids, which decreased moisture and minimized potential ice crystal formation. It also boosted vanilla flavor, since vanillin (the flavor compound in vanilla extract) is largely fat-soluble.

Not surprisingly, the two frozen yogurts that tasters favored most, from TCBY and Ben & Jerry's, each contained a combination of corn syrup, carrageenan (among other stabilizers), and cream. Tasters enjoyed both the "straightforward vanilla" flavor of TCBY and the recognizable yogurty "tang" of Ben & Jerry's Greek.

But even these frozen yogurts didn't elicit anything close to the rave reviews of a great ice cream—or a great fresh yogurt. Nevertheless, if you're looking for a low-fat frozen dessert with decent texture and reasonably good flavor (that may or may not be full of healthy bacteria), any of our recommended yogurts will do.

⇒ BY ANDREA GEARY, ANDREW JANJIGIAN, SARAH MULLINS & DAN SOUZA ⇐

Evaluating Iced Coffee Methods

A trendy new method for iced coffee based on the Japanese-developed pour-over brewing technique is making waves among coffee aficionados. It promises a complex brew in minutes, so we decided to try it. In the end, however, tasters preferred two classic methods. Both require planning ahead, but we think the results are worth it.

➤ POUR-OVER METHOD: FAST BUT WEAK

A small amount of nearly boiling water is poured over ground coffee in a slow stream to make a double-strength brew, and by brewing directly over ice, the coffee is chilled and diluted to the proper strength. Cooling the coffee immediately after brewing is said to lock in volatile aroma compounds that would normally drift into the air if the coffee were allowed to cool naturally, in theory delivering more complexity. However, because only a small amount of water passes through the ground coffee, the flavors aren't fully extracted, which we found led to weaker coffee.
Tasting Notes: Quite weak (albeit clean and fresh-tasting).

➤ TRADITIONAL METHOD: BOLD, BRIGHT, AND ACIDIC

Coffee is brewed hot following any standard method and then allowed to cool naturally before being iced. We used our favorite drip coffee maker from Technivorm and let the coffee cool for 45 minutes before icing and serving.
Tasting Notes: Ample bitterness, acidity, and complexity because a hot brewing temperature (195 to 205 degrees is optimal) extracts the most flavor compounds.

➤ COLD BREW METHOD: SMOOTH AND SUBTLE

Ground coffee is combined with cold or room-temperature water and allowed to sit for at least 8 hours (and up to several days); the infusion is strained and consumed as is, or diluted with additional water to a desired strength. (For our recipe, go to CooksIllustrated.com/coldbrewcoffee.)
Tasting Notes: Because the extraction is done at a much lower temperature (40 to 72 degrees), the coffee lacks the bitterness and acidity of a traditional hot brew. Instead, it boasts a more subtle, smooth flavor with hints of chocolate and fruit. –D.S.

An Even Easier Way to Stretch Pizza Dough

One of the most challenging aspects of making pizza is getting the dough to stretch into an even, thin crust without it tearing or springing back—a problem that results from the dough's strong gluten network. Our Thin-Crust Pizza recipe (January/February 2011) makes the task easier (and delivers more flavor, too) by calling for proofing the dough in the refrigerator for three days before shaping it into balls and then stretching, topping, and baking it. This longer proofing relaxes the gluten network, which makes it easier to stretch. But we've recently found a way to make the stretching process even easier for any cold-fermented pizza dough: Shape the proofed dough into balls and then return it to the fridge for 4 to 24 hours before stretching it. This allows natural enzymes in flour to continue to break down the gluten, helping it return to its relaxed state. –A.J.

CHILL BEFORE STRETCHING
Refrigerating balls of pizza dough for 4 to 24 hours makes stretching much easier.

A Sweet Release for Bundt Cakes

Recently we ran across an idea for giving Bundt cakes a crackly, sugary crust while they bake, saving the need to make a frosting or glaze. The idea is to coat the pan with sugar before adding the batter, so that in the heat of the oven it melts into a lacy crust. The challenge would be to create a sugary coating that would stick to the cake rather than fuse the cake to the pan. First we tried coating the pan with a hefty amount of vegetable oil spray before dusting it with granulated sugar. Unfortunately the spray's coating was too thin, and the cakes almost always stuck. Next we tried brushing the pan with melted butter and then dusting it with sugar. These cakes released easily, but there was no crunchy coating. Why? The sugar had dissolved in the water in the butter (butter is nearly 20 percent water).

SUGAR-COATED
Brushing a Bundt pan with vegetable oil and then dusting it with sugar before adding the batter creates a sweet, crackly crust.

In the end, we landed on brushing the pan with 1 tablespoon vegetable oil before coating it with ⅓ cup of sugar. It provided a thick coating of pure fat that was easy to brush on and guaranteed that the cake released with ease. What's more, the sugar turned into just the lacy, sweet coating on the cake that we were looking for. –S.M.

New Uses for Xanthan Gum

Recipes for gluten-free baked goods often call for xanthan gum to reinforce structure, but we found that this ingredient has a couple of other worthwhile uses.

SAUCE THICKENER

We often use a flour-and-fat roux to thicken gravies and sauces; xanthan gum will do the same thing and deliver a cleaner flavor while eliminating the fat (plus it's gluten-free). We compared a batch of gravy thickened with a roux (¼ cup of flour and 3 tablespoons of unsalted butter) with the same recipe thickened instead with ⅜ teaspoon of xanthan gum. The xanthan-gum batch tasted more clearly of meat and vegetables, while the roux-thickened gravy was more mellow, as the notable amount of flour and fat muted flavors.

ICE CREAM STABILIZER

Many ice cream manufacturers add xanthan gum to their products because it prevents the formation of large ice crystals during churning and storage. And that translates into a smoother ice cream. This can easily be done at home. Adding ⅛ teaspoon of xanthan gum to the base prior to churning had our ice cream starting out smoother and less noticeably icy than a control recipe made without the gum—and it stayed that way for more than a week.

HOW TO ADD IT

Xanthan gum has a tendency to clump when it comes in contact with liquids; here's how we ensure even incorporation.
Create a Vortex: Place ice cream base or finished gravy in tall, narrow container, leaving at least 4 inches of headspace. Insert immersion blender to bottom of container. With blender on high speed, create vortex in middle of liquid.
Sprinkle and Blend: Slowly sprinkle xanthan gum over vortex (⅜ teaspoon per 2 cups of gravy or sauce and ⅛ teaspoon per quart of churned ice cream), allowing it to be sucked down into blade of blender for at least 30 seconds to thoroughly combine. –D.S.

Better Care for Wood Tools

We've always used mineral oil to keep our wood cutting boards and utensils from drying and cracking, but lately we've been hearing about spoon butter, a mixture that you can prepare at home that is touted as a more durable, water-repellent option for wood kitchenware.

We made spoon butter in a Mason jar by combining mineral oil and chopped beeswax (ordered from a cheese-making store) in the recommended ratio of 3 to 1 and then placing the jar in a water-filled saucepan set over low heat to melt the beeswax. Once the mixture had cooled to room temperature, we rubbed it into several boards and utensils with a clean cloth. We let the tools sit for 24 hours and then buffed off the excess coating. For comparison we also applied straight mineral oil to a set of similar utensils and boards. After washing both sets 20 times, we found that the set treated with spoon butter was in noticeably better shape. Those treated with straight mineral oil looked ashen, with dried, rough spots, while the spoon butter set had a smooth finish and retained some protective coating. Making spoon butter takes a little more effort up front, but the long-lasting results are worth it. –S.M.

For a sandwich that's easy to eat, we wrap our Grilled Chicken Souvlaki (page 19) in aluminum foil. Start by placing the warm pita at one corner of a 12-inch square piece of foil, and then layer the sandwich ingredients on top of the pita, leaving a 1-inch border on all sides. After folding the sides of the pita over the filling, follow these simple steps to make a neatly bundled sandwich. –A.G.

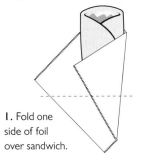

1. Fold one side of foil over sandwich.

2. Fold up bottom of foil.

3. Fold over other side of foil.

SCIENCE EXPERIMENT The Best Way to Use a Whisk

We've noticed that different cooks seem to favor different motions when using a whisk. Some prefer side-to-side strokes, others use circular stirring, and others like the looping action of beating that takes the whisk up and out of the bowl. That got us wondering: Is any one of these motions more effective than the others?

EXPERIMENT

We compared stirring, beating, and side-to-side motions in three core whisking applications: emulsifying vinaigrette and whipping small amounts of cream and egg whites. We timed how long the dressing stayed emulsified and how long it took us to whip cream and egg whites to stiff peaks.

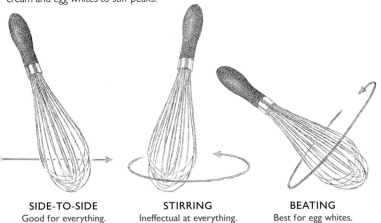

SIDE-TO-SIDE
Good for everything.

STIRRING
Ineffectual at everything.

BEATING
Best for egg whites.

RESULTS

In all cases, side-to-side whisking was highly effective. It kept the vinaigrette (made simply of oil and vinegar) fully emulsified for 15 minutes, and it speedily whipped cream to stiff peaks in 4 minutes and egg whites to stiff peaks in 5 minutes. Circular stirring was ineffectual across the board. It never fully emulsified the dressing, which remained thin and separated, and it took more than twice as long as side-to-side whisking to whip cream and egg whites (10 and 12 minutes, respectively). Beating was even less effective than stirring for emulsifying, and whipping cream dragged on with minimal effect for 8 minutes before we threw in the towel. Beating was only effective at whipping egg whites, creating stiff peaks in a record 4 minutes, surpassing the timing of side-to-side strokes.

EXPLANATION

So why does a side-to-side motion work so well—and the other actions, in the main, work so poorly? The first reason is that side-to-side whisking is simply an easier motion to execute quickly and aggressively—allowing you to carry out more and harder motions per minute than with the other strokes. Second, this action causes more of what scientists call "shear force" to be applied to the liquid. As the whisk moves in one direction across the bowl, the liquid starts to move with it. But then the whisk is dragged in the opposite direction, exerting force against the rest of the liquid still moving toward it. Because stirring and beating take the liquid in the same direction of the whisk, they produce less shear force.

In vinaigrette, the greater shear force of side-to-side whisking helps break oil into tinier droplets that stay suspended in vinegar, keeping the dressing emulsified longer. To create stiff peaks in cream and egg whites, shear force and efficiency are both key. As the tines are dragged through each liquid, they create channels that trap air. Since the faster the channels are created, the faster the cream or whites gain volume, rapid, aggressive side-to-side strokes are very effective. Their greater shear force is also better at keeping each type of foam stable. In cream, shear force disrupts the proteins surrounding the fat molecules, freeing them to form a protective coating around the air bubbles; in egg whites, shear force performs a similar function, unfolding proteins that then create a protective film around the bubbles.

In whipping egg whites, however, beating had an advantage even over side-to-side strokes. Because egg whites are very viscous, more of them will cling to the tines than cream, even at the beginning of whipping. This allows the whisk to create wider channels that trap more air. With side-to-side strokes, the reverse motion will disrupt some of the channels that were just created, slowing the process of trapping air and building volume. Since beating takes the whisk out of the liquid during some of its action, these larger channels can stay open longer, trapping more air. In this case, the effect is more important than shear force in quickly creating volume. –D.S.

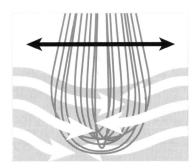

SHEAR FORCE IN LIQUID
The force exerted by a moving liquid (the liquid moved by the tines) against the adjacent liquid.

● **THE SCIENCE OF COOKING: USING A WHISK** Everyone knows the correct way to use a whisk, right? Wrong. Check out our latest science video where we pit three commonly used techniques against one another to find a winner.

⇒ BY HANNAH CROWLEY, AMY GRAVES, LAUREN SAVOIE & KATE SHANNON ⇐

UPDATE Mini Toaster Oven

Our top-rated toaster oven, the Smart Oven by Breville, sports simple, intuitive controls and five highly responsive quartz heating elements, which helped it out-toast, -roast, -bake, and -broil the nine other machines in our most recent testing. Nothing about it could be beat—except maybe the $249.95 price and its countertop-hogging size. For tighter spaces and budgets, Breville offers the roughly 25 percent smaller Mini Smart Oven with Element IQ, which features similar easy controls and the same quartz technology (in four elements) for $149.95. We used it to toast four slices of bread, roast two bone-in split chicken breasts, bake eight cookies, and heat a personal-size frozen pizza. In every case, the Mini Smart Oven aced our tests, preheating in 5 minutes or less and baking evenly. We also liked that this oven includes a button labeled "A Bit More," which lets you broil or toast food for just a few extra seconds or minutes. The Mini Smart Oven by Breville is a terrific choice for smaller spaces. –A.G.

COMPACT CHOICE
The Mini Smart Oven by Breville performs as well as its sibling, our top-rated toaster oven, in a smaller, cheaper package.

NEW Beverage Infusers

Beverage infusers promise to flavor drinks with fresh produce with little fuss. We brewed water with lemon, grapefruit, watermelon, strawberries, and blackberries in four models: three pitchers with removable infusing columns and an infusing ball for use in any pitcher. We struggled to find a pitcher wide enough for the Jokari Healthy Steps Water Infuser, which barely held a cup of produce and was awkward to fill. The pitcher-style infusers all brewed fruity-tasting water, but two had skimpy infusing chambers, and the lid of one pitcher fell off when we poured, while the other's column trapped liquid that leaked everywhere when we pulled it out, which you must do in order to pour. Only the Primula Flavor It Beverage System ($29.99) passed muster. It held nearly twice the fruit of the others, and with additional inserts for brewing tea and chilling drinks, it was also more versatile, making the investment a bit more worthwhile. (Otherwise we might just opt for a plain old pitcher and chunks of fruit to flavor our water.) –L.S.

INFUSION SOLUTION
The Primula Flavor It Beverage System delivers fruity-flavored beverages (and iced tea) while keeping cleanup easy.

UPDATE Seafood Scissors

Kitchen shears are ideal for butterflying chicken and snipping herbs but not so great for thick, curvy seafood shells. When we're cooking lobster, crab, or shrimp, we reach for seafood scissors, designed with small, curved blades that snip open shells without marring the seafood within. Our winning pair, Progressive International Seafood Scissors ($9.95), was recently redesigned, so we bought the updated version plus four new products ($6.55 to $14.99) and snipped our way through pounds of shellfish.

Sadly, the redesigned pair was a bust. While it had excellent blades, the new, smaller handles cramped even the most petite hands. Of the remaining models, two had either comfortable handles or strong, sharp blades—but not both. The final two contenders fared better, but the RSVP International Endurance Seafood Scissors ($14.99) were the clear winner. These scissors had comfortable, sturdy handles and strong, sharp blades that snipped through tough lobster claws and delicate shrimp shells with ease, leaving the meat within pristine and ready for plucking. –H.C.

SEAWORTHY
The RSVP International Endurance Seafood Scissors easily snipped through hard crab legs and delicate shrimp shells.

NEW Grill Grate Cleaning Block

The GrillStone Value Pack Cleaning Kit by Earthstone International ($9.99) promises to deliver a deeper clean than the typical grill brush. We used this pumice block (two are included in the kit), which is attached to a plastic handle, to clean messy charcoal and gas cooking grates. We routinely clean preheated grates just before we put on the food to cook, and this block's short handle put testers' hands too close to the heat. However, we found that this strong scrubber quickly stripped off all the accumulated gunk even from cold grates. As we scrubbed, the pumice wore into a grooved shape that conformed to that of the grates, allowing it to clean even more thoroughly. Because each block lasted for only three or four cleanings (replacement blocks cost $4.49), and it generated abundant pumice dust that had to be rinsed off before we could use the grate, we find that it's best used as a once-per-season grill grate reconditioning tool. Still, it's one that we'd recommend to get grates shining like new. –A.G.

GRATE MAKEOVER
The tough-scrubbing pumice block on the GrillStone Value Pack Cleaning Kit is ideal for the occasional grill grate deep cleaning.

NEW Microwave Pasta Cookers

It's time-consuming to bring a big pot of water to a boil, but it's not exactly hard to prepare pasta. Despite our skepticism, we tested three different microwave pasta cookers, priced from $12.95 to $35. We simply added pasta to each oblong plastic box, poured in enough cold water to cover,

EVEN EASIER PAS
The Fasta Pasta Microw Cooker simplifies an speeds up the pasta cooking process.

microwaved until done (no stirring), and then flipped to drain through the lid. Every model cooked both strand and shaped pasta properly in almost half of the time it took to cook the same amount in the traditional stovetop method from start to finish. Draining through one model's floppy lid was problematic: Its draining holes let small noodles slip through and it exposed our hands to steam and water burns. But the other two models won favor for sturdy, quick-cooling plastic handles and lids, with narrow slits that strained water away from our hands. Of the two, the Fasta Pasta Microwave Cooker ($12.95) got the edge for its low price. Foolproof for cooking up to four servings, it makes fast pasta dinners even faster. –K.S.

For complete testing results, go to CooksIllustrated.com/aug14.

Sources

Prices were current at press time and do not include shipping. Contact companies to confirm information or visit CooksIllustrated.com for updates.

PAGE 12: GRILL BRUSH
- Grill Wizard 18-Inch China Grill Brush: $31.50, item #B007A26BF4, Amazon (866-216-1072, **amazon.com**).

PAGE 25: ARTISANAL CREAM CHEESE
- Zingerman's Creamery Fresh Cream Cheese: $15 for 1-pound tub, Zingerman's (888-636-8162, **zingermans.com**).

PAGE 27: FOOD STORAGE BAGS
- Elkay Plastics Ziplock Heavy Weight Freezer Bag: $9.69 for 100 bags, item #130F41012K 100, webstaurantstore.com (717-392-7472, **webstaurantstore.com**).

PAGE 32: MINI TOASTER OVEN
- Breville Mini Smart Oven with Element IQ: $149.95, item #BOV450XL, Breville USA (866-273-8455, **brevilleusa.com**).

PAGE 32: BEVERAGE INFUSER
- Primula Flavor It Beverage System: $29.99, item #PFBK-3725, Primula Products (561-353-3900, **primulaproducts.com**).

PAGE 32: SEAFOOD SCISSORS
- RSVP International Endurance Seafood Scissors: $14.99, item #SEA-J, Amazon.

PAGE 32: GRILL GRATE CLEANING BLOCK
- GrillStone Value Pack Cleaning Kit by Earthstone International: $9.99, item #750-SHB, Earthstone International (888-994-6327, **earthstoneinternational.com**).

PAGE 32: MICROWAVE PASTA COOKER
- Fasta Pasta Microwave Cooker: $12.95, Fasta Pasta Cooker (810-845-8677, **fastapastacooker.com**).

INDEX
July & August 2014

FOLLOW US ON SOCIAL MEDIA

 facebook.com/CooksIllustrated

 twitter.com/TestKitchen

 pinterest.com/TestKitchen

 google.com/+AmericasTestKitchen

 instagram.com/TestKitchen

ONLINE EXCLUSIVES
Available free for 4 months at
CooksIllustrated.com/aug14

Grilled Chicken Souvlaki for Two
Grilled Napa Cabbage and Radicchio
   Topping
Grilled Scallion Topping
Grilled Shiitake Mushroom Topping
Pasta Frittata with Mushrooms
   and Gorgonzola
Singapore Noodles for Two
Tasting Artisanal Cream Cheese
Testing Beverage Infusers
Testing Grill Brushes
Testing Grill Grate Cleaning Block
Testing Microwave Pasta Cookers
Testing Mini Toaster Ovens
Testing Seafood Scissors
Zucchini Bread with Pistachios and Orange

WATCH NEW VIDEOS
Available free for 4 months at
CooksIllustrated.com/aug14

Cream Cheese Brownies
Eggplant Involtini
Grilled Chicken Souvlaki
Pasta Frittata with Sausage and Hot Peppers
Singapore Noodles
Smoky Pulled Pork on a Gas Grill
Spanish Chilled Almond and Garlic Soup
Tender, Juicy Grilled Burgers
Testing Food Storage Bags
The Science of Cooking: Using a Whisk
Tomatillo Salsa
Zucchini Bread

Grilled Chicken Souvlaki, 19

Smoky Pulled Pork on a Gas Grill, 12

Singapore Noodles, 15

Spanish Chilled Almond and Garlic Soup, 13

Zucchini Bread, 23

Cream Cheese Brownies, 25

Tender, Juicy Grilled Burgers, 7

Tomatillo Salsa, 22

Pasta Frittata with Sausage and Hot Peppers, 21

Eggplant Involtini, 9

PHOTOGRAPHY: CARL TREMBLAY; STYLING: MARIE PIRAINO

Champagne

Bull's
Blood

Chioggia

Golden

White

Red

BEETS

NUMBER 130

SEPTEMBER & OCTOBER 2014

COOK'S
ILLUSTRATED

Grilled Fish Tacos
Chilled Spice Paste Is Key

Mahogany Chicken
Dual Cooking Method

Broiled Pork Tenderloin

Testing Mixing Bowls
Cheaper Is Better

Step by Step to Authentic Baguettes

Perfect Latin Flan
New Caramel Technique

Prosciutto Tasting
The Best of Grab 'n' Go

The Science of Onions
Fresh Corn Side Dishes
Carne Asada
Roasted Fruit Desserts

CooksIllustrated.com
$6.95 U.S. & CANADA

7 25274 62805 6

10>

CONTENTS
September & October 2014

COOK'S ILLUSTRATED

Founder and Editor — Christopher Kimball
Editorial Director — Jack Bishop
Editorial Director, Magazines — John Willoughby
Executive Editor — Amanda Agee
Test Kitchen Director — Erin McMurrer
Managing Editor — Rebecca Hays
Executive Food Editor — Keith Dresser
Senior Editors — Hannah Crowley
Andrea Geary
Lisa McManus
Dan Souza
Senior Editors, Features — Elizabeth Bomze
Louise Emerick
Senior Copy Editor — Megan Ginsberg
Copy Editors — Nell Beram
Krista Magnuson
Associate Editors — Shannon Friedmann Hatch
Andrew Janjigian
Chris O'Connor
Test Cooks — Daniel Cellucci
Lan Lam
Assistant Editors — Lauren Savoie
Kate Shannon
Assistant Test Cooks — Cecelia Jenkins
Sarah Mullins
Executive Assistant — Christine Gordon
Assistant Test Kitchen Director — Leah Rovner
Senior Kitchen Assistants — Michelle Blodget
Alexxa Grattan
Kitchen Assistants — Maria Elena Delgado
Ena Gudiel
Executive Producer — Melissa Baldino
Co-Executive Producer — Stephanie Stender
Associate Producer — Kaitlin Hammond
Contributing Editor — Dawn Yanagihara
Science Editor — Guy Crosby, PhD

Managing Editor, Web — Christine Liu
Associate Editors, Web — Jill Fisher
Roger Metcalf
Assistant Editor, Web — Charlotte Wilder
Senior Video Editor — Nick Dakoulas
Product Manager, Cooking School — Anne Bartholomew
Senior Editor, Cooking School — Mari Levine

Design Director — Amy Klee
Photography Director — Julie Cote
Art Director — Susan Levin
Associate Art Director — Lindsey Timko
Art Director, Marketing — Jennifer Cox
Associate Art Director, Marketing — Melanie Gryboski
Designer, Marketing — Judy Blomquist
Staff Photographer — Daniel J. van Ackere
Associate Art Director, Photography — Steve Klise

Vice President, Marketing — David Mack
Circulation Director — Doug Wicinski
Circulation & Fulfillment Manager — Carrie Fethe
Partnership Marketing Manager — Pamela Putprush
Marketing Assistant — Marina Tomao

Chief Operating Officer — Rob Ristagno
VP, Digital Products — Fran Middleton
Production Director — Guy Rochford
Workflow & Digital Asset Manager — Andrew Mannone
Senior Color & Imaging Specialist — Lauren Pettapiece
Production & Imaging Specialists — Heather Dube
Lauren Robbins
Director, Project Management — Alice Carpenter
Development Manager — Mike Serio
Senior Controller — Theresa Peterson
Customer Loyalty & Support Manager — Amy Bootier
Customer Service Representatives — Jessica Haskin
Andrew Straaberg Finfrock
Juliet Tierney

VP, New Business Development — Michael Burton
Director of Sponsorship Sales — Anne Traficante
Client Services Manager — Kate Zebrowski

Director, Retail Book Program — Beth Ineson
Retail Sales & Marketing Director — Emily Logan
Human Resources Director — Adele Shapiro
Publicity — Deborah Broide

SPECIALTY PEARS Pears are divided into two groups: European and Asian. European pears tend to be tender, while Asian pears offer an apple-like crispness. A hint of vanilla distinguishes the long-necked CONCORDE's flavor. The WARREN pear boasts a tropical taste. The STARKRIMSON changes from deep crimson to a brighter cranberry color as it ripens, making it one of the few pears whose ripeness can be judged at a glance. Chinese YALI and FRAGRANT pears are plump and round. Both have a subtle sweetness and plenty of crunch, even when ripe. The skin of the Korean SHINGO pear is tough but thin. Store it with care—as with all Asian varieties, it doesn't soften when ripe, but it will bruise. The freckled 20TH CENTURY pear hails from Japan. Its flavor ranges from butterscotch at the exterior to green apple at the core.

COVER (Leeks): Robert Papp; BACK COVER (Specialty Pears): John Burgoyne

America's TEST KITCHEN
RECIPES THAT WORK®

America's Test Kitchen is a very real 2,500-square-foot kitchen located just outside Boston. It is the home of Cook's Illustrated and Cook's Country magazines and the workday destination of more than three dozen test cooks, editors, and cookware specialists. Our mission is to test recipes until we understand how and why they work and arrive at the best version. We also test kitchen equipment and supermarket ingredients in search of products that offer the best value and performance. You can watch us work by tuning in to America's Test Kitchen (AmericasTestKitchen.com) and Cook's Country from America's Test Kitchen (CooksCountry.com) on public television.

PRINTED IN THE USA

MOTHER DEAREST

My mother, Mary Alice, was a latter-day suffragette. A rumored Communist party member in the '30s (or, at the very least, a bang-up socialist), she was always fighting the system and for good reason. Her chosen profession, school psychologist, put her up against a bureaucracy that was rigged for men, semiprofessionals of a lower order: hidebound, territorial, and well fanged, much like encountering a group of particularly savage baboons in western Uganda, where we visited in 1967. In an academic setting, this savagery took its toll behind closed doors and over years, not minutes.

That led to an alternate life, one landscaped by organic gardens, a love of new age health advocates such as Bonnie Prudden and Adelle Davis (*Let's Eat Right to Keep Fit*), and a social group made up of New York misfits who visited the farm for summer outings. One of my most bizarre memories is of three nuns—Faith, Hope, and Charity—playing badminton on our lawn. Of course there were the folksingers; the fund-raising cocktail parties for Jack Kennedy and, later, Bobby; and all sorts of stray intellectuals—the sort that felt right at home in our ex-urban commune. Every summer evening was launched with gimlets and cheddar cheese on the porch until the mosquitoes ran amok.

Summers and weekends were a rich stew of creosote, pig manure, raw cow's milk, fly-stuffed barns, and the happy scent of molasses cookies, wood smoke, and yeast with a strong undercurrent of wet dog. Fence posts needed pounding; barbed wire had to be stretched; hay had to be cut, tedded, raked, and baled; pigs and Angus had to be chased up the road and back into fenced pasture. We sold our own Green River brand of pork and beef, which, when mixed together, made our signature burgers. As for the garden, the theory was survival of the fittest. A full quarter acre was planted every spring with no intention of further support (watering or weeding). There were always sufficient survivors to fill the root cellar and provide for bitter and fresh greens, tomatoes, and herbs throughout the season.

My sister Kate and I endured countless hours of slow Vermont conversation about the road commissioner, foundations, conservation easements, and property lines. It took years to get used to a people who spoke only when they had something to say, which was not all that often. (Bernie Squires, a neighbor, was once working in his yard when a stranger from the Vermont Bureau of Land Management came up inquiring after my mother. When asked if he knew where the Kimballs lived, he simply replied, "Yes," and slowly walked away.) And the characters in our childhood production were straight out of central casting: two Bentleys, Charlie and Floyd; Marie Briggs the baker; Herbie and Onie the summer farmhands; plus Daisy the collie and Bonnie the mutt. The other old-time families in town were Skidmores, Wilcoxes, Hurds, and Lombergs, but it was Mary Alice who was, for me, at the epicenter—a New York intellectual who had read everything from Proust to Trollope yet reveled in Bean boots, mud, crop rotations, animal husbandry, fly fishing, tractors, and the party line phone that needed cranking. She was born to one thing—she was married at the National Cathedral in Washington, D.C.—yet was happiest in another; a flock of chickens was almost family in the size of her affections. On Saturday nights, she got liquored up on Jack Daniels and drove a WWII surplus Jeep helter-skelter up the mountain, Kate and me hanging on for dear life, bugs smashing into our faces like grapeshot.

After I had my own family, we showed up at her farm at midday and the turkey was warming in a 175-degree oven per Adelle Davis's *sous vide* theory of cooking meat at its final resting temperature. Keenly aware that bacteria doubles every 20 minutes, my first act was to raise the oven temperature to 325 degrees, hoping not to lose a family member to an outbreak of salmonella. (In later years, I revealed my strategem and confronted her about the risk to our four small children. Her reply was, "Well, I haven't killed any of you yet," a retort that I always felt was evidence of good luck rather than good practice.)

And she was a tortured soul of contradictions. One Thanksgiving she extolled the virtues of the local redheaded minister and the next disavowed any knowledge of churchgoing. Having finished listening to a particularly damning polemic against sugary treats, I discovered a freezer full of Häagen-Dazs and a drawer full of English biscuits, the sweet kind. And she had an endless supply of organizational tools, from her personal day-by-day farm calendar (when to check your hoses, plant cover crops, clean your garden tools, and order your seeds) to dozens of yellow legal pads filled with to-do lists. The numbered items were but a paean to a nuts-and-bolts Protestant universe from a woman who thrived on intellectual heresy fed by a rich appreciation for right-brain chaos.

Mary Alice's legacy lives on in my latter-day root cellar: carrots and beets stored in sand and bushel baskets of Green Mountain potatoes with a good flow of cold air to keep them from rotting. (Always store apples in a separate area.) I learned to butcher beefers and pigs, milk a cow, shovel manure, raise bees, boil maple syrup, and throw hay bales. As for culinary adventure, I have eaten venison jerky and pickled cow's tongue out of a gallon-size jar filled with liquid the color of Oz on a dark, rainy day.

In later years, she turned to good topsoil, a 22 pistol to keep the bears out of the bird feeder, and an English shepherd named Dolly for solace. My last memory is a Sunday goodbye. She often waved us off, standing high above on her second-floor porch, her eyes moist, but the kids didn't notice. Their grandmother was beyond their known world, like the candy-cottage witch from Hansel and Gretel. In later years, they would remember a woman ahead of her time, who put local above global, who dug deep into the ground for nourishment.

When she died, I took the ancient birch and gut snowshoes; there is nothing better in deep snow. They are a reminder that Mary Alice was fond of gearing up to challenge the elements or whatever else stood in her way. She knew the secret of life, taking that first step.

Her legacy is still the garden, our family's hallowed ground. We plant every year with the hope of digging deep to find a life that is rich and unexpected.

FOR INQUIRIES, ORDERS, OR MORE INFORMATION

CooksIllustrated.com
At CooksIllustrated.com, you can order books and subscriptions, sign up for our free e-newsletter, or renew your magazine subscription. Join the website and gain access to 21 years of *Cook's Illustrated* recipes, equipment tests, and ingredient tastings, as well as companion videos for every recipe in this issue.

COOKBOOKS
We sell more than 50 cookbooks by the editors of *Cook's Illustrated*, including *The Cook's Illustrated Cookbook* and *The Science of Good Cooking*. To order, visit our bookstore at CooksIllustrated.com/bookstore.

COOK'S ILLUSTRATED MAGAZINE
Cook's Illustrated magazine (ISSN 1068-2821), number 130, is published bimonthly by Boston Common Press Limited Partnership, 17 Station St., Brookline, MA 02445. Copyright 2014 Boston Common Press Limited Partnership. Periodicals postage paid at Boston, MA, and additional mailing offices, USPS #012487. Publications Mail Agreement No. 40020778. Return undeliverable Canadian addresses to P.O. Box 875, Station A, Windsor, ON N9A 6P2. POSTMASTER: Send address changes to *Cook's Illustrated*, P.O. Box 6018, Harlan, IA 51593-1518. For subscription and gift subscription orders, subscription inquiries, or change of address notices, visit AmericasTestKitchen.com/support, call 800-526-8442 in the U.S. or 515-248-7684 from outside the U.S., or write to us at *Cook's Illustrated*, P.O. Box 6018, Harlan, IA 51593-1518.

FOR LIST RENTAL INFORMATION Contact Specialists Marketing Services, Inc., 777 Terrace Ave., 4th Floor, Hasbrouck Heights, NJ 07604; phone: 201-865-5800.

EDITORIAL OFFICE 17 Station St., Brookline, MA 02445; phone: 617-232-1000; fax: 617-232-1572. For subscription inquiries, visit AmericasTestKitchen.com/support or call 800-526-8442.

⇒ BY ANDREA GEARY, LAN LAM, SARAH MULLINS & DAN SOUZA ⇐

Making Stock with Skin–On Onions

My grandmother always left the skins on her onions when she made stock. Is there any advantage to this?

RODGER BRAM
SEATTLE, WASH.

➤ To determine what effect onion skins might have, we made two batches of simple chicken stock, one with peeled, chopped onions and the other with onions we chopped and added straight to the pot, papery skin and all. The two stocks looked quite similar as they cooked, but when they were strained, we noticed a marked difference in appearance: The stock made without skins was pale yellow, while the stock made with skins had an appealingly deep golden-brown color. But that difference turned out to be superficial: Tasters agreed that both stocks tasted virtually identical.

The bottom line: Chopping your onion, skin and all, is a nifty timesaver, and it can give richer, appealing color to stock or gravy, but it won't affect flavor. –A.G.

WITH ONION SKINS   **WITHOUT ONION SKINS**

Browning Salted Butter

Your recipes for brown butter sauces call for unsalted butter. Can I use salted butter in a pinch?

EULA LEE MILLER
DALLAS, TEXAS

➤ While we strongly recommend using unsalted butter for baking applications, where water content and variable salt content can alter results, your question made us curious. We always call for unsalted butter when browning so that we can control the seasoning, but perhaps we could brown and season at once with good results? We browned 4 tablespoons of salted butter in one skillet and the same amount of unsalted butter in another. Surprisingly, the salted butter appeared to yield more than twice the volume of browned particles as the unsalted butter. It was impressive visually, but when we tasted them we found that the browned salted butter was no deeper or richer in flavor than the unsalted. (When browning butter, the milk solids develop color during cooking and provide the rich, nutty flavor.) What was happening? Salted butter, after

all, is just unsalted butter with salt added; it doesn't contain more milk solids.

So we ran a second test. We calculated how much salt is in 4 tablespoons of salted butter and incorporated that amount into an equal amount of unsalted butter. We then browned both butters, strained the results, and compared them. This time, we ended up with exactly the same volume of browned solids. It turned out that the salt was being coated in the browned milk solids, adding bulk but not any flavor.

The salted butter also foams more than unsalted butter as it melts, which makes it hard to judge the color change.

So while it's possible to brown salted butter, you'll get no browned-milk-solid flavor benefit from it and it's actually more difficult to avoid burning salted butter compared with unsalted. Your best bet is to stick with using unsalted butter. –D.S.

Ammonia Odors in Cheese

When I unwrapped a recently purchased wheel of Brie, it smelled like ammonia. Was it spoiled?

DAVE CYKERT
CHARLESTON, S.C.

➤ We took your question to Ihsan Gurdal, coproprietor of Formaggio Kitchen, a shop in Cambridge, Massachusetts, that specializes in fine cheeses. He explained that during the cheese-making process young surface-ripened cheeses like Brie and Camembert are coated with live mold that acts on the milk proteins, transforming the cheese from chalky and bland to creamy, silky, and full-flavored. That mold also gives off metabolic byproducts. When the cheese is wrapped tightly (as with plastic wrap), these byproducts can be trapped and concentrated over time, resulting in unfamiliar or even unpleasant smells that can be quite strong when the cheese is first unwrapped. But, Gurdal says, letting the cheese sit unwrapped at room temperature for 1 hour before serving (which you should do, anyway, since the flavors are muted in chilled cheeses) should allow those smells to dissipate. However, if the ammonia smell persists after the cheese has aired for an hour, discard it. Other warning signs of spoilage are gray, orange, or brown spots of mold (inspect the edges and sides).

In sum: Pungent aromas are no cause for concern. To minimize the issue, don't store Brie (or any cheese for that matter) wrapped in plastic wrap. Cheese shops typically sell cheese wrapped in specialty paper that is optimal for keeping the cheese at its best. Alternatively, we recommend wrapping it tightly in waxed or parchment paper and then loosely in aluminum foil. –A.G.

Baking with Fresh Pumpkin

Baking recipes usually call for canned pumpkin, but I've received fresh pumpkins in my community-supported agriculture share. How can I substitute them?

JESSICA CARDA-AUTEN
DURHAM, N.C.

➤ For starters, make sure you're using a sugar pumpkin, which is about 8 to 10 inches in diameter and usually has a darker orange exterior compared with jack-o'-lantern pumpkins. Its flesh has more flavor and is also denser and drier than that of bigger pumpkins, so it will take less time to cook. However, it's still somewhat watery, so you can't simply cook it until soft and then puree it (see our instructions below).

Also, be aware that fresh pumpkin puree does not taste exactly like canned pumpkin. (Our favorite canned pumpkin from Libby's is made from a special variety called Dickinson.) In pumpkin bread, tasters found the fresh sample a bit more vegetal and less sweet, though definitely acceptable. In pumpkin pie, tasters preferred the fresh to canned. Though its more subdued orange hue made some hesitate, they observed that the fresh pumpkin contributed a pleasant squash flavor, compared with the pie made with canned, which tasted predominantly of the spices added to the pie.

To make homemade pumpkin puree, halve a sugar pumpkin from top to bottom and then scoop out the seeds and pulp. Place the halves cut side down on a parchment paper–lined rimmed baking sheet and roast in a 375-degree oven until the flesh can be easily pierced with a skewer, 45 to 60 minutes. Turn the halves over and continue to roast 30 minutes longer. Scoop the flesh from the skins and puree it in a food processor until smooth. Drain the puree in a fine-mesh strainer set over a bowl for at least 1 hour. To test the consistency, pack the puree into a small drinking glass and unmold it onto a plate. It should slump gently toward the base but otherwise hold its shape. Loosen as necessary with drained liquid, or return the puree to the strainer and continue to drain it if it is too loose. The puree can be refrigerated for up to four days or frozen in an airtight container with parchment pressed on its surface for up to two months. You can substitute this puree for an equal amount of the canned product. –A.G.

PERFECT PUREE
To be sure your homemade pumpkin puree is the proper consistency, pack it into a drinking glass and then unmold it onto a plate. It should slump slightly at its base.

Blue Ginger

Why does fresh ginger sometimes have a blue-gray color?

TED SCHANTZ
BOSTON, MASS.

➤ We've noticed that, too. After conferring with our science editor, we learned that when ginger is stored for a long period of time in a cold environment, it becomes less acidic, and this causes some of its anthocyanin pigments to change to a blue-gray color. It is still safe to eat, but we wondered if there was a difference in the flavor.

We started by finely grating some ginger that had changed color and some that had not and then squeezing out the juice from each and adding it to water (to make it palatable). The majority of our tasters found the flavor of the water with the blue ginger to be less potent and spicy than that containing the regular ginger. However, when we compared the two gingers in a soy dipping sauce and a gingerbread cake, no one could detect a difference due to all the competing flavors.

The takeaway? Ginger that has turned blue is perfectly safe to eat, and while its flavor is slightly milder, it's unlikely you'll notice when using it in a recipe. –S.M.

Artichokes and Wine

Wine can taste oddly sweet and one-dimensional when I drink it with dishes that include artichokes. Is there anything I can do?

DEVON ROYCE
ATLANTA, GA.

➤ A compound in artichokes called cynarin purportedly binds to sweet receptors on the tongue, temporarily shutting them off. As you sip your wine, the cynarin is pulled off of the receptor, reactivating it. At that moment, your tongue registers sweetness, and your wine tastes sweeter than it normally would. Not everyone experiences the phenomenon, but about 60 percent of people do. To compensate, wine experts recommend serving artichokes with wines that are highly acidic and contain little to no residual sugar, such as Sauvignon Blanc, Pinot Grigio, Grüner Veltliner, or Albariño.

But what if you don't have such a wine on hand? We asked several tasters (whom we'd prescreened to confirm that they experience this phenomenon) to sip Sauvignon Blanc and Chardonnay and then to sample each again after a bite of our Tagliatelle with Artichokes and Olive Oil (page 11). They noted that the wines tasted noticeably sweeter, with the Chardonnay being off-puttingly sweet. We then asked them to take another bite of the pasta dish and then to take a drink of water before sipping the wine. This time they noted that the wines tasted like their control version. Why? They had washed away the cynarin with the water.

While your best bet is to buy a highly acidic, dry wine, you can ensure that lower-acidity wines like Chardonnay won't taste overly sweet with artichokes if you take a drink of water before you sip your wine. –L.L.

Converting Layer Cakes to Bundt

I want to bake a layer cake batter in a Bundt pan. Do I need to make any adjustments to the recipe?

RACHAEL ROSSI
WORCESTER, MASS.

➤ We too have layer cake recipes we'd like to make less fussy by preparing them in a Bundt pan. Creating a picture-perfect layer cake takes time and effort, while a Bundt cake doesn't require much more than a simple glaze or dusting of powdered sugar once it's out of the pan. To answer your question, we baked the batters for three types of 9-inch round layer cake—yellow, chocolate, and carrot—in 15-cup Bundt pans and compared each to its original layer cake version.

We were happy to discover that all three worked well, though none were identical to their original counterparts. Because the batter wasn't divided into multiple thinner layers, the leavener had more work to do in the deeper Bundt pan and wasn't as effective. All three came out denser than their light and fluffy layer-cake counterparts, though the crumbs were still lighter than a classic Bundt cake's. Also, because they all required a longer baking time in the deeper Bundt pan (twice as long for the yellow and chocolate and three times as long for the carrot), they were all slightly drier toward the edges, though still acceptable. The cakes baked in Bundt pans also developed a thicker crust—just as you'd expect to find on a classic Bundt cake.

In sum, baking layer cake recipes in a Bundt pan will work fine. Just keep in mind that you'll need to bake the cake considerably longer (the cake is done when a skewer inserted into the center comes out with no crumbs attached), and the resulting texture will be a bit denser than the original, though not as heavy as a classic Bundt cake. –S.M.

NO ASSEMBLY REQUIRED
You can successfully bake the batter for two 9-inch layer cakes in a 15-cup Bundt pan—and you won't have to spend a lot of time assembling and frosting.

SEND US YOUR QUESTIONS We will provide a complimentary one-year subscription for each letter we print. Send your inquiry, name, address, and daytime telephone number to Notes from Readers, *Cook's Illustrated*, P.O. Box 470589, Brookline, MA 02447, or to NotesFromReaders@ AmericasTestKitchen.com.

WHAT IS IT?

I love pull-apart cloverleaf rolls and recall a tool that saves the trouble of shaping by hand. Have you heard of such an item?

LEO SKELLCHOCK
EXETER, N.H.

The pull-apart shape of cloverleaf rolls traditionally comes from rolling dough into ropes, cutting it into small pieces that are rolled into balls, and then snuggling three balls together in each cup of a muffin tin. But this takes time and effort. The timesaving tool you mention is the red plastic Kesco cloverleaf and fantail cutter, sold for a quarter from department stores around 1950. Bakers could simply drop rounds of dough into muffin cups and then push the cutter down to the bottom of each cup to create the roll they desired.

Using a simple yeasted-roll recipe, we gave the cloverleaf/fantail cutter a try, dropping a single portion of dough into each muffin cup and then stamping down with the cloverleaf side of the cutter (which we greased to prevent sticking). We found that the cuts it made were quite definitive, which meant the baked rolls came apart a bit more at the seams than rolls made following the classic method. However, they still held together sufficiently well and baked up just fine. We also gave the fantail side of the stamp a try. Once again the time savings were great, although the fan effect was subdued. Our verdict? If you're willing to sacrifice a bit on looks, a cutter like this will save you lots of time and effort and still give you rolls worthy of a place at the table. –Shannon Friedmann Hatch

SECOND IMPRESSIONS
Rolls made with this mid-century roll cutter aren't perfect, but they're presentable.

Quick Tips

⇒ COMPILED BY SHANNON FRIEDMANN HATCH ⇐

Quick-Pour Boxed Broth

When she's using an entire carton of boxed broth, Ashley Ratchford of Roxbury, Mass., speeds the usual slow glug of broth with this trick.

1. Open the spout, hold the container upside down, and begin to pour.

2. Using the tip of a paring knife, puncture a small hole in the bottom of the carton. The extra hole releases the pressure in the box, hastening the broth's exit through the spout.

Makeshift Bread Slicing Guide

Amanda Fuerst of Los Angeles, Calif., had trouble cutting evenly thick slices of homemade sandwich bread until she arrived at this tip: Let the loaf cool on its side on an oven rack. The rack's bars leave subtle vertical indentations that act as a template for evenly spaced slices.

Getting a Grip on Fresh Corn Prep

Bart McSpadden of Edmond, Okla., has found an easy way to remove the fine hairs from fresh corn: with a silicone potholder. By rubbing the grippy mat around the shucked ear from one end to the other, he loosens and grabs the silky strands.

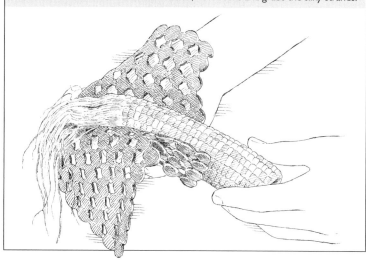

Homemade Wine Stain Remover

Robin Inman of Malden, Mass., offers this solution for removing red wine stains: Combine equal parts hydrogen peroxide and dish detergent. Pour on stain to saturate. The stain should disappear within an hour. (Be sure to test the solution on an inconspicuous spot first.)

Stand-In Strainer

We found that a key step to boosting the nutty flavor of the sesame seeds in our sesame-crusted salmon recipes (March/April 2014) was brining them. When Trip DuBard of Florence, S.C., was making the recipe for the first time, he realized that he didn't have a strainer fine enough to drain the small seeds. Instead, he grabbed a coffee filter (paper or mesh is fine), which worked just as well, so long as he poured slowly enough to let the water drain through the filter.

Improvised Egg Cups

Betsy Wise of Lubbock, Texas, a fan of soft-cooked eggs, invested in an egg topper to easily remove the tops of the shells—only to realize that she lacked egg cups to steady them as she sliced. Instead, she places the cooked eggs in empty shot glasses, which keep the top of the egg propped above the rim of the glass.

SEND US YOUR TIPS We will provide a complimentary one-year subscription for each tip we print. Send your tip, name, address, and daytime telephone number to Quick Tips, *Cook's Illustrated*, P.O. Box 470589, Brookline, MA 02447, or to QuickTips@AmericasTestKitchen.com.

ILLUSTRATION: JOHN BURGOYNE

Supersize Funnel

Diane Krenik of Nevada City, Calif., gets frustrated by standard-size funnels that are narrow and slow to drain, so she fashioned a wider, more efficient option from a sturdy plastic gallon juice jug (avoid flimsy plastic vessels like milk gallons). After cutting below the handle to remove the bottom, she upturns the top to use as the funnel and holds it steady with the jug handle.

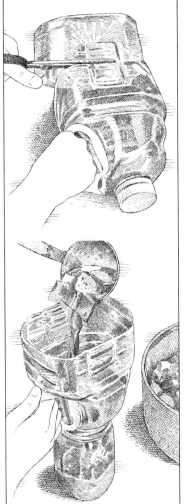

Easier Trash Can Liner

When you're fitting a trash can with a new garbage bag, air often becomes trapped inside the can and causes the bag to balloon inward, making it hard to secure and reducing the bag's capacity. To equalize the air pressure, Scott Muller of Montclair, N.J., drills three ¼-inch evenly spaced holes 2 inches up from the bottom of the can and one in the center of the can above the bottom holes. (The method works with metal or plastic cans. If you have a lidded can with a hard plastic liner, drill the holes in the liner.)

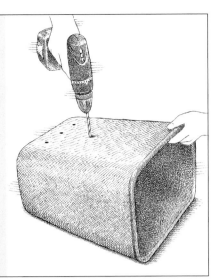

Build a Timer into Your Coffee Maker

Marcus Smith of Los Angeles, Calif., would like to wake up to fresh coffee, but his coffee maker lacks a built-in timer. Rather than spring for a new model, he purchased an inexpensive appliance timer (the kind that turns lights on and off when you go on vacation) at the local hardware store. He can set the brewing time before he goes to bed and also set a time for the machine to turn off, so he never worries that he left it on.

Handy Weight Chart

Greg Manning of Portland, Ore., sometimes forgets to tare his digital scale (i.e., zeroing out the weight of the empty container before adding ingredients). Instead of removing the ingredients from the container and reweighing, he references a bowl-weight chart he made and taped to the inside of a cabinet door. Determining the accurate weight is as easy as subtracting the recorded bowl weight from the total.

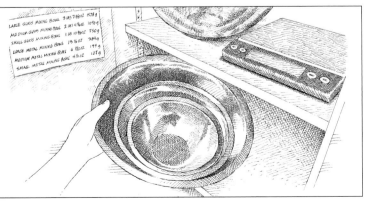

Dutch Oven Storage

Due to limited cabinet space, Martha Butterfield of Raritan, N.J., had to find an alternative option for storing her large Dutch oven. She discovered that affixing two sturdy coat hooks, spaced 3 inches apart, to the side of her cabinet allowed her to hang the pot by its handle on the lower hook and prop the lid on the top hooks.

Burn Blocker

After burning her hand one too many times on one of her electric stove's burners that hadn't fully cooled after use, Marie Louzon of Kintnersville, Pa., came up with this solution: She keeps a kettle on the stove and places it over the hot burner after use to shield the surface while it cools. (To prevent the bottom of the kettle from burning on the hot surface, make sure it has some water in it.)

Better Broiled Pork Tenderloin

Before we could perfect this easy dish, we had to figure out how broilers really work.

⇒ BY LAN LAM ⇐

What easier way to prepare a quick-cooking cut like pork tenderloin than to stick it under the broiler? Instead of the two-step approach of searing the roast on the stove and then transferring it to the oven, the intense heat of the broiler promises to deeply brown the exterior and cook the roast through in one fell swoop. But having worked with dozens of broilers over the course of my career, I know that using them isn't quite that straightforward.

The problem is that recipes calling for the broiler rely on a one-size-fits-all approach, when in reality no two behave exactly the same way. This became clear when I took a typical recipe for broiled pork tenderloin and made it in different ovens in the test kitchen. The results were all over the map—and none were perfect. One was beautifully browned but overcooked inside; another was burned in patches; a third came out tender and juicy inside but with an unappetizing drab gray exterior.

My goal was twofold: to create a recipe for richly browned, juicy pork tenderloin—and to figure out a way to minimize differences among broilers so every oven would produce consistent results.

Racking Up Answers

I began with a pair of 1-pound tenderloins to serve four. I wanted a simple weeknight dinner, so I decided to forgo brining or salting. To ensure even cooking, I folded the tenderloins' thinner tail ends underneath their middles, and I tied the meat at 2-inch intervals to give them a uniform shape. After brushing the roasts with oil and seasoning them with salt and pepper, I placed them on a baking sheet.

Though many recipes that I found instructed to get the meat as close to the element as possible, I knew from experience that closer was not necessarily better. Too close a position can not only exacerbate uneven browning but also leave the middle of the meat raw. The key would be to find the position where the exterior browned evenly and the interior

For a beautifully browned, juicy pork tenderloin under any broiler, first you've got to turn your oven to bake.

cooked through at roughly the same pace.

Indeed, when I roasted the tenderloins about 3 inches from the heat source, the top of each roast was partly pale and partly scorched by the time the meat cooked through. Roasts cooked close to the center of the oven browned somewhat more evenly, but they took so long to get deep color that the interiors overcooked. The best results came from cooking the roasts 4 to 5 inches from the broiler element; tenderloins cooked at that distance were lightly but evenly browned. And because the broiler's intense heat was causing the roasts' internal temperature to rise 15 to 25 degrees after cooking, I pulled them from the oven when they registered 125 to 130 degrees to ensure that they reached the ideal serving temperature (145 degrees) after a 10-minute rest.

Reflecting on the Problem

On to the next challenge: producing not only even browning but deep browning. We often use baking soda to help in this department. By creating an

alkaline environment, the soda accelerates the Maillard reaction, which browns food and creates numerous flavor and aroma compounds in the process. For even distribution, I made a paste with just ¼ teaspoon of baking soda, salt, and a little oil that was easy to spread over the roasts. This treatment boosted browning, but it was still not enough. I couldn't get the broiler any hotter, so what else could I do?

I took a break to think more about how broilers actually work. Unlike roasting or baking, in which a heating element heats the walls of the oven, which heats the air within, which in turn heats the food (a phenomenon called convection), broiling cooks food directly with invisible infrared light waves, or radiant heat. I realized that the broiler's heat waves weren't hitting just the pork but also the baking sheet, the oven racks, and the oven walls. What if I was able to direct more of those waves toward the meat?

With that in mind, I ditched the baking sheet for the taller sides of a 13 by 9-inch metal baking pan, which I lined with foil to reflect as much of the heat as possible. The roasts cooked in this pan were definitely deeper in color, but I knew I could do better still when my eyes landed on a disposable aluminum roasting pan. With 3-inch-high sides and a shiny surface that didn't require a foil lining, it seemed like a win. And sure enough, tenderloins broiled in it came out with beautiful browning on the top and the sides facing the reflective surface. For browning all the way around, I tried flipping the roasts halfway through broiling, but they overcooked. In the end, I found that deeply browning just the top portion of each roast achieved decent flavor. It seemed like a good point at which to try my recipe out under some other broilers.

Getting Warmed Up

Not at all surprisingly, some tenderloins cooked under other broilers came out just as my working recipe had, while many had subpar browning by the time they were cooked through. After poring over a stack of oven manuals, I pinpointed the source of the problem. Every manual had a different recommendation for preheating the broiler, from as long as 8 minutes (the length of time I'd been following) to as few as 2 minutes.

Avoid Overcooking

As the roasts rest, their internal temperature rises 10 to 15 degrees more than it would in a typical roasting recipe. For the ideal 145-degree serving temperature, take them out of the oven when they hit 125 degrees.

▶ Lan Beats the Broiler
Video available free for 4 months at CooksIllustrated.com/oct14

Broilers that were preheated for too long were likely shutting off midway through cooking. This is because most ovens these days are designed with a built-in maximum temperature (typically around 550 degrees). Once the air temperature rises beyond that point, the oven (and broiler) will automatically turn off, wait for the temperature to drop, and then turn back on again. Because the broiler was also heating up the air in the oven, this would mean that the meat could continue to cook in the residual heat (by convection)—but it wouldn't continue to brown under radiant heat from the broiler.

I could err on the side of caution and preheat the broiler for only a minute or two—but slower-to-heat broilers would still give me roasts that weren't browned enough. I suddenly had a radical thought:

What if I preheated the *oven* first and then switched on the broiler and slid in the meat? This would preheat the oven and also heat the broiler, which would narrow the jump the broiler had to make to fully come up to temperature. I settled on 325 degrees: Any higher and the ovens might still cycle on and off during broiling.

I preheated several ovens as I prepped more pork and then put the meat into the oven and switched on the broilers. I suspected that my new method was so effective that I would be able to brown the meat on both sides. After 5 minutes, I flipped the roasts and then removed them once they reached 125 to 130 degrees. Happily, every roast boasted rich browning—plus they were all equally tender and juicy.

I not only nailed a recipe for broiled pork tenderloin that would truly work in any oven but also walked away with a deeper knowledge of broilers in general—sure to make me a better cook down the road.

BROILED PORK TENDERLOIN
SERVES 4 TO 6

We prefer natural pork, but if you use enhanced pork (injected with a salt solution), reduce the salt in step 2 to 1½ teaspoons. A 3-inch-deep aluminum roasting pan is essential. Do not attempt this recipe with a drawer broiler. For more information on using your broiler, see page 31. If you like, serve the pork with our Sun-Dried Tomato and Basil Salsa (recipe follows). For our free recipes for Broiled Pork Tenderloin for Two and Mustard–Crème Fraîche Sauce, go to CooksIllustrated.com/oct14.

- 2 (1-pound) pork tenderloins, trimmed
- 2 teaspoons kosher salt
- 1¼ teaspoons vegetable oil
- ½ teaspoon pepper
- ¼ teaspoon baking soda
- 1 (13 by 9-inch) disposable aluminum roasting pan

1. Adjust oven rack 4 to 5 inches from broiler element and heat oven to 325 degrees. Fold thin tip of each tenderloin under about 2 inches to create uniformly shaped roast. Tie tenderloins crosswise with kitchen twine at 2-inch intervals, making sure folded tip is secured underneath. Trim excess twine close to meat to prevent it from scorching under broiler.

2. Mix salt, oil, and pepper in small bowl until salt is evenly coated with oil. Add baking soda and stir until well combined. Rub mixture evenly over pork. Place tenderloins in disposable pan, evenly spaced between sides of pan and each other.

3. Turn oven to broil. Immediately place meat in oven and broil tenderloins for 5 minutes. Flip tenderloins and continue to broil until golden brown and meat registers 125 to 130 degrees, 8 to 14 minutes. Remove disposable pan from oven, tent loosely with aluminum foil, and let rest for 10 minutes. Remove twine, slice tenderloins into ½-inch-thick slices, and serve.

SUN-DRIED TOMATO AND BASIL SALSA
MAKES ABOUT 1 CUP

We like the sweet flavor and pliable texture of oil-cured sun-dried tomatoes.

- ¼ cup oil-packed sun-dried tomatoes, rinsed and chopped fine
- ¼ cup chopped fresh basil
- ¼ cup chopped fresh parsley
- ¼ cup extra-virgin olive oil
- 2 tablespoons balsamic vinegar
- 1 small shallot, minced
  Salt and pepper

Combine all ingredients in bowl and season with salt and pepper to taste.

Understanding Broilers

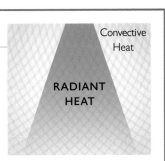

Convective Heat

RADIANT HEAT

To use a broiler effectively, it's important to understand how it differs from regular oven cooking. While roasting relies on convective heat (air molecules surround the food), a broiler cooks food primarily with radiant heat, a form of invisible infrared light waves. The broiler element can reach 2,000 degrees. This poses an inherent challenge in all broiling, and the way most broilers operate doesn't make it any easier. To learn more about broilers, go to CooksIllustrated.com/oct14.

➤ **Waves Must Hit the Food**
The waves should directly hit the food. The food should be just far enough away from the element that the heat is intense but also evenly hitting the food (for more detail, see "The Parchment Test: Finding the Broiler Sweet Spot," page 31).

➤ **Preheating Is Unreliable**
Most broilers have no ready signal, so you're left guessing when the broiler is preheated. Those that heat quickly may cycle off during cooking, while slow-to-heat broilers will be too cool and won't cook the food in the given time.

➤ **If a Broiler Cycles Off, Browning Suffers**
If the broiler is on for too long, most ovens will exceed a maximum air temperature and the broiler will temporarily switch off. The food will continue to cook by convection, but without radiant heat browning will slow dramatically.

Getting a Broiler to Work for Pork Tenderloin

For well-browned, perfectly cooked pork tenderloin, the key is eliminating the variables and catching more heat. Our solution works with every broiler.

HIT THE SWEET SPOT
Rack position terms like "upper-middle" can be interpreted differently from oven to oven. We set the rack 4 to 5 inches from the element for the best results for this recipe.

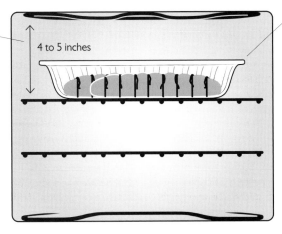

4 to 5 inches

USE A DEEP DISPOSABLE ALUMINUM ROASTING PAN
This reflects more radiant heat toward the pork, maximizing browning.

PREHEAT THE OVEN This brings not just the air in the oven but also the broiler element up to 325 degrees, narrowing the jump before the broiler element is fully preheated. Broilers that run hot won't cycle off, and broilers that run cool will be fully preheated.

Rice and Lentils with Crispy Onions

Our new method for frying onions delivers crispy, ultrasavory results that make this fragrantly spiced Middle Eastern classic—and many other dishes—richly satisfying.

⇒ BY ANDREW JANJIGIAN ⇐

Whenever I eat the Levantine rice and lentil pilaf known as *mujaddara* (pronounced "MOO-ha-druh"), I think of an anecdote that cookbook author Claudia Roden recounts in *A Book of Middle Eastern Food*. When her Egyptian aunt presented guests with this dish (which she called *megadarra*), she would ask them to excuse this food of the poor, to which they would reply: "Keep your food of kings and give us megadarra every day!"

That perfectly sums up my affection for the dish. Essentially the "rice and beans" of the Middle East, this might be the most spectacular example of how a few humble ingredients can add up to a dish that's satisfying, complex, and deeply savory. Though every household and restaurant differs in its approach, it's simple to throw together. Basically: Boil basmati rice and lentils together until each component is tender but intact, then work in warm spices such as coriander, cumin, cinnamon, allspice, and pepper, as well as a good measure of minced garlic. But the real showpiece of the dish is the onions—either fried or caramelized—which get stirred into and sprinkled over the pilaf just before serving. Their flavor is as deep as their mahogany color suggests, and they break up the starchy components. Finished

French Lentils? *Non Merci.*

Many lentil dishes benefit from the firm, distinct texture of the French variety known as *lentilles du Puy*. But in this dish, the softer (but still intact) texture of green or brown lentils is best because it pairs well with the tender grains of rice. A bonus: Green and brown lentils are also easier to find and cheaper than the French kind.

FIRM AND DISTINCT
Save small, firm French lentils for soups and salads.

SOFT AND CREAMY
Tender brown and green lentils work best for pilaf.

To brighten the dish's earthy and warm spice flavors, we finish the pilaf with a tangy mixture of yogurt, lemon juice, and garlic.

with a bracing garlicky yogurt sauce, this pilaf is comfort food at its best.

I had every intention of making this dish a regular weeknight main course in my house but, frankly, had been disappointed with the recipes I'd tried. They all could do a better job cooking the lentils and rice, which I've found either too firm or overcooked and mushy. And while the onions should be the best part, the ones I made were either leathery, cloyingly sweet, or too crunchy. I could—and would—do better.

A Staggered Start

For any other lentil recipe, my first test might be to figure out which variety was best for the job, but in this case I knew that ordinary brown or green lentils were the way to go. When cooked properly, they become tender while just holding their shape—a consistency that ensures that they meld well with the tender-chewy rice. The other option, French *lentilles du Puy*, would remain too firm and distinct.

So I moved on to the cooking method. Lentil cookery is simple: Bring water to a boil with lentils

(use a 4:1¼ ratio) and a dash of salt, reduce the heat to low and simmer until they're just tender, and drain.

But cooking lentils with rice was another matter, since I needed both components, which cook at different rates, to emerge evenly tender and also form a cohesive pilaf. I had two options: cook the rice and lentils in separate pots and fold them together or simmer them together in one pot, staggering their start times by parcooking the lentils until they are just tender, draining them, combining them with raw rice and a measured amount of water, and simmering until the liquid is absorbed. Or I could try a variation on the absorption approach, in which the rice and parcooked lentils are cooked pilaf-style—that is, toasted in fat before liquid is added.

After a battery of tests, it was clear that a combination of staggered and pilaf-style cooking was the way to go. Giving the lentils a 15-minute head start ensured that they finished cooking on pace with the rice. This step also allowed me to drain away their muddy cooking liquid before combining them with the rice, which made for a cleaner-looking dish. Toasting the rice in oil brought out the grain's nutty flavor and let me deepen the flavor of the spices and garlic by cooking them in the fat, too.

The one snag: Even after I parcooked the lentils, they still absorbed quite a bit of water, robbing the rice of the liquid it needed to cook through. Adding more water didn't help; the lentils simply soaked it up faster than the rice and turned mushy. Fortunately, I had a quick fix in mind—one that I'd applied to our Rice and Pasta Pilaf (May/June 2014) when the pasta was absorbing too much liquid and leaving the rice dry. I soaked the raw rice in hot water for 15 minutes (while the lentils simmered), which softened the grains' exteriors so that they could absorb water more easily. Plus, this step loosened and washed away some of the excess starches, helping the rice cook up fluffy, not sticky.

Oil and Water

On to those onions. I wanted to go the deep-fried route, as the onions' crispy-chewy texture would be the perfect contrast to the soft pilaf. And given that I'd be both stirring the fried onions into the dish and using them as a garnish (and, let's be honest, snacking on a few here and there), I'd start with a generous 2 pounds. That way, I'd have plenty even after the onions shrank way down during cooking.

The downsides of frying are the time it takes (multiple batches cooked for upwards of 30 minutes apiece) and the large amount of oil, so I made it my goal to cut down on both. Most of the cooking time is spent waiting for the water in the onions to boil away, so I thought about ways to rid the onions of some liquid before they hit the oil. The obvious answer: salt, the thirsty mineral we regularly use to pull water from vegetables.

So after cutting the onions into thin half-moons, I coated them with a couple of teaspoons of salt and let them sit. After 10 minutes, they'd shed a few tablespoons of water—encouraging results. I rinsed them to remove excess salt, dried them thoroughly, and fried them in two batches in a Dutch oven.

Frankly, the time savings were disappointing—just 5 minutes from each batch—so I took more drastic draining measures. After tossing the onions with the salt, I popped the bowl into the microwave for 5 minutes. Now I was getting somewhere: This two-step approach pulled more moisture from the slices and jump-started the cooking process. Still, batch frying was fussy and long; I was hovering over that pot of oil for more than 40 minutes, waiting for the heaps of onions to shrink and crisp.

That's when a thought occurred to me. The onions were initially piled high in the pot, but there was room to spare once they really started to cook down. Did I even need to bother with batch frying?

I sliced, salted, and microwaved another batch, this time piling all the onions into the pot at once, and turned the burner to high. Most of the onion slices started out well above the surface of the oil, but sure enough, they collapsed quickly and everything was soon fully submerged. About 25 minutes later, every last morsel was deeply golden and crispy with just a hint of chew. Not only that, but they were so far below the oil's surface that I felt bold and made another batch with just 1½ cups of oil—half the amount I'd been using. Happily, these were every bit as crispy and golden as the onions cooked in 3 cups of oil. I strained them and packed the onion-infused oil into a container to save, as it adds savory depth to salad dressings, sautés, and sauces.

In fact, why not swap the 3 tablespoons of oil that I was using for the pilaf for an equal amount of the reserved onion oil, boosting the savory flavor of the pilaf right from the start? I also added a touch of sugar to the rice and lentils to complement the warmth of the spices—a tweak I'd seen in a few mujaddara recipes. Many versions also suggested stirring in fresh herbs; I chose cilantro for its fresh, faintly citrusy flavor and bright color.

As I scooped myself a bowl of the fragrant pilaf; scattered a handful of crispy, supersavory onions on top; and dolloped on a quick-to-make garlicky yogurt sauce, I couldn't help thinking that this was in fact food fit for a king.

RICE AND LENTILS WITH CRISPY ONIONS (MUJADDARA)
SERVES 4 TO 6

Do not substitute smaller French lentils for the green or brown lentils. When preparing the Crispy Onions, be sure to reserve 3 tablespoons of the onion cooking oil for cooking the rice and lentils.

Yogurt Sauce
- 1 cup plain whole-milk yogurt
- 2 tablespoons lemon juice
- ½ teaspoon minced garlic
- ½ teaspoon salt

Rice and Lentils
- 8½ ounces (1¼ cups) green or brown lentils, picked over and rinsed
  Salt and pepper
- 1¼ cups basmati rice
- 1 recipe Crispy Onions, plus 3 tablespoons reserved oil (recipe follows)
- 3 garlic cloves, minced
- 1 teaspoon ground coriander
- 1 teaspoon ground cumin
- ½ teaspoon ground cinnamon
- ½ teaspoon ground allspice
- ⅛ teaspoon cayenne pepper
- 1 teaspoon sugar
- 3 tablespoons minced fresh cilantro

1. FOR THE YOGURT SAUCE: Whisk all ingredients together in bowl. Refrigerate while preparing rice and lentils.

2. FOR THE RICE AND LENTILS: Bring lentils, 4 cups water, and 1 teaspoon salt to boil in medium saucepan over high heat. Reduce heat to low and cook until lentils are tender, 15 to 17 minutes. Drain and set aside. While lentils cook, place rice in medium bowl and cover by 2 inches with hot tap water; let stand for 15 minutes.

3. Using your hands, gently swish rice grains to release excess starch. Carefully pour off water, leaving rice in bowl. Add cold tap water to rice and pour off water. Repeat adding and pouring off cold tap water 4 to 5 times, until water runs almost clear. Drain rice in fine-mesh strainer.

4. Heat reserved onion oil, garlic, coriander, cumin, cinnamon, allspice, ¼ teaspoon pepper, and cayenne in Dutch oven over medium heat until fragrant, about 2 minutes. Add rice and cook, stirring occasionally, until edges of rice begin to turn translucent, about 3 minutes. Add 2¼ cups water, sugar, and 1 teaspoon salt and bring to boil. Stir in lentils, reduce heat to low, cover, and cook until all liquid is absorbed, about 12 minutes.

5. Off heat, remove lid, fold dish towel in half, and place over pot; replace lid. Let stand for 10 minutes. Fluff rice and lentils with fork and stir in cilantro and half of crispy onions. Transfer to serving platter, top with remaining crispy onions, and serve, passing yogurt sauce separately.

The Garnish That Makes the Meal—and Many Others
Crispy onions, stirred into the pilaf and sprinkled over the top as a garnish, add concentrated, sweet-savory depth and textural contrast, making *mujaddara* an incredibly satisfying meatless meal. But the onions are also great sprinkled on salads and sandwiches and as a garnish for soups. And be sure to save the onion-flavored oil, which can give salad dressings, sautéed vegetables, eggs, and pasta sauces a savory boost.

CRISPY ONIONS
MAKES 1½ CUPS

It is crucial to thoroughly dry the microwaved onions after rinsing. The best way to accomplish this is to use a salad spinner. Reserve 3 tablespoons of oil when draining the onions to use in Rice and Lentils with Crispy Onions. Remaining oil may be stored in an airtight container and refrigerated up to 4 weeks.

- 2 pounds onions, halved and sliced crosswise into ¼-inch-thick pieces
- 2 teaspoons salt
- 1½ cups vegetable oil

1. Toss onions and salt together in large bowl. Microwave for 5 minutes. Rinse thoroughly, transfer to paper towel–lined baking sheet, and dry well.

2. Heat onions and oil in Dutch oven over high heat, stirring frequently, until onions are golden brown, 25 to 30 minutes. Drain onions in colander set in large bowl. Transfer onions to paper towel–lined baking sheet to drain. Serve.

▶ Mujaddara Step by Step
Video available free for 4 months at CooksIllustrated.com/oct14

Tagliatelle with Artichokes

Pasta paired with artichoke hearts is an Italian favorite. We'd love it, too, if we didn't have to trim, steam, and extract the hearts.

> BY LAN LAM

Artichokes have been cultivated in Italy since Roman times, and Italians have learned to cook the prized *carciofo*, the flower bud of a thistle plant, in almost every conceivable way. One of my favorite preparations is *pasta con carciofi*, a delicate pairing of herbal, nutty artichoke hearts with tender pasta. Unfortunately, to prepare the dish, you must trim, cook, and dismantle the artichokes to get to the fleshy hearts before you can even think about turning them into a sauce. I've always considered processed artichokes a poor substitute for the fresh kind, but if I could somehow transform their uninspired flavor, I knew I'd have the makings of a great weeknight dish.

To get my bearings, I made a handful of pasta sauce recipes calling for jarred or canned artichoke hearts. One required simmering the hearts in a pot with fresh tomato, onion, and dried herbs for almost 2 hours. A second called for tossing the hearts with broiled cherry tomatoes, olive oil, and oregano. Another required coating the hearts in a rich cream sauce laced with lemon and Parmesan. I even found a recipe that called for pureeing hearts into a slightly chunky, gray concoction that was then used to dress ravioli. While the recipes were easy to prepare, the artichoke flavor was lost in all of them. To succeed, my dish would need to highlight the unique subtleties of the artichoke—not force them to compete with lots of butter and cream or acidic ingredients like tomato.

Before examining the artichokes further, I decided to piece together a bare-bones sauce recipe. I brought a few quarts of water to a boil in a Dutch oven and dumped in 12 ounces of tagliatelle. (In preliminary tests, tasters expressed a strong preference for this egg pasta, whose richness was a nice counterpoint to the lean artichokes.) Meanwhile, I sautéed minced garlic, dried oregano, and red pepper flakes in extra-virgin olive oil in a skillet and then

To boost the flavor of jarred artichokes, we brown the hearts in a skillet and then build complexity with aromatics, wine, and a touch of cream.

poured in a splash of dry white wine and reduced the mixture. The tagliatelle was al dente by the time I had drained a couple of jars of water-packed baby artichokes (we found out early on that we much prefer this type of product to the canned, frozen, or marinated options; see "Shopping: Processed Artichoke Hearts") and added them to the sauce. I drained the pasta and combined it with the chunky sauce along with just enough starchy pasta water to pull the sauce together.

The good news: The artichoke flavor was no longer obscured by the other ingredients. The bad: The artichoke flavor that was present was compromised, tasting strongly of the citric and ascorbic acids that are added to the packing water during processing. I wanted a deeper artichoke flavor.

The Heart of the Matter
To enhance the positive flavor traits of the artichokes, I tried to brown them before building the sauce. But their irregular shape made browning difficult, plus the leaves had turned tough and

leathery by the time they finally picked up color. That said, the parts of the heart that had browned tasted fantastic. For the next go-round, I cut the leaves from the hearts and set them aside. I then halved each heart to create a flat side that would make good contact with the hot pan. I blotted off the excess brine and put the hearts into a hot skillet shimmering with olive oil. Sure enough, the hearts browned beautifully and took on a deep, rich taste that disguised the off-flavor from the additives.

I dealt with the leaves next, swirling them in a bowl of water before draining them and adding them to the sauce. I was hoping that the water bath would eliminate their less-than-appealing flavor, but tasters reported that it had endured.

I wondered if I could use baking soda to neutralize the acidity from the additives. In the test kitchen, we use soda to neutralize odors on cutting boards, so maybe it could block unwanted flavors in my artichokes. I briefly soaked some leaves in a mild baking soda solution and then drained and rinsed them. They definitely tasted less acidic, but alas, the soda dip had left behind a chemical flavor.

Instead of trying to neutralize the acid, maybe I just needed to try harder to wash it away. I prepped more artichoke leaves and left them to soak in water for various amounts of time. Five- and 10-minute

Why Egg Pasta?

When we're making a relatively lean sauce like this one, we like to pair it with a wider egg-based pasta. Wider, richer-tasting tagliatelle noodles give the dish a little extra heft.

PRIMO PASTA
Rich egg pasta complements our somewhat lean sauce.

▶ **See Why It Works**
Video available free for 4 months at CooksIllustrated.com/oct14

samples still hinted of brine. But 15 minutes was the ideal amount of time, after which only the subtle flavor of artichoke remained.

Finessing Flavor

Happy with the state of my artichokes, I was ready to perfect the rest of the dish. The aromatics, wine, olive oil, and artichokes needed just a splash of something rich to bring them together into a unified sauce. Stirring in a mere 2 tablespoons of cream with the wine did just that. I also tried adding small amounts of bacon and prosciutto for depth of flavor, but even two slices overwhelmed the artichokes with porkiness. Using a mere half of a slice of bacon was a possibility but seemed impractical, so I rooted through the test kitchen pantry for other options. I quickly landed on anchovies: Two fillets, added along with the aromatics, contributed a hint of savoriness, and none of my tasters picked out any fishiness.

When finished with chopped parsley, lemon zest, Parmesan, and a generous drizzle of extra-virgin olive oil, the pasta boasted a range of clear flavors—richness from touches of cream and cheese, brightness from the lemon and artichokes, and grassy notes from the herbs and olive oil.

The flavor of the dish was spot-on, but it was lacking a little textural contrast. That was nothing that some toasted bread crumbs couldn't fix. I pulsed two slices of sandwich bread in a food processor and then toasted the crumbs in a skillet. Just as they began to brown, I added a sprinkling of Parmesan and continued to cook the mixture until it was nicely toasted. Sprinkled on top of my pasta, the cheesy crumbs added pops of crunchiness.

With its tangy, creamy, cheesy, and crunchy elements—and genuine artichoke flavor—this dish is far more than something to turn to for a quick dinner. In fact, it's so good that I'd even make it for company.

IMPROVING JARRED ARTICHOKE HEARTS

Jarred artichokes have a sharp taste from the acids they are packed in. Here's how we tempered that quality.

CUT AWAY LEAVES
Separating the leaves from the hearts allows us to treat each component independently.

SOAK Soaking the leaves in water for 15 minutes takes away the sour taste while still leaving them well seasoned.

BROWN HEARTS IN OIL
Browning adds rich depth to the hearts (we skipped this step with the leaves, which turned tough).

TAGLIATELLE WITH ARTICHOKES AND OLIVE OIL

SERVES 4 TO 6

We prefer jarred artichoke hearts labeled "baby" or "cocktail" that are 1½ inches or shorter in length. Larger artichoke hearts tend to have fibrous leaves. If you are using larger hearts, trim the top ¼ to ½ inch from the leaves. Do not use marinated or oil-packed artichoke hearts. You'll need three 9.9-ounce jars of artichokes for this recipe. The anchovies add depth without imparting a fishy taste; don't omit them. Tagliatelle is a long, flat, dry egg pasta that is about ¼ inch wide. Pappardelle can be substituted for the tagliatelle. For our free recipe for Tagliatelle with Artichokes and Olive Oil for Two, go to CooksIllustrated.com/oct14.

- 3 cups jarred whole artichoke hearts packed in water, preferably baby or cocktail size
- 2 slices hearty white sandwich bread, torn into 1-inch pieces
- 3 tablespoons plus ¼ cup extra-virgin olive oil
- 1 ounce Parmesan cheese, grated (½ cup), plus extra for serving
  Salt and pepper
- 3 garlic cloves, minced
- 2 anchovy fillets, rinsed, patted dry, and minced
- ½ teaspoon dried oregano
- ⅛ teaspoon red pepper flakes
- ⅓ cup dry white wine
- 2 tablespoons heavy cream
- 12 ounces tagliatelle
- ¼ cup minced fresh parsley
- 1 teaspoon grated lemon zest

1. Cut leaves from artichoke hearts. Cut hearts in half and dry with paper towels. Place leaves in bowl and cover with water. Let leaves stand for 15 minutes. Drain well.

2. Pulse bread in food processor until finely ground, 10 to 15 pulses. Heat 2 tablespoons oil in 10-inch nonstick skillet over medium heat until shimmering. Add bread crumbs and cook, stirring constantly, until crumbs begin to brown, 3 to 5 minutes. Add ¼ cup Parmesan and continue to cook, stirring constantly, until crumbs are golden brown, 1 to 2 minutes. Transfer crumbs to bowl and season with salt and pepper to taste. Wipe out skillet.

3. Heat 1 tablespoon oil in now-empty skillet over medium-high heat until shimmering. Add artichoke hearts and ⅛ teaspoon salt; cook, stirring frequently, until hearts are spotty brown, 7 to 9 minutes. Add garlic, anchovies, oregano, and pepper flakes; cook, stirring constantly, until fragrant, about 30 seconds. Stir in wine and cream and bring to simmer. Remove skillet from heat and stir in artichoke leaves. Set aside.

4. Meanwhile, bring 4 quarts water to boil in large pot. Add pasta and 1 tablespoon salt and cook, stirring often, until al dente. Reserve 1 cup cooking water, then drain pasta and return it to pot. Stir in artichoke sauce, remaining ¼ cup Parmesan, ⅔ cup reserved cooking water, remaining ¼ cup oil, parsley, and lemon zest. Adjust consistency with remaining reserved cooking water as needed. Season with salt and pepper to taste. Serve, passing bread-crumb mixture and extra Parmesan separately.

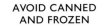

Really Good Grilled Fish Tacos

For a fish taco that doesn't require the mess of deep frying, we turned to the grill.

⇒ BY DAVID PAZMIÑO ⇐

Batter-fried Baja-style fish tacos have their place, but when I don't want to deal with a pot of hot oil—or be left with that heavy feeling you inevitably get after eating fried food—I go for the grilled kind. Nicely charred but moist fillets wrapped in tortillas with a few cool, crunchy garnishes and a squeeze of lime have the potential to be lighter on both the fuss and the stomach.

The problem is that this leaner preparation can also be light on flavor and complexity. For grilled fish tacos with more punch, I looked for inspiration in a preparation popular in the Yucatán Peninsula. Here they split whole fish in half lengthwise, bathe it in a deep-red chile-citrus marinade, and then grill it wrapped in banana leaves or in a grill basket. This flavor-packed fish is served on a platter whole, to be flaked off and eaten with tortillas and some simple sides. I wanted grilled fish tacos featuring a similarly bold flavor profile, but a simpler approach—no dealing with whole, skin-on fish—plus, I wanted a few complementary toppings to complete the package.

Fish is delicate, but that's no reason to hold back on heat. For great smoky-tasting char, we grill our fish over a mounded chimney of coals.

Keeping It Together

My first task was finding the best substitute for the whole fish. Traditional recipes usually start with a whole butterflied snapper or grouper. I knew I wanted to grill smaller portions, but a quick test in which I grilled both snapper and grouper fillets confirmed that they weren't going to work out. Keeping the skin on was key with these flakier fish to prevent sticking, and that meant at serving time almost all their charred flavor went into the trash with the skin. Relying on banana leaves or a grilling basket, as in the traditional recipes, would circumvent sticking, but tracking down such an obscure item or requiring special equipment was out of the question in my mind. I needed a different variety of fish.

All flaky fish, like cod and hake, were out for the same reason. Fish with a denser, meatier texture were more promising, so I gave mahi-mahi, tuna, swordfish, and halibut a chance. In the end, swordfish was the favorite. It's easy to find, it stands up well to flipping on the grill, and steaks that were 1 inch thick had enough time to pick up plenty of flavorful char before the interior cooked through. Cutting the fish into 1-inch-wide strips made it even easier to handle and also meant that the fish could go from grill to taco without any further prep.

In the Thick of Things

Some of the more modern recipes I found called for marinating the fish in lots of citrus juice with a hit of warm chile and other seasonings. Such a brightly flavored approach offered lots of appeal, but I quickly discovered that this sort of pretreatment created more problems than benefits. First, the flavor was lackluster since the fish spent only about 30 minutes in the marinade, and letting it sit long enough to make a noticeable difference led to fish that cooked in its high-acid bath (think ceviche). Worse, the significant amount of sugar in the fruit juice meant that, even with oil in the marinade, the fish had to be chiseled off the cooking grate. In the past, we've combated sticking and lack of flavor by using a postgrilling marinade, but in this case it left the spices tasting raw. I briefly considered putting a piece of foil between the fish and the grate, but aside from the fact this isn't recommended by some grill manufacturers, it prevented the fish from picking up

flavorful char. I moved on to option two.

Many of the traditional recipes I'd found called for coating the fish in a thick paste featuring ground annatto seeds (the same spice used to color yellow cheese) or ground dried chiles, various warm spices, and just enough citrus juice to make it spreadable. A trip to the supermarket spice aisle confirmed that I'd have to vary from tradition at least a little. Annatto seeds, which come from the tropical achiote tree, might be easy to find in Mexico, but they can be tough to ferret out stateside. Though I'd go without, I hoped that landing on the right mix of chiles and spices could make up for the loss of their earthy, peppery flavor.

Starting with whole dried chiles is the authentic approach, but the fuss of toasting them in a dry skillet or softening them in oil and then grinding them to a powder was more work (not to mention shopping effort) than I cared to deal with. At the other end of the spectrum—and also not an option in my mind—was generic chili powder. With its blend of ground chiles and other spices and herbs, it made a paste that was passable but not distinctive.

Instead, I created my own blend of chile powders and ground herbs, singling out ancho chile powder for its fruitiness and chipotle chile powder for smoky heat and earthiness, while some oregano and ground coriander boosted complexity. Blooming this mixture in oil, along with some minced garlic and salt, rounded out the flavors. But it still needed a bigger

Don't Flake Out

When grilling fish, avoid flaky varieties like grouper, hake, cod, or snapper, which will stick to the grill and fall apart when you try to flip them.

SHREDDED SNAPPER

For fillets that stay intact, choose a denser variety like swordfish, mahi-mahi, tuna, or halibut.

For grilled fish that's infused with flavor, it wasn't enough to simply create nice char marks. We also boosted flavor with a bold spice paste and a grilled-fruit salsa.

MAKE PASTE
A thick spice paste, brightened by lime and orange juices, adds complexity to the fish.

CHILL FISH
Refrigerating the paste-covered fish for at least 30 minutes allows the salt in the paste to penetrate and season the fish.

GRILL FISH, FRUIT, AND JALAPEÑO
The grill deepens the flavor of the pineapple and chile destined for the salsa.

WARM TORTILLAS
Grill the tortillas for about 30 seconds per side and then wrap them in a dish towel or foil to keep them warm.

FINISH SALSA
Finely chop the pineapple and jalapeño and then combine them with red bell pepper, cilantro, and lime juice.

---

punch of savory sweetness. Adding a few tablespoons of tomato paste took care of that.

The last component: the citrus juice. Looking back at the recipes I'd compiled, sour or Seville oranges appeared most frequently. Instead, I employed a commonly suggested substitute: orange juice with a little lime juice added to give it the right tart, bright acidity.

After coating the fish in the paste, I let it sit in the refrigerator while the grill heated up to give the salt time to penetrate and season the fish. Despite fish's reputation for delicacy, I found that there was no need to hold back on heat. A heaping chimney of charcoal (about 7 quarts) gave the coating great char that further deepened the swordfish's flavor and just cooked it through. I was also happy to find that as long as I thoroughly oiled the grate, the paste (helped no doubt by the grittiness of the chile powders and herbs) didn't exacerbate any issues with the fish sticking to the grate.

Topping Out

All that was left was coming up with the right combination of garnishes. Iceberg lettuce, for its crunchy freshness, and avocado, for its silky richness, were both in. A fresh fruit salsa also sounded promising. Mango and papaya both had potential, but pineapple won out for its acidity and sweetness, which balanced the spicy earthiness of the fish. A little jalapeño for some fresh heat and red bell pepper and cilantro for color and freshness rounded out the salsa.

Since there was plenty of room on the grill, I threw the pineapple and jalapeño on the cooking grate opposite the fish, an easy step that caramelized the fruit and deepened the chile's flavors and brought more of the smoky flavor of the grill to my tacos. Once the fish and salsa ingredients came off the grate, I quickly warmed the tortillas over the fire until they were nicely speckled with brown spots, and then wrapped them in foil to keep warm.

Loaded up with the smoky, boldly flavored fish, salsa, and garnishes, these tacos were satisfying yet still refreshingly light. They didn't need anything else but a cold beer to drink alongside.

GRILLED FISH TACOS
SERVES 6

Mahi-mahi, tuna, and halibut fillets are all suitable substitutes for the swordfish, but to ensure the best results buy 1-inch-thick fillets and cut them in a similar fashion to the swordfish.

- 3 tablespoons vegetable oil
- 1 tablespoon ancho chile powder
- 2 teaspoons chipotle chile powder
- 1 teaspoon dried oregano
- 1 teaspoon ground coriander
- 2 garlic cloves, minced
  Salt
- 2 tablespoons tomato paste
- ½ cup orange juice
- 6 tablespoons lime juice (3 limes)
- 2 pounds skinless swordfish steaks, 1 inch thick, cut lengthwise into 1-inch-wide strips
- 1 pineapple, peeled, quartered lengthwise, cored, and each quarter halved lengthwise
- 1 jalapeño chile
- 18 (6-inch) corn tortillas
- 1 red bell pepper, stemmed, seeded, and cut into ¼-inch pieces
- 2 tablespoons minced fresh cilantro, plus extra for serving
- ½ head iceberg lettuce (4½ ounces), cored and thinly sliced
- 1 avocado, halved, pitted, and sliced thin
  Lime wedges

1. Heat 2 tablespoons oil, ancho chile powder, and chipotle chile powder in 8-inch skillet over medium heat, stirring constantly, until fragrant and some bubbles form, 2 to 3 minutes. Add oregano, coriander, garlic, and 1 teaspoon salt and continue to cook until fragrant, about 30 seconds longer. Add tomato paste and, using spatula, mash tomato paste with spice mixture until combined, about 20 seconds. Stir in orange juice and 2 tablespoons lime juice. Cook, stirring constantly, until thoroughly mixed and reduced slightly, about 2 minutes.

Transfer chile mixture to large bowl and let cool for 15 minutes.

2. Add swordfish to bowl with chile mixture, and stir gently with rubber spatula to coat fish. Cover and refrigerate for at least 30 minutes or up to 2 hours.

3A. FOR A CHARCOAL GRILL: Open bottom vent completely. Light large chimney starter mounded with charcoal briquettes (7 quarts). When top coals are partially covered with ash, pour evenly over grill. Set cooking grate in place, cover, and open lid vent completely. Heat grill until hot, about 5 minutes.

3B. FOR A GAS GRILL: Turn all burners to high, cover, and heat grill until hot, about 15 minutes. Turn all burners to medium-high.

4. Clean cooking grate, then repeatedly brush grate with well-oiled paper towels until grate is black and glossy, 5 to 10 times. Brush both sides of pineapple with remaining 1 tablespoon oil. Place fish on half of grill. Place pineapple and jalapeño on other half. Cover and cook until fish, pineapple, and jalapeño have begun to brown, 3 to 5 minutes. Using thin spatula, flip fish, pineapple, and jalapeño over. Cover and continue to cook until second sides of pineapple and jalapeño are browned and swordfish registers 140 degrees, 3 to 5 minutes. Transfer fish to large platter, flake into pieces, and tent with aluminum foil. Transfer pineapple and jalapeño to cutting board.

5. Clean cooking grate. Place half of tortillas on grill. Grill until softened and speckled with brown spots, 30 to 45 seconds per side. Wrap tortillas in dish towel or foil to keep warm. Repeat with remaining tortillas.

6. When cool enough to handle, finely chop pineapple and jalapeño. Transfer to medium bowl and stir in bell pepper, cilantro, and remaining 4 tablespoons lime juice. Season with salt to taste. Top tortillas with flaked fish, salsa, lettuce, and avocado. Serve with lime wedges and extra cilantro.

▶ **Watch the Tacos Happen**
Video available free for 4 months at CooksIllustrated.com/oct14

Perfecting Carne Asada

Superthin, well-charred steaks define this Mexican favorite. To deliver maximum char as well as tender meat, we created an unusual grill setup.

⇒ BY DAN SOUZA ⇐

These days carne asada usually refers to a supercharred, thin steak, but traditionally the dish involves a platter of food. Created around 1940 at the Tampico Club in Mexico City, carne asada began as a plate of seared strips of lime-and-salt-seasoned beef jerky, folded enchiladas, beans, and *queso fresco*. At some point a fresh grilled or seared steak was swapped in and the number of sides was upped. Thus *carne asada de Tampico* was born.

For my version, I wanted to stick close to the original while keeping it approachable by the home cook. A juicy, thin, well-charred steak was a must, and I settled on two extras: a salsa that would complement the meat and some quick refried beans.

Meat of the Matter

Mexican cookbooks were divided on the best cut for the job. Some went the thriftier route, calling for chuck roast, but pricier tenderloin and strip steak appeared, too. I tested them all sliced or pounded to ¼ inch thick, marinated in salt and lime juice, and grilled until charred. Inexpensive chuck may have been ideal for the jerky version, but its tough connective tissue and pockets of sinew and fat made it a flop for the update. Supertender steaks didn't fare much better. While I wasn't cooking any of the steaks to well-done as a number of traditional recipes suggested, to get good charring on a thin steak, medium was the most realistic goal. Cooked to this degree, both tenderloin and strip were inevitably dry and mealy. Flank steak was better, but it was hard to pound thin enough, so it also fell out of the running.

Left at the top of the heap were skirt steak and sirloin steak tips. Not only do these cuts have a beefier flavor, but because of their muscle structure, they were tender when grilled to medium. In the end, skirt steak won out for both flavor and texture, and since it's inherently thin, all I needed to do was give it a few good whacks with a meat pounder.

After searing the skirt steak, we punch up its flavor with fresh garlic and lime and slice it thin.

Next I focused on the marinade. Purist recipes call for lime juice and maybe salt. Outside this circle, recipes went to the other extreme, calling for everything from wine, herbs, and garlic to cumin, chiles, and even soy sauce. I tried every combination that I found. The verdict? Steaks bathed in unexpected ingredients like red wine and soy sauce garnered few fans. My tasters liked simple—though not dead simple. While salt and lime alone were OK, a little warmth from cumin and sharpness from garlic were welcome. A 45-minute soak allowed the salt to penetrate the meat, helping make it more tender and juicy, but any longer and the acidic mixture broke down the structure and made the meat mushy. When the time was up, I removed the steaks from the marinade, patted them dry, and fired up the grill.

Order of Operations

For the grill setup, I needed a ripping-hot fire to ensure that the meat charred well before the interior overcooked. Loading a chimney starter full of coals (about 6 quarts of charcoal briquettes) was essential.

First I tried steeply banking the coals on one side to put concentrated heat close to the cooking grate, but with the coals packed into such a small footprint, I couldn't cook more than one steak at a time. I needed coals mounded into a relatively thick layer for intense heat but spread out just enough to cook all the steaks at once. Arranging them just so was too fussy; I needed something to corral the coals.

A disposable aluminum roasting pan seemed like just the answer, but even when I punched numerous holes in the bottom to allow for airflow, the heat was tempered too much. I eventually grabbed kitchen shears and cut the bottom out, leaving just the pan collar to contain the coals. This setup delivered the fastest browning yet—about 4 minutes per side—but I still ended up with overcooked meat. I had a hunch that my marinade might be part of the problem.

In order for browning to kick into high gear, the surface of a steak must dry out. The soaking step was introducing unwanted moisture, so I ditched the marinade and instead treated the steaks to a dry rub of salt, cumin, and minced garlic. I also refrigerated them uncovered on a wire rack for 45 minutes to further encourage a dry exterior before grilling. These steaks browned and crisped in record time—just longer than 2 minutes per side—leaving the interior moist and tender. To work in the lime flavor, I simply gave the grilled steaks a squeeze of citrus before serving. This all worked great, except that without added moisture the garlic in the rub burned. So I stole a technique often used for bruschetta: I took a smashed garlic clove and rubbed it over the steaks' charred crusts after they came off the grill. This simple step brought a burst of fresh garlic flavor and aroma to the meat.

Sidekicks

Many carne asada recipes call for a tomatillo salsa, but it was the versions that had a red chile salsa that really stuck with me. The chiles' fruity, slightly smoky flavor added incredible depth to the steak. I started by toasting dried guajillo chiles—which have the right bright, slightly tangy flavor with a hint of heat—in a hot skillet before grinding them in a blender. From there I added a can of fire-roasted

▶ **Dan Creates the Char**
Video available free for 4 months at CooksIllustrated.com/oct14

For Serious Char, Corral the Coals

Concentrating the charcoal directly under the steaks using an aluminum roasting pan was the first step toward getting a really hot fire. And since greater availability of oxygen translates into a fire that burns hotter, instead of poking a few holes in the pan, we maximized the airflow by cutting the bottom out of the pan completely.

Make a foil collar by cutting the bottom out of an aluminum roasting pan.

diced tomatoes, water, garlic, vinegar, oregano, pepper, clove, cumin, and salt. Punchy and intense, it complemented the charred steaks perfectly.

Finally, no carne asada platter would be complete without beans. I opted for creamy refried beans over the brothy boiled kind. A quick homemade version with canned pinto beans, onion, garlic, and rich meaty depth from bacon was easy to prepare and tasted far superior to the canned stuff. My recipe was streamlined and simple since I could prepare the salsa and beans in the time the meat sat in the refrigerator. Combined with the juicy, perfectly charred steak, this was carne asada that lived up to the Mexico City favorite.

MEXICAN-STYLE GRILLED STEAK (CARNE ASADA)
SERVES 4 TO 6

Two pounds of sirloin steak tips, also sold as flap meat, may be substituted for the skirt steak. In addition to Red Chile Salsa and Simple Refried Beans, another nice accompaniment is our Folded Enchiladas. For the free recipe, go to CooksIllustrated.com/oct14.

- 2 teaspoons kosher salt
- ¾ teaspoon ground cumin
- 1 (2-pound) skirt steak, trimmed, pounded ¼ inch thick and cut with grain into 4 equal steaks
- 1 (13 by 9-inch) disposable aluminum roasting pan (if using charcoal)
- 1 garlic clove, peeled and smashed
  Lime wedges

1. Combine salt and cumin in small bowl. Sprinkle salt mixture evenly over both sides of steaks. Transfer steaks to wire rack set in rimmed baking sheet and refrigerate, uncovered, for at least 45 minutes or up to 24 hours. Meanwhile, if using charcoal, use kitchen shears to remove bottom of disposable pan and discard, reserving pan collar.

2A. FOR A CHARCOAL GRILL: Open bottom vent completely. Light large chimney starter filled with charcoal briquettes (6 quarts). When top coals are partially covered with ash, place disposable pan collar in center of grill over bottom vent and pour coals into even layer in collar. Set cooking grate in place, cover, and open lid vent completely. Heat grill until hot, about 5 minutes.

2B. FOR A GAS GRILL: Turn all burners to high, cover, and heat grill until hot, about 15 minutes. Leave all burners on high.

3. Clean and oil cooking grate. Place steaks on grill (if using charcoal, arrange steaks over coals in collar) and cook, uncovered, until well browned on first side, 2 to 4 minutes. Flip steaks and continue to cook until well browned on second side and meat registers 130 degrees, 2 to 4 minutes longer. Transfer steaks to carving board, tent loosely with aluminum foil, and let rest for 5 minutes.

4. Rub garlic thoroughly over 1 side of steaks. Slice steaks against grain into ¼-inch-thick slices and serve with lime wedges.

RED CHILE SALSA
MAKES 2 CUPS

Guajillo chiles are tangy with just a bit of heat. Our favorite brand of fire-roasted tomatoes is DeLallo. Serve the salsa alongside the steak.

- 1¼ ounces dried guajillo chiles, wiped clean
- 1 (14.5-ounce) can fire-roasted diced tomatoes
- ¾ cup water
- ¾ teaspoon salt
- 1 garlic clove, peeled and smashed
- ½ teaspoon white vinegar
- ¼ teaspoon dried oregano
- ⅛ teaspoon pepper
  Pinch ground clove
  Pinch ground cumin

Toast guajillos in 10-inch nonstick skillet over medium-high heat until softened and fragrant, 1 to 2 minutes per side. Transfer to large plate and, when cool enough to handle, remove stems and seeds. Place guajillos in blender and process until finely ground, 60 to 90 seconds, scraping down sides of blender jar as needed. Add tomatoes and their juice, water, salt, garlic, vinegar, oregano, pepper, clove, and cumin to blender and process until very smooth, 60 to 90 seconds, scraping down sides of blender jar as needed. (Salsa can be stored in the refrigerator for up to 5 days or frozen for up to 1 month.)

SIMPLE REFRIED BEANS
MAKES ABOUT 1½ CUPS

- 2 slices bacon
- 1 small onion, chopped fine
- 2 garlic cloves, minced
- 1 (15-ounce) can pinto beans (do not rinse)
- ¼ cup water
  Kosher salt

Heat bacon in 10-inch nonstick skillet over medium-low heat until fat renders and bacon crisps, 7 to 10 minutes, flipping bacon halfway through. Remove bacon and reserve for another use. Increase heat to medium, add onion to fat in skillet, and cook until lightly browned, 5 to 7 minutes. Add garlic and cook until fragrant, about 30 seconds. Add beans and their liquid and water and bring to simmer. Cook, mashing beans with potato masher, until mixture is mostly smooth, 5 to 7 minutes. Season with salt to taste, and serve.

SCIENCE Medium-Rare? Not with This Steak

Cooking most steaks to 125 degrees, or medium-rare, delivers the juiciest, most tender results. But skirt steak is one exception. When a piece of beef is heated, its muscle fibers shrink in width, separating them from one another and making them easier to chew. For cuts like strip steak, which have comparatively thin fibers, the amount of shrinking, and thus tenderizing, that occurs when the meat is cooked to 125 degrees is sufficient. But skirt steak has wider muscle fibers that need to shrink further, and thus require cooking to 130 degrees, before they are acceptably tender.

However, this tenderizing effect doesn't continue the more you cook the steak. Once any cut of meat hits 140 degrees, muscle fibers begin to shrink not just in width but also in length, and that causes the meat to toughen again. This lengthwise shrinking also squeezes out juices, which means your steak will end up not just tough but also dry.

BEFORE COOKING: THICK, TOUGH FIBERS

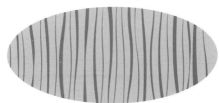

AFTER COOKING: THIN, TENDER FIBERS
Steaks like skirt steak, with comparatively thick muscle fibers, must be cooked to 130 degrees, or medium, before their fibers shrink enough to be acceptably tender.

The Science of Onions

Though flavor starts with the type of onion you buy at the supermarket, how you cut and cook it can have a dramatic impact on how it tastes. BY ELIZABETH BOMZE

TWO BASIC ONION TYPES

There are at least several hundred onion varieties, but all fall into two broad flavor categories: pungent and mild. Pungent onions contain more of the sulfur molecules that impart characteristic oniony flavor and—somewhat surprisingly—lots of sugars. The abundance of both kinds of flavor molecules translates into more complexity in cooking, making pungent onions the best choice for heated applications. Though mild onions have even more of the sugars glucose, fructose, and sucrose than pungent onions, they also have more water and far fewer sulfur molecules, for an overall weaker taste that makes them more suitable for raw applications.

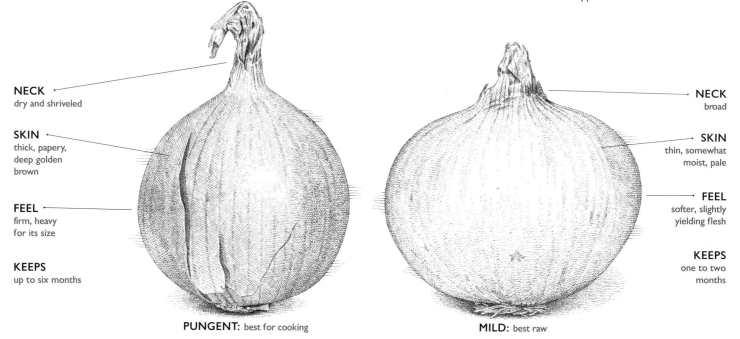

NECK
dry and shriveled

SKIN
thick, papery, deep golden brown

FEEL
firm, heavy for its size

KEEPS
up to six months

NECK
broad

SKIN
thin, somewhat moist, pale

FEEL
softer, slightly yielding flesh

KEEPS
one to two months

PUNGENT: best for cooking

MILD: best raw

SHOPPING TIPS

The only way to know for sure that you're getting a mild onion is to buy a trademarked mild variety, such as Vidalia or Walla Walla. That said, the following tips can still help you predict onion flavor.

DON'T RELY ON COLOR
Though the yellow onions in most supermarkets tend to be pungent, color is generally not a good indicator of pungency: Yellow, white, or red onions can be pungent as well as mild. To single out a pungent onion, inspect the shape of the neck, skin thickness, and firmness (see "Give It a Squeeze").

CHECK THE NECK (AND SKIN)
Most pungent onions will have drier, tighter necks and thicker skins compared with those of milder varieties. That's because pungent onions undergo a curing process that dries their outer scales and causes their necks to shrivel, sealing off the bulb to moisture and allowing it to keep longer. Mild onions tend to have broader necks and thinner skins, both of which make them more perishable.

GIVE IT A SQUEEZE
Because they generally have less water, pungent onions (held under the proper storage conditions) will often feel quite firm compared with mild varieties. In fact, a good way to pick a pungent onion is to gently squeeze it; the bulb should feel smooth, rock-hard, and heavy for its size. Onions that give a little when pressed are more likely to be mild. Either way, avoid onions that are soft only in spots, which indicates bruised, rotting flesh.

ONION DO'S AND DON'TS

➤ **DO keep them dry**
Moisture encourages rot, so keep onions in a dry, well-aerated place. We found that a colander in a pantry is ideal. Also keep them away from light, which can cause the onions to sprout.

➤ **DON'T store with potatoes**
Storing onions with produce that gives off a lot of moisture, such as potatoes or apples, will cause them to spoil faster. Onions can also pick up the flavor of other produce, and vice versa.

➤ **DON'T eat the sprout**
We found that the sprout not only tastes bitter but pulls sugar and moisture from the bulb, making the onion itself taste harsh and dull. Consider tossing a sprouted bulb—or if you decide to cook with it, be sure to remove the sprout.

➤ **DO cover your eyes**
Cutting an onion releases a tear-inducing compound called propanethial S-oxide. Of the 20-plus methods we tested to stave off tears, we found that wearing ski, swim, or specialty onion goggles, or contacts, will help protect your eyes.

➤ **DO light a flame**
Cutting an onion near a candle or a lit gas burner isn't as effective as covering your eyes, but we found that it does help. The flame completely oxidizes the sulfuric propanethial S-oxide that comes near the flame.

HOW ONION FLAVOR WORKS—AND HOW YOU CAN CONTROL IT

As soon as you cut an onion, you start its flavor in motion. The ruptured cell walls of both pungent and mild onions release odorless sulfur-containing molecules that react with an enzyme known as alliinase. The interaction transforms them into new compounds called thiosulfinates and thiosulfonates that are responsible for a raw onion's characteristic harsh flavor and odor. At that point, there are three factors that can further influence flavor: how finely the onion is cut; how long it is exposed to air when raw; and, most significant, how it's cooked.

PREPPING AND CUTTING

➤ **Avoid using an onion's core in raw applications.** We've found that the outer layers of an onion taste noticeably milder than the inner layers. When we consulted onion experts, they confirmed that the inner layers contain a higher concentration of flavor precursors than the outer layers do, and therefore have stronger flavor.

➤ **For fuller, more complex flavor in cooked applications, cut onions finely.** The more you process an onion, the more thiosulfinates and thiosulfonates will develop, and the more potential there will be for the development of complex flavor during cooking.

➤ **For milder flavor in raw applications, slice onions with the grain.** We sniffed and tasted eight onions sliced pole to pole (with the grain) and parallel to the equator (against the grain). Because slicing pole to pole ruptures fewer cell walls, thus leading to the creation of fewer sulfur molecules, we weren't surprised that these onions were clearly less pungent in taste and odor than those cut along the equator.

➤ **For even milder flavor, give them a soak.** Many sources recommend soaking chopped raw onions in milk or vinegar to remove sulfur compounds from their surface; we found that a 15-minute soak in plain water was just as effective. That said, if you like the flavor of lightly pickled onions, go ahead and soak them in vinegar instead.

➤ **Beware of cutting onions in advance.** Whether you're cutting pungent or mild onions, their flavor will degrade as they sit. We found that pungent onions can turn "sour," while mild onions can taste harsh. If you must cut onions in advance, store them in a zipper-lock bag, give them a quick rinse before using, and use them only in cooked applications.

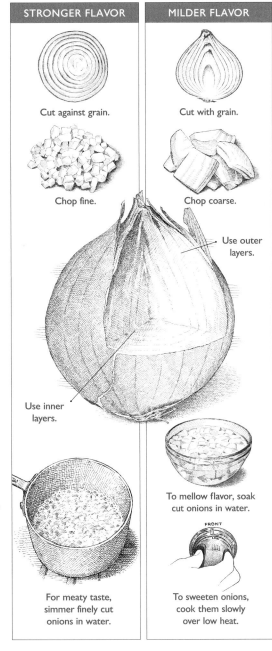

STRONGER FLAVOR
Cut against grain.
Chop fine.
Use inner layers.
For meaty taste, simmer finely cut onions in water.

MILDER FLAVOR
Cut with grain.
Chop coarse.
Use outer layers.
To mellow flavor, soak cut onions in water.
To sweeten onions, cook them slowly over low heat.

COOKING

➤ **For tenderness and even seasoning, salt onions during, not after, cooking.** Since salting onions draws moisture out of their cells and softens them, we wondered if salting onions at the outset of cooking—rather than after—would produce more tender onions. Sure enough, when we sautéed two batches of chopped onions for the same amount of time, the ones salted from the start were meltingly tender compared with the almost-crunchy batch that was salted postcooking. Not only that, but onions salted earlier were more deeply seasoned.

➤ **To boost meaty taste, cook onions in water.** When chopped, onions slowly form a water-soluble compound called 3-mercapto-2-methyl-pentan-1-ol, or MMP for short, that tastes meaty when a cut onion is heated in water. For meatless preparations that need a savory boost, such as vegetable stock, process the onions finely to release as much MMP as possible and use enough water so that the onion's cut surfaces are fully submerged.

➤ **For sweeter—and more complex—flavor, cook your onions low and slow.** High heat makes onions taste flat by deactivating the enzyme alliinase, thereby putting a halt to the formation of sulfur molecules. Low heat has the opposite effect. It not only encourages the creation of thiosulfinates and thiosulfonates but encourages these harsh-tasting molecules to transform into sweeter, mellower substances called disulfides and trisulfides.

TEST: To verify this bit of culinary science, we made two batches of tomato sauce, cooking one batch of the onions for 10 minutes over low heat and the other onions for 8 minutes over high heat. The low-and-slow-cooked-onion sauce, which tasters praised as "rich," "round," and "sweet," was the overwhelming favorite.

EXPERIMENT Is It OK to Cook with Mild Onions?

Thanks to their higher ratio of flavor-packed tissue to water and the potential to deliver more complex taste, pungent onions are typically referred to as cooking onions. But since mild onions have even more sugars, that, when caramelized, can contribute lots of new flavors, is it really so bad to cook with them?

TEST We made rice pilaf and French onion soup with both pungent and mild onions.
RESULTS In pilaf, where onions were sautéed until softened, tasters preferred the batch made with pungent onions, which tasted noticeably rounder and more complex, though the pilaf with mild onions was still acceptable. When we caramelized the onions for the soup, their differences were more apparent: The mild onions brought a one-dimensional sweetness to the soup, while the pungent onions contributed a deeper, richer sweetness. Furthermore, the mild onions cooked down about 15 percent more—which makes sense, since water takes up far more of their mass than it does in pungent onions.
BOTTOM LINE With mainly sugars contributing to their flavor during cooking, mild onions can't help but taste less complex, so it's best to stick with pungent ones.

Roasted Fruit Desserts

A two-stage cooking process yields tender, beautifully caramelized fruits.

> BY SARAH MULLINS

Everyone knows that pears, apples, and plums are terrific baked into a classic pie or crisp, but an equally appealing option is simply roasting the fruits. Without a crust or a crumble to shield the fruit from the heat of the oven, its exterior caramelizes into a rich, nutty foil to the subtly sweet interior. Another plus: Unlike with many fruit desserts, there is almost no prep work. Just halve the fruit (pears and apples are best peeled), remove the core or pit, and it's ready to go—no slicing required.

But even a faultless piece of roasted fruit needs some type of adornment to become a full-fledged dessert. My goal was to perfect a roasting technique and then gussy up the fruit so that it would make a thoroughly satisfying dessert.

Starting with pears, I peeled, halved, and cored a few Boscs and then tossed them in a baking dish with melted butter and sugar before roasting them at 450 degrees for half an hour. The pears were golden, but the sugar and butter had cooked into a sticky, chewy caramel that detracted from the tender pear flesh.

I ditched the sugar in the next go-round, causing the tacky caramel to disappear. But without sugar to soak up the juice that seeped from the pears during baking, the soggy pears failed to brown. Next, I preheated the baking dish in the oven before adding the fruit, hoping to jump-start evaporation. Unfortunately, this didn't offer much improvement.

What if I could drive off some of those juices prior to roasting? Switching to a skillet, I melted the butter, arranged the pears flat side down, and let them cook over medium-high heat until they started to brown, about 5 minutes. I transferred the skillet to the oven and roasted the pears until a fork easily pierced their flesh, about 30 minutes longer.

The pears were now gorgeously caramelized and perfectly tender, ready to be transformed into a dessert. Wanting to make use of the flavorful browned bits left in the pan after roasting the pears, I decided that a quick pan sauce would be a great way to jazz things up. I removed the pears from the skillet and poured in some apple cider (along with a pat of butter for silkiness) to deglaze the pan. After a few minutes of simmering, the sauce boasted a nice, thick consistency, but it lacked depth, featuring only a one-note sweetness. White wine (along with a little

sugar) seemed as though it might be a better choice than cider. Indeed, this was a definite step up, but to make it even more interesting, I added lemon juice and cardamom. Now the sauce had a citrus boost plus a spice kick that complemented the pears.

For textural contrast and extra sweetness, I thought dried apricots would be a good addition. Sure enough, a handful contributed just the right amount of fruity sweetness and tender chew. I also sprinkled on some chopped pistachios, which offered a contrasting crunch. Finally, I experimented with serving plain Greek yogurt or vanilla ice cream alongside the fruit, and both were hits with tasters.

With such pleasing results, I was ready to mix things up with other fruits. For one, I swapped the white wine for red and combined Gala apples with dried figs, walnuts, and black pepper. For another, I matched red plums with a complementary trio—dried cherries, almonds, and cinnamon. With deeply caramelized fresh fruit, chewy dried fruit, toasted nuts, and spice-scented wine sauces, these were sophisticated finishes to any meal.

▶ See the Caramelization
Video available free for 4 months at CooksIllustrated.com/oct14

ROASTED PEARS
WITH DRIED APRICOTS AND PISTACHIOS
SERVES 4 TO 6

Select pears that yield slightly when pressed. We prefer Bosc pears in this recipe, but Comice and Bartlett pears also work. The fruit can be served as is or with vanilla ice cream or plain Greek yogurt. For our free recipes for Roasted Apples with Dried Cranberries and Pecans and Roasted Pears with Golden Raisins and Hazelnuts, go to CooksIllustrated.com/oct14.

- 2½ tablespoons unsalted butter
- 4 ripe but firm Bosc pears (6 to 7 ounces each), peeled, halved, and cored
- 1¼ cups dry white wine
- ½ cup dried apricots, quartered
- ⅓ cup (2⅓ ounces) sugar
- ¼ teaspoon ground cardamom
- ⅛ teaspoon salt
- 1 teaspoon lemon juice
- ⅓ cup pistachios, toasted and chopped

1. Adjust oven rack to middle position and heat oven to 450 degrees. Melt 1½ tablespoons butter in ovensafe 12-inch skillet over medium-high heat. Place pear halves, cut side down, in skillet. Cook, without moving them, until pears are just beginning to brown, 3 to 5 minutes.

2. Transfer skillet to oven and roast pears for

After caramelizing the fruit, we build a pan sauce with the flavorful browned bits.

15 minutes. Using tongs, flip pears and continue to roast until fork easily pierces fruit, 10 to 15 minutes longer (skillet handle will be hot).

3. Using tongs, transfer pears to platter. Return skillet to medium-high heat and add wine, apricots, sugar, cardamom, salt, and remaining 1 tablespoon butter. Bring to vigorous simmer, whisking to scrape up any browned bits. Cook until sauce is reduced and has consistency of maple syrup, 7 to 10 minutes. Remove pan from heat and stir in lemon juice.

4. Pour sauce over pears, sprinkle with pistachios, and serve.

ROASTED APPLES
WITH DRIED FIGS AND WALNUTS

Substitute Gala apples for pears, red wine for white wine, dried figs for apricots, ¾ teaspoon pepper for cardamom, and walnuts for pistachios.

ROASTED PLUMS
WITH DRIED CHERRIES AND ALMONDS

Substitute unpeeled plums for pears, dried cherries for apricots, ground cinnamon for cardamom, and sliced almonds for pistachios. Reduce stovetop cooking time in step 1 to 3 minutes. Reduce oven roasting time in step 2 to 5 minutes per side.

Authentic Baguettes at Home

Most American baguettes are doughy and pale, and the recipes we found weren't much better. To get it right, we went to Paris to learn from the masters.

≥ BY ANDREW JANJIGIAN ≤

I think home cooks rarely make baguettes for two reasons: One, they are intimidated, and two, they don't know what they are missing. A great baguette is hard to come by, at least outside France. Those from the supermarket or the average U.S. bakery, with their pale, soft crust and fine crumb, are no comparison to the real thing. The ideal: a moist, wheaty interior punctuated with irregular holes and a deeply browned crust so crispy that it shatters into a shower of tiny shards (if it isn't messy, *c'est pas bon*). Even if a nearby bakery makes a great baguette, you have to buy one within hours of baking or else it's rock hard. If you want a great baguette, you should make it yourself.

But when I tested some promising recipes, not one produced loaves that attained that ideal. Many had a pale, soft crust and weak flavor; others were dense and uniform on the inside. I'd need to develop my own recipe—and what better place to begin than the baguette's home turf?

In Paris, I sampled as many worthy versions as I could find and even watched the best bakers at work. (For a full account of my trip to Paris, go to CooksIllustrated.com/parisbaguette.) I focused on winners of the Grand Prix de la Baguette de la Ville de Paris, the annual competition for the city's best baguette. (In addition to money and prestige, the prize guarantees that the winning baguette is served daily at the French president's table for a year.) Here's what I learned. The darker the crust, the deeper the flavor. Excess exterior flour will dull flavor and compromise crispiness. Irregular interior holes indicate that the dough has been handled gently and thus will have a tender crumb. Almond-shaped slashes that open wide also signify tenderness and a fully expanded interior, while color that changes from pale to dark within those cuts is a sign of complex flavor. A great baguette should have the flavor of sweet wheat, with just a subtle hint of tangy, complex fermented flavor.

The problem with recipes wasn't so much what they instructed me to do but how little instruction and explanation they provided. As I'd witnessed in France, so much of what goes into making a good baguette is in the mechanics of the thing—shaping, proofing, scoring, steaming in the oven—and this wasn't conveyed in recipes. My role was clear: Cull what I could from recipes and then apply what I learned in France to create a step-by-step, authentic baguette recipe for the home oven.

Wide-open slashes on the crust and both large and small holes within indicate a fully expanded, tender crumb.

Taking It Slow with the Dough

The standard baguette ingredient list is simple: flour, water, salt, and yeast. I settled on 1 pound of flour, 1 teaspoon of yeast, 1½ teaspoons of salt, and 12 ounces of water, enough for a moderately wet dough. (I also added a teaspoon of diastatic malt powder to help the loaf brown deeply; for more information on this ingredient, see "Baguette Baker's Kit.") As for mixing and kneading, I found that less is more. Using a stand mixer to do both jobs left the crumb too uniform and tight. Mixing by hand and then giving the dough several folds during the initial proofing to develop the structure gave me better results, but it was difficult to evenly combine the ingredients. I settled on mixing the dough in the machine and then folding the dough several times during the initial proofing.

Next up was fermentation, which is when the yeast consumes sugar and starches in the flour to produce gas and alcohol, giving the loaf both lift and flavor. The simplest approach calls for doing everything from mixing through baking in a single day, allowing 2 to 3 hours for fermentation. Another option is the sponge or pre-ferment method, in which a portion of the yeast, flour, and water are mixed and proofed for a few hours, and often overnight, before proceeding. And finally, there is the slow rise, or cold-fermentation method, in which the dough is placed in the fridge for a day or more before shaping and baking. The straight dough method gave me baguettes with little character. A pre-ferment produced a far better flavor, but the slow-rise baguettes were equally flavorful and offered another benefit: convenience. The dough needed at least 24 hours in the fridge, but it could sit for as long as 72 hours. Plus, this dough could be portioned out to make baguettes "on demand" as desired within that window.

When I used this method, the flavor was good, but my loaves were missing that wheaty taste that I'd experienced with the Parisian baguettes. I contacted French baking scholar James MacGuire for insight. He said that most of the flavor of a baguette's interior comes from yellow carotenoid pigments that naturally occur in wheat. But because much of the wheat grown in North America is destined for the Far East, where people want pure white dumplings and noodles, the growth of wheat varieties high in carotenoids is discouraged. In France, the best flours are high in carotenoid pigments. To mimic the more intense wheatiness of French flours, MacGuire suggested adding a bit of whole-wheat flour to my recipe.

So I tried substituting ¼ cup of whole-wheat flour for some of the white flour. Tasters welcomed the wheatiness, but they also noted a hint of bitterness and found these baguettes more dense and less crispy. The bran in the wheat flour was adding a bitter flavor and its sharp edges were cutting gluten strands, weakening the structure. Happily, there was a solution: Sifting the wheat flour removed some of

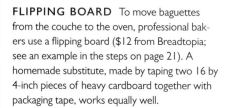

the larger pieces of bran (but not the germ). Subbing in this sifted flour gave me baguettes with the same texture as that of all-white-flour loaves, but with far better flavor.

Shape Shifting

Now that I had a dough I was happy with, I could focus on shaping. Too often my loaves had a dense, uniform crumb—or they had inappropriately giant holes—instead of a mix of small and large holes. I learned in Paris that shaping has a major impact here.

I knew that turning that mass of dough into a baguette shape gradually was critical. If done too quickly, you'll overwork the dough, or you won't get the right shape—or both. As I worked out my own step-by-step method, I found that the key was using a gentle touch and avoiding trapping large pockets of air. Borrowing from what I'd seen in Paris, I settled on a three-stage process—preshape, fold, stretch—and a few key tricks that ensured ideal results. For instance, pressing the dough into a square and then rolling it like a log was the gentlest way to start the shaping process, while moving the semi-formed loaf back and forth at the center until its ends widened, giving it a dog-bone shape, tightened the loaf and also pushed large air bubbles out either end.

I also learned that to score the loaves properly, I needed to keep the blade at a shallow angle. A *lame*, a traditional baguette scoring tool with a slightly curved blade, made producing slashes that baked up into the right almond-shaped openings easy, and it also created the proper ridge, or "ear," along one side of the slash that baked up deliciously crispy.

On Its Own Steam

It was time to move on to the crust, which was too thick, almost leathery. At bakeries, shaped loaves are proofed in the folds of a piece of heavy linen known as a *couche*. The couche has two core jobs: It helps the baguette retain its shape, and it wicks away moisture from the exterior to encourage a crispy crust. But the thick crusts on my loaves suggested that they might be losing a little too much moisture. Most bakeries make hundreds of baguettes at a time, and as loaves sit side by side on their large couches, the moisture that comes off them saturates the fabric and the air around it. With my small batch, the same effect wasn't possible. Misting the back of my couche lightly with water was a step in the right direction, but still the crust wasn't quite right.

Steam within the oven serves three important functions in bread baking. First, it keeps the exterior of the bread moist when it begins to bake, preventing the crust from hardening before the interior has fully expanded. Second, it ensures good color since the enzymes that convert some of the starches into sugars, which in turn lead to browning, need water

to function. And finally—and most important for my current concern—steam promotes crispiness. The remaining starches on the loaf's surface absorb the steam and cook into a crispy crust; without it, they simply dry out, leaving the crust dull and raw-tasting.

I had been creating steam using my go-to method: Just before putting the bread into the oven, I poured boiling water into a pan of preheated lava rocks sitting on the bottom shelf. Steam is most important at the start of the baking time, and as I watched a fair amount of it escape when I put baguettes into the oven, I began doubting my technique. With the standard *boule*, which requires about 45 minutes of baking, there is time to recover that steam without much impact, but with a baguette, which requires only 20 minutes or so of oven time, by the time the steam has been replaced, it's too late.

I recalled our Almost No-Knead Bread recipe (January/February 2008), which starts the bread in a covered pot, steaming the loaf by surrounding it in its own evaporating moisture. I wondered if a similar approach would work here. For my next test, I covered my baguettes with a pair of large, overturned disposable roasting pans (doubled up for a better seal). After 10 minutes, I pulled off the pans and continued to bake the baguettes. Tearing into a baguette confirmed it: It was shatteringly crispy. This was a baguette that could sit proudly on anyone's table, French president or otherwise.

Making Parisian Quality Baguettes

Gentle shaping is key for authentic texture. For the best flavor, here's what we do:
➤ Add some whole-wheat flour to mimic the wheatiness of French flours
➤ Use a long, cold fermentation to develop complex flavor
➤ Steam the loaves under aluminum pans to create a dark and flavorful crispy crust

---

AUTHENTIC BAGUETTES AT HOME
MAKES FOUR 15-INCH-LONG BAGUETTES

If you can't find King Arthur all-purpose flour, substitute bread flour. For best results, weigh your ingredients. This recipe makes enough dough for four loaves, which can be baked anytime during the 24- to 72-hour window after placing the dough in the fridge. For tips on folding and slashing, see pages 30 and 31. It's essential to watch our video on making baguettes at CooksIllustrated.com/oct14.

- ¼ cup (1⅓ ounces) whole-wheat flour
- 3 cups (15 ounces) King Arthur all-purpose flour
- 1½ teaspoons salt
- 1 teaspoon instant or rapid-rise yeast
- 1 teaspoon diastatic malt powder (optional)
- 1½ cups (12 ounces) water
- 2 (16 by 12-inch) disposable aluminum roasting pans

1. Sift whole-wheat flour through fine-mesh strainer into bowl of stand mixer; discard bran remaining in strainer. Add all-purpose flour, salt, yeast, and malt powder, if using, to mixer bowl. Fit stand mixer with dough hook, add water, and knead on low speed until cohesive dough forms and no dry flour remains, 5 to 7 minutes. Transfer dough

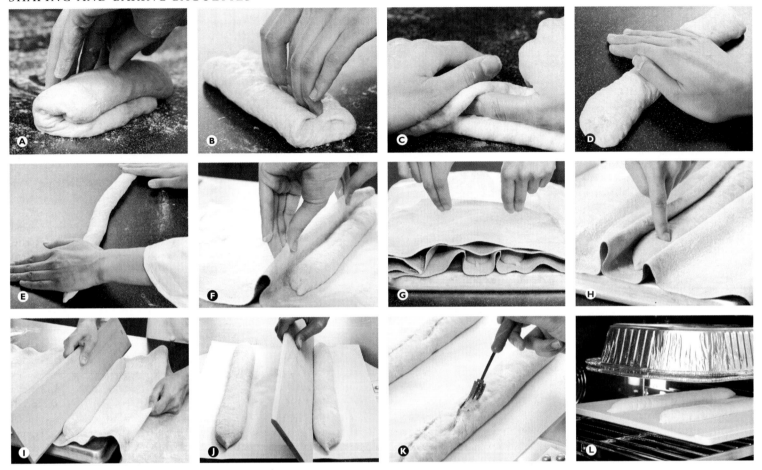

to lightly oiled large bowl, cover with plastic wrap, and let rest at room temperature for 30 minutes.

2. Holding edge of dough with your fingertips, fold dough over itself by gently lifting and folding edge of dough toward center (see page 30). Turn bowl 45 degrees; fold again. Turn bowl and fold dough 6 more times (total of 8 folds). Cover with plastic and let rise for 30 minutes. Repeat folding and rising every 30 minutes, 3 more times. After fourth set of folds, cover bowl tightly with plastic and refrigerate for at least 24 hours or up to 72 hours.

3. Transfer dough to lightly floured counter, pat into 8-inch square (do not deflate), and divide in half. Return 1 piece of dough to container, wrap tightly with plastic, and refrigerate (dough can be shaped and baked anytime within 72-hour window). Divide remaining dough in half crosswise, transfer to lightly floured rimmed baking sheet, and cover loosely with plastic. Let rest for 45 minutes.

Shaping and Baking

4. Ⓐ ▶ On lightly floured counter, roll each piece of dough into loose 3- to 4-inch-long cylinder; return to floured baking sheet and cover with plastic. Let rest at room temperature for 30 minutes.

5. Lightly mist underside of couche with water, drape over inverted baking sheet, and dust with flour. Gently press 1 piece of dough into 6 by 4-inch rectangle on lightly floured counter, with long edge facing you. Fold upper quarter of dough toward center and press gently to seal. **Ⓑ ▶** Rotate dough 180 degrees and repeat folding step to form 8 by 2-inch rectangle.

6. Ⓒ ▶ Fold dough in half toward you, using thumb of your other hand to create crease along center of dough, sealing with heel of your hand as you work your way along the loaf. Without pressing down on loaf, use heel of your hand to reinforce seal (do not seal ends of loaf).

7. Ⓓ ▶ Cup your hand over center of dough and roll dough back and forth gently to tighten (it should form dog-bone shape).

8. Starting at center of dough and working toward ends, gently and evenly roll and stretch dough until it measures 15 inches long by 1¼ inches wide. **Ⓔ ▶** Moving your hands in opposite directions, use back and forth motion to roll ends of loaf under your palms to form sharp points.

9. Transfer dough to floured couche, seam side up. **Ⓕ ▶** On either side of loaf, pinch edges of couche into pleat, then cover loosely with large plastic garbage bag.

10. Repeat steps 4 through 9 with second piece of dough and place on opposite side of pleat. **Ⓖ ▶** Fold edges of couche over loaves to cover completely, then carefully place sheet inside bag, and tie or fold under to enclose.

11. Ⓗ ▶ Let stand until loaves have nearly doubled in size and dough springs back minimally when poked gently with your fingertip, 45 to 60 minutes. While bread rises, adjust oven rack to middle position, place baking stone on rack, and heat oven to 500 degrees.

12. Line pizza peel with 16 by 12-inch piece of parchment paper with long edge perpendicular to handle. Unfold couche, pulling from ends to remove pleats. Gently pushing with side of flipping board, roll 1 loaf over, away from other loaf, so it is seam side down. **Ⓘ ▶** Using your hand, hold long edge of flipping board between loaf and couche at 45-degree angle, then lift couche with your other hand and flip loaf seam side up onto board.

13. Ⓙ ▶ Invert loaf onto parchment-lined peel, seam side down, about 2 inches from long edge of parchment, then use flipping board to straighten loaf. Repeat with remaining loaf, leaving at least 3 inches between loaves.

14. Ⓚ ▶ Holding lame concave side up at 30-degree angle to loaf, make series of three 4-inch-long, ½-inch-deep slashes along length of loaf, using swift, fluid motion, overlapping each slash slightly (see page 31). Repeat with second loaf.

15. Ⓛ ▶ Transfer loaves, on parchment, to baking stone, cover with stacked inverted disposable pans, and bake for 5 minutes. Carefully remove pans and bake until loaves are evenly browned, 12 to 15 minutes longer, rotating parchment halfway through baking. Transfer to cooling rack and let cool for at least 20 minutes before serving. Consume within 4 hours.

Mahogany Chicken Thighs

Chicken thighs can contain unappetizing pockets of fat and sinew. But what if you could turn those liabilities into texture-enhancing assets—and get crispy skin, too?

> ⇒ BY ANDREA GEARY ⇐

I'm a big fan of chicken thighs, but I'm aware that not everyone shares my enthusiasm. Even those who admit that a roasted thigh delivers more flavorful meat than a roasted breast might steer clear of the dark meat, lest they encounter the pockets of fat and chewy connective tissue that tend to hide beneath the crispy skin.

There is a cooking method that directly addresses those flaws: braising, which melts the fat and breaks down the connective tissue into soft gelatin. Both coat the muscle fibers and leave the meat moist and silky. The downside? Braised chicken thighs have flabby, pale skin. To tempt white-meat devotees to the dark side, I'd need a method that delivered the moist meat of braising—with no pockets of fat or connective tissue—and the crispy skin of roasting.

A hybrid approach seemed like the best bet. First I'd braise the chicken to render the skin's fat and melt down the sinew—and I'd do so with a flavorful liquid that would season the meat. Then I'd blast the chicken with dry heat to crisp that rendered skin.

Opting for a teriyaki flavor profile, I stirred together 1 cup of soy sauce and 6 smashed cloves of garlic in a Dutch oven. I nestled eight chicken thighs into the pot, skin side down to encourage the skin's fatty underbelly to render, and added 1½ cups of water. I brought it all to a simmer on the stove and then transferred the pot to a 350-degree oven for its gentler, more even heat.

After 40 minutes, the chicken had reached 175 degrees, the temperature at which I usually remove roasted chicken thighs from the oven. I transferred the pieces skin side up to a wire rack set in a rimmed baking sheet and returned them to the oven, this time setting them just below the broiler.

When I sampled the thighs, I noticed that the moist heat had melted some, though not all, of the fat and connective tissue, so the meat wasn't as tender as I'd have liked. Also, its flavor was one-dimensional. As for the skin, it wasn't quite crispy, but the soy sauce had dyed it a rich mahogany color.

To add complexity, I mixed in sherry, white vinegar, ginger, and sugar and molasses for sweetness (both would also caramelize and boost that mahogany hue). Turning the chicken skin side up halfway through braising allowed the skin to dry

▶ Watch Mahogany Happen
Video available free for 4 months at CooksIllustrated.com/oct14

For moist meat and crispy skin, braise—then broil.

before broiling, which helped it crisp more. I also swapped my Dutch oven for a 12-inch skillet, which I could use for both braising and broiling.

On to ridding the meat of the fatty, chewy bits and making it more tender. Forty minutes was ample time for the thighs to cook through, but their connective tissue was another matter. This part of the chicken needs plenty of time to break down.

Realizing that I needed to hold the meat longer in the collagen breakdown sweet spot—above 140 degrees but below the temperature at which the meat would be overcooked—I reduced the oven temperature by 50 degrees and increased the braising time to about an hour. I thought that the lower heat would prevent the meat's temperature from climbing too rapidly, but alarmingly, the braised pieces registered 195 degrees—before broiling. I was sure I'd way overshot my mark, but I finished the batch anyway.

But my mistake turned out to be a happy accident. Yes, the meat was overcooked according to our usual standards, but the extended braising time had broken down the connective tissue so thoroughly that there was loads of gelatin to bathe the muscle fibers, resulting in meat that was supple and juicy.

Now it was time to address the skin, which still wasn't perfectly crispy. It was an easy fix: I lowered the oven rack to the middle position, which put more

distance between the broiler and the meat, so the skin would brown and crisp more slowly and evenly.

I finished up by using some of the braising liquid to make a quick sauce. Now that I know how to get the best out of chicken thighs, I'm planning to convert plenty of white-meat fans into devotees.

MAHOGANY CHICKEN THIGHS
SERVES 4 TO 6

For the best results, trim all visible fat and skin from the underside of the thighs. Serve with steamed rice.

1½	cups water
1	cup soy sauce
¼	cup dry sherry
2	tablespoons sugar
2	tablespoons molasses
1	tablespoon distilled white vinegar
8	(5- to 7-ounce) bone-in chicken thighs, trimmed
1	(2-inch) piece ginger, peeled, halved, and smashed
6	garlic cloves, peeled and smashed
1	tablespoon cornstarch

1. Adjust oven rack to middle position and heat oven to 300 degrees. Whisk 1 cup water, soy sauce, sherry, sugar, molasses, and vinegar in ovensafe 12-inch skillet until sugar is dissolved. Arrange chicken, skin side down, in soy mixture and nestle ginger and garlic between pieces of chicken.

2. Bring soy mixture to simmer over medium heat and simmer for 5 minutes. Transfer skillet to oven and cook, uncovered, for 30 minutes.

3. Flip chicken skin side up and continue to cook, uncovered, until chicken registers 195 degrees, 20 to 30 minutes longer. Transfer chicken to platter, taking care not to tear skin. Pour cooking liquid through fine-mesh strainer into fat separator and let settle for 5 minutes. Turn oven to broil.

4. Whisk cornstarch and remaining ½ cup water together in bowl. Pour 1 cup defatted cooking liquid into now-empty skillet and bring to simmer over medium heat. Whisk cornstarch mixture into cooking liquid and simmer until thickened, about 1 minute. Pour sauce into bowl and set aside.

5. Return chicken skin side up to now-empty skillet and broil until well browned, about 4 minutes. Return chicken to platter and let rest for 5 minutes. Serve, passing reserved sauce separately.

Fresh Corn Side Dishes

There are many ways to cook fresh corn, but few produce rich, complex, sweet flavor.
We kept experimenting until the right method popped up.

> BY SANDRA WU <

There's nothing like fresh corn on the cob, simply boiled or grilled and then slathered with salted butter. But to take full advantage of fresh corn season, side dishes made with corn stripped off the cob are invaluable. I wanted recipes that could be made quickly on a weeknight but had sufficient character to elevate a simple accompanying protein like grilled chicken or steak.

Boiling whole shucked corn and then cooling it and stripping the kernels was too fussy. Instead, I cut the kernels from raw ears and experimented with cooking methods. Gently sautéing the corn in butter before simmering it in cream sounded like a good idea, but this made for an overly rich dish that wasn't conducive to flavor variations. Conversely, simply sautéing the kernels in neutral oil over moderate heat provided a clean flavor base but left little to rave about. I wanted something with more oomph.

I thought about the lightly charred, smoky flavor and satisfying texture of grilled corn and wondered if I could replicate those qualities here. After some tinkering, I found that the best results came from searing the corn in a small amount of oil in a hot nonstick skillet, with minimal stirring.

The benefits of this method were twofold: The caramelization of the corn contributed noticeable depth of flavor—a rich sweetness as well as a complex toasted quality—while the high heat meant that the corn cooked very quickly and retained some crunch. The key was being sure that the oil was shimmering before adding the corn in an even layer and then waiting—no touching—until the kernels began to make a popping sound before stirring.

To ensure that the dish wasn't overly sweet, it was critical to add enough salt and/or naturally savory ingredients and acid (in the form of citrus juice or vinegar) to bring the flavors in line.

For my first recipe, I went the Italian route and toasted sliced garlic cloves in oil before removing the crispy garlic chips and using the flavored oil to cook the corn. Crumbled ricotta salata, cherry tomatoes, fresh basil, and lemon juice completed the dish.

I got creative with variations, coming up with Southern-style corn with bacon and leeks; southwestern corn with bell pepper, black beans, and cilantro; and a Japanese-inspired corn with miso, scallions, and sesame seeds. Regardless of the flavor profile, the method remained the same: easy and quick enough to keep your kitchen cool on an already scorching summer day.

Browning the corn in a hot skillet develops complexity.

SAUTÉED CORN WITH CHERRY TOMATOES, RICOTTA SALATA, AND BASIL
SERVES 4 TO 6

If ricotta salata is unavailable, substitute feta cheese. Because fresh corn can vary in sweetness, we've called for seasoning with a range of lemon juice. For our free recipes for Sautéed Corn with Black Beans and Red Bell Pepper and Sautéed Corn with Miso and Scallions, go to CooksIllustrated.com/oct14.

- 2 tablespoons vegetable oil
- 3 garlic cloves, sliced thin
- 4 ears corn, kernels cut from cobs (4 cups)
  Salt and pepper
- 6 ounces cherry tomatoes, halved
- 1½ ounces ricotta salata cheese, crumbled (⅓ cup)
- ¼ cup shredded fresh basil
- 1–2 tablespoons lemon juice

1. Heat oil and garlic in 12-inch nonstick skillet over medium heat. Cook, stirring frequently, until garlic is light golden brown and fragrant, 2 to 3 minutes. Using slotted spoon, transfer garlic to large bowl, leaving oil in skillet.

2. Return skillet to medium-high heat and heat until oil is shimmering. Add corn and sprinkle with ½ teaspoon salt. Cook, without stirring, until corn is browned on bottom and beginning to pop, about 3 minutes. Stir and continue to cook, stirring once or twice, until corn is spotty brown all over, 2 to 3 minutes longer. Transfer corn to bowl with garlic.

3. Stir in tomatoes, half of ricotta salata, basil, 1 tablespoon lemon juice, and ¼ teaspoon pepper. Season with salt, pepper, and remaining lemon juice to taste. Sprinkle with remaining ricotta salata and serve.

SAUTÉED CORN WITH BACON AND LEEKS
SERVES 4 TO 6

Because fresh corn can vary in sweetness, we've called for seasoning with a range of cider vinegar.

- 6 slices bacon, cut into ½-inch pieces
- 1 pound leeks, white and light green parts only, halved lengthwise, sliced thin, and washed thoroughly
  Salt
- 4 ears corn, kernels cut from cobs (4 cups)
- ¼ cup minced fresh chives
- 1–2 tablespoons cider vinegar
  Pinch cayenne pepper

1. Cook bacon in 12-inch nonstick skillet over medium heat until crispy, 5 to 7 minutes. Transfer bacon to paper towel–lined plate. Pour off and reserve all but 2 tablespoons fat from skillet.

2. Add leeks and ¼ teaspoon salt to fat in skillet and cook over medium heat, stirring occasionally, until softened, 7 to 10 minutes. Transfer leeks to large bowl and wipe out skillet.

3. Heat 1 tablespoon reserved fat in now-empty skillet over medium-high heat until shimmering. Add corn and sprinkle with ¼ teaspoon salt. Cook, without stirring, until corn is browned on bottom and beginning to pop, about 3 minutes. Stir and continue to cook, stirring once or twice, until corn is spotty brown all over, 2 to 3 minutes longer. Transfer corn to bowl with leeks.

4. Stir in chives, 1 tablespoon vinegar, cayenne, and bacon. Season with salt and remaining vinegar to taste. Serve.

▶ **Look: It Pops**
Video available free for 4 months at CooksIllustrated.com/oct14

Perfect Latin Flan

This cousin to crème caramel boasts a denser, sweeter profile and rich toffee-like flavor. Too bad its star ingredient can also be its biggest liability.

> BY SARAH MULLINS <

Spain is known for flan that is creamy and lightly set—almost indistinguishable from French crème caramel—but I've always been partial to the versions served in Mexican and Cuban restaurants. Though they share the same layer of caramelized sugar glistening on top and pooling at the bottom, the Latin style of this baked custard isn't light and quivering like its European counterparts. It is far richer and more densely creamy, with a texture somewhere between pudding and cheesecake. It also boasts a more deeply caramelized, toffee-like flavor.

Paging through flan recipes claiming a Latin heritage, I got my first clue as to how the custard gets its thick, luxurious texture: In place of fresh dairy, all such recipes called for canned milk—evaporated as well as sweetened condensed. The cooking process that concentrates canned milks also causes their sugars and proteins to brown, which accounts for the light tan color and toffee flavor they lend to this style of the dessert.

I made a few recipes, cooking sugar with a little water on the stove to create a caramel that I poured into a mold (typically a round cake pan), adding eggs whisked together with the canned milks, baking the custard in a water bath, and inverting it onto a platter when chilled. The first things I noticed: Even more so than with crème caramel, much of the caramel stuck to the bottom of the pan. And often the custard was so dense that it was borderline stiff, with even thicker skin where the flan had been exposed to the direct heat of the oven.

Needless to say, this was not the dessert I had in mind, so I got to work on a version that was as dense and rich-tasting as it was creamy.

General Custard

I homed in on the recipe I'd made with the best taste: three whole eggs and five yolks whisked together with one can each of evaporated and sweetened condensed milk (plus a touch of vanilla and salt

Baking a flan in a narrow loaf pan, rather than in a wide cake pan, makes it easier to unmold without cracking.

for flavor) and baked in a water bath at 350 degrees for about an hour. It tasted appropriately rich and sweet, if overly eggy. The bigger issue was its texture, which was not only stiff but also uneven; while the exterior was rubbery, the core was pudding-like.

A review of how custards work seemed in order. At their most basic, all custards are cooked mixtures of eggs and dairy in which the eggs are largely the source of proteins and the dairy largely the source of water. When the proteins are heated, they link up and form a matrix that traps the water, giving the custard structure. The exact texture of a custard mainly depends on the ratio of eggs to dairy: The more the proteins are diluted with water (from the dairy), the looser the custard's consistency will be.

But in Latin flan, I had a hunch that the dairy was playing a different role. Since canned milks contain less water than fresh milk, they obviously had less to contribute to the custard. Not only that, but these concentrated forms of milk were without a doubt contributing far more protein to the custard than fresh milk does—though I didn't realize just how much

more until I took a look at their nutrition labels. Both products, in fact, contain at least twice as much protein per ounce as fresh milk.

Milking It

Knowing that an overload of protein was making my flan too stiff, I tried removing one whole egg. I knew I was on the right track when the next batch of flan turned out noticeably creamier (albeit still uneven from edge to center). Even better, this quick fix did away with the custard's distinct eggy flavor. But ideally the custard would still be a tad more loose.

Removing another egg was the obvious next step, but the test backfired. In exchange for the more-velvety texture I wanted, I was left with a custard that lacked richness. So I stuck with the two whole eggs and considered my alternatives. Cutting back on either the sweetened condensed or evaporated milk was one option, but I quickly dismissed it, realizing that this would not only reduce the volume of the custard but also leave me with a small amount of canned milk I would surely waste.

The other option would be to add some liquid to the mixture, and fresh milk was the obvious choice; in essence, I'd be merging the European and Latin versions of this dessert. Of course, I didn't want to dilute the protein network so much that the custard would buckle when I unmolded it, so I went with what I hoped was a judicious ½ cup of fresh milk, whisking it into the egg-and-canned-milk mixture and proceeding with the recipe as before.

This was the texture I had in mind: dense, but not stiff, and luxuriously creamy. The core was still gooey and there was still a thin skin on the very edge of the custard where it was exposed to heat, but I had fixes in mind. I wrapped the cake pan in aluminum foil before baking, which prevented that pesky skin. As for the undercooked center, I cooked the custard to a slightly higher temperature than I had been (180 degrees instead of 175 degrees) while also reducing the oven temperature to 300 degrees to ensure that the custard cooked evenly from edge to center.

Now my flan tasted great—but unfortunately, it wasn't looking so hot. When I unmolded the more-fragile custard, a crack inevitably developed on the surface.

▶ **Watch It Take Shape**
Video available free for 4 months at CooksIllustrated.com/oct14

When Goodness Comes (Mainly) from a Can

The advent of canned milk in Latin America in the late 1800s helped make flan, which was introduced by Spanish conquistadores 300 years earlier, even more popular. When refrigeration became widespread and shelf-stable milk was no longer as necessary, the practice of using the canned stuff stuck. And with good reason: Evaporated and sweetened condensed milks give flan a distinctively thick, luxurious texture and caramelized notes. (In some Latin American countries, this texture has given rise to the alternate name *quesillo*, or little cheesecake). But these milks can also have a negative effect, contributing to a stiff, almost rubbery consistency. This is because they have about twice as much protein as an equivalent amount of fresh dairy, which, when combined with egg proteins in the custard, can create an overly tight structure. Our solution? Add ½ cup of fresh milk, which loosens the texture without adding much protein of its own or diluting dairy flavor.

EVAPORATED

This canned milk is made by heating pasteurized fresh milk in two stages to drive off nearly half of its water, which also triggers some Maillard browning. Once sealed in a can, the milk is sterilized to become shelf-stable, a process that triggers more browning and the creation of subtle caramel flavors.

SWEETENED CONDENSED

Adding sucrose or glucose syrups to milk that's been evaporated (and undergone Maillard browning) results in this canned milk. In combination with the lactose naturally present in the milk, these added sugars make up more than 50 percent of its weight, rendering sterilization unnecessary.

Loafing Around and Loosening Up

It occurred to me that the cake pan I'd been using was not helping the problem, as it produced a wide, shallow flan that was clearly inclined to crack. Looking through the test kitchen's arsenal of baking vessels, I wondered if the deeper walls and narrower surface area of a loaf pan might produce a sturdier flan. That it did. Even better, this taller flan was more statuesque—a presentation bonus.

Now back to that caramel-sticking problem. I suspected that the lack of water in this style of flan was partly to blame, since the caramel relies on moisture from the custard to keep it fluid. Up until now, I'd been resting the flan for about 4 hours—enough time for it to thoroughly chill. But resting it longer would surely allow more of the custard's moisture to seep into the caramel, so I let the next batch sit overnight before I unmolded it. The longer rest was worth it, as the liquid did indeed dilute the caramel, so that more caramel traveled with the custard this time. This approach also put this flan squarely in the make-ahead dessert category, which I considered a plus.

And yet I wanted even more of the caramel to release with the custard, so I decided to address the issue more directly. After cooking one more batch of caramel, I swirled 2 tablespoons of water (warm—to prevent the caramel from seizing) into the sugar just as it turned reddish-amber and then poured it into the pan and proceeded as before. When I turned out the next flan and saw that it was covered with a substantial layer of runny caramel, I knew I'd hit the mark. Plus, the small amount of caramel left in the pan was soft enough to scrape out with a spatula.

Now that my version was a reliable showpiece that I'd want to make often, I created a few easy flavor variations by infusing the custard with orange and cardamom, as well as with typically Latin flavors: coffee and almond extract. That made four rich, densely creamy, make-ahead desserts —a profile that may have permanently stolen my allegiance from French custards.

PERFECT LATIN FLAN
SERVES 8 TO 10

This recipe should be made at least one day before serving. We recommend an 8½ by 4½-inch loaf pan for this recipe. If your pan is 9 by 5 inches, begin checking for doneness at 1 hour. You may substitute 2 percent milk for the whole milk, but do not use skim milk. Serve the flan on a platter with a raised rim to contain the liquid caramel.

- ⅔ cup (4⅔ ounces) sugar
- 2 large eggs plus 5 large yolks
- 1 (14-ounce) can sweetened condensed milk
- 1 (12-ounce) can evaporated milk
- ½ cup whole milk
- 1½ tablespoons vanilla extract
- ½ teaspoon salt

1. Stir together sugar and ¼ cup water in medium heavy saucepan until sugar is completely moistened. Bring to boil over medium-high heat, 3 to 5 minutes, and cook, without stirring, until mixture begins to turn golden, another 1 to 2 minutes. Gently swirling pan, continue to cook until sugar is color of peanut butter, 1 to 2 minutes. Remove from heat and swirl pan until sugar is reddish-amber and fragrant, 15 to 20 seconds. Carefully swirl in 2 tablespoons warm tap water until incorporated; mixture will bubble and steam. Pour caramel into 8½ by 4½-inch loaf pan; do not scrape out saucepan. Set loaf pan aside.

2. Adjust oven rack to middle position and heat oven to 300 degrees. Line bottom of 13 by 9-inch baking pan with dish towel, folding towel to fit smoothly, and set aside. Bring 2 quarts water to boil.

3. Whisk eggs and yolks in large bowl until combined. Add sweetened condensed milk, evaporated milk, whole milk, vanilla, and salt and whisk until incorporated. Strain mixture through fine-mesh strainer into prepared loaf pan.

4. Cover loaf pan tightly with aluminum foil and place in prepared baking pan. Place baking pan in oven and carefully pour all of boiling water into pan. Bake until center of custard jiggles slightly when shaken and custard registers 180 degrees, 1¼ to 1½ hours. Remove foil and leave custard in water bath until loaf pan has cooled completely. Remove loaf pan from water bath, wrap tightly with plastic wrap, and chill overnight or up to 4 days.

5. To unmold, slide paring knife around edges of pan. Invert serving platter on top of pan and turn pan and platter over. When flan is released, remove loaf pan. Using rubber spatula, scrape residual caramel onto flan. Slice and serve. (Leftover flan may be covered loosely with plastic wrap and refrigerated for up to 4 days.)

ALMOND LATIN FLAN

Reduce vanilla to 1 tablespoon and whisk 1 teaspoon almond extract into the egg-milk mixture.

COFFEE LATIN FLAN

Whisk 4 teaspoons of instant espresso powder into the egg-milk mixture until dissolved.

ORANGE-CARDAMOM LATIN FLAN

Whisk 2 tablespoons orange zest and ¼ teaspoon ground cardamom into the egg-milk mixture before straining.

Don't Let the Caramel Stick to the Pan

The rich layer of caramel on top of flan is the best part of the dessert—except when most of it sticks to the pan like glue. Adding a couple of tablespoons of water to the syrup after it's caramelized will dissolve some of the sugar and keep it runny. In addition, resting the flan overnight allows moisture from the custard to dissolve more of the sugar, ensuring that most of the caramel will release from the pan (and that what's left in the pan is soft and easy to remove).

CLINGY CARAMEL
To prevent the caramel from sticking to the pan, we add a little water.

Why a Good Mixing Bowl Matters

This most basic piece of cooking equipment might not seem worthy of scrutiny—until you have one that wobbles when you whisk, slips in your hand, or traps food in its crevices.

⇒ BY KATE SHANNON ⇐

They may not be as sexy as chef's knives or as cutting-edge as *sous vide* circulators, but when it comes to basic cooking tasks, plain old mixing bowls can't be beat. We reach for them any time we mix up pancake batter or vinaigrette, or when simply melting butter. A good bowl should be so steady, durable, and comfortable to handle that it goes almost unnoticed while you work.

For those reasons, we shop carefully when outfitting the test kitchen with mixing bowls. Our criteria start with size: At the very least, we need small, medium, and large bowls—by which we mean 1- to 1½-quart; 2½- to 3-quart; and 4- to 6-quart, respectively. We also find it useful to have a set in both stainless steel and glass: The lightness of metal makes it easy to use, but only glass can go in the microwave. Plastic and ceramic bowls just aren't practical: The former's porous surface scratches and retains oils, while the latter is so heavy that it's a detriment.

To single out a set of each, we scooped up three stainless-steel sets and four sets made of tempered glass (glass that has undergone a mechanical strengthening process to increase its impact and thermal resistance), all priced from $13.19 to $59.99. We bought nesting sets when possible and cobbled together a custom set if the sizes we wanted were available only as open stock. We then subjected the bowls to the core tasks that we think any mixing bowl should be able to handle. In each of the small bowls, we whisked oil into vinegar to make dressing. In the medium and large bowls we mixed up muffin and pancake batters. We also used the large bowls to mix bread dough and the medium bowls to melt chocolate in a jury-rigged double boiler, with the bowl set over a saucepan of simmering water.

Getting in Shape

Not all the bowls excelled at these basic functions. Some models even made easy work annoyingly difficult, thanks to a variety of design defects.

Take bowl height. A vessel's walls should neatly contain the food but be shallow enough that users—particularly shorter folks—don't have to strain to access the food. A side-by-side comparison of the 5-quart bowls from OXO and Vollrath illustrated this point: Standing nearly 5 inches tall, the OXO forced some testers to reach farther up and over its rim than felt comfortable, while the Vollrath, which was shorter by almost an inch, allowed easy access to the bowl's contents.

Vollrath, as well as Pyrex and Arc International, got the shape of the walls right, too. In relation to their bases, these bowls' sides curved gently, which made it comfortable for testers to not only reach into the bowls to stir but also hold the bowls aloft to pour and scrape ingredients out of them. Conversely, testers had to tilt bowls with steeper walls more dramatically if they wanted to scrape out every last bit of food, and once a bowl was nearly upside-down, it was awkward to maneuver a spatula around the inside. That's why some shorter testers found the relatively tall and narrow Cuisinart bowl set challenging to access, although, since those bowls were made of lightweight stainless steel, their shape was still manageable. The same couldn't be said for the Anchor Hocking glass bowls, a brutally heavy fleet with L-shaped walls and sharp corners that were hard to scrape clean. Testers observed that they looked more like storage containers than mixing bowls.

From Rim to Base

Whether a bowl had a rim also affected how comfortable—or not—it was to hold. The rimmed models, which included all the stainless-steel bowls as well as the Pyrex, offered roughly ¼ to ½ inch of grippable material. The alternative, the thickened collar that ringed the other glass bowls, was better than nothing, but not much. Grasping the 4-quart Anchor Hocking bowl, which weighed more than 3½ pounds empty, by its collar took some serious muscle. Its only perk: Its collar sloped smoothly down the inside of the bowl, whereas those on the Arc International and the Duralex bowls stuck out, trapping food in the crevices.

As for countertop stability, we used the vinaigrette test to determine how far each bowl moved as we vigorously whisked oil into the dressing. To our surprise, there were no clear advantages or disadvantages to using heavier glass or lighter-weight metal, nor to using bowls with broader or narrower base diameters. In fact, the bowl that traveled the farthest, from Anchor Hocking, was the heaviest and the broadest at its base. The only model that flat-out flunked the stability test was from OXO. Ironically, its supposed selling point—its rubber-coated base—was its downfall: Instead of keeping the bowl stable, the coating clung to the counter and caused the bowl to twirl to the point of tipping over. (The final blow to that set: OXO cautioned against using its bowl as part of a double boiler, since its exterior plastic coating could overheat.) In durability tests, one glass bowl cracked and another shattered, but all stainless bowls emerged unscathed.

Fortunately, the best models in both categories were also reasonably priced. The three from Vollrath's Economy Stainless line will set you back just $14.30, while the Pyrex Smart Essentials set of four glass bowls (and lids) is as functional as it is affordable at $13.19.

A Case for Both Metal and Glass

Our winning metal and glass bowls, from Vollrath and Pyrex, respectively, share traits that make them sturdy and easy to handle, but each material also offers benefits of its own.

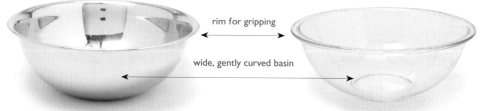

rim for gripping

wide, gently curved basin

STAINLESS STEEL

Why You Need It: Because lightweight stainless steel is so easy to handle and won't break, it's a default choice for most mixing tasks—particularly those for which a large bowl is needed, since metal will never get very heavy. Metal also conducts heat faster than glass, making it the better choice for a jury-rigged double boiler.

GLASS

Why You Need It: Tempered glass is a must for the microwave. Its transparency also lets you check for pockets of unmixed ingredients. Good glass bowls can also be surprisingly durable; our winners from Pyrex resisted chipping when knocked against a Dutch oven and even survived an 18-inch drop onto the counter.

▶ **See the Differences**
Video available free for 4 months at CooksIllustrated.com/oct14

TESTING MIXING BOWLS

We tested seven sets of mixing bowls, available in existing sets or from open stock; we singled out sizes closest to 1 to 1½ quarts, 2½ to 3 quarts, and 4 to 6 quarts. All bowls are dishwasher-safe and all glass bowls are microwave-safe. Prices shown were paid online. Sources for the winning metal and glass bowls appear on page 32.

PERFORMANCE We used the bowls to prepare vinaigrette, muffin and pancake batters, and bread dough and also in jury-rigged double boilers. Bowls rated highly if they were sturdy and minimized splashes and spills.

EASE OF USE We rated each set of bowls on how easy and comfortable they were to handle (including when holding them aloft and scraping the insides with a spatula), averaging the impressions of testers of varying heights, strengths, and skills.

DURABILITY We ran all sets through the dishwasher 15 times before inspecting them for clouding, chipping, and dents. We also bumped the bowls against Dutch ovens, dropped them from 18 inches onto the counter, and pushed them off the counter onto the floor, noting any cracks or breaks. We docked points from models that weren't safe for double boilers.

STAINLESS-STEEL BOWLS

HIGHLY RECOMMENDED

	CRITERIA		TESTERS' COMMENTS

VOLLRATH Economy Stainless Steel Mixing Bowls
Material: Stainless steel
Sold As: Open stock
Sizes Tested: 1½ qt ($2.90, model 47932); 3 qt ($4.50, model 47933); 5 qt ($6.90, model 47935)
Weights: 4⅝ oz (1½ qt); 6⅛ oz (3 qt); 8⅞ oz (5 qt)

Performance ★★★
Ease of Use ★★★
Durability ★★★

The broad, shallow shape of these inexpensive bowls put food within easy reach and allowed for wide turns of a spatula. These were also the lightest bowls in the lineup—the combined weight of all three that we tested was less than 1½ pounds—allowing us to comfortably lift, scrape, and pour.

RECOMMENDED

CUISINART Set of 3 Stainless Steel Mixing Bowls with Lids
Material: Stainless steel with plastic lids
Sold As: Three-bowl set ($29.99, model CTG-00-SMB)
Sizes Tested: 1½ qt; 3 qt; 5 qt
Weights: 9¾ oz (1½ qt); 13¾ oz (3 qt); 1 lb, 3⅝ oz (5 qt)

Performance ★★★
Ease of Use ★★
Durability ★★★

Though their relatively tall and narrow build made it a little challenging for shorter testers to access their contents, these bowls were lightweight and sported a generous rim—features that made them easy to grasp and hold while we scraped them clean.

NOT RECOMMENDED

OXO Good Grips Stainless Steel Mixing Bowl Set
Material: Stainless steel interior, white plastic exterior with nonskid Santoprene base
Sold As: Three-bowl set ($59.99, model 1107600V1)
Sizes Tested: 1½ qt; 3 qt; 5 qt
Weights: 11½ oz (1½ qt); 1 lb, 3 oz (3 qt); 1 lb, 10¾ oz (5 qt)

Performance ★
Ease of Use ★½
Durability ★★★

Apart from having wide rims, these bowls were not user-friendly—and certainly not worth the high price. Their small, Santoprene-coated bases caused them to spin and almost tip over as we mixed. Plus, the company does not recommend using them in a double boiler, lest the exterior plastic coating come in contact with the pot and overheat.

GLASS BOWLS

HIGHLY RECOMMENDED

PYREX Smart Essentials Mixing Bowl Set with Colored Lids
Material: Tempered glass with plastic lids
Sold As: Four-bowl set ($13.19, model 1086053)
Sizes Tested: 1 qt; 2½ qt; 4 qt
Weights: 1 lb, 3½ oz (1 qt); 2 lb, 4¼ oz (2½ qt); 3 lb, 7⅜ oz (4 qt)

Performance ★★★
Ease of Use ★★★
Durability ★★★

Even though these bowls were heavy, they never felt cumbersome to handle, thanks to their shallow, gently curved walls and easy-to-grip rims. Notably, they did not break when we dropped them. A bonus: Tight-fitting lids kept food well protected.

RECOMMENDED

ARC INTERNATIONAL Luminarc 10 Piece Stackable Bowl Set
Material: Tempered glass
Sold As: Ten-bowl set ($29.75, model E4371)
Sizes Tested: 1 qt (5½ in); 3 qt (9 in); 4½ qt (10¼ in)
Weights: 15⅛ oz (1 qt); 2 lb, 1⅛ oz (3 qt); 3 lb, ⅜ oz (4½ qt)

Performance ★★½
Ease of Use ★★
Durability ★★★

These shallow, wide bowls were easy to navigate with a whisk or a spatula. They were also one of the lighter glass sets, although they would have been easier to grip if they'd had rims instead of food-trapping collars. They survived the drop tests with minor scratches. A shopping note: Bowl sizes are listed by diameter, not volume.

NOT RECOMMENDED

DURALEX Lys Stackable Clear Bowls
Material: Tempered glass
Sold As: Open stock
Sizes Tested: 1½ qt ($6, model 2027AF06); 2½ qt ($8.25, model 2028AF06); 6 qt ($21, model 2030AF03)
Weights: 15½ oz (1½ qt); 2 lb, ⅝ oz (2½ qt); 4 lb, 5 oz (6 qt)

Performance ★
Ease of Use ★
Durability ★

We would have appreciated the capacity of the 6-quart bowl more if it wasn't unbearably heavy and hard to maneuver. The bowls' collars protruded so much that food stuck to them during mixing. Duralex made the only bowl to shatter during the drop tests.

ANCHOR HOCKING Mixing Bowls with Red Plastic Lids
Material: Tempered glass with plastic lids
Sold As: Four-bowl set ($21.99, model 918508K) or open stock
Sizes Tested: 1 qt; 2½ qt; 4 qt
Weights: 1 lb, 6⅜ oz (1 qt); 2 lb, 7⅝ oz (2½ qt); 3 lb, 9⅝ oz (4 qt)

Performance ★
Ease of Use ½
Durability ★½

As if the weight of these hefty bowls didn't make them challenging enough to handle, their shallow collars barely helped with gripping. Reaching over their high, practically vertical sides was a struggle. The base developed hairline cracks during the drop tests.

The Best Supermarket Prosciutto

A new surge of grab 'n' go packages means you no longer have to wait at the deli counter to have this cured pork sliced by hand. But does "convenience" prosciutto make the cut?

⋙ BY LISA McMANUS ⋘

Not too long ago, the only way to buy prosciutto was to find an Italian market and wait while someone sliced imported prosciutto di Parma or prosciutto di San Daniele by hand. What you get is sublime: rosy, supple slices of pork that are at once salty, tangy, and sweet and incredibly complex.

But since American and Canadian producers have gotten into the game, this cured pork is easier to come by. Many sell their prosciutto in supermarkets in grab 'n' go packages, making it as easy to buy as bologna.

Since it can be hard to find hand-sliced Italian prosciutto at smaller supermarkets, we were happy about the meat's wider availability. But we also couldn't help wondering if these presliced North American prosciutti retained the same depth of flavor and soft texture that we expect from Italian prosciutto that's sliced to order.

Price was also on our radar: Purchasing nine of these products confirmed that presliced non-Italian prosciutto is no bargain. The per-pound prices ranged from just over $19 to a whopping $58-and-change. The numbers are even more staggering when compared with the cost of prosciutto di Parma and prosciutto di San Daniele: about $23 and $20 per pound, respectively.

As for flavor, we tried them plain and also seared in chicken saltimbocca. The good news: We liked most of the samples. A few even boasted some of the complexity and silky texture that we expect from the Italian imports. The three we panned not only lacked porkiness but also carried a pronounced spice flavor that tasters compared to salami. To figure out what might separate the winners from the losers, we started by learning how prosciutto is made on its home turf.

It's in the Air

Italians have been curing ham for more than 2,000 years, most notably around Parma. (Why Parma? Go to CooksIllustrated.com/oct14 to learn more about the tradition of making prosciutto.) Producers in this city still make prosciutto under the eye of a consortium that sears Parma's crown icon onto every approved ham. Prosciutto di San Daniele, from the Friuli region, has its own consortium and ham leg–shaped icon. Both are designated "PDO"— Protected Designation of Origin—by the European Union, meaning they are exceptional regional products with exclusive rights to their names.

Producers in both regions use the same basic method: After slaughtering pigs, they salt and hang the legs for a minimum of 12 months. The meat's flavor concentrates with age, as prosciutto loses up to 30 percent of its weight in moisture during curing.

Age gave us our first clue as to the flavor differences among our non-Italian prosciuttos. Whereas the U.S. government requires that dry-cured ham from Italy be aged for at least 400 days (a little more than 13 months), it doesn't set a minimum age for ham dry-cured in North America. Two of the hams in our lineup were aged for less than 9 months—and tasters noticed, describing them as "not very complex."

Adding Up Additives

From there, we checked the ingredient labels for clues and homed in on a big difference between the three products that tanked and the ones we recommend. While our top six producers follow the Italians and use nothing but pork and salt, the makers of two of the losing products add nitrates—preservatives that turn the meat's color bright red and boost its savory flavor so that it tastes like "salami." Columbus and Dietz & Watson further muddy the flavor of their prosciutti by including unspecified "natural flavorings," sugar, sodium nitrite (another preservative and curing agent), sodium ascorbate (another preservative), and lactic acid starter culture.

That last ingredient turned out to be another important factor. Lactic acid–producing bacteria, or *lactobacillus*, launch the fermentation process that breaks down the meat's proteins into savory peptides and amino acids, which over time help develop the meat's famously complex depth. In a high-quality prosciutto, the bacteria is allowed to develop naturally over time. This produces a wide range of different bacteria that boost complexity. But some producers shortcut the process by adding lactic acid starter cultures containing a single strain of bacteria. Flavor suffers as a result, leading to the one-note tanginess we noticed in our least favorite brands.

Not surprisingly, sodium was another key factor in our likes and dislikes. Most of our favorite prosciutti (including our winner) were salty. What did surprise us was that the texture of the hams mattered at least as much as their flavor. The most telling examples were the two from La Quercia. Even though these prosciutti won raves for their "lush" pork flavor, they fell in the rankings. Why? These hams were among the driest and most thickly sliced—a fatal combination that made them taste "chewy" and "jerky-like." (Thicker-sliced hams with more moisture fared better.) Meanwhile, low-moisture hams that were sliced thinner delivered that ideal combination of complex flavor and supple texture.

Such was the case with our winner from Volpi (3 oz for $5.75/$30.67 per pound). Not only were these low-moisture slices among the thinnest of the lot, but this high-salt prosciutto with "porky complexity" was well worthy of any *salumi* plate and can be quickly picked up at any supermarket. Meanwhile, for convenience prosciutto that doesn't cost an arm and, um, a leg, our Best Buy from Del Duca (3 oz for $3.59/$19.15 per pound) boasts "supple" slices that taste "complex" and a bit less salty.

Presliced Prosciutto: A Cost-Benefit Analysis

When we compared our favorite presliced prosciutto from Volpi to imported prosciutti that we had sliced to order (we chose consortium-branded prosciutto di Parma and prosciutto di San Daniele, both aged 24 months) at a local Italian market, we found the presliced stuff plenty respectable, but noticeably less complex than the Italian hams. Still, besides convenience, there's another advantage to buying presliced prosciutto: You can purchase it well in advance—up to 120 days. That's because the packages are sealed without oxygen, and thus keep much longer than prosciutto that's sliced to order, which should be used within 24 hours. (Once a presliced package is opened, it, too, should be used quickly.)

The bigger trade-off with buying presliced is cost: All but one of the presliced products we bought cost more per pound than our favorite Italian prosciutto di Parma ($22.99 per pound). For complete tasting results, go to CooksIllustrated.com/oct14.

BETTER, CHEAPER, HARDER TO FIND
Prosciutto di Parma tastes best and costs less.

CONVENIENCE AT A PREMIUM
Pricey presliced prosciutto tastes less complex but lasts longer.

TASTING PRESLICED PROSCIUTTO

Twenty-one America's Test Kitchen staff members tasted nine North American–made prosciutti, sold presliced and packaged. We sampled them plain and in chicken saltimbocca to assess flavor, saltiness, texture, and overall appeal; we also measured the thickness of a slice from each package. An independent laboratory analyzed levels of sodium, fat, and moisture. Results were averaged and the products appear in order of preference.

RECOMMENDED

VOLPI Traditional Prosciutto

Price: 3 oz for $5.75 ($1.92 per oz/$30.67 per pound)
Made In: Missouri
Aged: 9 months
Ingredients: Pork, sea salt
Sodium: 771 mg per 1-oz serving **Fat:** 15.64%
Moisture: 45.91% **Slice Thickness:** 0.5 mm
Comments: "Tender" and "buttery" with a "very nice porky complexity" and a "salty punch" that came from having one of the highest sodium levels in the lineup, our top choice was "sweet, rich-tasting, and acorn-y." Tasters were wowed by its "silky," "ultrasupple" texture that was highlighted by the meat being sliced very thinly. Fried up in chicken saltimbocca, it continued to win fans: "The prosciutto really elevated the dish . . . with rich, meaty flavor."

DEL DUCA Prosciutto

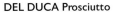

Price: 3 oz for $3.59 ($1.20 per oz/$19.15 per pound)
Made In: Rhode Island
Aged: Just over 1 year
Ingredients: Pork, salt
Sodium: 522 mg per 1-oz serving **Fat:** 12.58%
Moisture: 51.61% **Slice Thickness:** 0.9 mm
Comments: With a "nice porky sweetness" and "clean" but "intense" flavor, this prosciutto was one of the most thickly sliced in the lineup, but its ample moisture also gave it a "supple," "silky" texture. In saltimbocca, it was lauded for its "rich pork belly flavor." In sum: "Buttery, nutty, complex. This is good stuff."

CITTERIO All Natural Prosciutto

Price: 4 oz for $6.99 ($1.75 per oz/$27.96 per pound)
Made In: Pennsylvania
Aged: 9 to 11 months
Ingredients: Pork, sea salt
Sodium: 857 mg per 1-oz serving **Fat:** 9.90%
Moisture: 53.92% **Slice Thickness:** 0.58 mm
Comments: Tasters described this prosciutto as "so tender it practically disintegrates on the way to your mouth." Its "salty, sweet, oaky" flavor was deemed "classic" and "very pleasant." Citterio's thin slices became extra-crispy and "crunchy" when fried in chicken saltimbocca, and while its flavor contribution in that dish was considered "mild," it was good and salty.

BELLENTANI Prosciutto

Price: 3 oz for $6.49 ($2.16 per ounce/$34.61 per pound)
Made In: Pennsylvania
Aged: At least 200 days (6.6 months)
Ingredients: Ham, sea salt
Sodium: 363 mg per 1-oz serving **Fat:** 9.43%
Moisture: 55.51% **Slice Thickness:** 0.66 mm
Comments: These slices won fans for their "smooth," "moist," "soft, easy to eat" texture that helped tasters forgive their "supermild," "not very complex" taste, though a few deemed them "hammy" and "nutty-sweet." In saltimbocca, tasters noted "simple flavor," but the "crispy, chewy" slices provided "lovely texture."

LA QUERCIA Berkshire Prosciutto

Price: 4 oz for $8.99 plus shipping ($2.25 per ounce/$35.96 per pound)
Made In: Iowa
Aged: 9 to 12 months, depending on size of pig
Ingredients: Pork, sea salt
Sodium: 564 mg per 1-oz serving **Fat:** 14.42%
Moisture: 42.56% **Slice Thickness:** 0.82 mm
Comments: "Beautiful ruby color," raved tasters, giving this prosciutto "points for presentation." This color is a hallmark of Berkshire pork, which La Quercia makes from humanely raised Niman Ranch pigs. Tasters praised its "salty, gamy, nutty," "lush, full pork flavor" that boasted "real character." But its combination of low moisture and thick slices made it taste "chewy," or even "hard and stringy," which brought its score down in both tastings.

RECOMMENDED WITH RESERVATIONS

LA QUERCIA Prosciutto Americano

Price: 3 oz for $10.99 plus shipping ($3.66 per ounce/$58.61 per pound)
Made In: Iowa
Aged: 9 to 12 months
Ingredients: Pork, sea salt
Sodium: 384 mg per 1-oz serving **Fat:** 17.36%
Moisture: 44.12% **Slice Thickness:** 0.75 mm
Comments: There were near-unanimous raves for the complex flavor of this prosciutto, our former top pick: "so rich, with notes of toasty nuts, wine, and a lovely sweet finish," "meaty and quite sweet," and "an almost cheddar-y flavor." But as with its sibling, tasters found it "too dry—almost like a prosciutto jerky" as well as "tough" and "leathery"—whether plain or in saltimbocca. The company told us that it has tweaked its processing to produce a drier, less salty prosciutto since we tasted it last.

NOT RECOMMENDED

APPLEGATE Naturals Prosciutto

Price: 4 oz for $6.99 ($1.75 per oz/$27.96 per pound)
Made In: Canada
Aged: 6 to 9 months
Ingredients: Pork, salt, spice
Sodium: 729 mg per 1-oz serving **Fat:** 15.62%
Moisture: 49.09% **Slice Thickness:** 1 mm
Comments: "Chewy" was the oft-repeated description of this ham. While some tasters liked its "sweet porkiness," others found that it tasted "supermild" or "just OK," not to mention "a bit gummy," even "flabby." In saltimbocca, its inclusion of unspecified spice flavoring may have helped remind one taster of "Domino's pepperoni."

COLUMBUS Prosciutto

Price: 3 oz for $5.89 ($1.96 per oz/$31.41 per pound)
Made In: California
Aged: Company would not disclose
Ingredients: Pork ham, salt, and less than 2% of the following: sugar, sodium nitrate, natural flavorings, sodium ascorbate, sodium nitrite, lactic acid starter culture
Sodium: 358 mg per 1-oz serving **Fat:** 7.4%
Moisture: 58.49% **Slice Thickness:** 0.8 mm
Comments: This prosciutto's "tangy salami" flavor can likely be traced to its ingredient list. Its added lactic acid starter culture is known for producing a one-note tanginess not found in imported prosciutto. The other additives imparted flavor that tasted more like that of "hot dogs," "bologna," or "deli ham" than prosciutto. The texture was also too "lean," "wet," and "waxy."

DIETZ & WATSON Prosciutto

Price: 3 oz for $5.49 ($1.83 per oz/$29.28 per pound)
Made In: Pennsylvania
Aged: Up to 1 year
Ingredients: Pork ham, salt, contains less than 2% of sugar, sodium nitrate, natural flavorings, sodium ascorbate, sodium nitrite, lactic acid starter culture
Sodium: 397 mg per 1-oz serving **Fat:** 5.78%
Moisture: 58.49% **Slice Thickness:** 0.46 mm
Comments: The lactic acid starter culture, along with the inclusion of nitrates, doomed this prosciutto, too. One taster summed it up: "Too lean, and tastes funky and tangy like salami. [Tastes] nothing like the real thing!" High moisture and paper-thin slicing made its texture "wet" and "almost transparent," though it still crisped up well in saltimbocca.

DID YOU KNOW? All products reviewed by America's Test Kitchen, home of *Cook's Illustrated* and *Cook's Country* magazines, are independently chosen, researched, and reviewed by our editors. We buy products for testing at retail locations and do not accept unsolicited samples for testing. We do not accept or receive payment or consideration from product manufacturers or retailers. Manufacturers and retailers are not told in advance of publication which products we have recommended. We list suggested sources for recommended products as a convenience to our readers but do not endorse specific retailers.

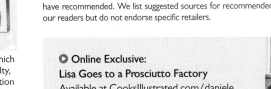

▶ **Online Exclusive:**
Lisa Goes to a Prosciutto Factory
Available at CooksIllustrated.com/daniele

SCIENCE Cooking Frozen Steaks

Conventional wisdom holds that frozen steaks should be thawed before cooking, but we wondered if steaks could be cooked straight from the freezer.

EXPERIMENT

We cut a strip loin into eight steaks, cut each steak in half crosswise, put the pieces in vacuum-sealed bags, and froze them. We then thawed half of each steak in the refrigerator overnight and kept the other half frozen. Using our preferred method, we seared both sets of steaks in a hot skillet for 90 seconds per side and then transferred them to a 275-degree oven until they reached 125 degrees, or medium-rare. To track moisture loss, we weighed each steak before and after cooking.

RESULTS

Not surprisingly, the frozen steaks took longer to finish cooking through in the oven (18 to 22 minutes versus 10 to 15 minutes for the thawed steaks). What was surprising was that the frozen steaks actually browned in the skillet just as well as, and in the same amount of time as, the thawed steaks. Furthermore, they had thinner bands of gray, overcooked meat directly under the crust than the thawed steaks had. We also found that these steaks lost on average 9 percent less moisture during cooking than the thawed steaks did. Sampling the steaks side by side, tasters unanimously preferred the cooked-from-frozen steaks to their thawed counterparts.

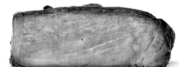

| **COOKED STRAIGHT FROM FREEZER** | **FROZEN, THAWED, THEN COOKED** |
| A frozen steak is less prone to overcook around its perimeter during searing. | A steak that goes into the pan warmer will overcook more around its perimeter. |

EXPLANATION

A fully frozen steak is extremely cold, which prevents overcooking while the surface reaches the very high temperatures necessary for browning reactions. As for the difference in moisture loss, we know that when meat is cooked to temperatures higher than 140 degrees, its muscle fibers begin to squeeze out a significant amount of moisture. As its slightly thicker gray band indicated, the steak that had been thawed had more overcooking around the edge, so it made sense that it also had greater moisture loss.

THE TAKEAWAY

While we prefer to start with steak that's never been frozen for the best texture, if we do have frozen steaks on hand, from now on we'll cook them straight from the freezer. Freeze steaks, uncovered, overnight on a baking sheet (this dries them out to prevent excess splattering during cooking), then wrap them tightly in plastic wrap, place in a zipper-lock bag, and return to freezer. To ensure that the steaks brown evenly, add oil to the skillet until it measures ⅛ inch deep. And because frozen steaks will splatter more during searing, use a large skillet. –D.S.

▶ THE SCIENCE OF COOKING: Searing Frozen Steak

Nothing beats a perfectly seared, juicy steak. Dan shows us all the best way to cook frozen steaks. Free for 4 months at CooksIllustrated.com/oct14.

Why Some Bread Doughs Are Folded

Some doughs are left alone during the rising stage, but for many rustic breads, including our Authentic Baguettes at Home (page 20), we interrupt the rising time by folding (or turning) the dough, gently folding the dough over itself several times as it rises. Like kneading, this process builds strength by bringing wayward sheets of gluten, the protein that gives bread structure once flour and water have been combined, into alignment. But folding is a more gentle process than kneading, and it works out large air pockets that can form as the dough rises, giving you a more even dough by the end of the rising time.

Recipes vary in the number of folds made and how many times the process is repeated, but the approach is generally the same. For our baguettes, we fold the dough instead of kneading, but other breads might knead the dough after mixing and fold fewer times. –A.J.

HOW TO FOLD

Using your fingertips, grab the edge of the dough and gently lift and fold it toward the middle. Turn the bowl and repeat, making folds as directed in recipe. If the dough is particularly sticky, use a lightly oiled bowl scraper or rubber spatula instead of your hands.

For Better Coconut Milk, Make Your Own

Homemade is almost always better than store-bought, and we wondered if that's the case with coconut milk made from scratch. We compared a homemade batch (see below for our recipe) with our favorite canned coconut milk, from Chaokoh, tasting it plain, as well as in a Thai chicken soup and a Thai curry.

The homemade coconut milk wasn't worth the effort in the curry, where there were competing flavors and textures, but tasters unanimously preferred the from-scratch milk when tasted both plain and in the soup. The homemade milk was thinner than the store-bought, though no one minded.

Without any stabilizers, our homemade version did tend to curdle if heated to a simmer, but we found a quick fix: Add a little baking soda, which makes the milk more alkaline and discourages milk proteins from clumping. –D.S.

HOMEMADE COCONUT MILK

MAKES 1¾ CUPS (THE EQUIVALENT OF ONE 13.5-OUNCE CAN COCONUT MILK)

Bring 1¾ cups water to near boiling (200 to 205 degrees) and add 1¾ cups unsweetened shredded coconut. Transfer to blender and process for 2 minutes. Transfer to fine-mesh strainer set over large measuring cup and press to extract as much liquid as possible; let cool for 15 minutes. Transfer shredded coconut to clean dish towel in large bowl. Gather sides of dish towel around coconut and squeeze remaining milk into measuring cup. Whisk ¼ teaspoon baking soda into milk. Discard shredded coconut and use milk as desired or refrigerate for up to 2 weeks. Recipe can be doubled.

The Parchment Test: Finding the Broiler Sweet Spot

As we learned with our Broiled Pork Tenderloin (page 7), the intense heat of the broiler can be great for cooking food through while also deeply browning the exterior. But the reflex to position the food as close to the broiler element as possible isn't necessarily—and in fact is rarely—the best approach. The key to success is finding the rack position that is the sweet spot (or, more accurately, the sweet zone), where even cooking and even browning are achieved simultaneously. This spot will vary from recipe to recipe, depending on the relative height and width of the food, and the desired level of doneness, but the general principle will always apply.

Finding the zone that produces even browning can be particularly tricky with electric broilers. Unlike gas broilers, where the flame heats a single ceramic plate at the top of the oven that then directs radiant heat to the food, electric broilers heat food via multiple rods that have gaps between them. This setup can create hot spots. Since radiant heat is a form of light wave, you can imagine that the rods of an electric broiler are spotlights whose waves diffuse and cover more area the farther from the source they go. To find the zone in your oven that delivers the most even browning, you can broil parchment at each position. Within any given oven there are likely two or three rack positions that will evenly brown the parchment (and your food); which one you should use will depend on the food you are cooking. –L.L.

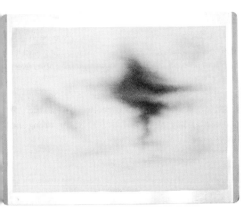 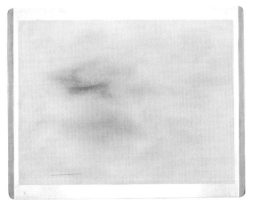 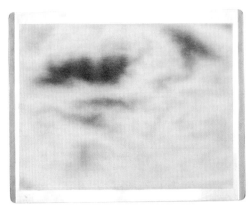

TOO CLOSE The radiant heat is too narrowly focused, so the browning on the parchment is concentrated in spots. By the time there is some browning, the areas directly under the rods will have burned.

SWEET SPOT The radiant heat waves broaden just enough to evenly cover the entire width of the parchment, delivering even browning.

TOO FAR The heat is so diffuse that it will take food so long to brown that it will likely overcook. And because of the longer time frame, reflected rays have a more noticeable impact, leading to uneven browning.

Giving Steaks a Garlic Boost

Mixing minced garlic into a steak rub might seem like a logical way to incorporate that flavor. But when the garlic in our Mexican-Style Grilled Steak (page 15) burned, we came up with an alternative approach: treating the steak like bruschetta. Rubbing a smashed garlic clove over the grilled meat's surface imparts a burst of flavor and aroma. Use the technique with any plain grilled or pan-seared steak. –D.S.

Advantages to Deep-Frying in a Wok

We've always used a Dutch oven for deep-frying, but we recently discovered that a wok can work just as well—and in some applications, such as French fries and doughnuts, can be more efficient.

In both cases, the shape of the wok—with its sloped sides and shallower depth (a 14-inch wok has a 3-inch wider diameter than a 7-quart Dutch oven)—made it easier to retrieve the food. And since lightweight foods like doughnuts float to the surface as they fry, the wok's broader surface allowed us to use about 30 percent less oil and still have sufficient space to do the job in the same number of batches. Note: Heavier foods, such as chicken, are not good candidates for frying in a wok, as they will sink and cluster in the vessel's narrow bottom. –A.J.

SAVE SOME OIL
When frying foods that float (such as doughnuts, beignets, and hush puppies), you'll need only about 4 cups of oil, compared with the 6 cups required for a Dutch oven.

Slashing Rustic Loaves

The slashes on rustic loaves, like our Authentic Baguettes at Home (page 20), aren't just about aesthetics. Slashes create weak spots in a loaf's surface, which allow the interior crumb to expand fully in the right direction. Without the slashes, the loaf will expand outward wherever it finds a random weak spot, resulting in an oddly shaped loaf and an uneven crumb.

Narrow baguettes and torpedo- or oval-shaped loaves should be scored along their length with long ½-inch-deep slashes made at a shallow, 30-degree angle (almost horizontal to the work surface). For even, smooth cuts, it's important to use swift, fluid motions. If the blade is held upright or the cut is too deep, it will close up during baking. Scoring of this type is most easily done with a curved-blade *lame* (our favorite is the Breadtopia Bread Lame, $9.50). This blade will produce broad, almond-shaped openings. Since the openings taper at the ends, the ends of each cut should overlap just slightly to ensure that the loaf expands evenly down its length. –A.J.

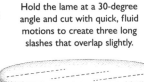

SWIFT SLASH
Hold the lame at a 30-degree angle and cut with quick, fluid motions to create three long slashes that overlap slightly.

Properly executed slashes bake up into almond-shaped openings with a flap on one side that curls into a crispy "ear" during baking.

EQUIPMENT CORNER

⇒ BY HANNAH CROWLEY, AMY GRAVES, LAUREN SAVOIE & KATE SHANNON ⇐

NEW Spiral Slicers

We were skeptical about spiral slicers, aka spiralizers, until we tried three models, priced from $21.99 to $35.96. Though one produced nothing but broken shreds, the other two, which held food on prongs against a blade while we turned a crank, quickly turned a variety of vegetables into strands and ribbons that could serve as more than garnishes. One model turned out gossamer-thin slices and spirals of beets and carrots, but it crushed a softer apple. Plus, foods had to be trimmed to no more than 3½ inches wide or long to fit in its small chamber. We were sold on the largest model we tested, which effortlessly produced long strands and wide ribbons from carrots and zucchini.

A NEW TWIST
The Paderno World Cuisine Tri-Blade Plastic Spiral Vegetable Slicer spooled out mounds of curly vegetable strands, lending appeal to steamed sides and fresh salads.

The Paderno World Cuisine Tri-Blade Plastic Spiral Vegetable Slicer ($35.96) transforms ordinary raw vegetables and firm fruit, adding texture and visual appeal to dishes with practically no pretrimming or waste. –A.G.

UPDATE Popover Pans

Unlike muffin tins, popover pans have an open design—typically six cups attached by metal wires—which allows heat to surround the batter. This is key to producing tall, airy rolls with a full cap that "pops" up high above each cup. Several years ago, we tested (and liked) the only popover pan widely available, the Chicago Metallic 6-Cup Popover Pan, Non-Stick ($13.21). Recently, we found three new pans (all nonstick). How did they stack up against our old favorite?

We compared how each model handled in and out of the oven, how well it released the baked goods, and, most important, how attractive the final results were. Cup shape and color proved essential. Tall cups with a gentle flare supported the batter as it expanded so that the tops of the rolls ballooned up properly. Two pans had optimally shaped cups, but our former favorite had a slight edge because of its darker finish, which conducted heat more efficiently, ensuring that batter cooked quickly to deliver the tallest, airiest popovers. Our former favorite, from Chicago Metallic, still turns out the most consistently impressive rolls. –H.C.

POP STAR
The Chicago Metallic 6-Cup Popover Pan, Non-Stick is still the best on the market.

UPDATE Home Seltzer Makers

Home seltzer makers transform tap water into sparkling, without the hassle and waste of store-bought bottles. A few years ago, we recommended the SodaStream Penguin Starter Kit ($199.95) as well as a cheaper model that has since been recalled. For a new, less expensive option, we tried two countertop machines, which carbonate with a few presses of a lever, and two handheld designs, which rely on a twist top to release the carbon dioxide into the bottle; they're priced from $49.99 to $129. All four models produced refreshing fizzy water, but we much preferred the countertop models. Their cartridges carbonate up to 60 liter-size bottles, and they made it easy to customize the level of carbonation. The handheld models were smaller and cost less up front but were fussier and more expensive over time since their cartridges can be used only once. Plus, they made it difficult to customize the level of carbonation. Our favorite countertop model, the SodaStream Source ($99.95), was easy to operate, and its display clearly indicated how much carbonation we'd added. Best of all, its empty cartridges can be exchanged for 50 percent off the price of new ones. We'll drink to that. –K.S.

FIZZY DRINKS
The SodaStream Source is an easy and affordable choice for making seltzer at home.

NEW Lid Pocket

If you've opened a slow cooker to stir or serve food, you've had this dilemma: Hold the lid and you're one-handed; put it down and not only does it take up a lot of space, but it leaves a puddle of condensation on the counter. The Lid Pocket ($9.99) aims to solve this problem. One end of the S-shaped piece of plastic hooks over the edge of the cooker and the other curves into a cupped slot in which the lid can sit upright, while collecting drips.

POCKET PERCH
It doesn't hold lids as securely as we'd like, but the Lid Pocket fit a range of slow cookers and solves a real problem.

We tried it with several sizes of slow cookers and found it fit all, but not as snugly as we'd like. That meant carelessly placed lids flopped too far back and fell off if the cooker was bumped hard. The Lid Pocket does provide a compact, convenient resting place for lids that frees up a hand and keeps the counter dry. (Lids fit back on the cooker without the need to remove the device.) We just wish it felt a bit more secure. –H.C.

NEW Burger Presses

We're always careful to shape patties gently since overworking the meat will turn it tough, but we wondered if a burger press could make the job easier and the results more consistent. We tried five models, priced from $6.90 to $22.17. Presses designed like a waffle iron or tortilla press—load ground meat and press down the top to produce the patty—squished the meat, and the resulting patties had to be peeled off. It was no surprise that these burgers cooked up tough.

BURGER BUST
Though it handled m◌ gently enough, the KitchenArt Adjust-A Burger was hard to cl◌ and ink from the plas rubbed off onto the m

The KitchenArt Adjust-A-Burger ($7.92) fared better. Made by the same manufacturer as our favorite adjustable measuring cup, its clear plastic barrel and plunger design works much the same way: Twist and lock the plunger to produce the desired-size burger, loosely pack meat into the barrel, and then push to eject the patty. This gentler handling produced tender burgers, but the plunger required significant force and meat clung to the crevices. Worse, ink markings on the plunger rubbed off onto our burgers. We'll pass on the press and just use our hands. –L.S.

For complete testing results, go to CooksIllustrated.com/oct14.

Sources:

PAGE 20: BREAD COUCHE
- San Francisco Baking Institute 18" Linen Canvas (Couche): $8, item #SWLINEN-P8C745, San Francisco Baking Institute (650-589-5784, sfbi.com).

PAGE 20: BREAD LAME
- Breadtopia Bread Lame: $9.50, Breadtopia (800-469-7989, breadtopia.com).

PAGE 27: MIXING BOWLS
- Vollrath Economy Stainless Steel Mixing Bowls: $2.90 for 1½ quart, item #47932; $4.50 for 3 quart, item #47933; $6.90 for 5 quart, item #47935, Webstaurantstore.com (717-392-7472, webstaurantstore.com).
- Pyrex Smart Essentials Mixing Bowl Set with Colored Lids: $13.19 for four-bowl set, item #B000FBUMLQ at Amazon (866-216-1072, amazon.com), or open stock 1 quart, 2½ quart and 4 quart at World Kitchen (800-999-3436, shopworldkitchen.com).

PAGE 32: SPIRAL SLICER
- Paderno World Cuisine Tri-Blade Plastic Spiral Vegetable Slicer: $35.96, item #A4982799, Amazon.

PAGE 32: POPOVER PAN
- Chicago Metallic 6-Cup Popover Pan, Non-Stick: $13.21, item #26562, Amazon.

PAGE 32: HOME SELTZER MAKER
- SodaStream Source Starter Kit: $99.95, item #1019511019, Amazon.

PAGE 32: LID POCKET
- Lid Pocket: $9.99, item #LP BLK, Lid Pocket (888-667-3988, lidpocket.com).

INDEX

September & October 2014

▶ RECIPE VIDEOS
Want to see how to make any of the
recipes in this issue? There's a video for that.

▶ MORE VIDEOS
Science of Cooking: Searing Frozen Steak
Testing Mixing Bowls

*Recipes, reviews, and videos available free for 4
months at* **CooksIllustrated.com/oct14**

▶ BEHIND THE SCENES
Andrew's Trip to Paris
CooksIllustrated.com/parisbaguette
Lisa Goes to a Prosciutto Factory
CooksIllustrated.com/daniele

FOLLOW US ON SOCIAL MEDIA
facebook.com/CooksIllustrated
twitter.com/TestKitchen
pinterest.com/TestKitchen
google.com/+AmericasTestKitchen
instagram.com/TestKitchen
youtube.com/AmericasTestKitchen

Authentic Baguettes at Home, 20

Roasted Pears with Apricots and Pistachios, 18

Rice and Lentils with Crispy Onions, 9

Tagliatelle with Artichokes and Olive Oil, 11

Mahogany Chicken Thighs, 22

Grilled Fish Tacos, 13

Perfect Latin Flan, 25

Sautéed Corn with Bacon and Leeks, 23

Mexican-Style Grilled Steak (Carne Asada), 15

Broiled Pork Tenderloin, 7

PHOTOGRAPHY: CARL TREMBLAY, KELLER + KELLER; STYLING: MARIE PIRAINO

Shingo

Fragrant

20th Century

Starkrimson

Yali

Concorde

Warren

SPECIALTY
PEARS

NUMBER 131   NOVEMBER & DECEMBER 2014

COOK'S
ILLUSTRATED

New Holiday Roast
Top Sirloin Goes Upscale

French Apple Tart
Easy Pat-in-Pan Crust

The Ultimate
Roast Turkey
How to Cook Heritage Birds

Crispy Salt and
Pepper Shrimp

Holiday Baking 911
Test Kitchen Rescues

Carbon-Steel Knives
Should You Buy One?

Best Chocolate
Crinkle Cookies

Crispy Pork Belly at Home
Pasta with Greens and Beans
All-New Hot Chocolate Mix

CooksIllustrated.com
$6.95 U.S. & CANADA

CONTENTS
November & December 2014

COOK'S ILLUSTRATED

Founder and Editor — Christopher Kimball
Editorial Director — Jack Bishop
Editorial Director, Magazines — John Willoughby
Executive Editor — Amanda Agee
Test Kitchen Director — Erin McMurrer
Managing Editor — Rebecca Hays
Executive Food Editor — Keith Dresser
Senior Editors — Hannah Crowley
Andrea Geary
Lisa McManus
Dan Souza
Senior Editors, Features — Elizabeth Bomze
Louise Emerick
Senior Copy Editor — Megan Ginsberg
Copy Editor — Krista Magnuson
Associate Editors — Shannon Friedmann Hatch
Andrew Janjigian
Chris O'Connor
Test Cooks — Daniel Cellucci
Lan Lam
Assistant Editors — Lauren Savoie
Kate Shannon
Assistant Test Cook — Cecelia Jenkins
Executive Assistant — Christine Gordon
Assistant Test Kitchen Director — Leah Rovner
Senior Kitchen Assistants — Michelle Blodget
Alexxa Grattan
Kitchen Assistants — Maria Elena Delgado
Ena Gudiel
Jason Roman
Executive Producer — Melissa Baldino
Co-Executive Producer — Stephanie Stender
Associate Producer — Kaitlin Hammond
Contributing Editor — Dawn Yanagihara
Science Editor — Guy Crosby, PhD

Managing Editor, Web — Christine Liu
Associate Editors, Web — Jill Fisher
Roger Metcalf
Assistant Editor, Web — Charlotte Wilder
Senior Video Editor — Nick Dakoulas
Product Manager, Cooking School — Anne Bartholomew
Senior Editor, Cooking School — Mari Levine

Design Director — Amy Klee
Photography Director — Julie Cote
Art Director — Susan Levin
Associate Art Director — Lindsey Timko
Art Director, Marketing — Jennifer Cox
Associate Art Director, Marketing — Melanie Gryboski
Staff Photographer — Daniel J. van Ackere
Associate Art Director, Photography — Steve Klise

Vice President, Marketing — David Mack
Circulation Director — Doug Wicinski
Circulation & Fulfillment Manager — Carrie Fethe
Partnership Marketing Manager — Pamela Putprush
Marketing Assistant — Marina Tomao

Chief Operating Officer — Rob Ristagno
VP, Digital Products — Fran Middleton
Production Director — Guy Rochford
Workflow & Digital Asset Manager — Andrew Mannone
Production & Imaging Specialists — Heather Dube
Dennis Noble
Lauren Robbins
Director, Project Management — Alice Carpenter
Development Manager — Mike Serio
Senior Controller — Theresa Peterson
Customer Loyalty & Support Manager — Amy Bootier
Customer Loyalty & Support Reps — Rebecca Kowalski
Andrew Straaberg Finfrock
Juliet Tierney

VP, New Business Development — Michael Burton
Client Services Manager — Kate Zebrowski

Director, Retail Book Program — Beth Ineson
Retail Sales & Marketing Director — Emily Logan
Human Resources Director — Adele Shapiro
Publicity — Deborah Broide

PRINTED IN THE USA

MEXICAN PANTRY BLACK BEANS and PINTO BEANS are often cooked with peppery EPAZOTE. Cooked HOMINY can be ground into masa and pressed into corn tortillas. Hominy is also found in posole, a hearty pork stew. CHIPOTLES IN ADOBO sauce are sold canned; these smoked jalapeño chiles pack plenty of heat. ACHIOTE PASTE—ground annatto seed sometimes seasoned with oregano, cloves, and cumin—adds earthiness to dishes. PILONCILLO is raw sugar pressed into pyramids as small as pencil erasers or as large as ice cream cones. Disks of MEXICAN CHOCOLATE have a sandy texture and never completely dissolve in hot beverages or mole sauce. CANELA quills are softer than cinnamon sticks sold in the United States and subtler in taste. Steeping DRIED JAMAICA FLOWERS, a member of the hibiscus family, releases their cranberry-like flavor. Sugar and lime juice are often added to make a refreshing drink. COVER (Pomegranates): Robert Papp; BACK COVER (Mexican Pantry): John Burgoyne

WHAT I AM SUPPOSED TO KNOW

I am frequently told that I am "supposed to know" how to act my age, close the refrigerator door, and keep my mouth shut. I am also supposed to know enough to plan ahead, chew slowly, and swallow my pride.

Instead, I know that rabbits run in circles (unless they hole up) and that if you see a deer at the edge of a field at twilight, it will probably be nearby in the morning. I know that you should mow a field just before the goldenrod goes to seed (but not before), that the best way to tell sugar maple from red is to examine the bark, and that divining for water actually works. I don't know for sure that dried nettles help with hay fever or that planting on a full moon speeds up germination, but I have been told they do. I don't believe that the planets rule our lives or that life is fair, but I do believe that what goes around comes around.

I am supposed to know the names of actors, divas, rap stars, and other celebrities, but all I remember is the name of the dog at Sherman's Country Store. I am told that I should keep up with politics but am more interested in why my daughter Caroline found three nuns in our raspberry patch and why our town keeps spending so much money on paving roads.

I am told that I am supposed to know myself.

I know that if an old car won't restart on a hot day, check the spark plug wires and the coil even though everyone tells you it's vapor lock. If your tractor won't turn over, clean the battery cables and posts. And if you have steam heat in your house, don't forget to drain off some of the water every week by the furnace; it gets sludgy.

But I don't know why there is no unified theory of the universe. I don't know what the president is told on his first day in office. I don't know why World War I became a world war. Most of all, I don't know why people drink kombucha and wear yoga clothes to the mall.

I also don't know why people look like their dogs.

I once knew that the best thing to do after making homemade peach ice cream was to eat the whole bucket. I also used to know that fruit cobbler is a main course when the berries are ripe and that eating a half-dozen ears of sweet corn in one sitting is perfectly respectable in mid-August. I also knew that the comic book ads for X-ray glasses were just a gimmick, but I still believed.

Yet I haven't forgotten that twilight was a time of childhood magic, as the branches of the Dutch elm outside my bedroom window rustled in the gloaming. Or that a swarm of honeybees moves across a

Christopher Kimball

hayfield in a swirling column. Or that to plunge into an ice-cold pond after haying with sunburned neck and hayseed eyes is a form of baptism. Or that watching crows land on the branches of a dead oak at the edge of our pasture was once a pastime. Or that there really is a Santa Claus; I saw his sleigh in the lower meadow one moonlit Christmas Eve.

When I am told something I don't know—that a coon can drown a dog, for example—then I know I still have a lot to learn. I still don't know who put the bomp in the bomp, bomp, bomp or whom to call for advice now that my parents are long gone. Some things I always have to look up: the real name of the Wicked Witch of the West (Elphaba), our assassinated presidents (Lincoln, Garfield, McKinley, and Kennedy), and the difference between a yawl and a ketch. And some things I don't care about, whether it is the Kardashians or what really happened at Area 51: If it really was the site of an alien crash landing, that's fine with me. I'm glad they landed in Nevada, not Vermont.

The problem is that I know too much for my own good. But that sounds a lot like an excuse.

As I said, I'm supposed to know better.

FOR INQUIRIES, ORDERS, OR MORE INFORMATION

CooksIllustrated.com
At CooksIllustrated.com, you can order books and subscriptions, sign up for our free e-newsletter, or renew your magazine subscription. Join the website and gain access to 22 years of *Cook's Illustrated* recipes, equipment tests, and ingredient tastings, as well as companion videos for every recipe in this issue.

COOKBOOKS
We sell more than 50 cookbooks by the editors of *Cook's Illustrated*, including *The Cook's Illustrated Cookbook* and *The Science of Good Cooking*. To order, visit our bookstore at CooksIllustrated.com/bookstore.

COOK'S ILLUSTRATED MAGAZINE
Cook's Illustrated magazine (ISSN 1068-2821), number 131, is published bimonthly by Boston Common Press Limited Partnership, 17 Station St., Brookline, MA 02445. Copyright 2014 Boston Common Press Limited Partnership. Periodicals postage paid at Boston, MA, and additional mailing offices, USPS #012487. Publications Mail Agreement No. 40020778. Return undeliverable Canadian addresses to P.O. Box 875, Station A, Windsor, ON N9A 6P2. POSTMASTER: Send address changes to *Cook's Illustrated*, P.O. Box 6018, Harlan, IA 51593-1518. For subscription and gift subscription orders, subscription inquiries, or change of address notices, visit AmericasTestKitchen.com/support, call 800-526-8442 in the U.S. or 515-248-7684 from outside the U.S., or write to us at *Cook's Illustrated*, P.O. 6018, Harlan, IA 51593-1518.

FOR LIST RENTAL INFORMATION Contact Specialists Marketing Services, Inc., 777 Terrace Ave., 4th Floor, Hasbrouck Heights, NJ 07604; phone: 201-865-5800.
EDITORIAL OFFICE 17 Station St., Brookline, MA 02445; 617-232-1000; fax: 617-232-1572. For subscription inquiries, visit AmericasTestKitchen.com/support or call 800-526-8442.

BY ANDREA GEARY, LAN LAM, SARAH MULLINS & DAN SOUZA

Removing Pomegranate Seeds

What's the best way to remove the seeds from a pomegranate?

CHERYL WILLIS
RICHMOND, VA.

While many sources recommend removing the seeds from a pomegranate by placing half of the fruit cut side down on a work surface and hitting the end with a rolling pin or wooden spoon, we've found an even better way that removes every seed without any mess.

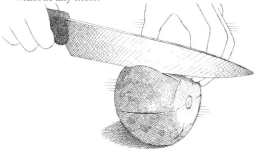

1. Cut off the bump on the blossom end and score the outside of the fruit from pole to pole into six sections.

2. Insert your thumbs into the blossom end and pull the fruit apart in sections.

3. Submerge the sections in a bowl of cold water and then bend the rind backward to release the seeds. Pull out any stragglers and let the seeds sink to the bottom of the bowl. Discard the rind and any bits of membrane that float to the surface and drain the seeds in a colander. The seeds can be refrigerated in an airtight container for up to five days. –A.G.

Sweet or Dry Marsala?

I have a recipe that calls for Marsala but doesn't specify sweet or dry. Which should I use?

GRACE CHOI
SEATTLE, WASH.

Marsala, an Italian fortified wine that originates from the port city of the same name, can be found in both sweet and dry styles, a classification based primarily on the residual sugar content of the wine. Aside from the obvious—sweet Marsala tasted sweeter than dry—tasters noted that the dry samples featured raisin and prune flavors balanced by sharp acidity and savory, nutty notes. The sweet Marsalas possessed those same dried fruit flavors but also featured hints of molasses and caramel, and they had a more syrupy consistency. Most tasters found sweet Marsala more palatable when sampled straight.

However, when we tried both styles in recipes for chicken Marsala, mushroom stuffing, and zabaglione, tasters preferred the dry style in all instances. Though both were acceptable, tasters found that dry Marsala offered more depth of flavor, while sweet Marsala added sweetness and some flavor but wasn't as complex.

The takeaway? For both savory and sweet applications, we suggest using dry Marsala if a recipe doesn't specify a style. –L.L.

Dust for a More Crisp Pie Crust?

I read in a baking book that sprinkling a layer of flour and sugar in a pie shell before adding the filling will prevent a soggy crust. Does it work?

ALICE PETERSON
SAGINAW, MICH.

We've read about this technique, most recently in the *Hoosier Mama Book of Pie* by Paula Haney of Chicago's eponymous pie shop. A layer of "crust dust," a mixture of equal parts granulated sugar and flour, is meant to form a barrier that prevents liquid in the filling from turning the crust soggy.

When we tried it with three of our own pie recipes (apple, blueberry, and pumpkin) and compared the results with a set made without the dusting, we found that the dust didn't make much of a difference—the crusts were equally crisp. This is because we take extra measures to remove excess moisture from fillings. However, when we tried crust dust with a coworker's family recipe, which didn't take any preventative steps to remove moisture, most tasters noticed an improvement in the crust's crispness, albeit a small one.

The bottom line: If you have a recipe that doesn't call for removing excess liquid, sprinkling the crust with a couple of tablespoons of crust dust before filling is a good precautionary measure. –A.G.

Naturally Sweet

Is natural cane sugar interchangeable with regular granulated sugar?

JOHN MOSS
ORLANDO, FLA.

Natural cane sugar is made from sugar cane, while conventional white granulated sugar may be made from either cane or sugar beets. Since both plants produce molecules of sucrose that are identical, this is not a significant distinction. Also, the "natural" tag is a bit of an oversell: Natural cane sugar is only slightly less processed than regular white sugar. That said, it retains a bit of a blond color, and some tasters found that it had slightly more depth of flavor compared with regular granulated sugar when they tasted both plain.

With such slight differences in the sugars, we weren't surprised that sugar cookies made with the natural sugar had a slightly deeper color but otherwise were no different from the batch made with conventional white sugar.

We had more of an issue with simple syrup. The natural cane sugar produced a liquid with a caramel tint rather than the traditional colorless syrup. While a brown syrup would be fine in iced tea, it might discolor lemonade or a pale cocktail. We also found natural sugar to be problematic in caramel sauce. The syrup in the pan was brown from the start, which made it hard to detect color changes. Furthermore, the impurities in the natural cane sugar caused foaming (to varying degrees depending on brand), in one case making it impossible to get an accurate temperature reading.

The takeaway? Natural cane sugar works in some—but not all—applications, particularly those in which its darker color is an issue. –A.G.

A More Effective Fridge Deodorizer

You've said that baking soda isn't great for deodorizing the refrigerator. Is there another option?

KRIS WIDICAN
WEST NEWTON, MASS.

We've found that baking soda is only moderately effective as an odor eliminator. It works by changing the structure of acidic molecules that it comes in contact with—which may make some stinky acidic molecules smell better but might simply make them smell different (but still bad). Furthermore, while most foods are at least slightly acidic, not all are. A little research informed us that so-called activated charcoal (a substance used in air filters, to clean the water in fish tanks, and to purify water) might be more effective. Because it is pure carbon, which absorbs almost all organic molecules, activated charcoal should potentially absorb—and thus remove from the air—almost all smelly molecules that it encounters. And because it's very porous, it has lots of surface area for smells to "stick" to.

To evaluate its effectiveness, we placed 1 cup of baking soda in an open container in one mini refrigerator and 1 cup of activated charcoal pellets in an identical fridge. During the course of a month, we placed various smelly items, including chopped onions, kimchi, Parmesan, and canned tuna, in each refrigerator and asked testers to evaluate how they compared. Throughout the testing, they agreed that the refrigerator with activated charcoal was significantly less stinky than the refrigerator with baking soda.

Activated charcoal can be found at pet and aquarium supply stores. For a full-size refrigerator, we recommend using 2 cups placed in an open container in the back of the fridge near an air vent. How often the charcoal needs to be replaced will vary depending on refrigerator size and contents, but based on our results, we predict that it will last at least one month and possibly much longer. –L.L.

Halloumi Cheese
Our supermarket recently started carrying halloumi cheese. What's the best way to use it?

ASHLEY HOWLE
DECATUR, GA.

➤ Halloumi is a firm brined cheese originally from Cyprus that's popular throughout the eastern Mediterranean. Made from cow's, sheep's, or goat's milk or even a combination of the three, it has a semifirm, springy texture that some of our tasters described as "squeaky" when sampled as is. Its dairy flavor is mild, but it is typically quite salty.

Because of how it's made, halloumi has a very strong protein network, which means that when it's heated, it softens but doesn't melt. Many recipes

TRY IT PAN-FRIED
Chunks of seared halloumi work well in a meze spread.

take advantage of this quality by calling for pan-frying or grilling cubes or slabs of the cheese, which gives it a crispy, flavorful exterior to contrast with the creamy interior. We tried both approaches. While grilling produced acceptable results, we found that the exterior dried out a bit more, and because this cheese is best eaten right off the heat, we preferred the easier approach of pan searing. Cook halloumi in a nonstick skillet with a small amount of oil over medium heat until it is well browned. Serve the cheese warm, drizzled with olive oil for an appetizer, or add it to grain or vegetable salads. –L.L.

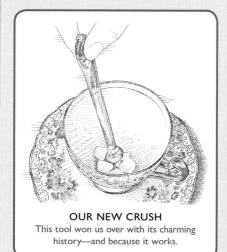
Making Quick Breads Without Eggs
I'm allergic to eggs, but I love muffins. Can you suggest an egg replacement that would work in muffin and quick bread recipes?

JESSICA FOX-WILSON
BELOIT, WIS.

➤ We tested five commonly suggested egg replacements in a handful of quick bread recipes: silken tofu; baking powder mixed with milk and distilled white vinegar; plain whole yogurt mixed with vegetable oil; ground chia seeds soaked in water; and a commercial egg-free alternative, Ener-G Egg Replacer (a powdered mix of starches, gums, and leaveners) mixed with water per the manufacturer's instructions.

In recipes calling for one or two eggs, the commercial egg replacer was the most successful, delivering muffins comparable to those made with real eggs. The tofu worked almost as well, and only a few tasters noticed a subtle soy flavor in the muffins. The yogurt-oil mixture placed third, producing somewhat dense muffins. These results made sense: The water in eggs provides moisture, while their protein provides structure. The tofu and the yogurt mixture are both similar to eggs in their water and protein composition. The other two substitutions failed outright.

None of the substitutes worked in our muffin recipe that calls for three eggs—they all came out dense and squat. Here's why: These recipes rely more heavily on eggs than on chemical leaveners for lift, and none of the egg replacers had enough boosting power.

In sum: If you want to make muffins or quick breads without eggs, stick to recipes that require one or two eggs and use Ener-G Egg Replacer or ¼ cup of silken tofu per egg. In a pinch, 2 ounces of plain whole-milk or low-fat yogurt mixed with ½ teaspoon of vegetable oil will work reasonably well. –S.M.

Worth Their Salt?
I've seen salt-roasted root vegetables on a number of menus recently. Is this worth doing at home?

OLIVER TOOTHAKER
MADRAS, ORE.

➤ Roasted in a hot oven, dense root vegetables can cook unevenly and dry out on the exterior before their interiors are tender. Salt-roasting—burying the vegetables in salt—is touted for being a more gentle approach due to the salt's insulating effect. It also has presentation appeal since the salt becomes a hardened crust that can be cracked open at the table. Still, we were skeptical. In the past, we've found that wrapping beets in foil for roasting does a pretty good job of gently cooking them evenly. The foil doesn't insulate as well as salt, but we wondered if we could get comparable results if we used a lower oven temperature and cooked foil-wrapped beets longer.

To find out, we compared beets buried in salt in a saucepan and roasted at 400 degrees to beets seasoned with salt, wrapped in foil, and roasted at 325 degrees. Both sets of beets were tender in 2 hours. Very few tasters found any differences between the two batches, including level of saltiness (which made sense since we roast beets skin on and peel them once cooked, which removes most of the seasoning).

Our takeaway? Salt-roasting may make for a showy tableside presentation, but it doesn't deliver a flavor or texture improvement over roasting beets gently in foil. Plus, checking for doneness is tricky, cleanup is messy, and it uses a copious amount of salt. –D.S.

Quick Tips

⇒ COMPILED BY SHANNON FRIEDMANN HATCH ⇐

Streamlining Dried Rice Noodle Prep

Rather than using a bowl and strainer to soak and drain dried rice noodles, Emily Fisher of Los Angeles, Calif., tackles both tasks in her salad spinner.

1. Place the dried noodles in the salad spinner basket, pour boiling water over to cover, and soak the noodles according to the recipe.

2. Lift the basket to drain the noodles.

Foiling Sticky Dough During Cleanup

The sticky, wet dough that clings to bowls after making bread also clings to sponges and collects in brush bristles during cleanup. Sian Roberts of Jersey City, N.J., scrubs the vessels with a crumpled sheet of aluminum foil before washing with soap and water. After removing the dough, the foil can be tossed in the trash.

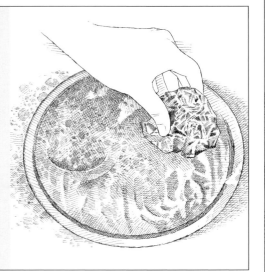

Dutch Oven Repair

When Pat McMurray of Indianapolis, Ind., noticed that the knob of her inexpensive Dutch oven was damaged, she found a replacement at the hardware store: a metal drawer knob with a short screw. It screws on easily and withstands the heat.

Keeping a Record of Rises

To keep track of which step he's on when making a bread recipe that calls for several folds and rises, William Lundy of Belleville, Ontario, jots notes with a marker on the plastic wrap covering the bowl of rising dough.

Alternative Drying Rack

When Elizabeth Silver of Scarsdale, N.Y., throws large dinner parties and doesn't have enough dish-rack space to dry numerous wineglasses, she turns to her cooling rack. Its large, flat surface holds at least a half-dozen glasses and allows air to flow freely around the glasses so they dry quickly and spot-free.

Bracelets That Do Double Duty

Denise Freitas of Leesburg, Ga., found a practical kitchen use for the many silicone bracelets she's collected over the years: slipping them around baking mats, flexible cutting boards, and tongs to keep them neatly rolled up for more efficient storage.

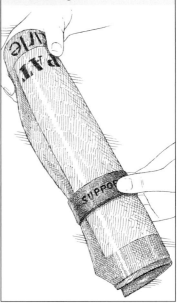

A Measuring Stick for Water

Dina MacDonald of Arcata, Calif., who often makes our Soft-Cooked Eggs (January/February 2013), devised a quick way to measure the ½ inch of water for the saucepan: Mark the level on a chopstick, hold it upright in the pan, and fill the water to the marked line.

Using a Pounder for Pressing

To evenly press dough into his tart pan, Philip Gordon of Mashpee, Mass., uses his meat pounder. Its flat, curved shape aligns nicely with the sides of the round vessel. (Just be sure to press lightly to avoid thinning out the dough too much.)

Sprinkling Streusel Neatly

No matter how carefully Marilyn Whitlock of Austin, Texas, tries to sprinkle streusel onto a batch of muffins, she ends up with a mess all over her muffin tin and countertop. To contain the crumbs, she cuts out the bottom of an empty 6-ounce yogurt container to create a funnel. The opening is about the same size as the muffin cup and the topping falls perfectly into place.

Making More Counter Space

Jan Wise of Des Moines, Iowa, has limited counter space, which is problematic when she's portioning cookie dough onto multiple baking sheets. She creates extra room by pulling out a cabinet drawer and resting a sheet on top.

Neater Nut Chopping

Chopping nuts with a chef's knife causes them to slip and scatter across the cutting board, so Louise Mermod of San Rafael, Calif., uses a serrated bread knife instead. Its scalloped edge grabs and keeps the nuts in place better than a straight edge does. (Note: A bread knife doesn't rock like a chef's blade, but it's still faster to use one than to chase nuts around the cutting board.)

Whipped Cream on the Go

When Alyssa Langer of Boston, Mass., brings a pie to someone's house for dessert, she likes to serve it with fresh whipped cream. Since this accompaniment doesn't travel well, she came up with an efficient way to transport cream and "whip" it all in one container.

1. Place ½ cup of heavy cream and 1½ teaspoons of sugar in a pint jar and secure the lid. Keep cool until ready to use.

2. Shake the jar until the contents double in volume, about 4 minutes. Serve immediately. (The volume will be a bit less than cream that's been whipped in a stand mixer.)

How to Cook Heritage Turkey

Heritage breeds promise juicier, more flavorful meat than do ordinary supermarket birds.
But to deliver on that promise, you have to devise a different cooking method.

⇒ BY DAN SOUZA ⇐

During the past few holiday seasons, we've become increasingly curious about heritage turkey. In 1997, these turkeys were nearly extinct in the United States, with only 1,335 breeding birds in existence. But a concerted effort by breeders and farmers brought them back: A 2006 census reported more than 10,000 breeding birds. The revival is understandable: As with heirloom produce (think tomatoes), heritage turkeys come from special stock that promises to be superior to its supermarket counterpart. These old-breed turkeys spend lots of time outdoors, eat a varied diet, and grow slowly. This purportedly translates to richly flavored meat.

I ordered a half-dozen heritage turkeys from farms across the country, each one boasting a slightly different pedigree. They did all have one thing in common: None looked like the familiar supermarket bird. They had notably longer legs and smaller breasts—so success using a standard cooking method seemed unlikely. Still, it was the logical place to start, so I forged ahead with a typical approach that started the bird at high heat and ended with low heat.

I cooked the birds breast side down at 400 degrees for 45 minutes and then breast side up at 325 degrees until the breast hit 165 degrees. Two things became clear. First, the flavor of the breast meat on these turkeys was richer than any white meat I'd ever tasted. And second, I had no idea how to cook these birds: The dark meat on some of them was so underdone that I had to separate the leg quarters and return them to the oven. Once fully cooked, however, the dark meat also proved exceptional—tender as well as deeply flavored.

Half-Baked

What I'd run into with that first round of testing was an extreme version of a problem we see with all poultry: Light and dark meat cook at different

After slow-roasting the bird, we let it rest for 30 to 60 minutes before giving it a final blast in a 500-degree oven to help its skin crisp and brown.

rates. I needed a technique that could deal with the unique build of these birds to deliver just-cooked white meat and well-done dark meat. I had an idea about how to do it.

One of the best ways to tenderize tough cuts of meat and poultry is a braise. A braising liquid quickly transfers heat to the meat because it is densely packed with molecules (which is where the heat is stored). The air in a hot oven, on the other hand, has comparatively few molecules and thus transfers heat more slowly. The upshot is that braising more efficiently breaks tough collagen down into lubricating gelatin. I wondered if I could take advantage of the disparity in speed between braising and roasting by submerging the back, legs, and wings of the turkey in broth while keeping the breast elevated (so that it would roast instead of braise). This seemed like a smart idea, until all of a sudden it didn't. There I was, standing in the kitchen in front of a roasting pan filled almost to the brim with a sea of chicken broth. Emerging like islands from the deep were the knee of each leg and only the top half of the breast. My plan had been

foiled by heritage turkey anatomy—because the breast was so shallow and the legs so long, there was no way to submerge the dark meat without covering much of the white in the process.

Or was there? I grabbed my knife and made slits between the breast and thigh on both sides of the turkey, allowing the legs to lie flatter so that I could add less liquid. My hope was that after braising I could truss the legs back into place and then roast the bird to finish cooking the breast and brown the skin. No dice. As the dark meat braised, the leg muscles contracted and hoisted the legs out of the liquid like surfacing submarines.

Out with the Old

I reworked my plan of attack. Breaking down the turkey would allow me to customize cooking the dark and white meat for the best possible results, but I wanted to keep it simple. I grabbed my knife and cut off both leg quarters. (At this point I also snapped off the backbone to create an attractive breast roast and because I could use the backbone to make the gravy.)

One immediate benefit of this quick butchering was ease of seasoning. Rubbing salt on the skin of a bird makes the skin salty, but if you want seasoned meat, you have to get under the skin and rub salt directly onto the breast and legs. My broken-down bird provided ample routes of entry for this endeavor. After seasoning the turkey parts, I let them rest overnight in the refrigerator, a step that leads to better-seasoned, more-tender meat, as well as drier skin that readily crisps and browns.

It was time to roast, and here I had a big decision to make. Should I start with high heat to brown the skin and then lower the oven to finish cooking gently, or do the reverse and go low to high? High to low turned out to be too fussy: After the browning stage, the breast, which had started cooking, had to be set aside while the dark meat got its jump start and then go back in. Low to high—starting the dark meat, adding the breast partway through, and then browning—was much more streamlined. I also noticed that the skin browned better and stayed more crisp when I saved the high-heat stage for the end.

I set the breast aside and placed the leg quarters,

▶ See What They Look Like
Video available free for 4 months
at CooksIllustrated.com/dec14

OLD-FASHIONED BIRD, NEW PREPPING AND COOKING METHOD

Since a heritage turkey's well-exercised legs require more time in the oven and its shallow breast is prone to overcooking, we separate the white and dark meat so that we can customize the cooking. We give the dark meat a head start before adding the breast, and we flip the meat partway through to ensure even cooking.

1. Using sharp knife, slice through skin between breast and thigh down to joint on both sides.

2. Pull leg quarter back to expose joint, then cut through hip joint and skin. Repeat on other side.

3. Slice through membrane connecting breast to backbone. Bend backbone, breaking where it meets rib cage. Use knife to remove.

4. Cook leg quarters skin side down in 250-degree oven until meat registers 140 degrees.

5. Turn leg quarters skin side up. Place breast on rack, skin side down, and cook for 1 hour.

6. Turn breast skin side up and cook until it registers 155 degrees and thighs register 175 degrees.

---

skin side down, in a 250-degree oven for their head start. I tested a flock of turkeys to determine the ideal temperature for the legs to reach before I flipped them over and added the breast: 140 degrees. This may seem like a big head start, given that the legs needed to reach only 175 degrees, but it actually made good sense. At 140 degrees collagen is just beginning to break down, and from there it happens very, very slowly so the temperature rises only gradually. By the time the breast was cooked through, the legs had finally fully tenderized. To ensure that the breast cooked evenly, I started it skin side down and then flipped it for the final couple of hours of cooking. After pulling the parts from the oven, I let them rest to allow the juices to redistribute and the meat to cool a bit so it wouldn't overcook during a final blast at 500 degrees. This setup did the trick. Just 10 minutes in the hot oven turned the skin brown, burnished, and crispy. The white meat was moist, the dark meat was tender and juicy, and the salting step had highlighted the bird's meaty, savory qualities.

While my turkey was slowly roasting, I put the reserved back and neck to work in a simple gravy. Since I didn't have any drippings (the gentle roasting temperature meant most of the juices stayed in the turkey), I browned the back and neck, built the gravy, and then reduced the mixture with the back and neck in the pot to eke out all their flavor before straining. Though, now that I'd tasted my heritage turkey, I wasn't so certain it needed gravy at all.

ROAST HERITAGE TURKEY
SERVES 8 TO 10

This recipe requires refrigerating the salted turkey for 24 to 48 hours before cooking. If you're making our Gravy for Roast Heritage Turkey (recipe follows), reserve the turkey backbone and neck. We prefer Mary's Free-Range Heritage Turkey (see page 28). See page 31 for details on reheating leftover turkey.

> 1 (10- to 12-pound) heritage breed turkey, neck removed
> Kosher salt

1. Place wire rack in rimmed baking sheet and lightly grease rack. With turkey breast side up, using sharp knife, slice through skin between breast and thigh down to joint on both sides. Using your hands, pull each leg quarter back to expose joint between leg and breast. Remove legs by cutting through hip joint and then skin. Slice through membrane connecting breast to backbone. Bend backbone away from breast to break where it meets rib cage; use knife to remove completely.

2. Using your fingers, gently loosen skin covering legs and breasts. Rub 1½ teaspoons salt evenly inside cavity of turkey breast, 1½ teaspoons salt under skin of each breast, and 1½ teaspoons salt under skin of each leg. Tuck wings underneath breast. Place turkey legs and breast, skin side up, on prepared wire rack.

Refrigerate turkey parts, uncovered, for at least 24 hours or up to 48 hours.

3. Adjust oven rack to lower-middle position and heat oven to 250 degrees. Transfer breast to large plate and set aside while leg quarters start roasting. Flip leg quarters skin side down and transfer to oven; roast until thighs register 140 degrees, 45 to 75 minutes.

4. Flip leg quarters skin side up and place breast, skin side down, on wire rack next to leg quarters. Return to oven and roast for 1 hour.

5. Flip breast skin side up and continue to roast until breast registers 155 degrees and thighs register 175 degrees, 1¼ to 2¼ hours longer. Remove turkey from oven and let rest for at least 30 minutes or up to 60 minutes.

6. While turkey is resting, increase oven temperature to 500 degrees. Stack turkey assembly on second baking sheet to prevent excess smoking. Return turkey to oven and roast until skin is golden brown and crispy, 10 to 15 minutes.

7. Transfer turkey to carving board and let rest for 20 minutes. Carve turkey and serve.

GRAVY FOR ROAST HERITAGE TURKEY
MAKES ABOUT 1 QUART

If the gravy reduces too quickly, add water and continue to cook for the full hour.

> 2 teaspoons vegetable oil
> Reserved turkey backbone and neck from Roast Heritage Turkey
> 4 tablespoons unsalted butter
> 1 small onion, sliced thin
> 1 celery rib, sliced thin
> ¼ cup all-purpose flour
> ½ cup dry white wine
> 4 cups chicken broth
> 3 cups water
> 3 bay leaves
> Salt and pepper

1. Heat oil in Dutch oven over medium heat until shimmering. Add reserved turkey backbone and neck and cook until well browned on all sides, 8 to 10 minutes. Transfer to large plate and set aside. Reduce heat to medium-low and add butter, onion, and celery. Cook, stirring frequently, until vegetables are softened and browned, 5 to 7 minutes. Stir in flour and cook, stirring constantly, until fragrant and lightly browned, about 1 minute. Whisk in wine and cook until thickened, about 1 minute. Whisking constantly, gradually add broth, water, and bay leaves. Return backbone and neck to pot and bring to simmer over high heat. Reduce heat to medium-low and simmer, uncovered, flipping backbone and neck occasionally, until liquid is thickened and measures about 1 quart, about 1 hour.

2. Discard backbone and neck. Strain gravy through fine-mesh strainer, pushing on solids to extract as much liquid as possible. Season with salt and pepper to taste.

A New Holiday Roast

Top sirloin offers great beefy flavor and decent tenderness, but this cheap cut also has its challenges. Our goal: figuring out how to make it worthy of the holiday table.

⇒ BY ANDREW JANJIGIAN ⇐

In many families, "holiday roast" means one thing: prime rib. It's a great cut of meat—both supremely tender and flavorful—and it's a knockout for presentation, but it's also a budget-buster and takes literally half a day if you want to cook it right. Others opt for the tenderloin, or Châteaubriand, which is the most tender cut there is but also one of the most costly, with a flavor that's somewhat mild. This year, I wanted to serve a roast that would be gentle on the wallet and not too time-consuming, but I didn't want to make sacrifices. My roast had to have a rich, beefy flavor and a tender, juicy interior. And, of course, it would have to present well at the table.

To meet my goal, I knew exactly where I should start: the sirloin. This section of the cow is located between the short loin (where the tenderloin comes from) and the leaner, tougher round end (home to the even more affordable, chewier cuts like the top round roast). The particular cut that I had in mind was the boneless top sirloin center-cut roast. It has plenty of beefy flavor, a reasonable amount of marbling, and an impressively tender texture. And at about $8 per pound, it filled most of my requirements.

That said, the top sirloin roast also has its share of flaws—which explains why it can be had on the cheap. First, it has an irregular profile, with two sides that slope and one that tapers into a narrower end, and it can be quite large, as much as 8 inches in diameter. That's fine if you are roasting or grilling it to serve for more run-of-the-mill entertaining, but these two traits make for less-than-beautiful, overly large slices that fall a bit short of true special-occasion standards. Second, this sirloin roast lacks a fat cap, which means it's frequently dry and doesn't brown as readily. Still, the pros were so promising that I knew this would be a holiday roast that could hold its own if I could just deal with the cons.

▶ See Sirloin's Virtues
Video available free for 4 months at CooksIllustrated.com/dec14

We halve the roast to ensure even cooking, but it also means we can cook one roast longer if some guests prefer more-well-done meat.

Fit to Be Tied

The shape problem, I realized, had a reasonably easy solution: Divide and conquer. Slicing a top sirloin center-cut roast in half down the center, following the grain, yielded two roasts with more compact profiles. These smaller roasts still looked a bit irregular, but tying them with kitchen twine every few inches turned them into almost perfectly round, attractive cylinders that were a much more reasonable 4 inches across.

From here, I followed a basic cooking method. I salted the two roasts and let them sit for a day in the refrigerator, uncovered, to season the meat and ensure maximum juiciness (salt helps proteins retain moisture when they cook). This also caused the exteriors to dry out, which would encourage browning. The next day I placed the roasts on a wire rack set in a baking sheet, a setup that would allow for even cooking, and roasted them in a 225-degree oven. This gentle temperature would prevent the exteriors from overcooking before the interiors cooked through. I pulled the roasts from the oven when

they were just shy of medium-rare at the center (although now that I had two roasts, I had the convenient option of cooking one roast longer if I had guests who were interested in more-well-done meat). The roasts rested while I waited for the oven to preheat to 500 degrees and then went back in the oven for 10 minutes to brown their exteriors and develop both flavor and visual appeal.

This first attempt wasn't bad at all. The roasts were juicy and tender and had great beefy flavor, and I was pleased to find that the narrow shape allowed them to reach medium-rare in less than 2 hours (a far cry from prime rib's 4-plus hours). That said, while a high-heat finish might be a great way to brown a prime rib or pork rib roast, it wasn't doing much for my top sirloin.

Looking Good

The fat cap on roasts like prime rib will readily brown in a hot oven, but these roasts—without any sort of fat cap—had barely a hint of browning in the 10 minutes I'd given them at 500 degrees. Roasting them longer eventually produced some appreciable browning but also created a substantial band of gray overcooked meat just beneath the surface.

A more effective approach was to quickly sear the roasts on all sides in a hot skillet before tying them and cooking them through, since searing them cold, rather than after they were cooked, helped minimize overcooking. This somewhat deepened the meaty flavor and improved the appearance, but still, top sirloin roast couldn't match a prime rib, whose fat cap isn't just visually pleasing but also adds richness and crisps up beautifully.

Adding a substantial amount of fat to the roasts myself—rubbing them liberally with either oil or butter before cooking—helped a little but not enough. These roasts needed something that would contribute to an elegant appearance and add flavor along with some textural contrast. What could achieve all three? I hoped the answer was a paste.

I started by reaching for a few intensely flavored kitchen staples: a handful of garlic cloves, since they would provide flavor and also give some substance to the paste; a half-dozen anchovy fillets, just enough to lend an umami meatiness without contributing

How Our Roast Measures Up to More Traditional Roasts

Though they have their pluses, two of the most classic holiday beef roasts—tenderloin and standing rib—have their minuses, too. After we turned top sirloin's drawbacks into assets by halving the roast, tying it, and adding a flavorful, attractive spice paste, there wasn't any reason to look elsewhere.

	BEEF TENDERLOIN	STANDING RIB ROAST	TOP SIRLOIN ROAST
Price	$$$$	$$$$	$$
Cooking Time	45 to 60 minutes	3½ to 5½ hours	2¼ to 2½ hours
Flavor	Mild	Beefy	Beefy
Marbling	Minimal	Ample	Decent

noticeable fishiness; rosemary; and red pepper flakes. I processed the ingredients plus ¼ cup of olive oil to a smooth paste in the food processor. I followed the same salting and cooking procedure as before, but this time when the roasts were resting, I spread the paste evenly over their exteriors. I came back around to the idea of a 10-minute high-heat finish, this time not with the goal of browning the meat but instead browning the paste. In terms of flavor, the results weren't bad, but it fell a bit flat. The paste also didn't brown particularly well, which meant it looked somewhat drab and wasn't adding any contrasting texture. Six anchovies and four garlic cloves may not seem like much, but I realized that their added moisture was the likely culprit.

I considered sautéing the paste to remove that moisture, but with my goal of keeping things easy in mind, I tried a simpler approach first. I applied the paste to the roasts before they went into the 225-degree oven. This was just the answer. The paste slowly dried out during the 2-hour cooking time, and once it hit the 500-degree oven, it quickly browned. A bite confirmed I'd hit the bull's-eye. The paste not only added texture and visual appeal but also had a more concentrated, complex flavor.

With their flavorful, attractive coating and tender, juicy interiors, these elegant roasts had it all—except of course for time-consuming steps and a hefty price tag.

DRESS IT UP WITH A SPICE PASTE

Because our roast lacks a fat cap, we cover it in a robustly flavored paste that browns in the oven, adding a boost of complex flavor, textural contrast, and visual appeal.

ROSEMARY-GARLIC TOP SIRLOIN ROAST
SERVES 8 TO 10

This recipe requires refrigerating the salted meat for at least 24 hours before cooking. The roast, also called a top sirloin roast, top butt roast, center-cut roast, spoon roast, shell roast, or shell sirloin roast, should not be confused with a whole top sirloin butt roast or top loin roast. Do not omit the anchovies; they provide great depth of flavor with no overt fishiness. Monitoring the roast with a meat-probe thermometer is best. If you use an instant-read thermometer, open the oven door as little as possible and remove the roast from the oven to take its temperature.

- 1 (5- to 6-pound) boneless top sirloin center-cut roast
- 2 tablespoons kosher salt
- 4 teaspoons plus ¼ cup extra-virgin olive oil
- 3 tablespoons chopped fresh rosemary
- 4 garlic cloves, minced
- 6 anchovy fillets, rinsed and patted dry
- 1 teaspoon pepper
- ¼ teaspoon red pepper flakes
  Coarse sea salt

1. Cut roast lengthwise along grain into 2 equal pieces. Rub 1 tablespoon kosher salt over each piece. Transfer to large plate and refrigerate, uncovered, for at least 24 hours or up to 4 days.

2. Adjust oven rack to middle position and heat oven to 225 degrees. Heat 2 teaspoons oil in 12-inch skillet over high heat until just smoking. Brown 1 roast on all sides, 6 to 8 minutes. Return browned roast to plate. Repeat with 2 teaspoons oil and remaining roast. Let cool for 10 minutes.

3. While roasts cool, process rosemary, garlic, anchovies, and remaining ¼ cup oil in food processor until smooth paste forms, about 30 seconds, scraping down sides of bowl as needed. Add pepper and pepper flakes and pulse to combine, 2 to 3 pulses.

4. Using 5 pieces of kitchen twine per roast, tie each roast crosswise at equal intervals into loaf shape. Transfer roasts to wire rack set in rimmed baking sheet and rub roasts evenly with paste.

5. Roast until meat registers 125 degrees for medium-rare or 130 degrees for medium, 2 to 2¼ hours. Remove roasts from oven, leaving on wire rack, and tent loosely with aluminum foil; let rest for at least 30 minutes or up to 40 minutes.

6. Heat oven to 500 degrees. Remove foil from roasts and cut and discard twine. Return roasts to oven and cook until exteriors of roasts are well browned, 6 to 8 minutes.

7. Transfer roasts to carving board. Slice meat ¼ inch thick. Season with sea salt to taste, and serve.

COFFEE-CHIPOTLE TOP SIRLOIN ROAST

Omit rosemary and red pepper flakes. Add 1 tablespoon ground coffee, 1 tablespoon minced canned chipotle chile in adobo sauce, 2 teaspoons ground coriander, 2 teaspoons paprika, 1 teaspoon unsweetened cocoa powder, and 1 teaspoon ground mustard to food processor with oil in step 3.

FENNEL-CORIANDER TOP SIRLOIN ROAST

Omit rosemary and red pepper flakes. Add 2 teaspoons ground fennel, 2 teaspoons ground coriander, 2 teaspoons paprika, and 1 teaspoon dried oregano to food processor with oil in step 3.

Shopping for the Right Roast

The boneless top sirloin center-cut roast comes from the hip of the cow, an area that may be called the sirloin (the term we use in the test kitchen) or the loin, depending on the butcher. To make sure you get the right cut, it helps to know exactly what to look for.

It should be about 8 inches square and 4 inches tall at the center, with one side that tapers into a narrower end and two sides that slope. Make sure there's no fat cap but there is a reasonable amount of marbling.

BONELESS TOP SIRLOIN CENTER-CUT ROAST
We buy a whole roast and cut it in two for even cooking.

Best Mushroom Bisque

Most versions have so much dairy that they could be cream of anything. We wanted the trademark silkiness of a bisque without drowning out the earthy mushrooms.

≥ BY ANDREA GEARY ≤

Mushroom bisque should be a far more sophisticated version of cream of mushroom soup: smoother, more luxurious, and with greater savory depth. And yet the abundance of dairy that gives a bisque its signature velvety texture can also mute its flavor. Decreasing the cream makes the soup more flavorful, but then it's too austere to merit the name "bisque." My goal was to reconcile an indulgent texture with robust mushroom flavor.

I made several recipes that began with cooking onions or leeks in butter or oil. I added mushrooms in widely varying amounts (anything from familiar white buttons to exotic foraged specimens), cooked them until they'd released most of their moisture, and browned them to concentrate their flavor. I poured in either chicken or vegetable broth and simmered the soups briefly before whizzing each to a smooth puree. Each was then enriched with a generous amount of cream, and some were finished with herbs and lemon juice.

All the soups, even those with an abundance of fungi, were surprisingly short on mushroom flavor. This round of testing was not a total loss, however. One of the recipes I'd tested was from Julia Child's *Mastering the Art of French Cooking*. Her soup featured only ¾ to 1 pound of mushrooms, so it lacked a deep woodsy flavor but boasted an ultrasatiny texture that managed not to completely obscure what mushroom flavor there was.

Instead of relying entirely on cream, this soup's velvety texture came from a combination of cream and egg yolks, an old-school French thickener known as a liaison. With less cream in the mix, more mushroom flavor could come to the fore. I'd keep

A garnish of cream and a sprinkle of chives complement the lush texture and rich woodsy flavor of the soup.

the liaison in mind when I was closer to finishing my soup, but for now I had to focus on seriously concentrating the mushroom flavor.

Mushrooms are 80 to 90 percent water, and I wanted to get rid of as much as I could for two reasons: First, the more moisture I removed, the more mushrooms (and therefore mushroom flavor) I could add to my bisque. Second, browning is an avenue to flavor, but mushrooms won't brown if they're wet. Most of the recipes I'd tried started with cooking the sliced mushrooms in the pot to

dehydrate them, but it took as long as 25 minutes for them to dry out enough to begin browning. I knew it would be quicker to move this part of the operation to the microwave.

I tossed 2 pounds of sliced button mushrooms (I'd test other varieties once I established my method) with a tablespoon of kosher salt to help draw out the liquid and microwaved them until they shrank down to about one-third of their original volume. This took 12 minutes, less than half the time that sautéing took. Worried that the alarmingly inky fluid the mushrooms gave off would discolor my soup, I discarded the liquid and transferred the mushrooms to the pot with some oil, where they began to brown in just 3 minutes.

As the mushrooms cooked, I reflected on the time savings: The microwave had definitely improved my efficiency, but it still took almost 15 minutes to slice the mushrooms. Curious if I could skip slicing altogether, I tossed 2 pounds of whole mushrooms with salt and tried again.

I was gratified to find that the whole mushrooms required exactly the same amount of time in the microwave as sliced mushrooms to shrink to one-third of their original volume. A mushroom-savvy colleague explained that fungi lack the thicker protective skin found on most vegetables that prevents evaporation, so they give up their moisture readily even when intact.

Wanting to keep the focus on the mushrooms, I added only a single finely chopped onion and a sprig of thyme to the browned mushrooms and cooked everything just a few minutes longer, after which I added 6 cups of chicken broth and simmered the soup for 20 minutes. I gave the soup a quick spin in

Lots of Mushrooms, Little Work

Our bisque contains a full 2 pounds of mushrooms, but we found that there's no need to slice or chop them. Because mushrooms lack a thick outer layer, they give up moisture readily even when left whole. We simply toss them with salt and microwave them until most of their liquid is released. Then we brown the shriveled mushrooms to deepen their flavor and use the reserved mushroom liquid to help form the base of the soup.

MEGA MUSHROOMS
A mix of white button, cremini, and shiitake mushrooms gives our soup woodsy depth.

SCIENCE Yoking Together Yolks for Silky—and Flavorful—Bisque

The abundance of cream in bisques gives them their lush consistency, but it also makes most versions taste flat. While the fat droplets in cream thicken a liquid by getting in the way of water molecules, slowing their movement, they also mute flavor by coating the tongue and preventing flavor molecules from reaching taste receptors.

For a bisque with both pleasing body and a more pronounced mushroom flavor, we turned instead to an old-school French thickener—a so-called liaison, which replaces a large portion of the cream with egg yolks. As the bisque heats, proteins in the yolks unfold and bond together into long, tangled strands that, like the fat in cream, interfere with the movement of water molecules. Egg yolks also contain the powerful emulsifier lecithin, which has a twofold effect: It breaks up the fat droplets into smaller particles that disperse more completely throughout the liquid, obstructing more water molecules, for an even thicker consistency. It also keeps the bisque smooth by holding the fat droplets suspended in the liquid so they don't separate out.

If yolks can do all this, why even use cream? Because the fat it contains provides an appealing mouthfeel that yolks alone can't match.

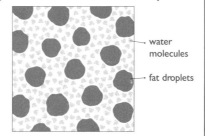

JUST CREAM
water molecules
fat droplets

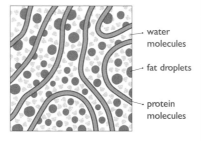

CREAM + YOLKS
water molecules
fat droplets
protein molecules

MUSHROOM BISQUE
SERVES 6 TO 10

Tying the thyme sprig with twine makes it easier to remove from the pot. For the smoothest result, use a conventional blender rather than an immersion blender. Our Fried Shallots can replace the garnish of cream and chopped chives. For our free recipe, go to CooksIllustrated.com/friedshallots.

- 1 pound white mushrooms, trimmed
- 8 ounces cremini mushrooms, trimmed
- 8 ounces shiitake mushrooms, stemmed
  Kosher salt and pepper
- 2 tablespoons vegetable oil
- 1 small onion, chopped fine
- 1 sprig fresh thyme, tied with kitchen twine
- 2 tablespoons dry sherry
- 4 cups water
- 3½ cups chicken broth
- ⅔ cup heavy cream, plus extra for serving
- 2 large egg yolks
- 1 teaspoon lemon juice
  Chopped fresh chives

1. Toss white mushrooms, cremini mushrooms, shiitake mushrooms, and 1 tablespoon salt together in large bowl. Cover with large plate and microwave, stirring every 4 minutes, until mushrooms have released their liquid and reduced to about one-third their original volume, about 12 minutes. Transfer mushrooms to colander set in second large bowl and drain well. Reserve liquid.

2. Heat oil in Dutch oven over medium heat until shimmering. Add mushrooms and cook, stirring occasionally, until mushrooms are browned and fond has formed on bottom of pot, about 8 minutes. Add onion, thyme sprig, and ¼ teaspoon pepper and cook, stirring occasionally, until onion is just softened, about 2 minutes. Add sherry and cook until evaporated. Stir in reserved mushroom liquid and cook, scraping up any browned bits. Stir in water and broth and bring to simmer. Reduce heat to low and simmer for 20 minutes.

3. Discard thyme sprig. Working in batches, process soup in blender until very smooth, 1½ to 2 minutes per batch. Return soup to now-empty pot. (Soup can be refrigerated for up to 2 days. Warm to 150 degrees before proceeding with recipe.)

4. Whisk cream and egg yolks together in medium bowl. Stirring slowly and constantly, add 2 cups soup to cream mixture. Stirring constantly, slowly pour cream mixture into simmering soup. Heat gently, stirring constantly, until soup registers 165 degrees (do not overheat). Stir in lemon juice and season with salt and pepper to taste. Serve immediately, garnishing each serving with 1 teaspoon extra cream and sprinkle of chives.

---

the blender along with 1¼ cups of cream (the average amount in the recipes I had tested) and a sprinkle of salt and pepper, and then I was ready to taste.

I had been hoping for elegant minimalism, but this soup was just plain bland. Despite having removed all that moisture in the microwave, I found the mushroom flavor faint, one-dimensional, and partially hidden by the chicken broth. Plus, the fatty texture was as cloying as it had been in my early tests.

The next time around, I paused to sip the murky-looking liquid I had drained from the microwaved mushrooms. It had a pleasant, earthy flavor, so I set it aside instead of discarding it. After adding the onion and thyme, I let the mushrooms and the bottom of the pot get good and brown and then I added a small amount of sherry. Not only is sherry a classic partner for mushrooms, but recent test kitchen experiments have shown that sherry contains compounds that subtly boost the complexity and savoriness of meaty-tasting foods. Like "umami bombs" soy sauce, tomato paste, and Worcestershire sauce (all ingredients I had seen in other recipes), sherry supports without stealing the show.

When it was time to add liquid to loosen the flavorful browned bits on the bottom of the pot, I asked myself: Why deglaze with chicken broth when you can use the mushrooms' own juice? Yes, it was ugly, but flavor was my main concern. I would worry about aesthetics later, so into the pot the juice went.

For the remaining liquid I used about 4 cups each of water and chicken broth. I pureed the soup in batches in the blender, running it for 2 minutes each time to make the soup as smooth as possible

What Is Bisque?

Consult a tome on classic French cookery and you'll learn that "bisque" traditionally refers to a rich, creamy soup made with shellfish. Nowadays, the word is used to describe any creamy soup, shellfish-based or not, that's a step up in flavor and refinement from plainer creamed soups.

(and to avoid the tiresome step of straining it). Then I mixed up the emulsifying liaison from Child's recipe: ⅔ cup of cream whisked with two egg yolks. I tempered the liaison with some hot broth and then added it to the soup and heated the mixture to 165 degrees to ensure that the egg yolks were sufficiently cooked. I stirred in just a bit of lemon juice to sharpen all the flavors.

This soup was a big improvement on the prior batch. It had a rich yet clean texture, and the mushroom flavor was right up front, with just a subtle hint of sherry, a bit of woodsy thyme providing support, and the lemon bringing everything into focus. And happily, the flavorful mushroom juice had not muddied the appearance of the soup. Now it was time to play with mushroom varieties.

Readily available white mushrooms are inexpensive and worked well in the soup, so I decided to keep them, but I decreased the amount to just 1 pound so I could bring in other varieties. Dried mushrooms have strong and distinctive flavors, which makes them great for boosting the intensity of sauces, but I found that they dominated my bisque. I would stick with fresh mushrooms.

One-half pound of oyster mushrooms contributed little, but cremini mushrooms provided earthiness, so they were in. The last addition: shiitakes, which are sometimes described as having a buttery flavor. They elevated the bisque without making it too rich.

This luxurious soup now had a deep, woodsy flavor worthy of a special occasion. A sprinkle of chives and a little cream and my work was done.

▶ Behold the Bisque
Video available free for 4 months at CooksIllustrated.com/dec14

Garlic-Parmesan Mashed Potatoes

For just the right balance, we started by examining how garlic flavor works.

≥ BY DAN SOUZA ≤

Whenever I want something more inspired than plain old mashed potatoes, I turn to potent additions like garlic and Parmesan. Achieving good cheese flavor is as simple as mixing in a handful of the freshly grated stuff, but the garlic is a different story. If it isn't too subtle, it's often overpowering—whether too sharp, too sweet, or even unpleasantly bitter. I envisioned moderately rich potatoes with complex, balanced garlic flavor accented by nutty Parmesan.

We've developed a lot of mashed potato recipes over the years. Dipping into our expansive archive, it didn't take me long to settle on a potato plan. I started with one of our favorite varieties for mashing: buttery-tasting, moderately starchy Yukon Golds (peeled and cut into ½-inch-thick slices for even cooking) simmered for about 20 minutes until tender. I drained the slices and then riced the potatoes back into the pot set over low heat. This move helped evaporate excess water, avoiding a soggy mash. Next I stirred in a modest amount of melted butter (4 tablespoons for 2 pounds of potatoes), salt and pepper, and, finally, ⅔ cup of warm whole milk.

Time for the garlic. The question is never as simple as how much to add, but what kind of flavor to develop. Here's why: Garlic cells do not develop the flavorful, aromatic compound called allicin until they are ruptured by cutting or smashing. What's more, the intensity of flavor depends on the size of the cut: The finer the cut (more broken cells and thus greater allicin production), the sharper the taste—slices or slivers will pack less of a punch than minced. You also have to pay attention to how (or if) the garlic is cooked. The fiery punch of raw garlic is tamed by heat, which converts allicin into mellower-tasting compounds. And what happens if you cook whole, uncut cloves? Allicin is never produced and only a sweet, mild taste emerges.

To get a handle on how the many faces of garlic play out in potatoes, I made four separate mashes. I added several whole roasted garlic cloves to one, a few cloves of minced sautéed garlic to another, and a touch of raw garlic paste to another. For the last batch I simmered a couple of whole cloves with the potatoes. Raw garlic boasted its signature assertive taste. The roasted cloves added a pronounced sweetness;

See Garlic Science
Video available free for 4 months at CooksIllustrated.com/dec14

A combination of fresh and powdered garlic produces full and complex—but not overwhelming—flavor.

the simmered ones only a faint sweetness. Finally, the sautéed minced garlic offered middle-of-the-road flavor. I would need to mix and match multiple preparations of garlic to develop my ideal blend.

I started by using a rasp-style grater to transform two garlic cloves into 1¼ teaspoons of a flavor-packed, ultrafine paste. I sautéed 1 teaspoon of the paste in the butter from my recipe and then added the remaining ¼ teaspoon raw to the mash. This fresh-cooked combo satisfied some, but the roasted devotees also wanted sweet, mellow notes. And yet I wasn't about to run my oven for an hour in pursuit of roasted garlic flavor. I wondered about another option that might provide the same taste with a lot less hassle: garlic powder. It's made by grinding and then drying garlic cloves to remove moisture, a process via which a mild roasted flavor develops. We don't use it much in the test kitchen aside from in spice rubs, but I thought it was worth a shot in my potatoes.

Eager to give it a try, I sprinkled a bit of the powder straight from the jar into the mash. When the results were harsh-tasting, I experimented with sautéing varying amounts in the butter along with the fresh stuff. No dice: Now the garlic flavor was wan. I did a little more research, and it turns out that although garlic powder still contains alliinase, the enzyme responsible for producing flavorful allicin, the dehydration process deactivates it. But alliinase can be reactivated

via rehydration. (Sautéing the powder in butter had destroyed the alliinase before it had time to develop flavor. For more on garlic powder, see page 30.) Armed with this information, I simply stirred water into the powder (I settled on ½ teaspoon) and let it sit for a minute before sautéing. Sure enough, the powder came to life, expressing the full garlic flavor I expected.

All that was left to do was to grab a hunk of Parmesan and grate until my tasters said stop. A savory depth that stood up to, and complemented, the sweet, sharp, and roasted garlic flavors was achieved using ¾ cup.

These garlicky, cheesy spuds are good enough for a special-occasion meal, but they're also so easy to make that I have a feeling I'll be serving them all the time.

GARLIC-PARMESAN MASHED POTATOES
SERVES 4 TO 6

Our favorite brand of garlic powder is Spice Islands. For our free recipe for Garlic-Parmesan Mashed Potatoes for Two, go to CooksIllustrated.com/dec14.

- 2 pounds Yukon Gold potatoes, peeled and sliced ½ inch thick
- ½ teaspoon garlic powder
- 4 tablespoons unsalted butter, cut into 4 pieces
- 1¼ teaspoons garlic, minced to paste
- 1½ ounces Parmesan cheese, grated (¾ cup)
  Salt and pepper
- ⅔ cup warm whole milk

1. Place potatoes in large saucepan and add cold water to cover by 1 inch. Bring water to simmer over medium-high heat. Adjust heat to maintain gentle simmer until paring knife can be slipped into and out of center of potatoes with no resistance, 18 to 22 minutes. Drain potatoes.

2. While potatoes cook, combine garlic powder and ½ teaspoon water in small bowl. Melt butter in 8-inch skillet over medium-low heat. Stir in 1 teaspoon garlic paste and garlic powder mixture; cook, stirring constantly, until fragrant and golden, about 1 minute. Transfer butter mixture to medium bowl and thoroughly stir in Parmesan, 1¼ teaspoons salt, ½ teaspoon pepper, and remaining ¼ teaspoon garlic paste.

3. Place now-empty saucepan over low heat; set ricer or food mill over saucepan. Working in batches, transfer potatoes to hopper and process. Using rubber spatula, stir in butter-Parmesan mixture until incorporated. Stir in warm milk until incorporated. Season with salt and pepper to taste; serve immediately.

French Apple Tart

Classic form and good looks are compulsory for a holiday centerpiece, but they don't matter if the dessert falls apart when you serve it. We wanted integrity with the beauty.

⇒ BY ANDREA GEARY ⇐

The word "elegant" is usually used to describe something that's exquisite and special occasion–worthy, like hand-cut crystal. But it can also refer to something that's ingeniously simple yet effective, like a mathematical proof. Both applications of the word fit the classic French apple tart, a visually stunning dessert that has intense fruit flavor and varied textures, yet is made with just a few basic ingredients.

Some variations feature extras like almonds or custard, but in its simplest form *tarte aux pommes* has a crisp pastry shell that's filled with a concentrated apple puree and then topped with a spiraling fan of paper-thin apple slices. It's usually finished with a delicate glaze, which caramelizes during baking, providing an extra layer of flavor and a distinctly European flair.

But dazzling looks quickly lose their appeal when there's no integrity backing them up: Poor structure is the fatal flaw of many a handsome apple tart. If the apple slices on top are tough, they resist the knife and the soft puree beneath squirts out under the pressure. That layer of puree also tends to make the crust sodden and mushy, while the dessert's overall flavor can be a bit one-dimensional.

Still, I was drawn to the idea of a showstopper dessert that could be made with a short list of pantry staples. My challenge would be perfecting each component to produce a tart with lively, intense apple flavor and a crust that stayed crisp. And I was unwilling to sacrifice integrity for beauty; I wanted both.

A Strong Foundation

For a dough that would hold its shape and maintain a crisp texture even after being filled with the puree, I started by preparing the three classic French pastry options and filling them with a placeholder puree: five peeled and cored Golden Delicious apples (widely available, and good quality year round) cooked with a splash of water until soft, mashed with a potato masher, and reduced until thick.

My first attempt was with puff pastry (frozen, since making puff pastry is a feat in and of itself), which is essentially many alternating layers of lean dough and butter. I lined the 9-inch tart pan with a sheet of the dough that I had rolled very thin,

To create complex caramelized flavor, we brush the top of the baked apple tart with apricot preserves and then briefly pass it under the broiler.

parbaked it to dry it out and firm it up, and then filled it with the puree. But it was a flop—literally. Despite parbaking it, the dough shrank. Its initially crisp texture also softened beneath the wet puree. On to the next.

Following a classic recipe for *pâte brisée* (essentially the French equivalent of flaky American pie dough), I buzzed 1⅓ cups of flour in the food processor with a touch each of salt and sugar and then pulsed 8 tablespoons of cold butter until the mixture formed a coarse meal strewn with lumps of butter. I drizzled in 3 tablespoons of water, pulsed the mixture until the dough formed a solid mass, chilled it, and then moved through a series of prebaking steps known as blind-baking: I rolled out the chilled dough, fit it into the tart pan, chilled it again, lined the dough with parchment, weighed it down with pie weights, parbaked it, removed the parchment and weights, and baked it until it was crisp.

The purpose of all that upfront work is to keep the dough from shrinking—and it paid off, as this shell held its shape nicely. The problem came when

I introduced the puree, which turned the pastry soggy.

Lastly, I tried a *pâte sucrée*. This pastry typically contains more sugar than the previous doughs, but the most significant difference is the degree to which the butter gets incorporated. Whereas most of the butter in pâte brisée is left in small chunks, here the butter is thoroughly worked into the flour, which limits the development of gluten—the strong elastic network that forms when flour proteins are moistened with water. Less gluten translates to pastry that is less prone to shrinking and that bakes up with a finer, shorter crumb.

I worked the butter into the dry ingredients until the mixture looked like sand, then bound it with an egg (typical in pâte sucrée recipes). I chilled, rolled, chilled, and baked as before—but I skipped the pie weights, since the dough wasn't likely to shrink.

Indeed, this crust baked up plenty sturdy. Even better, it didn't sog out when I filled it with the puree. Its texture was, however, a tad puffy, like a sugar cookie. And frankly, all that chilling and rolling was tiresome. Maybe there was an easier way to get the dough into the pan.

Crunch Time

I suspected that the cookie-like lift had something to do with the egg, so I eliminated it. But without the egg's moisture, how would I bind the dry ingredients with the cold butter?

I needed a liquid component but didn't want to add water, since that would encourage gluten development. That ruled out milk and cream, too. But what if I turned the butter (which contains very little water) into a liquid by melting it?

Stirring melted butter into the dry ingredients produced a cohesive, Play-Doh-like mass—so far so good. I considered rolling out this dough, but it was so malleable that I realized I could simply press it into the pan. Then I chilled it and baked it.

▶ **Look: A Thing of Beauty**
Video available free for 4 months
at CooksIllustrated.com/dec14

This was by far the easiest pastry I'd ever made, but I reserved any celebration until I saw the final result. To my delight, the crust baked up perfectly sturdy and, without the egg, was no longer puffed up like a sugar cookie, but crisp and delicate like shortbread. When I filled it with the puree, cut a slice, and heard a promising crunch as the knife passed through the still-crisp crust, I knew that this ultrasimple pastry was a game changer.

But it got even better: Subsequent streamlining tests showed that I didn't even have to chill this modified pâte sucrée before baking; the sides of the tart pan were shallow enough that the pastry didn't slump. Now to improve that placeholder puree.

Amping Up Applesauce

My apple filling had to meet two criteria: concentrated fruit flavor and enough body to hold its shape on a fork. The latter goal I'd almost met by cooking down the puree until it measured about 2 cups. The texture and the flavor were something of a cross between applesauce and apple butter. The only change I made was to move this operation from a saucepan to a covered skillet, the wide surface of which helped water from the fruit evaporate faster.

But for that European flair, I wanted the flavor to be more distinctive. I found just what I was looking for in Julia Child's recipe for tarte aux pommes, in which she adds butter and apricot preserves to her puree. I found that adding a few tablespoons of butter and ½ cup of the tangy fruit preserves to the apples yielded a richer, brighter-tasting filling. (A dash of salt boosted that flavor.) The preserves also contributed pectin, which helped the filling firm up even more.

Topping It Off

I'm a forbearing cook, but painstakingly shingling thin-sliced apples (for ease, I'd stick with Golden Delicious on the top as well) over the entire surface almost drove me over the edge. The outer ring looked uniform, but placement of the slices became more difficult and looked increasingly amateurish as I proceeded toward the center.

Hoping the tart would look better in its fully baked state, I briefly turned my attention to making

a glaze. The apricot preserves I was already using would add bright flavor and a dazzling sheen, so I microwaved them to make them fluid, strained them, gingerly painted a few tablespoons over the tart's surface (tricky, because the slightest drag of the brush could dislodge the delicate apples), and baked it.

What I pulled out of the oven 30 minutes later looked OK, if a bit pale. The bigger problem was that the apple slices never became tender enough for me to cut the tart without their resisting and becoming dislodged. I made a series of attempts to soften the fruit—baking the tart longer, brushing the slices with water or melted butter, covering the tart with foil for part of the baking time so the slices might soften in the trapped steam—none of which worked.

In the end, I swapped the wafer-thin apple slices for more generous slices and (since I was already using a skillet to make the apple puree) sautéed them for 10 minutes to jump-start the softening before placing them on the tart. As for the spiral shingling,

I decided to forgo this fussy tradition and devise a more easygoing, but still sophisticated, alternative. What I came up with: a rosette pattern made by placing the apple slices in concentric circles (see "Making a Rosette"). The parcooking had made the slices conveniently pliable, so there was no awkwardness toward the center of the arrangement; I simply bent the pieces and slipped them into place.

Once the tart was baked, I applied the glaze. Encouragingly, these sturdier pieces stayed put when I brushed them with the strained jam. Then I briefly ran the tart under the broiler to get the burnished finish that characterizes this French showpiece.

The rosette design of this tart made it look a bit different from the classic French apple tart, but it was every bit as elegant. And thanks to the now-tender glazed apple slices, the rich puree, and the crisp—not to mention utterly simple and foolproof—crust, every slice of the tart that I cut was picture-perfect, too.

Our Apple Tart: French Finesse Without the Fuss

Traditional *tarte aux pommes* looks impressive when whole, but is fussy to make and often falls apart when cut. Our version is easier to make, slices neatly, and boasts all the elegance of the original.

BRIGHT-TASTING GLAZE
Brushing strained apricot preserves over the top of the tart adds an extra burst of fruit flavor and a glossy sheen.

TENDER APPLE SLICES
Parcooking the sliced apples in a skillet makes them pliable enough to bend into place—and just soft enough to slice through once baked.

STURDY CRUST
Pastry made with melted (rather than cold) butter bakes up with a fine, crisp crumb and resists turning soggy.

CONCENTRATED PUREE
Apricot jam added to the apple puree brightens flavor, while butter contributes richness.

FRENCH APPLE TART
SERVES 8

You may have extra apple slices after arranging the apples in step 6. If you don't have a potato masher, you can puree the apples in a food processor. For the best flavor and texture, be sure to bake the crust thoroughly until it is deep golden brown. To ensure that the outer ring of the pan releases easily from the tart, avoid getting apple puree and apricot glaze on the crust. For a tip on easily unmolding the tart, see page 30. The tart is best served the day it is assembled.

Crust
1⅓	cups (6⅔ ounces) all-purpose flour
5	tablespoons (2¼ ounces) sugar
½	teaspoon salt
10	tablespoons unsalted butter, melted

Filling
10	Golden Delicious apples (8 ounces each), peeled and cored
3	tablespoons unsalted butter
1	tablespoon water
½	cup apricot preserves
¼	teaspoon salt

1. FOR THE CRUST: Adjust 1 oven rack to lowest position and second rack 5 to 6 inches from broiler element. Heat oven to 350 degrees. Whisk flour, sugar, and salt together in bowl. Add melted butter and stir with wooden spoon until dough forms. Using your hands, press two-thirds of dough into bottom of 9-inch tart pan with removable bottom. Press remaining dough into fluted sides of pan. Press and smooth dough with your hands to even thickness. Place pan on wire rack set in rimmed baking sheet and bake on lowest rack, until crust is deep golden brown and firm to touch, 30 to 35 minutes, rotating pan halfway through baking. Set aside until ready to fill.

2. FOR THE FILLING: Cut 5 apples lengthwise into quarters and cut each quarter lengthwise into 4 slices. Melt 1 tablespoon butter in 12-inch skillet over medium heat. Add apple slices and water and toss to combine. Cover and cook, stirring occasionally, until apples begin to turn translucent and are slightly pliable, 3 to 5 minutes. Transfer apples to large plate, spread into single layer, and set aside to cool. Do not clean skillet.

3. While apples cook, microwave apricot preserves until fluid, about 30 seconds. Strain preserves through fine-mesh strainer into small bowl, reserving solids. Set aside 3 tablespoons strained preserves for brushing tart.

4. Cut remaining 5 apples into ½-inch-thick wedges. Melt remaining 2 tablespoons butter in now-empty skillet over medium heat. Add remaining apricot preserves, reserved apricot solids, apple wedges, and salt. Cover and cook, stirring occasionally, until apples are very soft, about 10 minutes.

5. Mash apples to puree with potato masher. Continue to cook, stirring occasionally, until puree is reduced to 2 cups, about 5 minutes.

6. Transfer apple puree to baked tart shell and smooth surface. Select 5 thinnest slices of sautéed apple and set aside. Starting at outer edge of tart, arrange remaining slices, tightly overlapping, in concentric circles. Bend reserved slices to fit in center. Bake tart, still on wire rack in sheet, on lowest rack, for 30 minutes. Remove tart from oven and heat broiler.

7. While broiler heats, warm reserved preserves in microwave until fluid, about 20 seconds. Brush evenly over surface of apples, avoiding tart crust. Broil tart, checking every 30 seconds and turning as necessary, until apples are attractively caramelized, 1 to 3 minutes. Let tart cool for at least 1½ hours. Remove outer metal ring of tart pan, slide thin metal spatula between tart and pan bottom, and carefully slide tart onto serving platter. Cut into wedges and serve.

TO MAKE AHEAD: The baked crust, apple slices, and apple puree can be made up to 24 hours in advance. Apple slices and apple puree should be refrigerated separately in airtight containers. Assemble tart with refrigerated apple slices and puree and bake as directed, adding 5 minutes to baking time.

MAKING A ROSETTE

Briefly precooking the apple slices makes them pliable and easy to arrange in a rosette on top of the puree.

1. Gently cook the sliced apples with a little butter and water until just softened and translucent.

2. Arrange most of the slices in tightly overlapping concentric circles.

3. Bend the remaining slices to fit in the center.

Holiday Baking 911

The holidays are when you bake the most but also when time is short and do-overs are not an option. Here's our fix-it list for common baking emergencies. BY ELIZABETH BOMZE

Soften Cold Butter in a Hurry

Either of these tricks will quickly soften cold butter—which can typically take 30 minutes at room temperature—without oversoftening it. Both methods can also be applied to cream cheese.

Pound It
Place the butter in a plastic zipper-lock bag and use a rolling pin to pound it until soft.

Cut It
Slice the butter into tablespoon-size pieces and let it sit at room temperature while you measure the other ingredients.

Filling a Slumped Pie Shell

There's no reshaping slumped pie pastry, but holding back on some of the filling will prevent it from overflowing during baking. For shells that will be baked again after you fill them, such as pumpkin, leave ¼ inch of space at the top of the crust for the filling to expand. (No-bake fillings, such as those for cream pies, can be filled to the top of the crust.)

Prevent Overbaked Cookies

Rather than allow just-baked cookies to rest briefly on the baking sheet, which helps them set, immediately transfer them to a wire rack where there will be less carryover cooking.

Wrong Size Pan?

To switch between different sizes of cake, loaf, pie, and tart pans, you'll need to scale the recipe up or down or adjust the baking time. Here are some guidelines.

CAKES AND QUICK BREADS
Since standard-size cake and loaf pans usually measure within an inch of one another, and dividing leaveners and eggs can be tricky, it's better to adjust the baking time instead of the batter's yield. Add or subtract about 5 minutes from the baking time, and check the cake regularly for doneness. Note: In a larger vessel, the cake will be more squat.

PIES Any of our pie doughs meant to be rolled to 12 inches for a 9-inch pan can be rolled to 13½ inches to fit a 9½-inch (often labeled "deep dish") pan. To do the reverse, roll the dough to 12 inches.

TARTS The 2-inch difference between 9- and 11-inch pans is surprisingly substantial. We found that when using a 9-inch pan in a recipe that calls for an 11-inch one, or vice versa, it's necessary to scale the recipe down or up by 50 percent, respectively, to ensure that the pastry and filling are flush with the edge of the vessel.

Not Enough Cooling Racks?

Improvise with a pair of inverted empty egg cartons. Simply set them side by side to support the baking sheet.

Mend a Cracked Cheesecake

Loosening the sides of a baked cheesecake from the springform pan while it is still warm will prevent it from fusing to the pan and creating tension that causes cracking during cooling. But if the cake cracks during baking, you can seal up the fissure with this trick.

1. Remove sides from springform pan while cheesecake is warm. Wrap cloth ribbon snugly around cake, preferably one that covers sides completely.

2. Secure ribbon with binder clip; leave in place until cake is completely cooled.

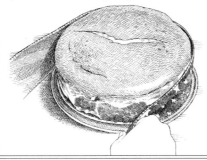

Muffin Tin MIA?

Foil muffin tin liners are sturdy enough to hold muffin (and cupcake) batters. Simply arrange the liners on a rimmed baking sheet and fill with batter.

Note: Unlike muffins baked in a muffin tin, only the bottoms (not the sides) will brown.

Tube Pan Troubleshooting

If your pan lacks feet, simply invert it over a bottle to cool the cake. And if it doesn't have a removable bottom, it's easy to prevent sticking by lining it with parchment paper as follows:

1. Place pan right side up on sheet of parchment paper and trace outside perimeter. Turn pan upside down and place parchment on top of pan bottom.

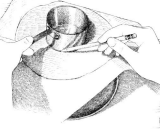

3. Fold parchment into quarters and cut out hole. Finally, cut out circle and line pan. When baked cake has cooled, gently peel away parchment.

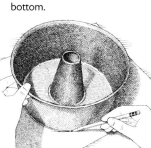

2. Place measuring cup that fits opening of center hole in middle of traced circle, where hole is. Use it as guide to trace center hole.

Parchment Paper Shortage?

If you run out of parchment paper when making cookies, don't grease the baking sheet or spray it with vegetable spray; the extra fat will cause the cookies to spread and bake unevenly. Waxed paper isn't a good option either, as heat can melt the wax coating. Ungreased aluminum foil is the best substitute. The cookies might stick a little, but you'll be able to gently lift them off the foil.

Save an Underdone Pie

Baked custard pies, like pumpkin or sweet potato, should be baked to 175 and 165 degrees, respectively, when the edges of the filling are set but the center is still a bit loose. (The pie fully sets as it cools.) But if you don't have an instant-read thermometer and you pulled the pie too early, rebake it in a preheated 275-degree oven for about 30 to 45 minutes (the filling should be set but not firm). If the pie has been in the refrigerator, let it sit at room temperature for 1 hour before rebaking.

Firm Up Too-Soft Butter

Butter that yields completely to pressure or is starting to melt can't support the air bubbles generated during creaming. To reestablish butter's structure, mix it with a few ice cubes and stir constantly until it firms up, about 1 minute. (The amount of water that leaks into the butter will be negligible.) We found that sugar cookies and buttercream frosting made with rehabbed butter were comparable to those made with butter that had been softened properly.

"Unwhip" Overwhipped Cream

There's no going back on cream you've whipped into butter, but here's our fix for loosening up whipped cream that's just a bit too stiff.

1. Add unwhipped heavy cream into overwhipped cream 1 tablespoon at a time.

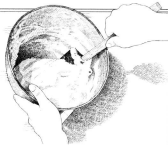

2. Gently fold mixture, adding more unwhipped cream until the desired consistency is reached.

Portion Without a Scoop

You can portion cookie dough with a measuring cup just as accurately as you would with a portion scoop. Fill a ¼-cup dry measuring cup (equal to 4 tablespoons) with dough and then divide it according to the desired size (e.g., halved for 2 tablespoons).

Pie Plates in a Pinch

If you don't own enough vessels for all the pies you want to bake during the holidays, these alternatives make good substitutes for the traditional 9-inch glass pie plate.

Disposable Pie Plate Disposable aluminum pie plates have relatively thin walls that don't hold or transfer heat as efficiently as our preferred glass pie plates do, so crusts don't brown or crisp as quickly. But we found that simply extending the baking time for pies baked in disposable pie plates can produce comparable results.

For empty crusts: Increase the time that the crust bakes with weights by up to 10 minutes, or until the crust turns golden brown and crisp.

For filled double-crust pies: Increase the baking time by up to 10 minutes, covering the top of the pie with aluminum foil if it starts to get too dark.

➤ **TIP:** It's especially important to bake pies in aluminum pie plates on a baking sheet—both to ensure a well-browned bottom crust and for stability when transporting the pies.

Cast-Iron Skillet
For double-crust pies, use a very well-seasoned cast-iron skillet that's 9 or 10 inches in diameter to keep the baking times consistent with the recipe. Because the pan is deeper than a pie plate, use 60 percent of the dough for the bottom crust so that it will reach up the sides. (Don't bake single-crust pies in a cast-iron skillet; the pan's relatively straight sides will cause the dough to slump.)

Crispy Salt and Pepper Shrimp

In this pungently spiced Chinese restaurant classic, the shells are every bit as important (and delicious) as the shrimp.

⪻ BY ANDREW JANJIGIAN ⪼

Shrimp that are dipped in a batter and fried until golden and crisp are undeniably good, but I'd argue that the Chinese take on frying these crustaceans—salt and pepper shrimp—boasts an exterior that's even more tempting. The key ingredient to that texture might surprise you: It's not a batter but simply the shrimp shells themselves. Instead of being removed before cooking, they're left intact on the meat. When the shrimp cook in the hot oil, the meat cooks up plump and moist, and the shells become as shatteringly crisp—and appealing to eat—as fried chicken skin.

That texture, along with the combination of pepper, garlic, and ginger (and, of course, salt) that gives this dish its killer savory-spicy profile, compels me to order salt and pepper shrimp anytime I'm in a Chinese restaurant. They're also what prompted me to look for recipes to make at home, so I gathered a half-dozen salt and pepper shrimp recipes (from Chinese as well as Vietnamese cookbooks, as the dish is hugely popular in both cuisines) and found that all followed the same basic approach: Salt the shrimp, dredge them in cornstarch or a simple batter (though some recipes actually call for leaving them plain), and then fry them in hot oil, adding the flavorings along the way.

Easy enough, I thought, until I tried a few of the recipes. It turns out that achieving shrimp shells with a delicately brittle texture, all the while ensuring that the meat inside remained tender and juicy, was no easy task. Most times, no matter how long I fried the shrimp, and whether or not I coated them, the shells came out leathery. So my goal was clear: a frying technique that produced juicy, tender meat encased in a shell so delicately crisp, even the shell-on naysayers wouldn't be able to pass it up.

A Shell Game
Though restaurant versions seem to be made with relatively small shrimp, I'd been following the lead

In addition to three types of dried pepper, we fry fresh jalapeño rings and serve the salty-spicy shrimp on a bed of cool shredded lettuce.

of published recipes, using larger shellfish that came 21 to 25 per pound. Maybe that was part of the problem, since bigger shrimp are also older—which might mean that they have thicker shells.

To test this theory, I compared batches of smaller 26- to 30-count and 31- to 40-count shrimp with the bigger crustaceans. For simplicity's sake, I cooked them plain in a pot of 350-degree vegetable oil for 5 minutes or so until they turned opaque. Sure enough, the shells on both batches of the smaller shrimp, while not perfectly crisp, developed spots where they were nicely browned and brittle. The shells on the 31- to 40-count batch seemed the most crispy, so I settled on this size.

Now that I was starting off with thinner shells, I wondered if a coating would help them crisp more uniformly. First I tried dipping them in a batter made of flour, egg white, and water. While the coating itself came out pleasantly brittle, it did little to help crisp up the shell it surrounded. In fact, the opposite was true: The batter-coated shrimp had the toughest shells of any I'd cooked yet. Simply dredging the

shrimp in cornstarch worked much better, leading to shells that were much crunchier than those in any of my previous batches.

When I researched the composition of shrimp shells, this result made a lot of sense. The main structural element in the shells of shrimp (and lobster) is a polysaccharide called chitin. Chitin does not break down when heated, which means that it doesn't soften or fall apart when cooked. However, chitin is flexible, thanks to its water content; thus, in order to make it crisp, it's necessary to drive off as much of that water as possible. While the batter formed a thick barrier that hindered moisture from escaping, and shells with no coating relied solely on the heat of the oil to drive off water, the cornstarch actively pulled moisture from the shells even before they hit the fryer.

I knew that getting—and keeping—the oil as hot as possible would aid in thoroughly drying out the shells. It also would dry them quickly so the shrimp wouldn't have a chance to overcook. We normally don't heat oil higher than 375 degrees, but I found that I could raise its temperature to 385 degrees without causing the oil to smoke. Adding too much food to the oil at one time is a sure way to drop the temperature, so I fried the shrimp in batches, holding the finished shrimp in a warm oven on a wire rack while the remainder fried. With all these adjustments, the shells were now as brittle and crisp as the best of any restaurant version I'd sampled.

Considering Salt and Other Flavorings
Of course salt and pepper shrimp wasn't about only the shells: It was time to focus on the meat beneath, which was a bit more tough and chewy than I wanted. To give the dish its signature salty punch, most recipes call for rubbing the raw shrimp with salt and letting them sit for about 10 minutes, a step that I knew would not only give the salt time to penetrate the flesh and thoroughly season it but also allow it to hold on to more of its juices. A few sources also called for tossing the shrimp with a couple of tablespoons of rice wine. This seemed like a great idea, since a little bit of this savory liquid would help the salt get under the shell to make contact with the meat and might contribute some flavor of its own. When I tried both approaches,

How Frying Makes Shrimp Shells Good Enough to Eat

Most of us peel shrimp before eating it—and for good reason. Made of an elastic substance known as chitin, the shell can be tough. But great salt and pepper shrimp feature a fried shell as crispy—and appealing to eat—as the skin on fried chicken.

Interestingly, the process by which poultry skin and shrimp shells become crisp and edible is somewhat different. Raw chicken skin is flabby because its fat molecules (which make up 50 percent of its weight) coat its proteins, preventing them from cross-linking and firming up the texture; it also contains a lot of water. The high heat of frying takes care of both issues: It causes the fat to render, allowing the proteins to cross-link and become more rigid, and it drives off water, turning the cross-linked proteins brittle.

Chitin, on the other hand, does not break down when exposed to heat. Furthermore, its rubbery texture is entirely caused by moisture. To crisp the shells, it is necessary to dehydrate them as much as possible—something that can be accomplished only by a dry heat method like frying. (Moist methods will leave the shells chewy and flexible; think shrimp boil.) For this reason, we eschew a wet batter and instead toss the shrimp in seasoned cornstarch. This light, dry coating helps pull moisture from the shells, which evaporates in the hot oil, leaving them brittle and crisp. Note: Since older, larger shrimp have thicker, tougher shells, it's also important to start with relatively small shrimp; we prefer 31- to 40-count specimens.

BOILED = TOUGH
Moist heat makes shrimp shells rubbery.

FRIED = CRISP
Dry heat dehydrates—and, thus, crisps—the shells.

tasters confirmed that the shrimp tossed with salt and rice wine was juicier as well as more flavorful. To ensure that the added moisture didn't affect frying, I patted the shrimp dry before coating them in starch.

It was time to incorporate the garlic and ginger that flavor the dish. I made an aromatic "paste" by reserving 2 tablespoons of the frying oil, cooking the minced garlic and ginger in it for around 45 seconds, and then dropping in the fried shrimp and briefly tossing them with the mixture before serving.

All that remained was to work in some trademark heat and pungency. Some recipes call for merely grinding black peppercorns over the fried shrimp before serving, but I preferred to add the pepper to the cornstarch before tossing the shrimp in it for better distribution. I was intrigued by recipes that also included Sichuan peppercorns, which have a distinctive piney, citrusy taste, so I introduced a

generous grind of these to the cornstarch as well, along with a little cayenne and sugar (which, like salt, can sharpen flavors). These heady flavors were even more evident when I set aside some of the seasoning mix and added it to the reserved frying oil with the garlic and ginger before tossing in the fried shrimp.

But I still wasn't quite satisfied. I wanted a bit more heat, as well as some herbal flavors. The solution: I thinly sliced a couple of fresh jalapeños, coated them in cornstarch, and quickly fried them after I'd removed the shrimp. I then sprinkled them over the finished dish. My tasters also approved of two final tweaks: sliced scallions added to the aromatic paste with the fried shrimp, and an extra ½ teaspoon of salt sprinkled into the oil at the same time.

With shrimp so moist and tender, shells so crisp, and such a heady spectrum of flavors, this was a dish that I'd be making again and again.

CRISPY SALT AND PEPPER SHRIMP
SERVES 4 TO 6

In this recipe the shrimp are meant to be eaten shell and all. To ensure that the shells fry up crisp, avoid using shrimp that are overly large or jumbo. We prefer 31- to 40-count shrimp, but 26- to 30-count may be substituted. Serve with steamed rice.

- 1½ pounds shell-on shrimp (31 to 40 per pound)
- 2 tablespoons Chinese rice wine or dry sherry
  Kosher salt
- 2½ teaspoons black peppercorns
- 2 teaspoons Sichuan peppercorns
- 2 teaspoons sugar
- ¼ teaspoon cayenne pepper
- 4 cups vegetable oil
- 5 tablespoons cornstarch
- 2 jalapeño chiles, stemmed, seeded, and sliced into ⅛-inch-thick rings
- 3 garlic cloves, minced
- 1 tablespoon grated fresh ginger
- 2 scallions, sliced thin on bias
- ¼ head iceberg lettuce, shredded (1½ cups)

1. Adjust oven rack to upper-middle position and heat oven to 225 degrees. Toss shrimp, rice wine, and 1 teaspoon salt together in large bowl and set aside for 10 to 15 minutes.

2. Grind black peppercorns and Sichuan peppercorns in spice grinder or mortar and pestle until coarsely ground. Transfer peppercorns to small bowl and stir in sugar and cayenne.

3. Heat oil in large Dutch oven over medium heat until oil registers 385 degrees. While oil is heating, drain shrimp and pat dry with paper towels. Transfer shrimp to bowl, add 3 tablespoons cornstarch and 1 tablespoon peppercorn mixture, and toss until well combined.

4. Carefully add one-third of shrimp to oil and fry, stirring occasionally to keep shrimp from sticking together, until light brown, 2 to 3 minutes. Using wire skimmer or slotted spoon, transfer shrimp to paper towel–lined plate. Once paper towels absorb any excess oil, transfer shrimp to wire rack set in rimmed baking sheet and place in oven. Return oil to 385 degrees and repeat in 2 more batches, tossing each batch thoroughly with coating mixture before frying.

5. Toss jalapeño rings and remaining 2 tablespoons cornstarch in medium bowl. Shaking off excess cornstarch, carefully add jalapeño rings to oil and fry until crispy, 1 to 2 minutes. Using wire skimmer or slotted spoon, transfer jalapeño rings to paper towel–lined plate. After frying, reserve 2 tablespoons frying oil.

6. Heat reserved oil in 12-inch skillet over medium-high heat until shimmering. Add garlic, ginger, and remaining peppercorn mixture and cook, stirring occasionally, until mixture is fragrant and just beginning to brown, about 45 seconds. Add shrimp, scallions, and ½ teaspoon salt and toss to coat. Line platter with lettuce. Transfer shrimp to platter, sprinkle with jalapeño rings, and serve immediately.

Roast Pork Belly at Home

Cure and smoke pork belly and you've got bacon. Roast the belly instead and you've got the ultimate pork entrée—provided the meat is tender and the skin stunningly crisp.

> BY DAN SOUZA <

When I'm dining out and in the mood for something that's richly satisfying, I often look for pork belly on the menu. This boneless cut features alternating layers of deeply flavorful, well-marbled meat and buttery fat, which, when properly cooked, turn silky and sumptuous. Even more appealing is the contrast between that luscious texture and the skin. Ideally, this top layer, which is dense and tough when raw, cooks up crisp, airy, and light-textured—just as it is in its more recognizable form: pork rinds.

Long a staple in Asian cuisines, this cut has become increasingly popular in upscale restaurants of all kinds and, more recently, has started showing up in supermarkets—though it's also worth noting that this cut is more familiar than you might think: Fresh pork belly is simply unsliced, uncured, unsmoked bacon.

I've always thought that pork belly would make a knockout centerpiece to serve during the holidays, particularly with a bright, acidic sauce to balance its richness. Another incentive: At $5 or $6 per pound, it's less expensive than almost any other holiday-worthy cut. My challenge was figuring out a cooking method that would create that ideal contrast between tender meat, silky fat, and airy, shatteringly crisp skin.

Full of Hot Air

Most restaurants either braise or slow-roast pork belly. Gentle cooking encourages tough collagen in the meat and fat to break down into softer gelatin that makes these components seem moist and supple. The latter would be my method of choice, as I would be using a skin-on cut and doing everything I could to dry out the exterior to encourage that puffed up, ultracrispy crown.

With a holiday dinner party in mind, I chose a 3-pound slab that would feed at least eight guests

> ● **See Bacon's Other Identity**
> Video available free for 4 months
> at CooksIllustrated.com/dec14

Because pork belly is rich, keep the portion size small—4 to 5 ounces per person—and serve it with a bright-tasting sauce, rice, and vegetables.

(small portions are plenty for this rich cut) and started with a very simple method: roasting it in a 250-degree oven for about 3 hours. By that time, the meat and fat had hit 195 degrees, turning velvety and supple; all they needed was a bit of seasoning. But the skin had a long way to go. Though dry on the surface, it was inedibly tough, tacky, and leathery.

I thought about slow-roasting other proteins with skin, like chicken, and how I crank the oven high for the final few minutes to brown and crisp the exterior. But a quick blast at 500 degrees did nothing to improve the pork belly skin. A longer 30-minute stint didn't do much more—and by that time the meat had started to dry out. Only when I turned the dial to broil did the skin start to puff and crisp, but only spottily and at the very surface. I was still far from that light, airy, pork rind–like crunch.

Come to think of it, knowing how pork rinds get that texture might give me a clue, so I queried a manufacturer of the pork skin snack. According to the company, three steps need to go right in order for pork skin to puff and crisp. First, the skin's rigid

collagen needs to be converted to soft, extensible gelatin. Second, the skin needs to shed most, but not all, of its water—from its starting point of about 50 percent down to around 10 to 15 percent. Finally, the skin needs to be heated to a high enough temperature to force the rest of the water to boil, creating steam that causes the skin to expand and the water to evaporate. Only once this happens can proteins in the skin set into the airy, rigid structure.

I was already breaking down plenty of collagen during the slow-roasting stage, but I knew I could help the skin lose more moisture. A salt rub, which we typically apply to the surface of meat to draw out moisture and thus encourage browning and crisping, was an obvious next step and would take care of the seasoning, too. I rubbed a couple of tablespoons each of kosher salt and brown sugar over the meat and skin, set the slab in an uncovered baking dish, and refrigerated it overnight, as air drying would wick away moisture. Then I proceeded as before, roasting the belly in a 250-degree oven for 3 or so hours.

Now I was getting somewhere. This skin wasn't just dry; it was desiccated. With the collagen breakdown and dehydration steps complete, I turned on the broiler for the crisping stage but hit two snags. One: The sugar in the rub caused the skin to burn—something I could easily fix by rubbing only salt on the skin. Two: While the

Bacon Before It's Bacon

Even if it sounds like something you've never cooked before, pork belly couldn't be more familiar. This unctuous, ultraflavorful cut with its alternating layers of meat and fat is nothing more than unsliced, uncured bacon. Slow-cooking approaches like braising and low roasting turn the meat and fat tender and sumptuous; the latter method is the best choice when you buy a skin-on cut, as it dries out the surface so that the skin can crisp.

COOKING PORK BELLY: SLOW-ROAST; THEN CRISP

Our mostly hands-off approach produces rich, tender meat capped with a layer of shatteringly crisp skin.

SPLIT IT LENGTHWISE
Cutting the pork belly into three strips provides more surface area for seasoning. The smaller pieces of meat and skin also cook more quickly and evenly.

GIVE IT A RUB
Seasoning the meat with salt and brown sugar adds flavor, encourages browning, and helps it retain moisture. Sprinkling salt on the skin (scored for deeper penetration) helps it dehydrate.

GIVE IT A REST
Letting the seasoned meat sit overnight in the refrigerator gives the rub time to penetrate. It also dries out the surface of the skin so that it can crisp.

ROAST IT SLOW
Slow roasting browns the meat and further dehydrates the skin while converting the rigid collagen in both to gelatin. Gelatin keeps the meat moist and helps the skin puff when crisped.

CRISP THE SKIN
Frying just the skin portion of the pork belly (start it in cold oil so that all the skin heats at the same pace) forces its remaining water to evaporate, leaving it puffed up and ultracrisp.

---

very surface of the skin had puffed and crisped dramatically, the underlayer remained dense and hard.

Fried to a Crisp
The problem with the oven, I now realized, was that crisping the skin required not only high heat, but a cooking method that would expose all the skin—from top to bottom—to that temperature. Frying was the obvious way to go: It would allow me to submerge the skin in oil hot enough to drive off the remaining moisture.

Deep frying was unnecessary, as I needed only about ½ inch or so of oil to submerge the skin. I simply combined the rendered fat from the roasted pork with enough vegetable oil to equal 1 cup; poured it into a 12-inch skillet, which provided enough surface area for the entire slab; brought the oil to a typical frying temperature of 375 degrees; and placed the pork skin side down in the fat. About 3 minutes later, the skin was perfectly crispy and golden across the surface—proof that frying was well worth it. But I wasn't in the clear yet, as one bite revealed that the hot oil hadn't had time to reach the center of the skin, which remained dense and chewy. Why? Because foods cook from the outside in, and as soon as the surface of the skin expanded and crisped, it put more distance between the center of the skin and the oil. What I needed was a way to get the skin to cook at the same rate from edge to center, so I made two easy changes to my method. First, I cut the belly into 2-inch-wide strips and scored the skin at ½-inch intervals, which allowed the fat to access more of the skin and seep in. Second, I didn't preheat the fat in the pan; that way, all the skin would heat up and puff at the same rate rather than heat faster on the exterior.

Now every bit of skin emerged dramatically puffed and golden—a perfect textural contrast to the soft, silky meat and fat. After a brief rest, I sliced the strips into ½-inch pieces and got to work on a few sauces. A spicy mustard concoction was the favorite. Plated and drizzled with sauce, my pork belly tasted as good as any restaurant preparation.

CRISPY SLOW-ROASTED PORK BELLY
SERVES 8 TO 10

This recipe requires seasoning and refrigerating the pork belly for at least 12 hours before cooking. Be sure to ask for a flat, rectangular center-cut section of skin-on pork belly that's 1½ inches thick with roughly equal amounts of meat and fat. Serve the meat in small portions with our Spicy Mustard Sauce (recipe follows), plus white rice and steamed greens or boiled potatoes and salad. For our free recipes for Sweet and Sour Chile Sauce and Tangy Hoisin Sauce, go to CooksIllustrated.com/dec14.

- 1 (3-pound) skin-on center-cut fresh pork belly, about 1½ inches thick
  Kosher salt
- 2 tablespoons packed dark brown sugar
  Vegetable oil

1. Using sharp chef's knife, slice pork belly lengthwise into 3 strips about 2 inches wide, then make ¼-inch-deep crosswise cuts through skin and into fat spaced ½ inch apart. Combine 2 tablespoons salt and brown sugar in small bowl. Rub salt mixture into bottom and sides of pork belly (do not rub into skin). Season skin of each strip evenly with ½ teaspoon salt. Place pork belly, skin side up, in 13 by 9-inch baking dish and refrigerate, uncovered, for at least 12 hours or up to 24 hours.

2. Adjust oven rack to middle position and heat oven to 250 degrees. Transfer pork belly, skin side up, to lightly greased wire rack set in rimmed baking sheet. Roast pork belly until meat registers 195 degrees and paring knife inserted in meat meets little resistance, 3 to 3½ hours, rotating sheet halfway through roasting.

3. Transfer pork belly, skin side up, to large plate. (Pork belly can be held at room temperature for up to 1 hour.) Pour fat from sheet into 1-cup liquid measuring cup. Add vegetable oil as needed to equal 1 cup and transfer to 12-inch skillet. Arrange pork belly, skin side down, in skillet (strips can be sliced in half crosswise if skillet won't fit strips whole) and place over medium heat until bubbles form around pork belly. Continue to fry, tilting skillet occasionally to even out hot spots, until skin puffs, crisps, and turns golden, 6 to 10 minutes. Transfer pork belly, skin side up, to carving board and let rest for 5 minutes. Flip pork belly skin side down and slice ½ inch thick (being sure to slice through original score marks). Reinvert slices and serve.

SPICY MUSTARD SAUCE
MAKES ABOUT 1 CUP

- ⅔ cup Dijon mustard
- ⅓ cup cider vinegar
- ¼ cup packed dark brown sugar
- 1 tablespoon hot sauce
- 1 teaspoon Worcestershire sauce

Whisk all ingredients together in bowl.

Skin So Crisp It Crackles

Though dense and tough when raw, pork belly skin becomes light-textured and ultracrisp when fried and is a treat in many cuisines—think English crackling, Latin *chicharrón*, and Southern pork rinds.

PORK BELLY SUPREME
We cut this slab into ½-inch-thick slices to serve.

Hearty Pasta, Greens, and Beans

Most versions of this one-dish meal throw a key ingredient down the drain.

≥ BY ANDREA GEARY ≤

Recipes for pasta with beans and greens abound—and are generally unremarkable. Most feature cannellini beans, plus sausage for heft, while everything from kale to spinach is fair game for the greens. And the sauce? There really aren't guidelines, but it's typically bare-bones. Yet even with numerous variations on the theme, the results are the same: a bland mix of thrown-together ingredients. It's no surprise, then, that I've never given the dish a second thought, at least not until I went to Italy. There I had a robust, flavorful bowl of pasta, beans, and greens that was a revelation.

One key to its success was its choice of beans. It featured borlotti, a staple in Italian cooking, which are creamy like cannellini but also wonderfully meaty. Despite a lack of sausage (which let the beans stay center stage), the sauce had a meaty depth, and it possessed a stew-like consistency that brought it all together. This was an exceptional, simple meal—one I'd prepare back home if I could re-create it.

Red-speckled borlotti beans (part of the cranberry bean family) aren't readily available at the average American supermarket, so I needed a substitute. Cannellini would be fine for simulating borlotti creaminess, and to provide the right meaty flavor, I'd also use an equal amount of pintos.

As for canned versus dried beans, we recently discovered that canned cannellini are often a good alternative, and not just because they are convenient. The best have a uniform tenderness that dried beans can lack. And because canned beans are simply dried beans sealed in cans with salted water (along with a few benign additives) and cooked under pressure, the canning liquid is pretty much the same mixture of bean starch and water that you get when you cook dried beans. While nearly every recipe using canned beans calls for draining and rinsing said beans, I would do no such thing. That starchy canning liquid would lend richness and body to my sauce.

For the greens, I settled on Swiss chard: I finely chopped its hearty stems to cook at the outset, and I chopped the tender leaves and set them aside to add toward the end. I sautéed an onion and the

Finishing cooking the chard and pasta off heat gently wilts the chard and lets the pasta soak up flavor.

Don't Drain the Beans

Most recipes call for draining and rinsing canned beans. That starchy liquid is the key to a great sauce consistency; be sure to add the bean liquid to the pot.

chard stems with garlic, red pepper flakes, and rosemary, and then I added 1½ cups of water and one can each of cannellini and pinto beans, scraping all their liquid and starch into the pot. Knowing that the Swiss chard leaves would turn mushy if overcooked, I took a more gentle approach. After simmering the mixture for 10 minutes to let the flavors meld, I spread the chard leaves over the surface, covered the pot, and allowed them to steam off heat for about 5 minutes. I then stirred in some penne, which I'd cooked separately, and sprinkled Parmesan on top.

I was on the right track, but the flavor was somewhat blah. The next time I started by sautéing 3 ounces of pancetta, not enough to become a primary ingredient but I hoped sufficient to provide a meaty backbone. I also tossed in the rind from my Parmesan when I added the beans. For the pasta, I switched to fusilli since the deep grooves of its spiral shape would better capture what I hoped would be a delicious broth. I also decided to cook the pasta less this time, to just shy of al dente, so that I could finish cooking it through in the broth, allowing it to soak up flavor. When the short simmer was done, I stirred in the pasta, sprinkled the chard on top as before, and left it to finish, covered and off heat.

The sauce was wonderfully flavorful, and the pasta had absorbed its meaty depth. The sauce also had the right creamy consistency, especially after I stirred in some Parmesan. The rosemary had faded a bit, so I stirred in some more after cooking to bolster its flavor, and then seasoned with vinegar. Simple, hearty, and flavorful, this was a dinner that I would savor.

PASTA WITH BEANS, CHARD, AND ROSEMARY
SERVES 6

The sauce will thicken as it cools. For our free recipe for Pasta with Beans, Chard, and Rosemary for Two, go to CooksIllustrated.com/dec14.

- 2 tablespoons vegetable oil
- 3 ounces pancetta, diced
- 1 onion, chopped fine
- 10 ounces Swiss chard, stems chopped fine, leaves chopped coarse
- 2 teaspoons minced fresh rosemary
- 1 garlic clove, minced to paste
- ¼ teaspoon red pepper flakes
- 1 (15-ounce) can cannellini beans (do not drain)
- 1 (15-ounce) can pinto beans (do not drain)
- 1 Parmesan cheese rind (optional), plus 1 ounce Parmesan, grated (½ cup), plus extra for serving
- 8 ounces (2½ cups) fusilli
  Salt
- 1 tablespoon red wine vinegar

1. Heat oil in Dutch oven over medium-high heat until smoking. Add pancetta and cook, stirring occasionally, until pancetta begins to brown, 2 to 3 minutes. Stir in onion and chard stems and cook, stirring occasionally, until slightly softened, about 3 minutes. Add 1 teaspoon rosemary, garlic, and pepper flakes and cook until fragrant, about 1 minute. Stir in beans and their liquid, 1½ cups water, and Parmesan rind, if using, and bring to boil. Reduce heat to medium-low and simmer for 10 minutes.

2. Meanwhile, bring 2 quarts water to boil in large saucepan. Add pasta and 1½ teaspoons salt and cook until pasta is just shy of al dente. Drain. Stir pasta into beans and spread chard leaves on top. Cover, remove from heat, and let sit until pasta is fully cooked and chard leaves are wilted, 5 to 7 minutes. Discard Parmesan rind, if using. Stir in remaining 1 teaspoon rosemary, ½ cup Parmesan, and vinegar. Season with salt to taste, and serve, passing extra Parmesan separately.

▶ See the Sauce Texture
Video available free for 4 months at CooksIllustrated.com/dec14

The Best Hot Chocolate Mix

Hot chocolate mixes often disappoint. We wanted a thick, chocolaty, indulgent drink.

≥ BY KEITH DRESSER ≤

Like many, I outgrew mass-market hot chocolate mixes years ago. With overwhelming sweetness and barely a hint of chocolate, they don't come close to satisfying my adult tastes. So how about high-end mixes with descriptions like "rich," "indulgent," and "intense"? Their aim is to mimic European sipping chocolate, a decadent version typically served in tiny 4-ounce portions. I wanted some of the superconcentrated flavor and luxurious body of this style—but not so much that I couldn't drink an entire mugful. But when I tried a handful of these deluxe mixes, adding enough milk to make 8 ounces, none came even close to boasting the deep flavor or lush texture I was after. Not to mention that all were exorbitantly priced. For a grown-up cup of hot chocolate, I would have to concoct my own premium mix.

Before mass market or upscale mixes came on the scene, the traditional way to make hot chocolate was to add either unsweetened cocoa powder or finely chopped unsweetened bar chocolate to hot milk, along with sugar. I tried both approaches, using high-quality cocoa powder and chocolate, and neither was exactly right. The cocoa powder sample was thick and boasted potent chocolate flavor, but it suffered from a chalky aftertaste. The unsweetened chocolate version was thinner but also smoother, and it offered only moderate chocolate flavor.

These results made sense. Cocoa powder is made up largely of cocoa solids, followed by starch, fiber, and, lastly, cocoa butter. It possesses considerable chocolate flavor and a nice viscosity, but it can also be experienced as dry and gritty. The unsweetened bar chocolate I was using, on the other hand, was nearly 50 percent cocoa solids and 50 percent cocoa butter, leading to a drink that was exceptionally smooth but, without the starch, not very thick and definitely not chocolaty enough.

Clearly the key to an ideal cup of hot chocolate would be to use both forms of chocolate. I started with a good amount of cocoa powder to give the beverage a deep chocolaty flavor and then added unsweetened chocolate, with its high proportion of cocoa butter, to lend creaminess. I then added sugar for sweetness. And so it went, on and on, as I tinkered with different amounts of these ingredients.

▶ See It Come Together
Video available free for 4 months at CooksIllustrated.com/dec14

The dry mix we created to make this rich, lush drink can be stored in an airtight container for two months.

After dozens of tests, I arrived at the ultimate blend: 1 tablespoon plus 1 teaspoon each of cocoa powder and sugar and ½ ounce of finely chopped unsweetened chocolate per 8 ounces of hot whole milk. To this mixture I also added 2 teaspoons of nonfat dry milk powder, which introduced a creamy sweetness and, with the help of the milk's protein, coated the fiber to mask any chalkiness. The extra protein in the milk powder also made the drink a little thicker, enhancing the perception of smoothness.

I was close. I had nailed rich chocolate flavor and a smooth consistency, but the beverage was still somewhat thin. I tried edging up on the cocoa powder, but that made the drink a little grainy. So why not use a classic thickener like cornstarch? As it turned out, that did the trick, developing body in the drink. Supporting flavors—a pinch of salt and splash of vanilla—heightened the chocolate's flavor.

My final task was to scale up the ingredients to create a 12-serving batch that could be used as needed. Whizzing everything to a fine powder in the food processor ensured that the mix would stay combined during storage. It also facilitated the addition of flavorings. I incorporated malted milk powder and bold ingredients like Mexican spices, mint extract, instant espresso powder, and orange zest. These packed big flavor without compromising the texture of my perfectly rich and chocolaty mug.

HOT CHOCOLATE MIX
MAKES 3 CUPS; ENOUGH FOR TWELVE 1-CUP SERVINGS

Our preferred unsweetened chocolate is Hershey's Unsweetened Baking Bar. Both natural and Dutch-processed cocoa will work in this recipe. Our favorite natural cocoa powder is Hershey's Natural Cocoa Unsweetened; our favorite Dutch-processed cocoa powder is Droste Cocoa. For more information on cocoa powder, see page 30. For one serving of hot chocolate, heat 1 cup of whole, 2 percent low-fat, or 1 percent low-fat milk in a small saucepan over medium heat until it starts to steam and bubbles appear around the edge of the saucepan. Add ¼ cup of hot chocolate mix and continue to heat, whisking constantly, until simmering, 2 to 3 minutes longer. Pour the hot chocolate into a mug and serve. For our free recipe for Orange Hot Chocolate Mix, go to CooksIllustrated.com/dec14.

- 1   cup (7 ounces) sugar
- 6   ounces unsweetened chocolate, chopped fine
- 1   cup (3 ounces) unsweetened cocoa powder
- ½   cup (1½ ounces) nonfat dry milk powder
- 5   teaspoons cornstarch
- 1   teaspoon vanilla extract
- ¾   teaspoon kosher salt

Process all ingredients in food processor until ground to powder, 30 to 60 seconds. Transfer to airtight container and store at room temperature for up to 2 months.

MALTED HOT CHOCOLATE MIX

Substitute malted milk powder for nonfat dry milk powder and reduce sugar to ¾ cup.

MEXICAN HOT CHOCOLATE MIX

Add 1 teaspoon ground cinnamon, ¾ teaspoon ancho chile powder, and pinch cayenne pepper to processor with other ingredients.

MINT HOT CHOCOLATE MIX

Substitute mint extract for vanilla.

MOCHA HOT CHOCOLATE MIX

Add ⅓ cup instant espresso powder to processor with other ingredients.

Chocolate Crinkle Cookies

These eye-catching cookies are as much about looks as they are about flavor. The problem is, most are neither chocolaty nor crinkly.

⇒ BY SARAH MULLINS ⇐

Rolled in powdered sugar before going into the oven, chocolate crinkle cookies (aka earthquakes) feature dark chocolaty fissures that break through the bright white surface during baking. They have a striking appearance, with an irresistible chocolaty richness to back it up.

Or at least that's how I think they should be. Before my days as a test cook, I worked at a bakery where I made batch after batch of chocolate crinkle cookies. These cookies were popular, but I always thought there was room for improvement. They were a little too sweet, the chocolate flavor was underwhelming, and the cracks were sparse and more like gaping chasms than fissures. And because the confectioners' sugar coating all but vanished in the oven, those few cracks weren't even that noticeable. I wanted a cookie with deep chocolate flavor and only enough sweetness to balance the chocolate's bitterness, a moist and tender—but not gooey—interior, and plenty of small irregular crinkly fissures breaking through a bright-white surface.

Dough Details

I started by trying a handful of published recipes, limiting myself to those that called for preparing the dough by hand—no stand mixer required—since the melted chocolate and melted butter should make this a loose, easy-to-stir dough. To my surprise, no matter what type of chocolate a recipe called for (and these were all over the map, from unsweetened, bittersweet, and semisweet bar chocolate to cocoa powder) or how much sugar was used, the results were all strikingly similar to the bakery cookies: They were too sweet, with muted chocolate flavor. Furthermore, they all had cracks that were too wide yet few in number.

The most promising recipe of the bunch achieved decent chocolate flavor from 3 ounces of unsweetened chocolate, 3 ounces of bittersweet bar chocolate, and ¼ cup of cocoa powder. Since these cookies were too sweet, my

A combination of unsweetened chocolate, cocoa powder, and espresso powder delivers cookies with serious chocolate flavor.

Minus One

Our recipe makes 22 cookies, not the usual two dozen. Here's how to space 11 cookies on each baking sheet.

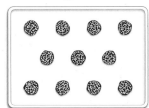

first decision was to drop the bittersweet chocolate because it contains added sugar. In its place, I upped the unsweetened chocolate to 4 ounces and the cocoa powder to ½ cup. I decided to see how these changes fared and left the sugar alone, at 1¾ cups. I didn't go into sugar shock at this first attempt, but the cookies were still a bit cloying and not chocolaty enough. Dropping the sugar down to 1½ cups helped bring the chocolate flavor to the fore and put the sweetness in an acceptable range.

My cookies were impressively chocolaty now, but I felt that they could taste even better. Taking a cue from one of the recipes I'd tested, I substituted brown sugar for the granulated, since it would lend a more complex sweetness, with a molasses undertone that would complement the chocolate. After I added some espresso powder, which helps heighten

chocolate flavor, my cookies really hit the mark for bold chocolate taste. It was time to move on to issues of appearance.

Cracking the Code

Just as I'd seen in the initial recipe tests, the cracks on my cookies were too few and too wide, and the cookies weren't spreading enough—they looked a bit humped. In the past, we've found that leaveners not only contribute to rise and spread in cookies but also help create a more crackly, fissured surface. Before a cookie sets in the oven, bubbles produced by the leavener rise to the surface and burst, leaving fissures. In our Gingersnaps recipe (November/December 2011) we found that baking soda alone was most effective, while our Chewy Sugar Cookies (November/December 2010) benefited from both baking powder and baking soda. I'd started my testing with baking powder since it was the most commonly used leavener in the recipes I'd seen, but baking soda, which requires an acidic ingredient to work, was also an option since my recipe included brown sugar and espresso powder.

Cookies with baking soda alone weren't impressive. Using ¼ teaspoon didn't provide enough leavening power, and ½ teaspoon gave the cookies a metallic aftertaste. Baking powder, as I already knew, did a decent job by itself, but a combination of baking powder and baking soda proved to be the winner. These cookies spread nicely, without any hump, and they had a more crackly surface than anything I'd produced thus far. However, the cracks still gaped and were fewer in number than I had hoped for.

Maximizing Chocolate Flavor

Both unsweetened bar chocolate and cocoa powder add chocolate flavor to our cookies because they contain cocoa solids, but they each have another less obvious way to boost the chocolate. Cocoa's starch content allows us to cut back on flour, while the chocolate's cocoa butter means we can use fewer tablespoons of dairy butter. And that translates to bigger, undiluted chocolate flavor. To amplify it further, we also add several teaspoons of espresso powder.

A Crack in the System

Most crinkle cookies miss the mark, with gaping, sparse cracks and a white coating that doesn't stay put.

**NO CRINKLES. NO COATING.
NO THANKS.**

I wondered if the temperature of the dough was playing a role. Because it was too fluid to work with right after I mixed it, I had been refrigerating the dough overnight before portioning the cookies and baking them. This is a common crinkle cookie step, but maybe it was doing more harm than good. To find out, I baked two more batches—one after refrigerating the dough for 4 hours and another after letting the dough sit at room temperature until the melted chocolate and butter cooled just enough to make the dough workable, which took only 10 minutes—and compared these with my current recipe that had the refrigerated overnight rest. My hunch was right. The cookies made after the 10-minute rest were the best of the group, with finer and more numerous cracks than the other two batches (and it didn't hurt that I didn't have to wait as long to enjoy them either).

What was happening? The cookies made with refrigerated dough were cold in the center and thus hadn't spread much by the time the heat of the oven had dried out their exteriors. This meant that these cookies did almost all their spreading after that dried exterior had formed, forcing the cracks to open wide as the cookies spread. Meanwhile, the room-temperature dough had already spread somewhat by the time the exterior dried in the oven. Minimal spreading once the exterior had dried meant smaller, more numerous cracks. Though I wondered if the cracks could be even more fine and numerous, they were looking pretty good—certainly the best yet—so I decided to turn my attention to the signature sugar coating.

Sugar Coated

As with the cookies I'd made at the bakery, the coating of confectioners' sugar on these cookies was faded. I recalled that some of the recipes in my early tests, flawed as they were, produced cookies with a picture-perfect bright-white exterior. I realized that they all called for rolling the cookies in granulated sugar before the powdered sugar. When I added this step to my recipe, not only did the powdered sugar stay put, but the cracking improved significantly. These cookies had my ideal fine cracks all over the surface.

How could a tweak as simple as this lead to such big changes? A likely explanation for the improved bright-white appearance was that the heavy coating of granulated sugar created a barrier that kept the fine-grained confectioners' sugar from dissolving and disappearing into the dough. As for the increase in fine cracks, our science editor explained that the crystalline structure of granulated sugar was key. Because sugar (in any form) is hygroscopic, a layer on the outside of the cookie will pull moisture from the inside, drying out the cookie surface so it is more prone to cracking. And granulated sugar is more effective than powdered sugar. The crystals in granulated sugar dissolve as they draw out moisture but then rapidly recrystallize as that moisture burns off in the heat of the oven. And once recrystallized, the sugar continues to pull more water from the cookie, creating a very dry top surface that breaks into numerous fine cracks as the cookie spreads.

Finally I had the cookie I'd always pictured. Combined with their deep chocolate flavor, these chocolate crinkle cookies were all they were cracked up to be.

CHOCOLATE CRINKLE COOKIES
MAKES 22 COOKIES

Both natural and Dutch-processed cocoa will work in this recipe. Our favorite natural cocoa is Hershey's Natural Cocoa Unsweetened; our favorite Dutch-processed cocoa is Droste Cocoa. For more information on cocoa powder, see page 30. Our preferred unsweetened chocolate is Hershey's Unsweetened Baking Bar. See "Minus One" for a tip on arranging the dough balls on the baking sheet.

1	cup (5 ounces) all-purpose flour
½	cup (1½ ounces) unsweetened cocoa powder
1	teaspoon baking powder
¼	teaspoon baking soda
½	teaspoon salt
1½	cups packed (10½ ounces) brown sugar
3	large eggs
4	teaspoons instant espresso powder (optional)
1	teaspoon vanilla extract
4	ounces unsweetened chocolate, chopped
4	tablespoons unsalted butter
½	cup (3½ ounces) granulated sugar
½	cup (2 ounces) confectioners' sugar

1. Adjust oven rack to middle position and heat oven to 325 degrees. Line 2 baking sheets with parchment paper. Whisk flour, cocoa, baking powder, baking soda, and salt together in bowl.

2. Whisk brown sugar; eggs; espresso powder, if using; and vanilla together in large bowl. Combine chocolate and butter in bowl and microwave at 50 percent power, stirring occasionally, until melted, 2 to 3 minutes.

3. Whisk chocolate mixture into egg mixture until combined. Fold in flour mixture until no dry streaks remain. Let dough sit at room temperature for 10 minutes.

4. Place granulated sugar and confectioners' sugar in separate shallow dishes. Working with 2 tablespoons dough (or use #30 scoop) at a time, roll into balls. Drop dough balls directly into granulated sugar and roll to coat. Transfer dough balls to confectioners' sugar and roll to coat evenly. Evenly space dough balls on prepared sheets, 11 per sheet.

5. Bake cookies, 1 sheet at a time, until puffed and cracked and edges have begun to set but centers are still soft (cookies will look raw between cracks and seem underdone), about 12 minutes, rotating sheet halfway through baking. Let cool completely on sheet before serving.

▶ See the Crinkles Form
Video available free for 4 months at CooksIllustrated.com/dec14

SCIENCE How Granulated Sugar Creates More Crinkles

Most cookies have top crusts that remain relatively soft and flexible as the cookies set during baking. However, if the top surface dries out before the cookie is finished spreading and rising, it hardens, cracks, and pulls apart, producing an attractive crinkly, cracked exterior. While we found that multiple factors can affect how quickly the top dries out and thus how many cracks are formed (including the temperature of the dough and how rapidly it spreads in the oven), a simple tweak turned out to be key to producing a maximum number of fissures: rolling the balls of dough in granulated sugar before rolling them in powdered sugar.

Coating the cookies with either type of sugar draws out moisture from their surface, promoting cracks by drying out their tops before the interiors set. But granulated sugar does so more efficiently because of its coarse, crystalline structure. As the crystals absorb moisture, some—but not all—dissolve into a syrup. As the cookies continue to bake, the moisture evaporates, and the sugar begins to recrystallize, a process that is accelerated by the undissolved sugar crystals, which act as "seed" crystals. When enough new crystals form, they begin drawing out moisture once again. The upshot: a cookie with a faster-drying surface that is more prone to cracking.

Demystifying Carbon-Steel Knives

Carbon-steel enthusiasts have long considered these knives sharper and more durable than stainless. But do they really perform better—and are they worth the upkeep?

⇒ BY HANNAH CROWLEY ⇐

As serious cooks, we've always been intrigued by knives made from carbon steel. This alloy is considered superior to stainless steel by many chefs and knife enthusiasts because it is believed to be harder and stronger and able to take on—and retain—a keener edge. But as practical cooks, we've been a bit skeptical. Carbon steel is a high-maintenance metal that rusts if not kept dry, so the makers of carbon-steel knives recommend drying the blade immediately after washing it; some even suggest wiping the blade dry between cutting tasks or occasionally coating it with mineral oil to ward off excessive oxidation, which corrodes the metal. Given that our longtime favorite stainless-steel chef's knife, from Victorinox, is virtually maintenance-free, that's asking a lot.

Still, we wanted to know if carbon steel was truly a cut above stainless. We singled out eight carbon-steel chef's knives, a mixture of Western- and Japanese-made blades, priced from $72.99 to a staggering $299.95. We recruited seven testers of various abilities to put the knives through our standard cutting tests: mincing parsley, dicing onions, quartering butternut squash, and butchering whole raw chickens. Before and after each round of tests, we sliced through sheets of copy paper; whether the blade cleaved smoothly or dragged indicated how well its edge held up. And all the while, we noted the overall user-friendliness of each model, particularly with regard to the handle.

Battle of the Blades

Some knives—namely the R. Murphy and the Sabatier—had sharp spines or handles that pressed painfully into our palms and caused fatigue. Better grips offered what ergonomists call "affordance": a shape and texture that allow multiple grips, so hands of all sizes feel comfortable and secure.

As for the meat of our testing—the blade—we homed in on sharpness, which is determined by two factors. First, the thinness of the edge, which

▶ See How They Match Up
Video available free for 4 months
at CooksIllustrated.com/dec14

Bonus Exclusive: Hannah visits MIT
Available at CooksIllustrated.com/MITcarbonsteel

is measured by its V-shaped angle. Simply put, the narrower the angle, the cleaner and more precise the cuts. Our top-ranking knives, which were sharpened to between 10 and 15 degrees on either side of the blade, slid through food, while we had to use more force with wider blades that were sharpened to 20 (or more) degrees on either side.

The second determining factor, the strength of the metal, depends on the type of steel that's used and how it is heat-treated. Manufacturers wouldn't disclose this information but did share their blades' Rockwell scale ratings—a measurement of the metal's strength in a unit called HRC (HR stands for Hardness Rockwell, and strong metals like these are in the "C" class). Sure enough, the highest and lowest Rockwell ratings—60 and above, and as low as 52, respectively—corresponded to the blades' performances. In fact, the bottom-ranking Sabatier was dull out of the box, with testers comparing it to "cutting with a spoon," and quickly lost what little edge it had.

To understand why harder blades performed better, we took copies of the knives to Mike Tarkanian at the Massachusetts Institute of Technology's Department of Materials Science and Engineering. Using a high-powered digital microscope, he zoomed in on the edges of the Sabatier and the top-performing blade, the Bob Kramer knife by Henckels, which had the lowest and one of the highest HRC ratings, respectively. Immediately we could see why the Sabatier failed: Even new, its edge looked rounded and dull. Conversely, the Kramer's edge looked as taut as fishing wire, which explained its razor-sharp performance.

Knowing how the carbon-steel knives stacked up against one another, we circled back to our original question: Can carbon steel actually perform better than stainless steel? We decided to pit the Kramer against our favorite Victorinox stainless-steel knife. We took a brand-new copy of each and tested blade durability by placing a plastic cutting board on a scale (to ensure that each cut would incur the same amount of pressure), making rocking cuts, and repeating the paper cutting test every 10 strokes to track changes. When both blades were still equally sharp after 5,000 cuts, we cut up five more whole raw chickens and butternut squashes with each and then sliced delicate tomatoes. Again, it was nearly impossible to pick a winner. Only after we repeated the scale test on a glass cutting board—hazardous to knife blades—did the knives start to wear down. The Kramer edged out the Victorinox (which has a Rockwell rating of 56 and a 15-degree edge), but

---

Zooming In on Steel Quality

Knife experts have long asserted that carbon-steel blades take and hold an edge better than stainless-steel blades do. That's because stainless steel contains a

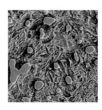

BOB KRAMER BY HENCKELS

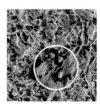

VICTORINOX
The chromium carbides visible in the Victorinox blade were too tiny to affect the steel's strength.

higher percentage of chromium—a metal that prevents rusting but also tends to cause the formation of largish brittle clumps called chromium carbides that weaken the metal's grain structure. But when our favorite stainless-steel knife, from Victorinox, held its edge almost as well as the winning Bob Kramer carbon-steel blade made by Zwilling J. A. Henckels, we took copies of both knives to the Boston University Photonics Center, where Anlee Krupp and Ryan Eriksen used a high-powered microscope to magnify the blades. The images showed that the two blades have similarly fine, tight grain structures.

---

only slightly; both knives still sliced onions with ease.

Their near-identical performance made us strongly suspect that how the metal is manufactured is more important than whether it's carbon or stainless—a hunch that was confirmed by images of the metals' grain structures taken at the Boston University Photonics Center. Both looked similarly fine and tight, indicating strong, durable blades. (For more, see "Zooming In on Steel Quality.")

Given our findings, we can't justify buying a carbon-steel knife—especially since the Victorinox is a bargain ($39.95) and requires no fussy upkeep. But if you are willing to pay a premium ($299.95) and care for carbon steel, the Kramer is a showstopper. Its razor-sharp blade, sloping ergonomic handle, and good looks make it both visually stunning and a pleasure to use. Our Best Buy, the Togiharu Virgin Carbon Steel Gyutou from Korin ($98.50), is a shade less sharp than the Kramer, but still impressive.

TESTING CARBON-STEEL CHEF'S KNIVES

Seven test kitchen staffers subjected eight chef's knives (with blades as close to 8 inches as possible), priced from $72.99 to $299.95, to a battery of kitchen tasks to assess sharpness, comfort, and overall performance. Manufacturers supplied Rockwell ratings (a measurement of the metal's hardness in a unit called HRC) and blade angles. Scores from each test were averaged to get the overall rating; knives are listed below in order of preference. Prices were paid online. A source for the winner appears on page 32.

CUTTING: We minced parsley, diced onions, quartered butternut squash, and butchered whole chickens, carrying out each task 70 times per knife. Narrow, razor-sharp blades that cut swiftly and evenly rated highest.

COMFORT: Knives with smooth, nonangular handles of medium width and length rated highest. We also preferred blades with rounded top spines that didn't dig into our fingers.

EDGE RETENTION: We sliced through paper before and after each round of cutting tests. Blades that kept their original sharpness rated highest.

RECOMMENDED

	CRITERIA		TESTERS' COMMENTS
BOB KRAMER 8" Carbon Steel Chef's Knife by Zwilling J.A. Henckels Price: $299.95 Model: 789693 Rockwell: 61 HRC Blade Angle: 10° to 15°	Cutting Comfort Edge Retention	★★★ ★★★ ★★★	With this knife's "precise" tip and "samurai-sharp," ultrathin blade, parsley "jumped to pieces" and whole chickens seemed to butcher themselves. More impressively, it maintained that edge throughout testing. Its ultracomfortable handle was also a gorgeous piece of craftsmanship.
TSUKIJI Masamoto Gyuto, 8¼" Price: $258 Model: N/A Rockwell: 62 to 63 HRC Blade Angle: 12° to 15°	Cutting Comfort Edge Retention	★★★ ★★½ ★★★	This "razor-sharp" knife—crafted in a seventh-generation shop at Tokyo's famous Tsukiji Fish Market—sliced through food "like butter." Its handle was smooth and comfortable, though a few testers wished it had a bit more heft.
TOGIHARU Virgin Carbon Steel Gyutou, 8.2" *(BEST BUY)* Price: $98.50 Model: HTO-HCGY Rockwell: 62 HRC Blade Angle: 12° to 15°	Cutting Comfort Edge Retention	★★½ ★★★ ★★★	An impressive knife for the price, this Japanese model was just as strong and almost as narrow as our winner but felt a shade less sharp. Testers praised its "agile," "precise," and "clean" handling and balanced, medium-size blade.
MISONO Swedish Carbon Steel Gyutou, 8.2" Price: $119 Model: 112 Rockwell: 60 HRC Blade Angle: 12° to 15°	Cutting Comfort Edge Retention	★★½ ★★½ ★★★	This "light," "maneuverable" Japanese blade "springs through" food with ease, testers said. Where it fell short was its narrow handle; some testers complained that the grip felt "unsubstantial" compared with that of other knives.
MASAMOTO SOHONTEN Virgin Carbon Steel Gyutou, 8.2" Price: $195 Model: HMA-VSGY Rockwell: 61 to 62 HRC Blade Angle: 12° to 15°	Cutting Comfort Edge Retention	★★ ★★★ ★★	Though this knife boasted "solid," "balanced" weight and a comfortable handle with enough girth to grip, the business end—the blade—just wasn't as sharp as those of higher-ranking knives. As a result, testers complained that it made them work harder.

RECOMMENDED WITH RESERVATIONS

	CRITERIA		TESTERS' COMMENTS
MESSERMEISTER Park Plaza Carbon 8 Inch Chef's Knife Price: $75 Model: 8107-8 Rockwell: 57 HRC Blade Angle: 20°	Cutting Comfort Edge Retention	★½ ★★★ ★★	The best part of this knife was its smooth, rounded handle. The blade, on the other hand, was not as sharp as others, probably due to its 20-degree edge and lower Rockwell rating, so testers had to "use more force" when cutting.

NOT RECOMMENDED

	CRITERIA		TESTERS' COMMENTS
R. MURPHY Chef's Select 8 Inch Carbon Steel Chef's Knife Price: $90 Model: CH8CIIHO Rockwell: 58 to 60 HRC Blade Angle: 12° to 15°	Cutting Comfort Edge Retention	★½ ★½ ★★★	Despite this blade's strong steel and narrow edge, its bevel was short, making it feel dull; testers reported needing to exert "three times the force" as they did with other knives. Its handle had "boxy," "sharp angles" that caused hand fatigue.
SABATIER Mexeur et Cie 8" Chef Price: $72.99 Model: 23688 Rockwell: 52 to 54 HRC Blade Angle: 20° to 25°	Cutting Comfort Edge Retention	★ ★ ★	This French knife's low Rockwell rating and wide-angle blade explained why it was the softest and dullest knife we tested. "I feel like I'm using a spoon," said one tester. The blade's sharp spine dug into hands, and because it was short (from spine to edge), testers' knuckles hit the cutting board.

Still Our Top Choice

Our stainless-steel favorite, the Victorinox 8" Swiss Army Fibrox Chef's Knife ($39.95), remained almost as sharp as the Henckels' Bob Kramer carbon-steel knife after more than 5,000 cuts—and at a fraction of the cost.

The Ultimate Thanksgiving Bird?

Heritage turkeys forage for food and live twice as long as modern birds. They can also cost 10 times as much. Do they taste great enough to command their premium price?

≥ BY LISA McMANUS ≤

Eating turkey on Thanksgiving is an American tradition, but today's supermarket turkeys barely resemble those enjoyed by early settlers. Starting in the 1950s, turkey breeders, catering to consumer preferences for white meat, started breeding turkeys to have big breasts and small legs. These birds could grow to full size on less feed and in half the time as the old-breed turkeys could—making turkey cheaper than ever before. Farmers also started raising the birds indoors and introduced artificial insemination, which made a turkey dinner a year-round option (in nature, turkeys hatch in the spring and reach "eating size" by late fall—not coincidentally, around Thanksgiving).

While supermarket turkey can taste great if it's carefully cooked, something has been lost. Near extinction not so long ago—and still on the "priority" list of the Livestock Conservancy—old-breed heritage turkeys have had a renaissance in the past decade, with a handful of farmers putting in the extra time, expense, and effort to raise these colorfully plumed birds that, unlike modern commercial turkeys, can fly, roam freely, and breed on their own. (For more detail, see "Heritage Turkey Defined.") Could turning back the clock bring back the flavor that's disappeared from modern turkeys?

To find out, we bought heritage turkeys from seven farms scattered across the United States. Breeds included Standard Bronze, American Bronze, and Bourbon Red, as well as a bird whose label reads "parent stock includes five different heritage breeds" and even an Eastern wild turkey raised in semicaptivity. All were pastured, meaning they were free to range outdoors and forage to supplement their feed.

The turkeys we unpacked were a far cry from the usual round, pale, plump supermarket turkey. All featured startlingly long legs and wings, a more angular breast and high keel bone, almost bluish-purple dark meat (a sign of well-exercised birds), and traces of dark pinfeathers in the skin around the tail. When we cooked one set according to a standard method, we also found their flavor worlds apart from ordinary turkey—far more rich and flavorful. We then roasted all seven types of birds again according to our new recipe customized to their unusual anatomy (see page 7), and their flavor was even more extraordinary.

Tasters raved about the "buttery," "nutty-sweet," "incredibly satisfying, rich flavor" of the meat. The biggest revelation was the white meat. Tasters found their favorite samples "amazing," "unctuous and silky," with "sweet, succulent flavor," and a texture that was "perfectly tender" and "really moist." So what was it about these birds that made them, as one taster put it, "the turkey of my dreams"?

Seeing the Light

During carving, we'd noticed a distinct layer of fat under the skin on the breast—more than what we've seen on a supermarket turkey. We know that fat not only adds flavor but also helps keep meat of all kinds moist during cooking. But, as Scott Beyer, extension poultry specialist at Kansas State University, explained, the fat under turkey skin is especially important. "If you peel off the skin, you strip most of the fat right off with it," he explained, noting that turkey meat doesn't become marbled with fat like beef. Our science editor also pointed out that the moistness and lubrication from fat reduces friction as you bite through the meat, making it more tender.

But how much of a difference was it, really? To find out, we sent samples from each heritage turkey to a lab to analyze the fat in both skin-on dark and skin-on white meat (uncooked). We also sent the lab a Broad Breasted White from Butterball, the largest producer of turkey products in the United States.

The results were convincing. The Butterball turkey had just 1.24 percent fat in its breast meat and skin, while breast-meat fat levels for the heritage birds ranged from a low of 4.56 percent in the wild turkey to a high of 10.63 percent in the bird from Good Shepherd Poultry Ranch. (In the dark meat, heritage birds' legs and thighs were actually slightly leaner than supermarket turkeys'. This was not surprising since they are more physically active, but overall the heritage birds still had far more fat.) No wonder tasters found the heritage turkeys so moist and tender.

So why would heritage turkey contain more fat? "Age," said turkey breeder Frank Reese Jr. of Good Shepherd Poultry Ranch in Lindsborg, Kansas, who has been raising heritage turkeys since the 1950s and sells breeding stock to other farms. (Reese is widely acknowledged as the "dean" of heritage turkeys.) According to Reese, commercial growers can raise a 20-pound turkey in 12 weeks, whereas "it would take six months with a heritage bird. And if a turkey lives to be six to seven months old, it has lived long enough to start putting on that fat."

A longer life has some other benefits, too. Beyer notes, "Inside [the fat and meat] is the accumulation over months and months of minor things from the feed and changes to the animal's biochemistry; proteins and lipids that aren't there in younger turkey that may be detectable as enhanced flavor." According to Reese, their foraged food would also contribute flavor.

Older birds also have much thicker skin, which helps shield the meat and trap moisture, "like putting

---

Heritage Turkey Defined

In the 1500s, Spanish explorers took some wild North American turkeys back to Europe and domesticated them. Then European colonists brought these breeds—what we know now as heritage—back to North America in the 1600s. Heritage turkey (also called "Standard Bred" turkey) is not just a matter of colorful feathers or romantic breed names like Narragansett or Bourbon Red; the Livestock Conservancy and the American Poultry Association agree that a heritage turkey is defined by these three criteria:

1. Heritage turkeys must have a long productive lifespan—five to seven years for breeding hens, three to five years for breeding toms—and have a genetic ability to withstand the environmental rigors of outdoor production systems.
2. Heritage turkey must have a slow to moderate rate of growth, reaching marketable weight in about 28 weeks, giving the birds time to develop a strong skeletal structure and healthy organs before building muscle mass. Commercial turkeys grow to full size in only 12 to 14 weeks.
3. Unlike commercial turkeys that must be artificially inseminated, heritage birds are the result of naturally mating pairs of both grandparent and parent stock. –L.M.

STANDARD BRONZE TURKEYS

TASTING HERITAGE TURKEYS

We tasted six heritage turkeys, prepared using our recipe for Roast Heritage Turkey (page 7). An independent laboratory measured fat and protein in light and dark meat (including skin). Prices are what we paid to mail-order a single turkey (shipping was extra). A source for the top-ranked turkey is on page 32. (Note: To avoid shipping costs for our winning turkey, check marysturkeys.com for information on stores across the country that carry the fresh birds during the holiday months.)

HIGHLY RECOMMENDED

MARY'S Free-Range Heritage Turkey
Price: $166.72 for 7- to 14-lb bird, plus shipping
Raised In: California
Breed: Standard Bronze
Fat in White Meat: 5.75%
Fat in Dark Meat: 7.25%
Comments: Our top pick was "richly flavored," with "great texture and moisture," and exquisitely "crisp" skin. This big turkey (just over 14 pounds) was "quite fatty," with "remarkably tender, moist white meat that tastes like poultry, not just wet fiber. Dark meat is dee-lish and also very tender." Tasters raved about its "good scent" and "nutty-sweet poultry flavor. Even the skin tastes meatier than [that of] most [other] turkey." One taster summed it up: "Amazing."

RECOMMENDED

ELMWOOD STOCK FARM Organic Heritage Turkey
Price: $149 for 9- to 10.9-lb bird, plus shipping
Raised In: Kentucky
Breed: Narragansett, Slate, or Bourbon Red (farm decides for you)
Fat in White Meat: 8.03%
Fat in Dark Meat: 5.21%
Comments: This turkey was "supertender and juicy," with white meat "so rich in flavor that it tastes like dark meat." The dark meat was even more tender and flavorful, prompting one taster to ask, "Is this dark turkey or pulled pork? So fall-apart tender that it's almost shredding itself." "Rich without gamy notes," the meat had a "texture like velvet."

GOOD SHEPHERD POULTRY RANCH Heritage Turkey
Price: $119 for 12- to 14-pound bird, plus shipping
Raised In: Kansas
Breed: Standard Bronze
Fat in White Meat: 10.63%
Fat in Dark Meat: 6.34%
Comments: Tasters enthused about this generously sized heritage bird, raised by the dean of heritage turkey breeders, Frank Reese. They praised its "very, very moist and intensely sweet breast meat," that was "moist but not wet," with "substantial turkey flavor," and dark meat that was "rich, almost fatty, in a good way, like duck," and "incredibly tender, quite fat-streaked." Indeed, lab results showed that it had one of the highest fat percentages of all the turkeys we tasted.

RECOMMENDED CONTINUED

HERITAGE TURKEY FARM Heritage Turkey
Price: $85 for 10- to 13-lb bird, plus shipping
Raised In: Wisconsin
Breed: American Bronze
Fat in White Meat: 5.10%
Fat in Dark Meat: 3.82%
Comments: "A fine specimen of turkey here," one taster wrote, and others agreed: "plenty moist and tender" "but not mushy," "fantastic," "perfectly juicy," and "full of turkey taste." The "lovely" dark meat was praised for being "packed with meaty flavor," "supple," and "richly flavored." A taster concluded: "Overall, unique enough that I'd spend money for this."

BEST BUY

RECOMMENDED WITH RESERVATIONS

EBERLY Heritage Turkey
Price: $84 for 8- to 9-lb bird, plus shipping
Raised In: Pennsylvania
Breed: Bourbon Red
Fat in White Meat: 8.25%
Fat in Dark Meat: 9.15%
Comments: This smaller bird's "white meat is moist, with a nice, unexpected sweetness." Tasters praised its "crispy" skin and "tender, savory" meat. But they were divided on their opinion of the dark meat: While some rated it "excellent—smooth and flavorful," "rich," and "acorn-y"—several others found it "a bit liver-y." "This one's an acquired taste," wrote one taster.

BN RANCH Heritage Turkey
Price: $138.98 for 10- to 12-lb bird, plus shipping
Raised In: California
Breed: Mixed, with "parent stock from five heritage breeds"
Fat in White Meat: 5.34%
Fat in Dark Meat: 6.99%
Comments: While this turkey, raised in a new venture by Bill Niman, founder of Niman Ranch, was "wildly moist," some tasters found it "lighter on turkey flavor, with the dark meat tasting almost of white." "One of the less impressive white meat samples," wrote one taster. "Quite moist but bland," agreed others, like "typical turkey breast." While there was nothing wrong with this bird, a turkey that costs this much should be perfect.

---

it in a Baggie," Beyer said. Meanwhile, most young, lean supermarket turkeys contain added flavor- and moisture-enhancing liquid. Our Butterball's label said it "contains up to 8% of a solution of water, salt, spices, and natural flavor."

Finally, turkey breed may have played a part in our preferences. In first and third place were Standard Bronze turkeys (both from Frank Reese's breeding stock). The bird with a "mixed" parentage was unremarkable, according to our tasters, and while flavorful, the wild turkey meat was somewhat tough.

Paying for Flavor
There's no denying that price is a big factor when considering heritage turkeys. Supermarket turkeys averaged $1.72 per pound nationwide last Thanksgiving, and promotional prices often dip well below $1 per pound. Heritage turkeys can cost upwards of $10 per pound; plus, required overnight or two-day shipping can nearly double the price. Also,

farms aren't charging a per-pound price but rather a flat price for a range of weights, such as 6 to 9 pounds, 7 to 14 pounds, and so on (similarly, you may be looking for a particular weight but sometimes smaller or larger birds are the only choices available). While we have a quibble with this pricing structure, farmers aren't getting rich; their rare, slow-growing, odd-size birds are far more expensive to raise and process.

A heritage bird is a centerpiece for a special occasion, like beef tenderloin or prime rib (which can cost $75 to $100 at the supermarket). Our top pick was Mary's Free-Range Heritage Turkey ($166.72 for a 7- to 14-pound bird, plus shipping), from a large family-owned farm in California that also produces our winning brand of chicken. It has everything we're looking for in turkey, with rich, full flavor and naturally moist meat. We'll be happy to splurge on this and other recommended heritage birds for the holidays—not just to save them from extinction, but for the great taste they bring to our Thanksgiving table.

What About Wild?

Native to North America and distinct from heritage breeds, wild turkeys come from unknown lineage (think wolf versus domesticated dog). We were curious how the ancestor to heritage breeds compared, so we ordered a wild turkey to include in our tasting.

The D'Artagnan Wild Turkey ($82.99 for a 5- to 7-pound bird, plus shipping) was smaller and more angular looking than the heritage turkeys, and it was even leaner too, with 4.56 percent fat in the white meat and 7.23 percent in the dark. Tasters weren't as wowed by it as by heritage turkeys. The meat's texture was "fibrous, dense, and chewy," and its flavor, while "good," left a "funky aftertaste." We're not convinced a wild bird is worth the expense.

KITCHEN NOTES

⇒ BY ANDREA GEARY, ANDREW JANJIGIAN & DAN SOUZA ⇐

EXPERIMENT
Bringing Out the Best in Garlic Powder

Garlic powder, which is simply dehydrated garlic that's ground to a powder, has never jumped out at us as a particularly potent form of garlic flavor, but when we were developing our Garlic-Parmesan Mashed Potatoes (page 12), we decided to explore all our options, including this ingredient. Knowing that the primary flavor in garlic is not only water-soluble but fat-soluble, we devised a quick test to find out if we could coax more flavor from garlic powder by treating it as we would a spice: blooming it in fat before adding it to the recipe.

EXPERIMENT For one batch of mashed potatoes, we added ½ teaspoon of garlic powder straight from the jar. For the second batch, we sautéed an equal amount of garlic powder in butter and then stirred it into the potatoes. We asked tasters to compare the garlic in each sample.

RESULTS The potatoes with untreated garlic powder tasted harsh and garlicky but not particularly complex, similar to what you'd find with raw minced garlic, while the batch with garlic powder that had been sautéed in butter had almost no garlic flavor at all. How could it be that sautéing the powder in butter not only didn't lead to more complex flavor but seemed to lessen its flavor?

EXPLANATION A little research informed us that there was more going on here than the garlic flavor's solubility in water and fat. Garlic develops flavor when its cells are ruptured, releasing an odorless sulfur-containing amino acid called alliin and the enzyme alliinase. These two react to produce the primary flavor component in garlic: allicin (which is soluble in both fat and water). Garlic powder producers are careful to dry garlic at temperatures low enough to remove water without destroying alliinase, which will happen at temperatures higher than 140 degrees. Once the water has been removed, the enzyme exists in an inactive state. Only with the reintroduction of water does alliinase "wake up" and begin producing allicin.

Adding garlic powder as-is to the mashed potatoes allowed the powder to hydrate in the potatoes' natural moisture, so allicin was able to form. The sample with garlic powder sautéed in butter, on the other hand, tasted dull because the alliinase had been exposed to high heat and thus any chance of allicin forming was eliminated.

TAKEAWAY It's important to first "wake up" the dormant flavor-producing enzyme in garlic powder by hydrating it—and to avoid heating the powder before doing so since that will destroy the enzyme.

With this in mind, we came up with the following approach to bringing out the most flavor from garlic powder for our mashed potatoes: We first hydrated ½ teaspoon of garlic powder in an equal amount of water, which reactivated the alliinase and allowed allicin to form, and then sautéed the hydrated powder in butter before stirring it into the potatoes, which contributed the most complex garlic flavor.

In sum, when using garlic powder, for the fullest flavor hydrate it in an equal amount of water and then sauté it in fat before adding it to your dish. –D.S.

⊙ SCIENCE OF COOKING:
Crinkly Cookies
Love the fissures and cracks atop crinkle cookies and ginger snaps? Learn the science of how to achieve the look every time. Free for 4 months at CooksIllustrated.com/dec14.

TART UNMOLDING MADE EASY

Lifting up the removable tart pan bottom in our French Apple Tart (page 15) with your hand causes the outer pan ring to slide down your arm like a hula hoop. To remove the pan ring easily, place a wide can, such as a 28-ounce can of tomatoes, on the counter and set the cooled tart pan on top of the can. Hold the pan ring and gently pull it downward. –A.G.

Are Dutched and Natural Cocoa Interchangeable?

In the world of cocoa powder, there are two main categories: Dutched and natural. The natural product is made mainly of unsweetened cocoa solids that have had much of their fat removed and are then dried and ground to a powder. Dutching refers to the step of adding an alkali to neutralize the powder's acidity and to mellow its astringent notes (it also darkens the color).

While some recipes don't specify whether you should use Dutched or natural cocoa, others do and then go on to strongly caution against swapping one for the other. We were curious how interchangeable natural and Dutched cocoa are, so we tested a half-dozen recipes, including our Hot Chocolate Mix (page 23) and Chocolate Crinkle Cookies (page 25), side by side, using both types of cocoa in each recipe.

NATURAL
Straightforward chocolate flavor with some acidity; produces a lighter color, drier crumb, and less spread.

DUTCH-PROCESSED
Fruity, bitter chocolate flavor; produces a darker color and moister, fudgier crumb.

The biggest finding was that none of the recipes, even those with a high proportion of cocoa powder—and thus with the potential to be most strongly affected—failed. But that didn't mean there weren't differences in appearance, texture, and flavor. Not surprisingly, Dutch-processed cocoa always produced cakes, cookies, and hot cocoa with a darker color than the versions made with natural cocoa. In terms of texture, natural cocoa produced slightly drier baked goods as well as cookies with less spread than did Dutch-processed. Finally, we found that baked goods and hot chocolate made with Dutch-processed cocoa displayed more of the fruity, bitter notes of dark chocolate, while natural cocoa delivered a more straightforward chocolate flavor.

The takeaway? Both natural and Dutched cocoa will work in recipes; use whichever fits your preferences in terms of flavor, appearance, and texture. –D.S.

Our recipe for Authentic Baguettes at Home (September/October 2014) walks you through the shaping and scoring technique that produces the classic long, skinny loaves, but there's another option. An *epi*, or *pain d'epi*, uses a technique to produce a loaf that resembles a stalk of wheat. Instead of being scored, the loaf is cut into angled, attached lobes. The dough preparation and baking process are exactly the same. –A.J.

1. After baguette has been stretched to 15-inch length, cut into loaf at 45-degree angle, about 3 inches from end of loaf, nearly but not all the way through loaf.

2. Arrange cut section at 30-degree angle in either direction.

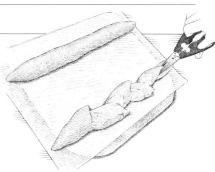

3. Repeat every 3 inches, pulling sections out toward alternating sides to create wheat stalk shape.

Carbon-Steel Knives: Why a Patina Matters

While researching carbon-steel knives (see our testing on page 26), we learned that they require more care than stainless-steel knives because they can oxidize in two ways. Hematite—rust—is an aggressive form of oxidation that eats into the metal, creating a flaky, orange surface. Magnetite is a mild form of oxidation that affects only the outer surface of the metal; its presence actually prevents further corrosion. Magnetite turns carbon-steel knives a charcoal gray, giving them what we call a patina.

Both types of oxidation occur when carbon steel comes in contact with oxygen and moisture (reactions that are sped up in the presence of salt). If water is left in contact with the blade for an extended period of time (for instance, if a wet knife is allowed to dry naturally), rusty spots will quickly form. Magnetite will form when exposure to oxygen and water is limited.

We found that if a knife developed a light charcoal-gray patina naturally over time, it was less likely to rust if left wet. To put this protection in place quickly, some manufacturers suggest forcing a patina to develop on the blade. We tried one method: soaking the blade in vinegar (a low pH environment favors the production of magnetite) and then washing it and wiping it dry. The approach gave the knife a matte, grippy finish that created undesirable drag in food, and more important, the blade ended up rusting more easily. The upshot? The best way to develop a protective patina and avoid rust is to use your carbon-steel knife regularly, to wipe it dry continually during use, and to rinse and dry it thoroughly as soon as you've finished a cutting task. (Look for our testing in an upcoming issue for the best method for removing rust from carbon-steel knives.) –D.S.

Shaping free-form breads is as much about creating a smooth skin on the exterior as it is about producing the proper shape. A taut exterior helps the loaf expand evenly, and the resistance created between the work surface and the dough plays a critical role. As you are working the dough, that resistance between the counter and the dough will allow you to produce that essential tight skin. To do the job, the loaf shouldn't slide around freely or be so tacky that it sticks and tears. The best way to achieve this slightly dry state is to avoid flouring the work surface itself—it's too easy to overflour—and instead flour an adjacent area to create a flouring station, where you can transfer the loaf for flouring as needed. –A.J.

Lightly flour area adjacent to work surface. Gently press unshaped dough into flour once or twice to coat underside, then transfer to work surface and shape. Press dough lightly in floured area as needed to prevent sticking.

Reheating Leftover Turkey

Leftover turkey is a fact of life during the holidays, but reheating lean breast meat (and to a slightly lesser degree, legs and thighs) can easily lead to dry, stringy results, not to mention leathery or flabby skin. Our gentle method helps ensure that as much moisture as possible stays in the meat and crisps the skin.

Wrap the leftover portions in aluminum foil, stacking any sliced pieces, and place them on a wire rack set in a rimmed baking sheet. Transfer them to a 275-degree oven and heat them until the meat registers 130 degrees, a temperature warm enough for serving but not so hot that it drives off more moisture. (Sliced turkey should be warm throughout; if the slices are relatively thick, you can insert the probe into the meat just as you would with bone-in pieces.) This gentle oven temperature also means that the meat comes up to temperature slowly and evenly. Note that timing will vary greatly based on the shape and size of the leftover turkey pieces. For a crosswise-cut half breast, we found 35 to 45 minutes to be sufficient.

Finally, place any large skin-on pieces skin side down in a lightly oiled skillet over medium-high heat, heating until the skin recrisps. –D.S.

CRISPY LEFTOVERS
After gently warming the meat in a low oven, crisp the skin in a lightly oiled skillet.

Sodium in the Water, Not the Pasta

Adding salt to pasta's cooking water ensures that the pasta is flavorful. Throughout the years we've zeroed in on a preferred ratio of 1 tablespoon of table salt to 4 quarts of cooking water per pound of pasta for the most well-seasoned pasta of any shape or size.

We were curious to find out exactly how much sodium actually makes it into the pasta, so we sent samples of six different shapes—spaghetti, linguine, penne, rigatoni, campanelle, and orzo—all cooked al dente according to our method, to an independent lab for analysis.

The results ? Give or take a few milligrams of sodium, all the shapes absorbed about the same amount of salt: $\frac{1}{16}$ teaspoon per 4-ounce serving or a total of $\frac{1}{4}$ teaspoon per pound of pasta. The Dietary Guidelines for Americans recommend less than 2,300 milligrams daily for people under 51 and less than 1,500 milligrams for those 51 and older, so even if you are watching your sodium intake, the amount pasta actually absorbs is so small that it's probably not an issue. –D.S.

⇒ BY LAUREN SAVOIE, SARAH SEITZ & KATE SHANNON ⇐

UPDATE Sous Vide Machines

For *sous vide* cooking, vacuum-sealed food is immersed in a water bath that is heated to the food's final serving temperature (e.g., 125 degrees for salmon). The method is slow and gentle and the cooking is remarkably uniform, with minimal moisture loss, making it ideal for lean foods as well as for tough cuts that need tenderizing.

A few years ago we recommended the Sous Vide Supreme ($429), the first home version of this restaurant appliance, but since then, cheaper, smaller models have come out. We tested five of them, priced from $199 to $329: two in the water-oven style (basically an insulated box) like the Supreme, and three stick models, which can attach to any large vessel and will heat and circulate the water within. (Note: A vacuum sealer wasn't included with any of the models; one must be purchased separately, or food can be put in a zipper-lock bag.)

One water oven was problematic from the start, with a very limited capacity and temperatures that fluctuated 20 degrees. The other water oven delivered nicely cooked eggs, salmon, and pork belly, but it lost out to the stick-style models, which brought the water to the desired temperature more quickly and offered the flexibility of attaching to any container, large or small. This did bring our attention to one drawback—attaching to open vessels meant evaporation was an issue when cooking at high temperatures or for 12 hours or more (a problem since circulators will stop operating without enough water). But it's a minor point since these situations aren't all that common. Plus, the sticks are cheaper and easier to store.

Our favorite, the Anova One ($199), was the cheapest, quickest, and quietest model we tried. It required topping off the water only once during a 48-hour stint cooking pork belly, and its big touch-screen display was easy to use. (Note: At press time, the company announced a newer model, which we will test when it launches.) –L.S.

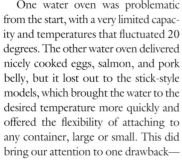

SOLD ON SOUS VIDE
The Anova One makes *sous vide* cooking at home easy and more affordable.

NEW Chef's Knives for Kids

Kids love helping in the kitchen, but letting them use sharp blades can be worrisome. After giving three scaled-down chef's knives for kids a quick trial run ourselves, we asked testers ages 5, 11, and 12 to use the blades to cut celery, apples, blocks of cheese, and grilled cheese sandwiches. We also had them perform the same tasks using a table knife and a plastic knife. While all three chef's knives bested the stand-ins, the 5½-inch serrated plastic knife by Curious Chef ($3.99) was a little too thick and blunt even for our 5-year-old. This young tester found the cute dog-shaped Kuhn Rikon Kinderkitchen Dog Knife ($10), with its 2-inch-long rounded metal blade and soft grip, a perfect match. The older kids were impressed by the Opinel Le Petit Chef + Finger Guard ($39.95), which has a sturdy wooden handle, a sharp 4-inch-long stainless-steel blade with a rounded tip, and nice "training wheel" features: a finger loop on the handle for proper hand position and a plastic guard to protect fingers on the other hand. Both the Kuhn Rikon and Opinel are great choices for future chefs. –S.S.

FOR YOUNG CHEFS
Opinel's Le Petit Chef is a real chef's knife, scaled down for kids.

NEW Marinating Stick

We've found that marinades generally don't go much farther than skin deep, which is why Mary's Marinating Stick ($24.90 for two) grabbed our attention. Each perforated 10-inch stainless-steel tube can be filled with seasoning and inserted into any piece of meat with the idea that the food will be seasoned thoroughly from the inside. But at only ½ inch wide, each tube held very little seasoning—less than ½ ounce of garlic, herbs, and citrus zest. And when used with a 3-pound pork loin, even potent garlic and rosemary failed to permeate beyond a ¼-inch area surrounding the stick—a far cry from the claim that it can flavor up to 6 pounds of protein. We also skewered a turkey breast with two salt-filled marinating sticks, but the seasoning was no better than a breast we'd simply salted before cooking. Once removed, the sticks leave behind unsightly "bullet holes," and the 132 tiny perforations are difficult to clean, even after a trip through the dishwasher. –K.S.

STICKING OUT
Mary's Marinating Stick didn't add much flavor to pork loin or turkey; plus, it left gaping holes.

UPDATE Insulated Food Carriers

Insulated food carriers are designed to keep casseroles hot en route to a potluck, picnic, or holiday dinner. Since our old favorite by Pyrex was redesigned, we tested its replacement, plus four others (priced from $27 to $40) designed to carry 13 by 9-inch baking dishes. We evaluated their heat retention and stain resistance. We also tested their design and sturdiness by walking around the block and driving over 5 miles of bumpy roads with them.

One carrier was too big—our lasagna dish shifted inside—but two contenders, including our winner, offered a snug fit; plus, they expanded to include extra dishes.

But heat retention was the biggest factor. We want food ready to serve on arrival—no reheating necessary. Additionally, the longer food stays piping hot, the safer it is (the U.S. Department of Agriculture recommends not holding food at temperatures below 140 degrees for more than 2 hours). In four of the five carriers, macaroni and cheese dipped from 180 degrees (fresh out of the oven) to 140 degrees in less than an hour. The new Pyrex model (which has insulation half as thick as its predecessor's) dropped below the minimum in just 12 minutes. Compare that with our new favorite, the Rachael Ray Expandable Lasagna Lugger ($26.95), which kept macaroni and cheese above 140 degrees for more than 3 hours. Our only quibble—that it wasn't as easy to clean as the others—is a small trade-off given that no other carrier matched its heat retention. –L.S.

CARRIED AWAY
Travel more than 2 hours and still arrive with your prize-winning casserole piping hot with the Rachael Ray Expandable Lasagna Lugger.

For complete testing results, go to CooksIllustrated.com/dec14.

Sources

Prices were current at press time and do not include shipping. Contact companies to confirm information or visit CooksIllustrated.com for updates.

PAGE 19: SICHUAN PEPPERCORNS
• Dean & DeLuca Szechuan Peppercorns: $6.25 for 1-ounce tin, Dean & DeLuca (800-221-7714, deandeluca.com).

PAGE 27: CARBON-STEEL CHEF'S KNIVES
• Bob Kramer 8" Carbon Steel Chef's Knife by Zwilling J.A. Henckels: $299.95, model 789693, Sur La Table (800-243-0852, surlatable.com).
• Togiharu Virgin Carbon Steel Gyutou: $98.50, model HTO-HCGY, Korin (800-626-2172, korin.com).

PAGE 29: HERITAGE TURKEYS
• Mary's Free-Range Heritage Turkey, 7 to 14 lbs: $166.72, Mary's Free-Range Turkeys (888-666-8244, marysturkeys.com).
• Elmwood Stock Farm Organic Heritage Turkey, 9 to 10.9 lbs: $149, Local Harvest (831-515-5602, localharvest.org).

PAGE 32: SOUS VIDE MACHINE
• Anova One: $199, model 120V, Anova Culinary (281-980-1236, anovaculinary.com).

PAGE 32: CHEF'S KNIVES FOR KIDS
• Opinel Le Petit Chef + Finger Guard: $39.95, model 001744, Opinel USA (877-982-0924, opinel-usa.com).
• Kuhn Rikon Kinderkitchen Dog Knife: $10, model 22277, J.L. Hufford (877-554-8336, jlhufford.com).

PAGE 32: INSULATED FOOD CARRIER
• Rachael Ray Expandable Lasagna Lugger: $26.95, model 297540, Amazon (amazon.com).

INDEX
November & December 2014

Follow us on social media
facebook.com/CooksIllustrated
twitter.com/TestKitchen
pinterest.com/TestKitchen
google.com/+AmericasTestKitchen
instagram.com/TestKitchen
youtube.com/AmericasTestKitchen

▶ RECIPE VIDEOS
Want to see how to make any of the recipes in this issue? There's a video for that.

▶ MORE VIDEOS
Science of Cooking: Crinkly Cookies
Testing Carbon-Steel Knives

Recipes, reviews, and videos available free for 4 months at **CooksIllustrated.com/ dec14**

BEHIND THE SCENES
Hannah Visits MIT
CooksIllustrated.com/MITcarbonsteel

Hot Chocolate Mix, 23

Rosemary-Garlic Top Sirloin Roast, 9

Chocolate Crinkle Cookies, 25

French Apple Tart, 15

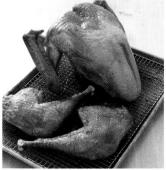
Roast Heritage Turkey, 7

Crispy Slow-Roasted Pork Belly, 21

Crispy Salt and Pepper Shrimp, 19

Mushroom Bisque, 11

Garlic-Parmesan Mashed Potatoes, 12

Pasta with Beans, Chard, and Rosemary, 22

PHOTOGRAPHY: CARL TREMBLAY; STYLING: MARIE PIRAINO

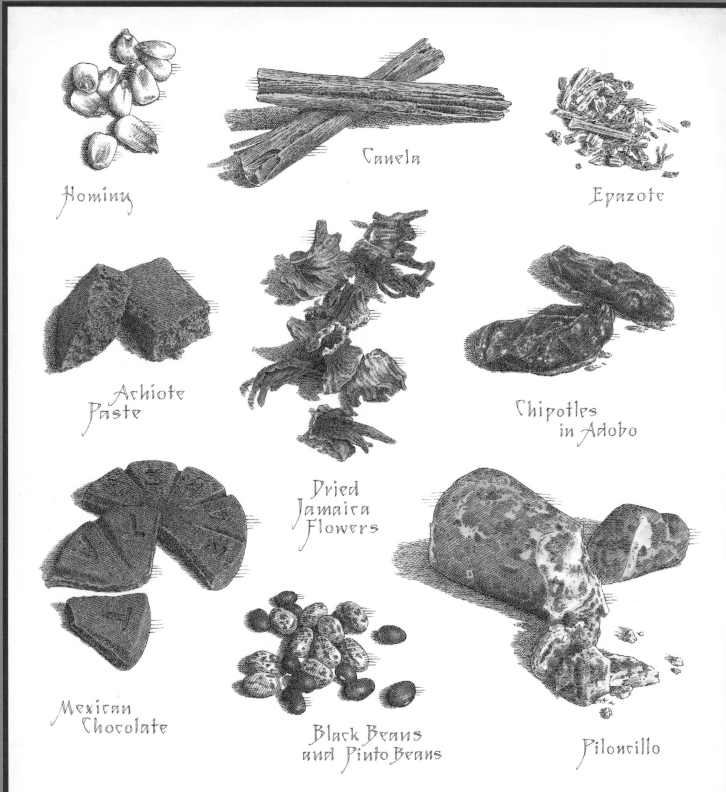

Hominy

Canela

Epazote

Achiote Paste

Dried Jamaica Flowers

Chipotles in Adobo

Mexican Chocolate

Black Beans and Pinto Beans

Piloncillo

MEXICAN PANTRY